THE OXFORD HANDBOOK OF

ORGANIZATION
THEORY

THE OXFORD HANDBOOK OF

ORGANIZATION THEORY

Edited by

HARIDIMOS TSOUKAS

AND

CHRISTIAN KNUDSEN

OXFORD

UNIVERSITY PRESS

OXFORD
UNIVERSITY PRESS

Great Clarendon Street, Oxford OX2 6DP

Oxford University Press is a department of the University of Oxford.
It furthers the University's objective of excellence in research, scholarship,
and education by publishing worldwide in

Oxford New York

Auckland Bangkok Buenos Aires Cape Town Chennai
Dar es Salaam Delhi Hong Kong Istanbul Karachi Kolkata
Kuala Lumpur Madrid Melbourne Mexico City Mumbai Nairobi
São Paulo Shanghai Taipei Tokyo Toronto

Oxford is a registered trade mark of Oxford University Press
in the UK and in certain other countries

Published in the United States
by Oxford University Press Inc., New York

British Library Cataloguing in Publication Data

Data available

Library of Congress Cataloging in Publication Data

The Oxford handbook of organization theory / edited by
Haridimos Tsoukas and Christian Knudsen.
p. cm.
1. Organization.   2. Management.   I. Title: Handbook of organization theory.
II. Tsoukas, Haridimos.   III. Knudsen, Christian.   IV. Oxford University Press.
HD31 .O94 2003   302.3′5—dc21   2002035573

ISBN 0–19–925832–5

1 3 5 7 9 10 8 6 4 2

Typeset by Kolam Information Services Pvt. Ltd., Pondicherry, India
Printed in Great Britain on acid-free paper by
T.J. International Ltd., Padstow, Cornwall

For Efi

'a madness most discreet /
A choking gall, and a preserving sweet'

H.T.

ACKNOWLEDGEMENTS

The idea for this handbook came initially from David Musson, the Business and Management Editor at Oxford University Press. In July 1999, at the 15th EGOS Colloquium, University of Warwick, Haridimos Tsoukas was an organizer (with Jean-Claude Thoenig) of one of the streams of the Colloquium, entitled 'Organization Theory as Science: Prospects and Limitations', in which Christian Knudsen presented a paper. David liked the topic of the stream as well as several of the papers presented and suggested that we edit an Oxford Handbook on Organization Theory with an explicitly meta-theoretical focus. Since both of us had been individually (and jointly) researching meta-theoretical issues in OT for several years, we were more than delighted to have this marvellous opportunity to put together a number of high-quality contributions by some of the field's most distinguished academics.

We would like to thank David Musson for this opportunity. Without his stimulating encouragement and keen eye for spotting interesting debates in management and business studies, this volume probably would not have been produced. We would also like to thank his team at the Oxford University Press for their professionalism, especially Lynn Childress for her thorough and meticulous copyediting. Last, but not least, we would like to express our gratitude to the contributors to this volume for the enthusiasm with which they embraced the idea of the present handbook, and their energy and patience in going through seemingly endless rounds of commentaries and revisions. This volume is what it is thanks to their high standards of scholarship and their passion for reflective dialogue. Thank you all.

Haridimos Tsoukas and Christian Knudsen

Contents

PART I ORGANIZATION THEORY AS SCIENCE

PART II THE CONSTRUCTION OF ORGANIZATION THEORY

PART III META-THEORETICAL CONTROVERSIES IN ORGANIZATION THEORY

PART IV ORGANIZATION THEORY AS A POLICY SCIENCE

PART V THE FUTURE OF ORGANIZATION THEORY

FIGURES

Tables

LIST OF CONTRIBUTORS

Chris Argyris is the James Bryant Conant Professor Emeritus, Harvard University. His books include *Overcoming Organizational Defenses* (1990), *Knowledge for Action* (1993), *Flawed Advice* (2000), *Theory in Practice* (1994), and *Organizational Learning II* (1996), both with Donald Schön, and *Action Science* (1985) with Diana Smith and Robert Putnam.

Gibson Burrell is Professor of Organization Theory at the University of Essex, UK, having previously been at the Universities of Warwick and Lancaster. He is Editor of the journal *Organization*. Over many long years he has published a small number of books, edited collections, and articles. Some of this material has even been read. He is currently working on a co-authored book entitled *Architecture, Space and Organization*. email: gibsonb@essex.ac.uk

Marta B. Calás is Associate Professor of Organization Studies and International Management at the Isenberg School of Management of the University of Massachusetts-Amherst. She was born in Cuba and has lived and done academic and scholarly work in several countries. She teaches International Management, Organization Theory, and a doctoral seminar in Conceptual Foundations of Organization Studies. Her earlier scholarly writing centered on cross-cultural organizational behavior, but in recent years she has been pursuing cultural and critical perspectives on organization and management. Her various publications, often co-authored with Linda Smircich, apply insights from cultural studies, postmodern, feminist, and post-colonial theorizing to interrogate organizational topics such as leadership, business ethics, and globalization. She is co-editor of the international, interdisciplinary journal *Organization*, along with Gibson Burrell, Mike Reed, and Linda Smircich. email: marta@mgmt.umass.edu

Robert Chia is Professor of Strategy and Organization at the School of Business and Economics, University of Exeter. He is the author of several books and journal articles on Organization Theory and Management and has presented conference papers at the American Academy of Management, the British Academy of Management, as well as other international conferences in Management and Organization Studies. Prior to entering academia, he worked for sixteen years in aircraft maintenance engineering, manufacturing management, and human resource management and was Group Human Resource Manager of Metal Box Asia Pacific based in

Singapore. His main research interests revolve around the application of process philosophy for the study of organization; strategic foresight; complexity and creativity; East–West management attitudes, and postmodernism.

Stewart Clegg is Professor at the University of Technology, Sydney. Born in Bradford, England, he migrated to Australia in 1976, after completing a first degree at the University of Aston (1971) and a Doctorate at Bradford University (1974). Previously he has held Professorial positions at the University of New England (1985–1989); University of St. Andrews (1990–1993), Scotland; and University of Western Sydney (1993–1996). He has produced over thirty books, including *Frameworks of Power* (1989) and over a hundred journal and other refereed publications, writing extensively on power, organizations, and related matters. His most recent books are *Trends in Japanese Management: Continuing Strengths, Current Problems and Changing Priorities*, co-authored with Toyohiro Kono (2001) and *Paradoxes of Management and Organizations*. Additionally, he has prepared an eight-volume collection on *Central Currents in Organization Studies*. He is perhaps best known for the *Handbook of Organization Studies*, which he co-edited with Cynthia Hardy and Walter Nord (1996), and which won the Academy of Management George R. Terry Best Book Award in 1997. He has been a Fellow of the Academy of the Social Sciences in Australia since 1988.

Barbara Czarniawska holds a Skandia Chair in Management Studies at the Gothenburg Research Institute, School of Economics and Commercial Law, Gothenburg University, Sweden. Her research focuses on control processes in complex organizations, most recently in the field of big city management. In terms of methodological approach, she combines institutional theory with the narrative approach. She has published in the area of business and public administration in Polish, her native language, as well as in Swedish, Italian, and English, the most recent positions being *Narrating the Organization: Dramas of Institutional Identity* (1997), *A Narrative Approach to Organization Studies* (1998), *Writing Management* (1999), and *A City Reframed: Managing Warsaw in the 1990s* (2000). A member of Royal Swedish Academy of Sciences since 2000, a member of Royal Swedish Academy of Engineering Sciences since 2001.

Lex Donaldson is a Professor in the Australian Graduate School of Management of the Universities of New South Wales and Sydney. He was previously a Senior Research Officer at London Business School and has been a visitor at the universities of Iowa, Maryland, Northwestern, and Stanford. Lex Donaldson holds a B.Sc. (Aston) and a Ph.D. (London). He has published a series of books defending and developing functionalist and positivist organizational theory: *In Defence of Organization Theory: A Reply to the Critics* (1985), *American Anti-Management Theories of Organization: A Critique of Paradigm Proliferation* (1995), *For Positivist Organization Theory: Proving the Hard Core* (1996), *Performance-Driven Organizational Change:*

The Organizational Portfolio (1999), and *The Contingency Theory of Organizations* (2001). email: lexd@agsm.edu.au

Silvia Gherardi is full Professor of Sociology of Organization at the Faculty of Sociology of the University of Trento, Italy, where she coordinates the Research Unit on Cognition and Organizational Learning. Areas of interest include the exploration of different 'soft' aspects of knowing in organizations, with a particular emphasis on cognitive, emotional, symbolic, and linguistic aspects of organizational process. To the theme of gender and organizational cultures is devoted her last book *Gender, Symbolism and Organizational Cultures* (1995), several articles in *Human Relations, Gender, Work and Organization, Journal of World Business*, and a book on ethnography and entrepreneurship is forthcoming by Stanford University Press.

Mary Jo Hatch (Ph.D., Stanford, 1985) is Professor of Commerce at the McIntire School of Commerce, University of Virginia (USA). Her current research interests include organizational culture and identity, corporate branding, and aesthetic approaches to organization theory. Her publications appear in journals such as *Academy of Management Review, Administrative Science Quarterly, European Journal of Marketing, Harvard Business Review, Human Relations, Journal of Management Inquiry, Organization, Organization Science and Organization Studies*. Among others, she sits on the editorial boards of *Academy of Management Review* and *Human Relations*. Her textbook *Organization Theory: Modern, Symbolic, and Postmodern Perspectives* (1997) is available from Oxford University Press, which also published *The Expressive Organization: Linking Identity, Reputation and the Corporate Brand* (2000), co-edited with Majken Schultz and Mogens Holten Larsen. email mjhatch@virginia.edu

Christian Knudsen is a professor at Copenhagen Business School. He has published extensively on the methodology of economics, theories of the firm, and strategy. Among his more recent books are *Rationality, Institutions and Economic Methodology* (with Mäki and Gustafsson) and *Towards a Competence Theory of the Firm* (with Foss). His research interests include economic methodology, theories of the firm, and organizational sociology. email: ck.ivs@cbs.dk

Arie Lewin is Professor of Business Administration and Sociology at Duke University. He is the Director of the Center for International Business Education and Research (CIBER) and of the recently established Center for Research on New Organization Forms (NOFIA). He is the Editor-in-Chief of the *Journal of International Business Studies, JIBS*. Professor Lewin was Program Director for Decision, Risk and Management Science at the National Science Foundation (1986–1988); Department Editor of *Management Science* for the department of Organization Analysis, Performance and Design (1974–1987); founding Editor-in-Chief of *Organization Science* (1989–1998); DKB Visiting Professor at the Keio University Graduate

School of Business (Spring 1993); and Visiting Research Professor at the Institute for Business Research, Hitotsubashi University (1994–1995). Professor Lewin's primary research interests involve the analysis of organization effectiveness and the design of organizations. Current research is focused on new forms of organizations distinguished by new adaptive capabilities. He leads a major long-term cross-cultural—Germany, Japan, Korea, Sweden, Switzerland, United Kingdom, and United States of America—comparative study of strategic reorientations and organization restructurings. email: aylewin@attglobal.net

William McKinley received his Ph.D. in organizational sociology from Columbia University, and is currently a Professor of Management at Southern Illinois University at Carbondale, USA. His research interests are organizational restructuring and downsizing, organizational change, organizational decline, epistemological issues in organizational research, and the sociology and philosophy of organization science. His publications have appeared in *Administrative Science Quarterly, Academy of Management Journal, Academy of Management Review, Academy of Management Executive, Journal of Management Inquiry, Organization, Organization Science, Accounting, Organizations and Society, Advances in Strategic Management, Management International Review, Journal of Engineering and Technology Management, Business Horizons,* and other outlets. email: decline@siu.edu

Iain L. Mangham is Professor Emeritus at the University of Bath where he was previously Professor of Organizational Behaviour and Head of the School of Management. He is currently a Senior Visiting Research Fellow at the Management Centre, King's College London. His books include *Power and Performance in Organisations* (1986), *Organisations as Theatre* (with Michael Overington, 1986), and *The Doing of Management* (with Annie Pye, 1981). email: ILMangham@aol.com

Joanne Martin is the Fred H. Merrill Professor of Organizational Behavior at the Graduate School of Business, Stanford University. She holds a BA from Smith College, a Ph.D. from the Department of Psychology and Social Relations at Harvard University, and an Honorary Doctorate in Economics and Business Administration from the Copenhagen Business School. She recently received the Distinguished Educator award from the Academy of Management and the Centennial Medal for 'contributions to society' from the Graduate School of Arts and Sciences at Harvard. She serves on the Board of Directors of CPP, Inc., a test and book publisher, and on the Advisory Board of the International Centre for Research in Organizational Discourse, Strategy, and Change for the Universities of Melbourne, Sydney, London, and McGill. She has published many articles and five books including *Cultures in Organizations: Three Perspectives* (1992) and *Organizational Culture: Mapping the Terrain* (2002).

Mark A. Mone, Ph.D., is Professor of Management and Associate Dean, Executive Programs, School of Business Administration, University of Wisconsin-Milwaukee.

His research areas include philosophical and quantitative research methods issues, organizational downsizing, retrenchment, and turnaround, and antecedents and consequences of personal goals. He is serving on the editorial board of the *Academy of Management Review*, and his publications have appeared there, in addition to *Journal of Applied Psychology, Strategic Management Journal, Personnel Psychology, Journal of Management, Human Relations, Organization, Journal of Management Inquiry*, and in other journals.

Richard P. Nielsen is Professor, Organization Studies Department, Carroll School of Management, Boston College. He is also a Visiting Professor at the Athens Laboratory of Business Administration in Greece. His areas of interest include organizational ethics and corruption reform methods, negotiating, leadership, change and transformation methods. His publications include *The Politics of Ethics: Methods for Acting, Learning, and Sometimes Fighting, with Others in Addressing Ethics Problems in Organizational Life* (1996). Related articles include 'The Politics of Long-Term Corruption Reform: A Combined Social Movement and Action-Learning Approach', *Business Ethics Quarterly* (2000); 'Business Citizenship and United States "Investor Capitalism": A Critical Analysis', in R. Edward Freeman and Sankaran Venkataraman (eds.), *Ethics and Entrepreneurship*, The Ruffin Series No. 3, A Publication of the Society for Business Ethics (2001); 'Can Ethical Character Be Stimulated and Enabled? An Action-Learning Approach to Teaching and Learning Organization Ethics', *Business Ethics Quarterly* (1998); and Richard P. Nielsen and Jean M. Bartunek, 'Opening Narrow, Routinized Schemata to Ethical Stakeholder Consciousness and Action', *Business and Society* (1996). In addition, he has published many articles in journals such as *Academy of Management Review, Academy of Management Executive, American Journal of Economics and Sociology, Business Ethics Quarterly, Business Ethics: A European Review, Business and Society, California Management Review, CULTURES, Human Resources Management, Journal of Applied Behavioral Science, Journal of Business Ethics, Journal of Management Inquiry*, and *Strategic Management Journal*. He has consulted and done executive training work with many business, government, and nonprofit institutions in Europe, North America, Latin America, and Asia. He is also a member of the Society of Friends.

Michael Reed was a Professor of Organization Theory and Associate Dean for Research, Department of Behaviour in Organizations, Lancaster University Management School. His books include *Redirections in Organizational Analysis* (1985), *The Sociology of Management* (1989), *The Sociology of Organizations* (1992), *Rethinking Organization* (1992), and *Organizing Modernity* (1994). He is one of the editors of the organization theory journal *Organization*. As of 1 September 2002, he is a Professor of Organization Theory, Cardiff Business School, Cardiff University.

Andreas Georg Scherer holds the chair for Foundations of Business Administration and Theories of the Firm at the University of Zurich (Switzerland). He earned his Ph.D.s in Strategic Management (1994) and in International Management (2000) both from the University of Erlangen-Nuremberg (Germany). From 2000–2002 he was associate Professor for Public Administration and General Management at the University of Constance (Germany). His research interests are in Business Ethics, International Management, Organization Theory, Philosophy of Science, Strategic Management. Dr Scherer has published six books. His work appeared in journals such as *Academy of Management Review, Advances in Strategic Management, Journal of Business Ethics, Management, Management International Review, Organization, Organization Studies*, and in numerous German journals and volumes. In 1998 he was guest editor of a special issue of the journal *Organization*. email: Andreas.Scherer@ifbf.unizh.ch

Yehouda Shenhav has written extensively and critically on rationality, the transformation of capitalism, and the birth of modern management. Among his books are: *Manufacturing Rationality: The Engineering Foundations of the Managerial Revolution (1999); The Organization Machine (1995)*; and *The Arab Jews: A Postcolonial Reading of Nationalism, Ethnicity and Religion* (2002). Shenhav teaches sociology at Tel Aviv University—where he also served as chair of the department (1995–1998)—and has taught in the past in several universities in the United States including Stanford University, University of Wisconsin-Madison, and University of Iowa. He is currently the editor of *Theory and Criticism*.

Linda Smircich is Professor of Organization Studies and past Chair of the Management Department at the Isenberg School of Management at the University of Massachusetts at Amherst. She teaches Organizational Alternative Paradigms. Her earlier scholarly writing centered on organizational culture, but now she would describe herself as pursuing a cultural and critical perspective on organization and management. Her various publications, often co-authored with Marta Calás, apply insights from cultural studies, postmodern, feminist, and post-colonial theorizing to interrogate organizational topics such as leadership, business ethics, and globalization. She is co-editor of the international, interdisciplinary journal *Organization,* along with Gibson Burrell, Marta Calás, and Mike Reed. email: smircich@mgmt.umass.edu

William Starbuck is the ITT Professor of Creative Management in the Stern School of Business at New York University. He has held academic positions in seven countries, edited *Administrative Science Quarterly,* chaired the screening committee for senior Fulbright awards in business management, directed the doctoral program in business administration at New York University, and been the President of the Academy of Management. He is a fellow of the Academy of Management, the American Psychological Association, the American Psychological Society, the British Academy of Management, and the Society for Industrial and Organizational Psychology. He has published numerous articles on accounting, bargaining, business strategy, computer programming, computer simulation, forecasting, decision-making, human-computer interaction, learning, organizational design, organizational growth and development, perception, scientific methods, and social revolutions. email: bill_starbuck@msn.com or bill_starbuck@attglobal.net

Richard Swedberg is Professor of Sociology at Cornell University and co-direcor of its Center on Economy and Society. His specialty is economic sociology, and he is the author of *Economics and Sociology* (1990), *Schumpeter – A Biography* (1991), *Max Weber and the Idea of Economic Sociology* (1998), and *Principles of Economic Sociology* (forthcoming). He is also co-editor (with Neil Smelser) of *The Handbook of Economic Sociology* (1994); (with Mark Granovetter) of *The Economic Sociology of Economic Life* (1992, 2001); and (with Victor Nee) of the *Economic Sociology of Capitalism.*

Haridimos Tsoukas is the George D. Mavros Research Professor of Organization and Management at the Athens Laboratory of Business Administration (ALBA), Greece and a Professor of Organization Theory and Behaviour at the Graduate School of Business, University of Strathclyde, UK. He has published widely in several leading academic journals such as *Academy of Management Review, Strategic Management Journal, Organization Science, Organization Studies, Journal of Management Studies, Organization,* and *Human Relations.* As of 1 September 2003 he will be the Editor-in-Chief of *Organization Studies,* and now sits on the editorial board of *Organization Science, Strategic Organization, Human Relations,* and *Emergence.* email: htsoukas@alba.edu.gr

Henk Volberda is Professor of Strategic Management and Business Policy and Chairman of the Department of Strategic Management & Business Environment of the Rotterdam School of Management, Erasmus University. He has been a visiting scholar at the Wharton School at the University of Pennsylvania and City University Business School, London. Professor Volberda obtained his doctorate *cum laude* in Business Administration at the University of Groningen. His research on organizational flexibility and strategic change received the NCD Award 1987, the ERASM Research Award 1994, the Erasmus University Research Award 1997, and the Igor Ansoff Strategic Management Award 1993. His work on strategic renewal, coevolution, and new organizational forms has been published in many refereed books and journals. Professor Volberda has worked as a consultant for many large European corporations. He is director of the Erasmus Strategic Renewal Centre (ESRC), program director of the Erasmus Institute of Management (ERIM), board member of the Rotterdam School of Management, and Advisor of Stroeve Stockbrokers. He is also editor-in-chief of *M&O* and *Management Select,* senior editor-in-chief of the *Journal of International Business Studies and Long Range Planning,* and member of the Editorial Board of *Organization Science, Accounting,* and

Maanblad voor Accountancy en Bedrijfseconomie (MAB). His book *Building the Flexible Firm: How to Remain Competitive* (1998) received wide acclaim. Recently, his new book together with Tom Elfring *Rethinking Strategy* appeared (2001).

Karl E. Weick is the Rensis Likert Distinguished University Professor of Organizational Behavior and Psychology at the University of Michigan. His current work is focused on wildland firefighter fatalities, the role of handoffs in medical errors, and distributed sensemaking in the diagnosis of anomalous infections. His books include *Managing the Unexpected* (2001, co-authored with Kathleen Sutcliffe), *Making Sense of the Organization* (2001), *Sensemaking in Organizations* (1995), and *The Social Psychology of Organizing* (2nd edn., 1979).

Hugh Willmott is Diageo Professor of Management Studies in the Judge Institute of Management at the University of Cambridge and a Visiting Professor at the Universities of Lund and Cranfield. He is currently working on a number of projects whose common theme is the changing organization and management of work. His books include *Critical Management Studies* (1992, co-edited), *Making Sense of Management: A Critical Introduction* (1996, co-authored), and *Management Lives* (1999, co-authored). He has served on the editorial boards of a number of journals including *Administrative Science Quarterly, Organization, Organization Studies* and *Accounting, Organizations and Society*. Further details can be found on his homepage: http://dspace.dial.pipex.com/town/close/hr22/hcwhome

Dvora Yanow (Ph.D., MIT, 1982) is Professor and Chair of the Department of Public Administration, California State University, Hayward (US). Her research is shaped by an overall interest in the communication of meaning in organizational and public policy settings. She has written on organizational learning from an interpretive-cultural perspective, the role of built space in communicating meaning, and public policies as collective identity stories, as well as on organizational metaphors, myths, and culture, and interpretive philosophies and research methods. She is the author of *How Does a Policy Mean? Interpreting Policy and Organizational Actions* (1996), *Conducting Interpretive Policy Analysis* (2000), and *Constructing 'Race and Ethnicity' in America: Category-making in Public Policy and Administration* (2002). Her articles have been published in such journals as *Administration & Society, Administrative Theory & Praxis*, the *Journal of Architectural and Planning Research*, the *Journal of Management Inquiry*, the *Journal of Public Administration Research and Theory, Organization, Organization Science*, and *Policy Sciences*, and *Political Research Quarterly*. Her editorial activities include four years as editor of one of the sections of the *Journal of Management Inquiry* and editorial board service for *Administrative Theory & Praxis*, the *American Review of Public Administration, Management Learning*, the *Journal of Public Affairs Education*, and *Qualitative Inquiry*. She is also a Contributing Editor for the quarterly *Judaism*, a pianist and violinist-fiddler, a folk dancer and singer, and gardener. email DYanow@csuhayward.edu

INTRODUCTION: THE NEED FOR META-THEORETICAL REFLECTION IN ORGANIZATION THEORY

HARIDIMOS TSOUKAS
CHRISTIAN KNUDSEN

WHY THIS HANDBOOK?

THIS handbook provides a forum for leading scholars in Organization Theory (OT) to engage in meta-theoretical reflection on the historical development, present state, and future prospects of OT. The central question that is explored is the following: *What is the status of OT as a social science discipline?* Notice that this is a *meta-theoretical* question: the object of analysis and debate in this volume is not a set of organizational phenomena, but OT itself. The book aims at reviewing and evaluating important epistemological developments in OT, especially issues related to the kinds of knowledge claims put forward in OT and the controversies surrounding the generation, validation, and utilization of such knowledge. Before we proceed, however, a few words of clarification are needed as to what is meant by 'Organization Theory'.

In this volume we have taken a sociological perspective on science, namely to view it as a historically situated activity, largely carried out in academic and research institutions, in which its practitioners are in the business of making knowledge claims about the phenomena they investigate (Whitley 2000). Those knowledge claims are subject to the assessment of their fellow practitioners, following certain methodological canons and conceptions of truth that prevail at a particular point in time. A science that is as practically oriented as OT is—that is, a science aiming at generating knowledge with the explicit aim that it be of direct utility to an identifiable body of practitioners—is a 'policy science' (Whitley 1984). Finally, instead of adopting the demarcation between Organization Behaviour and Organization Theory, widely encountered in North America—a demarcation that roughly corresponds to an exploration of micro and macro organizational phenomena, respectively—a broad notion of OT has been adopted in this handbook. Organization Theory is seen as the academic field specializing in the study of organizational phenomena (both micro and macro) and for this reason OT is used here as a synonym for Organization Studies. Although in some of the chapters included in this handbook there is a slant towards more macro phenomena, the term OT is intended here to be comprehensive in its coverage.

Although OT is a relatively new scientific field, in its sixty or so years of existence it has reflected most of the major trends and shifts that have emerged in the social sciences at large. All the major epistemological debates that have broken out in the social sciences have also been played out in OT (Burrell and Morgan 1979; Deetz 1996; Morgan 1983; Tsoukas 1994; Scherer and Steinmann 1999). The publication that undoubtedly, more than any other, kicked off serious epistemological debate in OT has been Burrell and Morgan's *Sociological Paradigms and Organizational Analysis*, published in 1979. Drawing on the most influential philosophical vocabularies of the time—notably, the Kuhnian notion of 'paradigm' and the notion of 'radical change' inspired by Marxism—Burrell and Morgan mapped out OT in terms of four paradigms. Other interesting attempts to provide an epistemological route map to the field has been the work of Astley and Van de Ven (1983), and Pfeffer (1982).

What is interesting to note from the early meta-theoretical attempts is their concern with creating typologies: they aimed at providing a map of the main theories of the field, teasing out their epistemological assumptions, rather than philosophically, historically, and sociologically scrutinizing key categories implicated in organizational research. Judged in their own terms, such attempts have been successful and furnished us with a helpful vocabulary in terms of which we may comprehend theoretical developments in the field. At the same time, it is interesting to note that some of the early controversies concerning, for example, qualitative vs. quantitative approaches (Morgan and Smircich 1980) have somewhat faded. It is now broadly accepted that each one of these approaches has its merits. Moreover, we do not seem to care very much about narrowly methodological controversies today, such as inductivism vs. deductivism, which exercised some organizational researchers in the past (Mintzberg 1979).

Other controversies, however, keep resurfacing from time to time. The notion of 'paradigm', for example, has not gone away, and how paradigms relate to one another, as well as the validity of the competing knowledge claims they help generate, have preoccupied several researchers until recently (Czarniawska 1998; Donaldson 1998; Jackson and Carter 1991; Kaghan and Phillips 1998; McKinley and Mone 1998; Scherer and Steinmann 1999; Scherer 1998; Willmott 1993). Similarly, the time-old questions surrounding the applicability of OT knowledge has resurfaced as a result of new philosophical developments in hermeneutics (such as the emergence of neo-Aristotelianism—see MacIntyre 1985; Toulmin 1990; Tsoukas and Cummings 1997), pragmatism (Wicks and Freeman 1998), critical theory and postmodern philosophy (Alvesson and Deetz 1996; Gergen and Thatchenkery 1998; Alvesson and Willmott 1992). Consequently, the very notion of 'practical reason' has undergone new definitions.

Meanwhile, new issues have cropped up, mainly as a result of fresh developments in the philosophy, sociology, and history of science. The critique of representationalism and the concomitant 'linguistic turn' in the philosophy of science have raised new questions about the very idea of 'knowledge', its modes of justification, and its relation to action (Rorty 1989, 1991; Tsoukas 1998). Recent developments in the philosophy of science make it possible to provide fresh insights into old controversies in OT, such as agency vs. structure, voluntarism vs. determinism, and micro vs. macro approaches, and help us refine our understanding of explanation. Similarly, recent research in the sociology and history of science enables us to understand now, better than before, the broader socio-cultural factors that are implicated in the production of OT knowledge (Knorr 1981; Latour and Woolgar 1986; Mirowski 1989; Pickering 1992). Questions regarding the role of gender, race, ethnicity, the state, and professional bodies in the production of OT knowledge, as well as the rhetorical function of OT discourse to persuade particular audiences, have come to the fore in a way that early meta-theoretical accounts had not quite anticipated (Czarniawska 1999; Guillen 1994; Martin 1990, 1994; Nkomo 1992; Shenhav 1999).

Contributors to the present handbook engage in meta-theoretical reflection on the epistemological status of OT by taking stock, on the one hand, of related debates in the past and, on the other hand, of new developments in OT and in the philosophy, sociology, and history of science. Five sets of questions are raised in the handbook, each one of which is addressed in a separate part:

(1) What is the status of OT as science? What counts as valid knowledge in OT and why? How do different paradigms view OT? (Part I)
(2) How has OT developed over time, and what structure has the field taken? What assumptions does knowledge produced in OT incorporate, and what forms do its knowledge claims take as they are put forward for public adoption? (Part II)
(3) How have certain well-known controversies in OT, such as for example, the structure/agency dilemma, the study of organizational culture, the different modes of explanation, the micro/macro controversy, and the different explanations produced by organizational economists and sociologists, been dealt with? (Part III)
(4) How, and in what ways, is knowledge generated in OT related to action and policy? What features must OT knowledge have in order to be actionable, and of relevance to the world 'out there'? How have ethical concerns been taken into account in OT? (Part IV)
(5) What is the future of OT? What direction should the field take? What must change in the way research is conceptualized and conducted so that OT enhances its capacity to generate valid and relevant knowledge? (Part V)

No doubt the above questions do not exhaust the list of meta-theoretical issues that could be explored in OT, although they are a good start. We are aware of certain omissions in the present handbook which, ideally, we would not have allowed. The question of race in OT, for example, is not covered, as is not the question of time. We would have liked to have included more material on organizational economics and psychology, on theory building, on comparative OT, and on the institutional influences on the formation of OT in different societies. We would have done more in an ideal world. Alas, as we will argue below, if knowledge production is viewed as a *practical activity*, it is never produced in ideal-world conditions; we had to cope with all the uncertainty and incompleteness that surrounds practical, real-world projects. We hope, however, that what is provided in this handbook is stimulating enough to contribute to our collective learning as organizational scholars and to pave the way for other similar books in the future.

WHAT IS TO BE GAINED FROM A META-THEORETICAL PERSPECTIVE ON OT?

Why should meta-theoretical reflection be necessary in OT? What is to be gained? At first glance, the number one problem in OT has been suggested to be the fragmentation of the field into so many, often unconnected, perspectives and paradigms. This is a problem, it has been alleged, for it makes the field less influential among policy makers; less capable of obtaining resources; it obstructs communication within the field; and, ultimately, it makes scientific progress difficult, if not impossible (Miner 1984; Pfeffer 1993; Webster and Starbuck 1988; Zammuto and Connolly 1984). OT, it has been alleged, appears to be close to becoming a tower of Babel (Burrell 1996: 644; Kaghan and Phillips 1998) and this cannot be good for anyone. Add to this concern the perennial anxiety regarding the extent to which a policy science such as OT is indeed relevant to practitioners (Abrahamson and Eisenman 2001; Lawler *et al.* 1999; Mowday 1997; Pettigrew 2001; Starkey and Madan 2001; Tranfield and Starkey 1998) and you have the making of a crisis of self-confidence: how good are we as a field to develop valid knowledge which is of relevance to practitioners?

The moment such questions are raised, meta-theoretical reflection (i.e. reflexivity) begins. What is valid knowledge and how is it to be generated? To whom exactly should it be made relevant? For what purpose? What does 'relevant' mean anyway, and how is 'relevant' knowledge best produced? How should competing knowledge claims be evaluated? Raising such questions implies taking a step back from ordinary theoretical activity to reflect on what the latter should be aiming at and how it ought to be conducted—it is for this reason that such reflection is called '*meta*-theoretical'. By raising those 'meta' questions the purpose is not to generate theory about particular organizational topics but to make the generation of theory itself an object of analysis (see Figure 0.1).

Notice, however, the paradox here, a paradox intrinsic to all acts of reflexivity. Ordinarily we go about doing our theoretical work (i.e. trying to make sense of a particular organizational phenomenon) without too much concern for what theory is and how it is best generated—as *practitioners* engaged in the generation of theoretical knowledge, we normally take such things for granted. The moment, however, we step back to inquire about theory—the moment, that is, we stop being practitioners and become, instead, *observers* of our theoretical practice (our research)—we are faced with questions which cannot be conclusively answered. Meta-theoretical questions have an air of undecidability about them and this explains the inconclusive arguments concerning paradigm incommensurability among organizational theorists.

The reason for this inconclusiveness—the reason, in other words, for not being able to arrive at a rational consensus concerning the validity claims of knowledge produced within different paradigms—is not only the intrinsically high degree of difficulty in answering such questions anyway, stemming in large measure from the ambiguity of, and the controversy surrounding, key concepts, but, principally, the abstract and de-contextualized manner in which such questions are raised. If, for example, we ask *in abstracto*, 'is organizational structure best explained by contingency or political models?' (see respectively Donaldson 1996; Pfeffer 1981), we will find it very difficult to demonstrate the superiority of one or the other position

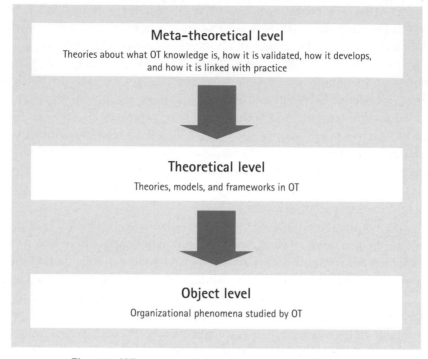

Fig. 0.1 What meta-theoretical reflection is about

(McKinley, Mone, and Moon 1999) (which is not to deny that some arguments in defense of one or the other position may be more *persuasive* than others). The reason is that, putting the question in purely abstract terms, assumes that all we need to do is to engage in a process of abstract reasoning in which we, as observers, scrutinize and compare different paradigmatic assumptions. When such assumptions widely differ, as they normally do, how are we to choose? We would need to step back and seek another set of paradigmatically neutral meta-assumptions that would enable us to adjudicate between the rival sets of assumptions we began with. But this would involve us in infinite regress: since no such set of meta-assumptions exists, we would need to step further back, and so on. This process of abstract reasoning is inconclusive, since there is no ultimate conceptual common ground upon which we may stand to make paradigmatic comparisons (MacIntyre 1985: ch. 2)—hence incommensurability (Burrell and Morgan 1979; Burrell 1996; Jackson and Carter 1991; Scherer and Steinmann 1999: 525; Tsoukas 1994).

As researchers we are both participants in the field and observers of our actions. Echoing Kierkegaard, Weick (2002) remarks that the way we live when we are engaged in our research practice is different from the way we live when we subsequently reflect on it. Acting in the world is necessarily somewhat opaque; we increase our awareness of what our acting has involved when we reflect *ex post facto* on the way we habitually act. Reflexivity enables us to detect the biases that creep into our research—biases which constitute likely threats to the validity of our knowledge claims—and hopefully try to overcome them next time we engage in research. As Weick (2002) remarks, 'We are reminded in no uncertain terms of the ways in which our culture, ideology, race, gender, class, language, advocacy, and assumed basis of authority limit, if not destroy, any claim our work has to validity in some interpretive community. These threats to validity are treated as objects that can be labeled, separated, differentiated, and treated as decisive flaws.'

It is the participant-observer duality that creates the paradox mentioned earlier: to carry out our theoretical work effectively we cannot afford to wonder too much about its key categories; but to improve it, to increase the validity of our knowledge claims, we need to reflect on what we do and how we do it. But the more we do so, the more we risk engaging in inconclusive meta-theoretical quandaries—we may end up infinitely regressing in search of some Archimedean original point. Reflexivity can easily turn into self-obsession and narcissism (Weick 2002). Indeed, most of the debate on incommensurability in OT could be seen in that light—an excessive preoccupation with our own practice rather than with the practice of those we study. It is perhaps for this reason that Weick makes a plea for 'disciplined reflexivity' (Weick 1999). Polanyi would certainly agree. 'Unbridled speculation' for him is detrimental to the effective carrying out of science (Polanyi 1962). But how should we view our work in OT so that we do justice to both its tacit component (the taken-for-granted assumptions which our research practice necessarily incorporates) and the possibility of meaningfully elucidating our research practice in order to reduce the likely threats to the validity of knowledge claims we make? We will explore this question in the next section.

ORGANIZATION THEORY AS A PRACTICAL SOCIAL ACTIVITY

Saying that the production of academic knowledge is a social activity is perhaps stating the obvious. The generation of knowledge involves both work and communicative interaction (Habermas 1972; Sayer 1992). By 'work' we mean the transformation of matter and/or symbols for human purposes. For an object of study to reveal itself to the researcher, it needs to be probed and such probing takes the form of several kinds of interventions (i.e. work), such as experiments, surveys, and/or fieldwork. By 'communicative interaction' we mean the sharing of meaning in a community of inquirers, typically through learning a particular scientific language and a set of procedures for thinking and arguing about the object of study (Sayer

1992: 17–22). Both work and communicative interaction are necessary and one cannot be reduced to the other, although in real life they are closely interwoven. Researchers act on their object of study through following a set of communication protocols, which they learn as members of a particular academic community.

The production of academic knowledge is a collective effort, embedded in historical time: to carry out his/her inquiry, a researcher draws on the conceptual resources and modes of thinking and arguing of a historically developed language community. Given that in OT the object of study is a *social* object, the relationship between the researcher and his/her object is also a social one (Weber 1993: 63). We do not stand in a social relationship to a tree or a planet, but we do so vis-à-vis an organization. The latter is a concept-dependent object; what it is depends on the particular self-interpretations and sets of meanings it incorporates. Unlike non-social objects, which are impervious to the meanings inquirers attach to them, social objects are socially defined—they are constituted by certain distinctions of worth marked in a conceptual space (Taylor 1985a, b). Since organizations are social objects of study they constitute language communities. There is a conceptual symmetry between a research community and a social object of study (see Figure 0.2), insofar as they are both constituted by language (Giddens 1993). As shown in Figure 0.2, developing new knowledge is a *practical* activity in which a researcher, drawing on the conceptual, symbolic, and material resources of his/her language community, attempts to account for what is going on in another language community by probing it in particular ways.

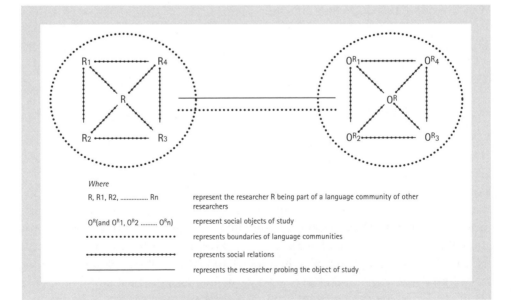

Fig. 0.2 Social research as a practical activity

Source: Adapted from Sayer, 1992: 27

Accepting that knowledge production is a practical social activity puts it on the same level with any other practical social activity: for work to be carried out effectively, a set of procedures, principles, and assumptions need to be internalized and unreflectively practiced—they need, in other words, to enter the pre-theoretical praxis, the lifeworld, of a community (Winogrand and Flores 1987; Scherer and Steinmann 1999: 527; Polanyi 1962; Tsoukas and Vladimirou 2001). Since research is a form of work, its practitioners have internalized a host of particulars (assumptions), of which they normally are not aware, while at work. Only when researchers reflexively raise the question of any likely threats to the validity of their knowledge claims, will they become aware of, and start scrutinizing, their assumptions, thus engaging in meta-theoretical reflection.

The point here is that, over time, OT practitioners will improve the validity of their knowledge claims by systematically thinking about the way they habitually think about their objects of study (Antonacopoulou and Tsoukas 2002). What sort of unreflective biases (what phenomenologists and interpretive philosophers call 'prejudgements', see Gadamer 1989) such as, for example, those concerning 'gender', 'race', and 'class', has OT research manifested over time? What are the historically contingent institutional arrangements and dominant societal and metaphysical understandings that have influenced research in a particular direction? What forms of explanation have dominated the field, and why? How have human agency and social structure—two time-old issues in social theory—been treated in OT? What modes of arguing and what rhetorical forms have been considered appropriate? What notions of 'practicality' and 'usefulness' have been put forward or implied in OT? How have normative principles of ethics been considered in relation to the descriptive-explanatory knowledge produced in OT? Most of these questions are explored in the current handbook.

HOW SHOULD WE MAKE SENSE OF THE DEVELOPMENT OF ORGANIZATION THEORY?

Notice that while it is important that the preceding questions are articulated and discussed, since by doing so we become more aware of the taken-for-granted assumptions we have unreflectively followed, the conceptual dilemmas they engender cannot be settled *in abstracto*. To the extent, however, we have become convinced of the importance of certain issues, hitherto underestimated—for example, of the boundedness of rationality; the conflict-ridden nature of organizations; the cultural context of organizing, etc.—we cannot go on pretending as if we did not know. Over time, our new awareness enters our pre-theoretical (tacit) stock of knowledge—it joins the internalized assumptions we take for granted. Put in those terms, it is possible to picture OT as a field which has been becoming ever more complex in its assumptions and investigations over time. As March and Olsen (1986: 28) have remarked with reference to organizational decision-making, 'theories of limited rationality relaxed the assumptions about cognitive capacities and knowledge. Theories of conflict relaxed the assumptions about the unity of objectives. Theories of ambiguity and temporal order relax the assumptions about the clarity of objectives and causality, as well as the centrality of decisions to the process of decision-making.'

The movement from initially rigid and limited assumptions to ever more realistic and complex assumptions has been one of the most encouraging features of the field. While, initially, organizations were viewed as rationally designed systems, it is now accepted that organizations are historically constituted social collectivities, embedded in their environments (Scott 1987). From this realization, now more or less taken for granted, stem most new investigations, such as those exploring the social embeddedness of organizations (Granovetter 1992; Granovetter and Swedberg 1992; Scott and Christensen 1995; Scott *et al.* 1994; Whitley 1992); the profoundly cultural aspects of organizations (Kunda 1992; Frost *et al.* 1991); the social construction of organizational identity (Brown 1997; Whetten and Godfrey 1998); the irreducibly emergent texture of organizing (Stacey, Griffin, and Shaw 2000; Taylor and Van Every 2000; Weick and Roberts 1993); the importance of history in accounting for aspects of organizations (Dobbin 1995; Kieser 1998; Roe 1994; Zald 1996); the processes through which sensemaking in organizations takes place (Weick 2001); the centrality of learning and knowledge to organizational functioning (Cohen and Sproull 1996; Grant 1996; Spender 1996; Tsoukas 1996); the importance of power and the significance of gender in organizational life (Calás and Smircich 1996; Gherardi 1995; Martin 1990); and the influence of unconscious processes and psychic needs on organizational functioning (Gabriel 1999).

What all these admittedly diverse perspectives have in common is the assumption about the profoundly social, historically shaped, and context-cum-time-dependent nature of organizing, which they approach from different angles, focusing on different levels of analysis. In other words, in the early steps of the field, individuals and organizational environments were 'given' to organizations, with the latter being seen, in quasi-algorithmic terms, as 'abstract systems' (Barnard 1968: 74) geared towards the optimization of certain key variables (typically the maximization of performance, the minimization of uncertainty or transaction costs) (Donaldson 2001; Thompson 1967; Williamson 1998). Following the 'Newtonian style' of analysis (Cohen 1994: 76; Toulmin 1990), organization theorists were supposed to uncover the calculus of organization. As Barnard (1976: p. xlvi) revealingly put it, 'abstract principles of structure may be discerned in organizations of great variety, and that ultimately it may be possible to state principles of general organization' (see also Thompson 1956/57). In other words, if the contingent, historical, time-dependent, contextual influences on organizations were somehow to be discarded, the essence of organizations, their invariant properties across space and time, would be revealed.

Over time, however, the limits of such an analysis became apparent. If nothing else, the Newtonian style of inquiry hardly illuminated what common experience told practitioners was important: organizations vary widely across time and space; history matters; extra-organizational institutions matter too; gender, race, and ethnicity are hot issues at the workplace; there are multiple rationalities in an organization; sensemaking is an important part of action; decision-making and strategy-making do not quite happen as formal theories prescribe. It is precisely the divergence between OT knowledge produced by following the Newtonian style and the common experience of practitioners that accounts, to a large extent, for the perception some practitioners have that OT is 'irrelevant' to their practice (Argyris 1980; Pfeffer 1993; Mowday 1997; Lawler *et al.* 1999; Webster and Starbuck 1988; cf. Nowotny, Scott, and Gibbons 2001). Indeed, one of the challenges for OT is to find ways in which practitioners' lived experiences may be incorporated, rather than ignored as 'unscientific', into OT accounts. This is where the 'ecological' style of analysis (to use Toulmin's (1990: 193—4) apt term) comes in.

Gradually, individuals and environments have been 'brought into' organizational analysis, and a whole new set of questions has opened up: how do individuals make sense of their tasks, with what consequences? What exactly do people do when they work in organizations? What makes a group of people working together an organization? How do organizational members sustain a sense of community? How do gender and ethnicity influence organizational politics? How are organizational objectives and policies set, by whom, with what consequences? How does the environment, as it changes over time, influence what is going on in organizations? What is the impact of history on key organizational features? Such questions purport to explain organizations in a *substantive* way by embracing the complexity of the issues involved, rather than abstracting them away for the sake of analytical rigor.

Viewing research as a practical social activity makes us see more clearly than before that researchers rarely are idealistic paradigm warriors but, more realistically, while they certainly do have certain paradigmatic predilections, they remain open to borrowing from other paradigms and perspectives as they see fit and are subjected to normative institutional criteria regarding the evaluation of their work. In other words, in order to get their work done, researchers are, to some extent, *bricoleurs* (Brown and Duguid 1991): they purposefully work with whatever conceptual resources are available. Their work is shaped by their own paradigmatic preferences, the prevailing *zeitgeist*, and the institutional frameworks and norms within which their work takes place. Insofar as we *work* with others within certain institutional and cultural contexts, our work rarely adheres to idealized paradigms.

Sometimes paradigms are erroneously given an anthropomorphic status, which obscures the obvious fact that it is not paradigms that do the research, but researchers. It is not paradigms which 'cannot speak unto each other', for example, as Burrell (1996: 648) asserts, for paradigms have no voice. It is researchers engaged in practical work, interacting with other researchers, who influence and are influenced by others in what they do and, to the extent this happens, there is a certain inevitable osmosis between paradigms. Child, for example, one of the most important contributors to the contingency theory of organizational structure, has revised his views to formulate a strategic-choice perspective, which gave a more prominent role to managers as agents exercising choice within certain contexts than contingency theory would allow for (Child 1997). Similarly, in his four desiderata for a 'dynamic theory of strategy' Porter (1991) has shown an appreciation for the limits of an industrial economics approach to the firm, arguing for the need for theories of strategic management to take into account, among other things, endogenous change, creative action, and historical accident and chance. Finally, responding to the ascendance of interpretive OT in the 1970s and 1980s, in which meaning and human agency are strongly highlighted, positivist accounts have expanded their scope to include aspects of agency and meaning, such as cognition and culture, into their agenda (Tenbrunsel *et al.* 1996).

This should not be surprising. Insofar as interaction and dialogue goes on among researchers, new syntheses are likely to come up. We learn more about new research agendas and cross-paradigmatic exchange by looking at what OT practitioners *do* rather than by hypostastizing paradigms and then getting ourselves caught into conceptual traps regarding paradigmatic 'incommensurability'. Paradigms appear incommensurable only to an observer who, seeking *in abstracto* a neutral set of 'translation rules', cannot find any and proclaims that, well, there aren't any (Burrell 1996: 650). Instead, paradigms do provide challenges for thinking and learning to anyone engaged in research *in concreto*.

For example, reflecting on his own work, Deetz (1996: 200) remarks as follows:

I often draw on conceptions from critical and dialogic writings. For me, critical theory conceptions of ideology and distorted communication provide useful *sensitizing* concepts and an analytic framework for looking for micro-practices of control, discursive closure, conflict suppression, and skewed representation in organizational sites. But rarely are these conceptions closely tied to the full critical theory agenda. They require considerable *reworking* in specific sites, and the results of my studies aim more at finding and giving suppressed positions a means of expression than realizing an ideal speech situation or reaching a purer consensus. What is important is not whether I am a late-modern critical theorist or a dialogic post-modernist, but rather the meaning and implications of concepts that I draw from these two competitive orientations. My degree of consistency is of less interest than how I handle the tension and whether the two conceptual resources provide an interesting analysis or intervention. (references omitted; emphasis added)

In this passage Deetz draws attention to the fact that a researcher may have multiple paradigmatic sympathies and, at any rate, subscribing to a paradigm means that one is more likely to be inspired and sensitized by it, than to be buying wholesale into it. It is surprising how often it is forgotten that paradigms are our own constructions—artifacts we have invented *ex post facto* to make sense of competing sets of assumptions social scientists habitually make—and, as such, they are somewhat idealized descriptions. When we engage in research we do not necessarily buy into an entire paradigm; more realistically, we are oriented by it to explore particular kinds of questions. Moreover, the effective carrying out of research into particular topics of interest entails the 'reworking' of key paradigmatic assumptions *in concreto* ('in specific sites') and this reworking may well bring about new concepts and syntheses (Moldoveanu and Baum 2002).

Like any other kind of work, empirical research is not a matter of mere 'application' of a given set of paradigmatic assumptions, but of active determination of those assumptions *in practice* (cf. Boden 1994: 19). Researchers do not so much 'apply' or 'follow' paradigms in their work as they explore particular topics, in particular sites and, having to cope coherently with all the puzzles and tensions stemming from the complexity of the phenomena they investigate, they extend, synthesize, and/or invent concepts (cf. Rorty 1991: 93–110). Paradigmatic exchange occurs before our nose, but we do not recognize it as such until well after such exchange has led to new concepts and conceptual syntheses. Certain insights from Silverman's (1971) interpretive critique of positivist OT in the 1970s and Weick's (1979) phenomenological model of organizing have been 'translated' into other research traditions and have led to interesting developments in, for example, the institutional school of OT and the cognitive perspective on organizations. Conceptual translation 'on the ground' inevitably takes place, all the time, and this is what makes intellectual developments so potentially interesting.

WHAT IS OT KNOWLEDGE FOR?

Figure 0.2 shows the double relationship that exists between a researcher and an object of study. The researcher probes the object (the solid line in Figure 0.2) and, at the same time, he/she is involved in a social relationship with it (the dotted-cum-solid line). What Figure 0.2 is not showing is that these two relationships occur in *time*. Probing an object of study means using systems of representation, such as vocabularies and conceptual frameworks, and certain research techniques and modes of thinking, such as ideal-type models, *ceteris paribus* clauses, surveys, experiments, and fieldwork, whereby the salient features of an object of study may be revealed and explained (Searle 1995: 151).

Acts of probing are acts of construction: they *bring forth* aspects of the object under investigation. There are several vocabularies, conceptual frameworks, and modes of thinking to be used, and which ones are chosen is bound, to some extent, to depend on contingent institutional arrangements, the material and symbolic resources available, and the historical and cultural context. While an object of study is often independent of the researcher and his/her vocabulary, the moment it is framed in a particular language it acquires a *contingent* existence—systems of representation contain particular distinctions of worth, they are loaded with particular values, and approach the study object from only certain angles. In that sense, theories in OT, and in the social sciences in general, are *generative* of meaning (Gergen 1994: ch.3): they provide practitioners with certain symbolic resources for making sense of their situation.

Moreover, systems of representation incorporate certain assumptions concerning how they are related to their objects and to the users of the knowledge produced, and locate their object within a wider social and political vision (Heilbroner and Milberg 1995). For example, a positivist epistemology assumes that the language of the researcher more clearly represents than lay language what is really going on in an object of study (cf. Deetz 1996: 196; McKelvey 1997). Moreover, the knowledge produced by a positivist epistemology is thought to be external to its users, by whom it is instrumentally used in order to optimize a particular performance variable, and is devoid of any intrinsic ethical commitments (cf. Tsoukas and Cummings 1997). To be precise, ethics enters the scene in the way knowledge is *used* rather than in the manner and the form it is produced. A positivist epistemology aims at enhancing the effectiveness of formal organizations in the context of a rationalized society (Burrell 1996; Marsden and Townley 1996; Reed 1996). It is that distinctly modern socio-political vision that animates positivist work in OT. Moreover, each paradigm in OT has its own particular assumptions about these matters.

The social relationship between the OT research community and its object of study implies that knowledge produced is fed back to its users, altering their beliefs and understandings. This is profoundly important for two reasons. First, because it shows that practitioners may change their behavior in a non-instrumental manner: simply by changing the vocabulary in terms of which they think of themselves and of what they do, they may alter their practice. Think, for example, how the notions of 'Total Quality Management', 'Business Process Reengineering', 'organizational competences', 'strategic learning', and 'chaos', as well as the rhetoric of 'business excellence', have influenced how practitioners view organizations and their role in them (Abrahamson and Fairchild 1999). In this sense academic knowledge is profoundly political and rhetorical (Astley 1985; Astley and Zammuto 1992; Czarniawska 1999). As van Maanen (1995: 135) remarks, 'the discourse we produce as organization theory has an action component which seeks to induce belief among our readers. Our writing is then something of a performance with a persuasive aim. In this sense, when our theories are well received they do practical work. Rather than mirror reality, our theories help generate reality for readers.'

Secondly, an intrinsic relationship between theory and action implies that any regularities organization theorists uncover are bound to be perishable, since, as soon as they are announced to practitioners, the latter will probably modify their beliefs and expectations, thus altering those very regularities (Bhaskar 1978; Tsoukas 1992). As Numagami (1998: 10) has persuasively shown in his game-theoretical models of OT knowledge dissemination, provided we accept that practitioners are reflective agents, the search for invariant laws in OT is futile in most cases (the only exception is when a game with a dominant strategy can be established). This is far from denying the presence of observable regularities, but to merely point out that such regularities do not rest upon invariant social laws, but upon the stability of the beliefs and expectations of the actors involved.

Numagami (1998: 10) has put it convincingly as follows:

What we must not forget, however, is that stable macro patterns in social phenomena are stable not because they are supported by inhuman forces, but because they are reproduced by human conduct. Most observable stability and universality are not generated by invariant and universal laws, but are supported by the stability of knowledge and beliefs shared steadily and universally.... If practitioners and researchers are able to predict the future course of events, it may not be because they know any invariant laws but because they have a good understanding of what the agents involved would expect in a specific situation and excellent skills in synthesizing the actions, and/or because they are powerful enough to redefine the original situation into a game structure that has a dominant equilibrium. That is, for a person to predict the future course of events, he or she should at least have either knowledge or power.

If the search for invariant laws in OT is futile, what should OT be aiming at? It should be aiming at generating 'reflective dialogue', says Numagami (1998: 11–12) (see also Flyvbjerg 2001; Gergen and Thatchenkery 1998; Tsoukas and Knudsen 2002). Espousing a hermeneutical model of knowledge, Numagami points out that OT knowledge should aim at producing explanations (re-descriptions) of organizational phenomena which must include references to actors' meanings and conceptual schemata, for it is only then that we as researchers understand what generates the regularities we have noticed. Moreover, such explanations will be, in principle, useful to practitioners, since they invite them to engage in 'sympathetic emulation' (p. 11) of the situation described in the explanandum, thus stimulating their thinking. In other words, a hermeneutical model of knowledge does not pretend to be able to offer practitioners universal generalizations and invariant laws, since such knowledge is logically impossible to be attained. It does, however, empower practitioners by enabling them to make links with and reflect on others' experiences (i.e. the explananda organizational theorists re-describe), thus leading practitioners to undertake potentially novel forms of action. By re-entering the world of practitioners hermeneutically, OT knowledge may connect with practitioners' concrete experiences, thus inviting them to reflect on their circumstances in novel ways (Tsoukas and Knudsen 2002: 432). Hermeneutically conceived, OT knowledge does not tell practitioners how things universally are, but how they locally become.

A Review of the Handbook

Part I ('Organization Theory as Science') includes four chapters, each one of which approaches OT from a different paradigmatic angle. The overarching question underlying Part I is this: how do different paradigms view OT as a science? Or, to put it differently, what is considered as valid knowledge from the perspective of each paradigm?

In Chapter 1 ('Organization Theory as a Positive Science'), Lex Donaldson offers a robust and lucid defense of a positivist OT. Continuing his long-standing defense of positivism, Donaldson summarizes the main tenets of positivism in general, and in OT in particular, to highlight the links between positivism and functionalism (with the latter considered as a sub-species of the former). Moreover, Donaldson critically considers some of the philosophical objections to positivism, which he dismisses, and offers some thoughts on the future of positivist OT.

Chapter 1 is a model of expositional clarity. For Donaldson, a positivist OT is a naturalist science: it ought to be concerned with the generation of causal theories, as far general in scope as possible, aiming at neutrally explaining social facts via other social facts, thus circumventing any reference to actors' subjective states of mind. This is possible, he argues, echoing Durkheim and Blau, since organizational actors are constrained by 'situational imperatives': in any situation actors eventually choose the structure that fits that situation, given the performance requirement for organizational efficiency. It is not that actors do not have subjective states of mind, but that these are explanatorily redundant—eventually the situational imperative tends to prevail, no matter what individuals think or feel. Explaining 'social facts' (e.g. organizational structure) by other 'social facts' (e.g. organizational size) enables researchers to avoid the perils of reductionism, namely the research strategy whereby organizational phenomena are explained by the individuals who participate in them. This is not a reliable strategy, argues Donaldson, because individual motivational states of mind as well as individual political self-interests tend to be private, opaque, and usually inaccessible to outside observers. For him, the best kind of positivist OT that succeeds in explanatorily getting rid of the 'individual' is functionalism—the explanation of structure in terms of its beneficial consequences for the survival of the organization—whose benefits he illustrates by drawing on relevant empirical research in OT (see Scherer in this volume for a discussion of the different modes of explanation in OT).

What Donaldson denies, namely the subjective states of mind, Mary Jo Hatch and Dvora Yanow, openly embrace. In Chapter 2 ('Organization Theory as an Interpretive Science'), they set out the main tenets of an interpretive approach to OT. The contrast between Donaldson's account and that of Hatch and Yanow, could not have been clearer. There are no 'social facts', they say, if by that we mean sense data of the same kind as in the natural sciences. What sets the social world apart is *meaning*, hence the prime epistemic task of the social sciences is *understanding*. If one accepts this, one ought to take the next logical step and acknowledge that it is not only social phenomena that embody meaning, but that particular approaches to social phenomena—styles or modes of inquiry—embody meaning too; social scientific knowledge is crucially framed (or mediated) by the self-understandings of communities of inquirers. It is for this reason that Hatch and Yanow talk about the significance of 'apriori knowledge' (value systems, national culture, education systems, professional codes, state policies, etc), that shapes what one apprehends, and point out the situated and socially constructed character of all human know-ledge (on this, see the papers by Starbuck, Shenhav, and Gherardi, in this volume). Incidentally, notice the difference between Donadson and Hatch and Yanow in the way they use the term 'situated': for Donaldson it indicates an objective state that cannot be ignored; for Hatch and Yanow it indicates locality, contingency, and Heideggerian 'thrownness' (on the latter, see Weick's chapter in this volume). Discussing how meanings maybe studied, the authors point out that meaning is embedded in (or projected onto) artifacts by their creators; thus meaning can be inferred indirectly by studying those artifacts. Moreover, the hallmark of the interpretive paradigm is to treat social reality as a text, whose meaning needs to be deciphered. The textual metaphor and, by extension, the central role of language in constructing and communicating meaning, is the most distinguishing feature of the interpretive paradigm.

According to Hatch and Yanow, interpretive approaches to organizational phenomena have developed since the 1970s. The authors single out three overlapping areas of interpretive organizational research: studies of organizational culture, symbolism and aesthetics; process-based theorizing about interpretation; and analyses of writing and storytelling in 'narrating' organizational studies. That organizational culture, symbolism, and aesthetics would be a central part in the agenda of interpretive OT seems pretty obvious—this is, par excellence, the phenomena interpretive organization theorists would be interested in. Process-based theorizing derives from the crucial role assigned to meaning-making in interpretive OT. If meaning is so important, and since it is people who make meaning, then *how* they do so is an important object of study. Hence the double interest in meaning-making both as the process through which organizational members make sense of reality and, recursively, in how organization theorists make sense of the reality organizational members make sense. This helps explain the third area of interpretive research, namely the focus on storytelling and narration. From an interest in the symbolic-cultural dimension of organizations, interpretive OT research has moved on to embrace more literary approaches, focusing on storytelling in organizations, both in terms of content (the stories themselves) and the process (the performance of telling stories). Moreover, an interest in storytelling invites reflection on how the author relates his/her knowledge to the reader—how the author constructs his/her own storytelling—which, in turn, implies an interest in reflexive theorizing and the rhetorical character of social scientific writing (on the latter, see Czarniawska's chapter in this volume).

Neither positivism nor interpretivism are good enough, argues Hugh Willmott, since none of them deals with the power relationships within which knowledge and forms of understanding develop. In Chapter 3 ('Organization Theory as a Critical Science?: Forms of Analysis and "New Organizational Forms"') Willmott describes what are the distinctive features of a 'critical OT'. The adjective 'critical' has been used in all sorts of ways in the social sciences and philosophy, ranging from Popper's 'critical rationalism', through Bhaskar's 'critical realism', to the 'critique' employed by neo-Marxist students of the labour process. Willmott, however, uses the term in a particular way drawing on 'critical theory' developed by the German philosophers of the Frankfurt School, especially Jürgen Habermas.

The problem with positivism, argues Willmott, is that it lacks an appreciation of the conditions within which knowledge is produced: rather than scientific knowledge mirroring objectively and value-neutrally the world, it is inescapably produced, transmitted, and legitimized within power-laden contexts. There is no value-free knowledge, because there are no value-free social contexts of knowledge production and transmission. While interpretivism is right in highlighting the importance of meanings embedded in artifacts, practices, and institutions, it fails, according to Willmott, to deal with the power relationships within which forms of understanding are developed and, thus, in unmasking 'unnecessary oppression'.

Drawing on Habermas's theory of cognitive interests, Willmott describes knowledge production as being driven by three cognitive interests: a technical interest in production and control (the main concern of positivism); a practical interest in mutual understanding (the chief preoccupation of interpretivism); and an interest in emancipation (the focus of critical social science). Of course, human action involves the mobilization of all cognitive interests. However, each type of interest generates a different kind of knowledge, whose form and consequences Willmott very informatively surveys in OT, illustrating his arguments with relevant organizational examples, drawn especially from the literature on new organizational forms. The technical and practical interests are understood to arise by the human capacity to act intentionally towards the world (natural and social alike). In contrast, the emancipatory interest is conceived to be stimulated by the consequences flowing from the actions generated by the other two cognitive interests. The emancipatory interest seeks to unmask 'unnecessary structures of domination' and to subject social practices and institutions (Donaldson's 'situational imperatives') to critical reason in order to expose unequal power relationships, with the view to changing them. Although Willmott does not explicitly say so, it is interesting to note that, from a critical perspective, neither positivism nor interpretivism are rejected as such, since they both help generate knowledge which is 'transcendentally' necessary—that is, knowledge that stems from the intrinsically human desire to, respectively, control and understand nature and society. But if this is so, it is not immediately apparent whether the emancipatory interest is merely a logical complement in the Habermasian typology of knowledge, or whether it seeks to subvert, replace, or merely modify the technical and practical types of knowledge. Whatever the answer may be, it is the case that the critical perspective does sharpen our awareness of the social conditions within which both formal OT knowledge and organizational members' understandings are formed, and invites us to reflect on possible alternatives.

In Chapter 4 ('Organization Theory as a Postmodern Science'), Robert Chia offers a refreshing view of what OT should be concerned with, if it were to adopt a postmodern perspective. Keen to avoid the charges of cynicism and nihilism, often thrown at postmodern theorists, Chia insightfully shows how a postmodern OT helps us see more clearly the roots of western metaphysics upon which OT has historically been predicated so that, by reworking them, we can get a better understanding of both organization and OT. Modern thought, argues Chia, has historically privileged form over process, being over becoming, stability over change, identity over deferral. Postmodern thought, by contrast, seeks to rehabilitate the second term of these pairs. OT has historically followed a representationalist epistemology, whereby reality is sought to be adequately captured and symbolically represented through the use of abstract categories, concepts, and schemas. Such an epistemology entails the breaking down, fixing, locating, and naming of all experienced phenomena, and privileges the abstract over the concrete, the general over the particular, and the timeless over the timely.

A postmodern OT does not get fixated on organizations as distinct, bounded entities, but is determined to show, more broadly, how the process of organizing is enacted. Organizing is a world-making activity, argues Chia, in the sense that it involves the regularization of human exchanges and the development of predictable patterns of interactions. Through the process of organization—'the will to order'— objects of knowledge acquire distinctive identities and are located in systems of representations, thus enabling us to treat them as entities existing independently of our perceptions. Consequently, a postmodern OT should be concerned with how systems of representation are produced and causality is imputed; how the flux and variability of social life are tamed; how systems of signification are used to carve up reality with what consequences; how individual identities are established and social entities created; the effects of tacit and often unpresentable forms of knowledge; how stability is generated out of endless change. What, in other words, is so distinctive of postmodern OT is the second-order concern with how we know and order (the two are intimately linked).

It is worth noting that Chia's 'post'-modern OT is to some extent a recovery of 'pre'-modern ways of thinking. A Heraclitean at heart, Chia is at pains to show that a postmodern OT ought to concern itself with broader and more fundamental questions—how form, stability, and identity are constructed; how order is achieved; and how what we accept as reality is an outcome of an essentially organizational process of fixing, differentiating, classifying, locating, and representing.

Part II ('The Construction of Organization Theory') includes five chapters that present very different perspectives on the evolution of OT. In doing so Part II reflects the gradual convergence that has taken place between philosophy of science and history of science, following the publication of Thomas Kuhn's (Kuhn 1962) influential book on *The Structure of Scientific Revolutions* in 1962. This convergence has later been followed up by a renewed interest in areas such as the sociology of science and the rhetoric of science, when studying the evolution of a field.

In Chapter 5 ('The Origins of Organization Theory'), William Starbuck attempts to set up a broad understanding of the external conditions that made it possible for OT to become an intellectual field. He starts his account of OT by noting that theoretical writings about management have existed for more than 4,000 years and that writings about bureaucratic organizations have existed for more than 3,000 years. He then argues that the essential educational, occupational, and techno-logical conditions for the existence of large-scale organizations and OT gradually escalated through the sixteenth to the nineteenth century, and then accelerated rapidly after 1850. It was also during this timeframe that the term 'organization' first came to be used to name social systems that possess some degree of 'organization' and that organizations obtained legal status as corporate persons distinct from the persons working in them.

Starbuck proceeds to a discussion of how OT has taken roots in a mechanistic tradition and how the early writers in OT converged on two major themes: (a) bureaucracy has defects, and (b) organizations can operate more effectively. During the late 1940s and early 1950s the first of these themes, which was mainly of a sociological nature, merged with the second more managerial theme. At about the same time, writers in OT started to refer to the empirical basis of their theories. For Starbuck this marked the birth of OT as an intellectual field.

While Starbuck's chapter gives the grand view of how theorizing about organiza-tions emerged in the western world, Shenhav's contribution in Chapter 6 ('The Historical and Epistemological Foundations of Organization Theory: Fusing Sociological Theory with Engineering Discourse') focuses on an explanation of how OT was institutionalized as a separate scientific field in the United States. In his influential book *Organizations: Rational, Natural and Open Systems*, Scott (1987) argued that OT emerged as a scientific field in the mid-1940s, shortly after the translation of Weber's work in English. A few years later, some of Robert Merton's students were involved in the development and testing of generalizations dealing with organizations as separate social systems, and earlier contributions by Taylor, Barnard, and Mayo were rediscovered by the emerging academic community. It was these efforts that, according to Scott, gave rise to the identification of OT as a separate intellectual field of study.

It is this genealogy of OT that Shenhav sets out to criticize and replace with an alternative genealogy. First, he argues that OT as a scientific field emerged earlier than postulated by Scott, since a comprehensive engineering/managerial discourse about organizations existed much earlier. Second, Shenhav argues that Weber's work was not only translated, but also accommodated into the American engineering and managerial discourses to fit their language and epistemology. According to Shenhav, such a historical account gives a much more adequate understanding of how the engineering and the sociological discourses merged, creating the embryo of what we consider as OT today.

In Chapter 7 ('Feminist Theory and Organization Theory: A Dialogue on New Bases') Silvia Gherardi usefully identifies the different ways that feminist theory and OT have interacted and enriched each other since 1970. Gherardi starts by identifying different feminist approaches, drawing on the work of Calás and Smircich (1996): liberal theory, radical theory, psychoanalytic theory, Marxist theory, social theory, poststructuralist/postmodern theory, and third world/post-colonial theory. With reference to each theory, Gherardi shows how they represent the relation between gender and organization. Based upon this analysis she then argues that Feminist Theory and OT may converge on a research program that centers on the politics of knowledge.

While Chapters 5 and 6 approach OT from the perspective of sociology of science, in Chapter 8 ('The Styles and the Stylists of Organization Theory'), Barbara Czarniawska insightfully analyzes the field from a rhetorical point of view. Such a perspective in the study of intellectual fields became popular during the 1980s, mainly after the publication of McCloskey's (1985) influential book *The Rhetoric of Economics*. Among the different styles that Czarniawska identifies in OT, is the 'scientistic style' used by Thompson (1967), the 'poetic style' used by Weick (1979), the 'revolutionary style' used by Burrell (1997), the 'philosophical style' used by March (1988), the 'educational style' employed by Silverman (1971) and, finally, the 'ethnographic style' exemplified by Van Maanen (1988). Having identified different styles in OT, Czarniawska discusses the following questions. Can a specific style be imitated? What implications do the different styles have for OT? How does a style influence how outsiders view a field like OT? And how can a stylist provide justifications for how to imitate a specific style?

Whereas Chapters 5 and 6 focus mainly on the making of OT as a distinct intellectual field, in Chapter 9 ('Pluralism, Scientific Progress, and the Structure of Organization Theory') Christian Knudsen is oriented more toward the explanation of OT after its establishment as a relatively autonomous intellectual field. Knudsen takes his point of departure in Whitley's (2000) comparative analysis of how intellectual fields are structured as reputational organizations. He then argues that OT has moved away from a bureaucratic structure during the hegemony of the structural contingency research program in the 1960s and 1970s to a polycentric oligarchy in the 1980s, due to the emergence of several new research programs. Besides the structural contingency program, these new programs include programs such as population ecology, institutional theory, resource-dependency theory, and transaction cost economics. The emergence of these new theoretical alternatives, which in some cases have their own distinct empirical methodologies, have increased what Whitley (2000) calls the 'task' and 'strategic uncertainty' in the field of OT. Knudsen argues that, during the 1990s, the developments toward more uncertainty have continued in European OT and that the polycentric form has been replaced with a fragmented adhocracy while the polycentric oligarchy has stabilized in American OT.

Knudsen suggests that Whitley's static framework of how different fields are organized should be extended in order to be able to analyze how different structures of a reputational organization either restricts or promotes scientific progress. Inspired by the organizational learning literature, Knudsen argues that intellectual fields (like other kinds of organizations) need to find a reasonable balance between innovation and tradition, or avoid falling into either a 'fragmentation trap' or a 'specialization tap'. Finally, he argues that the structure that is best suited to uphold a balance between innovation and tradition and, therefore, to avoid the fragmentation and specialization traps is the polycentric oligarchy.

Part III consists of five chapters, each one of which addresses a different meta-theoretical controversy in OT. In Chapter 10 ('The Agency/Structure Dilemma in Organization Theory: Open Doors and Brick Walls') Mike Reed discusses one of the oldest meta-theoretical questions in social and organization theory: how are agency and structure related? Organizations are commonly thought of as structures, while agency is increasingly recognized as being extremely important for accounting for creative organizational action. At a time in which innovation and creativity are highly valued as key features of effective organizations, clearly agency acquires renewed significance. But how is agency exercised? What are the conditions within which it is realized and how much, if at all, is it influenced by structure? Or, to put it differently, to what extent, and in what ways, is structure influenceable and changeable by actors?

Reed offers a comprehensive review of the relevant literature by distinguishing three schools of thought (reductionism, determinism, conflationism), which he critiques as problematic, while offering a fourth (relationism), which he recommends as being better able to account for the relation between structure and agency. Reductionism, argues Reed, tends to reduce structure to agency: collective entities, such as organizations, are typically thought of as aggregations of individual constituents. Determinism exaggerates the importance of structure, which is assumed to dictate to agency. Conflationism rejects the analytical dualism of both reductionism and determinism, and insists on the mutual and equal co-determination of agency and structure. This is not the right solution to the structure/agency dilemma, argues Reed, since by assigning to structure a 'virtual existence', it denies it of causal influence. By contrast, relationism, does pay attention to the causal efficacy of objective structures and to the creative role of human agency. The capacity for human agency is grounded in relatively enduring social structures and relations that unavoidably constrain human action. Both agency and structure possess independent causal properties that can exert a strong influence on organizational life. Although Reed does recognize both the danger inherent in relationism—principally, the possibility of reverting to some form of determinism—and the difficulty in achieving consensus on any particular conception of the structure/agency relationship, he does rightly emphasize the need to be clear and consistent in our meta-theoretical choices, and mindful of their theoretical and social consequences.

In Chapter 11 ('Modes of Explanation in Organization Theory') Andreas Georg Scherer offers an informative review of the different modes of explanation encountered in OT. Starting with the acknowledgement that it is important that organization theorists reflect on their research practice in the same way that they reflect on the practices of the organizations they study, Scherer lucidly describes six modes of explanation: the deductive-nomological (DN) model, interpretivism, critical theory, postmodernism, functionalism, and rational choice theory (RCT). In a nutshell, the DN model seeks to apply to the study of organizational phenomena the same epistemological principles applied in the natural sciences; interpretivism, critical theory, and postmodernism reject this, arguing instead for the irreducibility of actors's meanings, which ought to be incorporated in the explanations produced. These perspectives, however, differ from one another in important respects: critical theorists argue that merely attaining mutual understanding is not enough but, instead, normative critique must be included in social scientific accounts, while postmodernists are not so much preoccupied with explanation per se as with revealing and defending the 'local truths' that are normally suppressed by meta-narratives and 'consensual' institutional arrangements. Finally, functionalism and RCT address the relationship between individual behavior and social institutions, providing widely different templates for explanation. While for functionalists there are only objective 'social facts' to be explained by other 'social facts' (typically 'functions'), for RC theorists institutions are aggregates of individual behaviors and, consequently, they need to be explained by taking recourse to individual preferences and actions. Scherer's chapter usefully complements those in Part I as well as the chapter by Swedberg in this Part.

In Chapter 12 ('Micro and Macro Perspectives in Organization Theory: A Tale of Incommensurability'), William McKinley and Mark A. Mone, offer an enlightening survey of five of the most prominent micro and macro perspectives to be found in OT. Adopting the North American definition of OT (what in Europe would most likely be called macro-OB), the authors define the micro level of analysis as single organizations adapting to their individual task environments, while the macro level refers to populations of organizations and to multi-organizational fields or sectors. McKinley and Mone critically review three micro perspectives (neo-contingency theory, resource dependence theory, and transaction costs theory) and two macro perspectives (population ecology theory and neo-institutional theory). Explaining why each school is categorized as a micro or macro perspective, and describing the theoretical propositions as well as the underlying logic of each school, the authors proceed to offer a meta-theoretical critique of each school.

The main point McKinley and Mone make, in this highly readable chapter, is that each school is founded on ambiguous theoretical constructs, which, while fostering creativity in empirical research, also preclude conclusive empirical testing and make the schools incommensurable with one another. For example, the concept of 'fit', a key concept in neo-contingency theory, has been ambiguously defined by those using it, to the effect that it impedes the falsifiability of their theory. This incommensurability, founded on construct ambiguity, has serious implications for the conceptual integration of the field that is envisaged by some theorists. It is worth reading McKinley and Mone's chapter in the light of recent debates in OT regarding the integration and impact of OT, as well as in the light of the arguments advanced in Part I by proponents of different paradigms.

If McKinley and Mone are right, knowledge generation in OT lacks the secure foundations to make it a cumulative enterprise, since, on the one hand, OT theories are founded on ambiguous constructs and, on the other hand, their hard core is protected by theorists who compete in the academic market for reputations and resources. Lack of cumulative progress, however, should not stop us from trying to learn from different paradigms and perspectives, and drawing new distinctions, which resolve old conflicts and permit selective borrowing. In other words, there are, indeed, several competing ways for looking at organizations and it is precisely because of such conceptual diversity that learning and conceptual innovation are possible.

In Chapter 13 ('Economic versus Sociological Approaches to Organization Theory'), Richard Swedberg, offers an enlightening discussion of the different ways in which economists and sociologists have conceptualized business organizations. Although OT is interdisciplinary, remarks Swedberg, most of the research is carried out within the boundaries and assumptions set by single disciplines. Economics and sociology have long been the disciplines from within which some of the most significant contributions to OT have come. For economists, as is typically shown in transaction cost analysis, agency theory, and evolutionary, game theoretical and property rights perspectives, firms represent profitable solutions to coordination problems emanating mainly from self-regarding behavior on the part of rational individuals.

By contrast, for sociologists, especially Weberian ones, business organizations are seen as the carriers of the modernization process, incorporating structures of meaning from the societies within which they are embedded. Typically, whereas for economists economic interests and instrumental action are taken for granted and form the foundational assumption of elegant formal modeling, for sociologists instrumental action and economic interests are social constructions in need of historical elucidation. While economists focus on the single firm, sociologists, typically, place the firm in larger contexts, be they business groups and systems, networks, populations, or fields. Economic theories of organization tend to be rigorous over highly stylized and delimited areas of economic behaviour, while sociological theories are more descriptive (lacking the precision and analytical rigor of economic models) over larger areas of economic behavior. Swedberg is not particularly optimistic that both camps will find a common language, although he points at entrepreneurship as an area over which supporters of both camps could stand and converse. At any rate, a comprehensive theory of firms will have to unite the two key ideas in economics and sociology, respectively: economic interests and social structures. That will not be easy, but that is the way to go, remarks Swedberg.

In Chapter 14 ('Meta-theoretical Controversies in Studying Organizational Culture'), Joanne Martin provides a thorough and lucid overview of meta-theoretical debates in organizational culture research. Intellectual controversies in the study of culture have ranged over a number of issues, which Martin critically examines in her chapter. These are: objectivity and subjectivity; etic (outsider) and emic (insider) research; generalizable and context-specific research; focus and breadth; and level of depth. Drawing on variety of sources, including anthropology, philosophy, and, of course, OT, Martin advances a balanced and open-minded argument which, while it acknowledges the controversial nature of these issues, it does want, through drawing subtle distinctions, to reformulate them in order to show that quite often in academic debates, certain dichotomies are unnecessarily overdrawn. It is no accident that she frames the above controversies not as struggles between opposing terms ('this versus that') but, more positively, as a coexistence of different ways of looking at culture ('this and that').

Her empathic writing style and her willingness to draw on and learn from a variety of perspectives are indicative of the stance Martin takes towards the meta-theoretical controversies in organizational culture research: we should always try to enhance our understanding of different viewpoints; looks for ways in which conceptual oppositions may be reconciled without denying differences (for example, culture is both an objective and subjective construction; the boundaries between etic and emic research are blurred; context-specific knowledge cannot escape abstraction, etc). In short, we should try to learn to enrich our ideas by engaging with those of others. Building consensus is not realistic, while enforcing conformity to elite preferences is undesirable; but learning may be possible.

Part IV consists of four chapters, all of which deal with the relationship between theory and practice in OT and, more broadly, the nature of practical reason. In Chapter 15 ('Actionable Knowledge'), Chris Argyris, summarizes, with his custom-ary lucidity and directness, his lifetime's work regarding the prerequisites for OT to produce actionable knowledge. Being a policy science, says Argyris, OT is in the business of generating propositions that are actionable. Actionable knowledge is knowledge that actors can use to implement effectively their intentions. Such knowledge is important not only to practitioners, but to researchers too, since actionable knowledge required for intervention mandates that we specify causal propositions about how to bring change about. A strong and passionate believer in Lewin's dictum that unless you try to change something, you do not really under-stand it, Argyris makes the important point that when we try to change the organizations we allow data to surface which otherwise would not have surfaced.

Before setting out to describe Models I and II, for which Argyris has been best known, he sets out to survey the fundamental norms and rules about producing knowledge in OT (and in the policy sciences in general) that tend to inhibit the production of valid actionable knowledge. These are: (a) the importance traditionally attached to description and explanation; (b) the unintended gaps and inconsistencies that the emphasis to description and explanation produces; (c) the misplaced importance given to epistemological pluralism; and (d) the emphasis placed on internal and external validity. It is worth pointing out Argyris's stance on epistemological pluralism. Of course pluralism is a good thing, he remarks, but it does not help us a great deal to solve organizational problems, for two reasons. First because even the critics of positivism (the 'humanists' as Argyris calls them) do not get close enough to their objects of study, since they eschew interventions. And secondly, when the objective is to produce actionable know-ledge, epistemological pluralism is not necessarily superior to monism: the strategy of producing different descriptions of a phenomenon may meet the needs of researchers but not necessarily those of practitioners and, at any rate, since it does not attempt to change the status quo it deprives itself of depth. In fact, argues Argyris, when change interventions are attempted, one finds that *both* 'positivist' and 'humanist' assumptions are relevant. Passionate about actionability and eman-cipatory change, Argyris critiques both Habermasian critical theory and psycho-analysis for not specifying explicitly the causal processes required to produce effective action. Enhanced awareness is not good enough, observes Argyris; action is the key criterion for the validity of awareness.

While Argyris is concerned with showing how actionable knowledge may be produced, in Chapter 16 ('Theory and Practice in the Real World'), Karl Weick undertakes a broader task: to examine how theory and practice are related in the real world. 'Theory' and 'practice' are qualitatively different, argues Weick in his thoughtful and stimulating paper. The central question he addresses relates to how theory and practice may be reconciled. The whole chapter can be seen as Weick's attempt to elucidate Kierkegaard's remark that life is understood backwards but it must be lived forwards. Reviewing eight different ways in which organizational theorists have tried to reconcile theory with practice, Weick draws on Heidegger to distinguish three different modes of living: the 'ready-to-hand' mode in which individuals find themselves 'thrown' at the world, are immersed in particular tasks, and are aware of the world holistically, contextually, and unreflectively; the 'unready-to-hand' mode, in which problematic aspects of a task that produced an interruption stand out, although individuals still do not become aware of context-free objects; and the 'present-at-hand' mode in which individuals step back from their involvement in a task to reflect on it. This is the mode of theoretical reflection.

Theorists, remarks Weick, tend to explain organizational phenomena by using 'present-to-hand' images, thus simplifying the complex, intertwined lifeworld understandings embedded in the 'ready-to-hand' mode of living, which practitioners inhabit. The gap between theory and practice is the gap between different modes of engagement with the world—between the 'ready-to-hand' mode and the 'present-at-hand' mode. Weick argues that this gap may be reduced when both practitioners and theorists scrutinize those moments where 'backward' and 'forward' views meet, namely unready-to-hand moments. Such moments are usually interruptions, accidents, and breakdowns. During those moments practitioners are partly disengaged from their tasks and are in need of looking backwards for abstractions, models, and theories. At the same time, interruptions present theorists with opportunities to sense more of the world as it is experienced by practitioners. During interruptions both engaged understanding and disengaged explanation come together. Weick insightfully illustrates his argument of unready-to-hand theorizing by analyzing the case of an accident in which two US Air Force F-15 fighter planes misidentified, over Northern Iraq, two US Army helicopters as Russian Hind aircraft and shot them down.

Although in the academic division of labor OT is a separate discipline from Business Ethics, it is impossible, as Richard Nielsen powerfully argues in Chapter 17 ('Organization Theory and Ethics: Varieties and Dynamics of Constrained Optimization'), to separate the two. Just as it is not possible to have a particular organizational form without an at least implicit ethical or normative foundation, it is also not possible to actualize social ethics without organizational form. The prescriptions of a policy science such as OT necessarily involve ethical commitments and normative orientations. For example, the regular exhortations to firms to embrace continuous innovation and change, or the current critique of the bureaucratic organization, are underlain by certain ethical preferences.

The central organizing concept of this insightful paper is that of 'constrained optimization'. Distinct organizational forms optimize distinct variables (e.g. shareholder value, efficiency, power and influence, etc.) under certain constrains (e.g. the well-being of local communities, etc.). What is optimized and what is constrained has varied enormously across historical periods, types of organizations, and social traditions. Ethics issues and conflicts arise in the spaces between what is optimized and what is constrained. Nielsen considers six historically different types of constrained optimization, and discusses both the change processes through which varieties of constrained optimization evolve, and the epistemological question of how 'normative' questions are interwoven with 'scientific' assertions.

While Nielsen traces the ethical commitments implied by particular organizational forms, Iain Mangham explores, in Chapter 18 ('Character and Virtue in an Era of Turbulent Capitalism'), the impact of unregulated ('turbo') capitalism on the ethical climate, both within and beyond organizations, by focusing on the Aristotelian notions of 'character' and 'virtue'. Prompted by Richard Sennett's (1998) widely acclaimed *The Corrosion of Character*, Mangham draws his empirical material from two ethnographies of life in the City of London, before and after the Big Bang. His argument in this provocative essay is that the greatest influence on the ethical climate of our times is not so much exerted by particular forms of organization as by particular forms of capitalism. Unregulated capitalism produces a different ethical climate from regulated capitalism. Moreover, while the concepts of character and virtue, says Mangham, are helpful for understanding what occurred in the era of 'gentlemanly capitalism', they are less so in the era of 'impatient capitalism'. Mangham draws attention to the strong links between morality and social context arguing, in a MacIntyrian fashion, that character is not idiosyncratic, nor a matter of merely 'individual' choice, but is irreducibly social and emerges from ritualized habituation.

Finally, Part V ('The Future of Organization Theory') consists of five chapters whose authors reflect on the prospects of OT. The overall question they attempt to answer is this: what direction should research in OT take? As you would expect, answers differ widely, reflecting authors' onto-epistemological commitments and theoretical predilections.

In Chapter 19 ('The Future of Organization Theory: Prospects and Limitations') Gibson Burrell addresses two questions. First, 'What new research issues should OT try to tackle?'; and secondly, 'What methodological and epistemological positions need to be adopted in OT?' He answers the first question with another question: 'who do we write for?' He argues that much of OT has been written for middle managers. In his answer to the second question he rejects the 'anatomizing urge' that haunts most sciences. Later he discusses the recent interest in 'critical realism' among some OT scholars, and compares several possible methodologies such as naïve empiricism, analytical empiricism, conventionalism, and orthodox realism. His argument is that we will always have to rely on some form of 'logic of invention', a position that brings him close to some form of conventionalism. Finally, he interestingly argues for opening OT to what he calls 'neo-disciplinarity', which implies opening the field to younger scholars and to notions of organizations stemming from outside the North Atlantic area. He concludes by pointing out that OT needs to look at a particular group, the peasantry, which has always been outside the domain of western notions of organization.

In Chapter 20 ('Managing Organization Futures in a Changing World of Power/ Knowledge') Stewart Clegg explores some of the changes OT will likely go through in the immediate future. He argues that, contrary to what one would expect, it would be organizational researchers, above all other specialists, that would be developing new paradigms, when essential business conditions change. However, OT and business practice have been largely decoupled from each other as two separate institutional spheres. While the academic knowledge of OT intends to be universal and global, the working knowledge of business practice is specific and local. Despite this separation, Clegg insightfully argues that business practice has considerable implications for OT, though in ways that traditional universities have not conceived.

In Chapter 21 ('The Future of Organization Studies: Beyond the Selection-Adaptation Debate'), Arie Lewin and Henk Volberda first informatively present the key research traditions that have either argued for an adaptation or a selection view of how organizations are formed. Second, they convincingly argue that the co-evolutionary perspective has the potential to resolve this duality between adaptation and selection by integrating micro- and macro-level evolution within a unifying framework. In the co-evolutionary framework, they point out, change is not just seen as an outcome of managerial adaptation or market selection but, rather, the joint outcome of strategic decisions and environmental effects.

In Chapter 22 ('At Home from Mars to Somalia: Recounting Organization Studies'), Marta B. Calás and Linda Smircich offer a provocative and passionate account of how they see the future of OT. Commenting on two sets of vignettes culled from the news—the failed attempts by NASA to locate water and, through it, forms of life on Mars; and the plight of two women in Africa in their desperate attempts to escape famine and drought—Calás and Smircich ask the question why, despite a plethora of critical analyses, OT has contributed so little innovation when it comes to producing institutions to tackle world problems. Their answer is that OT has been a prisoner of dominant western understandings concerning what constitutes 'modernization' and, consequently, it has been unable to think outside the box. To do that organization theorists would need to think much wider than they have done so far and engage with heterodox theoretical discourses such as Third World feminist analyses, post-colonial theorizing, and the anthropology of technology. By drawing on these perspectives, Calás and Smircich demonstrate how such radical rethinking may be done and what it would involve.

The authors share with critical organization theorists the belief that OT (and social science at large) needs to engage in emancipatory theorizing, but they are more inclined to take their cues from Foucauldian-inspired historical analyses of 'subjugated knowledges' rather than Habermasian arguments concerning 'ideal speech', although the two are not necessarily at odds with one another. Drawing on Latour, the prospect of OT, argue Calás and Smircich, should be to rethink modern institutions as 'hybrid forums' and 'space for co-researching'. Dismissing the distinction between experts and non-experts, the authors side with Latour in their claim that all people are 'co-researchers' and, one way or another, we are all engaged into the collective experiments that make up our lives on the planet. Although Calás and Smircich do not specify what exactly this 'co-researching' is and how it is to be achieved—is it, for example, different from the collaborative vision of science offered by Nowotny, Scott, and Gibbons (2001)?—they do imply that what is important for organization theorists is to escape the modernist conceptual and institutional limits of western science, which have come to historically privilege certain forms of life and conceptions of rationality over others, and open up towards the Other.

Finally, in Chapter 23 ('New Times, Fresh Challenges: Reflections on the Past and the Future of Organization Theory'), Haridimos Tsoukas adopts a Wittgensteinian perspective on OT, and puts forward four claims: First, OT has, over time, become more complex in some of its assumptions, seeking to incorporate real-world complexity in its models. However, it has been limited in its focus by being heavily concerned with the study of formal organizations as opposed to the broader phenomenon of *organization*. Second, along with the rest of social sciences, the mode of inquiry that has mainly underpinned OT is intellectualism and ontological atomism, which have prevented OT from fully grasping the inherent sociality of organizational phenomena. Third, the main task of OT has tended to be the causal, especially contingency, explanation of organizational behavior, whereas it should be the elucidation of reasons for organizational behavior. And fourth, OT has often been trapped by certain dualisms of its own making, such as stability vs. change, routines vs. creativity, failing to appreciate that such phenomena are mutually constituted. Arguing for a discursive turn in OT, Tsoukas suggests that the proper focus of OT should not so much be the study of authoritatively coordinated action as, more broadly, the study of patterned interaction; organizational theorists, he argues, should not be searching for some invariant logic of organizing but they ought to be exploring the discursive patterns involved in organizing.

As you will see in the chapters that follow, there is no shortage of debate or controversy in this handbook, and that is a sign of the vitality of OT as a social science discipline. At the same time, for the debate to be stimulating and productive it must be, to paraphrase Weick (1999), a 'disciplined debate'—organization theorists, we suggest, are not in the business of arguing for the sake of it, but only insofar as they want to make clearer sense of the activity they are engaged in. We would like to think of the present handbook as providing a coherent rationale and structure so that such a meta-theoretical debate may be lucid in its conduct and fruitful in its outcomes. No, we do not believe that a consensus will emerge, nor do we necessarily desire one. But we do want to help enhance collective learning, and hope this handbook will contribute to such a process. We keep learning by keeping conversing, and reflecting on how we do so. The present handbook is a modest contribution to the ongoing meta-theoretical conversation in our field.

REFERENCES

ABRAHAMSON, E., and EISENMAN, M. (2001). 'Why Management Scholars must Intervene Strategically in the Management Knowledge Market'. *Human Relations*, 54: 67–75.
——and FAIRCHILD, G. (1999). 'Management Fashion: Life Cycle, Triggers and Collective Learning Processes'. *Administrative Science Quarterly*, 44: 708–40.
ALVESSON, M., and DEETZ, S. (1996). 'Critical Theory and Postmodern Approaches to Organization Studies', in S. R. Clegg, C. Hardy, and W. R. Nord (eds.), *Handbook of Organization Studies*. London: Sage.
——and WILLMOTT, H. (eds.) (1992). *Critical Management Studies*. London: Sage.
ANTONACOPOULOU, E., and TSOUKAS, H. (2002). 'Time and Reflexivity in Organization Studies: An Introduction'. *Organization Studies*, in press.
ARGYRIS, C. (1980). *Inner Contradictions of Rigorous Research*. San Diego, Calif.: Academic Press.
ASTLEY, W. G. (1985). 'Administrative Science as Socially Constructed Truth'. *Administrative Science Quarterly*, 30: 497–513.
——and VAN DE VEN, A. H. (1983). 'Central Perspectives and Debates in Organization Theory'. *Administrative Science Quarterly*, 28: 245–73.
——and ZAMMUTO, R. F. (1992). 'Organization Science, Managers, and Language Games'. *Organization Science*, 3: 443–60.
BARNARD, C. (1968). *The Functions of the Executive*. Cambridge, Mass.: Harvard University Press.
——(1976). 'Foreword', in H. Simon, *Administrative Behavior*. New York: Free Press.
BHASKAR, R. (1978). *A Realist Theory of Science*. Hertfordshire: Harvester Wheatsheaf.
BODEN, D. (1994). *The Business of Talk*. Cambridge: Polity Press.
BROWN, A. (1997). 'Narcissism, Identity and Legitimacy'. *Academy of Management Review*, 22: 643–86.
BROWN, J. S., and DUGUID, P. (1991). 'Organizational Learning and Communities of Practice: Toward a Unifying View of Working, Learning and Innovation'. *Organization Science*, 2: 40–57.
BURRELL, G. (1996). 'Normal Science, Paradigms, Metaphors, Discourse and Genealogies of Analysis', in S. R. Clegg, C. Hardy, and W. R. Nord (eds.), *Handbook of Organization Studies*. London: Sage.
——(1997). *Pandemonium*. London: Sage.
——and MORGAN, G. (1979). *Sociological Paradigms and Organizational Analysis*. London: Heinemann.

CALÁS, M., and SMIRCICH, L. (1996). 'From 'the Woman's' Point of View: Feminist Approaches to Organization Studies', in S. R. Clegg, C. Hardy, and W. R. Nord (eds.), *Handbook of Organization Studies.* London: Sage.

CHILD, J. (1997). 'From the Aston Programme to Strategic Choice: A Journey from Concepts to Theory', in T. Clark (ed.), *Advancement in Organizational Behaviour.* Aldershot: Ashgate.

COHEN, I. B. (1994). 'Newton and the Social Sciences, with Special Reference to Economics, or the Case of the Missing Paradigm', in P. Mirowski (ed.), *Natural Images in Economic Thought.* Cambridge: Cambridge University Press.

COHEN, M. D., and SPROULL, L. S. (eds.) (1996). *Organizational Learning.* Thousand Oaks, Calif.: Sage.

CZARNIAWSKA, B. (1998). 'Who is Afraid of Incommensurability?' *Organization*, 5: 273–5.

—— (1999). *Writing Management.* Oxford: Oxford University Press.

DEETZ, S. (1996). 'Describing Differences in Approaches to Organization Science: Rethinking Burrell and Morgan and their Legacy'. *Organization Science*, 7: 190–207.

DOBBIN, F. (1995). 'The Origins of Economic Principles: Railway Entrepreneurs and Public Policy in 19th-Century America', in W. R. Scott and S. Christensen (eds.), *The Institutional Construction of Organizations.* Thousand Oaks, Calif.: Sage.

DONALDSON, L. (1996). *For Positivist Organization Theory.* London: Sage.

—— (1998). 'The Myth of Paradigm Incommensurability in Management Studies: Comments by an Integrationist'. *Organization*, 5: 267–72.

—— (2001). *The Contingency Theory of Organizations.* Thousand Oaks, Calif.: Sage.

FLYVBJERG, B. (2001). *Making Social Science Matter.* Cambridge: Cambridge University Press.

FROST, P. J., MOORE, L. F., LOUIS, M. R., LUNDBERG, C. C., and MARTIN, J. (1991). *Reframing Organizational Culture.* Newbury Park, Calif.: Sage.

GABRIEL, Y. (1999). *Organizations in Depth.* London: Sage.

GADAMER, H. G. (1989). *Truth and Method* (2nd edn). London: Sheed & Ward.

GERGEN, K. (1994). *Toward Transformation in Social Knowledge* (2nd edn). London: Sage.

—— and THATCHENKERY, T. J. (1998). 'Organizational Science in a Postmodern Context', in R. Chia (ed.), *In the Realm of Organization.* London: Routledge.

GHERARDI, S. (1995). *Gender, Symbolism and Organizational Culture.* London: Sage.

GIDDENS, A. (1993). *New Rules of Sociological Method* (2nd edn). Oxford: Polity.

GRANOVETTER, M. (1992). 'Problems of Explanation in Economic Sociology', in N. Nohria and R. G. Eccles (eds.), *Networks and Organizations.* Boston: Harvard Business School Press.

—— and SWEDBERG, R. (1992). *The Sociology of Economic Life.* Boulder, Colo.: Westview Press.

GRANT, R. M. (1996). 'Toward a Knowledge-Based Theory of the Firm'. *Strategic Management Journal*, 17 Special Winter Issue: 109–22.

GUILLEN, M. F. (1994). *Models of Management.* Chicago: University of Chicago Press.

HABERMAS, J. (1972). *Knowledge and Human Interests.* London: Heinemann.

HEILBRONER, R., and MILBERG, W. (1995). *The Crisis of Vision in Modern Economic Thought.* Cambridge: Cambridge University Press.

JACKSON, N., and CARTER, P. (1991). 'In Defense of Paradigm Incommensurability'. *Organization Studies*, 12: 109–27.

KAGHAN, W., and PHILLIPS, N. (1998). 'Building the Tower of Babel: Communities of Practice and Paradigmatic Pluralism in Organization Studies'. *Organization*, 5: 191–215.

KIESER, A. (1998). 'From Freemasons to Industrious Patriots: Organizing and Disciplining in 18th-Century Germany'. *Organization Studies*, 19: 47–71.

KNORR, K. (1981). *The Manufacture of Knowledge*. Oxford: Pergamon.

KUHN, T. (1962). *The Structure of Scientific Revolutions*. Chicago: University of Chicago Press.

KUNDA, G. (1992). *Engineering Culture*. Philadelphia: Temple University Press.

LATOUR, B., and WOOLGAR, S. (1986). *Laboratory Life*. Princeton: Princeton University Press.

LAWLER, E. E., MOHRMAN, A. M., MOHRMAN, S. A., LEDFORD, G. E., CUMMINGS, T. G., and Associates (1999). *Doing Research that is Useful for Theory and Practice* (2nd edn). Lanham, Md.: Lexington Books.

McCLOSKEY, D. N. (1985). *The Rhetoric of Economics*. Madison: University of Wisconsin Press.

MacINTYRE, A. (1985). *After Virtue* (2nd edn). London: Duckworth.

McKELVEY, B. (1997). 'Quasi-natural Organizational Science'. *Organization Science*, 8: 352–80.

McKINLEY, W., and MONE, M. A. (1998). 'The Re-construction of Organization Studies: Wrestling with Incommensurability'. *Organization*, 5: 169–89.

——— ——— and MOON, G. (1999). 'Determinants and Development of Schools in Organization Theory'. *Academy of Management Review*, 24: 634–48.

MARCH, J. G. (1988). *Decisions and Organizations*. Oxford: Blackwell.

—— and OLSEN, J. (1986). 'Garbage Can Models of Decision-Making in Organizations', in J. March and R. Weissinger-Baylon (eds.), *Ambiguity and Command*. Marshfield, Mass.: Pitman.

MARSDEN, R., and TOWNLEY, B. (1996). 'The Owl of Minerva: Reflections on Theory in Practice', in S. R. Clegg, C. Hardy, and W. R. Nord (eds.), *Handbook of Organization Studies*. London: Sage.

MARTIN, J. (1990). 'Deconstructing Organizational Taboos: The Suppression of Gender Conflict in Organizations'. *Organization Science*, 1: 339–59.

MINER, J. B. (1984). 'The Validity and Usefulness of Theories in an Emerging Organizational Science'. *Academy of Management Review*, 9: 296–306.

MINTZBERG, H. (1979). 'An Emerging Strategy of "Direct" Research'. *Administrative Science Quarterly*, 24: 582–9.

MIROWSKI, P. (1989). *More Heat Than Light*. Cambridge: Cambridge University Press.

MOLDOVEANU, M. C., and BAUM, J. A. C. (2002). 'Contemporary Debates in Organizational Epistemology', in J. A. C. Baum (ed.), *The Blackwell Companion to Organizations*. Oxford: Blackwell.

MORGAN, G. (ed.) (1983). *Beyond Method*, Beverly Hills, Calif.: Sage.

—— and SMIRCICH, L. (1980). 'The Case for Qualitative Research'. *Academy of Management Review*, 5: 491–500.

MOWDAY, R. T. (1997). 'Presidential Address: Reaffirming our Scholarly Values'. *Academy of Management Review*, 22: 335–45.

NKOMO, S. (1992). 'The Emperor Has No Clothes: Rewriting "race in organizations"'. *Academy of Management Review*, 17: 487–513.

NOWOTNY, H., SCOTT, P., and GIBBONS, M. (2001). *Re-Thinking Science*. Cambridge: Polity.

NUMAGAMI, T. (1998). 'The Infeasibility of Invariant Laws in Management Studies: A Reflective Dialogue in Defense of Case Studies'. *Organization Science*, 9: 1–15.

PETTIGREW, A. (2001). 'Management Research after Modernism'. *British Journal of Management*, 12/Special Issue: S61–S70.

PFEFFER, J. (1981). *Power in Organizations*. Marshfield, Mass.: Pitman.

—— (1982). *Organizations and Organization Theory*. Boston: Pitman.

—— (1993). 'Barriers to the Advance of Organizational Science: Paradigm Development as a Dependent Variable'. *Academy of Management Review*, 18: 599–620.

PICKERING, A. (1992). *Science as Practice and Culture*. Chicago: University of Chicago Press.

POLANYI, M. (1962). *Personal Knowledge*. Chicago: University of Chicago Press.

PORTER, M. (1991). 'Towards a Dynamic Theory of Strategy'. *Strategic Management Journal*, 12: 95–117.

REED, M. (1996). 'Organizational Theorizing: A Historically Contested Terrain', in S. R. Clegg, C. Hardy, and W. R. Nord (eds.), *Handbook of Organization Studies*. London: Sage.

ROE, M. J. (1994). *Strong Managers, Weak Owners*. Princeton: Princeton University Press.

RORTY, R. (1989). *Contingency, Irony, and Solidarity*. Cambridge: Cambridge University Press.

—— (1991). *Objectivity, Relativism, and Truth*. Cambridge: Cambridge University Press.

SAYER, A. (1992). *Method in Social Science* (2nd edn). London: Routledge.

SCHERER, A. G. (1998). 'Pluralism and Incommensurability in Strategic Management and Organization Theory: A Problem in Search of a Solution'. *Organization*, 5: 147–68.

—— and STEINMANN, H. (1999). 'Some Remarks on the Problem of Incommensurability in Organization Studies'. *Organization Studies*, 20: 519–44.

SCOTT, W. R. (1987). *Organizations: Rational, Natural, and Open Systems*. Englewood Cliffs, NJ: Prentice-Hall International.

—— and CHRISTENSEN S. (eds.) (1995). *The Institutional Construction of Organizations*. Thousand Oaks, Calif.: Sage.

—— MEYER, J. W., and Associates (1994). *Institutional Environments and Organizations*. Thousand Oaks, Calif.: Sage.

SEARLE, J. R. (1995). *The Construction of Social Reality*. London: Allen Lane.

SENNETT, R. (1998). *The Corrosion of Character*. New York: W.W. Norton.

SHENHAV, Y. (1999). *Manufacturing Rationality*. Oxford: Oxford University Press.

SILVERMAN, D. (1971). *The Theory of Organizations*. London: Heinemann.

SPENDER, J.-C. (1996). 'Making Knowledge the Basis for a Dynamic Theory of the Firm'. *Strategic Management Journal*, 17/Special Winter Issue: 45–62.

STACEY, R. D., GRIFFIN, D., and SHAW, P. (2000). *Complexity and Management*. London: Routledge.

STARKEY, K., and MADAN, P. (2001). 'Bridging the Relevance Gap: Aligning Stakeholders in the Future of Management Research'. *British Journal of Management*, 12/Special Issue: S3–S26.

TAYLOR, C. (1985a). *Human Agency and Language: Philosophical Papers*, i. Cambridge: Cambridge University Press.

—— (1985b). *Philosophy and the Human Sciences: Philosophical Papers*, ii. Cambridge: Cambridge University Press.

TAYLOR, J. R., and VAN EVERY E. J. (2000). *The Emergent Organization*. Mahwah, NJ: Lawrence Erlbaum.

TENBRUNSEL, A. E., GALVIN, T., NEALE, M. A., and BAZERMAN, M. (1996). 'Cognition in Organizations', in S. R. Clegg, C. Hardy, and W. R. Nord (eds.), *Handbook of Organization Studies*. London: Sage.

THOMPSON, J. D. (1956–57). 'On Building an Administrative Science'. *Administrative Science Quarterly*, 1: 102–11.

—— (1967). *Organizations in Action*. New York: McGraw-Hill.

TOULMIN, S. (1990). *Cosmopolis*. Chicago: University of Chicago Press.

TRANFIELD, D., and STARKEY, K. (1998). 'The Nature, Social Organization and Promotion of Management Research: Towards Policy'. *British Journal of Management*, 9: 341–53.

TSOUKAS, H. (1992). 'The Relativity of Organizing: Its Knowledge Presuppositions and its Pedagogical Implications for Comparative Management'. *Journal of Management Education*, 16/Special Issue: S147–S162.

—— (1994). 'Refining Common Sense: Types of Knowledge in Management Studies'. *Journal of Management Studies*, 31: 761–80.

—— (1996). 'The Firm as a Distributed Knowledge System: A Constructionist Approach'. *Strategic Management Journal*, 17/Special Winter Issue: 11–26.

—— (1998). 'The World and the Word: A Critique of Representationalism in Management Research'. *International Journal of Public Administration*, 21: 781–817.

—— and CUMMINGS, S. (1997). 'Marginalization and Recovery: The Emergence of Aristotelian Themes in Organization Studies'. *Organization Studies*, 18: 655–83.

—— and KNUDSEN, C. (2002). 'The Conduct of Strategy Research', in A. Pettigrew, H. Thomas, and R. Whittington (eds.), *Handbook of Strategy and Management*. London: Sage.

—— and VLADIMIROU, E. (2001). 'What is Organizational Knowledge?' *Journal of Management Studies*, 38: 973–94.

VAN MAANEN, J. (1988). *Tales of the Field*. Chicago: University of Chicago Press.

—— (1995). 'Style as Theory'. *Organization Science*, 6: 133–43.

WEBER, M. (1993). *Basic Concepts in Sociology*. New York: Citadel Press.

WEBSTER, J., and STARBUCK, W. H. (1988). 'Theory Building in Industrial and Organizational Psychology', in C. L. Cooper and I. Robertson (eds.), *International Review of Industrial and Organizational Psychology* 1988. London: Wiley.

WEICK, K. (1979). *The Social Psychology of Organizing* (2nd edn). New York: McGraw-Hill.

—— (1999). 'Theory Construction as Disciplined Reflexivity: Tradeoffs in the 1990s'. *Academy of Management Review*, 24: 797–806.

—— (2001). *Making Sense of the Organization*. Oxford: Blackwell.

—— (2002). 'Real-Time Reflexivity: Prods to Reflection'. *Organization Studies*, in press.

—— and ROBERTS, K. (1993). 'Collective Mind in Organizations: Heedful Interrelating on Flight Decks'. *Administrative Science Quarterly*, 38: 357–81.

WHETTEN, D., and GODFREY, P. (eds.) (1998). *Identity in Organizations*. Thousand Oaks: Sage.

WHITLEY, R. (1984). 'The Scientific Status of Management Research as a Practically-Oriented Social Science'. *Journal of Management Studies*, 21: 369–90.

—— (1992). *Business Systems in East Asia*. London:Sage.

—— (2000). *The Intellectual and Social Organization of the Sciences* (2nd edn). Oxford: Oxford University Press.

WICKS, A. C., and FREEMAN, R. E. (1998). 'Organization Studies and the New Pragmatism: Positivism, Anti-positivism, and the Search for Ethics'. *Organization Science*, 9: 123–40.

WILLIAMSON, O. (1998). 'Transaction Cost Economics and Organization Theory', in G. Dossi, D. J. Teece, and J. Chytry (eds.), *Technology, Organization, and Competitiveness*. Oxford: Oxford University Press.

WILLMOTT, H. (1993). 'Breaking the Paradigm Mentality'. *Organization Studies*, 14: 681–719.

WINOGRAND, T., and FLORES, F. (1987). *Understanding Computers and Cognition*. Reading, Mass.: Addison-Wesley.

ZALD, M. N. (1996). 'More Fragmentation? Unfinished Business in Linking the Social Sciences and the Humanities'. *Administrative Science Quarterly*, 41: 251–61.

ZAMMUTO, R. F., and CONNOLLY, T. (1984). 'Coping with Disciplinary Fragmentation'. *Organizational Behavior Teaching Review*, 9: 30–7.

PART I

ORGANIZATION THEORY AS SCIENCE

CHAPTER 1

ORGANIZATION THEORY AS A POSITIVE SCIENCE

LEX DONALDSON

POSITIVE science applied to organizations seeks to build a body of knowledge that consists of general causal theories about organizations and their members. These theories are empirically validated through scientific methods. The theories are positive in that they explain how the world works, rather than being normative, that is, prescribing what ought to occur. In positivist organizational science, organizations are explained as being driven by the environment. Organizational science has made considerable progress to date through using the positivist approach. Moreover, there is the potential for organizational theory to make even more progress in future, through continuing to be pursued positivistically.

1.1 POSITIVISM IN SOCIAL SCIENCE

Science is a body of knowledge that consists of general explanations (Toulmin 1962). It is pursued through the systematic study of phenomena, which involves constructing theories and comparing them against empirical evidence (Chalmers 1999). The application of this approach in the natural sciences has led to great increases in knowledge (Boorstin 1983). Positivism holds that the same approach applied to society will increase knowledge about human affairs (Comte 1853). Thus positivism takes the natural sciences as a role model. This modeling means that aspects of methods used in the natural science are adopted by social science (Phillips 1992). It also means that aspects of the theory and world view of the natural sciences are adopted by social science (Burrell and Morgan 1979).

The natural sciences have revealed that underlying the surface appearance of the natural world there are deeper structures of regularities of causes and effects (Boorstin 1983). Some of these underlying mechanisms are simple, though some are complex. Biological and other scientific theories are often functionalist, in that they explain the occurrence of an attribute by its beneficial outcome, e.g. survival. The view of human beings is of animals that struggle for existence within their environments. As their environment changes over time, so too must the human beings. Darwinian selection operates against those humans who do not fit their environment and so fail to survive. However, human adaptation also occurs through problem-solving, so that some behavior is changed through human choice. Nevertheless, the generalized capacity for adaptive problem-solving is intelligence, and so Darwinian selection tends to favor intelligence. This biological view is rather tough-minded, in that it includes some processes that are unappealing and contrary to values, e.g. infanticide to control population numbers. The emphasis of the biological view is upon revealing the mechanisms that actually occur, even if they go against values.

Positivism seeks to transfer many of these aspects of the natural sciences across to the study of society and thereby to create a social science. The orientation to the objects of inquiry (i.e. societies and their members) is objective, in that they are observed from without by detached observers. The aim is to identify social facts, that is, causes that stand apart from people and constrain them, forcing them to behave in certain ways—even sometimes regardless of the ideas in the minds of the people involved (Durkheim 1938). A prominent type of sociological theory is functionalism, which holds that the social structure is shaped by the imperative to adapt so as to provide fundamental societal needs (Parsons 1966). The benefits of some aspects of the social structure are not apparent to societal members, i.e. they are latent functions (Merton 1949), so that the functions are objective characteristics. Harris (1977) offers objectivist, positivist, functionalist explanations of phenomena that seem not to be explicable positivistically, such as cultural taboos, e.g. cow worship in India removes the temptation to eat, and thus lose, an enduringly valuable source of milk, cooking fuel, and traction for the farmer.

Social science, however, has long been marked by debate between positivism and anti-positivism. The main anti-positivist philosophy regarding the study of human society is ideationalism (Burrell and Morgan 1979). In its boldest form this rejects the suggestion that the natural sciences can be applied to human society. Ideation-alism emphasizes the role of ideas and values as causal influences, and sees human actions as the results of choices based on free will (Schreyögg 1980). Reality is seen as being socially constructed (Berger and Luckmann 1966). Ideationalism also empha-sizes that the phenomena to be explained include consciousness, cognition, feelings, and symbols, which lie, to a great degree, within the human mind, and so involve subjectivity (Berger and Pullberg 1966; Schutz 1967). Much of subjective experience is bound up with language, so that language becomes a focus of inquiry. Ideation-alists therefore tend to liken social research to learning a language, rather than doing natural science. Thus ideationalism tends to see the humanities as the more appropriate role model. Given that a language tends to be specific to a society, the tendency of ideationalists is towards understanding particular people in a locale, including their language, art, and culture (e.g. laws, customs, humor, etc.). Idea-tionalism explains human behavior as action whose meaning is known to the actor and to the people of that culture. These actions are oriented to attaining the ends that the individual values (Rex 1961). The respect for language can extend to philosophical arguments that all human motivation is context-specific and local-ized, so that broad general psychological theories about motivation are held to be unsound (Winch 1958). Thus ideationalism differs from positivism in fundamental regards and can become anti-positivist by rejecting, or casting doubt upon, posi-tivist precepts such as generalization, objectivism, determinism, and causation being external to the mind of the individual (Burrell and Morgan 1979).

1.2 Positivism in Organizational Science

Positivism in organizational science seeks to create general theories about organiza-tions and their members, which are reminiscent of the powerful universal laws found in the natural sciences. The aim is to reveal causal regularities that underlie surface reality. Explanation is primarily in terms of causes that determine effects. The formal logic of the explanation is that an independent variable, x, causes y, the dependent variable (Blalock 1961). The preference is for simple theories, though recourse may be had to more complex theories for those phenomena for which simple theories prove inadequate. Thus in formal terms, the explanation may be made more complex by saying that besides x causing y, there is another variable, u, that is also a cause of y (Blalock 1961). Also, the explanation may be made more complex by saying that x causes more than y, by x being also a cause of another dependent variable, *v*. Again, the explanation may be made more complex by including a moderator, such as saying that *x* causes *y* where the moderator *z* has a high value, but not where *z* is low (Galtung 1967). Alternatively, the explanation may be made more complex by including a mediator, such as saying that *x* causes *y* through the mediating variable, *w*, so that the more complete causal model is that *x* causes *w* causes *y* (Galtung 1967). A causal explanation may contain both moderator and mediating variables, and may contain many causes and effects, so that complexity of the explanation is increased. In organizational positivism, as in all positivism, such theorizing is accompanied by empirical study, to test and refine the theories (Galtung 1967). The empirical work makes use of scientific methods, such as quantitative variables, statistical analyses and controls for confounding causes, in order to validly assess whether the theoretical causal models accord with the empirical evidence (Blalock 1961; Cook and Campbell 1979).

Organizational science aims to create valid explanations that capture how the organizational world really operates, rather than to broadcast views that may better accord with values but which are not accurate characterizations of the world as it exists. Thus organizational science is value-free and may be quite tough-minded in some of its aspects. Positivism makes a distinction between positive science, that is, positive statements that describe the actual world and its causation, and normative science that makes prescriptions based on value judgments (Friedman 1953; Simon 1997). Positive science states that factor, *x* causes *y*. As such it can inform prescription (i.e. normative science), in that a person who wishes to attain *y* will know to do *x*. However, the preference for *y* comes from outside of science and reflects values and so is not itself the province of science (Weber 1968). In this way, positivism draws on the philosophical distinction between facts and values, which linguistically is the difference between propositions about 'is' and 'ought'.

Sociological positivism holds that phenomena, or social facts, should be explained by other social facts, i.e. objective conditions, rather than in the consciousness of social actors (Durkheim 1938). Positivist social theories explain human behavior by causes that lie in the situation and constrain the individual to act in certain ways, thereby conforming to the pressures of the environment. In organizational theory, positivism explains aspects of the organization or its members by the environing situation. In particular, in structural contingency theory, the environment (*e*) causes a certain level of the contingency variable (*c*), which in turn causes the organization to adopt a certain structure (*s*); hence in formal terms *e* causes *c* causes *s*. Thus, the degree of uncertainty in the environment (*e*) affects task uncertainty (*c*), which causes organizations to alter the degree of differentiation and integration (*s*) of their organizational structures (Lawrence and Lorsch 1967). Failure to conform to the situational requirements posed by the environment leads to reduced functionality for the organizations, forcing them and their managers to adapt. In this way causality comes from outside of the individual organizational member.

An exemplar of sociological positivism, in organizational theory, is the theory of structural differentiation in organizations propounded by Blau (1970, 1972), which is positivist both in its theory and methods. The phenomenon being explained, structural differentiation, is the tendency for an organization, as it grows in size, to become composed of progressively more and more specialized subunits. This concept (and its name 'differentiation') strongly echoes the biological concept of the same name. The theory is highly general, potentially applying to any organization in any setting. The theory is put forth in a series of propositions, with subordinate propositions being deduced from major propositions and assumptions, in the manner of a formal theory in the natural sciences (Blau 1970, 1972). The explanatory mechanisms are cause and effect. A major cause is size, which is the number of members of the organization, which is an objective, situational characteristic, rather than a subjective idea. The mechanisms are functionalist, promoting organizational efficiency.

Blau and Schoenherr (1971) present evidence supporting the theory from studies that measure variables and compare across organizations, using multivariate statistical analysis. Subsequent studies in other organizations (Blau 1972) and other countries have, in the main, supported the theory, showing generality across different types of organization and nations. For instance, the positive relationship between organizational size and vertical structural differentiation (the number of levels in the hierarchy) has been found in over thirty empirical studies of organizations (Donaldson 1996a: 135–7). These studies range in types of organization across governmental (Beyer and Trice 1979), insurance (Agarwal 1979), manufacturing organizations (Grinyer and Yasai-Ardekani 1981), and labor unions (Donaldson and Warner 1974). These studies also range in nations across Germany (Child and Kieser 1979), Hong Kong (Wong and Birnbaum-More 1994), India (Shenoy 1981), Jordan (Ayoubi 1981), Poland (Kuc, Hickson, and McMillan 1981), and the United Kingdom (Child 1973). While many studies have established correlations through cross-sectional research, some have studied change across time and thereby provided evidence of the causal effect of size on structural differentiation (Meyer 1972; Marsh and Mannari 1989).

The theory goes beyond surface appearance by revealing that structural differentiation increases at a declining rate as organizations increase in size (Blau 1970, 1972). It also shows that the ratio of managers to employees declines as size increases (Blau 1970, 1972), thereby contradicting the erroneous, commonsense, impression that this ratio must rise with size, because bigger organizations have taller managerial hierarchies. The decreasing proportion of managers to size (i.e. total employees) as size increases, means that the cost of administration is decreasing with size growth, so that there are economies of scale in administration, which is a functionalist outcome from the changes in organizational structure as size grows. The situational causation that Blau and Schoenherr (1971) argue theoretically, and show empirical support for, is that the environment, the size of the population in a state of the United States, causes the size of a governmental organization in that state, which causes its structural differentiation (for further discussion, see Donaldson 2001: 112–14).

1.3 POSITIVISM AND FUNCTIONALISM

Blau (1972: 13 fn.) is explicit that his theory of the effect of size on structural differentiation is positivist, in the tradition of Durkheim's rules of sociological method:

Another assumption is implied here: the prevailing characteristics of organizations, as distinguished from those in particular organizations, can be explained in terms of the influence of antecedent conditions in organizations (or their environment) without reference to the psychological preferences or decisions of individual managers, because these social conditions greatly restrict the options of managers who pursue an interest in efficient operations. This principle derives from Durkheim (1938: 110): 'The determining cause of a social fact should be sought among the social facts preceding it and not among the state of individual consciousness.'

In positivist organizational theory, the reason why the ideas in the minds of the social actors make no independent contribution to the explanation is not that they have no effect, but rather lies in the logic of functionalism. Clearly, most organizational changes occur because of decisions by the management or other parties. Thus ideas in the minds of these social actors are part of the process that produces the changes. The decision-makers may consider a range of choices and then choose between them. However, as Blau (1972: 13 fn.) insightfully states, the decision-makers will choose the option that is most effective. Given that only one option is the most effective, then it is predetermined that the decision-makers will choose that one. Thus positivism gains force when united with functionalism, so that the option that is chosen has to be chosen because of its functionality, that is, with respect to its beneficial outcomes. If all options are equal in their outcomes, then decision-makers seeking functionality could choose any option without detriment. However, in variants of functionalism such as structural contingency theory, the optimal outcome is produced only by the structure that fits the contingency, i.e. the situation (e.g. Lawrence and Lorsch 1967). Thus, in any situation, to attain the best outcome, the decision-makers must choose the structure that fits that situation. In this way the situation causes the structure, with the ideas of the decision-makers making no independent contribution to the explanation of the structure. Hence the positivist premise that explanation lies in situational causation, with the consciousness of the actors being superfluous, is made cogent when joined with functionalism. In particular, where functionalism is of the type that holds that optimal functionality arises from fitting the organization to its situation, then there is a situational, effectiveness-based, imperative that forces the choice.

Of course, the choice is forced because only one option leads to organizational effectiveness and the decision-makers are using organizational effectiveness as the criterion to choose between the options. Thus the decision-makers are placing a high value on organizational effectiveness. This is a value in their minds. Therefore, in that sense, the positivist, functionalist argument may be said to be predicated upon a condition of the ideationalist type. Blau (1972: 13 fn.) makes this explicit with his statement that the organizational managers value efficiency. However, if the organizational decision-makers fail to choose the option that best fits the situation and produces the best outcomes, then the organization will suffer sub-optimal performance. The objective consequences that would follow from not choosing the option that best fits the organization to its situation creates pressures on organizational managers that tend to force them to choose the option that fits. Severely low performance would cause the organization not to survive, if it is in a competitive situation, as are many business firms (the most numerous type of organization). Thus organizations that fail to adopt the most effective option tend to be eliminated from the population, and so management have an incentive to avoid such a catastrophe. Sub-optimal performance by a firm would leave it vulnerable to takeover, which provides an inducement to incumbent management to choose the effective option. Again, sub-optimal performance by managers of firms leaves them open to sanctioning, and possible replacement, by their superordinate managers or directors. While imperfections in control, or the presence of organizational slack, may allow the managers of an organization to delay adoption of the most effective option, so that misfit can exist for some time, eventually the situational imperative will tend to prevail. Thus among the population of extant organizations, there will be an irresistible tendency for organizational managers to choose options that conform to the situational imperative. Thus the situation will determine the structure with no moderation by managerial ideas.

In this way functionalism explains why positivism works, and provides a theoretical rationale that gives credence to the contention of Durkheim (1938) that causality lies outside the consciousness of people. In his terms, the social fact of the organizational structure that decision-makers choose is caused by two social facts:

(1) that only one structure objectively fits the situation in that only it will produce the most functional outcomes; and

(2) that organizational decision-makers are under situational pressures (from competition, head office, directors, takeover threat, etc.) to give priority to attaining the most functional outcome for their organization.

Thus the argument that Blau (1972: 13 fn.) makes contains an important theoretical point that applies generally to organizational positivism, providing it with a functionalist rationale.

Going further, because organizational decision-makers are forced by the situation and the performance imperative to adopt a particular option, they may do so even if it runs counter to their thinking. Thus their attitudes and values may incline them to prefer another option, which, nevertheless, fits the situation less well and so would produce less organizational effectiveness. Despite these initial preferences, the situational imperative is strong enough to override them, so that decision-makers acquiesce to the option that is dictated by the situation (Donaldson 1996a: 172–3). While the reluctantly chosen option is the immediate cause of the organizational change, it would not have been predictable from the initial attitudes and values of the decision-makers. Thus the consciousness of the decision-makers, independent of the situation, is not the cause of the option eventually put into practice. This conceptual point gives added meaning to the positivist proposition that the determining cause of the option chosen is in the situation and not in 'the state of individual consciousness' (Durkheim 1938: 110).

Positivism in social science draws on the biological view of humans to depict them as struggling for existence in a challenging environment, often competitively with one and other, and as being forced to adapt or perish. Applied to organizations, this leads to the positivist view of organizations as being shaped by their environments through either adaptation or selection.

1.3.1 Adaptation in Organizational Positivism

In organizational science, positivist theories of organizational adaptation include the theory of organizational adaptation in structural contingency theory (Donaldson 1995a, 1996b, 2001). This explains organizational structure by the need to fit the contingencies, such as organizational size (Child 1975; Khandwalla 1973) or technology (Woodward 1965). Fit of organizational structure to the contingencies leads to higher performance, whereas misfit leads to lower performance (Keller 1994). To avoid the damage caused by continuing low performance, organizations in misfit make adaptive changes, by adopting a new organizational structure that brings them into fit (Donaldson 2001). This process of organizational adaptation to the situation is seen in positivist studies of strategy and structure.

Strategy has been said to lead to structure (Chandler 1962). Strategy means an intention, that is, an idea, in the mind of managers, particularly the senior managers of an organization, and is therefore an ideationalist phenomenon. However, by acting on these ideas, managers make actual changes to organizations, such as increasing the range of their products, i.e. diversification (Chandler 1962). The

degree of diversification actually achieved causes divisionalization, in that diversified firms replace their existing structures, such as the functional structures with
divisional structures (Chandler 1962). This is an adaptation, in that the functional
structures fitted the pre-existing, non-diversified state, but misfit the new, diversified state, whereas divisional structures fit the new, diversified state. Thus the
explanation is of the functionalist type, by reference to beneficial outcomes.

Empirical support comes from case studies and comparative, quantitative statistical studies of corporations. Studies show a positive relationship between diversification and divisionalization in the United States (Chandler 1962; Rumelt 1974;
Fligstein 1985; Palmer et al. 1987; Mahoney 1992; Palmer, Jennings, and Zhou
1993). Other studies show that the relationship generalizes, by also holding in
other countries: Australia (Chenhall 1979; Capon et al. 1987), Canada (Khandwalla
1977), France (Dyas and Thanheiser 1976), Germany (Dyas and Thanheiser 1976),
Italy (Pavan 1976), Japan (Suzuki 1980), New Zealand (Hamilton and Shergill 1992,
1993), and the United Kingdom (Channon 1973, 1978). As Pfeffer (1997: 161)
remarks, some of these studies show not merely correlation between diversification
and divisionalization, but also that diversification precedes divisionalization, cor-
roborating that diversification is a cause of divisionalization. Moreover, the fit
between diversification and divisionalization has been shown to be beneficial for
performance (Donaldson 1987; Hamilton and Shergill 1993)—supporting the functionalist theory. Again, the poor performance of firms that are in misfit, through
retaining a functional structure when diversified, has been shown to be a trigger for
the adoption of the new, better fitting structure (Donaldson 1987). This empirically
supports the positivist view that firms are forced to adapt to their changing
circumstances in order to limit injurious outcomes (i.e. low performance).
Among large firms, the empirical evidence is that adaptive change is overwhelmingly through individual, ongoing firms changing their strategies and structures
(Donaldson 1995b: 73–5, 2001: 168–70).

1.3.2 Selection in Organizational Positivism

The other wing of organizational positivism stresses not adaptive change by ongoing organizations, but changes in the population, through selection. The selection mechanism for attaining organizational change is that organizations that misfit
their ecological niche fail to survive and newly founded organizations better fit their
ecological niche, i.e. functionalism. Organizational ecology has drawn on modern-
day evolutionary biology to explain the rates at which organizations in an industry
are founded and disbanded in terms of the number of organizations in that
industry (the 'population density') (Hannan and Freeman 1977). The vital (i.e.
founding and disbanding) rates in one sub-population can affect the vital rates in

another sub-population. Also founding rates can be affected by prior founding rates (Hannan and Freeman 1989). Organizational age also affects organizational mortality rates (Hannan and Freeman 1989). Furthermore, there is evidence that fit of organizational strategies to the ecological niches affects disbanding rates, such that specialists fit fine-grained and generalists fit coarse-grained niches (Hannan and Freeman 1989). There is empirical evidence of validity and generality from studies that feature the development and use of scientific methods (Hannan and Freeman 1989). The theory and methods of organizational ecology combine to make it a case of positivism in one of its strongest forms in organization studies (albeit with some limitations (Donaldson 1995b)). An empirical study of the changing organizational forms of gasoline stations shows that this is caused both by cases of adaptation of ongoing stations and by disbandings and new foundings among the population (Usher and Evans 1996). This provides support for both the positivist mechanisms, adaptation and selection, through which the situation molds organizations, and suggests that both may operate simultaneously in some populations of organizations.

In sum, positivist organizational theory shows that organizations are molded by their situation. This is seen in the organizational theories of structural contingency theory and organizational ecology. The processes whereby the situation molds the organization are functionalist: adaptation and selection. Other organizational sociologists, however, follow non-positivist approaches, such as interpretist, conflict, critical, postmodern, power, or social action theories, or social constructionism (Aldrich 1992; Alvesson and Deetz 1996; Clegg, Hardy, and Nord 1996). Organizational sociology has been subject to a vigorous debate between ideationalist, anti-positivism (e.g. Bourgeois 1984; Clegg 1988; Silverman 1968, 1970; Turner 1977; Whittington 1989) and positivism (Donaldson 1985, 1996a).

1.4 PHILOSOPHICAL ISSUES IN ORGANIZATIONAL POSITIVISM

The social sciences have been subject to discussions of their philosophical bases that claim to be damagingly critical. Such critical discussions purport to find fundamental philosophical difficulties even with 'The Idea of a Social Science' itself, as expressed by Winch (1958), in a book of this title. Thus the program of building a social science has been declared naive and invalid a priori (Winch 1958). This type of philosophically-based critique has been deployed in organizational studies, to declare invalid any attempt to construct a science of organizations, especially of the positivist type (e.g. Silverman 1968, 1970; Clegg and Dunkerley 1980; Turner 1977; Whitley 1977).

Some philosophers of science, however, have presented philosophical arguments that social science is not negated philosophically and is feasible (Kincaid 1996; Phillips 1992). They defend the thesis of naturalism (Kincaid 1996; Phillips 1992), which is that social sciences can be like the natural sciences, the view taken here. More specifically, philosophical defenses are offered of positivism and functionalism (Kincaid 1996). Whereas philosophical critics of social science are wont to question—and indeed dismiss—whole branches of social science based only on very broad characterizations of those branches (e.g. Winch 1958), Kincaid (1996) instead presents a philosophical analysis of social sciences that includes detailed analyses of actual social scientific research. His conclusion is that there is no impediment to building social sciences, similar to the natural sciences (Kincaid 1996). Indeed he argues that the difficulties in creating social science are just the ordinary practical problems faced in doing any good science, such as adequately controlling for confounding influences (Kincaid 1996). These problems are exactly those that positivist social and organizational sciences seek to overcome in their methodology and practice (Cook and Campbell 1979). Thus the implication is that positivism should continue with its traditional agenda rather than halting out of fear that it transgresses some philosophical strictures.

In particular, Kincaid (1996: 131–5) examines organizational research in one of its most positivist forms, organizational ecology (Hannan and Freeman 1989), and finds this to be good science. Kincaid (1996: 135–6) concludes of organizational ecology: 'Hannan and Freeman's work is thus an exemplary piece of social research, and it shows that good functionalist social science is possible in practice . . . Far from being pseudoscience, this functional explanation is arguably as well confirmed as good work in the non-experimental natural sciences. Those who claim that the social sciences are doomed to failure have a lot of explaining (away) to do.'

The philosophical analyses of Phillips (1992) and Kincaid (1996) present a major counter to the philosophical critiques of social science (e.g. Winch 1958). By extension, they provide an effective counter to the derived philosophically-based criticisms of positivist organizational science that have been presented by some organizational theorists (e.g. Silverman 1968, 1970; Clegg and Dunkerley 1980). The trenchant defenses of positivism provided by these philosophers (Kincaid 1996; Phillips 1992) furnish strong reinforcement to the earlier defense of organizational science against philosophically-based criticisms (Donaldson 1985). We turn now to an examination of some philosophical objections to social and organizational science:

- the argument that logical positivism is invalid and therefore so too is positivism
- the argument that functionalism is invalid

- the argument that positivism entails problematic ontological assumptions
- the argument that positivism fails because it does not use the hermeneutic method.

1.4.1 Positivism is Not Logical Positivism

Positivism is sometimes confused with logical positivism, but many positivists are not adherents of logical positivism. Logical positivism is the epistemological doctrine that science can only deal in observables and that any proposition dealing with unobservables is metaphysical nonsense (Ayer 1936; Bohman 1991). Popper (1959), a philosopher influential on positivism, rejected logical positivism by arguing that unobservables, such as scientific concepts like the atom, are meaningful. From such concepts can be deduced hypotheses about observables, which can be tested against empirical evidence, thereby subjecting the theory to falsification. This view of science as a hypothetico-deductive activity is probably the epistemology that is most common among contemporary positivists.

Falsifying the hypotheses does not necessarily mean, however, that the theory from which they are deduced is invalid. Hypotheses depend not only on the theory but also other, auxiliary sciences, such as the technologies used in measuring the observations (Feyerabend 1975). Therefore falsification of hypotheses may lead to improvements in the auxiliary sciences, which subsequently show the hypotheses to be supported. Thus initial disconfirmation of hypotheses can spur fruitful work to improve the auxiliary science, as part of the research program, rather than falsification of the theory (Lakatos 1974; Kuhn 1970). Thus the requirement that a theory be logically falsifiable is not the same as requiring that every failure of its hypotheses must lead to the theory being viewed as false.

Logical positivism influenced the social sciences, particularly psychology where it helped create behaviorism (Schlagel 1979), which sought theories of behavior that made no mention of unobservable states such as thinking or feeling. Behaviorism explains behavior as being shaped by the reinforcement coming from the environment (Skinner 1971). Thus adaptive learning can take place because of its association with outcomes beneficial for the organism. This is a kind of functionalism and marks a connection with biology. However, logical positivism has been largely supplanted in the philosophy of science by views that see unobservable concepts as legitimate (Chalmers 1999). This has fostered the development of non-behavioristic psychology and 'the cognitive revolution' (Harré and Gillett 1994). In organizational behavior, this turn towards cognition has led, *inter alia*, to the view of people as possessing intentions, setting goals, and self-regulating (Bandura 1986). In related moves in the study of human resource management, emphasis has shifted, from the study of the details of task behaviors, to general mental abilities, as the bases of personnel selection tools (Schmidt and Hunter 1998). The rise and fall of logical positivism is an example of shifts in epistemological doctrines within the philosophy of science that have affected organizational science.

Modern positivism in organizational science follows neither logical positivism nor behaviorism. Theoretical concepts are seen as legitimately being abstract and therefore unobservable. Also thinking and feelings and other unobservable processes are accepted as existing and being legitimate topics of study, though this must perforce be through their manifestation in observables, e.g. interview protocol or questionnaire response. Because unobservables have to be inferred indirectly from observables, they may be less reliable than observables and so treated accordingly. Hence positivism seeks objectivity, which is to say high levels of inter-subjective agreement between two or more observers (Popper 1959), and this tends to inhere in observables or other data that are colloquially called objective. This leads to the positivist strategy of seeking to study phenomena by studying objective social facts and then approaching more subjective aspects within that framework (Donaldson 1997). However, this modern positivist caution about the reliability of subjective data is far removed from the blanket disavowal of subjectivity by behaviorism that was spurred by logical positivism. The de-emphasis of subjective states in organizational positivism is because they are not the keys to explanation, which, instead, lie in the objective situational causes. Thus the focus on objective conditions in positivism is theoretical, rather than philosophical, in nature.

The problem of the unreliability of some observation statements is a reason for avoiding reductionism and instead favoring the holistic, or macro-scopic, approach of sociological positivism. In organizational science, reductionism holds that theories about organizations should be explained by the behavior of the individuals who compose, or interact with, the organizations. The notion is to provide a supposedly firm base for macro-organizational science by grounding it in the behavior of individuals. This could take the form of psychological reductionism, whereby macro-organizational phenomena are reduced to explanations about the motivations of individuals. However, there is a problem about how far an outside observer can have accurate knowledge about the psychological motivations of an individual. Such motivational states are inherently subjective and private, and the individual may not wish to fully disclose them to an observer. It is one thing for a manager to tell a social scientist about his or her need for achievement (McClelland 1961), but he or she may be coy about fully disclosing his or her needs for money, power, or sex, which may be less socially or organizationally legitimate. Moreover, some strands of psychology hold that individuals deny and are unconscious of some of their important motives (Freud 1925). Also, organizational colleagues may vary in their assessments of the motivations of an individual according to whether they are friends or rivals. Thus there is no secure foundation in psychological, motivational analyses of individuals on which to ground macro-organizational science.

Equally, political analyses explain organizations by their constituent individuals each pursuing their own self-interest. But how is an observer to know what is the real self-interest that the individual privately, subjectively perceives, when political theories hold that people acting politically consciously seek to conceal their true objectives in order to better play the political game (Pettigrew 1973)? Thus the reduction of macro-organizational phenomena to explanations by political models of individuals and their self-interests is as fraught with unreliability as is psychological reductionism.

Given these problems with reductionism, it is best avoided. Instead a better path is the positivist one of seeking to study the social facts, that is, phenomena such as structure or other public organizational characteristics, which are explained by other social facts, such as organizational size or environmental competition that are publicly observable. Both cause and effect are objective characteristics that can be measured reliably, thus providing a secure foundation for organizational science. The variables are at the macro-scopic level of the organization and its environment. Thus positivist organizational theory eschews seeking insight in the minds of the individuals and instead seeks what may be termed 'outsight', i.e. understanding how the organization results from the pressures of the situation.

It should be noted that while modern philosophers of social science are generally highly critical of logical positivism (e.g. Bohman 1991), some accept sociological positivism, which is being advocated in this chapter, as being valid, i.e. holistic or macrosocial (Rosenberg 1995) or functionalist or macrosociological (Kincaid 1996) explanation.

1.4.2 Functionalism is Valid

As we saw above, positivism gains much of its force in organizational science by being underpinned theoretically by functionalism. However, functionalism in sociology has attracted a lot of criticism (e.g. Silverman 1968, 1970), but much of it is misplaced (see Donaldson 1985). Philosophical problems are seen by some to be inherent in functionalism in social science. Functionalist explanation may be criticized as being teleology without a knowing subject (Elster 1983). Teleology refers to explanations of present states of affairs by a purpose that will be realized in the future. However, where the present state of affairs is sustained by a purpose about the future, the purpose can be held by people who are acting in the present. For example, the managers of an organization may do something now with the purpose of improving the effectiveness of the organization in the future (Etzioni 1968). In this case there is a knowing subject, so there is no mystical, disembodied purpose (Hegel 1953) involved in such a functionalist explanation in organizational sociology.

Sociological functionalism posits that the consequences, such as the functions of a social structure, are the causes of that structure. By cause is meant mainly that the functions explain the persistence of the structure (Kincaid 1996). While causes in science usually precede their consequences, the functionalist kind of explanation is not teleological, and has been termed telecausal (Isajiw 1968). In the case of organizational structures in functionalist organizational theory, the functional consequence of the structure feeds back to cause the structure to persist through human intention or Darwinian selection. A manager may see that the structure of his or her organization is producing beneficial outcomes and retain the structure for that reason, so that it persists. Again, a manager observing the outcomes of his or her organization's structure may change the structure to obtain more beneficial outcomes in future. In these cases, of both persistence and change, the manager is acting on the feedback effect of the consequences of present structures, to affect future structure for the purpose of securing future outcomes that are beneficial. Moreover, empirical research supports the functionalist theory that organizational structures change because of the feedback from organizational performance (Donaldson 1987; Ezzamel and Hilton 1980), as a result of managerial perceptions about such problems (Hill and Pickering 1986).

Going further, an entrepreneur may bring into being an organization that he or she intends will produce some beneficial function (e.g. serving a new market). In this way human intention can provide a functionalist explanation for the origins of a new organization. Similarly, human intention to increase the functionality can provide a functionalist explanation of how new organizational structures originate, e.g. the invention of the multidivisional structure by the managers at DuPont (Chandler 1962). Thus, through human intention, functionalism can explain not only the persistence of, and change in, existing structures, but also their origins.

Where organizational outcomes are severely dysfunctional, then that organization may fail to survive, so that the remaining organizations in the population are more functional (Hannan and Freeman 1989). In this Darwinian way, more, rather than less, functional organizational structures (or forms) can persist without any managerial intention or other human purpose being entailed.

Thus there is nothing philosophically or logically invalid about functionalist explanations of organizations. Moreover, by pursuing the functionalist theoretical agenda, through showing empirically the performance consequences of structures and their feedback effects (Donaldson 1987; Ezzamel and Hilton 1980; Hill and Pickering 1986; Hamilton and Shergill 1992, 1993), organizational theory research is providing the kind of evidence that skeptical critics of functionalism demand (Elster 1983: 61).

In formal terms functionalism involves the following logical structure:

x causes f

Where *x* is some attribute of an organization or one of its individual members and *f* is a function, that is, an outcome of *x*, which is of value to the organization, member or society.

and f causes x

Where the functional outcome, *f*, feeds back to cause *x* (or the organization itself) to exist, or *x* to be increased so as to increase *f*, or the organization to not survive because of a low value of *f*. Or where the human intention of attaining *f* causes *x* (or the organization itself) to exist, or *x* to be increased so as to increase *f*.

This formal statement includes both causality by feedback and by intention about the future. Human intentions about the future are, of course, not always borne out in the future. What actually occurs is also influenced by many factors other than intention, such as knowledge, judgment, capability, and luck. Insofar as human intentions are shaping the organization, they will explain the organization in a functionalist way only to the extent that the intentions about producing functions are realized in practice in the future. Otherwise the explanation is one by human intention shaping the organization but not in a way that is functionalist.

1.4.3 No Problematic Ontological Assumptions

In referring to external situational causes, such as 'the size of the population in a state of the United States', no claim is being made that such a factor necessarily exists. In philosophical terms, there is no ontological claim being made. Nor is there a presumption about ontology being made that is some kind of presupposition upon which the validity of positivist theory stands or falls. The external situational causes used in positivist theories are constructs, like those in any theory. As constructs, these causes are concepts used in the explanation. They may or may not exist. The question of their ontology is distinguishable from the question of their validity as explanations, which hangs on their ability to coherently account for patterns in the empirical data.

Within epistemology, the nominalist or instrumentalist account of science holds that scientific concepts are adequate if they meet tests of coherency and the explanation of data, without having also to pass tests of ontology (such as can the concept be seen, touched, etc.) (Chalmers 1999). The contrary epistemology of realism holds that theoretical concepts corresponds to entities that exist in the real world, so that the causes posited by positivist theories would be required to exist and entail ontology. Thus, on philosophical grounds, there is room for a range of views about how far the external situational causes of positivism exist or not. The key point is that the nominalist or instrumentalist epistemology allows positivism to speak about external situational causes without thereby having also to hold that such causes exist. Therefore there is no obligation on positivist research to show that such external situational causes pass tests of existence (i.e. ontology). Instead, the explanations by reference to external situational causes proffered by positivism are to be subject to tests of their validity as explanations, the same as any theory, i.e. tests of logical coherency and consistency with data.

1.4.4 Strong Hermeneutics Not Required

As we have seen, positivist social science is sometimes mistakenly equated with behaviorism, that is, studying observable human behavior and ignoring that people have a private inner world of consciousness. Yet almost all of what is interesting about organizations and organizational behavior involves action, that is, the behavior *and* the meanings that people give to their behaviors and those of other people. Meaning involves language and consciousness. They are what define a piece of behavior as 'making a decision', or 'exercising authority'. Thus even if studying organizational structural phenomena such as centralization of decision-making, the analyst is studying meaningful action involving the subjective meanings held by the organizational members. Mutually shared meanings between actors produce the interactions between roles that constitute organizational structures such as a hierarchy of authority. More importantly, the shared meanings of people interacting together create 'the organization'. In this sense organizational studies, like almost all social science, is weakly hermeneutic (i.e. entails the interpretations of the social actors). For example, to say of an organization that its size is a thousand members is only valid if those people see themselves as members of that organization. However, as Phillips (1992) states, social research can be hermeneutic in the definition of its variables without requiring that the relationships it studies between those variables be purely hermeneutic, i.e. be the interpretations given by the actors who are being studied. An external analyst can take these same variables and come up with different relationships among them and interpret them by a theory that is different from the theory that is believed by the actors. In Phillips's (1992) terms, social research is weakly hermeneutic, but does not all have to be strongly hermeneutic. In particular, positivist organizational science is weakly, but not strongly, hermeneutic. The phenomena and variables of organizational science entail subjective meanings, and in that sense are weakly hermeneutic. However, the relationships among the variables are explained by positivist theories constructed by an external analyst and can be different from the interpretations of the organizational members, i.e. not be strongly hermeneutic.

1.5 THE FUTURE OF POSITIVIST ORGANIZATIONAL SCIENCE

Continuing with positivism can make further progress in organizational science in the future. As we have seen, positivism can explain organizational change as bringing into alignment the organizational structure with the situational contingencies, so that adaptation occurs. However, this adaptive process is subject to time lags, which might seem to indicate limitations in the scope of the positivist explanation of organizational change. Yet, positivism can be extended to offer an explanation of when adaptive organizational changes will occur.

The adaptation of the organization to its environment allows it to perform more highly. However, the adaptive process is itself driven by organizational performance in a positivist way, in that the level of performance feeds back to foster or postpone adaptive organizational change. An organization in misfit with its environment or situation consequently suffers lower performance (Hamilton and Shergill 1992, 1993; Keller 1994). However, it is only when performance drops to the point of being low that adaptation is triggered (Child 1972; Donaldson 1987; Ezzamel and Hilton 1980; Hill and Pickering 1986). This is consistent with the theory that managerial decision-making under ambiguity is boundedly rational, i.e. problem-solving that is triggered when outcomes have become unacceptable (Simon 1997). The ensuing crisis of low performance impels adaptive organizational change. Organizational performance is the result of the fits or misfits (e.g. in organizational structure) between the organization and its situation, together with other causes of organizational performance (Child 1972). Such other causes of organizational performance include the business cycle, competition, directors, and divestment (Donaldson 1999). The interaction of these other causes of organizational performance with misfit determines whether organizational performance drops low enough for adaptation to occur, or not (Donaldson 1999).

Use may be made of portfolio theory from finance (Sharpe 1970), to construct, by analogy, an organizational portfolio theory (Donaldson 1999). Each cause of performance is a factor in the organizational portfolio. Each organizational portfolio factor has a certain variance and a certain covariance with misfit. Those factors with high variance that are positively correlated with fit, so that they depress organizational performance when the organization is in misfit, drive down organizational performance and so promote organizational adaptation. In contrast, those factors that are negatively correlated with fit, so that they buoy up organizational performance when the organization is in misfit, tend to maintain satisfactory organizational performance and so postpone organizational adaptation. Thus the key to facilitating needed organizational changes lies not so much in the minds of managers (where it is usually sought), but in the objective situation they face and which forces them to act: the performance level of their organization. This, of course, is consistent with the positivist theory that causation lies in the external situational conditions, rather than in the minds of organizational members, and that situational imperatives determine the organization, rather than that individuals exercise a free choice. Organizational portfolio theory provides an analytical framework for modeling performance-driven organizational change at both the organizational and divisional levels (Donaldson 1999). Thus positivism can further the explanation of organizational change by studying it through the lens of organizational portfolio theory. In this way, organizational positivism may illuminate not only long-term causal relationships that align the environment, contingencies, and structure, but also the short-run dynamics that explain when change will, and will not, occur. It is a task for future research to empirically test organizational portfolio theory and ascertain its validity more comprehensively than has occurred to date.

To the degree that organizational portfolio theory is corroborated in future research, it may shed light beyond that presently available from traditional, non-positivist analyses of organizational change. It could eventually help take practice beyond the more customary, ideationalist approach, of trying to change organizations by seeking 'to change managerial thinking'. Instead, positivism holds that adaptive organizational change is fostered by altering organizations so that, periodically, they have episodes of low performance when they are in misfit. This state is attained by altering the organizational portfolio factors that affect how the organization is impacted by its environment and so affect its performance levels (Donaldson 1999). It is also partly attained by altering the external environment of the organizations, such as by government policies on competition and taxation, which affect organizational performance, either directly or through the organizational portfolio factors (Donaldson 2000). This is consistent with the positivist approach that organizational change is caused by the objective, situational conditions, so that fostering change entails changing those conditions.

References

Agarwal, Naresh C. (1979). 'Nature of Size–Structure Relationship: Some Further Evidence'. *Human Relations*, 32/6: 441–50.

Aldrich, Howard (1992). 'Incommensurable Paradigms? Vital Signs from Three Perspectives', in Michael Reed and Michael Hughes (eds.), *Rethinking Organization: New Directions in Organization Theory and Analysis*. London: Sage Publications.

Alvesson, Mats, and Deetz, Stanley (1996). 'Critical Theory and Postmodernism Approaches to Organizational Studies', in S. R. Clegg, C. Hardy, and W. Nord (eds.), *Handbook of Organization Studies*. London: Sage Publications.

Ayer, A. J. (1936). *Language, Truth and Logic*. London: Gollancz.

AYOUBI, Z. M. (1981). 'Technology, Size and Organization Structure in a Developing Country: Jordan', in D. J. Hickson and C. J. McMillan (eds.), *Organization and Nation: The Aston Programme IV.* Farnborough, Hants.: Gower.

BANDURA, A. (1986). *Social Foundations of Thought and Action: A Social Cognitive Theory.* Englewood Cliffs, NJ: Prentice-Hall.

BERGER, PETER L., and LUCKMANN, T. (1966). *The Social Construction of Reality: A Treatise in the Sociology of Knowledge.* Garden City, NY: Doubleday.

—— and PULLBERG, S. (1966). 'Reification and the Sociological Critique of Consciousness'. *New Left Review*, 35: 56–71.

BEYER, J. M., and TRICE, H. M. (1979). 'A Reexamination of the Relations between Size and Various Components of Organizational Complexity'. *Administrative Science Quarterly*, 24/1: 48–64.

BLALOCK, HUBERT M. (1961). *Causal Inference in Nonexperimental Research.* Chapel Hill: University of North Carolina Press.

BLAU, PETER M. (1970). 'A Formal Theory of Differentiation in Organizations'. *American Sociological Review*, 35/2: 201–18.

—— (1972). 'Interdependence and Hierarchy in Organizations'. *Social Science Research*, 1: 1–24.

—— and SCHOENHERR, P. A. (1971). *The Structure of Organizations.* New York: Basic Books.

BOHMAN, JAMES (1991). *New Philosophy of Social Science: Problems of Indeterminacy.* Cambridge: Polity Press.

BOORSTIN, DANIEL J. (1983). *The Discoverers.* New York: Random House.

BOURGEOIS III, L. J. (1984). 'Strategic Management and Determinism'. *Academy of Management Review*, 9/4: 586–96.

BURRELL, GIBSON, and MORGAN, GARETH (1979). *Sociological Paradigms and Organisational Analysis: Elements of the Sociology of Corporate Life.* London: Heinemann.

CAPON, N., CHRISTODOLOU, C., FARLEY, JOHN U., and HULBERT, JAMES M. (1987). 'A Comparative Analysis of the Strategy and Structure of United States and Australian Corporations'. *Journal of International Business Studies*, 18/1: 51–74.

CHALMERS, A. F. (1999). *What is This Thing Called Science? An Assessment of the Nature and Status of Science and its Methods* (3rd edn). St Lucia: University of Queensland Press.

CHANDLER, ALFRED D., Jr. (1962). *Strategy and Structure: Chapters in the History of the Industrial Enterprise.* Cambridge, Mass.: MIT Press.

CHANNON, DEREK F. (1973). *The Strategy and Structure of British Enterprise.* London: Macmillan.

—— (1978). *The Service Industries: Strategy, Structure, and Financial Performance.* London: Macmillan.

CHENHALL, ROBERT H. (1979). 'Some Elements of Organizational Control in Australian Divisionalized Firms'. *Australian Journal of Management*, Supplement to 4: 1–36.

CHILD, JOHN (1972). 'Organizational Structure, Environment and Performance: The Role of Strategic Choice'. *Sociology*, 6/1: 1–22.

—— (1973). 'Predicting and Understanding Organization Structure'. *Administrative Science Quarterly*, 18/2: 168–85.

—— (1975). 'Managerial and Organizational Factors Associated with Company Performance, Part 2: A Contingency Analysis'. *Journal of Management Studies*, 12/1: 12–27.

—— and KIESER, ALFRED (1979). 'Organizational and Managerial Roles in British and West German Companies: An Examination of the Culture-free Thesis', in C. J. Lammers and D. J. Hickson (eds.), *Organizations Alike and Unlike*. London: Routledge & Kegan Paul.

CLEGG, STEWART (1988). 'The Good, the Bad and the Ugly'. *Organization Studies*, 9/1: 7–13.

—— and DUNKERLEY, DAVID (1980). *Organization, Class and Control*. London: Routledge & Kegan Paul.

—— HARDY, C., and NORD, W. (eds.) (1996). *Handbook of Organization Studies*. London: Sage Publications.

COMTE, AUGUSTE (1853). *The Positivist Philosophy*, i, trans. H. Martineau. London: Chapman.

COOK, THOMAS D., and CAMPBELL, DONALD T. (1979). *Quasi-experimentation: Design and Analysis Issues for Field Settings*. Chicago: Rand McNally College Pub Co.

DONALDSON, LEX (1985). *In Defence of Organization Theory: A Reply to the Critics*. Cambridge: Cambridge University Press.

—— (1987). 'Strategy and Structural Adjustment to Regain Fit and Performance: In Defense of Contingency Theory'. *Journal of Management Studies*, 24/1: 1–24.

—— (1995a). *Contingency Theory*, ix, in *History of Management Thought Series*, Aldershot: Dartmouth Publishing Company.

—— (1995b). *American Anti-Management Theories of Organization: A Critique of Paradigm Proliferation*. Cambridge: Cambridge University Press.

—— (1996a). *For Positivist Organization Theory: Proving the Hard Core*. London: Sage Publications.

—— (1996b). 'The Normal Science of Structural Contingency Theory', in S. R. Clegg, C. Hardy, and W. Nord (eds.), *The Handbook of Organization Studies*. London: Sage Publications.

—— (1997). 'A Positivist Alternative to the Structure-Action Approach'. *Organization Studies*, 18/1: 77–92.

—— (1999). *Performance-Driven Organizational Change: The Organizational Portfolio*. Thousand Oaks, Calif.: Sage Publications.

—— (2000). 'Organizational Portfolio Theory: Performance-Driven Organizational Change'. *Contemporary Economic Policy*, 18/4: 386–96.

—— (2001). *The Contingency Theory of Organizations*. Thousand Oaks, Calif.: Sage Publications.

—— and WARNER, MALCOLM (1974). 'Structure of Organizations in Occupational Interest Associations'. *Human Relations*, 27/8: 721–38.

DURKHEIM, ÉMILE (1938). *The Rules of Sociological Method*. Glencoe, Ill.: Free Press.

DYAS, GARETH P., and THANHEISER, HEINZ T. (1976). *The Emerging European Enterprise: Strategy and Structure in French and German Industry*. London: Macmillan.

ELSTER, JON (1983). *Explaining Technical Change: A Case Study in the Philosophy of Science*. Cambridge: Cambridge University Press.

ETZIONI, AMITAI (1968). *The Active Society: A Theory of Societal and Political Processes*. New York: Free Press.

EZZAMEL, M. A., and HILTON, K. (1980). 'Divisionalisation in British Industry: A Preliminary Study'. *Accounting and Business Research*, 10: 197–214.

FEYERABEND, P. (1975). *Against Method: Outline of an Anarchistic Theory of Knowledge*. London: New Left Books.

FLIGSTEIN, NEIL (1985). 'The Spread of the Multidivisional Form among Large Firms, 1919–1979'. *American Sociological Review*, 50: 377–91.

FREUD, SIGMUND (1925). 'The Unconscious', in *Collected Papers*. London: L. and V. Woolf.

FRIEDMAN, MILTON (1953). 'The Methodology of Positive Economics', in Milton Friedman, *Essays in Positive Economics*. Chicago: Chicago University Press.

GALTUNG, JOHAN (1967). *Theory and Methods of Social Research*. London: George Allen & Unwin.

GRINYER, PETER H., and YASAI-ARDEKANI, MASOUD (1981). 'Strategy, Structure, Size and Bureaucracy'. *Academy of Management Journal*, 24/3: 471–86.

HAMILTON, R. T., and SHERGILL, G. S. (1992). 'The Relationship between Strategy–Structure Fit and Financial Performance in New Zealand: Evidence of Generality and Validity with Enhanced Controls'. *Journal of Management Studies*, 29/1: 95–113.

—— —— (1993). *The Logic of New Zealand Business: Strategy, Structure, and Performance*. Auckland, New Zealand: Oxford University Press.

HANNAN, MICHAEL T., and FREEMAN, JOHN (1977). 'The Population Ecology of Organizations'. *American Journal of Sociology*, 82/5: 929–64.

—— (1989). *Organizational Ecology*. Cambridge, Mass.: Harvard University Press.

HARRÉ, ROM, and GILLETT, GRANT (1994). *The Discursive Mind*. Thousand Oaks, Calif.: Sage Publications.

HARRIS, MARVIN (1977). *Cows, Pigs, Wars and Witches: The Riddles of Culture*. London: Fontana.

HEGEL, G. W. F. (1953). *Reason in History*, trans. Robert S. Hartman. New York: Bobbs-Merrill.

HILL, CHARLES W. L., and PICKERING, J. F. (1986). 'Divisionalization, Decentralization and Performance of Large United Kingdom Companies'. *Journal of Management Studies*, 23/1: 26–50.

ISAJIW, WSEVOLOD W. (1968). *Causation and Functionalism in Sociology*. London: Routledge & Kegan Paul.

KELLER, ROBERT T. (1994). 'Technology-Information Processing Fit and the Performance of R&D Project Groups: A Test of Contingency Theory'. *Academy of Management Journal*, 37/1: 167–79.

KHANDWALLA, PRADIP N. (1973). 'Viable and Effective Organizational Designs of Firms'. *Academy of Management Journal*, 16/3: 481–95.

—— (1977). *The Design of Organizations*. New York: Harcourt Brace Janovich.

KINCAID, HAROLD (1996). *Philosophy Foundations of the Social Sciences: Analyzing Controversies in Social Research*. Cambridge: Cambridge University Press.

KUC, B., HICKSON, D. J., and MCMILLAN, C. J. (1981). 'Centrally Planned Development: A Comparison of Polish Factories with Equivalents in Britain, Japan and Sweden', in D. J. Hickson and C. J. McMillan (eds.), *Organization and Nation: The Aston Programme IV*. Farnborough, Hants.: Gower.

KUHN, THOMAS S. (1970). *The Structure of Scientific Revolutions* (2nd enlarged edn). Chicago: University of Chicago Press.

LAKATOS, I. (1974). 'Falsification and the Methodology of Scientific Research Programmes', in I. Lakatos and A. Musgrave (eds.), *Criticism and the Growth of Knowledge*. Cambridge: Cambridge University Press.

LAWRENCE, PAUL R., and LORSCH, JAY W. (1967). *Organization and Environment: Managing Differentiation and Integration*. Boston: Division of Research, Graduate School of Business Administration, Harvard University.

MCCLELLAND, D. C. (1961). *The Achieving Society*. New York: Free Press.

MAHONEY, JOSEPH T. (1992). 'The Adoption of the Multidivisional Form of Organization: A Contingency Model'. *Journal of Management Studies*, 29/1: 49–72.

MARSH, ROBERT M., and MANNARI, HIROSHI (1989). 'The Size Imperative? Longitudinal Tests'. *Organization Studies*, 10/1: 83–95.

MERTON, R. K. (1949). *Social Theory and Social Structure*. Chicago: Free Press.

MEYER, MARSHALL W. (1972). 'Size and the Structure of Organizations: A Causal Analysis'. *American Sociological Review*, 37: 434–41.

PALMER, D., JENNINGS, P. DEVEREAUX, and ZHOU, X. (1993). 'Late Adoption of the Multidivisional Form by Large U.S. Corporations: Institutional, Political, and Economic Accounts', *Administrative Science Quarterly*, 38/1: 100–31.

—— FRIEDLAND, R., JENNINGS, P. D., and POWERS, M. E. (1987). 'The Economics and Politics of Structure: The Multidivisional Form and Large U.S. Corporation'. *Administrative Science Quarterly*, 32/1: 25–48.

PARSONS, TALCOTT (1966). *Societies: Evolutionary and Comparative Perspectives*. Englewood Cliffs, NJ: Prentice-Hall.

PAVAN, ROBERT J. (1976). 'Strategy and Structure: The Italian Experience'. *Journal of Economics and Business*, 28/3: 254–60.

PETTIGREW, ANDREW M. (1973). *The Politics of Organizational Decision-Making*. London: Tavistock.

PFEFFER, JEFFREY (1997). *New Directions for Organization Theory: Problems and Prospects*. New York: Oxford University Press.

PHILLIPS, D. C. (1992). *The Social Scientist's Bestiary: A Guide to Fabled Threats to, and Defenses of, Naturalistic Social Science*. Oxford: Pergammon Press.

POPPER, K. R. (1959). *The Logic of Scientific Discovery*. New York: Harper & Row.

REX, JOHN. (1961). *Key Problems of Sociological Theory*. London: Routledge & Kegan Paul.

ROSENBERG, ALEXANDER (1995). *Philosophy of Social Science* (2nd edn). Boulder, Colo.: Westview Press.

RUMELT, RICHARD P. (1974). *Strategy, Structure and Economic Performance*. Boston: Division of Research, Graduate School of Business Administration, Harvard University.

SCHLAGEL, RICHARD H. (1979). 'Revolution in the Philosophy of Science: Implications for Method and Theory in Psychology', Invited Address at the meeting of the American Psychological Association, New York.

SCHMIDT, FRANK L., and HUNTER, JOHN E. (1998). 'The Validity and Utility of Selection Methods in Personnel Psychology: Practical and Theoretical Implications of 85 Years of Research Findings'. *Psychological Bulletin*, 124/2: 262–74.

SCHREYÖGG, GEORG (1980). 'Contingency and Choice in Organization Theory'. *Organization Studies*, 1/4: 305–26.

SCHUTZ, A. (1967). *The Phenomenology of the Social World*, trans. G. Walsh and F. Lehnert. Evanston, Ill.: Northwestern University Press.

SHARPE, WILLIAM F. (1970). *Portfolio Theory and Capital Markets*. New York: McGraw-Hill.

SHENOY, S. (1981). 'Organization Structure and Context: A Replication of the Aston Study in India', in D. J. Hickson, and C. J. McMillan (eds.), *Organization and Nation: The Aston Programme IV*, Farnborough, Hants.: Gower.

SILVERMAN, DAVID (1968). 'Formal Organizations or Industrial Sociology: Towards a Social Action Analysis of Organizations', *Sociology*, 2: 221–38.

—— (1970). *The Theory of Organizations*. London: Heinemann.

SIMON, HERBERT A. (1997). *Administrative Behavior: A Study of Decision-Making Processes in Administrative Organizations* (4th edn). New York: Free Press.

SKINNER, BURRHUS F. (1971). *Beyond Freedom and Dignity.* New York: Knopf.

SUZUKI, Y. (1980). 'The Strategy and Structure of Top 100 Japanese Industrial Enterprises 1950–1970'. *Strategic Management Journal,* 1/3: 265–91.

TOULMIN, S. E. (1962). *The Philosophy of Science.* London: Arrow.

TURNER, STEPHEN D. (1977). 'Blau's Theory of Differentiation: Is it Explanatory?', in J. Kenneth Benson (ed.), *Organizational Analysis: Critique and Innovation,* Sage Contemporary Social Science Issues 37. Beverly Hills: Sage Publications.

USHER, JOHN M., and EVANS, MARTIN G. (1996). 'Life and Death along Gasoline Alley: Darwinian and Lamarkian Processes in a Differentiating Population'. *Academy of Management Journal,* 39/5: 1428–66.

WEBER, MAX (1968). *Economy and Society: An Outline of Interpretive Sociology,* ed. Guenther Roth and Claus Wittich. New York: Bedminster Press.

WHITLEY, R. D. (1977). 'Concepts of Organization and Power in the Study of Organizations'. *Personnel Review,* 6/1: 54–9.

WHITTINGTON, RICHARD (1989). *Corporate Strategies in Recession and Recovery: Social Structure and Strategic Choice.* London: Allen & Unwin.

WINCH, P. (1958). *The Idea of a Social Science.* London: Routledge & Kegan Paul.

WONG, GILBERT Y. Y., and BIRNBAUM-MORE, PHILIP H. (1994). 'Culture, Context and Structure: A Test on Hong Kong Banks'. *Organization Studies,* 15/1: 99–123.

WOODWARD, JOAN (1965). *Industrial Organization: Theory and Practice.* London: Oxford University Press.

CHAPTER 2

....

ORGANIZATION THEORY AS AN INTERPRETIVE SCIENCE

....

MARY JO HATCH
DVORA YANOW

INTERPRETIVE approaches to science are found in many social sciences, including organizational studies. They trace their antecedents, sometimes consciously, sometimes by implication, to a set of philosophical arguments that developed largely in the first part of the twentieth century in Europe (initially in Germany, at mid-century in France, with the occasional involvement of English philosophers). These arguments have even earlier roots—in the eighteenth-century work of Kant, in the ancient Greek philosophers, and in 1,500-year-old Jewish textual practices.

To talk about 'science' is to ask certain kinds of questions, involving claims-making about the subject(s) of study. A colleague, student, or client can reasonably inquire about the bases for these claims, 'How do you know that which you are claiming about this organization? What is the foundation (or "truth value", in philosophical language) for your claim(s)?' Answers to such epistemological questions themselves rest on ontological claims about the reality status of the subject of study: How does its character, as an entity in the social world, affect our ability to know it? Is an organization real in the same way that a table is real? The answers also entail methodological matters: claims about the character of an organization's reality and about the knowability of that reality implicate certain procedures of discovery, which themselves establish and undergird truth value claims.

As interpretive philosophies developed in dialogue with other nineteenth- and twentieth-century philosophical arguments about similar questions and claims, we begin this essay with a brief overview of the context out of which they grew, touch on their central ideas, and then turn to their manifestations in organizational studies.

2.1 HISTORICAL BACKGROUND

Imagine: you are sitting under a tree and an apple falls on your head. How do you explain that event? In Rome in 239 you might have answered, 'Zeus and Hera were throwing thunderbolts; one hit the tree and it knocked the apple off.' In 1739 in London, thanks to Newton, you would likely no longer appeal to such metaphysical explanations, offering instead a 'scientific law'—gravity—for your explanation. Newton's observations and those of other late fifteenth to early eighteenth-century thinkers, such as Copernicus and Galileo, laid the foundation for a conception of 'science' that replaced religion as the source of certain knowledge. That conception still holds today.

It rests, first, on the understanding that humans possess powers of reasoning that they can apply systematically to the world surrounding them: they need not rely on the authority of tradition (or charisma, in a Weberian view) vested in religious or monarchic leaders. Second, the application of that reasoning yields a set of 'laws' or principles that are considered to be universal—that is, holding at all places at all times for all persons (i.e. regardless of class or religion, race or gender, paving the way for non-Protestants, non-Europeans, and women to be understood as having personhood). Third, this universality means that a certain regularity or order inheres in natural and physical events (discoverable through the application of human reason, point one above). This, in turn, means that these events can be predicted—and, hence, controlled (see Bernstein 1976, 1983; Dallmayr and McCarthy 1977; Rabinow and Sullivan 1979).

By the early 1800s, a set of philosophical principles began to emerge based on the premise that if universal laws can be 'discovered' for the physical and natural world, they can also be found for the social or human world. This argument, known as social positivism, was reformulated mid-1800s as evolutionary positivism, and toward the end of the century evolved into critical positivism (or empiriocriticism). The latter emphasized the certainty of knowledge based only on the senses (sight, sound, touch, taste, smell) and limited science to sense descriptions of experience in order to eliminate error. Largely fading from view after that, this line of thinking enjoyed a resurgence in the early twentieth century (especially strong between the two World Wars) under the name logical positivism (also known as the 'Vienna Circle' because of its proponents' main location; see Abbagnano 1967; Passmore 1967; Polkinghorne 1983).

It was primarily against the claims of the logical positivists that interpretive philosophies developed (see DeHaven-Smith 1988; Hawkesworth 1988; Jennings 1983, 1987). While it is not our intention to provide a history of positivist thought, this short summary is important as background for reading interpretive organizational studies, many of whose authors, in critiquing 'positivism', are addressing only or primarily logical positivism or subsuming four different, albeit related, schools of thought under the one name.

We will commit a similar 'fallacy' in this chapter, using 'interpretive' as an umbrella term subsuming several different schools of thought, including phenomenology, hermeneutics, (some) Frankfurt School critical theory, symbolic interaction, and ethnomethodology. Many of these ideas dovetail with late nineteenth- and early twentieth-century pragmatism[1] and later twentieth-century feminist epistemology and research methods (e.g. Falco 1987; Harding 1989, 1990; Hartsock 1987, Hawkesworth 1989; Heldke 1989; Miller 1986; Modleski 1986) and science studies (e.g. Harding 1991; Latour 1987; Longino 1990), although we will note these only in passing. We will treat the philosophical presuppositions that these several schools hold in common which distinguish them from the positivist presuppositions with which they took issue.

2.2 CENTRAL IDEAS FROM INTERPRETIVE PHILOSOPHIES

Interpretive scholars argue that the social world cannot be understood in the same way as the natural and physical worlds. Unlike rocks and atoms, humans make

[1] James credited Pierce with the coinage of the term, although Pierce did not like James's formulation of the philosophy and himself called it 'pragmaticism'. The points of similarity are pronounced in Mead's and Dewey's work, among them the emphasis on the context-specificity of knowledge and the extent to which the Self is constituted in interaction within society and its themes. See Menand (1997, 2001).

meaning, and so a human (or social) science needs to be able to address what is meaningful to people in the social situation under study. This requires understanding how groups, and individuals within them, develop, express, and communicate meaning, something that objective, unmediated observation (if that were even possible) cannot yield.

In addressing the question of how things might be known, early interpretive thinkers (e.g. Droysen, Rickert, Windelband, Simmel) turned to Kant's central idea that knowing depends on a priori knowledge (and so interpretive thought is sometimes referred to as neo-Kantian or neo-Idealist, as Kant's ideas were part of the German Idealist movement). Admitting prior knowledge into the realm of scientific inquiry implies a source other than one of the five senses. Rickert even argued for linking meaning with human values, themselves not sense-based. As to the purpose of science, Droysen, for example, argued that whereas for the physical sciences it was to explain, human sciences' purpose was to understand, an idea developed by Weber in his writings on *Verstehen* (understanding; see Beam and Simpson 1984; Fay 1975; Filmer *et al.* 1972; Polkinghorne 1988).

Different neo-Kantians argued for different elements as the proper focus of study. The debate is encapsulated in distinctions between phenomenology and hermeneutics. Phenomenologists favored an analytic focus on experience: Dilthey, for example, argued that social scientists should study the lived experience (or life world: *Lebenswelt*) of human actors in (or members of) the setting under analysis, in terms of the meaning(s) they made of those experiences. Hermeneuticists, among them Rickert, argued that the appropriate subject of study was the cultural artifacts people created and imbued with their values. Simmel advanced an argument in favor of content *and* form: studying both meaning (the values, beliefs, and feelings of lived experience) and the artifacts that embody meaning.

Both schools agreed on one central implication of Kant's thinking: if a knower comes to a study with a priori knowledge and that shapes or filters what she apprehends, then the knowledge process cannot be said to be objective, as positivist philosopher-scientists had argued, and knowing cannot be said to proceed through direct, unmediated observation alone. Something intercedes between sense-based perception and 'sense data' (the thing being perceived). The term *Verstehen* developed against the notion that the sense-based 'facts' of nature, seen by positivists as external to human actors, could simply be grasped (*Begreifen*, in Weber's terminology). According to Weber and others, human acts and other artifacts are the projections or embodiments of human meaning. They are not, then, completely external to the world of their creators or of others engaging them (including researchers), and so their meaning must be understood (or interpreted); it cannot merely be grasped.

Phenomenologists, among them Husserl and Schutz, referred to this entity interceding between event-experience and understanding as mind or consciousness. Other terms such as lens, frame, paradigm, world view or *weltanschauung* capture aspects of the same idea. As developed in phenomenology, each knower comes to his subject with prior knowledge that has grown out of past experience, education, training, family-community-regional-national (and so on) background, and personality. These constitute, for each of us, the contexts of our lived experience; and this lived experience, in turn, shapes the way that we understand our 'Selves' and the world within which we live (Schutz 1967, 1973). This holds, too, for social scientists with respect to their subjects of study.

What we claim as knowledge of this social world comes from *interpreting* our sense perceptions, not from an uninterpreted grasping of them. The cones in our eyes, for example, might be excited by the colors of a sunset; but sensing that sunset as 'beautiful' or 'moving' requires more than sight alone. This sense-making requires interpretation, which we do in the context of the event or experience, informed by prior knowledge. Both researcher and researched are, then, situated entities: their meaning-making and meaning is contextualized by prior knowledge and by history and surrounding elements (other events, other experiences), a position shared by critical theorists and echoed in feminist 'standpoint theory' (e.g. Hartsock 1987; Hawkesworth 1989). The implication of this argument is not only that universal, objective laws are not possible, but that social 'reality' may be construed differently by different people: the social world we inhabit and experience is potentially a world of multiple realities, multiple interpretations. Discovery of some external singular reality, a requisite of positivist science, is not possible in this view.

Hermeneutic philosophers, such as Dilthey and Gadamer, argued that meaning is not expressed or known directly. Rather, meaning is embedded in (or projected onto) artifacts by their creators; it can be known through interpreting these artifacts. As hermeneutics developed originally as a form of interpreting Biblical texts, the initial focus in its application to the social world more broadly was on texts and text-like objects seen as the sorts of artifacts into which their human creators projected meaning: language, both written (e.g. fiction, poetry, non-fiction) and oral (e.g. conversations, speeches); art; architecture; film. Later thinkers extended this reasoning to argue that in seeking to understand daily behavior, we treat human acts *as if* they were texts (Ricoeur 1971; Taylor 1971). This greatly expanded the realm of human artifacts to which hermeneutic methods could be applied. For example, we rarely discuss explicitly, in common everyday encounters, what our values are. One might strike up a conversation with someone waiting in line at the supermarket and infer what she values or what is meaningful to him from the words spoken, the tone of voice, and other elements of nonverbal language, including dress, bearing, and facial expressions. Similarly, we might infer an organization's values from the design or use of the building in which it is located. Researchers seeking to understand human meaning, then, cannot access it directly. All we can have direct access to is artifacts, inferring from them their underlying meanings (an idea central to interpretive methodologies and methods).

These arguments link directly to three American schools of thought that can be seen as applications or extensions of European interpretive philosophies: ethnomethodological analysis, in both its strands—conversation and event analysis, developed by Garfinkel (1977) in the mid-1900s; symbolic interactionist theory developed by Goffman (1959, 1974; building on Mead 1934); and the dramaturgic analysis developed by Burke (1969/1945; 1989) extending literary analysis to interpretations of everyday life.

Although twentieth-century hermeneutic scholars did not treat it as such, it is clear that the relationship between meanings and artifacts is a symbolic one: artifacts come to stand in for, to represent, their embedded meanings. This relationship is dynamic: every time an artifact is engaged or used, its underlying meaning is maintained and reinforced, or revised and changed. Arguing that meanings cannot be apperceived or accessed directly, but only through interpreting their artifactual representations, leads to the basic methods of data access used in interpretive analyses: observing (with whatever degree of participation), conversational (or 'in-depth') interviewing, and the close reading of documents. The argument opens the door to two sorts of questions about the relationship among data, methods of access and analysis, and interpretation. One concerns the certainty of knowledge; the other, the ability to make this knowledge explicit.

Questions may be raised about the certainty with which one can claim to know what artifacts mean, especially when one is studying artifacts and meanings of people other than oneself and societies, cultures, or organizations other than one's own. A theoretical answer is suggested by the dual sense in which Kuhn (1970; see also 1977) used the term 'paradigm' in his analysis of scientific practices. He meant both the framing of knowledge about or approach to a scientific problem, and the community of scientists sharing that frame. Phenomenologists show us that the two are inseparable: the process by which a problem comes to be framed is the same process that creates a community—of scientists or other interpreters. It is a process of creating intersubjective understandings, in which members come to share a set of practices, knowledge about those practices, about one another, about how to address new situations, and so on. They become an interpretive community who, within this context at least, share a frame—a view of how to approach and interpret new situations (see e.g. the description of this process in Berger and Luckmann 1966: Part II; see also Latour 1987). Interpretation, then, rests on a community of meaning.

The same intertwined duality is implied by the hermeneutic circle. The hermeneutic circle refers to the process of developing understanding in interpreting texts: one starts from whatever point of understanding one already has, studies more (often together with others), thereby adding further understanding; studies more, adding even further understanding; and so on, each new insight revising prior (and therefore provisional) interpretations that overlap in an ever-circular process of making meaning. It also refers to the communal character of knowing:

that modes of interpreting (or 'making') meaning are developed among a group of people—a community of interpreters, a circle—acting and interacting together in that process, thereby coming to share an approach to understanding a problem. One of Gadamer's departures from Dilthey was his observation that this described not just a mode of understanding texts, but the way humans make sense of any new situation, including everyday life.

Social realities, in this view, are constructed by the actors in those situations, acting together; and these acts can only be understood through interpretation. In this sense, knowing and understanding are subjective processes—understood from the viewpoint of the subject acting (and interacting) in and interpreting the situation; they are not 'objective' processes, understood from the outside through sense-based observation alone. Phenomenologists and hermeneutic thinkers alike emphasize the context-specificity of knowledge: it is created *in* a situation and is *of* that situation. The certainty of knowledge about the social world being observed, in other words, cannot lie within that world. Judgments about the 'goodness' of that knowledge rest within the community that has established procedural rules for generating interpretations. There is no external authority— no king, no religious leader, no deity, no universal and independent set of rules—to which one can appeal for verification. There is only the collective sense-making of the interpretive community—whether scholars or citizens—observing, inter- preting, theorizing, and reporting about these observations in the rhetorical style developed and accepted by that community (see Bruner 1990; Fish 1980; Geertz 1973, 1983).

The second set of concerns deriving from the argument that meanings cannot be apperceived or accessed directly has to do with how much one can articulate what one knows, and whether one can claim knowledge of something without being able to articulate it. Logical positivism, influenced by the analytic philosophy of Russell and the early writings of Wittgenstein, argued for the possibility of an unambiguous correlation between language and its referents, insisting that all knowledge must be rational—the product of reason (rather than emotion)—and capable of being made explicit. Moral and value statements, for example, were seen as products of emotion and hence beyond the realm of science.

Polanyi (1966; Polanyi and Prosch 1975), however, argued that there is a realm of knowability aside from the explicit: there is much that humans know, in his view, but cannot say. Drawing on his example of bicycle-riding, one might ask which way a rider turns the front wheel when falling to the right. If you claim to know how to ride a bicycle, you know the answer to this question; otherwise, you would always be falling. But most bicycle riders asked this question cannot articulate their know- ledge. Furthermore, even if they could, they could not write a manual naming all the rules for riding a bicycle. Moreover, even if they could write such a manual, no novice could read it, get on a bicycle, and ride off without falling—without learning the 'tacit knowledge' that experienced riders know but cannot articulate.

In shifting the focus of study to human meaning and dropping the insistence on the transparent correlation between words and their signifiers, interpretive science opens to the possibility of tacit knowledge. This is accomplished in recognizing the need to access meanings through their artifactual representations. Ethnomethodological analysis of conversations presents an illustration. Many examples show two (or more) people engaging each other at length in ways that the parties to the conversation clearly understand but which are opaque to an onlooker. While analysis can reveal the 'missing' pieces of the exchange—the added details that reveal the participants' sense-making to the observer—the parties themselves feel little need to do so. Participants make sense of situations, events, interactions, and so on by relying on tacit knowledge that is nonetheless shared among members of an interpretive community—without having to make that knowledge explicit (see e.g. Charon 1985). Describing such sense-making is one task that interpretive researchers take on.

Interpretive science's appreciation for the multiplicities of possible meaning and attendant ambiguities has refocused attention on the perspectival, and even rhetorical, character of scientific writing (concerns of feminist theory and science studies also), leading to an appreciation for the narrative or storied character of both scientific and everyday communication. Attention to the persuasive elements of language brings in considerations of power and power relations, as well as privileged speech and silences in collective, public discourses. While interpretive philosophies have been critiqued by some critical theorists for their disengaged contemplation, including inattention to questions of power, this criticism seems less founded when these discourses are applied to actual practices—in organizations, for example. To put this point somewhat differently, DNA science does not tell genes what to do; but interpretive organizational (or other social) science of necessity engages a social world that acts and responds—to its own meaning-making, potentially to scientific meaning-making—and such action perforce involves interpretive science with political and other engaged concerns. Used in organizations, communities, public policies, and other 'applied' settings, an interpretive approach tends toward the democratic: it accords the status of expertise to local knowledge possessed by situational actors, not just to the technical expertise of researchers (Dryzek 1990; Schneider and Ingram 1997).

In sum, interpretive science focuses on meaning and meaning-making in specific situational contexts and on processes of sense-making more broadly; it is concerned with understanding the lifeworld of the actor in the situation(s) being studied; and it engages the role of language and other artifacts in constructing and communicating meaning and social relationships. The researcher engages these meanings through various methods that allow access to actors' meanings. Interpretation operates at several levels: that of the situational actor *and/or* the researcher experiencing and interpreting an event or setting; of the researcher interpreting conversational interviews with situational actors and organizational or related documents and extending those interpretations in preparing a report; and of the reader or audience interpreting the written or oral report. In this view, all knowledge is interpretive, and interpretation (of acts, language, and objects) is the only method appropriate to the human, social world.

2.3 Interpretive Perspectives in Organizational Studies

Since the field's inception, many organizational studies scholars have addressed matters of meaning, understanding, and interpretation. Weber, whose work (1924/1947) is centrally significant in this regard, is one of the few who both developed interpretive philosophical ideas and applied them to organizational settings. Roethlisberger and Dickson (1939) discovered how an interpretive community of workers defied then-accepted knowledge about the 'laws' of human behavior. Barnard (1938/1968) analyzed the role of symbolic communication in coordinating systems of action; Selznick (1949) studied how people's interpretations provide meaning and significance to organizations and their leaders; Boulding (1956) described organizations as symbol-processing social systems. None of these presented themselves as 'interpretive' scholars per se; yet the interpretive themes sketched above are apparent in reading their work today.

Explicit interest in interpretive perspectives developed within organizational studies in the 1970s and matured in the 1980s and 1990s. Silverman's (1970) textbook, Schon's Reith lectures (1971), the works of Turner, Weick, and Van Maanen (see below), together with excursions into cultural anthropology, interpretive sociology, and, later, literary theory provided concepts and position statements that eventually grew into the interpretive perspectives in organizational studies that we know today. These have developed within three overlapping areas: (1) studies of organizational culture, symbolism, and aesthetics, (2) process-based theorizing about interpretation, and (3) analyses of writing and storytelling in 'narrating' organizational realities.

2.3.1 Organizational Culture, Symbolism, and Aesthetics

The topics of organizational culture and symbolism provided the broadest initial exploration of interpretive perspectives within organizational studies. Jaques (1951) and Turner (1971) anticipated the development of organizational culture studies, as did some of the early work of the institutional school in the sociology of organizations (e.g. Selznick 1949; Kaufman 1960). Inspired by then-recently published critiques of structural-functionalist anthropology, Turner approached organizations from a perspective informed by involvement in their cultural processes and with their situated actors. In the book's preface he explained (1971: pp. vii–viii):

I believed that the sociology of industrial organizations ought to concern itself with discovering the way in which people in industry define their life-positions, with learning the sets of symbolism which they adopt in their definitions, and with examining the collective or organizational consequences of these views which they hold of themselves. But, at that time, this belief was formulated only enough to allow me to choose a mode of inquiry—the mode of informal, slow, qualitative field observation and discussion... In carrying out these studies, I attempted to 'get under the skin' of an organization by informal interviewing and by just 'being around'...

This cultural approach led Turner to develop qualitative research methods, particularly grounded theory (1981, 1983); the concept of safety cultures (1976, 1978); and notions of organizational symbolism (1986, 1990a, b). In all of this work he promoted studying the lived experience of organizational actors with a view toward grounding organizational action in the understanding such a perspective made possible.

Turner's early formulation of a cultural framework positioned him as a key figure within the Europe-based academic community that became the Standing Conference on Organizational Symbolism (SCOS) whose 'manifesto' articulated the research interests of the symbolic-interpretive organizational culture school:

Our starting point is the realization that an organization is a cultural and therefore symbolic reality in the life process of its members. This realization has meant that categories and discourse appropriate to the study of culture now emerge as central in this approach to our study of organizations. Thus organizations may be seen in terms of their rituals, traditions, ceremonies and 'myths', or their 'cults' and 'clans', their styles, symbols and cultural identities and so forth. The possibilities are as rich and various as culture itself... (Call for papers, First International Conference on Organization Symbolism and Corporate Culture, Lund, Sweden, 26–30 June 1984)

SCOS members were joined by other interpretively-oriented researchers who explored the role in meaning-making of linguistic artifacts (e.g. stories, myths, heroes and villains, jargon, metaphors, jokes, proverbs), acts (e.g. rituals, ceremonies, gestures, taboos), and objects (e.g. products, logos, signs, headquarters architecture). They emphasized the context-specific meanings (values, beliefs, feelings) held by organizational members and other organizationally relevant publics that underlie such artifacts, as well as researchers' interpretations of those meanings (for a taste of this literature, see compendiums edited by Pondy et al. 1983; Frost et al. 1985, 1991; Jones, Moore, and Snyder 1988; Turner 1990a; Gagliardi 1990; see also Smircich 1983).

The different approaches to reasoning, methods, and scholarly writing influenced by positivist and interpretive scholars were manifested early on in organizational culture writings (Martin and Frost 1996; Yanow and Adams 1997). One of the central differences involved the question of whether culture was a unitary phenomenon, seen, typically, as having been designed by organizational founders and executed by top executives (e.g. Schein 1985/1992; Sergiovanni and Corbally 1984), or whether culture was experienced differently at different levels or within different parts of the organization (hierarchical, occupational, etc.), including the possibility of subcultures and even countercultures (e.g. Gregory 1983; Louis 1985; Siehl and Martin 1984; Van Maanen and Barley 1984; Young 1986; Yanow 1996). Reflecting on this divergence, some came to see culture more as an attribute of researchers' perceptions than of any characteristic inhering in the organization under study (e.g. Meyerson and Martin 1987; Martin 1992), leading to an increased awareness of the role of the researcher-as-writer in constructing, rather than mirroring, organizational cultures (Smircich 1995; Yanow 1995).

Interpretive perspectives also differed concerning the universality of research findings. Many researchers, particularly those oriented toward consulting, prescribed the widespread use of cultural artifacts as if these could be designed at random or imported from other organizations and as if organizational cultures could be categorized according to a universal, generalizable schema and compared cross-nationally (e.g. Deal and Kennedy 1982; Hofstede 1980; Ouchi 1981; Peters and Waterman 1982; Kilmann, Saxton, and Serpa 1985). Interpretive-oriented researchers saw cultural artifacts as rooted in their organizational settings, growing out of their specific values, beliefs, and/or feelings—that is, out of whatever was meaningful to members situated in those contexts, emerging from the lived experience within those settings (e.g. Ingersoll and Adams 1986, 1992; Hirsch 1986; Van Maanen 1973, 1974, 1978, 1982, 1991; Putnam and Pacanowsky 1983; Rosen 2000; Kunda 1992; Czarniawska-Joerges 1988; Schultz 1991, 1994; Yanow 1996).

A third, related distinction concerned the matter of control. The focus on meaning-making led critically-oriented interpretive scholars to examine how power and domination were socially constructed. In culture studies, the attribution of agency to all situational actors encouraged scholars to study how interpretive processes are involved in managerial oppression and resistance to it (e.g. Collinson 1988; Kunda 1992; Knights and Willmott 1989; Willmott 1993).

As organizational culture research matured, it developed into several subfields. For instance, one group of researchers was concerned with the role of tacit knowledge in the communication of meaning. Opening consideration beyond the requirement for explicit meaning statements renewed interest in non-verbal modes of communication and the role of physical artifacts in this process (e.g. Hatch 1997a on irony; Berg and Kreiner 1990, Hatch 1990, other essays in Gagliardi 1990, Yanow 1998 on built spaces; Boje 1991, Ingersoll and Adams 1992). Another focused on silence in organizational discourse (e.g. Calás and Smircich 1991; Martin

1990). Still other researchers explored the ways in which symbols express meaning both emotionally and aesthetically. These interests eventually led to aesthetic philosophy and an aesthetics of organization (e.g. Gagliardi 1990, 1996; Strati 1992, 1999; Guillet de Monthoux 1996; Ottensmeyer 1996; Linstead and Hopfl 1999).

These later developments within organizational culture studies carried many interpretive organizational culture scholars beyond interpretive perspectives. In a way, Calás and Smircich (1987) anticipated a shift away from interpretive organizational culture studies when they asked provocatively: 'Is organization culture dominant but dead?' Their paper presented 'culture' as a limited vehicle for postpositivist concerns as the result of having tied the concept irrevocably to interpretive philosophical foundations. As Calás and Smircich and a host of interpretive scholars moved on to postmodernism, others stayed to continue developing the theoretical side of interpretive perspectives.

2.3.2 Theorizing about Interpretation

As interpretive sociology, cultural anthropology, and other fields were sources for organizational culture, they were also sources for theorizing about meaning-making more broadly. Much of this theorizing drew on the language of frames, lenses, metaphors, and paradigms, reflecting the phenomenological-pragmatist idea (e.g. Goffman 1974) of the situatedness of knowledge (e.g. Astley 1985; Gray, Bougon, and Donnellon 1985; Jacobson and Jacques 1990). One of the most influential of these works was Burrell and Morgan (1979), which distinguished interpretive from functionalist, radical structuralist, and radical humanist perspectives on organizational studies. Subsequent work also embodied the interpretive idea that theory development and organizational analysis reflect multiple researcher perspectives, rather than any singular, objective truth (e.g. Morgan 1986; Schmidt 1987; Yanow 1987; Bolman and Deal 1991; Martin 1992; Hatch 1997*b*; Dennard 1989). Other theoretical work reflects such interpretive ideas as the difference of human 'systems' (Vickers 1965, 1973) and Berger and Luckmann's (1966) delineation of social construction processes (e.g. Shotter 1993; Weick 1969/1979, 1995). Weick, in particular, grasped the processual nature of social constructionist thought, arguing for a shift from organiza*tion* to organiz*ing*.

In Chia's (1997) view, the shift to process-based thinking most differentiates interpretive theorizing from positivistic thinking, which is predicated on static notions of outcomes and entities—mainstays of causal logic. Drawing on Bergson (1913) and Whitehead (1929), Chia (1997: 696) argued for a 'process-based becoming ontology' in which 'The actual world is fundamentally in a process of becoming so that every phenomenon of which we are aware—...from human societies and families of crystals to nursery rhymes and creational myths—each exists only as a stabilized moment in an interminable process of becoming' (1997: 696).

One of the most influential process-based theories to appear in organization studies is Weick's (1969/1979) *Social Psychology of Organizing*, in which he focused on lived experience and socially constructed reality: 'many of the ways of thinking about organizing that will be introduced in this book . . . [imply] that there is not an underlying "reality" waiting to be discovered. Rather, organizations are viewed as the inventions of people, inventions superimposed on flows of experience and momentarily imposing some order on these streams' (1979: 11–12). Weick's commitment to understanding interpretation and to describing how reality is socially constructed by organizational participants through their social interactions was clear: 'Organizing is first of all grounded in agreements concerning what is real and illusory' (1979: 3).

Weick (1979) introduced a set of concepts for addressing aspects of organizing which are consonant with interpretive views, among them retrospective reconstruction, enactment, causal chains, double interacts, equivocality, and loose coupling. His subsequent empirical studies illustrate these concepts (e.g. Bougon, Weick and Binkhorst 1977; Weick 1987; Weick and Roberts 1993). Later, he made explicit his interpretive assumptions that sense-making is social, intersubjective, and composed of multiple realities, and proposed a theory that organizational sense-making emerges from continuous processes of renegotiating and reconciling understandings (Weick 1995).

Following Weick's lead, but also in conversation with the SCOS community of which she was a member, Hatch (1993, 2000) theorized about organizational culture using a Weick-inspired, process-based model that made use of hermeneutic reasoning. In her theory she included interpretation and symbolization as processes that shape the meanings underlying an organization's culture. Adding symbols to Schein's (1985/1992) model of culture as artifacts, values, and assumptions, Hatch (2000: 252) described how interpretation and symbolization, along with manifestation and realization, 'describe a continuous dynamic state within which members forge their cultural influences and respond to them'. Referring to a diagram of the cultural dynamics model, she showed how the four processes link assumptions, values, artifacts, and symbols together in a circular (hermeneutic) stream of mutual influence. In a subsequent empirical study Hatch (1997*a*) presented the interpretive processes at play in the ironic humor of a management team, applying a hermeneutic approach to theorizing how meaning underpins and is expressed by artifacts and demonstrating the use of interpretive reasoning to theorize interpretation. She also illustrated interpretivism's subjective and reflexive elements by commenting self-reflexively on the hermeneutics (and irony) of using interpretive methods to study interpretation and by treating her own interpretive processes as part of the data for studying interpretation.

Also drawing on Weick's contributions, Van Maanen (1995) proposed to make interpretive theorizing a question of language use (e.g. Weick's use of concepts like 'organizing' and 'enactment' to stimulate processual thinking). He characterized the linguistic turn as 'promot[ing] language in the scheme of things and revers[ing] the relationship typically thought to obtain between a description and the object of description' (133–4):

This language-first switch produces a culturally relative version of reality and suggests that perception is as much a product of imagination as imagination is a product of perception. Reality thus emerges from the interplay of imaginative perception and perceptive imagination. Language (and text) provide the symbolic representations required for both the construction and communication of conceptions of reality and thus make the notions of thought and culture inseparable. (Van Maanen 1995: 141)

In this way, Van Maanen harnessed culture researchers' interests in linguistic artifacts to Weickian modes of theorizing, while at the same time helping to introduce the linguistic (and narrative) turn into organizational studies (see below).

Theorizing about interpretation intertwined with empirical research into its processes is also found in collective-interpretive approaches to organizational learning (e.g. Blackler 1995; Blackler, Crump, and McDonald 2000; Cook and Yanow 1993; Engestrom 2000; Gherardi 2000a, b; Gherardi, Nicolini, and Odella 1998; Yanow 2000a) and to organizational identity (e.g. Albert and Whetten 1985; Dutton and Dukerich 1991; Hatch and Schultz 2000, 2002). They reflect such interpretive ideas as organizational learning as context-specific meaning-making and organizational identity as socially constructed in interaction with other members of a group.

2.3.3 Narrative Turns

Interpretive perspectives also grew in organizational studies under the influence of developments in literary theory that spread across many social sciences, moving from a linguistic to a narrative and from a rhetorical to a reflexive turn. This movement joined interpretive organizational culture scholars' interests in linguistic artifacts and sense-making theorists' increasing awareness that researchers' own situatedness shaped the ways in which they constructed organizational realities in their writing (e.g. White 1999). Attention to the role of metaphor, not just in framing theories, but in shaping managerial and others' perceptions and subsequent actions, already existed (Gusfield 1976; Manning 1979; D. Miller 1985; Pondy 1983; Rein and Schon 1977; Schon 1979; Smith and Simmons 1983). The 'linguistic-narrative-rhetorical-reflexive' turn directed attention toward writing and storytelling.

Van Maanen's (1983, 1988, 1995) interest in ethnographic description and his reflections on his own storytelling craft and language use led interpretive organizational studies toward the linguistic-narrative turn. As a cultural anthropologist, Van Maanen had studied policework, training at a police academy and riding along on patrol to observe policework from the inside. Like other organizational culture researchers, he recorded what happened to him or what he witnessed, and the significance of his police research lay initially in his reporting of the patrolmen's own language in describing their lives and their work. In *Tales of the Field* (1988), Van Maanen returned to his police data in a more reflexive mood that explored writing as method.

There, he articulated the researcher's interpretive role as he or she constructs the rich description that readers confront in the written text. He presented three types of tales—realist, confessional, and impressionist—distinguishable on several bases, including their different degrees of authorial presence and styles of expression. Van Maanen's typology offers insight not only into how interpretive accounts are written, but also into the mindset that an interpretive perspective requires. Interpretive narratives recognize that knowledge is situated in the person doing the knowing. To relate knowledge from one person (the author) to another (the reader) requires that the author make herself known. This is done implicitly in the realist tale, overtly in the confessional tale, and in a more literary fashion in the impressionist tale.

Van Maanen's reflexive theorizing, together with work in other social sciences on their own rhetorical practices (e.g. Brown 1976; McCloskey 1985), led to analytic interest in scholarly narratives and writing. An initial focus was the ways in which organizational culture writings constructed the organizational worlds that were presented as objective reports (e.g. Smircich 1995; Yanow 1995). The understanding that scientific writing constructs organizational realities led to explicit attention to writerly practices as rhetorical acts intended to persuade readers of an argument's veracity (Golden-Biddle and Locke 1993, 1997; O'Connor 1995; Hatch 1996; Yanow 1998; Czarniawska 1999; Abma 1999; and Brower, Abolafia, and Carr 2000, among others). Golden-Biddle and Locke (1997), for example, described how writers anticipate the interpretations their reader/reviewers will give their papers and work these anticipations into their writing. Other areas within organizational studies have similarly treated the activities they study as texts, among them accounting (e.g. Boland 1989; Czarniawska-Joerges 1992).

In addition to the contribution *Tales of the Field* made to methodology debates and to reflexivity in writing, it promoted the budding field of story and storytelling research. As noted earlier, interest in organizational stories first appeared in the organizational culture literature, as artifacts to be interpreted in order to understand cultural meanings and values (e.g. Martin 1982; Martin *et al.* 1983; Wilkins 1983). The linguistic-narrative turn moved this research from symbolic-cultural to more literary approaches. Key to this transformation was a shift from collecting stories to observing story*telling*, brought about largely by Boje (1991; see also Boland 1989; Gabriel 1995, 2000; Hummel 1992; Maynard-Moody 1993).

Following the lead of the folklorist Georges (1980), Boje (1991:107–9) criticized researchers for interpreting organizational stories out of context, arguing that studying story*telling* is the proper analytical focus for interpretive approaches:

Text research does not capture basic aspects of the situated language performance, such as how the story is introduced into the ongoing interaction, how listeners react to the story, and how the story affects subsequent dialogue . . . because stories are contextually embedded, their meaning unfolds through the storytelling performance event . . . Stories can therefore be correctly interpreted only to the extent that the researcher grasps the story in situ.

With this approach Boje shifted the emphasis from content (the stories themselves) to process (the performance of telling stories), paralleling Weick's efforts to move organizational studies from its focus on structure (organiza*tion*) to process (organiz*ing*).

In his study Boje (1991) showed how a small office-supply firm in Southern California constructed itself through continuous (re)tellings of organizational stories. In his view collective acts of storytelling and interpretation are acts of sense-making that give a firm its distinctive character. Boje also made connections to the study of emotion in organizations (e.g. Fineman 1993; see especially Hopfl and Linstead 1993), observing, 'We all tell stories, and during better performances we feel the adrenalin pump as word pictures dance in our intellect and we begin to live the episode vicariously or recall similar life events.' Drawing from literary theory, Boje (1991: 110) also raised the issue of the role of the listener:

As listeners, we are co-producers with the teller of the story performance. It is an embedded and fragmented process in which we fill in the blanks and gaps between the lines with our own experience in response to cues, like 'You know the story!' Because of what is not said, and yet shared, the audible story is only a fraction of the connections between people in their co-production performance.

This last observation introduced one of the key findings of Boje's study—that organizational storytelling entails missing elements, their narrators giving little detail. Storytelling, in other words, involves tacit knowledge, a central argument of interpretive philosophy for which this study provided compelling empirical support.

Czarniawska (1997) showed how organizational stories, taken in the context of their telling, are embedded in sequences that unfold over time along lines comparable to serial television (the soap opera). This comparison offered a new interpretive frame for addressing ongoing organizational activities on the level of lived experience. In providing serialized accounts of how members of the Swedish social insurance agencies experienced change, Czarniawska performed her own narrative. This can be seen in the format of her book, which differentiated Czarniawska's own voice as narrator from the voices of her subjects, who are acting out the changes even as they speak of them. In this respect Czarniawska simultaneously presented an interpretive study of the Swedish public sector and a reflexive portrayal of herself as narrator, combining ethnographic organizational culture studies with narrative theory.

2.4 CONCLUDING THOUGHTS

Interpretive organizational studies are increasingly found at major conferences, in the pages of mainstream journals, and in curricula. The depth and breadth of the philosophical underpinnings of interpretive approaches are becoming more widely known, and scholars increasingly understand that interpretive work is supported on its own merits, rather than merely in relation to positivist thought. As a consequence, interpretive research methods for accessing and analyzing data (e.g. observing, interviewing, content analysis, semiotics, ethnomethodology, metaphor analysis) are themselves becoming better understood and judged according to their own presuppositions, rather than against positivist scientific criteria for validity and reliability which they cannot meet (e.g. Golden-Biddle and Locke 1993; Erlandson et al. 1993; Feldman 1994; Yanow 2000b).

Some argue that the tenets of interpretive philosophy place its applications outside science, better situated within the realm of the humanities. While we agree with the tenor of this claim—understanding it as an argument that interpretive research can never meet the standards of positivist research and its normative scientific method—we maintain that interpretive work can be, and is, scientific, if 'science' is understood as a systematic mode of observing and explaining. For rhetorical-political reasons we wish not to relinquish the claim to science: its status in Western societies still commands respect (and funding). We maintain that interpretive science *is* a science, seeking to expand the terms of engagement rather than walk away from positivist challenges to its scientific claims. In doing so, we yield much of the desire to predict and control upon which positivist science rests its claims; but we still contend that interpretive perspectives offer a path to understanding in a systematic, methodical way.

REFERENCES

ABBAGNANO, NICOLA (1967). 'Positivism', in *Encyclopedia of Philosophy*, vol. 6 New York: Macmillan.

ABMA, TINEKE (ed.) (1999). *Telling Tales*. Advances in Program Evaluation, vol. 6 Stamford, Conn: JAI Press.

ALBERT, S., and WHETTEN, D. A. (1985). 'Organizational Identity', in L. L. Cummings and M. M. Staw (eds.), *Research in Organizational Behavior*, 7: 263–95.

ASTLEY, W. GRAHAM (1985). 'Administrative Science as Socially Constructed Truth'. *Administrative Science Quarterly*, 30: 497–513.

BARNARD, CHESTER (1938/1968). *The Functions of the Executive*. Cambridge, Mass.: Harvard University Press.

BEAM, GEORGE, and SIMPSON, DICK (1984). *Political Action*. Chicago: Swallow Press.

BERG, P. O., and KREINER, KRISTIAN (1990). 'Corporate Architecture', in P. Gagliardi (ed.), *Symbols and Artifacts*. New York: Aldine de Gruyter.

BERGER, PETER L., and LUCKMANN, THOMAS (1966). *The Social Construction of Reality*. New York: Anchor.

BERGSON, HENRI (1913). *An Introduction to Metaphysics*. London: Macmillan.

BERNSTEIN, RICHARD J. (1976). *The Restructuring of Social and Political Theory*. Philadelphia: University of Pennsylvania.

—— (1983). *Beyond Objectivism and Relativism*. Philadelphia: University of Pennsylvania.

BLACKLER, FRANK (1995). 'Knowledge, Knowledge Work, and Organizations'. *Organizational Studies*, 16: 1021–46.

—— CRUMP, NORMAN, and McDONALD, SEONAIDH (2000). 'Organizing Processes in Complex Activity Networks'. *Organization*, 7: 247–68.

BOJE, DAVID M. (1991). 'The Storytelling Organization'. *Administrative Science Quarterly*, 36: 106–26.

BOLAND, RICHARD J., Jr. (1989). 'Beyond the Objectivist and the Subjectivist'. *Accounting, Organizations and Society*, 14: 591–604.

BOLMAN, LEE G., and DEAL, TERRENCE E. (1991). *Reframing Organizations*. San Francisco: Jossey-Bass.

BOUGON, M. G., WEICK, K. E., and BINKHORST, D. (1977). 'Cognition in Organizations'. *Administrative Science Quarterly*, 22: 606–39.

BOULDING, KENNETH (1956). 'General Systems Theory'. *Management Science*, 2: 197–208.

BROWER, RALPH S., ABOLAFIA, MITCHEL Y., and CARR, JERED B. (2000). 'On Improving Qualitative Methods in Public Administration Research'. *Administration and Society*, 32: 363–97.

BROWN, RICHARD H. (1976). 'Social Theory as Metaphor'. *Theory and Society*, 3: 169–97.

BRUNER, JEROME (1990). *Acts of Meaning*. Cambridge, Mass.: Harvard University Press.

BURKE, KENNETH (1969/1945). *A Grammar of Motives*. Berkeley: University of California Press.

—— (1989). *On Symbols and Society*, ed. Joseph R. Gusfield. Chicago: University of Chicago.

BURRELL, GIBSON, and MORGAN, GARETH (1979). *Sociological Paradigms and Organisational Analysis*. Portsmouth, NH: Heinemann.

CALÁS, MARTA, and SMIRCICH, LINDA (1987). 'Post-Culture: Is the Organizational Culture Literature Dominant but Dead?' Paper presented at the International Standing Conference on Organizational Symbolism and Corporate Culture, Milan, Italy.

—— —— (1991). 'Voicing Seduction to Silence Leadership'. *Organization Studies*, 12: 567–602.

CHARON, JOEL M. (1985). *Symbolic Interactionism*, (2nd edn). Englewood Cliffs, NJ: Prentice-Hall.

CHIA, ROBERT (1997). 'Essai: Thirty Years On'. *Organization Studies*, 18: 685–707.

COLLINSON, DAVID (1988). 'Engineering Humor, Masculinity, Joking and Conflict in Shopfloor Relations'. *Organization Studies*, 9: 181–99.

COOK, SCOTT, and YANOW, DVORA (1993). 'Culture and Organizational Learning'. *Journal of Management Inquiry*, 2: 373–90.

CZARNIAWSKA-JOERGES, BARBARA (1988). *Ideological Control in Nonideological Organizations*. New York: Praeger.

—— (1992). 'Budgets as Texts'. *Accounting, Management & Information Technology*, 2: 221–39.

CZARNIAWSKA, BARBARA (1997). *Narrating the Organization*. Chicago: University of Chicago Press.

—— (1999). *Writing Management*. Oxford: Oxford University Press.

DALLMAYR, FRED R., and McCARTHY, THOMAS A. (eds.) (1977). *Understanding and Social Inquiry*. Notre Dame, Ind.: University of Notre Dame Press.

DEAL, TERRENCE E., and KENNEDY, ALLEN A. (1982). *Corporate Cultures*. Reading, Mass.: Addison-Wesley.

DEHAVEN-SMITH, LANCE (1988). *Philosophical Critiques of Policy Analysis*. Gainesville: University of Florida Press.

DENNARD, LINDA (1989). 'The Three Bears and Goldilocks Meet Burrell and Morgan'. *Administration and Society*, 21: 384–6.

DRYZEK, JOHN S. (1990). *Discursive Democracy*. Cambridge: Cambridge University Press.

DUTTON, J., and DUKERICH, J. (1991). 'Keeping an Eye on the Mirror: Image and Identity in Organizational Adaptation'. *Academy of Management Journal*, 34: 517–54.

ENGESTRÖM, YRJÖ (2000). 'Comment on Blackler et al'. *Organization*, 7: 301–10.

ERLANDSON, DAVID A., HARRIS, EDWARD L., SKIPPER, BARBARA L., ALLEN, STEVE D. (1993). *Doing Naturalistic Inquiry*. Newbury Park, Calif:. Sage.

FALCO, MARIA J. (ed.) (1987). *Feminism and Epistemology*. New York: Haworth.

FAY, BRIAN (1975). *Social Theory and Political Practice*. Boston: George Allen & Unwin.

FELDMAN, MARTHA S. (1994). *Some Interpretive Techniques for Analyzing Qualitative Data*. Beverly Hills, Calif.: Sage.

FILMER, PAUL, PHILLIPSON, MICHAEL, SILVERMAN, DAVID, and WALSH, DAVID (1972). *New Directions in Sociological Theory*. London: Collier-Macmillan.

FINEMAN, STEPHEN (ed.) (1993). *Emotion in Organizations*. London: Sage.

FISH, STANLEY (1980). *Is There a Text in This Class?* Cambridge, Mass.: Harvard University Press.

FROST, P., MORGAN, G., and DANDRIDGE, T. (eds.) (1983). *Organizational Symbolism*. Greenwich, Conn.: JAI Press.

——, MOORE, LARRY F., LOUIS, MERYL REIS, LUNDBERG, CRAIG C., MARTIN, JOANNE (1985). *Organizational Culture*. Newbury Park, Calif.: Sage.

—— —— —— —— (1991). *Reframing Organizational Culture*. Newbury Park, Calif.: Sage.

GABRIEL, YIANNIS (1995). 'The Unmanaged Organization'. *Organizational Studies*, 16: 477–501.

—— (2000). *Storytelling in Organizations*. Oxford: Oxford University Press.

GAGLIARDI, PASQUALE (ed.) (1990). *Symbols and Artifacts*. New York: Aldine de Gruyter.

—— (1996). 'Exploring the Aesthetic Side of Organizational Life', in S. R. Clegg, C. Hardy, and W. R. Nord (eds.), *Handbook of Organizational Studies*. London: Sage, 565–80.

GARFINKEL, HAROLD (1977). 'What is Ethnomethodology?' in Fred R. Dallmayr and Thomas A. McCarthy (eds.), *Understanding and Social Inquiry*. Notre Dame: University of Notre Dame Press, 240–61.

GEERTZ, CLIFFORD (1973). *The Interpretation of Cultures*. New York: Basic Books.

GEERTZ, CLIFFORD (1983). *Local Knowledge*. New York: Basic Books.

GEORGES, ROBERT (1980). 'A Folklorist's View of Storytelling'. *Humanities in Society*, 3: 317–26.

GHERARDI, SILVIA (2000a). 'Practice-Based Theorizing on Learning and Knowing in Organizations'. *Organization*, 7: 211–23.

—— (ed.) (2000b). Special issue on 'Knowing in Practice'. *Organization*, 7: 2.

——NICOLINI, DAVIDE, and ODELLA, FRANCESCA (1998). 'Toward a Social Understanding of How People Learn in Organizations'. *Management Learning*, 29: 273–98.

GOFFMAN, ERVING (1959). *The Presentation of Self in Everyday Life*. New York: Doubleday Anchor.

—— (1974). *Frame Analysis*. New York: Harper & Row.

GOLDEN-BIDDLE, KAREN, and LOCKE, KAREN (1993). 'Appealing Work'. *Organization Science*, 4: 595–616.

—— —— (1997). *Composing Qualitative Research*. Thousand Oaks, Calif.: Sage.

GRAY, BARBARA, BOUGON, MICHEL G., and DONNELLON, ANNE (1985). 'Organizations as Constructions and Destructions of Meaning'. *Journal of Management*, 11: 83–98.

GREGORY, KATHLEEN L. (1983). 'Native-View Paradigms'. *Administrative Science Quarterly*, 28: 359–76.

GUILLET DE MONTHOUX, PIERRE (1996). 'The Theatre of War'. *Studies in Cultures, Organizations and Societies*, 2: 147–60.

GUSFIELD, JOSEPH (1976). 'The Literary Rhetoric of Science'. *American Sociological Review*, 41: 16–34.

HARDING, SANDRA (1989). 'Feminist Justificatory Strategies', in Ann Garry and Marilyn Pearsall (eds.), *Women, Knowledge, and Reality*. Boston: Unwin, Hyman.

—— (1990). 'Feminism, Science, and the Anti-Enlightenment Critiques', in Linda J. Nicholson, *Feminism/Postmodernism*. New York: Routledge.

—— (1991). *Whose Science? Whose Knowledge?* Ithaca, NY: Cornell University Press.

HARTSOCK, NANCY C. M. (1987). 'The Feminist Standpoint', in Sandra Harding (ed.), *Feminism & Methodology*. Bloomington: Indiana University Press.

HATCH, M. J. (1990). 'The Symbolics of Office Design', in P. Gagliardi (ed.), *Symbols and Artifacts*. New York: Aldine de Gruyter.

—— (1993). 'The Dynamics of Organizational Culture'. *Academy of Management Review*, 18: 657–93.

—— (1996). 'The Role of the Researcher: An Analysis of Narrative Position in Organization Theory'. *Journal of Management Inquiry*, 5: 359–74.

—— (1997a). 'Irony and the Social Construction of Contradiction in the Humor of a Management Team'. *Organization Science*, 8: 275–88.

—— (1997b). *Organization Theory*. New York: Oxford University Press.

—— (2000). 'The Cultural Dynamics of Organizing and Change', in N. Ashkanasy, C. Wilderom, and M. Peterson (eds.), *Handbook of Organizational Culture and Climate*. Thousand Oaks, Calif.: Sage.

—— and SCHULTZ, M. (2000). 'Scaling the Tower of Babel: Relational Differences between Identity, Image and Culture in Organizations', in M. Schultz, M. J. Hatch, and M. H. Larsen, (eds.), *The Expressive Organization: Linking Identity, Reputation, and the Corporate Brand*. Oxford: Oxford University Press, 13–35.

—— —— (2002). 'The Dynamics of Organizational Identity'. *Human Relations*.

HAWKESWORTH, M. E. (1988). *Theoretical Issues in Policy Analysis*. Albany, New York: SUNY Press.

—— (1989). 'Knowers, Knowing, Known', in M. R. Malson *et al.* (eds.), *Feminist Theory in Practice and Process*. Chicago: University of Chicago.

HELDKE, LISA (1989). 'John Dewey and Evelyn Fox Keller: A Shared Epistemological Tradition', in Nancy Tuana (ed.), *Feminism & Science*. Bloomington: Indiana University Press.

HIRSCH, PAUL S. (1986). 'From Ambushes to Golden Parachutes'. *American Journal of Sociology*, 91: 800–37.

HOFSTEDE, GEERT (1980). *Culture's Consequences*. Beverly Hills, Calif.: Sage.

HOPFL, H., and LINSTEAD, S. (1993). 'Passion and Performance: Suffering and the Carrying of Organizational Roles', in S. Fineman (ed.), *Emotion in Organizations*. London: Sage.

HUMMEL, RALPH. P. (1992). 'Stories Managers Tell'. *Public Administration Review*, 51: 31–41.

INGERSOLL, VIRGINIA HILL, and ADAMS, GUY (1986). 'Beyond Organizational Boundaries'. *Administration and Society*, 18: 360–81.

—— —— (1992). *The Tacit Organization*. Greenwich, Conn.: JAI Press.

JACOBSON, SARAH, and JACQUES, ROY (1990). 'Of Knowers, Knowing and the Known'. Presented to the Academy of Management Annual Meeting (August).

JAQUES, ELLIOTT (1951). *The Changing Culture of a Factory*. London: Tavistock.

JENNINGS, BRUCE (1983). 'Interpretive Social Science and Policy Analysis', in Daniel Callahan and Bruce Jennings (eds.), *Ethics, the Social Sciences, and Policy Analysis*. New York: Plenum.

—— (1987). 'Interpretation and the Practice of Policy Analysis', in Frank Fischer and John Forester (eds.), *Confronting Values in Policy Analysis*. Newbury Park, Calif.: Sage, 128–52.

JONES, M. O., MOORE, M. D., and SNYDER, R. C. (1988). *Inside Organizations*. Newbury Park, Calif.: Sage.

KAUFMAN, HERBERT (1960). *The Forest Ranger*. Baltimore: Johns Hopkins Press.

KILMANN, RALPH K., SAXTON, MARY J., SERPA, ROY, and Associates (1985). *Gaining Control of the Corporate Culture*. San Francisco: Jossey-Bass.

KNIGHTS, DAVID, and WILLMOTT, HUGH (1989). 'Power and Subjectivity at Work'. *Sociology*, 23: 535–58.

KUHN, THOMAS S. (1970). *The Structure of Scientific Revolutions* (2nd edn, enlarged). Chicago: University of Chicago Press.

—— (1977). *The Essential Tension*. Chicago: University of Chicago Press.

KUNDA, GIDEON (1992). *Engineering Culture*. Philadelphia: Temple University.

LATOUR, BRUNO (1987). *Science in Action*. Cambridge, Mass.: Harvard University Press.

LINSTEAD, STEPHEN, and HOPFL, HEATHER (eds.) (1999). *The Aesthetics of Organization*. London: Sage.

LONGINO, HELEN (1990). *Science as Social Knowledge*. Princeton: Princeton University Press.

LOUIS, MERYL REISS (1985). 'Sourcing Workplace Cultures', in Ralph H. Kilmann, Mary J. Saxton, Roy Serpa, and Associates, *Gaining Control of the Corporate Culture*. San Francisco: Jossey-Bass.

McCLOSKEY, DONALD (1985). *The Rhetoric of Economics*. Madison: University of Wisconsin.

MANNING, PETER K. (1979). 'Metaphors of the Field'. *Administrative Science Quarterly*, 24: 660–71.

MARTIN, JOANNE (1982). 'Stories and Scripts in Organizational Settings', in A. H. Hastorf and A. M. Isen (eds.), *Cognitive Social Psychology*. New York: North Holland-Elsevier, 165–94.

—— (1990). 'Deconstructing Organizational Taboos'. *Organization Science*, 11: 339–59.

—— (1992). *Cultures in Organizations: Three Perspectives*. New York: Oxford University Press.

—— FELDMAN, M., HATCH, M. J., and SITKIN, S. (1983). 'The Uniqueness Paradox in Organizational Stories'. *Administrative Science Quarterly*, 28: 438–53.

—— and FROST, PETER (1996). 'The Organizational Culture War Games', in S. Clegg, C. Hardy, and W. Nord (eds.), *Handbook of Organizational Studies*. London: Sage.

MAYNARD-MOODY, STEVEN (1993). 'Stories Managers Tell', in Barry Bozeman (ed.), *Public Management*. San Francisco: Jossey-Bass.

MEAD, GEORGE HERBERT (1934). *Mind, Self, and Society*. Chicago: University of Chicago Press.

MENAND, LOUIS (1997). *A Pragmatism Reader*. New York: Vintage.

—— (2001). *The Metaphysical Club*. New York: Farrar, Straus and Giroux.

MEYERSON, D., and MARTIN, J. (1987). 'Cultural Change'. *Journal of Management Studies*, 24: 623–47.

MILLER, DONALD F. (1985). 'Social Policy: An Exercise in Metaphor'. *Knowledge*, 7: 191–215.

MILLER, NANCY K. (1986). 'Changing the Subject', in Teresa de Lauretis (ed.), *Feminist Studies/Critical Studies*. Bloomington: Indiana University.

MODLESKI, TANIA (1986). 'Feminism and the Power of Interpretation', in Teresa de Lauretis (ed.), *Feminist Studies/Critical Studies*. Bloomington: Indiana University.

MORGAN, GARETH (1986). *Images of Organization*. Beverly Hills, Calif.: Sage.

O'CONNOR, ELLEN S. (1995). 'Paradoxes of Participation'. *Organization Studies*, 16: 769–803.

OTTENSMEYER, EDWARD (1996). 'Too Strong to Stop, Too Sweet to Lose'. *Organization*, 3: 189–94.

OUCHI, WILLIAM (1981). *Theory Z*. Reading, Mass.: Addison-Wesley.

PASSMORE, JOHN (1967). 'Logical Positivism'. *Encyclopedia of Philosophy*, Vol. 5. New York: Macmillan.

PETERS, THOMAS, and WATERMAN, ROBERT H. (1982). *In Search of Excellence*. New York: Harper & Row.

PINDER, C. C., and BOURGEOIS, V. W. (1982). 'Controlling Tropes in Administrative Science'. *Administrative Science Quarterly*, 27: 641–52.

POLANYI, MICHAEL (1966). *The Tacit Dimension*. New York: Doubleday.

—— and PROSCH, HARRY (1975). *Meaning*. Chicago: University of Chicago Press.

POLKINGHORNE, DONALD (1983). *Methodology for the Human Sciences*. Albany, NY: SUNY.

—— (1988). *Narrative Knowing and the Human Sciences*. Albany, New York: SUNY.

PONDY, LOUIS R. (1983). 'The Role of Metaphors and Myths in Organization and in the Facilitation of Change', in L. Pondy, P. Frost, G. Morgan, and T. Dandridge, (eds.), *Organizational Symbolism*. Greenwich, Conn.: JAI Press, 157–66.

PUTNAM, LINDA L., and PACANOWSKY, MICHAEL E. (eds.) (1983). *Communication and Organizations: An Interpretive Approach*. Newbury Park, Calif.: Sage.

RABINOW, PAUL, and SULLIVAN, WILLIAM M., (eds.) (1979). *Interpretive Social Science*. Berkeley: University of California.

REIN, MARTIN, and SCHON, DONALD (1977). 'Problem Setting in Policy Research', in Carol Weiss (ed.), *Using Social Research in Policy Making*. Lexington, Mass.: Lexington Books.

RICOEUR, PAUL (1971). 'The Model of the Text'. *Social Research*, 38: 529–62.

ROETHLISBERGER, F. J., and DICKSON, W. J. (1939). *Management and the Worker*. Cambridge, Mass.: Harvard University Press.

ROSEN, MICHAEL (2000). *Turning Worlds, Spinning Worlds*. Amsterdam: Harwood Academic Press.

SCHEIN, EDGAR (1985/1992). *Organizational Culture and Leadership*. San Francisco: Jossey-Bass.

SCHMIDT, VIVIEN (1987). 'Four Approaches to Science and Their Implications for Organizational Theory and Research'. *Knowledge*, 9: 19–41.

SCHNEIDER, ANNE LARASON, and INGRAM, HELEN (1997). *Policy Design for Democracy*. Lawrence: University Press of Kansas.

SCHON, DONALD A. (1971). *Beyond the Stable State*. New York: W. W. Norton.

—— (1979). 'Generative Metaphor', in Andrew Ortony, *Metaphor and Thought*. Cambridge: Cambridge University Press.

SCHULTZ, MAJKEN (1991). 'Transitions between Symbolic Domains in Organizations'. *Organizational Studies*, 12: 489–506.

—— (1994). *On Studying Organizational Cultures*. Berlin: Walter de Gruyter.

SCHUTZ, ALFRED (1967). *The Phenomenology of the Social World*. Evanston, Ill.: Northwestern University Press.

—— (1973). 'Concept and Theory Formation in the Social Sciences', in *Collected Papers*, Vol. 1, ed. Maurice Natanson. The Hague: Martinus Nijhoff, 48–66.

SELZNICK, PHILIP (1949). *TVA and the Grass Roots*. New York: Harper & Row.

SERGIOVANNI, THOMAS J., and CORBALLY, JOHN E. (1984). *Leadership and Organization Culture*. Urbana: University of Illinois.

SHOTTER, JOHN (1993). *Conversational Realities*. Thousand Oaks, Calif.: Sage.

SIEHL, KAREN, and MARTIN, JOANNE (1984). 'The Role of Symbolic Management', in J. D. Hunt, D. Hosking, C. Schriesheim, and R. Steward (eds.), *Leaders and Managers*. New York: Pergamon, 227–39.

SILVERMAN, DAVID (1970). *The Theory of Organizations*. London: Heinemann.

SMIRCICH, LINDA (1983). 'Concepts of Culture and Organizational Analysis'. *Administrative Science Quarterly*, 28/3: 339–58.

—— (1995). 'Writing Organizational Tales: Reflections on Three Books on Organizational Culture. *Organization Science*, 6: 232–7.

SMITH, K. K., and SIMMONS, V. M. (1983). 'A Rumpelstiltskin Organization'. *Administrative Science Quarterly*, 28: 377–92.

STRATI, ANTONIO (1992). 'Aesthetic Understanding of Organizational Life'. *Academy of Management Review*, 17: 568–81.

—— (1999). *Organization and Aesthetics*. London: Sage.

TAYLOR, CHARLES (1971). 'Interpretation and the Sciences of Man', *Review of Metaphysics*, 25: 3–51.

TURNER, BARRY A. (1971). *Exploring the Industrial Subculture*. London: Macmillan.

—— (1976). 'The Organizational and Interorganizational Development of Disasters'. *Administrative Science Quarterly*, 21: 378–97.

—— (1978). *Man-Made Disasters*. London: Wykeham Press.

—— (1981). 'Some Practical Aspects of Qualitative Data Analysis. *Quality and Quantity*, 15: 225–47.

—— (1983). 'The Use of Grounded Theory for the Qualitative Analysis of Organizational Behavior'. *Journal of Management Studies*, 20: 333–48.

—— (1986). 'Sociological Aspects of Organizational Symbolism'. *Organizational Studies*, 7: 101–15.

—— (ed.) (1990*a*). *Organizational Symbolism*, New York: Aldine de Gruyter.

—— (1990*b*). 'The Rise of Organizational Symbolism', in J. Hassard and D. Pym (eds.), *The Theory and Philosophy of Organizations*. London: Routledge, 83–96.

VAN MAANEN, JOHN (1973). 'Observations on the Making of Policemen'. *Human Organization*, 32: 407–18.

—— (1974). 'Working the Street', in H. Jacob (ed.), *The Potential for Reform or Criminal Justice*. Beverly Hills: Sage.

—— (1978). 'The Asshole', in P. K. Manning and J. Van Maanen (eds.), *Policing: A View from the Streets*. Santa Monica, Calif.: Goodyear.

—— (1982). 'Fieldwork on the Beat', in J. Van Maanen, J. Dabbs, and R. Faulkner, *Varieties of Qualitative Research*. Beverly Hills: Sage.

—— (1983). *Qualitative Methods*. Beverly Hills: Sage.

—— (1988). *Tales of the Field*. Chicago: University of Chicago Press.

—— (1991). 'The Smile Factory', in P. J. Frost, L. F. Moore, M. R. Louis, C. C. Lundberg, and J. Martin (eds.), *Reframing Organizational Culture*. London: Sage.

—— (1995). 'Style as Theory'. *Organization Science*, 6/1: 133–43.

—— and BARLEY, STEPHEN R. (1984). 'Occupational Communities: Culture and Control in Organizations', in B. M. Staw and L. L. Cummings (eds.), *Research in Organizational Behavior*. Greenwich, Conn.: JAI Press.

VICKERS, GEOFFREY (1965). *The Art of Judgment*. New York: Basic Books.

—— (1973). *Making Institutions Work*. London: Associated Business Programmes.

WEBER, MAX (1924/1947). *The Theory of Social and Economic Organization*, ed. A. H. Henderson and T. Parsons. Glencoe, Ill.: Free Press.

WEICK, KARL E. (1969/1979). *The Social Psychology of Organizing*. Menlo Park, Calif.: Addison-Wesley.

—— (1987). 'Substitutes for Corporate Strategy', in D. Teece (ed.), *The Competitive Challenge*. Cambridge, Mass.: Ballinger, 22–33.

—— (1995). *Sensemaking in Organizations*. Thousand Oaks, Calif.: Sage.

—— and ROBERTS, KARLENE (1993). 'Collective Mind in Organizations'. *Administrative Science Quarterly*, 38: 357–81.

WHITE, JAY (1999). *Taking Language Seriously*. Washington, DC: Georgetown University.

WHITEHEAD, A. N. (1929). *Process and Reality*. New York: Free Press.

WILKINS, ALAN (1983). 'Organizational Stories as Symbols which Control the Organization', in P. Frost *et al.* (eds.), *Organizational Culture*. Beverly Hills: Sage, 81–91.

WILLMOTT, HUGH (1993). 'Strength is Ignorance; Slavery is Freedom: Managing Culture in Modern Organizations'. *Journal of Management Studies*, 30: 515–52.

YANOW, DVORA (1987). 'Ontological and Interpretive Logics in Organizational Studies'. *Methods* 1: 73–90.

—— (1995). 'Writing Organizational Tales'. *Organization Science*, 6: 225–26.

—— (1996). *How Does a Policy Mean? Interpreting Policy and Organizational Actions.* Washington, DC: Georgetown University.

—— (1998). 'Space Stories; Or, Studying Museum Buildings as Organizational Spaces, while Reflecting on Interpretive Methods and their Narration'. *Journal of Management Inquiry*, 7/3: 215–39.

—— (2000*a*). 'Seeing Organizational Learning'. *Organization*, 7: 247–68.

—— (2000*b*). *Conducting Interpretive Policy Analysis.* Newbury Park, Calif.: Sage.

—— and ADAMS, GUY B. (1997). 'Organizational Culture'. *International Encyclopedia of Public Policy and Administration.* New York: Henry Holt.

YOUNG, ED (1986/1991). 'On Naming the Rose: Interests and Multiple Meanings as Elements of Organizational Change', in P. J. Frost, L. F. Moore, M. R. Louis, C. C. Lundberg, and J. Martin (eds.), *Reframing Organizational Culture.* London: Sage.

CHAPTER 3

....

ORGANIZATION THEORY AS A CRITICAL SCIENCE?

FORMS OF ANALYSIS AND 'NEW ORGANIZATIONAL FORMS'

....

HUGH WILLMOTT

> Science as a productive force can work in a salutary way when it is infused
> by science as an emancipatory force . . . The enlightenment which does
> not break the (mythic) spell dialectically, but instead winds the veil of a
> halfway rationalization only more tightly around us, makes the world
> divested of deities itself into a myth! (Habermas 1974: 281)

An earlier version of this chapter was presented in the Department of Management at the University of
Keele. I would like to thank participants in this seminar, and especially Simon Lilley, for their
comments and criticisms.

Sections of this chapter draw upon Willmott (1997) and Alvesson and Willmott (1996). The three-
year research project associated with this paper is funded by the UK Economic and Social Research
Council Future of Work Programme, grant number L212252038. The project is investigating 'changing
organizational forms and the reshaping of work'. It involves a number of in-depth case studies of a
variety of organizational forms, including franchises, employment agencies, Private Finance Initiatives, partnerships, supply chain relationships, and outsourcing. The full research team is Mick
Marchington, Jill Rubery, Hugh Willmott, Jill Earnshaw, Damian Grimshaw, Irena Grugulis, John
Hassard, Marilyn Carroll, Fang Lee Cooke, Gail Hebson, and Steven Vincent.

As knowledge production in the management disciplines has expanded in volume and increased in theoretical sophistication, doubts have grown about the coherence and viability of a conception of science that represents scientific knowledge as unified, authoritative, and/or value-free. These concerns are dramatically articulated in the claim that organizational analysis comprises four incompatible and indeed hostile paradigms founded upon polarized sets of assumptions about science as well as society (Burrell and Morgan 1979; see Willmott 1993; see also *Organization Studies* 1988).

Critical Theory is identified by Burrell and Morgan as a major, and perhaps the central, tradition within the radical humanist paradigm wherein 'the notion that the individual creates the world in which he lives' is subjected to critique by drawing upon and seeking to combine and develop the insights of diverse radical thinkers, notably Marx, Freud, and Husserl but also, in Habermas's thinking, those who have recognized the importance of language as a focus for social analysis (see Alvesson and Willmott 1996: ch. 3 for an overview). For Critical Theorists, and especially in the work of Habermas who is the leading contemporary exponent of Critical Theory, the critique of ideology has been a recurrent focus. In Habermas's writings, his attention has been directed to the role of science and technology, in the form of the domination of instrumental rationality in modern societies.

This chapter presents and applies insights developed by Critical Theory to offer a heuristic framework for appreciating and accommodating the existence of competing conceptions of scientific knowledge. Specifically, the chapter commends the contribution of Habermas's theory of cognitive interests for the development of our self-understanding of (our knowledge of) management and organization. This theory is illustrated by reference to established areas of organizational analysis as well as to more recent research on 'new organizational forms' (NOFs).[1]

The thinking of Critical Theorists, and Habermas's theory of cognitive interests more specifically, has been largely overlooked in management and organization studies (but see Alvesson and Willmott 1992; Lyytinen and Klein 1985; Stablein and Nord 1985); or, if vaguely known about, Habermas's theory of cognitive interests is regarded as somewhat 'old hat', having allegedly been superseded in Habermas's subsequent work, a criticism that is addressed later in the chapter. For the moment it is relevant to keep in mind Burrell's (1994) observation that for the past thirty years and more, Habermas 'has fought in a variety of ways against "the present mood" and all attempts to bring about the downfall of Western rationality... Habermas stands against all varieties of totalizing critique which lead to despair.

---

[1] The term 'new organizational form' has emerged as a way of announcing the claimed presence of emergent and distinctive (e.g. 'post-bureaucratic') organizing practices that depart from established, 'older' forms of organizing (Daft and Lewin 1993) which view the old virtues of specialization and clarity as inhibitors of responsiveness to rapidly changing opportunities and demands.

For him, the philosopher as "guardian of reason" is also the sentinel of, and for, human hope' (p. 5).

Habermas's theory of cognitive interests has continuing relevance for illuminating at least three important concerns in organization studies:

- the aspiration of management knowledge to be scientific
- the fragmentation of methodologies within organization studies
- the scope for recognizing and combining the distinctive contributions of different forms of knowledge.

The theory of knowledge-constitutive interests can be taken seriously without necessarily accepting that Critical Theory in general, or Habermas's thinking in particular, offers the most plausible or coherent account of the 'interested' production of knowledge. The more modest requirement is a willingness to contemplate the possibility that Habermas's theory of knowledge-constitutive interests may be helpful in advancing the *self-understanding* of management knowledge as a product of scientific investigation.

The chapter begins by locating the claims of Critical Theory in relation to traditions of 'systemic modernism' and 'postmodernism' (Cooper and Burrell 1988) as a basis for showing how Critical Theory illuminates the normativity of knowledge production (and consumption). A plurality of methodologies within organization studies is then identified and reviewed, using the literature on mainstream management theory, employee participation as well as 'new organizational forms' to illustrate the analysis. In a discussion section, attention is then drawn to a number of criticisms levelled against Habermas's cognitive interests theory before indicating how these have been addressed by Habermas and others. In conclusion, some affinities between elements of Habermas's thinking and poststructuralist analysis advanced by Foucault and by Laclau and Mouffe are signalled.

3.1 MANAGEMENT SCIENCE AND EPISTEMOLOGICAL ANGST

3.1.1 The Claims of Systemic Modernism

Critical Theory has repeatedly assailed the received understanding that science is unified, authoritative, and value-free, is underpinned by the assumption that reality is 'out there' (e.g. Horkheimer 1937), and that scientific knowledge can capture this reality in *value-neutral* ways that facilitate its effective manipulation. This value-free conception of science harbours no doubts about the ethics of scientific practice, once the decision to embrace the values of science has been made (Weber 1949; for a critique, see Alvesson and Willmott 1996: ch. 2). In contrast, those who challenge what Cooper and Burrell (1988) characterize as the claims of 'systemic modernism' argue that 'scientific' knowledge is inescapably produced, transmitted, and legitim-ized through a variety of *power-laden* mechanisms of production and control (e.g. resource allocations and refereeing procedures)—mechanisms that discipline the research process and condition what is to count as 'value-free knowledge' (Hales 1974; Wood and Kelly 1978). According to Whitley (1984),

topic selection and assessment criteria are affected by individual and collective values so that *what is seen as constituting scientific knowledge is dependent upon preferences and interests.* Secondly, the existence of internal relationships between descriptions of phenomena con-stituted by everyday meanings and values means that *all descriptions and explanations are inevitably permeated by values.* (ibid. 384, emphasis added)

3.1.2 Anyone for Postmodernism?

A strong postmodernist position contends that modernist analysis harbours inher-ently oppressive grand narratives that constrain the possibilities of 'conflict, sur-prise and unpredictability' (Power 1990: 117). At the heart of this critique is the objection that taken for granted, modernist truths of 'objective knowledge', 'rigor-ous analysis', 'independent scrutiny', etc., aspire to be totalizing. Postmodernist thinking unsettles the 'truths' of modernism in

a way that, in a sense, returns to reality what is repressed by its rationalist vision . . . Postmodernism is thus associated with the recognition and celebration of the value of diverse rationalities and, relatedly, with the charge that the one-dimensional application of a supposedly authoritative (scientific) rationality is indefensible . . . the discourse of postmodernism draws much of its plausibility from the inevitable 'failure' of modernism to eliminate indeterminacy and multiplicity. (Willmott 1992: 59–60)

The modernist rejoinder to such criticisms is that the most strenuous of efforts are made to refine and purify their research methods, thereby ensuring that biases ascribed to 'individual and collective values' are minimized and eventually elimin-ated. What this defence declines to acknowledge, however, is that the very methods of detecting and demonstrating the reduction of bias are themselves subject to the processes identified by Whitley (see above)—namely, the permeation of scientific by particular 'ethnocentric', rather than universal values, preferences, and interests. As a consequence, it is not surprising to find that, despite the best efforts of the Canutes of systemic modernism (e.g. Donaldson 1985; Bacharach 1989) who struggle valiantly to stem the delinquent tide of 'irrationalism' and 'subjectivism' (as they might characterize the diverse assaults on the citadel of Science, see Bernstein 1976), their defences have been breached (see Marsden 1993) and the waves are not receding.

3.1.3 The Critical Modernist Alternative

'*Critical* modernists', Habermas included, share a postmodern scepticism about value-free knowledge, yet seek to retain and revive the spirit of the Enlightenment in the face of what are regarded as the perversions of Reason, including the power invested in Scientific Authority by systemic modernism. The rosy view of science as the benevolent agent of enlightenment is challenged by the understanding that modern civilization is mesmerized by the power of a one-sided, instrumental conception of reason (see quotation that opens this chapter). Beguiled by successes in conquering and harnessing nature, the inhabitants of modern societies are seen to be prisoners of a nexus of systemic modernism that is no less constraining, and is in many ways much more destructive, than the myopia and deprivations of pre-modern traditions. Yet, it is of course these traditions that the enlightening advance of science aspires to replace: 'In the most general sense of progressive thought, the Enlightenment has always aimed at liberating men from fear and establishing their sovereignty.' Yet continue 'the fully enlightened earth radiates disaster triumphant' (Horkheimer and Adorno 1947: 3). Symptomatic of this disaster is the relentless and mechanized effort to dominate nature and the widespread environmental destruction and pollution associated with the ruthless exploitation of scarce natural resources.

By deploying the debunking capacities of *critical* Reason (e.g. to unmask racist or sexist claims about the innate superiority of particular groups), critical modernists anticipate a progressive demystification and rationalization of communication that moves beyond the 'halfway rationalization' (Habermas 1974: 281) that is (arguably) consequent upon the equating of science with a technical interest in prediction and control. According to critical modernists, the connection of scientific knowledge to an interest in 'liberating men from fear' (Horkheimer and Adorno 1947: 3) is weakened as science becomes an instrument of political and economic domination. When decisions are dominated by a technical interest in refining means, based upon seeming incontrovertible 'facts', fundamental questions about politics and ethics are marginalized. Ends are taken as given or beyond rational determination as they are represented as a matter of arbitrary value-choice.

In opposition to an exclusively instrumentalist conception of science, critical modernists seek to mobilize reflective Reason to expose 'unreason', or distorted forms of Reason, and thereby facilitate an overcoming of 'the totalizing control of systemic logic' (Cooper and Burrell 1988: 97). This logic is seen to spawn an incipiently technocratic form of life based upon seemingly objective information produced by experts, rather than a democracy fashioned through an ideal of universal participation in open debate. Critical modernism counterposes to technical reason the practical rationality of the institutional frameworks in which technical reason is embedded, and which can be mobilized to contest processes of (technocratic) rationalization.

3.2 CRITICAL THEORY AND HABERMAS'S THEORY OF COGNITIVE INTERESTS

This section places Habermas's thinking on science in the context of the development of Critical Theory. Each type of knowledge-constitutive interest is briefly summarized. They are then illustrated by reference to studies that focus upon 'new organizational forms' in addition to more generalist literatures.

3.2.1 Critical Theory

Having its institutional origins in the Institute of Social Research at Frankfurt University, Critical Theory developed by members of the Frankfurt School, as they have become known, aims to combine social science and philosophy to advance politically and practically committed social philosophy. This mission, as we noted in the previous section, includes a fundamental questioning of the claim that social science can and would produce objective, value-free knowledge of social reality. Instead of feeling obliged to discover universal, invariant regularities and law-like patterns in social behaviour (or at least to dress up empirical findings in these terms), members of the Frankfurt School have sought to show how seemingly 'given' patterns of activity (e.g. consumerism, authoritarianism) take shape within specific historical and societal contexts, and that the methods of representing these patterns are themselves inextricably embedded within and coloured by these contexts.

A strong thread links the ideas of the Frankfurt School to the views of left-Hegelians whose most influential member was Marx (see Jay 1973). Members of the School have identified themselves with the critical, emancipatory *intent* of the Marxian tradition. But, instead of focusing upon the revolutionary potential ascribed by Marx to the working class of which they were sceptical, their attention has been directed to any and all individuals who—feeling frustrated, oppressed, and confused by the contradictory claims, perverse priorities, and divisive effects of modern capitalist societies—are potentially receptive to the revitalization of an Enlightenment conception of Critical Reason as a means of exposing and removing forms of mystification and oppression engendered by a modern, scientistic culture.

3.2.2 Knowledge and Human Interests

According to Habermas, a forgetting of the critical, emancipatory role of modern science in discrediting prescientific dogmas is symptomatic of a contemporary failure to appreciate how scientific activity is embedded in the human 'self-formation process' through which different kinds of 'interest' guide the generation of knowledge. 'The methodology of the sciences', Habermas (1972: 5) argues, is inextricably 'intertwined with the objective self-formation process' made possible by humanity's cultural break with nature. Released from the secure tyranny of instinctual demands, human beings are compelled to organize forms of knowledge or 'cognition' through which a precarious 'management' of social and natural phenomena is accomplished.

The interests that are constitutive of knowledge are described by Habermas as 'quasi-transcendental'. On the one hand, their origin is understood to lie in the universal, transcendental human condition of world-openness; but, on the other hand, their realization is historically and culturally mediated within immanent social institutions. Habermas's usage of the term 'cognitive interests' refers to the human species' (transcendent) capacities, and not to the historically contingent (immanent) interests of any particular social group. His theory of cognitive interests accommodates and values diverse forms of knowledge production,[2] and Habermas argues that the most basic challenge for contemporary scientific endeavour is to re-member the *diverse* cognitive interests released by the cultural break with nature; and then to mobilize these interests in the emancipatory project of developing more fully, as contrasted with 'halfway' (see earlier), rational social institutions and relations.

Three cognitive interests, Habermas contends, underpin the production of distinctive forms of knowledge (and associated types of science): a technical interest in production and control; a practical (historical-hermeneutic) interest in mutual understanding; and finally an interest in emancipation (See Table 3.1). Everyday human action is understood to involve combinations of these cognitive interests. For heuristic and emancipatory purposes, however, it is helpful to appreciate how human interests are constitutive of different kinds of knowledge. More particularly,

---

[2] It is not developed for, or directly relevant to, the rather different, but also important sociological task of explaining how knowledge is socially organized, sponsored, and appropriated (Whitley 1984).

Table 3.1 Habermas's three knowledge–constitutive interests

Cognitive interest	Type of science	Purpose	Focus	Orientation	Projected outcome
Technical	Empirical-analytic	Enhance prediction and control	Identification and manipulation of variables	Calculation	Removal of irrationality within means–ends relationships
Practical	Historical-hermeneutic	Improve mutual understanding	Interpretation of symbolic communication	Appreciation	Removal of misunderstanding
Emancipatory	Critical	Development of more rational social institutions and relations	Exposure of domination and exploitation	Transformation	Removal of relations of domination and exploitation that repress without necessity

the partitioning of human interests facilitates an appreciation of how the three cognitive interests—technical, practical, and emancipatory and related types of science—contribute more fully and self-consciously to the human self-formation process.

3.3 THE THREE KNOWLEDGE-CONSTITUTIVE INTERESTS AND THEIR ARTICULATION AS ORGANIZATION THEORY

3.3.1 The Technical Interest

When the technical interest is engaged or articulated, it impels the production of knowledge in a way that improves the efficiency and/or effectiveness of the means of fulfilling current ends. The world is then represented as a set of given, objectified elements and processes over which human beings seek to establish and extend their control. When motivated by a 'technical' interest, these elements and processes are apprehended as independent phenomena that can be manipulated in a continuous process of design, intervention, and feedback. In its scientific manifestation, the technical cognitive interest represents the world as a complex set of interdependent variables. Wage-payment systems, for example, are a typical product of such knowledge in which material and symbolic rewards are geared to the measured outputs of productive effort. It is understood that increases in productivity can, in principle, be predicted and controlled—for example, by changing the reward system, or by refining the organization of internal labour markets. Such interventions may achieve the desired results. However, from the perspective of the practical interest (see below), this is because such interventions are consistent with the particular meanings attributed by employees to (changes in) their work, and not as a direct consequence of the redesign of their jobs. A vast literature has been spawned by a technical interest in enhancing the *prediction and control* of people in work organizations. It comprises two key strands. The first is overtly problem-solving and prescriptive; the second is ostensibly investigative and descriptive.

The most celebrated example of the *overtly prescriptive* literature is Taylor's *Principles of Scientific Management* (1911), a model of instrumental reason that has been reinvented or recast by numerous other management thinkers, including the contemporary champions of business process re-engineering. A more thoughtful and penetrating example of prescriptivism is Barnard's *The Functions of the*

Executive (1934) whose ghost haunts so much 'progressive' management thinking, including the influential Excellence literature (e.g. Peters and Waterman 1982). This strand of prescriptionism identifies a 'new' factor—'culture'—that, when managed effectively, is deemed to ensure predictable and continuing improvements in performance. More recently, recipes for managing 'chaos' have joined, and are perhaps poised to supplant, prescriptions for controlling 'culture':

Today scientists are developing powerful descriptions of the ways complex systems—from swarms of mosquitoes to computer programs to futures traders in commodity markets—cope effectively with uncertainty and rapid change... The new rules of complex behaviour that cutting-edge scientific research describes have intriguing parallels with the organizational behaviours many companies are trying to encourage. (Freedman 1992: 26)

An emergent prescriptive literature on 'new organizational forms' advises managers to pursue particular courses of action—generally couched in terms of the need to remove 'old' rigid, bureaucratic practices—as a means of enhancing performance. 'Flexibility' is widely canvassed as the key to success in a 'hypercompetitive' environment (Volberda 1996). The 'transgression of boundaries is commended as a means of allowing greater fluidity of movement throughout the organization' (Ashkenas *et al.* 1995: 4). In each case, managers are enjoined to identify a critical variable that, once controlled effectively, will yield the predicted improvements in performance.

We now turn to consider a second major strand of thinking, also guided by a technical interest, that is more scholarly and less explicitly prescriptive. Here we find literature concerned with the construction and testing of theory that is *ostensibly* distanced from 'the real world' preoccupations of organizational design and performance improvement. The *Hawthorne* experiments, for example, correlated employee productivity with changes in various 'environmental factors'. Likewise, the *Aston* studies measured and compared the performance of organizations operating in different contexts with different structures and patterns of behaviour (Pugh and Hickson 1968), where the latter are understood to be reactive to the contingencies of the former. An opposing, 'action theoretic' stance ascribes adaptations of structure and behaviour to the particularities of the accumulated competencies and recipes that inform *pro-active*, strategic choices (Child 1972) made by managers who enact and shape the contexts of their actions—for example, by entering into alliances.

More recently, students of 'new organizational forms' have called for the combining of 'reactive' and 'proactive' models of change in a 'co-evolutionary' framework that considers 'the joint outcomes of managerial adaptation and environmental selection' where the emergence of new forms of organization are examined as an interaction of managerial intentionality and environmental effects (Lewin and Volberda 1999: 523). The call is for research that abandons the focus upon unidirectional causalities founded upon a dependent-independent variable distinction in favour of a framework that studies how 'changes in any one variable may be caused endogenously by changes in others' (ibid. 527). However, the preoccupation with mapping and measuring variables that will render organizations more predictable and controllable is extended rather than suspended.

The call to abandon research aimed at discovering unidirectional causalities points towards an alternative approach where the concern to appreciate how people in organizations actively interpret, construct, negotiate, and accomplish their organizing practices, including those practices identified as exemplifying 'new organizational forms'. Such research addresses the question of how knowledge of 'organizations' as well as their 'environments' is developed within particular schema that are productive of the very distinctions and relations—between 'organizations' and 'environments', for example—that they aspire to illuminate. Some limited attention to this process is evident in Dijksterhuis and Van den Bosch's 'Where Do New Organizational Forms Come From?' (1999), in which it is argued that '*perceived* environment characteristics derived from shared schemas of top management trigger strategic design actions that may lead to new organization forms' (ibid. 571, emphasis added); and where it is suggested that this 'shared set of beliefs' comprising the schema not only 'functions as a context' for strategic design actions but 'is also reproduced in these actions' (ibid.). This formulation of the relationship between 'environments', 'strategic design actions' and 'forms' incorporates some appreciation of how 'schemas' are productive of the characteristics ascribed to environments; and also notes how design actions are at once 'triggered' by the schemas and reproductive of them. Such analysis does not, however, extend to an appreciation of how the *identification* of 'forms' and 'strategic actions' by managers and commentators is itself an expression of a particular interpretive framework, and not a more or less accurate reflection of the reality that such sensemaking seeks to penetrate and conquer. The analysis remains rooted in an empirical-analytic conception of knowledge production in which the self-evidence of the distinctions made between 'environment', 'design actions', and 'forms' is assumed; and in which minimal attention is paid to the question of how the existence ascribed to 'forms' and 'strategic actions' is enacted. To consider how knowledge of organizations, or organizing processes, including their allegedly 'new' forms, can be differently constituted, it is necessary to consider research guided by an alternative, practical interest in mutual understanding.

3.3.2 The Practical Interest

The practical interest anticipates and pursues the possibility of attaining mutual understanding between people. When knowledge production is guided by this interest, the pressing concern is not to predict or control but, rather, to facilitate communication so that mutual understanding is reached, or at least advanced. This interest is termed 'practical' because *the process of making sense of the world is understood to be a precondition of any form of social action*, including the prediction and control of objectified processes (see previous section). The identification and measurement of variables, it is argued, is irremediably dependent upon 'the prior frame of reference to which they are affixed' (Habermas 1972: 308). Knowledge guided by the practical interest addresses the question of how 'variables' are identified and operationalized in order to develop insights into the social organization of empirical-analytic knowledge production.[3] The type of science that discloses and appreciates, rather than takes for granted, such socially organized frames of reference is termed 'historical-hermeneutic' because such 'practical' knowledge necessitates the mobilization of historically mediated processes of inter-pretation.

When addressing the issue of employee participation, for example, knowledge guided by a practical interest in mutual understanding might begin with the question of how employees currently make sense of their work, and then explore how such sensemaking is historically and culturally embedded within a wider set of social practices, norms, and values (e.g. Gouldner 1954; Dalton 1959; Watson 1994). It may be shown how increased participation, for example, is viewed by employees in different and shifting ways—as a means of removing petty rules and/or as a more subtle form of management control, for example. The purpose of knowledge guided by a practical knowledge is to appreciate how persons enact their situation(s), and thereby aspire to develop a better understanding of their respective orientations.

In the 'new organizational forms' literature, Sydow and Windeler (1998), for example, call for an approach to their study, and more specifically the development of inter-firm networks, that 'focuses on organizational and interorganizational *practices* and, at the same time, takes the interplay of action and structure, as well as power, *sense-making* and legitimacy issues involved in economic practices into account' (ibid. 265, emphases added). Sydow and Windeler examine the network practices of a group of 900 financial advisors, led by MLP-Finanzdienstleistungen AG, Heidelberg, who offer financial services to high income customers.[4] The branches not only provide support services for the advisors but 'are strongly involved in the process in which the symbols, interpretive schemes, knowledge, norms, understandings and ways of doing business are reproduced' (ibid. 267). It is to an exploration and explication of these 'schemes, knowledge, norms, under-standings and ways of doing business' that the practical interest in mutual understanding is directed. The schemes, etc. are understood to be media of organizing, as are appeals to values and ostensibly rational courses of action signalled by

---

[3] This form of knowledge may also be directed at gaining a better, reflexive understanding of how its own form(s) of knowledge (e.g. about the practices of empirical-analytic science) are accomplished.

[4] In addition to the advisers, the hub firm of MLP includes its own life insurer and an information services provider as well as stable relationships with insurance companies, banks, and investment funds.

concepts such as 'profitability, return on capital, stockholder value, fairness, reputation, innovativeness, adaptive capacity', etc. They all serve to evoke a context within and through which action is accomplished.[5]

3.3.3 The Emancipatory Interest

Whereas the technical and practical interests are conceived to be endemic to human existence, the emancipatory interest is understood to be stimulated by consequences flowing from ideas and actions guided by the other two cognitive interests. This interest is provoked when, for example, employees resist techniques and lampoon ideologies that purport to 'empower' them, yet are experienced as an intensification of their work without appropriate or sufficient compensation. In elucidating the emancipatory interest, Habermas (1986) explains that

what I mean is an attitude which is formed in the experience of suffering from something man-made, which can be abolished and should be abolished. This is not just a contingent value-postulate: that people want to get rid of certain sufferings. No, it is something so profoundly ingrained in the structure of human societies—the calling into question, and deep-seated wish to throw off, relations which repress you without necessity—so intimately built into the reproduction of human life that I don't think it can be regarded as just a subjective attitude which may or may not guide this or that piece of scientific research. It is more. (ibid. 198)

Habermas points to the experience of (unnecessary) frustration and suffering which, he contends, stimulates, yet also frustrates, a desire to 'throw off relations' that '*repress without necessity*' (my emphasis). For Habermas, critical science resonates with, and indeed is fuelled by, a desire to assert (the possibility of) greater autonomy and responsibility[6] in the face of institutions and practices that are sensed to impede unnecessarily their contemporary expression and extension. In contrast to the 'empirical-analytic' and 'historical-hermeneutic' sciences, which each regard existing social formations and patterns of meaning as *given* objects of prediction and control or of interpretation, critical science strives to expose *the unreasoned, political basis of this givenness*. For example, instead of seeking to identify covariance between observable events (the project of empirical-analytic science) or striving to interpret the development of particular meanings (the concern of historical-hermeneutic science), critical science is concerned to reveal

---

[5] The study incorporates consideration of the practical, negotiated process of organizational reality production as a means of advancing our understanding of how 'organizational and interorganizational practices' are accomplished. Criteria used for evaluating organizations and interorganizational networks are, from this perspective, 'necessarily contextually embedded *social constructions*' (ibid. 273, emphasis in original). There is, however, disappointingly little illumination of how these sensemaking processes are learned, developed, and changed through processes of communication.

[6] Later, I question Habermas's unreflective use of these terms.

how patterns of behaviour and meaning are embedded in oppressive structures of domination that, potentially, are open to challenge and change. In Habermas's (1972) words, critical social science seeks 'to determine when theoretical statements grasp invariant regularities of social action as such and when they express ideologically frozen relations of dependence that can in principle be transformed' (ibid. 310).

To consider once more the case of employee participation, knowledge guided by an emancipatory interest goes beyond the 'mere' appreciation of employee orientations (e.g. towards participation) to show how these understandings are structured within relations of power and domination—relations that are potentially open to (radical) transformation that dissolve 'frozen relations of dependence' and thereby eliminate forms of socially unnecessary suffering associated with these relations. From this perspective, findings that indicate employee indifference or hostility towards a participation scheme may be interpreted as symptomatic of a structure of social and industrial relations where, historically, participation has either been excluded (e.g. by the adoption of a top-down approach to organization and job design) or introduced cynically as a means of achieving some other, often undisclosed, purpose—such as greater flexibility. Employee hostility towards, or scepticism about, participation schemes is then viewed, from the standpoint of critical science, not as evidence of worker apathy or negativity per se but, rather indicative of institutionalized relations of dependence in which employees have been historically excluded from participation in key decisions. Precisely because such attitudes are located in a particular structure of dependency relations, they are understood to be mutable: they can be changed by transforming the structures in which such attitudes are fostered and reproduced.

An academic body of knowledge guided primarily by an emancipatory interest has emerged only comparatively recently in the field of management and organization studies. Forester (1992), for example, applies Habermas's analysis of the pragmatics of communicative action 'to show how much more than instrumental action...takes place in ordinary practice and what difference this makes for questions of power and powerlessness, community and autonomy' (ibid. 47). Forester's analysis illuminates how hierarchy operates to exclude or marginalize the contribution of subordinate actors to decision-making processes, thereby depriving them of full involvement in the institutions through which their sense of identity and purpose is constituted. This deprivation is understood not just as a loss to the individual, but simultaneously as a loss for the group or community. The wider community forfeits the benefit of subordinates' immediate contribution; there is also a loss of the future benefits of skills and a sense of collective responsibility that can develop through active participation in decision-making.

In Forester's analysis, capitalists (e.g. property developers), senior planners, and managers are identified as (highly compensated) participants in a structure of power relations that they struggle to secure and sustain. Highlighting the interdependence of individuals and the wider community, he shows how those who are understood to occupy privileged positions of relative autonomy and power are themselves frequently oppressed by a burden of responsibility which they routinely contrive to evade. Superficially, this representation of the privileged as victims would seem to affirm conservative arguments for further compensatory hikes in their material and symbolic compensation. However, critical analysis turns this proposal on its head. The (critically) rational solution to problems of irresponsibility and apathy ascribed to disadvantaged citizens and employees, on the one side, and the excessive responsibility and stress suffered by an elite of decision-makers, on the other side, it is argued, is not to strengthen the existing system of control and rewards. Rather, the more enlightened way forward is to promote a wider diffusion of power and responsibility through the democratization of economic, as well as political, institutions.

Turning, finally, to consider studies of 'new organizational forms', it is relevant to take up once more Sydow and Windeler's (1998) study of organizing and evaluating inter-firm networks. Network performance measures applied to the financial advisers studied by Sydow and Windeler included 'the ratios of prospective clients, of prospective to actual customers, and of the revenue realized to the revenue planned' (Sydow and Windeler 1998: 275). Of particular relevance is their observation that evaluations of the performance and effectiveness of the MLP network were not the product of impartial calculations so much as the outcome of political processes of domination that presented themselves as rational decision-making. Resources at the command of those occupying the hub firm of the MLP network are seen to be mobilized to establish and institutionalize particular criteria of evaluation, including the acceptability or normalcy of criteria supportive of the reproduction of their position of dominance within the network. To the extent that there is compliance amongst network members with the evaluation criteria, then the use of resources to marshal and maintain the network serves to augment the assets at the disposal of the hub, thereby stabilizing the structure of domination. It is noted, for example, how what can be made to count as '*the* adequate information' is dependent upon agents' 'power to impose the corresponding concept on the individual, on the organization or on the network'.[7] 'Network effectiveness', Sydow and Windeler (ibid. 275) contend, is thus 'an expression of distinct modes of domination, inherent in the organizing practices'. From a critical standpoint, network effectiveness is not simply a matter of reducing inefficiencies, facilitating expansion, or negotiating

---

[7] There is, however, little consideration of how the process of 'imposition' is accomplished or indeed how certain kinds of information are privileged (and widely accepted?) as reliable and legitimate indicators of effectiveness. Within what interpretive frameworks are such demands placed, and how are these frameworks forged and reproduced? Sydow and Windeler are largely silent on such issues, despite their contention that 'studying inter-firm networks in general and strategic networks in particular requires the analysis of concrete, contextually embedded (network) practices' in a way that 'renounces conventional hypothesis-testing' (1998: 280).

a shared definition of the situation wherein the evaluation criteria are viewed as normal and reasonable. More fundamentally, it is about organizing forms of economic activity that maintain a situation in which 'the greater proportion' of the surplus generated by the network as a whole is 'appropriated by the hub firm' (ibid. 276).

This darker side of new organizational forms has been noted by Victor and Stephens (1994) who acknowledge that they may be effective at generating surplus, reducing costs, leveraging competitive advantage, etc., but that their 'radical design . . . entails losses as well as costs'. They note, for example, how the security of a role anchored in an organization with a well-defined boundary and codified in a job description is being supplanted by stress-ridden, 'hyperflexible workplaces' where roles are defined by the task of the moment, and where rights become ephemeral as everything is driven by the demand to be adaptive and innovative. These 'high velocity' workplaces, Victor and Stephens contend, 'offer no ongoing relationships, no safe haven, no personal space' (1994: 481). Everything is negotiable and disposable.

This unremittingly dark picture tends to overlook how the very existence and exploitation of relations of dependence ferments the possibility of counter-discourses and practices that expose and challenge oppressive institutions. Hints of this are present when Sydow and Windeler describe network processes being 'full of tensions and contradictions and a dialectic of control that only to some extent and for some time can be tamed by an appropriate governance structure' (1998: 280). They note, for example, that the hub firm is 'highly interested that the advisors see themselves as "independent"' (sic) even though their scope for acting independently of the network is, in some respects at least, 'almost as restricted as that of some employees in vertically integrated firms' (ibid. 272). It is implied that those in the hub firm mobilize their resources to promote a definition of the advisers' situation that is intended to distance the self-understanding of the latter from that of employees. This stratagem proved to be contradictory, however, when the advisers exercised their sense of independence to mount a successful challenge to pressures to change their client quota. In this way, the attribution of independence that was intended, according to Sydow and Windeler, to obfuscate their capture by the network's performance indicators had the contradictory consequence of emboldening advisers to exercise their power as key players within the network upon whose continued cooperation and delivery of client revenues the hub firm depended.

When knowledge is guided by an emancipatory interest, questions are posed that bring to the surface the suffering—in terms of anxiety and stress, for example—that are associated, in Sydow and Windeler's study, with the use of performance indicators and the means of maintaining the subordination of the advisers within the network. Is it asked, for example, if the measures devised jointly and democratically by those to whom they were applied, or were they imposed by fiat by the hub firm?

To the extent that advisers complied with, or even consented to, the application of the performance indicators, does this imply that their cooperation was a consequence of making an informed decision, or was it because they calculated that the benefits (e.g. opportunity to earn bonuses) associated with advisory work outweighed the costs (pressures, job insecurity)? To what extent had the methods and criteria of assessing the job of advisers been conditioned by the high value placed upon material wealth in our society? The thrust of the emancipatory interest is to raise questions of this kind as a way of problematizing what is suspected to be an unreasoned basis for decision-making, such as career choice. Upon reflection, the conclusion may be reached that compliance with, or even consent to, evaluation procedures institutionalized within the MLP network is an 'expression of ideologically frozen relations of dependence' (Habermas 1972: 310)—of advisers on the hub firm in particular—that can be transformed.

One kind of transformation would be for a group of advisers to establish their own, rival network. A more radical transformation might involve pressures from advisers to transform the network into a mutual company or a cooperative in which decisions about the distribution of the surplus are made by the policy-holders or by the partners within the cooperative. Less ambitiously, advisers might organize to shift the centre of gravity away from the hub firm towards the advisers by organizing 'microemancipatory' forms of resistance to the repressive and/or precariously maintained pressures to produce a surplus. As Sydow and Windeler (1998: 275) usefully point out, the place of those occupying a dominant position within a hierarchy is rarely, if ever, unassailable. Changes of circumstances, such as shifts in distribution mechanisms (e.g. moves towards the remote distribution of financial services through the internet), can disturb prevailing structures of domination and relations of power; and ultimately those occupying such positions are dependent upon others who generate the surpluses. It was this dependence that enabled some MLP advisers—presumably, the ones with the most affluent client base—successfully to resist pressures by the hub firm to change the average number of clients that an adviser was allowed to serve. One may speculate that the prospect of disaffected advisers and their possible departure (with their clients) to establish a competitor network to MLP was sufficient to dissuade those in the hub to persist in their efforts to renegotiate the client quota.

3.4 DISCUSSION

It would be inconsistent to conclude this chapter without briefly addressing some criticisms of Habermas's Critical Theoretic Formulation of cognitive interests.

Criticism has been directed at his characterization of the ontological status of human interests as 'quasi-transcendental'. When responding to the criticism that he fudges his position by refusing to say whether the interests are historical (immanent) or universal (transcendental), Habermas defends his original, ambivalent formulation of the dialectical development of human nature and its interests: the interests, he contends, are a *condition* of 'the cultural break with nature' (see earlier), but they are *also* a *consequence* of this break. Without interests in either understanding or controlling nature and society, knowledge that facilitates the realization of this project would not be generated. But the realization of these interests is always mediated by the specific contexts of their articulation. It is therefore erroneous to suggest that the interests are transcendental *or* immanent since, in practice, they are both.

Second, Habermas has been criticized for his representation of the self-understanding of the empirical-analytic sciences. The objection is that his account relies upon an outdated, idealized representation of natural scientific practice (Hesse 1982). It can be readily conceded, as Habermas (1982: 274 *et seq.*) has done, that not all empirical-analytic scientists are unreflective empiricists in the way that his representation of their work may suggest. Fortunately, this admission is not particularly damaging to Habermas's theory of cognitive interests. It is possible to acknowledge the existence of post-empiricist *philosophies* of (social) science whilst, at the same time, contending that in many fields of investigation, including the field of management, the *conduct* of 'normal science' proceeds, for the most part, blissfully unaware of and/or unconcerned by post-empiricist philosophical debates. It is precisely this complacent sleep that the theory of cognitive interests aspires to disturb—a prospect that is not diminished by Habermas's positive valuing of empirical-analytic science within this theory.[8]

Habermas has also sought to strengthen the basis of his argument by abandoning a philosophy of consciousness in favour of a philosophy of language.[9] It is worth stressing that this 'linguistic turn' does not nullify the theory of cognitive interests or make it 'old hat'.[10] By rooting his analysis in the universal properties of language, Habermas attempts to show—although not persuasively, in my view—how the very (transcendental) structures of language anticipate a consensus based upon dialogue rather than force.[11]

[8] With specific reference to empirical-analytic science, Habermas has argued that 'no matter how perverted', its findings 'remain a piece with committed reason' (Habermas 1974: 270).

[9] The basic difference between these formulations is that, in the philosophy of language, Habermas's claims are grounded *inter*subjectively in what he terms the 'universal pragmatics' of language use, rather than *intra*subjectively in the consciousness of each human being.

[10] Burrell (1994 : 8) has noted how, in Habermas's later work, including *The Theory of Communicative Action*, 'some of the key conceptualization of knowledge interests not only remain but grow in importance. They are part and parcel of Habermas's linguistic turn . . .'. See also White, 1988 : 27 and Honneth and Joas, 1991 : 19.

[11] That said, the plausibility or otherwise of Habermas's claims is of relevance for my argument. This chapter is not concerned primarily with the role of the theory of cognitive interests in providing a

I am not persuaded that it is possible to separate knowledge from relations of power within an 'ideal speech situation' in the manner that Habermas (counter-factually) claims. Instead, I am drawn to a Nietzschean or postmodernist position which warns that there can be no escape from power relations; and that despite all the fine words surrounding Critical Theory, its proponents' refusal to fully acknowledge that the idea of emancipatory reason is historically constructed, not onto-logically given, leads to a suppression of pluralism and playfulness as its authority is uncritically privileged. In response to this criticism, Habermas retorts that post-modernist thinking leads inexorably to nihilism and despair. Deeply sceptical about the progressive claims of postmodernists (e.g. Lyotard 1986), Habermas (1987b) argues that the postmodern inclination to relativize (modernist) rationality de-values and squanders the emancipatory potential of Reason as a resource for exposing and removing forms of mystification and oppression.

Against Habermas's criticism of postmodernist thinking, it can be questioned whether his aspiration to provide a rational grounding for normative standards is a coherent project. Its coherence is suspect if all forms of knowledge—including the idea of the ideal speech situation and communicative action—are articulations of power and, inescapably, exert a subjugating effect upon those who identify them as truth. The objection here is that the Habermasian position is insufficiently self-reflective and self-critical about his own preconceptions—notably, the assumption that (radical humanist) ideas about 'autonomy' and 'responsibility' are unequivo-cally propitious for humankind. Such a view is also potentially dangerous, insofar as it implies that what is done in the name of emancipation is somehow exempt from (its own kinds of) oppressive effects (Knights and Willmott 2002). The risk is one of 'reason' being invoked to deny or mystify forms of subjection that ostensibly it claims to expose and remove.

Habermas's response to this criticism has been to concede that Critical Theory cannot escape this risk. He then seeks to turn the tables on his critics (see Poster 1989) by inviting them to reflect upon what, for him, are the far more serious consequences of abandoning any basis for differentiating the true from the false, and the rational from the irrational. In its absence, Habermas (1992: 209) argues, 'All validity claims become immanent to particular discourses. They are simultaneously absorbed into the totality of some one [sic] of the blindly occurring discourses and left at the mercy of the "hazardous play" amongst these discourses as each over-powers the other.' In part, Habermas seems to be responding constructively to the poststructuralist contention that consideration must be given to the consequences of adopting particular kinds of discourse, and not just to the way their claims are grounded. Habermas's defence of Critical Theory is based on the claim that efforts to differentiate the truth from the false are less damaging in their, apparently

foundation for Critical Theory. My concern is instead with the heuristic value of this theory in differentiating types of science.

conservative, effects than either a refusal to do so and/or a commitment to showing how such distinctions are solely 'immanent to particular discourses' rather than in any way being a condition of all forms of discourse (Freundlieb 1989; see also Power 1990).

However, if it is the case that what passes for truth is historically contingent, at least until 'the ideal speech situation' has been realized rather than simply invoked as a counter-factual, then the plausibility of truth claims is conditional upon the context of their assessment, and not upon their alleged universal veracity. If this point is accepted, it then follows that even if we were to be convinced by Habermas's theory of universal pragmatics, our conviction would tell us more about the strength of our cultural receptivity to such ideas—which, of course, does not logically exclude the possibility of the theory being true—than about their veracity. In which case, forms of critical thinking that reject a Habermasian (transcendental) preoccupation with grounding truth claims become more appealing. More specifically, such scepticism enhances the appeal of approaches that attend to, and build upon, the (immanent) identification of opportunities for exposing and dissolving forms of oppression; and this is not least because they are compatible with commending Habermas's theory of cognitive interests as a *heuristic device* for appreciating the presence and potentially emancipatory contribution of different forms of science.

From a (self-critically) critical modernist perspective, postmodernist analysis may have the beneficial consequence of renewing and extending the critical strand of modernism. By prompting reflection upon assumptions and methods that are otherwise shielded from scrutiny by disciplinary complacency, blinkered self-referentiality, and/or intellectual pride, it may encourage deeper questioning of whether, for example, Critical Theory, and the work of Habermas especially, is excessively preoccupied with the universal justification of its own truth claims, to the neglect of exploring what can be done to challenge everyday forms of subjugation, oppression, and repression by appealing to extant local understandings and traditions (Alvesson and Willmott 1996). To this extent, at least, there is some common cause in postmodernist and critical modernist critiques of systemic modernism; and in this regard, it is worth quoting briefly from the (later) writings of Foucault who, though often identified with the postmodern camp, arguably straddles the critical modernism–postmodernism divide: 'the thread that may connect us with the Enlightenment is . . . the permanent reactivation of an attitude—that is, of a philosophical ethos that could be described as a permanent critique of our historical era' (Foucault 1984: 42). Foucault's understanding of (the) Enlightenment, which he prefers to characterize as an attitude rather than as a period or a project, is remarkably similar to that of Habermas. But a key point of difference remains: profound Foucauldian scepticism that there is *an authoritative basis* for critique and transformation. This anti-foundationalism denies the need to make highly problematical claims about an essential human autonomy or even the embeddedness of autonomy in the structure of language. *Contra* Habermas, the pursuit of freedom and equality is not, as it were, guaranteed or privileged by a foundational principle, whether its location is posited in the structure of language or in the depths of human nature. Rather, as in Laclau and Mouffe's (1985) thinking, the possibility of freedom and equality is understood to be conditional upon the development and continuing existence of discourses that attribute value to ideas of freedom and equality and the institutions that support their articulation and facilitate their realization. As Laclau and Mouffe (1990: 124) note, the absence of any apodeictic certainty that one type of society (or organization) is better than 'another' does not prevent us from reasoning politically and of preferring, for a variety of reasons, certain political positions to others. In a passage that echoes Habermas's anticipation of the ideal speech situation, without becoming encumbered by the baggage that seeks to justify it as a touchstone of objective truth, Laclau and Mouffe commend an approach to the production of knowledge and the transformation of relations that

tries to found itself upon the verisimilitude of its conclusions, is essentially pluralist, because it needs to make reference to other arguments and, since the process is essentially open, these can always be contested and refuted. The logic of verisimilitude is, in this sense, essentially public and democratic. (Laclau and Mouffe 1990: 125)

From this perspective, it makes little sense to deny that methodologies favoured by critical science exert disciplinary effects that can be constraining as well as enabling—an observation that takes on board elements of the postmodernist critique of Critical Theory.

3.5 CONCLUSION

With the benefit of Habermas's theory of cognitive interests, it is possible to appreciate how, for example, a technical interest in prediction and control dominates the production of knowledge about management and organization. Ideas about improved quality of working life, better communications, employee involvement and empowerment, for example, are routinely formulated in terms of their contribution to organizational effectiveness, to the exclusion of their contribution to a questioning of established objectives and priorities, or to the development and application of knowledge that reaches out beyond these limits. Commenting upon the weakness of the (acknowledged) connection between knowledge and praxis within empirical-analytic science, Habermas (1974: 254–5) observes:

Emancipation by means of enlightenment is replaced by instruction in control over object-ive or objectified forces. Socially effective theory is no longer directed towards the con-sciousness of human beings who live together and discuss matters with each other, but to the behaviour of human beings who manipulate. As a productive force of industrial develop-ment, it changes the basis of human life, but it no longer reaches out critically beyond this basis to raise life itself, for the sake of life, to another level.

Nevertheless, and crucially, Habermas's theory of cognitive interests admits and celebrates the (yet to be fully realized) potential of the technical interest in predic-tion and control to enable human beings to develop ways of organizing and managing that are safer and less wasteful of human and natural resources. Haber-masian thinking does not deny the value and power of empirical-analytic science but, rather, seeks to recall its critical, emancipatory potential. Habermas's theory of cognitive interests also recalls and celebrates how the capacity to develop mutual understanding through the use of language can enable people to cooperate more effectively.

In the absence of the catalyst of critical reflection upon the historical conditions in which technical and practical knowledge is generated and applied, however, knowledge remains the servant, rather than the debunker, of power (Baritz 1960). Movement away from a narrowly instrumental, politically conservative, socially divisive and ecologically destructive use of knowledge, as Fischer (1990) has argued, demands the adoption of 'a methodological framework that not only includes but logically transcends empirical analysis by interpreting the meaning of its data in both the context of action and a larger critique of society' (p. 217).

Habermas's exploration of the connectedness of knowledge and human interests is of considerable value in exposing and changing the division of science from ethics and the damaging consequences, social and ecological, of ascribing neutrality to the principles and practices of management that embody and sustain this division. As the Enlightenment connection of scientific knowledge with the reduction of suffering is remembered, it may be hoped that the calamitous illusion of ethically neutral value-free knowledge will be progressively dispelled.

Those unsympathetic to such a project have complained that it contravenes the understanding that 'decisions about good and evil and the meaning of the universe cannot have any scientific foundation' (Kolakowski 1978: 394, cited in Tsoukas 1992: 643). Even if it is the case that moral positions can never be conclusively validated, Habermas's theory of cognitive interests, and the recogni-tion and pursuit of critical science in particular, can nonetheless help us to identify, question, and hopefully dissolve some of the prejudices which place unnecessary constraints upon our collective capacity to wrestle with moral and metaphysical questions. The claim here is not that rationality should be redesigned from scratch or that it should replace morality that has developed through a process of cultural evolution (see Tsoukas 1992: 644). Rather, the more modest hope is that the human reason of modernity has been, and can continue to be, a force in the critique and transformation of moral rules—for example, the rules that legitimize and sustain the sanctity of managerial prerogatives, the necessity of functional imperatives and/ or the inevitability of patriarchal power relations.

REFERENCES

ALVESSON, M., and WILLMOTT, H. C. (eds.) (1992). *Critical Management Studies*. London: Sage.

—————— (1996). *Making Sense of Management*. London: Sage.

ASHKENAS, R., ULRICH, D., JICK, T., and KERR, S. (1995). *The Boundaryless Organization: Breaking the Chains of Organizational Structure*. San Francisco: Jossey-Bass.

BACHARACH, S. B. (1989). 'Organizational Theories: Some Criteria for Evaluation'. *Academy of Management Review*, 14/4: 496–515.

BARITZ, L. (1960). *The Servants of Power*. New York: Wiley.

BARNARD, C. (1934). *The Functions of the Executive*. Cambridge, Mass.: Harvard University Press.

BERNSTEIN, R. J. (1976). *The Restructuring of Social and Political Theory*. London: Methuen.

BURRELL, G. (1994). 'Modernism, Postmodernism and Organizational Analysis 4: The Contribution of Jurgen Habermas'. *Organization Studies*, 15/1: 1–19.

—— and MORGAN, G. (1979). *Sociological Paradigms and Organizational Analysis*. London: Heinemann.

CHILD, J. (1972). 'Organizational Structure, Environment and Performance: The Role of Strategic Choice', *Sociology*, 6: 1–22.

COOPER, D. J., and HOPPER, T. (eds.) (1989). *Critical Accounts*. London: Macmillan.

COOPER, R., and BURRELL, G. (1988). 'Modernism, Postmodernism and Organizational Analysis'. *Organization Studies*, 9: 81–112.

DAFT, R., and LEWIN, A. (1993). ' "Where Are the Theories for the New Organizational Forms?" An Editorial Essay', *Organization Science*, 4/4: i–iv.

DALTON, M. (1959). *Men Who Manage*. New York: Wiley.

DAVIDOW, W. H., and MALONE, M. S. (1992). *The Virtual Conception*. New York: Harper.

DIJKSTERHUIS, M. S., and VANDEN BOSCH, F. A. J. (1999). 'Where Do New Organisational Forms Come From? Management Logics as a Source of Co-evolution'. *Organization Science*, 10/5: 569–82.

DONALDSON, L. (1985). *In Defence of Organization Theory*. Cambridge: Cambridge University Press.

FISCHER, F. (1990). *Technocracy and the Politics of Expertise*. London: Sage.

FORESTER, J. (1992). 'Critical Ethnography: On Fieldwork in a Habermasian Way', in M. Alvesson and H. C. Willmott (eds.), *Critical Management Studies*. London: Sage.

FOUCAULT, M. (1984). 'What is Enlightenment?', in P. Rabinow (ed.), *The Foucault Reader*. Harmondsworth: Peregrine.

FREEDMAN, D. H. (1992). 'Is Management Still a Science?', *Harvard Business Review*, November–December: 26–38.

FREUNDLIEB, D. (1989). 'Rationalism v. Irrationalism? Habermas's Response to Foucault'. *Inquiry*, 31: 171–92.

GOULDNER, A. W. (1954). *Patterns of Industrial Bureaucracy*. Glencoe, Ill.: Free Press.

HABERMAS, J. (1972). *Knowledge and Human Interests*. London: Heinemann.

—— (1974). *Theory and Practice*. London: Heinemann.

—— (1982). 'A Reply to My Critics', in J. B. Thompson and D. Held (eds.), *Habermas: Critical Debates*. London: Macmillan.

—— (1984). *The Theory of Communicative Action*, i. Boston: Beacon Press.

—— (1986). 'Life Forms, Morality and the Task of the Philosopher', in P. Dews (ed.), *Habermas: Autonomy and Solidarity*. London: Verso.

—— (1987a). *The Theory of Communicative Action*, ii Boston: Beacon Press.

—— (1987b). *Lectures on the Philosophical Discourse of Modernity*. Cambridge, Mass.: MIT Press.

—— (1992). *Postmetaphysical Thinking: Philosophical Essays*. Cambridge: Cambridge University Press.

HALES, M. (1974). 'Management Science and the Second Industrial Revolution'. *Radical Science Journal*, 1: 5–28.

HESSE, M. (1982). 'Science and Objectivity', in J. B. Thompson and D. Held (eds.), *Habermas: Critical Debates*. London: Macmillan.

HONNETH, A., and JOAS, H. (eds.) (1991). *Communicative Action: Essays on Jürgen Habermas's The Theory of Communicative Action*. Cambridge, Mass.: MIT Press.

HORKHEIMER, M. (1937). 'Traditional and Critical Theory', in P. Connerton (ed.), *Critical Sociology*. Harmondsworth: Penguin (1976).

—— and ADORNO, T. (1947). *The Dialectics of Enlightenment*. London: Verso (1979).

JAY, M. (1973). *The Dialectical Imagination: A History of the Frankfurt School and the Institute of Social Research 1923–50*, Berkeley: University of California Press.

KNIGHTS, D., and WILLMOTT, H. C. (2002). 'Autonomy as Utopia and Dystopia', in M. Parker (ed.), *Utopia and Organization*. Oxford: Blackwell.

KOLAKOWSKI, L. (1978). *Main Currents of Marxism*, iii. Oxford: Clarendon Press.

LACLAU, E., and MOUFFE, C. (1985). *Hegemony and Socialist Strategy: Towards a Radical Democratic Politics*. London: Verso.

—— —— (1990). 'Post-Marxism Without Apologies', in E. Laclau, *New Reflections on the Revolution of Our Time*. London: Verso.

LEWIN, A. Y., and VOLBERDA, H. W. (1999). 'Prolegomena on Coevolution: Framework for Research on Strategy and New Organizational Forms', *Organization Science*, 10/5: 519–34.

LYOTARD, J.-F. (1986). *The Postmodern Condition*. Manchester: Manchester University Press.

LYYTINEN, K. J., and KLEIN, H. K. (1985). 'The Critical Theory of Jürgen Habermas as a Basis for a Theory of Information Systems', in E. Mumford, R. Hirschheim, and G. Fitzgerald (eds.), *Research Methods in Information Systems*. North Holland: Amsterdam.

MARSDEN, R. (1993). 'The Politics of Organizational Analysis'. *Organization Studies*, 14/1: 93–124.

Organization Studies (1988). 9/1.

PETERS, T. J., and WATERMAN, R. H. (1982). *In Search of Excellence: Lessons from America's Best-Run Companies*. New York: Harper & Row.

PFEFFER, J. (1993). 'Barriers to the Advance of Organization Science: Paradigm Development as a Dependent Variable'. *Academy of Management Review*, 18/4: 599–620.

POSTER, M. (1989). *Critical Theory & Poststructuralism: In Search of Context*. Ithaca, NY: Cornell University Press.

POWER, M. (1990). 'Modernism, Postmodernism and Organization', in J. Hassard and D. Pym (eds.), *The Theory and Philosophy of Organization*. London: Routledge.

PUGH, D. S., and HICKSON, D. J. (1968). 'The Comparative Study of Organizations', in D. Pym (ed.), *Industrial Society*. Harmondsworth: Penguin.

STABLEIN, R., and NORD, W. (1985). 'Practical and Emancipatory Interests in Organizational Symbolism: A Review and Evaluation'. *Journal of Management*, 11/2: 13–28.

SYDOW, J., and WINDELER, A. (1998). 'Organizing and Evaluating Interfirm Networks: A Structurationist Perspective on Network Processes and Effectiveness'. *Organization Science*, 9/3: 265–84.

TAYLOR, F. (1911). *Principles of Scientific Management*. New York: Harper & Row.

TSOUKAS, H. (1992). 'Panoptic Reason and the Search for Totality: A Critical Assessment of the Critical Systems Perspective'. *Human Relations*, 45/7: 637–57.

VICTOR, B., and STEPHENS, C. (1994). 'The Dark Side of the New Organizational Form'. *Organization Science*, 5/4: 479–82.

VOLBERDA, H. W. (1996). 'Toward the Flexible Firm: How to Remain Vital in Hypercompetitive Environments', *Organization Science*, 7/4: 359–74.

WATSON, T. (1994). *In Search of Management*. London: Routledge.

WEBER, M. (1949). *The Methodology of the Social Sciences*, New York: Free Press.

WHITE, S. (1988). *The Recent Work of J. Habermas*. Cambridge: Cambridge University Press.

WHITLEY, R. (1984). 'The Scientific Status of Management Research as a Practically-Oriented Social Science'. *Journal of Management Studies*, 21/4: 369–90.

WILLMOTT, H. C. (1983). 'Paradigms for Accounting Research: Critical Reflections On Tomkins and Groves' "Everyday Accountant and Researching His Reality"'. *Accounting, Organizations and Society*, 8: 389–405.

—— (1992). 'Postmodernism and Excellence: The De-differentiation of Economy and Culture'. *Journal of Organizational Change Management*, 5/1: 58–68.

—— (1993). 'Breaking the Paradigm Mentality'. *Organization Studies*, 14/5: 681–720.

—— (1997). 'Management and Organization Studies as Science? Methodologies of OR in Critical Perspective', *Organization*, 4/3: 309–44.

WOOD, S., and KELLY, J. (1978). 'Towards a Critical Management Science', *Journal of Management Studies*, February: 1–24.

CHAPTER 4

ORGANIZATION THEORY AS A POSTMODERN SCIENCE

ROBERT CHIA

In each period there is a general form of the forms of thought; and, like the air we breath, such a form is so translucent, and so pervading, and so seemingly necessary, that only by extreme effort can we become aware of it.

(Alfred North Whitehead 1933: 21)

I must start by underlining just how much I admire the work of M. Einstein....I believe that we are being presented here not only with a new realm of physics, but also, in a certain respect, a new way of thinking.

(H. Bergson 1922: 102)

Whereas the mechanistic picture regarded discrete objects as the primary reality...I suggest that the unbroken movements of enfolding and unfolding...is primary while the apparently discrete objects are secondary phenomena....Whereas modern physics has tried to understand the whole reductively by beginning with the most elementary parts, I am proposing a postmodern physics which begins with the whole.

(D. Bohm 1988: 66)

THIS chapter seeks to offer a comprehensive and critical exposition of the post-modern imperative and its implications both for our understanding of organization as a theoretical object and its consequences for Organization Theory (OT) as an academic discipline. The central argument made here is that postmodernism must not be understood as a cynical or nihilistic tendency in contemporary thought but as a subtle and complex attempt at reworking the metaphysical bases of modern knowledge. We begin by examining the roots of Western metaphysics and the manner in which it has shaped modern scientific thought especially in relation to our contemporary privileging of form, being, order, stability, identity, and presence over becoming, formlessness, flux, difference, deferral, and change. We then identify the key axioms and imperatives associated with the modernist impulse especially the ideas of differentiation, simple-location, classification, and representation. Against this modernist tendency we counterpose a postmodern metaphysics in which the Heraclitean primacy accorded to process, movement, interpenetration, and incessant change are emphasized. From this process ontology, order, form, and identity are viewed as humanly imposed patterns of comprehension and not immutable structures existing independently in an external world. Organization is fundamentally an ongoing aggregative world-making activity not a solid and static thing. Such a view of organization leads us to reconceptualize OT, not as a study of organizational forms, identities, and attributes, but as a sustained analysis of the inextricable relationship between broader civilizational trends and forms of social order, and between metaphysical orientations and managerial imperatives. Thus, the study of dominant modes of thought, processes of individuation and identity creation, strategies of objectification and institutionalization, the development of codes of behaviour, social mannerisms, rules of law, and disciplines of knowledge all form a part of this extended field of inquiry. It is this radical reworking of the function and contribution of OT that is implied by the advent of a postmodern science.

4.1 THE METAPHYSICAL ROOTS OF MODERN WESTERN THOUGHT

Contemporary modes of thought are circumscribed by two opposing and enduring metaphysical presuppositions. Heraclitus, a native of Ephesus in ancient Greece emphasized the primacy of a fluxing, changeable, and emergent world whilst Parmenides his successor insisted upon the permanent and unchangeable nature of reality. One emphasized reality as inclusively processual the other privileged a homeostatic and entitative conception of reality. This seemingly intractable opposition between a Heraclitean ontology of *becoming* and a Parmenidean ontology of *being* provides us with the key for understanding contemporary debates between modernism and postmodernism and their consequences for OT. Although there is clear evidence of a resurgence in Heraclitean-type thinking in recent years, it is the Parmenidean-inspired mindset that has decisively prevailed in the West over the past five hundred years or so. According to this neo-Parmenidean modernist world view, ultimate reality is atomistic, stable, and relatively unchanging. Atomism presupposes that reality is made up of individual discrete particles with identifiable properties and characteristics that combine together to produce the multifarious life-sized phenomena of our experiences. Wholes are in principle reducible to 'parts' and are, in practice, aggregate outcomes of individual elements.

Furthermore, the belief that individual atoms are stable and thing-like leads to the assumption that each aspect of reality that presents itself to us can be observed, differentiated, recorded, identified, and classified in a comprehensive system of representation. Experienced phenomena are deemed to be reducible to aggregate elements possessing distinct boundaries, definable shapes, and clear spatial integrity that endure through time. From this metaphysical mindset, it then becomes possible to postulate the existence of a universal pattern of ordering through which the multitude of phenomena can be predictably related to each other in a hierarchical system of causal relations. Thus, it is believed that through this systematic process of observation, recording, classification, analysis, and causal attribution, the goal of ultimate predictability and absolute control is attainable. Moreover, the contemporary neo-Parmenidean world view does accept the reality of change. However, such changes are importantly assumed to be epi-phenomena of primary stable entities. When changing objects are analysed, it is their attributes that are deemed to have changed, but 'that which underlies the attributes, what the attributes are attributes *of*' (Cobb 1993: 170) is assumed to remain strictly the same. Thus, any change observed is explained in terms of the *locomotion* of entities; i.e. 'things' moving through space from one location to another. There is no acknowledgement of an internal *becoming* and transformation in these atomistic individuals.

Such a privileging of an entitative conception of reality was much inspired by the introduction of the Phoenician-invented alphabetic system into Grecian thought some three thousand years ago. This is because the phonetic alphabet, as a system of communication, works by breaking up the seamless flow of speech into arbitrary consonants and individual sound syllables. The sound heard and the word seen are distinctly different experiences. In the former, like listening to a continuous melody, the individual sounds melt into one another and there are no clear distinctions separating each note of the music. On the other hand, the phonetically-based alphabet clearly delineates one syllable from another, one word from another, and one sentence from another, and each are treated as distinct entities to be manipulated and dealt with in isolation (McLuhan and McLuhan 1988). Car-others (1959: 31) maintains that Western thought, because of its overwhelming influence by the alphabet, has developed a dominant mode of perception which is 'overwhelmingly visual and which elevated the universal, the abstract and the static over the fluxing and concrete particular'.

In sum, the alphabet precipitated the analytical breaking-up and objectification of phenomena for the purpose of analysis, and by reducing all our senses into visual and pictorial or enclosed space, inspired the rise of the Euclidean sensibility that has dominated our thought processes for over two thousand years. This privileging of a static and atomistic world view has paved the way for the emergence of a mechanistic, clock-work view of the universe and the elevation of mathematics as the quintessential tool for investigating and explicating the properties of the physical world (Shapin 1994). As Shapin writes, the link between a mechanistic world view and the use of mathematical technique was taken 'as a matter "of course"' (p. 318) during the period of the Enlightenment. For instance Robert Boyle, like many of his contemporaries 'propagated a mechanical conception of nature' and 'elaborated a matter-theory couched in mathematical concepts' (p. 333). This is especially evident in an essay he wrote on the *Usefulness of Mathematics for Natural Philosophy*, where he urged the application of mathematics in the analysis of nature. It is this clock-work mechanistic view of the universe that has led to the modernist obsession with *representing* reality, since the latter is now believed to be made up of precise, stable, and discrete component parts that have been assembled together by universal forces.

4.2 REPRESENTATIONALISM: THE BASIC EPISTEMOLOGICAL STRATEGY OF MODERNISM

Although the alphabetic system is clearly responsible for the development of an abstractive and visually-based form of knowledge, it took the invention of the printing press over two and a half thousand years later for the modernist mindset to finally emerge (McLuhan 1967; Eisenstein 1980). The invention of the printing press promoted a widespread typesetting mentality through its emphasis on combining and recombining the otherwise discrete and individual characters of the alphabet. Because of the astonishing capacity of this new technology coupled with the flexibility of the alphabetic system we are able to produce impressive combinations of syllables, words, sentences, and paragraphs to create the seemingly inexhaustible libraries of books and genres we find all around us. The idea that all phenomena can be similarly dealt with by breaking them up into component parts and then reassembling them as needs be, rapidly became the overpowering metaphor for modern analysis (Fisher 1991; McArthur 1986). As Fisher shows, mining was one of the first systematic attempt to de-constitute and reconstitute the natural world into a series of resources for our use: 'It is in mining that the world first appears as broken lumps of pure matter' (Fisher 1991: 223). It is this typographic 'assemblage' metaphor that serves as the organizing template for modern thought. It led Descartes in his *Discourse on Method* to insist upon dividing each of the difficulties that he encountered 'into as many parts as might be possible and necessary in order best to solve it' (Descartes 1628/1968: 41).

One major consequence of this analytical and typographic mindset was the development of an obsession with the creation of taxonomies, tables, hierarchies, and classificatory schemas for representing both nature and the social world. Linnaeus's *Systema Naturae*, written in the early eighteenth century provides one of the clearest examples of this taxonomic obsession. In the broader social realm, this same preoccupation was to be found in the work of John Wilkins and Thomas Sprat, both founding members of the Royal Society. For both Sprat and Wilkins, modern knowledge is to be based upon pre-established symbols, taxonomies, and hierarchies. Thus, in this scheme of things, 'you do not *call* a thing by its name, which would be arbitrary. No, you *use* the name to designate the thing's location in a taxonomic chart' (Kenner 1987: 87, emphasis original). Through this system of differentiation, classification, and representational ordering, Wilkins and Sprat sought to create an exaggeratedly formal and ordered social world that could thereby be more precisely described, analysed, and controlled. It is this taxonomic strategy of representation that provides the leitmotif for the modernist mindset.

This taxonomic impulse, first initiated by Aristotle and rediscovered by the invention of the printing press, precipitated the modern emphasis on what we now call a 'representationalist epistemology': the idea that reality can be adequately captured and symbolically represented through the use of established terms, categories, concepts, and explanatory schemas. Such a predisposition, however, is predicated upon an unexamined belief in the stability and fixity of phenomena under investigation. For it is only when portions of reality are assumed to be discrete, identifiable, and fixable in space-time, and that they remain relatively unchanging, that words, symbols, and concepts can be deemed to adequately represent the world of phenomena including the underlying forces and generative mechanisms associated with them. Such an epistemological strategy entails the *breaking down*, *fixing*, *locating*, and *naming* of all phenomena. Knowing, thus, entails the ability to say what a thing 'is' or what it 'is not'. Knowledge is therefore predicational judgement in that by identifying what a thing 'is' or what it 'is not', we fix the focus of our attention and attribute a general property or condition with the object of study. This is deemed to be possible precisely because it is believed that the world has a logical structure and hence lends itself to the grasp of language. All proper knowledge is, therefore, generalizable knowledge and not knowledge of the particular since the particular is always subsumed by the wider predicate term. Thus, ' "red" and "wine" are not individual "thises", but universal classifications pointing to the original intuition of the individually observed thing' (Carter 1990: 26). They refer to common properties rather than specific experiences.

All this implies that modernist thought places more importance on generalized concepts and categories than on the actual particulars of experience. The latter is inevitably subsumed under the former. As a consequence, visible *end-states* and *outcomes* are elevated over processes of change. Only the *fixed* within the *flow* of lived experience and the *universal* in the *particular* are accorded legitimate knowledge status. It is this basic epistemological assumption that provides the inspiration for the scientific obsession with precision, accuracy, and parsimony in representing and explaining social phenomena such as organization (Sandelands and Drazin 1989; Pfeffer 1993). Such an approach to theory-building inevitably privileges *being* over *becoming*; the *already formed* over the *unformed*; the *visible* over the *invisible*; *presence* over *absence*; *consciousness* over the *unconscious*; *identity* over *relational clusters*; *literal meanings* over *metaphorical allusions*; the *analytical breaking-up* and *decontextualizing* of experience over its *wholesome, deeply contextual* encounter; the use of *rational causal explanation* as the *sine que non* of intellectual analysis over a reliance on the immediate and dynamic *intuition of things*. It is these interlocking sets of philosophical assumptions that continue to shape the modernist approach to organizational analysis.

4.3 KEY ASSUMPTIONS OF MODERN ORGANIZATION THEORY

Six key meta-theoretical assumptions, with varying accentuation, underpin the epistemological project of modern OT. These are *objectivity, self-identity, individual intentionality, local causality, homeostatic change*, and *linguistic adequacy*. Each of these reflect enduring value strands woven into the epistemological fabric of modernity.

Objectivity: First, organizations whether socially constructed or otherwise are viewed as concrete social entities with fixed locations, clear identities, and describable attributes (Hannan and Freeman 1977; Pfeffer and Salancik 1978; Scott 1992;

Aldrich 1992; Donaldson 1996). Even though it may be readily acknowledged that organizations are 'human products' resulting from 'processes of habitualization', they are nevertheless 'experienced as an objective reality' (Berger and Luckmann 1966: 77) by the individual. They 'resist his attempts to change or evade them. They have coercive power over him . . . by the sheer force of their facticity' (ibid.). Thus, even from a first-order social constructionist view (Steier 1991), an organization is deemed to exist relatively independently of the individual actors associated with it and therefore forms an appropriate theoretical object of analysis. Solidity, thing-likeness, and identity are attributed to the phenomenon of organization. It has relatively distinct boundaries that can be temporarily and geographically located in space and time. Moreover, organizations are given a certain degree of causal power. They can 'act' and create effects that would not be otherwise possible if they were merely the disaggregate actions of uncoordinated individuals. Alternatively, they may produce 'unintended' effects and consequences that can nevertheless still be attributable to their presence. Whichever the case, both views regard it as axiomatic to attribute causal power to organizations in the way we commonly attribute 'gravity' as the reason for falling objects and 'the weather' as a reason for our choice of clothing.

Self-Identity: Secondly, for many organization theorists, organizations possess identifiable characteristics including especially purposefulness and direction (Donaldson 1987; Robbins 1989), stability and configuration (Mintzberg 1979; Scott 1992), culture and values (Deal and Kennedy 1982; Frost *et al.* 1985; Schein 1992; Martin 1992), goals and functions (Perrow 1967; Blau 1970; Child 1984) that are often believed to be visible, comparable, and/or measurable in the research process. Moreover, the identity and distinctiveness of an organization is not believed to be relationally derived. Instead, it is its own unique configuration that gives it its organizational character. Thus it is possible to talk about an organization's structure, strategy, culture, values, and goals and to relate these attributes to perceived organizational actions. Such a macro-orientation is also favoured by those forms of institutionally-based analyses that take economic rationality as the driving force behind organizational configuration and action (Powell and DiMaggio 1991). Here the organization is thought of as interacting relatively freely with its 'environment' much in the same way we think commonsensically of biological species adapting and interacting with their surroundings in an effort to survive. Each has the capacity to influence and be influenced by the external world. Organizations are widely conceived as open but bounded *systems* (Scott 1992) interacting with their environments. Systems, whether open or closed, have clearly defined forms and boundaries. They are relatively stable and endure through time so that their identity and attributes can be clearly established. Their 'survival' and 'growth' are linked to internal adaptability, the efficacy of sense-making processes, their capacity for learning, the extent of structural realignments achieved, and their capacity for innovation and renewal. In all these instances, the organization is treated as a concrete and relatively autonomous social entity with humanized capacities.

Individual Intentionality: Thirdly, for an increasingly influential number of organizational theorists who eschew the tendency to reify organizations, the primacy and autonomy of individual actors are taken as a given starting point (Weick 1969; Silverman 1970; Sandelands and Drazin 1989). Atomicity and the aggregation of individual actions into a collective effort are emphasized. Individual actors are believed to make meaningful and conscious choices so much so that purposefulness, control, and causal attribution can be duly assigned even if the eventual outcomes are not always what were intended. Such outcomes are either loosely or 'tightly-coupled' to intended actions on the part of individual actors so much so that the organization as a whole is assigned a secondary 'reified' status. Organizational realities are very much a product of the subjective *enactments* or social constructions of individual actors. They do not exist independently of our perceptions.

In an important discussion of the way language affects our ways of thinking and theorizing about organization, Sandelands and Drazin rightly criticize the widespread use of *achievement* verbs such as 'shape', 'determine', 'select', and so on, to loosely refer to concrete organizational processes. When this happens organizational theorists tend to mystify organizational processes 'in a welter of misbegotten abstractions' (Sandelands and Drazin 1989: 458). For Sandelands and Drazin, words that refer to objects or processes that cannot be observed or verified should be questioned. Organizations on this view are reified abstractions: an emergent property of 'phenomenally given actions of individuals' (ibid.). They develop from the interactions of concrete individuals much in the same way as 'snowflakes or ice-crystals develop from interactions of water molecules, or melodies develop from the interplay of notes' (Sandelands and Drazin 1989: 473). On this atomistic view the status and identity of individuals as autonomous actors remains unquestioned. Thus deliberate, conscious, and purposeful action on the part of individual actors is emphasized. This means that organizational studies, instead of focusing on the larger organizational unit should instead concentrate on individual meanings and intentions, interpretations, and sensemaking, to throw fresh light onto the reality of organizational life. Ethnographies, narratives, discourse analysis, and storytelling (Van Maanen 1988; Deetz and Mumby 1990; Czarniawska-Joerges 1994) therefore provide the rich tapestry of inputs for this type of organizational theorizing. However, contrary to popular perceptions of postmodernism and OT, these interpretive emphases DO NOT reach at the heart of the postmodern agenda. In so far as these accounts focus on and hence privilege the consciousness, intentionality, and collective meaning of actors within circumscribed units called 'organizations', they do not, in principle, depart from the modernist mindset.

Local Causality: Fourthly, organizations are deemed to change primarily through active intervention: either internally by wilful actors or externally through agents of change (Miller and Friessen 1980; Van de Ven 1987; Tichy 1983; Kanter, Stein, and Jick 1992). Local, tightly coupled causality is presupposed. Causality as an explanatory tool for linking otherwise disparate objects and events in space-time is an archetypal modernist concept. What is crucial in the typical use of causal explanation is the need for the observable conjunction of two otherwise separate events. In its minimalist Humean sense, to say that event 'A' is the cause of event 'B' is really to maintain that an event precedent and contiguous to another is 'so united with it in the imagination, that the idea of one determines the mind to form the idea of the other, and the impression of one to form a more lively idea of the other' (Hume 1740/1992: 172). Thus, observed 'contiguity', 'priority', and 'constancy of relations' constitute the founding basis for the attribution of causality in the classic positivistic sense. Whenever two otherwise unrelated events follow each other in a way such that a consistent pattern of relationship appears to exist, then the antecedent event is deemed to be the efficient cause of the succeeding event.

Aristotle also had much to say about the notion of causality and his ideas remain influential in modern science. His understanding of the causes of change is somewhat more elaborate and qualitatively different from Hume's idea of constant conjunction. For Aristotle, there are four types of causes: the formal, the material, the efficient, and the final cause. To take an extremely simple example—the production of a statue from a piece of marble—the *formal cause* is the initial shape given the marble, the *material cause* is the marble itself, the *efficient cause* is the sculptor, and the *final cause* is the purpose for which the statue is produced (Lindberg 1992: 53). Modern OT, however, following the classical sciences and the positivistic tradition, have tended to emphasize only the efficient cause and either ignored or downplayed the other three Aristotelian causes. This is because the idea of efficient cause accentuates the active interventional role of the agent of change and gives it a more tightly coupled relationship with its effect. By overemphasizing agency and choice, it exaggerates the sense of mastery and control in our world of affairs.

It is this model of 'tightly-coupled' causality that is assumed in the modernist explanatory schema. This model is widely deployed in the analysis of organizational change and in the prescriptive literature that abounds in OT (Tushman and Romanelli 1985; Kanter, Stein, and Jick 1992; Van de Ven and Poole 1995).

Homeostatic Change: Moreover, change, according to the modernist schema, is something exceptional because equilibrium is presumed to be the natural state. It is that which momentarily upsets the balance of an otherwise stable and organized state. Because systems are inherently stable, what is required for change to occur is some kind of intervening force, whether internally applied or externally enforced. Thus environmental pressures or internal agency by way of choices and decisions taken provide the impetus for changes to take place. From this perspective of change, undermining stasis, overcoming inertia, and unsettling equilibrium provide the *modus operandi* for successful organizational change and transformation initiatives (Lewin 1951; Miller and Friessen 1980; Tushman and Romanelli 1985; Pettigrew 1987; Van de Ven and Poole 1995). The need for active, visible, and very often external intervention is presumed. Repositioning, diversification, re-engineering, culture change, mergers, takeovers, acquisitions, strategic alliances, etc., form a part of the dominant vocabulary that presupposes the need for such overt and purposive intervention. Organizations are deemed to operate within a socio-economic context which includes markets, an immediate external environment, local national laws and regulations, and international practices and agreements all of which impact upon the survival of the organization itself. Market pressures, mission statements, culture change imperatives, and technological imperatives therefore provide the necessary justificatory bases for initiating change efforts. Change is not regarded as immanent in organizational processes. Rather change must be *initiated* and very often externally enforced.

Linguistic Adequacy: The idea that words are adequate for expressing thought and more importantly that all proper knowing entails conscious thought that can be suitably expressed through language provides the epistemological platform for the legitimization of modern knowledge. For the modern mind, 'to know a thing is to name it, and to name it is to attach one or usually more universal predicates to it' (Carter 1990: 26). Knowledge itself, thus, becomes very much like a product or commodity that can be 'accumulated', 'stored', and 'transferred' in the form of unique word configurations that we call a theory. The current popular notion of 'knowledge management' (Drucker 1993; Nonaka 1994) is very much tied to this modernist view of knowledge. A theory is, thus, a coherent system of explicit linguistic expressions woven together in an identifiable pattern that purportedly mirrors the going-ons in the real world. If, according to the modernist view, knowledge is predicational judgement precisely because the world is assumed to be logical and lends itself to the grasp of language, then proper knowing becomes a linguistic matter and not a matter of sensation or experience. For modern OT, therefore, symbols, names, concepts, categories, linguistic expressions, and theories are the basic raw material needed for theory-building. Accordingly, we need to be especially vigilant about issues of meaning, precision, and parsimony in organizational knowledge creation. It is this emphasis on the adequacy of language in expressing our innermost thoughts and understandings which fuels the project of 'theory-building' and the even-more obsessive practices of data collection and computerized storage of information. The most controversial of these in modern science is perhaps the current human genome project.

These six metaphysical assumptions shape much of the research agenda of organizational theorists. What remains unchallenged and unquestioned are:

(a) the notion of 'organizations' as solid entities with clear identities and attributes that provide the legitimate focus for OT; (b) the idea of 'individuals' and their conscious meanings and 'intentions' as the basis for understanding the subjective aspects of organizational life; (c) the view of change as an epi-phenomena of basically fixed entities; (d) the tightly coupled and/or localized notion of causality; and (e) the unquestioned belief in the adequacy of language, and particularly the written word, in expressing our knowledge of the world and ourselves. These form an interlocking web of values and beliefs that support and justify the project of modern OT.

The idea that organizing could be more productively thought of as a generic existential strategy for subjugating the immanent forces of change: that organization is really a loosely coordinated but precarious 'world-making' attempt to regularize human exchanges and to develop a predictable pattern of interactions for the purposes of minimizing effort; that language is the quintessential organizing technology that enables us to selectively abstract from the otherwise intractable flux of raw experiences; that management is more about the taming of chance, uncertainty, and ambiguity than about choice; and that individuals themselves are always already effects of organizational forces: all these escape the traditional organization theorist. Thus, the broader organizational questions of how social order is achieved; how the flux and flow of our lifeworlds are rendered coherent and plausible; how individual identities are established and social entities created; how taxonomies and systems of classification are produced and with what effects; how causal relations are imputed and with what consequences; how systems of signification are used to arbitrarily carve up reality and with what outcomes; these are left unanswered by traditional OT.

Yet it is increasingly clear that such a broader form of societal understanding is unquestionably necessary for today's reflective management practitioners and policy-makers to act effectively and sensitively within the context of a global economy. More and more the world of practical affairs is being rendered inordinately complex and changeable by a panoply of competing ideologies, shifting societal trends, emerging social movements, clashes of global/local cultures, and the advances of telecommunication and the internet that promises to revolutionize our social lives on a scale parallel if not exceeding that of the invention of the alphabetic system and the advent of the printing press. Within such a postmodern context, a deep and abiding philosophic appreciation of the complex flux of the variety and diversity of human societies and an 'unspecialised aptitude for eliciting generalizations from particulars and for seeing the divergent illustration of generalities in diverse circumstances' (Whitehead 1933: 120) is what is urgently needed both in the practitioner world of business and in the realm of state governance. The ability to understand the origins and limitations of our own habits of thought; to remain concretely sensitive to local societal attitudes and aspirations; to detect deeply unconscious cultural idiosyncrasies; to be able to track emergent technological trends and their consequences; to understand shifting political affiliations and public perceptions; to grasp the prevalent social moods, inclinations, and capacities: these are all highly prized facets of the effective postmodern business manager and policy-maker. In a reference to this need for a postmodern prescience in successfully negotiating the world of affairs, Alfred North Whitehead, in a lecture given at Harvard Business School during the depths of the Great Depression, maintained that a society can only prosper and retain its greatness if 'its men of business think greatly of their function. Low thoughts mean low behaviour, and after a brief orgy of exploitation, low behaviour means a descending standard of life' (Whitehead 1933: 120). Space does not permit a more extensive treatment of how exactly a postmodern attitude can directly lead to effective managerial action. Suffice to say that the postmodern as articulated in these pages is not so much a call for the celebration of diversity and plurality, but a call for the return to a re-grounding of theory on the primacy of lived experience. The cultivation of this wider societal vision and understanding of management is what a truly postmodern theory of organization engenders.

4.4 POSTMODERN PHILOSOPHY AND SCIENCE

The term 'postmodern' made its first appearance in the title of a book, *Postmodernism and Other Essays* written by Bernard Iddings Bell as early as 1926. It was subsequently picked up and used by Arnold Toynbee in 1939 in volume v of his massive tome *A Study of History* where he used the term 'post-modern' to describe the end of the modern era beginning from about the third quarter of the nineteenth century. In the 1950s the poet Charles Olson began using the term to describe an anti-modernist strain in the then contemporary poetry, including especially his own work and that of other so-called Black Mountain poets. From then on the use of the term began to proliferate and multiply although there is little continuity between these early uses and the more recent debates on postmodernism beginning from the early 1960s. Thus, it was not until Lyotard's (1984, but originally published in 1979) publication of a report entitled *The Postmodern Condition* that wider public attention was drawn into the debate between modernism and postmodernism and their implications for the status of knowledge.

One consequence of the rapid eruption in its usage over the last two decades, is that the term 'postmodern', has been increasingly loosely employed in much of the academic literature in art, science, literary criticism, philosophy, sociology, politics, and even in management and organization studies. Its use has tended to evoke vastly contrasting reactions. On the one hand, postmodernism is frequently dismissed as an extremely simplistic and cynical tendency towards nihilism within contemporary culture and, on the other, it is regarded as an extremely subtle and complex philosophical attempt at reworking the metaphysical bases of modern knowledge. The word 'postmodern' is therefore, characterized, from its very inception, by an essential ambiguity; a certain '*semantic* instability' (Hassan 1985: 121) that prevents clear consensus about its meaning and effects.

The postmodern, however, may be most productively invoked as an alternative *style of thought*—a new way of thinking—which attempts to more adequately comprehend *and* deconstruct the almost-inexorable complexification of science and modern society with all its attendant social and societal ramifications. The possibility of such a new way of thinking was arguably inaugurated during a seminal meeting between Albert Einstein and Henri Bergson hosted by the *Société de Philosophie* of Paris on 6 April 1922. It is not my purpose here to delve into the details of the exchange that ensued.[1] However, it is important to note that, in this intellectual encounter, which revolved around Einstein's special theory of relativity, Bergson proceeded to examine its wider philosophical implications in terms of the distinction between lived time and clock time and their consequences for our modes of theorizing.

In his special theory of relativity, Einstein had calculated how time, in a particular reference system that is moving away from the observer at a constant velocity, appears to slow down when viewed from another system at rest relative to it. Subsequently, in his general theory of relativity proposed in 1916, he extended the theory and came to the conclusion that 'every reference body has its own particular time' (Einstein 1916/1952: 26) thereby relativizing the idea of a universal clock time. The theory of relativity had the effect of 'figuratively...placing a clock in every gravitational field in the universe' (Kern 1983: 19). This whole argument ran counter to the then prevailing belief that clock time was a universal phenomenon.

Bergson was clearly not attempting to refute or downplay Einstein's findings in the realm of theoretical physics. Rather his intention was to critically reflect on the wider philosophical implications of the theory and to point to the need for radically revamping our dominant habits of thought. As Robin Durie (1999) very persuasively argues, this was something that even Einstein failed to fully appreciate in his momentus discussion with Bergson. The result was Einstein's hasty dismissal of Bergson's argument that the special theory of relativity, contrary to Einstein's conclusion, in fact confirmed our deeply held intuition of a universal and irreversible *lived* time, a *durée*, that cannot be fixed and/or reduced to the supposed

[1] For a comprehensive analysis of the debate which ensued between Einstein and Bergson, the reader is encouraged to refer to Robin Durie's (1999) *Duration and Simultaneity: Bergson and the Einsteinian Universe.* This is an excellent teasing out of the key differences and the subsequent misunderstandings that occurred both on the parts of Einstein and Bergson.

plurality of clock times implied by the special theory of relativity. Bergson states his position clearly in his introduction to *Duration and Simultaneity*:

Our admiration for this physicist (Einstein), our conviction that he was giving us not only a new physics but also certain news way of thinking, our belief that science and philosophy are unlike disciplines but are meant to implement each other, all this imbued us with the desire and even impressed us with the duty of proceeding to a confrontation (with the wider implications of Einsteins' theory of relativity). (Bergson, in Durie (trans.), 1999: xxvii)

As Murphy (1999: 70) points out, Bergson's philosophical critique of Einstein anticipated Bohm and Hiley's (1993) 'ontological' interpretation of quantum mechanics which, following Bohr's 'Copenhagen Interpretation' of quantum theory and Heisenberg's principle of 'complementary indeterminacy' with regards to position and velocity, gave rise to the central notion of *non-locality* in theoretical physics.[2] Non-locality posits apparently instantaneous communication and real simultaneous determination between objects widely separate in space-time. It confuses location, presence, and hence representation by making the absent present and the present absent. In Derridean (Derrida 1981) terms, it is the *différance* that 'consists in deferring by means of delay, delegation, reprieve, referral, detour, postponement, reserving' (Derrida 1981: 8). *Différance* instantiates a perpetual 'de-centering' (i.e. non-locatable) movement that resists attempts to fix and represent objects in space-time. Like Whitehead's (1926/1985: 61–3) critique of 'simple location' and Bohm and Hiley's ontological interpretation of quantum theory, Derrida's *différance* can be seen as a parallel attempt to deconstruct the 'metaphysics of presence', or logocentrism which underpins much of Western scientific thought. According to this metaphysics of presence, reality is readily amenable to symbolic representation and can be made to *present* itself to us in all its immediacy through linguistic representations. Clearly, the notions of non-locatability, *différance*, and Whitehead's critique of 'simple-location' resist this simplifying tendency in modernist thought.

It is this belief that the theory of relativity and subsequently that of quantum theory offers not just a new physics but a whole new way of thinking that underpins the more contemporary effort to formulate a postmodern science. One that is more in keeping with the leading-edge advances of theoretical physics (see, for instance, David Bohm's (1980) *Wholeness and the Implicate Order* and Ilya Prigogine's (1996) *The End of Certainty*) and a postmodern philosophy (Serres 1981; Deleuze and Guattari 1988; Rorty 1991).

The postmodern critique of modernist theories therefore arises from a complex combination of the growing disaffection with the adverse consequences of modernity and the subsequent realization of the limitations of classical science even

---

[2] For a more detailed argument of this ontological critique of quantum theory, see Murphy (1999) in J. Mullarkey (ed.), *The New Bergson*, 66–81.

within the most hallowed domain of theoretical physics. It inspired a relentless search for a more adequate and scientifically-based comprehension of the inherent complexities of both the natural and social worlds we currently inhabit. According to this postmodern view, therefore, modern societal evolution and progress seems to have proceeded 'of its own accord' with an 'autonomous motoricity that is independent of us' (Lyotard 1992: 66). It is the nature and character of this strange 'autonomous motoricity' that postmodern analysis sought to render more transparent and comprehensible.

Understood thus, the postmodern critique attempts to reveal modern rationality as the consequent effect of a reductionistic operation whereby the phenomenal flux of lived experience are forcibly carved up, conceptually fixed, and systematically subjugated by the widely practised organizing impulses of division, naming, classification, and representation. Through this method of reduction and representation our otherwise intractable and amorphous life experiences are then made more amenable to instrumental manipulation and control. Modern rationality, and hence representation, is thus a method of thinking, ordering, and social construction that creates distinct and legitimate objects of knowledge for a knowing subject. The perceived objectivity, solidity, and regularity of our all-too-familiar social world are, therefore, arbitrarily socially constructed rather than the result of inexorable progress, immutable laws, and universal principles. Postmodernists argue that it is the structured nature of language that creates the impression that reality itself is stable, pre-organized, and law-like in character. It insists that without the social acts of differentiating, identifying, naming, classifying, and the creation of a subject-predicate structure through language, lived reality is but a 'shapeless and indistinct mass' (Saussure 1966: 111). Language, thus, provides one of the first systematic ordering impulses and is intimately linked to the rise of human civilizations throughout the world.

In the process of conventional languaging, however, significant portions of our tacit and embodied forms of knowing are suppressed, marginalized, or denied legitimacy in the modernist scheme of things. This is a loss that must not be underestimated. For, we know far more than we can tell (Polanyi 1966). There is an extensive realm of subliminal comprehension that resists and defies linguistic translation. Such subliminal and oftentimes subconscious forms of knowing can only be accessed indirectly and alluded to elliptically. For this reason, much of what is written within this postmodern awareness oftentimes seem unnecessarily obscure to the uninitiated. However, it is this refusal to capitulate to the reductionistic instincts of modernism that defines the postmodern project. *The postmodern, then, is centrally concerned with giving voice and legitimacy to those tacit and oftentimes unpresentable forms of knowledge that modern epistemologies inevitably depend upon yet conveniently overlook or gloss over in the process of knowledge creation.* This is the real purpose and value of the postmodern critique.

4.5 POSTMODERN AXIOMS AND IMPERATIVES

Four intellectual axioms and imperatives are detectable in the postmodern approach to research and analysis. First, in place of the modernist emphasis on the ontological primacy of substance, stability, identity, order, regularity, and form, postmodern analyses seek to emphasize the Heraclitean primacy accorded to process, indeterminacy, flux, interpenetration, formlessness, and incessant change. This Heraclitean emphasis is evident in Jacques Derrida's (1981) *différance*, in Michel Serres's (1981) notion of *homeorrhesis*, in Deleuze's (1993; Deleuze and Guattari 1988) notions of the *nomadic*, the *labryinth*, the *fold*, and the *rhizome*. Notwithstanding their vastly different styles and approaches, these writers return again and again to the problem of trying to convey the sense of fluidity, movement, flux, and change immanent in reality. Such a processual orientation must not be equated with the commonsensical idea of the process that a system is deemed to undergo in transition. Rather it is a metaphysical orientation that emphasizes an ontological primacy in the *becoming* of things; that sees things as always already momentary outcomes or effects of historical processes. As Tim Ingold, paraphrasing Ortega y Gasset, puts it well: 'We are not things but dramas; we have no nature, only history; we *are* not, though we *live*' (Ingold 1986: 117, emphasis original). Such a *becoming* orientation rejects what Rescher (1996) calls the *process reducibility thesis* whereby processes are often assumed to be processes *of* primary 'things'. Instead, it insists that 'things', social entities, generative mechanisms etc., are no more than 'stability waves in a sea of process' (Rescher 1996: 53). This process ontology promotes a decentred and dispersive view of reality as a heterogeneous concatenation of atomic event-occurrences that cannot be adequately captured by static symbols and representations. For process ontology the basic unit of reality is not an atom or thing but an 'event-cluster' forming a relatively stable pattern of relations. Correspondingly, postmodern science, which is based upon this processual mode of thought, eschews atomistic thinking in favour of a flowing undifferentiated wholeness in which the ultimate unit of reality is not an atom but 'pulses of energy bound together by a thread of "memory"' (Gunter 1993: 137). What we call an 'atom' is nothing more than a 'certain form in the field of movement' (Bohm 1988: 62).

Second, from this commitment to a *becoming* ontology, it follows that language, and in particular the activities of *naming* and *symbolic representation*, provide the first ordering impulse for the systematic fixing and structuring of our human lifeworlds. Language, and in particular the alphabetic system, are technologies of organization that help us portion off, fix, locate, and represent different aspects of our phenomenal experiences to ourselves. They do not, in any way mirror the going-ons in the world. Postmodernists therefore reject the kind of representationalist epistemology championed by modern science. For postmodernists, theories are viewed more pragmatically as selective and useful instruments or devices that help us to negotiate our way through the world (Rorty 1991). They are eminently useful even if they do not necessarily tell us how that world really is. In other words, theories may be *workable*, but may not be timelessly *true*. Moreover, because all theories are manifestly selective and hence incomplete, there will always be parts of reality that are ignored or not accounted for in our dominant scheme of interpretation.

This realization of the intrinsic inadequacy of language leads postmodernists to a third preoccupation: the attempt to explore and sensitively articulate tacit and oftentimes unconscious forms of knowing in a manner that remains faithful to the subtle nuances of the gestalt processes of comprehension. Ordinarily, the emphasis in gestalt psychology, for instance, is on bisecting the visual field into significant 'figure' and insignificant 'ground'. Analysing this overwhelming tendency in *The Hidden Order of Art*, Ehrenzweig (1967) shows that the really accomplished modern artist cannot afford to attend only to the gestalt figure and ignore the ground. Instead, for the artist, what is needed is a kind of 'undifferentiated attention akin to syncretistic vision which . . . holds the total structure of the work of art in a single undifferentiated view' (Ehrenzweig 1967: 23). Modern artistic vision entails the cultivation of a certain quality of 'eye-wandering' (Ehrenzweig 1965: 22–3) that runs counter to traditional painting. Traditional painting excludes this eye-wandering effect by the good gestalt it presents. What the modern artist is taught, however, 'amounts to a technique of perception *against* the gestalt principle' (Ehrenzweig 1965: 28). He/she is advised to watch not only the outline of the object being drawn, but also the *negative form* that the figure cuts out from the background. This attention to the 'invisible' negative form sensitizes the artist to the unconsciously perceived process of gestalt formation. It is a kind of *unconscious scanning* that produces knowing that is inherently unreachable through the modern scientific approach with its emphasis on visibility and presence and its overwhelming reliance on precise and rigid terms, concepts, and categories. This 'full' emptiness of the unconsciousness scanning process occurs in nearly all forms of creative works. Thus: 'the artist's vacant unfocused stare pays attention to the smallest detail however far removed from the consciously perceived figure. The uncompromising democracy which refuses to make any distinction between the significance of the elements building the work of art, belongs to the essence of artistic rigor' (Ehrenzweig 1967: 29). It is this insistence on holding judgement in abeyance and the resistance to prematurely making straightforward distinctions between figure and ground that characterizes this form of unconscious scanning. This is the kind of subliminal awareness that postmodernists draw our attention to.

Realizing the need for extending our powers of comprehension beyond the level of conscious perception, postmodernism attempts to modify the conceptual asymmetry that surreptitiously privileges consciousness and intentionality over the unconscious scanning process. The elevation of rationality, intentionality, and choice in the modernist explanatory schema conspire to underplay the role of such unconscious nomadic forces in shaping planned action and outcomes. Postmodern analyses, on the other hand, emphasize the vaguely intuited, heterogeneous, multiple, and *alinear* character of real-world happenings. It draws attention to the fact that events in the real world, as we experience it, do not unfold in a conscious, homogeneous, linear, and predictable manner (Deleuze and Guattari 1988). Instead they 'leak in insensibly' (James 1909/1996: 399). Human action and motives must, therefore, not be simply understood in terms of actors' intentions or even the result of underlying generative mechanisms, but rather in terms of unconscious metaphysics, embedded contextual experiences, accumulated memories, and entrenched cultural traditions that create and define the very possibilities for interpretation and action. This is not to suggest a kind of crude structural determinism whereby agency is entirely explained away in terms of structure. Rather, it is an attempt to show that action is a resultant effect of the ongoing tension and contestation between an immanent tendency towards *repetition* and a centrifugal drive towards novelty and *otherness*. Every existential action, in this postmodern sense is an experimental action reaching out into the not-yet-known. Outcomes are a particular unfolding of innate potentialities yet the manner of their specific manifestations remains essentially indeterminate. Surprise and the unexpected are the real order of things. Against the grand narratives of universal truths, total control, and predictability that defines the modernist agenda, postmodernism advocates a more tentative and modest attitude towards the status of our current forms of knowledge.

Finally, instead of thinking in terms of tightly coupled causal explanations that attempt to deterministically link observed phenomena with underlying tendencies, postmodernism privileges the ideas of reminiscence, resonance, recursion, and resemblance as more adequate expressions for describing the 'loosely coupled' and non-locally defined web of event-clusters constituting real-world happenings (Foucault 1970, 1979). These more elliptical descriptions of a more subliminal form of causality point us more and more towards thinking in terms of the language of complexity science. Thus, recently introduced concepts such as *self-similarity*, *non-local* causality, strange *attractors*, and the *butterfly effect* are more intellectually productive in that they all allude to a form of dispersive and loosely coupled causality that resonates more with our comprehension of reality. Consequently, it is argued that thinking in this more allusive and elliptical manner helps us to better appreciate how social phenomena such as 'individuals' and 'organizations', can be more productively viewed as temporarily stabilized event-clusters. These are microcosms of the civilizing process rather than concrete, isolatable systems and entities with distinct and definable boundaries. Postmodern analyses, thus, seek to disabuse us of the stubbornly held idea that reality, including especially our sense of self, is invariably objective, stable, orderly, and 'systemic' and hence predictable in character.

These four theoretical emphases in the postmodern approach provide a fertile alternative basis for redefining the focus of organization studies and for reframing research priorities. It is one that emphasizes the role of social organizing forces and the logic and technology of societal orderings as the more appropriate theoretical foci for OT, and elevates the impact of creativity, chance, novelty, and happenstance in our explanatory schemas. As Michel Foucault puts it very succinctly:

> it is to identify the accidents, the minute deviations—or conversely, the complete reversals—the errors, the false appraisals, and the faulty calculations that gave birth to those things that continue to exist and have value for us; it is to discover that truth or being does not lie at the root of what we know and what we are, but the exteriority of accidents. (Foucault 1984: 81)

If only for this emphasis alone, Foucault must be considered a precursor of postmodern OT in the sense elicited in these pages.

4.6 ORGANIZATION THEORY AS POSTMODERN SCIENCE

According to a postmodern perspective, change is a pervasive phenomena whilst organization and order represents the cumulative productive efforts of human intervention to temporarily stave off the nomadic and immanent forces of change. Contrary to the commonly held view, order and organization do not reflect the law of things but their *exception*. They are the outcome of our existential 'Will to Order'. Without organization and the stability and regularity it forges, and hence the predictability it earns, human life would be chaotic and eminently unliveable. Yet the seeming stability and solidity of such a socially constructed world is always precarious and continuously threatened by the restlessness of an inexorable change and the surprise that it brings with it. Beneath the seeming stability of our organized social life lie the restless and nomadic forces of change. This accounts for why even our best made plans are thwarted or often fail. What is called 'organizations', therefore, is nothing more than islands of relatively stabilized relational orders in a sea of ceaseless change. Organization and change are intrinsically opposing, not complementary, forces. Moreover, change does not take place in a linear manner. Instead real change is quintessentially 'rhizomic' in character taking place through variations, restless expansion, opportunistic conquests, sudden captures, and offshoots. Real change is anti-genealogical in nature. Unlike the predictable 'tree-like' structure of genealogy with its accompanying binary logic that fixes a linear order, rhizomic expansion and change is subtle, agglomerative, and often subterranean in nature. It spreads like a patch of oil.

On the other hand, organization is a constructive counter-movement aimed at fixing, ordering, routinizing, and regularizing changes through human interactions so that a degree of predictability and productivity in social exchange is attainable. In this sense organization as a 'world-making' activity is pivotal to a civilizational process that 'works from a start of more or less randomness towards increasing coherence, and that moves from amorphousness towards definiteness, from fumbling trails to decision' (Kroeber 1963: 23). The emergence of modern forms of organized social life and systems of governance follows a trail that leads from 'bands to tribes, tribes to chiefdoms, and chiefdoms to city-states' (Ingold 1986: 71). Through organization we come to acquire our structure of relations, individual identities, codes of behaviour, habits of thought, social preferences, and our ideals and aspirations.

As generic forms of social ordering through space-time, organization inevitably influences, amongst other things: how the flux and flow of our lifeworlds are structured, given identities, and made into objects of knowledge; how such objects of knowledge are causally linked in a coherent system of ordering; how taxonomies and hierarchies help create a system of priorities that influence perceptions and values; how values shape aspirations, choices, and decision-making; and how we are socialized to relate to one another in the greater scheme of things that we call 'society'. These are what ultimately inspired the ideologies that gave rise to the peculiarly western form of capitalism analysed and promoted by Adam Smith. It helped define the goals and functions of modern management, shapes managerial orientations, and overwhelmingly influences managerial priorities and practices.

It is this second-order concern with the organization of our forms of social life, our ways of seeing, our modes of understanding, and our methods of knowledge creation that constitutes the basis for an alternative postmodern OT. One that invariably emphasizes the reality-constituting and reality-maintaining character of organization. What is significantly overlooked in much of conventional OT, therefore, is a rigorous and critical reflection on the underlying social, cultural, and historical forces shaping the way we see, think, and act within the institutionalized and organized structures of the modern world. Against this restricted and restrictive view of OT as an economic-administrative discipline an expanded *Postmodern Theory of Organization* seeks to critically examine the underlying logic of modern rationality and the consequent societal and institutional strategies associated with it. A number of sub-themes and theoretical preoccupations can be associated with this postmodern science of organization.

4.6.1 Organizing Analysis: From Atomistic Individualism to Enfolded Organicism

The organizational order that modern science has employed with such overwhelming effectiveness is the order of differentiation, fragmentation, and representation. The dominance of visually-based forms of knowledge (e.g. 'seeing is believing') brought about by the alphabetization of the western world has meant that language has been assigned a literal role. One point of the image on our retina corresponds to one set of letters or words in our system of comprehension. In this way, everything observed is deemed to be reducible to pre-established symbols. This habit of analysis has affected us greatly suggesting implicitly that everything is reducible to points and can be reconstituted therefrom. This is the basis for the kind of atomistic thinking underpinning modern science. It provides a powerful and convenient method for effectively dealing with an otherwise amorphous and intractably fluxing reality. Such a method works in contrast to the kind of processual thinking advocated by postmodernism. Atomistic thinking, however, is not simply the opposite of processual thinking. Rather, the crucial difference lies more with the *direction of derivation* (Ingold 1986: 43) in our thought processes than it is about static differences. In an atomistic conception, every phenomenon is constituted by the aggregation and interaction of discrete individual part-elements. Each of these exists as a stable, independent entity prior to its incorporation. In a processual view, however, the individual elements have no real existence apart from the process of which they are but particular points of emergence. In short: the atomistic individual 'is *constituted* by its parts, not by its position in a wider system of relationship' (Ingold 1986: 44). Its identity derives from the sum features of its component parts. In a more enfolded and unfolded organismic view of the individual, however, the individual is inextricably linked and relationally defined. Indeed as Bohm (1980: 149) insists, the external order is 'enfolded or *implicate*' in every single element we might abstract from it. Thus, the individual organism is more a vehicle whose singular impetus is to 'receive life and pass it on, to act as a temporary vehicle for the projection of past into future' (Ingold 1986: 106). The individual is but an ephemeral vector of a creative evolutionary process. Life is like a current passing from germ to germ so much so that 'the living being is above all a thoroughfare, along which the impulsion of life is transmitted. And as each individual, like a relay runner, takes up this impulsion and passes it on, as each generation must lean over and touch the next, so how can we tell exactly where one individual ends and another begins' (Bergson 1911/1992: 45). This is the real empirical facticity of living encounters. As social beings, we do not suddenly appear as already-formed individuals with established identities that then proceed to engage in social intercourse. Instead individual identities are historically shaped outcomes of the *becoming* processes of individuation, identification, and institutionalization. Our personality and character is nothing more than 'the condensation of the history that we have lived from our birth'. Hence, 'It is with our entire past...that we desire, will and act' (pp. 5–7). As such the idea of individual intentionality and purposeful action must be tempered with the recognition that as one deals more and more with social 'persons' and not composite individual entities,[3] immanent or 'final cause' rather than the efficient cause becomes decidedly more appropriate. Regularity and predictability increasingly eludes us (Griffin 1988: 25).

4.6.2 Organizational Complexity and the Unconscious

In keeping with the recognition of an immanent and enfolded notion of reality, postmodern OT finds resonance with the contemporary preoccupations of Complexity Science in their search for more adequate causal explanations that do not overly rely on the kind of localized and tightly coupled causality proffered by classical science. It is therefore not surprising to see a recent burgeoning infusion of complexity concepts such as 'bifurcation', 'self-similiarity', 'strange attractors', 'butterfly effects', and so on, into organizational theorizing both in Europe and the United States. Such an expansive orientation has been precipitated by an increasing acceptance of the central idea of *non-locality* brought about by the advent of a more ontologically informed interpretation of quantum theory (Bohm and Hiley 1993). The broader implications of this understanding and its relationship with postmodernism have been productively explored by a number of important thinkers especially David Bohm (1980, 1988), Ilya Prigogine (1996; Prigogine and Stengers 1984), J. S. Bell (1993), and Paul Cilliers (1998). Elsewhere (Chia 1998), I have attempted to show how such a complexity awareness could be expanded to approach the core concerns of postmodernism.

Additionally, a heightened awareness of the inherent limitations of language has led to the examination of alternative ways of theorizing knowledge and organization. Thus, interest in issues relating to the unconscious such as Freudian and Lacanian psychoanalysis and the associated question of 'tacit' knowledge (Polanyi 1958, 1966) form another cluster of interests actively promoted by a postmodern 'turn' in organizational theorizing. Postmodernism's revelation of the inherent inadequacies of language points us to a realm of knowing beyond the grasp of representationalist epistemology. This is something that Lyotard, in particular, viewed as the singular, most important project of postmodernism. For him, postmodern analysis is that which 'in the modern, invokes the unpresentable in presentation itself...that which searches for new presentations, not in order to enjoy them but in order to impart a stronger sense of the unpresentable' (Lyotard

---

[3] For a thorough discussion of this important distinction, see Ingold 1986: 105–8.

1992: 15). For Lyotard and other postmodern writers, the real purpose of concepts and representations is not so much to discover a better set of representations that will enable us to mirror the going-ons in the world. Rather, it is to point us to an unconscious realm of knowing which lies beyond words but which, nevertheless, has a performative impact upon our lives.

By disabusing us of the seductions of dominant representations, postmodern analyses create the necessary conceptual vacuum for us to directly intuit that realm of concrete experiences that constitutes an essential part of our knowing and living. In this way it seeks to cultivate greater sensitivity and awareness of the human condition in general and the complexities and paradoxes of organizational situations in particular. What is advocated in a postmodern OT, therefore, is the radical abandonment of 'the organization' as a legitimate object of knowledge and its substitution by organization as a generic process of 'world-making'. In this regard, both complexity science and studies of unconscious desire and knowing must be applied, not so much to circumscribed economic-administrative units called 'organizations', but to all forms of social order such as that proposed in this chapter.

4.6.3 The Logic of Organization

In his thoughtful study of the nature and logic of capitalism, Robert Heilbroner (1985) makes the important point that what drove seminal thinkers such as Adam Smith and Karl Marx to formulate their wide-ranging principles and critiques of the causes and consequences of capitalism was the belief in the presence of enduring but hidden forces underlying the ordinary world of everyday affairs; a kind of 'netherworld' that impels us towards some destination not of our own making. For Smith it was the notion of the Invisible Hand which guided us towards the Deity whilst for Marx it was the 'internal dialectic' that provided the driving force for transformations in the socio-economic order. Both notions, however, harboured essentialist overtones and underplayed a more historically informed understanding of the intimate link between civilization and the socio-economic configuration it produces. This is something that the French historian Fernand Braudel (1981) so persuasively articulated in his book *Capitalism and Civilisation*. Viewed from this latter perspective, our present-day ordering impulses are by no means immutable principles, but are rather derived from a historically evolved logic of organization that has been transformed over the centuries through the civilizing process. As we have tried to show earlier in this chapter, the invention of the alphabetic system of representation, as well as the later development of typography has had much to do with the shaping of this dominant logic of organization underpinning everyday social and economic transactions. How this has come to pass becomes a central preoccupation of postmodern organizational analyses. In this regard, Weber's lifelong study of the gradual systematization and disenchantment of modern societies (Gerth and Mills 1948: 51–2), Schoenwald's (1973) fascinating depiction of the Victorian order and its effects on our sense of identity and self-perception, as well as Foucault's (1979) detailed excavation of the processes of individuation; all these become legitimate domains of analysis in an expanded theory of organization. Postmodern OT then creates an 'open field' of thought that draws liberally from the whole gamut of philosophy, art, and the social sciences to illuminate and inform the world of management practice.

4.7 CONCLUSION: ORGANIZATION AS 'WORLD-MAKING'

Human organizing creates order and predictability out of an otherwise inchoate and amorphous lifeworld. It consists of an interlocking sequence of ontological acts of differentiating, isolating, fixing, and identifying of portions of lived experience. These actions are central to the self's attempt to detach itself from its surroundings in order to attain a measure of autonomy and independence. The object of organization, therefore, is the 'preparation of objects by means of which the system can then distinguish itself from its primary subject and, therefore, be certain of itself' (Cooper 1987: 408). In other words, organization works to construct legitimate objects of knowledge for a knowing subject: 'dirt', 'notes of a musical score', 'food', 'pupils', 'the weather', 'culture', 'gravity', and so on. Through this process of organization, objects of knowledge acquire distinctive identities that allow us to treat them as existing independently of our perceptions. In this fundamental sense organization is a world-making activity. It is a ceaseless process of reality construction and maintenance that enables us to carve out our otherwise amorphous lifeworlds into manageable parts so that we can act purposefully and productively amidst a flood of competing and attention-seeking stimuli. The narrowing of focus, simplification, and the consequent economizing of effort in action are thus the ultimate aim of the impulse to organize. Through organization, the various aspects of our lived experiences, including especially our experience of self, acquire a familiar and seemingly unproblematic identity.

Approaching the question of organization from this postmodern perspective opens up radically new ways for rethinking the role and function of OT. Organization theory, according to this expanded postmodern understanding, thus, becomes one of critically examining the oftentimes subterranean societal and institutional strategies that help shape our habits of thought, our sense of self-identity, our perceptions and expectations of social life as well as our values, beliefs, and aspirations. In this way postmodern OT draws our attention to the need for practitioner managers and policy-makers to be made more deeply aware of the underlying societal forces shaping societal moods and capacities as well as managerial mindsets, and hence priorities and practices. This is the real potential contribution of a postmodern science of organization.

REFERENCES

ALDRICH, H. (1992). 'Incommensurable Paradigms? Vital Signs from Three Perspectives', in M. Reed and M. Hughes (eds.), *Rethinking Organization.* London: Sage.

BELL, B. I. (1926). *Postmodernism and Other Essays.* Milwaukee: Morehouse Publishing.

BELL, J. S. (1993). *Speakable and Unspeakable in Quantum Mechanics.* Cambridge: Cambridge University Press.

BERGER, P., and LUCKMANN, T. (1966). *The Social Construction of Reality.* Harmondsworth: Penguin.

BERGSON, H. (1911/1992). *The Creative Mind.* New York: Citadel Press.

—— (1922/1999). 'Discussion with Einstein'. *Bulletin des Société française de Philosophie.* 22/3 (July 1922): 102–13. Reprinted in R. Durie (ed.), *Duration and Simultaneity: Bergson and the Einsteinian Universe.* Manchester: Clinamen Press, P. xxvii.

BLAU, P. (1970). 'A Formal Theory of Differentiation in Organizations', *American Sociological Review.* 35/2: 201–18.

BOHM, D. (1980). *Wholeness and the Implicate Order.* London: Routledge & Kegan Paul.

—— (1988). 'Postmodern Science and the Postmodern World', in D. R. Griffin (ed.), *The Reenchantment of Science.* New York: State University of New York Press.

—— and HILEY, B. (1993). *The Undivided Universe: An Ontological Interpretation of Quantum Theory.* New York: Routledge.

BRAUDEL, F. (1981). *Capitalism and Civilisation.* New York: Harper & Row.

CAROTHERS, J. C. (1959). 'Culture, Psychiatry and the Written Word'. *Psychiatry.* Nov.: 18–34.

CARTER, R. E. (1990). *The Nothingness Beyond God.* New York: Paragon House.

CHIA, R. (1998). 'From Complexity Science to Complex Thinking: Organization as Simple-Location'. *Organization.* 5/3 (Aug.): 341–69.

CHILD, J. (1984). *Organization: A Guide to Problems and Practices.* London: Harper & Row.

CILLIERS, P. (1998). *Complexity and Postmodernism.* London: Routledge.

COBB, J. (1993). 'Alfred North Whitehead', in D. R. Griffin *et al.* (eds.), *Founders of Constructive Postmodern Philosophy.* New York: State University of New York Press.

COOPER, R. (1987). 'Information, Communication and Organization: A Poststructural Revision'. *Journal of Mind and Behaviour,* 8/3: 395–416.

CZARNIAWSKA-JOERGES, B. (1994). 'Narratives of Individual and Organizational Identities', in S. A. Deetz (ed.), *Communication Yearbook.* 17. Thousand Oaks, Calif.: Sage.

DEAL, T. E., and KENNEDY, A. A. (1982). *Corporate Cultures: The Rites and Rituals of Corporate Life.* Reading, Mass.: Addison-Wesley.

DEETZ, S., and MUMBY, D. (1990). 'Power, Discourse, and the Workplace: Reclaiming the Critical Tradition in Communication Studies in Organizations', in J. Anderson (ed.), *Communication Yearbook*, 13. Newbury Park, Calif.: Sage.

DELEUZE, G. (1993). *The Fold*. Minneapolis: University of Minnesota Press.

—— and GUATTARI, F. (1988). *A Thousand Plateaus: Capitalism and Schizophrenia*. London: Athlone Press.

DERRIDA, J. (1981). *Positions*, trans. A. Bass. Chicago: University of Chicago Press.

DESCARTES, R. (1628/1968). *Discourse on Method and Other Writings*. Harmondsworth: Penguin.

DONALDSON, L. (1987). 'Strategy and Structural Adjustment to Regain Fit and Performance: In Defence of Contingency Theory'. *Journal of Management Studies*. 24/1: 1–24.

—— (1996). 'The Normal Science of Structural Contingency Theory', in S. Clegg, C. Hardy, and W. Nord (eds.), *Handbook of Organization Studies*. London: Sage.

DRUCKER, P. (1993). *Post-Capitalist Society*. Oxford: Butterworth Heinemann.

DURIE, R. (ed.) (1999). *Duration and Simultaneity: Bergson and the Einsteinian Universe*. Manchester: Clinamen Press.

EHRENZWEIG, A. (1965). *The Psychoanalysis of Artistic Vision*. New York: George Braziller.

—— (1967). *The Hidden Order of Art*. Berkeley: University of California Press.

EINSTEIN, A. (1916/52). *Relativity: The Special and General Theory*. New York: Three Rivers Press.

EISENSTEIN, E. (1980). *The Printing Press as an Agent of Change*. Cambridge: Cambridge University Press.

FISHER, P. (1991). *Making and Effacing Art*. New York: Oxford University Press.

FOUCAULT, M. (1970). *The Order of Things*. London: Tavistock.

—— (1979). *Discipline and Punish*, trans. A. Sheridan. London: Penguin.

FROST, P., MOORE, L., LOUIS, M., LUNDBERG, C., and MARTIN, J. (1985). *Organizational Culture*. Beverly Hills, Calif.: Sage.

GERTH, H. H., and MILLS, C. W. (1948). *From Max Weber*. London: Routledge.

GRIFFIN, D. R. (1988). *The Reenchantment of Science: Postmodern Proposals*. New York: State University of New York Press.

GUNTER, P. A. Y. (1993). 'Henri Bergson', in D. R. Griffin *et al.* (eds.), *Founders of Constructive Postmodern Philosophy*. New York: State University of New York Press.

HANNAN, M. T., and FREEMAN, J. H. (1997). 'The Population Ecology of Organizations'. *American Journal of Sociology*, 82: 929–64.

HASSAN, I. (1985). 'The Culture of Postmodernism'. *Theory, Culture & Society*, 2/3: 119–31.

HEILBRONER, R. (1985). *The Nature and Logic of Capitalism*. New York: W.W. Norton & Co.

HUME, D. (1740/1992). *A Treatise of Human Nature*, ed. L. A. Selby-Bigge. Oxford: Clarendon Press.

INGOLD, T. (1986). *Evolution and Social Life*. Cambridge: Cambridge University Press.

JAMES, W. (1909/1996). *A Pluralistic Universe*. Lincoln and London: University of Nebraska Press.

KANTER, R. M., STEIN, B. A., and JICK, T. D. (1992). *The Challenge of Organizational Change*. New York: Free Press.

KENNER, H. (1987). *The Mechanical Muse*. New York: Oxford University Press.

KERN, S. (1983). *The Culture of Time and Space 1880–1918*. Cambridge, Mass.: Harvard University Press.

KROEBER, A. L. (1963). *An Anthropology Looks at History.* Berkeley: University of California Press.

LEWIN, K. (1951). *Field Theory in Social Science.* New York: Harper & Row.

LINDBERG, D. C. (1992). *The Beginnings of Western Science.* Chicago: University of Chicago Press.

LYOTARD, J. F. (1984). *The Postmodern Condition: A Report on Knowledge.* Minneapolis: University of Minnesota Press.

—— (1992). *The Postmodern Explained.* Minneapolis: University of Minnesota Press.

McARTHUR, T. (1986). *Worlds of Reference.* Cambridge: Cambridge University Press.

McLUHAN, M. (1967). *The Gutenberg Galaxy.* Toronto: University of Toronto Press.

—— and McLUHAN, E. (1988). *Laws of Media.* Toronto: University of Toronto Press.

MARTIN, J. (1992). *Cultures in Organizations: Three Perspectives.* New York: Oxford University Press.

MILLER, D., and FRIESSEN, P. H. (1980). 'Momentum and Revolution in Organizational Adaptation'. *Academy of Management Journal,* 23: 591–614.

MINTZBERG, H. (1979). *The Structuring of Organizations,* Englewood Cliffs, NJ: Prentice-Hall.

MURPHY, T. S. (1999). 'Beneath Relativity: Bergson and Bohm on Absolute Time', in J. Mullarkey (ed.), *The New Bergson.* Manchester: Manchester University Press.

NONAKA, I. (1994). 'A Dynamic Theory of Organizational Knowledge Creation'. *Organization Science,* 5/1: 14–37.

—— and TAKEUCHI, H. (1995). *The Knowledge-Creating Company.* New York and Oxford: Oxford University Press.

PERROW, C. (1967). 'A Framework for the Comparative Analysis of Organizations'. *American Sociological Review,* 32/3: 194–208.

PETTIGREW, A. M. (1987). *The Management of Strategic Change.* Oxford: Blackwell.

PFEFFER, J. (1993). 'Barriers to the Advance of Organizational Science: Paradigm Development as a Dependent Variable'. *Academy of Management Review,* 18/4: 499–520.

—— and SALANCIK, G. R. (1978). *The External Control of Organizations: A Resource-Dependence Perspective.* New York: Harper & Row.

POLANYI, M. (1958). *Personal Knowledge.* Chicago: University of Chicago Press.

—— (1966). *The Tacit Dimension.* London: Routledge & Kegan Paul.

POWELL, W. W., and DIMAGGIO, P. J. (1991). *The New Institutionalism in Organizational Analysis.* Chicago: University of Chicago Press.

PRIGOGINE, I. (1996). *The End of Certainty.* New York: Free Press.

—— and STENGERS, I. (1984). *Order out of Chaos.* London: Fontana.

RESCHER, N. (1996). *Process Metaphysics.* New York: State University of New York Press.

ROBBINS, S. (1989). *Organization Theory: Structure, Design, and Applications.* Englewood Cliffs, NJ: Prentice-Hall.

RORTY, R. (1991). *Objectivity, Relativism and Truth.* Cambridge: Cambridge University Press.

SANDELANDS, L., and DRAZIN, R. (1989). 'On the Language of Organization Theory'. *Organization Studies,* 10/4: 457–78.

SAUSSURE, F. DE (1966). *Course in General Linguistics.* New York: McGraw-Hill.

SCHEIN, E. H. (1992). *Organizational Culture and Leadership* (2nd edn). San Francisco: Jossey-Bass.

SCHOENWALD, R. (1973). 'Training Urban Man', in H. J. Dyos and M. Wolff (eds.), *The Victorian City: Images and Ideals*, ii. London: Routledge & Kegan Paul.

SCOTT, W. R. (1992). *Organizations: Rational, Natural and Open Systems*, Englewood Cliffs, NJ: Prentice-Hall.

SERRES, M. (1981). *Hermes: Literature, Science, Philosophy*. Baltimore: Johns Hopkins Press.

SHAPIN, S. (1994). *A Social History of Truth: Civility and Science in Seventeenth-Century England*. Chicago: University of Chicago Press.

SILVERMAN, D. (1970). *The Theory of Organizations*. London: Heinemann.

STEIER, F. (1991). *Research and Reflexivity*. London: Sage.

TICHY, N. M. (1983). *Managing Strategic Change*. New York: Wiley.

TOYNBEE, A. (1939). *A Study of History*, v. Oxford: Oxford University Press.

TUSHMAN, M. L., and ROMANELLI, E. (1985). 'Organizational Evolution: A Metamorphosis Model of Convergence and Reorientation', in L. L. Cummings and B. Staw (eds.), *Research in Organizational Behavior*, vii. Greenwich, Conn.: JAI Press.

VAN DE VEN, A. H. (1987). 'Review Essay: Four Requirements for Processual Analysis', in A. M. Pettigrew (ed.), *The Management of Strategic Change*. Oxford: Blackwell.

—— and POOLE, M. S. (1995). 'Explaining Development and Change in Organizations'. *Academy of Management Review*, 20/3: 510–40.

VAN MAANEN, J. (1988). *Tales of the Field: On Writing Ethnography*. Chicago: University of Chicago Press.

WEICK, K. E. (1969). *The Social Psychology of Organizing*. Reading, Mass. Addison-Wesley.

WHITEHEAD, A. N. (1926/1985). *Science and the Modern World*. London: Free Association Books.

—— (1933). *Adventures of Ideas*. Harmondsworth: Penguin.

PART II

THE CONSTRUCTION OF ORGANIZATION THEORY

CHAPTER 5

THE ORIGINS OF ORGANIZATION THEORY

WILLIAM H. STARBUCK

ACCORDING to *Webster's Third International Dictionary*, theory is 'a coherent group of general propositions used as principles of explanation'. Organization theory is a collection of general propositions about organizations. Although people have been creating organizations for many thousands, perhaps tens of thousands of years, generalizations about organizations—contributions to organization theory—are almost entirely products of the last half of the twentieth century. People proposed very few generalizations about organizations before 1850, when a trickle of such propositions began. Propositions about organizations remained infrequent until the late 1940s, and they did not become prevalent until the 1960s.

The history of organization theory contrasts with the history of managerial thought. When people began to compose texts about organized activities, between 2,000 and 3,000 years before the Christian era (BCE), they focused on managerial practices rather than on organizations as such. Several writers proposed general principles for managerial practice before 1000 BCE, so one can say that theories about managing have existed for at least 3,000 years. These writings often said nothing about the organizational contexts in which managing was to occur. When the writers did make statements about organizations, they did not generalize. They wrote about specific organizations.

This chapter argues that contemporary organization theory owes its existence to social and technological changes that occurred during the last half of the nineteenth century and first half of the twentieth century. These changes created both a basis for theorizing and an audience for theories about organizations. They stimulated an explosion in the numbers of large, formalized organizations, they made organizations relevant to many more people, and they made many more people interested in and capable of understanding theoretical propositions. This chapter reviews the developments that made organization theory possible and interesting.

The idea may have originated with Gulick's (1937) phrase 'the theory of organization', but it appears to have been Simon (1950, 1952–3, 1952) who most actively promoted the actual phrase 'organization theory'. Simon (1952) envisaged 'organization theory' as a broad category that included scientific management, industrial engineering, industrial psychology, the psychology of small groups, human-resources management, and strategy. He said his ideas reflected his participation in two conferences, and the programs of these conferences show that organization theory had a very broad meaning in the early 1950s. A conference at the Rand Corporation in August 1951 brought together social psychologists who discussed interactions among small groups, roboticists who discussed automata, and economists who discussed mathematical models of choice and information (Flood 1951). The second conference, at Princeton University in June 1952, assembled more than thirty scholars from a dozen universities to discuss the 'Theory of Organization'. The presentations at this conference focused mainly on intraorganizational behaviors: morale, leadership, the effects of organizations on their members, decision-making.

Despite the broad concepts of organization theory during the 1950s, intraorganizational topics are generally not included in the present-day meaning of 'organization theory'. In 1950, Princeton University received a grant to strengthen its social sciences, and it used this grant for an 'Organizational Behavior Project'. The Princeton scholars chose the topic 'organizational behavior' because it would embrace very diverse studies and encourage interdisciplinary research (Princeton University 1950–4). By 1960, however, many academics were making a distinction between 'organization theory' and 'organizational behavior', and the latter term had come to denote intraorganizational activities that focus on individual workers and small groups (Argyris 1957, 1960). A few years later, strategic management emerged as another partly distinct domain. Although the dividing lines remain very fuzzy and they may actually interfere with understanding, there now exists general agreement among academics that 'organization theory' somehow differs from both 'organizational behavior' and from 'strategic management'. This chapter assumes that 'organization theory' has this restricted contemporary domain, which involves looking at (a) single organizations as integrated systems, (b) many organizations that resemble each other, or (c) interactions among groups of organizations. The chapter explicitly excludes intraorganizational issues such as work design, industrial psychology, compensation, human relations, leadership, decision-making by individuals, and strategizing. In doing so, the chapter imposes esoteric, academic distinctions that appeared after 1960 on real-world events occurring long ago.

The chapter follows a loosely chronological itinerary. It begins by taking note that theoretical writing about management began more than 4,000 years ago, and that some organizations had the essential properties of bureaucracy more than 3,000 years ago. Next, the chapter surveys the educational, occupational, and technological changes that laid foundations for a new, organizational perspective. These changes escalated gradually through the sixteenth to nineteenth centuries, and then accelerated rapidly after 1850. Ensuing sections of the chapter examine changes in how people thought about organizations. The term 'organization' evolved from a Roman medical term into a perceived property of societies, and then came to denote both a property of diverse social systems and medium-sized social systems that possess some degree of 'organization'. Organizational forms such as company and corporation emerged and gained status, not as mere labels for their collective members, but as legal persons distinct from their members.

Although the term 'organization' arose from a philosophical tradition that saw social systems as history-dependent organisms, the earliest contributions to organization theory portrayed organizations as machine-like systems and they said little about how organizations might reflect history or temporary environmental conditions. Some of these early contributions protested against bureaucracies' deficiencies or against threats that bureaucracies posed; others hailed organizations' virtues or opportunities that organizations offered; the latter had a prescriptive tone. These themes began to merge during the late 1940s. Also around that time, writings about organizations started to acquire a character that its proponents described as more 'scientific'.

The chapter ends sometime around 1960, as other chapters in this book discuss the subsequent events in detail. At that time, many studies were appearing and organization theory was acquiring a different kind of existence as an autonomous academic domain. Organization theory had arrived, but it now had to contend with pressures to fragment and to become self-absorbed and irrelevant to its environment.

As with any historical study, this one has biases created by the availability of records, my limitations, and my choices about what to report. History has often been a harsh editor of itself, with the result that surviving documents represent only a small fraction of those that once existed, and people chose this surviving fraction to support political or religious goals. Where no documents survive, understanding derives from later interpretations that incorporate the cultural and personal biases of the interpreters. As a resident of the United States, I have had much better access to documents in the English language, and although colleagues in other nations gave valuable assistance, this chapter's cultural and linguistic biases are still obvious.[1] The chapter expresses a cognitive and social-constructionist view of science; it emphasizes people's perceptions and their choices of perceptual frameworks. The resulting description of the origins of organization theory is rather phenomenological and atheoretic. It does not rest on a theoretical framework, and it does not purport to describe the development of social theories other than organization theory.

5.1 PREMODERN WRITINGS ABOUT MANAGEMENT

5.1.1 In the Beginning, there was the Boss

The most conspicuous property of the oldest writings is their emphasis on superior–subordinate relations (Rindova and Starbuck 1997a). Probably the oldest surviving advice about managerial practices, a Mesopotamian version of the ark and flood, explains why leaders have to deceive their followers and how they can do so. The ark-builder asks one of his gods how to persuade other people to help him construct the ark: they will not help him if he discloses that the ark is intended to save him while a great flood drowns everyone else, including those who helped him build the ark. His god advises the ark-builder how he can tell the literal truth but do so in a way that deceives the workers.

Ancient texts from China, Egypt, Greece, India, and Mesopotamia describe uncomfortable and wary relations between leaders and followers, relations filled with ambivalence and fear. Superiors distrusted their subordinates, and subordinates distrusted their superiors, yet each had to depend on the other. People were concerned about (a) whether leaders and followers did or should trust each other and speak forthrightly to each other, (b) how leaders did or could manipulate followers and followers could control leaders, (c) how much followers did or should respect leaders and leaders respect followers, (d) whether status differences were justified, and (e) when leaders could be trusted to act appropriately. All strategies for controlling subordinates entail advantages and disadvantages, as do all strategies for acting as a subordinate. Ancient people saw these trade-offs and recognized their complexity.

---

[1] This chapter would contain even stronger biases had I not received help from Michel Anteby, Mie Augier, Mike Barnett, Barbara Czarniawska, Roger Dunbar, Wolf Heydebrand, Geoff Hodgson, Sten Jönsson, Alfred Kieser, Lee Kam-hon, Christian Knudsen, Jim March, Derek Pugh, Jacques Rojot, Haridimos Tsoukas, and Malcolm Warner.

Some writers sought to render superiors and subordinates more compatible. They urged superiors to restrain their exercise of power, to focus on behaving properly themselves, to be just and considerate, and to cultivate support of the populace over the long run. They urged subordinates to accept subordination, to demonstrate respect, to act honestly and forthrightly, and to pursue their superiors' best interests rather than their own. Other writers advised superiors to be suspicious of their subordinates, to deal harshly with dissenters and rebels, to pit subordinates against one another, and to manipulate subordinates by means of rewards and punishments. Control of armed force permitted superiors to seize property, to alter people's statuses, and to inflict death, so their subjects had reason to avoid actions that might arouse superiors' displeasure. Because many superiors had power of life or death over their subordinates and corporal punishment was prevalent, subordinates took pains to appear obedient and they stood ready to perform very diverse services if their superiors asked them to do so.

Superior–subordinate relations did elicit theorizing. One very old Chinese text, 'The Great Plan', spells out precepts about leadership that resemble some contingency theories of the late twentieth century (Rindova and Starbuck 1997*b*). This document and others not only stated prescriptions about how superiors and subordinates should behave but also articulated philosophies that explicitly related superior–subordinate relations to the structures of societies more generally. However, theories about organizations, if they existed, have not survived. In fact, the few documents that do survive from before 2000 BCE do not even discuss organizations as such. Organizations did exist, of course. There were armies, businesses, construction projects, and royal households. But, it appears that people did not regard themselves as working for or in organizations. They perceived themselves primarily as subordinates of specific individuals—such as kings, ministers, or owners of businesses. Their exact job assignments were secondary because their first responsibility was to do whatever their superiors asked of them.

5.1.2 Then Came Bureaucracy

The surviving documents indicate that some organizations became clearly bureaucratic during the second millennium BCE. Evidence from before 2000 BCE shows that organizations kept written records and had well-defined hierarchies of authority and rules about the rights and duties associated with positions, but not that they had other properties of bureaucracy. By 1100–1200 BCE, however, documents from China and Egypt and archeological remains from Mycenae testify that some organizations had also acquired division of labor based on functional specialization, work procedures, impersonal relations among people performing roles, and promotion and employment based on technical competence. Thus, these organizations exhibited the key properties of bureaucracy (Hall 1963).

Probably the most complete and interesting example of ancient bureaucratic practices is 'The Officials of Chou', which was written around 1100 BCE (Rindova and Starbuck 1997b). This document describes an elaborate organizational structure for the 'royal domain', which was a combination of the government and the king's household staff. This document gives a long, exhaustive, and detailed list of job descriptions for the many officials in the king's service, ranging from the prime minister to household servants (Biot 1851; Gingell 1852). However, 'The Officials of Chou' does not generalize about organizations. It describes only one specific organization, and when it states principles, it does not indicate that they also apply to other organizations. Likewise, after several years of searching documents from other regions, I have found only documents that focus on specific organizations, none that state generalizations about organizations. This dearth contrasts strikingly with the multitude of generalizations about managing that various people generated over four millennia.

This bifurcated pattern persisted over the next 3,000 years. Ideas about how to manage evolved and many authors proposed generalizations about managing. These generalizations were relevant to organizations in that they focused on activities that managers or organizations performed—on rule, military strategy, military logistics, motivation, compensation, role performance, money making, occupational and task specialization, and the ever-present issues posed by superior–subordinate relations. The generalizations dealt with how to organize or how to make organized activities effective, yet they did not speak to the properties of organizations as distinctive, integrated social systems—different from small, informal groups and different from very large societies. Evidently, people saw the results of organized activities as being products of actions taken by individuals, so they formulated prescriptions about actions individuals should take.

Large, formalized organizations existed, but they were rare. Many nations had well-organized governments. The Chinese and the Romans, for example, operated imperial governments that spanned several thousand miles and hundreds of administrative subunits. Hundreds of cities had large civic governments. On various occasions, people formed large armies that carried out complex missions over long periods, Alexander the Great and Genghis Khan being two examples. Some organized activities involved hundreds or thousands of workers—for instance, the Chinese Wall, the Egyptian pyramids and temples, the vast network of Roman roads, mines in many locations throughout history, the English and Dutch East India Companies, and the Hudson's Bay Company. Some organizations had very long lives. The Roman Catholic Church has been operating for two millennia. Stora Enso Oyj, a mining company founded in 1288, continues in business today as one of the world's largest paper and timber companies. Striking as these examples were, they may have been too idiosyncratic and too extraordinary to inspire generalizations. I have been able to find only a few authors who proposed generalizations about organizations as distinctive social systems before the late nineteenth century.

One organizationally relevant theme that did elicit theoretical generalizations was division of labor, specialization, and mass production. People have understood the value of division of labor, specialization, and mass production for many thousands of years. People have had specialized occupations for as long as written records exist, and the bureaucratization that occurred in the second millennium BCE depended on specialization and division of labor. Archeological remains testify to the use of mass production techniques for glass-blowing and pottery-making as early as 500 BCE. Around 400 BCE, Plato remarked that specialization can increase productivity. Around 300 BCE, the Chinese philosopher Mencius discussed division of labor. Greek and Roman soldiers received training to standardize and coordinate their fighting techniques. In the early 1400s, the Arsenal of Venice was using an assembly line with about 2,000 workers to equip ships for fighting, and to make this process effective, the arsenal used standardized armaments and standardized components for the ships (George 1968; Lane 1934). Nevertheless, theorizing on these topics remained very sparse until European countries began to industrialize. Adam Smith (1776) put a spotlight on the economic benefits of specialization, division of labor, and mass production. Melchiorre Gioia (1815) and Charles Babbage (1832) sought to articulate principles for making mass production effective. Then these topics became the foci of the Scientific Management movement in the late nineteenth century (Merkle 1980).

Two men collaborated inadvertently in the seventeenth and eighteenth centuries to contribute a pair of insights to modern organization theory. In 1665 King Louis XIV appointed Jean-Bapiste Colbert his Comptroller General of Finance. At that time, the French economy was in turmoil. Colbert prosecuted corrupt officials and reorganized commerce and industry according to the economic principles known as mercantilism. To assure the populace that the government was going to act fairly, he demanded that officials abide by rules and apply them uniformly to everyone (Wolin 1960: 271). About eighty years later, in 1751, Jean-Claude Marie Vincent de Gournay became France's Administrator of Commerce. An outraged Gournay railed against the numerous governmental regulations that he judged to be suppressing business activity. To symbolize a government run by insensitive rule-makers and rule-enforcers who did not understand or care about the consequences of their actions, he coined the sarcastic term 'bureau-cratie'—government by desks.

Another forerunner of modern organization theorists was Andrew Ure, a professor of chemistry. An enthusiastic proponent of 'the factory system', Ure (1835) took a step beyond Adam Smith. Whereas Smith's pin factory was solely an example of division of labor, Ure pointed out that a factory poses organizational challenges. He asserted that every factory incorporates 'three principles of action, or three organic systems': (a) a 'mechanical' system that integrates production processes, (b) a 'moral' system that motivates and satisfies the needs of workers, and (c) a 'commercial' system that seeks to sustain the firm through financial management and marketing. Harmonizing these three systems, said Ure, was the responsibility of managers.

5.2 ORGANIZATIONS BECOME TOPICS OF DISCUSSION

5.2.1 Education, Specialization, and Technology Create the Concept of an Organization

Theories about organizations began to attract much more attention after 1850, as several long-term trends accelerated abruptly, making the concept of 'organizations' relevant to many people and preparing them to appreciate generalizations about organizations.

The societal changes that have greatly affected organizations and organization theory seem to have occurred mainly in education, occupational and task specialization, and technologies (George 1968; Shafritz and Ott 1996; Wren 1994). The people of 3,000 years ago had very well thought-out ideas about hierarchical control, superior–subordinate relations, motivational techniques, and compensation. However, they provided only rather basic education, and that for only small fractions of the populace; they generally drew fuzzy distinctions among occupations; they made little use of mass production; and they lacked access to technologies such as electricity, business machines, telecommunications, and flight that have had pervasive effects on procedures, strategies, and logistics.

5.2.2 Education Makes it Possible for Large Organizations to Proliferate and to Work Effectively

Over the centuries, education gradually grew more elaborate, especially after the invention of printing reduced the cost and increased the availability of study materials. However, education did not become widely available until the nineteenth century. Prussia led the movement toward universal education: in 1810, it began to require every child to receive three years of education. By 1850, well over 90 percent of the Prussian residents had become literate, and in 1868, Prussia began to require that every child receive eight years of education. Other countries followed Prussia's example. Sweden made education compulsory in 1842, Australia and New Zealand during the 1870s, Switzerland in 1874, Britain in 1876, the Netherlands in 1878, France in 1882, Serbia in 1888, and Ireland in 1892. The American states took almost seventy years to introduce compulsory schooling, starting with Massachusetts in 1852 and ending with Mississippi in 1918. For reasons political or religious, universal education came much later or not at all in Austria, Belgium, Italy, Portugal, Russia, and Spain (Bowen 1981).

Three factors drove the expansion of education in the nineteenth century. First, the Enlightenment period created an enthusiasm for rationality and a belief in the perfectibility of mankind. For example, in 1812, James Mill published a pamphlet titled 'Schools for All, in Preference to Schools for Churchmen Only'. Second, during the middle of the nineteenth century, while industrialization was creating employment for women and older children, many nations and states placed restrictions of the use of child labor. For example, Britain's Factory Act of 1833 forbade the employment of children less than 9 years of age. They shortly thereafter discovered that they needed to remove the young children from the streets. Third, industrialization created white-collar jobs that demanded literate workers. White-collar jobs quadrupled in England during the 1860s and 1870s.

As opportunities for white-collar employment multiplied during the last half of the nineteenth century, the graduates of elementary schools stayed in school to study accountancy and law. In America, the Land Grant Act following the Civil War encouraged the founding of many universities that embraced practical subject matter such as agriculture, engineering, and commerce. Merkle (1980) inferred that the Scientific Management movement contributed significantly to the expansion of managerial activity after 1880.

Then at the turn of the century, business-related studies acquired much higher status as curricula in elite universities. The University of Pennsylvania began teaching accounting and business law in 1881. Several prestigious universities created business schools around 1900. Harvard University launched a business school at the graduate level in 1908. These programs did not require that students take courses about management, but such courses were popular electives (Chandler 1977).

Education continued to spread and to grow more elaborate through the twentieth century. In the United States, in 1900, 24 percent of the population had less than five years of schooling. This percentage dropped to 11 percent in 1950, and to 1.6 percent in 1998. Similarly, in 1900, only 14 percent of adults had completed twelve years of schooling. By 1950, 33 percent of adults had completed twelve years of schooling, and by 1998, 83 percent.

Education disseminates literacy and arithmetic skills widely. Literacy and arithmetic skills have long been associated with organizations because they constitute foundations for consistent procedures, public accountability, coordination through written communication, and the enforcement of contracts.[2] The writing process shapes rationality by forcing authors to identify specific foci of attention and to arrange these foci in sequences. Thus, writing teaches people how to decompose complex tasks into sequences of elementary components, and this skill is a step toward dividing collective labor into sequential steps (Kallinikos 1996). Although written texts are distinctly artificial constructions, they are constructions that facilitate organizing (Ong 1982). Likewise, arithmetic facilitates the perception of individuals as substitutable units, the ordering and aggregation of divided labor, and commercial transactions (Hoskin and Macve 1986). As they grew larger and more systematic, organizations developed more complex and nuanced numerical methods (Edwards and Newell 1991).

Formal, public education also tends to emphasize generalizations because teachers try to make lessons meaningful to almost all students. Education emphasizes abstraction because lessons typically use in-principle discussions in classrooms rather than on-the-job experience. And such teaching also asserts the usefulness of abstract generalizations and gives students practice in applying generalizations to concrete instances. Thus, formal, public education creates a foundation for discussing abstract concepts such as 'an organization', 'bureaucracy', or 'role' and for seeing such concepts as useful.

Dreeben (1968) argued persuasively that one major function of schools is to transform people from junior and dependent members of small families into autonomous participants in multiple large organizations and social institutions. Schools teach 'principles of conduct' that include the proper behaviors of organizational membership—distinctions between roles and role incumbents, respect for bureaucratic authority, respect for standardized procedures, and accountability for task performance. In a similar vein, Foucault (1975) portrayed schools as systems for evaluating people and placing them into homogeneous categories, and in the process, teaching the use of numerical performance measures. However, Dreeben's and Foucault's observations may not describe all cultures. For example, the expatriate Chinese have built their business firms around families and their business relationships have emphasized personal networks (Chan 1998).

---

[2] One consequence of the association between writing and organization has been the destruction of historical documents that described organizations. Conquerors and rebels usually destroyed the records of the governments they overthrew.

5.2.3 Growing Populations and New Technologies Make Large Organizations Efficient and Increase the Benefits of White-Collar Work

Occupational and task specialization developed gradually until the last half of the nineteenth century. Very likely, the slowness of this development reflected the small scale of non-agricultural production. Although people have understood the advantages of mass production for thousands of years, small populations and slow, difficult transportation had kept markets small and had restricted the potential returns to scale.

World population grew slowly until approximately 1600, and then the rate of population increase began to rise. By the late seventeenth century, the world population was increasing by roughly twelve times its average rate during the previous 2,000 years, and it continued to increase at this rate until the twentieth century, although the populations of Europe and the Americas grew more rapidly than the rest of the world during the nineteenth century. Population growth accelerated even further in the twentieth century. By 1950, the world population was increasing more than twice as rapidly as it had during the nineteenth century and almost four times as rapidly as it had during the eighteenth century. As a result, the world population grew 60 percent between 1750 and 1850, and more than 100 percent between 1850 and 1950. By 1987 the earth held ten times as many people as it had in 1650 (Cameron 1993; Reinhard, Armengaud, and Dupaquier 1968; United Nations 1998; Wrigley 1969).

Population increases both resulted from and stimulated technological changes. Better sanitation, better diets, and better housing reduced infant mortality and lengthened lifespans. Other technological changes lowered the costs and risks of transport, accelerated the speed of transport, and extended the distances over which trading occurred. In 1754 the 200-mile trip across England took four days, largely because the roads were terrible; and robbers often preyed on persons who attempted such a journey (Boulton 1931). The eighteenth century brought improved roads, more bridges, and a few canals, but such heavy construction remained difficult and infrequent until steam engines became available. Similarly, although continuous improvements in sailing ships encouraged Europeans to explore the world and to build empires, truly dramatic changes did not occur until boats and ships acquired steam power. Inventors began to experiment with steam power in the late 1700s; a few steam-powered boats came into use during the early 1800s; and steam power was coming into wide use by the mid-1800s. However, steam power was dangerous. Not until the mid-1880s did people understand why steam engines exploded, and explosions continued to be frequent into the twentieth century (Petroski 1996; Ward 1989). When it did become reliable, steam power made many new technologies possible: large ocean-going ships, long railway lines, large bridges, tunnels, paved roads, and massive earth moving. During the early years of the twentieth century, internal combustion engines added to the available options and made automobiles, trucks, and aircraft practical. Manufacturers could obtain raw materials from afar and send their products long distances. Firms could manage plants that were far apart. Chandler (1980) argued that the especially rapid growth of American markets caused the United States to become a first-mover toward managerial capitalism.

Numerous large construction projects such as canals and railroads required numerous large organizations. As large markets materialized, the returns available from standardized, high-speed production led to the creation of thousands of large factories. As these new organizations imitated each other, they created a substantial population of similar social systems, and these similarities stimulated generalizations. It became useful for observers to think about general principles for categories of organizations instead of focusing on the idiosyncrasies of specific organizations. The new prevalence of large organizations also made people more aware of the distinctive problems and opportunities that they pose. Although such problems and opportunities had been occurring since antiquity, they had been unusual and easily ignored; now they became prevalent and very evident. Managers, who had earlier received low pay and disrespect, now gained value as problem solvers and opportunity pursuers (Pollard 1965). Large organizations created markets for consistent procedures and business machines to automate them. Business machines in turn reinforced the usefulness of consistent procedures (Elbourne 1934).

Although manufacturing has never dominated employment, the advent of factories had dramatic social effects that framed the birth of organization theory. Specialization and division of labor made work more efficient and less demanding physically but less satisfying. Women and children became more employable. Compliance received larger rewards, and ability received smaller ones. Social and economic differences between skilled and unskilled workers decreased, mainly by the devaluing of skill. Skilled workers began to form trade unions.

Frederick W. Taylor demonstrated how business could extract monetary value from white-collar activities—industrial engineering—that emphasized measurement and calculation and that possessed the avant-garde and respectable aura of 'science'. Greatly increased productivity made it possible for owners to reap large profits, and a lack of government regulation allowed predatory business behavior, with one result being creation of a class of very wealthy capitalists (Veblen 1904). Strife between business owners and employees gave impetus to the Scientific Management movement, which claimed to ameliorate conflict by increasing productivity and allowing higher wages (Merkle 1980; Shenhav 1995).

Strife between business owners and employees also spawned much controversy. Karl Marx (1867) railed against working conditions in factories, arguing that division of labor created unsatisfying jobs and allowed capitalists to dominate and take advantage of workers. Business organizations thus served as battlegrounds for conflict between working classes and capitalist ones. Marx also criticized the idea that managerial activity deserved special status; he opined that anyone could perform administrative tasks if these tasks were divided into sufficiently elementary components. He did not discuss who would decide what administrative tasks were needed, who would assign administrative tasks, or who would revise these assignments when circumstances changed. Marx's close colleague, Frederick Engels (1872) remarked, 'Everywhere combined action, the complication of processes dependent upon each other, displaces independent action by individuals. But whoever mentions combined action speaks of organization; now, is it possible to have organization without authority?' He responded to this rhetorical question by saying, 'The automatic machinery of the big factory is much more despotic than the small capitalists who employ workers ever have been. . . . If man, by dint of his knowledge and inventive genius, has subdued the forces of nature, the latter avenge themselves upon him by subjecting him, in so far as he employs them, to a veritable despotism independent of all social organization.' Presumably, Engels never met the clerk at the Bank of England who had to sign his seven-letter name on 5,300 new bank notes during an eleven-hour work shift (Babbage 1832).

Throughout the twentieth century, more affluent countries moved away from agriculture and manufacturing and toward service and information activities (Machlup 1962; Rubin and Huber 1986). Among white-collar workers, the fastest growing occupations were clerical, professional, and technical workers, and managers and administrators. In the United States, jobs in manufacturing fell from 27 percent in 1920 to 13 percent in 1999. Six factors contributed to this shift, which accelerated throughout the century. First, third-world and developing economies did more manufacturing while so-called advanced societies shifted toward services. Second, knowledge-intense and information-intense products and services grew, and production of traditional products made more intensive use of information and knowledge. Third, business invested in equipment to support information work. Fourth, within manufacturing, knowledge workers and information workers replaced manual production workers. Fifth, workers gained more education and information-processing skills. Sixth, new kinds of knowledge-intense and information-intense organizations emerged that focused on production, processing, and distribution of information (Laudon and Starbuck 2001).

5.2.4 The Term 'Organization' Evolves and Splits into Several Concepts

Linguistic practices support the inference that people began to see organizations as a general category around the turn of the century. Usage of 'organization' to denote voluntary associations appears to have begun late in the nineteenth century, and by the 1920s, some people had started to use 'organization' as a general term denoting the general category of formally constituted medium-sized social systems.

The word 'organization' derives from an ancient Indo-European root that also spawned the words 'organ' and 'work'. The Roman verb 'organizare' meant initially 'to furnish with organs so as to create a complete human being', but later Romans gave it the broader meaning 'to endow with a coordinated structure'. *Organizare* migrated from Latin into Old French. In 1488, the French language included the word 'organization', which an ancient dictionary defined self-reflexively as 'the state of an organized body'. At that time, people probably reserved the term for biological bodies.

Although dictionaries published between 1750 and 1840 do not mention this usage explicitly, around 1800 some writers began to use 'organization' to describe a property of societies. Dohrn-van Rossum (1977) attributed this new usage to proponents of the French Revolution. For example, in 1789, in a pamphlet that played an important role in initiating the French Revolution, Emmanuel-Joseph Sieyès declared: 'it is necessary to prove further that the noble order does not enter at all into the social organization; that it may indeed be a burden upon the nation.' But six years earlier, in 1783, Justus Möser, a German historian, wrote of 'the better organization of our political body', so it may be that this usage was inspired by the Romantic Movement, which fed the French Revolution but also appeared in every European country, the United States, and Latin America.

During disorder following the French Revolution, Claude-Henri Saint-Simon (1976) wrote about the dangers posed by uncontrolled individualism. He argued that superior social organization makes humans superior to other animals and enables humans to exploit their environment and to live at a high standard of prosperity. But, organization and equality are mutually inconsistent, he said, because organization requires hierarchy, subordination, and authority. He advocated reorganization of society by scientists and industrialists, to create a scientifically optimal division of labor that would produce social harmony, productivity, efficiency, and technological innovation. John Stuart Mill also spoke of societal-level social organization in 1829, as did Auguste Comte in 1865. Influenced by Herbert Spencer's (1862, 1876) ideas about societal evolution, Alfred Marshall (1892) explained that 'industrial organization' entails both differentiation and integration of economic activities. A French progress report dated 1840 used the phrase 'organization of work' to indicate production methods.

Two significant changes began during the late nineteenth century. First, people recognized that social groups smaller than societies may exhibit organization. Second, people started to use 'organization' to denote not a property of a social group, but the social group itself. Initially, however, the label 'organization' may have been restricted to voluntary associations: The *Durham University Journal* of 7 November 1894 said 'We now have in the University... somewhere about fifty-three different "Organisations," athletic, intellectual, literary, social, and religious.' Likewise, the *Century Dictionary* of 1902 said that organization meant either the act of organizing or something that is organized 'specifically—an organized body of persons, as a literary society, club, corporation, etc.' The *Catalogue Générale de la Librairie Française* had no entries for 'organization' in 1912, included voluntary scientific 'organizations' in 1915, and listed many kinds of 'organizations' in 1921. In 1920, the [American] National Association of Commercial Organization Secretaries published a text titled *Commercial Organizations* that is devoted to voluntary associations for business executives (Bruce 1920). Certainly, not many people were giving 'organization' the broad meaning it has in today's phrase 'organization theory'. The *Encyclopædia Britannica* of 1910 used the term only in the context of biology; early organization theorists such as Michels (1911) and Weber (1910–14) did not speak of organizations but of bureaucracies; Fayol (1916) spoke of 'social bodies'; and Urwick (1933*a*) spoke of 'governmental, ecclesiastical, military and business *structures*' (emphasis added).

Some people were giving 'organization' its contemporary meaning as a broad category of formally constituted social groups by the 1920s. Gutjahr (1920) observed that the word 'organization' has both a concrete meaning and an abstract one, the concrete meaning being exemplified by a commercial enterprise, the State, the Church, or the Army. Gutjahr also pointed out that whereas the components of some organizations were almost entirely human, a commercial enterprise combines people with equipment. Similarly, Davis (1928), the *Pitman Dictionary of Industrial Administration* (Lee 1928), and Mooney and Reiley (1931) explained 'organization' could mean a business firm.

5.2.5 Companies and Corporations become Immortal Persons

In one of the most implausible social constructions of the nineteenth and twentieth centuries, business and voluntary organizations changed from temporary special-purpose coalitions of specific owners into immortal legal persons having rights independently from their owners, members, or other stakeholders.

In Europe up to the late nineteenth century, almost all business organizations were sole proprietorships or partnerships, and a business entity was regarded as indistinguishable from its owners: any owner could unilaterally dissolve a business or make agreements on behalf of their businesses, and owners were liable for all debts incurred by their businesses and for any legal violations committed by their businesses. Indeed, under Greco-Roman law, partners in bankrupt businesses could be imprisoned or sold into slavery, so partners needed to have very great confidence in each other (Baskin and Miranti 1997). Such ownership imposed growing risks as enterprises grew larger and extended their geographic ranges.

Alternative forms of shared control emerged between the tenth and fifteenth centuries. First, to raise capital for expensive ventures, some partnerships sold transferable ownership shares. Small groups of senior partners controlled such partnerships. Second, Italian merchants invented a variety of ownership contracts for ventures encompassing a few voyages or short periods; the nouns 'company', 'college', and 'fraternity' derive from these arrangements. Later, the term 'company' denoted a partnership having a royal charter that granted it fixed-term monopoly rights for a specific form of manufacture or trade. Starting in the mid-1500s, some companies sold transferable ownership shares. These 'joint-stock companies' were usually ones that undertook expensive, risky ventures. Third, the label 'corporation', which had emerged originally to describe the Roman Catholic Church's claimed status as the embodiment of Jesus Christ, gradually spread to other collective bodies—monasteries, universities, craft guilds, municipalities, and the British Parliament. Corporations could own property and they had papal or royal charters that enabled them to persist indefinitely despite changes in the specific people who composed them. Thus, by the sixteenth century, companies were partnerships that engaged in manufacture or trade for fixed periods whereas corporations were collectivities that could legally exist indefinitely.

Improvements in sailing technology led European countries to expand their empires between the sixteenth and eighteen centuries, and joint-stock companies played important roles in these expansions (Arrighi, Barr, and Hisaeda 1999; Law 1986). By spreading risk across many people, joint-stock companies enabled the raising of large amounts of capital, and thus the constructing of multi-ship convoys and trading forts in remote lands. However, joint-stock companies remained quite unusual because they required royal charters. In this period, corporations, which also required royal charters, were often created to carry out public projects such as the construction and maintenance of roads.

By 1800, considerable variety had developed in forms of ownership, but proprietorships and partnerships vastly outnumbered joint-stock companies and corporations. The general perception seems to have been that joint-stock companies and corporations differed little from partnerships (Lamoreaux 2000). Legal decisions concerning joint-stock companies or corporations used plural pronouns and verbs just as did decisions concerning partnerships. Each company or corporation required a unique charter and, during the early part of the nineteenth century, these charters generally did not limit the liability of owners.

The nineteenth century brought many changes (Lamoreaux 2000). The American states competed with each other to attract businesses, and one medium for competition was legislation about business organization. More and more charters gave owners limited liability. The distinction disappeared between joint-stock companies and corporations. Legislatures stopped requiring each new enterprise to obtain a unique charter and, instead, they set up procedures by which people could create business corporations by filing standardized forms.

Most corporations were small, but the construction of railroads spurred the creation of corporations so large that they could not have been partnerships. British legislation also changed, culminating in a major revision in 1856 that made it much easier to form joint-stock companies (Wilson 1995). The number of British stockbrokerages more than tripled between 1800 and 1870 (Killick and Thomas 1970).

Confusion continued well into the twentieth century regarding the differences between corporations and partnerships. A focal issue was whether corporations were aggregates of their owners or were distinct from their owners. For instance, Machen (1911) asserted that a house could not be 'merely the sum of the bricks that compose it' for one could 'change many of the bricks without changing the identity of the house'. Gierke (1868–1913) put forth the idea that each corporation possesses a distinctive personality, and this notion progressively won supporters in Germany, then in France and Italy, and around the turn of the century in Britain and the United States. Legal decisions about corporations began to use singular pronouns and verbs, unlike decisions concerning partnerships (Laski 1916). Gradually, there came growing agreement in Europe and North America that a corporation possessed 'personhood' and was distinct from its owners (Lamoreaux 2000; Mark 1987). Rathenau (1917) proposed that many corporations no longer had permanent owners: 'The claims to ownership are subdivided in such a fashion, and are so mobile, that the enterprise assumes an independent life, as if it belonged to no one; it takes an objective existence, such as in earlier days was embodied only in state and church, in a municipal corporation, in the life of a guild or a religious order.'

The logical next step occurred during the 1930s, when some observers remarked that managers of corporations often act in ways that are inconsistent with the interests of stockholders. Berle and Means (1932: 313) surmised, 'The rise of the modern corporation has brought a concentration of economic power which can compete on equal terms with the modern state.' They reported that some corporations had grown so large that by 1930 the 200 largest ones controlled half of all corporate assets and a quarter of American assets. At the same time, stock ownership had been greatly dispersed and nearly all stockholders held very small fractions of the stock, with the result that stockholders of about half of the largest corporations could not exert effective control. Thus, in many cases, it was no longer realistic to think of managers as agents who were running businesses in the interest of owners:

On the one hand, the owners of passive property, by surrendering control and responsibility over the active property, have surrendered the right that the corporation should be operated in their sole interest.... At the same time, the controlling groups [managers], by means of the extension of corporate powers, have in their own interest broken the bars of tradition which require that the corporation be operated solely for the benefit of the owners of passive property. (1932: 311–12)

5.3 ORGANIZATION THEORY EMERGES

5.3.1 Organization Theory Takes Root in a Mechanistic Philosophical Tradition

Proposed generalizations about organizations began to appear shortly after 1850. At that time, scholars had recourse to two contradictory philosophical traditions regarding societies and their development (Mirowski 1994; Schumpeter 1912; Toulmin 1990). An older tradition characterized societies as history-dependent organisms, analogous to the bodies of animals. Social systems should not be regarded as mere aggregates of individuals for not only do individuals interact but societies contain many interacting subsystems. Occurrences blend concepts about what should happen with external factors such as accidents and temporary conditions, so explanations need to allow for the specifics of particular cases. Theories should describe the diversity of observed phenomena and fit them into evolutionary analytic frameworks. People are integrated creatures; human thinking occurs in human bodies; people have motives of which they are unconscious, and human actions are not always rational. Because people are not machines, it is both unrealistic and immoral to treat them as substitutable components in factories or bureaucracies.

A more 'modern' tradition that rose to prominence during the seventeenth century regarded societies as machine-like. This mechanistic tradition saw the natural universe as a system of clockwork that follows timeless and immutable laws and sought theories that describe these causal laws. Abstract generalizations are better than concrete descriptions because they focus on durable essentials. Although the animal nature of humans corrupts their behavior, people should isolate and suppress their animalistic urges and strive to act solely on the basis of rational thought, which gives human reason a machine-like quality. Factories and bureaucracies achieve high productivity and reliability by training people to behave uniformly and consistently and treating them as substitutable components. By using their rationality, people can create stable and effective social systems.

The mechanistic tradition gained popularity during the nineteenth century, which was a period of mechanical invention and of fascination with mechanical contrivances. Especially toward the end of the century, the proliferation of new machines and the successes of physical and chemical science sparked interest in theories that depicted people and social groups as mechanical systems. In the very first issue of the *American Journal of Psychology* in 1887, Charles S. Peirce addressed the then controversial topic of whether logical machines would be able to replicate human thought. Irving Fisher's doctoral dissertation of 1892 drew analogies between competitive economies and hydraulic systems.

A persistent topic of debate through many centuries has been the degree to which humans could exercise choice or control events, and both of the philosophic traditions made ambiguous statements regarding this issue. Mechanistic views of societies said people have very limited freedom to do what they please, but they also said people do not value freedom of choice because they act rationally and they can predict the consequences of their actions. Organismic views said societies can accommodate peculiarities and temporary deviations, but they also said societies must satisfy requirements about completeness and harmony. As a result, both traditions struggled to reconcile contradictions between societies' predictability and their controllability, between the stability of social arrangements and humans' ability to engineer them. A mechanistic system is very predictable because human intervention cannot affect it much. If people could control social arrangements, they would be able to turn the causal processes into unpredicted directions. Perhaps this debate explains the slowness with which observers came to see organization members as decision-makers. Not until the late 1930s did anyone—Barnard (1937/1938), as it turned out—assert that decision-making is an important activity within organizations; and decision-making remained a marginal theme in organization theory until the late 1950s.

A few thinkers explored the middle ground between these polar philosophical traditions. John Stuart Mill, for example, drew distinctions between the more permanent and the more volatile economic laws, and Karl Marx asserted that 'natural laws' are no more than descriptions of temporary social relations that happen to exist at a particular time. However, the two traditions are sufficiently dissimilar that it was and remains quite difficult to integrate them.

Wolin (1960) took it as significant that Simon (1952) used mechanical language to describe organizations; he interpreted this as a sign that Simon was attributing rationality to organizations. In this, Wolin may have been placing too much emphasis on Simon's personal input. Even the earliest generalizations about organizations tended to treat organizations as almost-mechanistic systems, and rational behavior has long been a component of the mechanistic philosophical tradition.

From the 1860s to the 1960s, two themes dominated organization-theoretic writings. One theme was 'Bureaucracy has defects.' The earliest organizational writings by sociologists and economists focused on governmental bureaucracies, and they paid much attention to how bureaucratic governments affect societies. They expressed particular concern about bureaucracies' propensity to ignore their environments. The second theme was 'How can organizations operate more effectively?' The earliest organizational writings by consultants and former managers discussed factories and other businesses, and they concentrated on identifying structural properties that influence organizations' productivity and responsiveness to top managers. The mechanistic orientations of the consultants and former managers are easier to understand because almost all these people expressed admiration for Scientific Management and mechanistic conceptions seemed to make it feasible to analyze organizations and to render them more efficient or effective. The mechanistic orientations of the early sociologists are more mysterious, since many of them had studied in academic traditions that viewed societies as history-dependent organisms.

Thus, organization theory's birth was motivated by both perceived threats and perceived opportunities. Those who wrote about bureaucracy generally saw it as a repulsive threat to something—good government, control by rulers, individual freedom. Those who wrote about organization design generally saw organizations as offering attractive opportunities for something—efficient production, control by owners, cooperative effort.

5.3.2 Theme 1: Bureaucracy has Defects, some of which Generalize to other Organizations

Given that Gournay defined bureaucracy as an undesirable form of government administration, it is not too surprising that 'bureaucracy' has generally had a bad connotation. Nearly everyone who has written about bureaucracy has complained about it; almost the only authors who found value in bureaucracy were German economists and sociologists writing between 1870 and 1915. It is also not too surprising that the authors who have pointed to bureaucracy's deficiencies have each defined it differently. Bureaucracy has tended to mean not a specific form of organization so much as some undesirable aspects of any organization.

In 1861 John Stuart Mill contrasted representative democracy with several governmental forms, including monarchical, aristocratic, and bureaucratic. He defined bureaucracy as government by trained officials, but he did not even mention bureaucracy in his chapter about the 'executive functionaries' in a representative democracy even though he discussed the education and selection of such personnel at length, so he evidently saw bureaucracy as a government without elected personnel. Mill asserted that bureaucracy exhibits higher political skill and ability than any other governmental form except representative democracy. Bureaucracy 'accumulates experience, acquires well-tried and well-considered traditional maxims, and makes provision for appropriate practical knowledge in those who have the actual conduct of affairs' (1861: 122). But bureaucracies are burdened 'by the immutability of their maxims; and still more, by the universal law that whatever becomes a routine loses its vital principle, and...goes on revolving mechanically'. Bureaucracy's weakness arises from its internal consistency; 'conflicting influences are required to keep one another alive and efficient' (1861: 123–4).

The economic historian Gustav Friedrich von Schmoller (1898) lauded the achievements of the Prussian government, which, he concluded, had been able to overcome feudal traditions and to bring about reforms because its administrators had stood above the selfish interests of social classes. He emphasized that in the Prussian state, government administrators were professionals with specialized training who were pursuing careers as civil servants, and they operated within a legal framework that defined their rights and duties. Such administration depends, he said, on the existence of a well-developed educational system. There was, however, risk that the professional administrators might act inconsistently with the will of the state's ruler and that they might form a new social class with its own selfish interests.

During the 1910s, the sociologists Robert Michels and Max Weber extrapolated the notion of bureaucracy from governmental units to other kinds of organizations. But, their bureaucracies were rather restricted organizations, being no more than administrative hierarchies that performed well-defined tasks.

In 1884 the Italian political scientist Gaetano Mosca published a book arguing that an effective organized political minority could dominate an unorganized majority. Michels took Mosca's idea an additional step (Albertoni 1987). Using arguments that reflect the German tradition of dialectic reasoning, Michels (1911/1999) pointed out that voluntary associations, such as political parties and labor unions, develop bureaucracies that become ends in themselves. To act rapidly and efficiently, bureaucracies create 'a certain administrative unity' and they tend not to listen to their constituents. Since bureaucracies' centralizing tendencies conflict with the democratic norms of voluntary associations, the associations have both centralizing and decentralizing tendencies. '[T]he various tendencies towards decentralization . . . , while they suffice to prevent the formation of a single gigantic oligarchy, result merely in the creation of a number of smaller oligarchies, each of which is no less powerful within its own sphere' (1911/1999: 202). On the one hand, 'Democracy is inconceivable without organization' (p. 61); and on the other hand, there are 'immanent oligarchical tendencies in every kind of human organization which strives for the attainment of definite ends' (p. 50).

Scholars have made divergent interpretations of Weber's writings, which use complex language that contains ambiguity and inconsistency. Weber (1910–14) attempted to understand social phenomena in terms of idealized groups of mutually reinforcing properties that he called 'ideal-types'. One of these ideal-types was bureaucracy. Thus, Weber saw bureaucracy as an idealization of a type of organization rather than as a description of actual organizations, yet he applied this label to a very wide range of contemporary and historic organizations that did not necessarily possess all properties of the ideal-type. Because he emphasized the technical virtues of bureaucracy and described its deficiencies as contingent possibilities, his characterizations resemble prescriptions for how to organize effectively. The examples that Weber cited included many ancient organizations—such as the Egyptian army, the late Roman government, the treasury of the Norman state—but he also argued that 'modern bureaucracy' was a new and pervasive organizational form that was especially well suited to meet the complex administrative challenges posed by a capitalist industrial society (Heydebrand 1994). According to Weber, bureaucratic administrative practices gained impetus from the spread of democracy, from demands for fast accurate business transactions, and from increases in public services such as police, roads, waterways, and railroads. He expressed a fear that the spread of bureaucratic practices would create an 'iron cage' of rational thought and impersonal relationships that would make human life less enjoyable.

The properties that Weber attributed to modern bureaucracy include: (a) division of labor into assigned areas of authority, (b) clear hierarchy of authority, (c) administrative actions based on formal rules rather than personal relationships, (d) written documents, (e) functional specialization, and (f) full-time jobs that convert administration into a vocation. He said the combination of a secure salary, career prospects, cohesion among colleagues, and vulnerability to public criticism compels bureaucrats to apply rules impersonally and mechanistically, but these properties also make bureaucracies resist change and make governmental bureaucracies resist control by parliaments or rulers. Weber stated:

> The decisive reason for the development of bureaucratic organization has always been its purely technical superiority over every other form. A fully developed bureaucratic apparatus compares to other forms as do mechanical to non-mechanical modes of production. Precision, speed, clarity, accessibility of files, continuity, discretion, unity, strict subordination, avoidance of friction and material and personal expenses—all these attain an optimal level under bureaucratic... forms of administration and by means of trained individual officials.... (Heydebrand 1994: 77–8)

What made 'modern bureaucracy' distinctively modern, Weber said, was that functional specialization 'presumes a thorough training in an area of specialization' (1994: 61). As a qualitative statement, this rationale for modernity makes no sense, because clerical workers and administrators have been receiving training and serving apprenticeships more than 4,000 years. However, there is no question that after the mid-1800s, much higher percentages of the populace were literate, were learning law, accounting, and clerical skills, and were attending schools of business.

The economist Alfred Marshall (1919: 850) asserted that bureaucracy was more appropriate to Germany than to Britain: 'although the semi-military organization of Imperial Germany was well adapted for the methods of bureaucratic control, other methods are needed by a nation which governs its own Government.' Even though 'each of the numerous Government offices in Westminster is in some measure bureaucratic', these partial bureaucracies were rule-bound impediments to innovation. Thus, Marshall observed that the effectiveness of organizational forms relates to their societal contexts, and that different organizational forms produce different consequences, but he did not discuss these relationships.

By the 1930s and 1940s, complaints about governmental bureaucracies could be heard in France, Germany, the United Kingdom, and the United States. Mannheim (1935) protested that societies were falling increasingly under the monopolistic control of administrative bureaucracies staffed by isolated administrative castes. He observed 'universal alarm at the growth of bureaucracy' based on 'the old belief that institutions and organizations are perfectly rigid, and incapable of developing new attitudes of mind' (1940: 325). Mannheim expressed particularly distress over the 'cold impersonal atmosphere' in 'the new bureaucracy', yet he advocated a new form of 'objective justice' such that 'emotion becomes attached to the handling of the case and not to the individual who is helped' (1940: 322).

Warnotte (1937) also remarked on bureaucracy's dreadful reputation. He observed that French dictionaries assigned two meanings to the word 'bureaucracy', one being the spreading influence of government officials upon business firms, the other being abusive actions by administrators. 'Administration, in the minds of those who are governed, is something ugly, incomprehensible, mysterious, irritating, and incompetent. Bureaucracy owes the birth of this sentiment in the populace to its frequent and unexpected intrusions into the life of citizens, to its ambition to observe all rules, without daring to risk diverse experiences and impeding innovation with an excessive lethargy' (1937: 258). Warnotte blamed the abusive actions on adherence to rules, conformity to precedents, and officials' acclimatization to their jobs, 'la déformation professionelle du fonctionnaire'.

Merton and Selznick restated the foregoing ideas in more formal language. Merton (1940) articulated three processes that had been identified by Michels, Mannheim, and Warnotte. First, an emphasis on reliability fosters adherence to rules. Rules become ends in themselves and lose their relationship to the purposes for which they originated. As a result, bureaucracies resist changes and have trouble adapting. Second, similarities among colleagues keep them from competing with each other and promote *esprit de corps*. As a result, the entrenched interests of bureaucrats take precedence over their concern for clients or their responsiveness to superiors. Third, depersonalized relationships with clients and general, abstract rules cause bureaucrats to ignore the peculiarities of individual cases. As a result, bureaucrats appear arrogant and haughty. Selznick (1943) contributed a formal restatement of Michels's ideas about how bureaucracies take actions that contradict their espoused norms. He emphasized the idea that organizations informally modify their procedures to obtain 'operationally relevant solutions' to problems that arise daily. The need for cooperative effort induces organizations to delegate functions to officials. Nominally, officials are supposed to be agents for someone else—members of voluntary associations, owners of firms, the citizenry—but the interests of officials do not always align with the interests of those they represent. The officials are able to deflect organizations' goals because they control bureaucracies and they have more expertise than do the people they represent.

Von Mises (1944: 1) observed that nearly everyone interpreted the term 'bureaucracy' as a 'disparaging criticism'. 'Even in Prussia, the paragon of authoritarian government, nobody wanted to be called a bureaucrat.' He (1944: 2) offered his

opinion that even though 'everyone seems to agree that bureaucracy is an evil,...
nobody has ever tried to determine in unambiguous language what bureaucracy
really means.' After much debate, he finally defined bureaucratic management as
'management in strict accordance with the law and the budget' (p. 43), and he said
that people resort to bureaucratic management to handle 'affairs which cannot be
checked by economic calculation' (p. 47). He devoted most of his book to bureaucratic management's undesirable effects, including complacency and regrettable
psychological effects.

World War II produced expansions of central governments and so made more
people aware of bureaucratic behaviors. Thus, the postwar period brought more
commentaries about bureaucracy. However, bureaucracies were not the only organizations that elicited complaints. By the late 1950s, complaints about organizations had extended beyond governmental bureaucracies. One of the most widely
read and influential documents of the 1950s was Whyte's (1956) best-selling and
influential critique of American corporate society. Whyte asserted that America was
in the grip of a troubling 'Social Ethic'. He said, 'Its major propositions are three: a
belief in the group as the source of creativity; a belief in "belongingness" as the
ultimate need of the individual; and a belief in the application of science to achieve
the belongingness.' As a result, many employees, at all levels of management and in
technical specialties, were allowing their employing organizations to dominate their
lives and the lives of their families. Organizations were telling employees how to
dress and to behave. They were cutting off employees' roots in communities by
moving them and their families frequently. They were shaping employees' personalities.

In a book that influenced many academics, Argyris (1957) shifted the discussion
from sociology to psychology when he spelled out some potential effects of organizations on employees' personalities. Young children, he said, are passive, dependent, subordinates who lack self-awareness and who have limited behavior
repertoires, short-term interests, and short time horizons. Through their lifetimes,
people ought to be maturing into active, independent adults who have self-
awareness, diverse behavior repertoires, long-term interests, and long time
horizons. But, organizations give workers minimal control over their activities,
encourage the use of superficial abilities, and require workers to be passive,
dependent, and subordinate and to have short time horizons. Thus, organizations
impede people's development and foster unhealthy personalities. Argyris called for
more academic research into 'organizational behavior' to counteract these unfortunate effects of organizations.

Thus, bureaucracy motivated organization theory with both propulsion and
repulsion. Some writers sought to describe bureaucracy's attractive qualities;
many writers sought to describe its deficiencies and harmful effects. Since more
admirers wrote earlier and more critics wrote later, the general trend was to
formulate organization theory as the study of tribulations.

5.3.3 Theme 2: How can Organizations Operate more Effectively?

Weber's research method was to think of examples a specific type of organization, the bureaucracy, and to try to infer what was similar or dissimilar about these examples. Other writers used much the same method during the 1920s and 1930s to look for properties common to organizations of all kinds. Like Michels and Weber, most of them took a limited view of organizations as being merely administrative hierarchies with well-defined tasks to perform, and they thought they were creating rigorous, scientific theories (e.g. Urwick 1933*b*). But unlike Michels and Weber, they used the plain language of managers, they rarely attempted to compare organizations from different eras, and they focused their thinking on how to make organizations more effective: How should organizations be organized? Their prescriptions resemble 'The Officials of Chou', but unlike the authors of 'The Officials of Chou', they sought to generalize across many organizations and they explicitly recognized that administrative hierarchies function as integrated systems.

Textbooks written during the very early years of the twentieth century talked about alternative ways to organize administrative hierarchies and to standardize procedures (Elbourne 1914; Kimball 1913), but they devoted little attention to organizations as integrated systems. These books often spoke of 'systems', but when they did so, they were talking about the need for organizations to have explicit procedures.[3] However, a gradual change took place, and documents written during the 1920s began to view organizations as integrated systems and to discuss the structures of these systems. In one of the earliest of these works, Gutjahr (1920) devoted a chapter to ways in which a commercial enterprise can or should adapt to its economic environment. He discussed product specialization, the failure of unsuccessful businesses, horizontal and vertical integration, alliances and joint ownership, choice of location, and advertising.

Child (1969) credited Frederick W. Taylor and Henri Fayol with rousing interest in the merits of different organizational structures (also see Urwick 1956). A highly influential and controversial author and speaker, Taylor focused his attention on work design and related topics that lie outside the domain of this chapter. But, he (1903) did experiment with 'functional management', in which each supervisor concentrated on a narrow range of 'functions' and each worker had no less than eight supervisors who attended to different aspects of the worker's job.

A retired business executive, Fayol became involved in the reorganization of government agencies, and as a result, he formulated prescriptions that he believed to be generally applicable in all kinds of organizations. According to Fayol (1923),

---

[3] Shenhav (1995) argued that industrial and mechanical engineers were treating organizations as systems between 1900 and 1920. As I read those works, they were talking about the need for systematic (efficient, consistent, orderly) procedures.

the word 'administration' had meant only government officials in 1910 when people met for the First International Congress of Administrative Science. Fayol saw himself as broadening the meaning of 'administration' to encompass, 'not only the public service but enterprises of every size and description, of every form and purpose. All undertakings require planning, organization, command, co-ordination and control, and in order to function properly, all must observe the same general principles' (1937: 101).[4]

Both Fayol and Taylor had enthusiastic adherents in France, and so Chevalier (1928) sought to reconcile the two viewpoints, arguing that they proposed complementary principles rather than contradictory ones. He also debated the generalizability of organizational prescriptions across cultures: he speculated about the implications of his stereotypes about the Americans, English, and Germans, and he proposed that the French would appreciate methods of rational organization that respect workers' individuality. French workers do not resist following orders, he said; they only resist following bad orders.

An early management text by Ralph C. Davis (1928) recognized that an organization includes workers as well as executives, and it took a rather broad view of organizational properties that should concern managers. For example, Davis observed that assignments of responsibilities typically take account of managers' personal abilities, personalities, experience, family connections, ambitions, and intraorganizational politics. He also said organizations benefit from *esprit de corps*, and 'this, in turn, depends on the creation of an ideal for which the whole organization is striving' (1928: 43). He described five basic 'organization types', as well as various subtypes, but he restricted these to alternative hierarchical arrangements.

Dennison (1931) expressed skepticism about the general validity of 'principles of organization structure'. Tasks change. Some tasks impose restrictions on organizational forms whereas other tasks can be performed well by very diverse organizations. In addition, organizations tend to grow more rigid as they grow older and larger, with the result that they become insensitive to gradual changes. One implication is that organizations need to reorganize, to evolve continuously.

---

[4] Despite Fayol's belief that 'administration' had meant only government officials in 1910, just four years later Elbourne (1914) published a large book titled *Factory Administration and Accounts* that assumed readers well understood the usage of 'administration' in the context of factories. However, Lewis's (1896) book on *The Commercial Organisation of Factories* says nothing about 'administration'.

Fayol (1916) formulated a prescriptive 'Administrative Theory' that focused on five functions performed by a managerial hierarchy: planning, organization, coordination, command, and control. He asserted that managers with adequate knowledge of this Administrative Theory could successfully manage organizations of every type. Almost three decades later, Edward H. Litchfield (1956) advocated very similar ideas as the dean of Cornell's Graduate School of Business and Public Administration. Litchfield had been successful as a military, business, and academic administrator. He argued that administration is the same 'in industrial, commercial, educational, military, and hospital organizations'. He launched *Administrative Science Quarterly* to promote the development of a general theory of the 'administrative process', in which he included decision-making, programming, communications, controlling, and evaluating.

A second implication is that organizations need to balance mobility with stability, flexibility with equilibrium.

The automobile executive James Mooney and Alan Reiley (1931) inquired what functions do organizations need to perform in order to operate effectively. They sought to identify the common properties of all kinds of organizations, the properties that make them distinctive social entities. They selected three key properties, which they called principles: coordination, hierarchy, and functional differentiation. Following Anderson's (1929) prescriptions for logic, they developed a systems theory of organization that assigned to each principle a causal process and an effect. In an effort to marshal empirical evidence that was unusually systematic for its time, they then discussed evidence about these principles in governments, the Roman Catholic Church, military organizations, and industrial firms.

Several other authors followed the lead of Fayol, Davis, and Mooney and Reiley in searching for general properties of organizations that could lead to prescriptions: Graicunas (1933) analyzed the combinatorial implications of different spans of control. Urwick (1933a, 1933b, 1934) contrasted the contributions of Fayol and Mooney and Reiley, and offered his thoughts on methods of coordination, spans of control, and especially relations between line and staff. Elbourne (1934) listed many principles that should guide organizations or managers; particularly interesting are his principles for treating organizational arrangements as experiments. Gaus (1936: 90) reviewed various organizational principles and concluded limply that organizing should be 'a relating of individuals so that their efforts may be more effective'. Gulick (1937) also offered prescriptions regarding spans of control, relations between line and staff, and methods of coordination, and analyzed the merits of alternative forms of decentralization (purpose, product, clientele, location).

Chester Barnard (1937/1938: p. ix), a retired executive, protested that

the social scientists—from whatever side they approached—just reached the edge of organization as I experienced it, and retreated. Rarely did they seem to me to sense the processes of coordination and decision that underlie a large part at least of the phenomena they described. More important, there was lacking much recognition of formal organization as a most important characteristic of social life, and as being the principle structural aspect of society itself.

In particular, Barnard complained that theories rooted in observations about governmental and church organizations had overstated the importance of formal authority, and that theories rooted in economics had overstated the importance of 'intellectual' processes as distinguished from emotional and physiological ones. In comparison with prior authors, Barnard's analyses exhibit more complexity and much more awareness of psychological factors. He defined an organization as any consciously coordinated system of cooperative activities, and argued that every organization needs willing participants, purpose, communication, effectiveness, and efficiency. Large, complex organizations, he said, are composed of many

small organizations involving from two to twenty persons, some of them constituted formally and others informally. The component organizations must be small
enough that people are able to communicate and lead effectively. Barnard proceeded to discuss (a) alternative bases for specialization, (b) the economy of
inducements that organizations offer members and the contributions they receive
from members, (c) the properties of authoritative communications, and (d) the
properties of organizational decision-making. He ended his analysis by discussing
various functions performed by executives, the key element being that executives do
'the specialized work of *maintaining* the organization in operation' (1937/1938: 215).

Barnard introduced the then novel ideas that decision-making is an important
activity performed by executives and that organizations influence executives' decisions. Simon (1944, 1947), a professor with strong interest in the academic implications of actual administrative practices, spelled out some ways in which
organizations affect decision-making. The inputs to decisions include authority,
organizational loyalties, efficiency criteria, intraorganizational communications,
and plans, and then after they are made, decisions become subject to review for
their correctness. Both Barnard and Simon were characterizing organizations as
settings for dynamic processes and they were asserting the relevance of social
psychology for understanding these processes. Before 1950, Barnard and Simon
were the only writers who paid much attention to decision-making or information-
processing in organizations. Theories of leadership did not discuss decision-making
skills or communication skills. Although economists portrayed firms as choosing
prices or output quantities, they assumed that firms had perfect information and
unlimited analytic abilities; some economists even argued that the decision-making
and information-processing within firms could not matter because any firm that
took suboptimal actions would go bankrupt. Changes began during the 1940s and
1950s, when some economists began to talk about possible limitations on economists' theories, and some social psychologists studied problem-solving by small
groups, in which different group members played different roles. In addition, in the
1950s, a few psychologists began to use computer programs as models of human
problem-solving (Laudon and Starbuck 2001; Salgado, Starbuck, and Mezias 2002).

Barnard and Simon described organizations as settings in which individuals
make decisions; they did not describe organizations as decision-making systems.
In fact, the ideas that organizations per se process information and make decisions
did not appear until the late 1950s and early 1960s. A conceptual shift became visible
in 1958 when Forrester and March and Simon described organizations as information processors. Then in 1963, Cyert and March portrayed organizations as
systems that learn and they described some organizational decision processes in
detail. The contributions by Forrester, March and Simon, and Cyert and March
emphasized the importance of rules in organizational behavior: organizations are
understandable and predictable because they behave consistently, because they act
like machines.

In contrast with the writings about bureaucracy, the prescriptive literature said little about organizations' deficiencies and generally portrayed organizations as offering opportunities. Most of the prescriptive writers sought to raise productivity, efficiency, or morale, but Barnard and Simon saw organizations as offering opportunities to apply social psychology.

5.3.4 The Themes Merge, Organizational Research becomes more 'Scientific', and Empirical Methods become more Public

The late 1940s and early 1950s saw two changes in the character of writings about organization theory, and Selznick participated significantly in both developments. For one thing, the two streams of thought about organizations—sociological writings about bureaucracy and managerial writings about organizational effect-iveness—discovered each other. For another thing, authors began to speak about the empirical bases for their theories.

Selznick (1948) led the integration of sociological and managerial streams of thought. Acknowledging influence by the writings of Barnard, Dennison, Gaus, Mooney and Reiley, and Urwick, he departed from the sociological focus on 'bureaucracy' and framed his discussions in more general language about 'organiza-tions' and 'formal organizations'. He acknowledged as well influence by Parsons, Malinowski, MacIver, and Merton upon his discussion of 'structural-functional analysis', and his overall discussion had a distinctly sociological flavor. Another step in the direction of integration was taken by the *Reader in Bureaucracy* (Merton *et al.* 1952), which drew excerpts from many different sources. March and Simon (1958) pushed integration even farther by drawing ideas and findings from artificial intelligence, cognitive psychology, economics, human-resources management, industrial engineering, industrial psychology, political science, public administra-tion, the psychology of small groups, scientific management, sociology, and strategic management.

As some were integrating the managerial and bureaucracy streams of thought, others were attempting to introduce new themes. Barnard and Simon had advo-cated the relevance of social psychology, and Simon (1946, 1947) had voiced a need for more 'scientific' studies of organizations. In particular, Simon attacked the idea that principles of organization and management are useful, and he pointed out that every principle seemed to contradict an equally plausible principle. He asserted that a more 'scientific' approach to the study of organizations would eliminate the contradictions. Simon spelled out this idea of a 'scientific' organization theory in three more articles and a book. First, he (1950: 4) predicted, 'we are in time going to have theory in management—theory of the kind that predicts reality, and not the kind that is contrasted with practice'. As examples of the kinds of theorizing he deemed relevant, he cited game theory, linear programming, servomechanisms, computers, and laboratory experiments with small group communication. Second, Simon, Smithburg, and Thompson (1950) produced a textbook about governmental organizations that discussed many of the topics that have attracted research in the second half of the twentieth century: centralization–decentralization, teamwork, communication, intergroup relations, environmental change, and need for support from external stakeholders. Third, Simon (1952) sketched his vision of the scope of organization theory: decision-making in organizations, power in organizations, rational and nonrational behavior in organizations, stability and change in organizations, specialization and division of work, and relations between organizations and their environments. Finally, he (1952–3) published an algebraic analysis that compared the economic theory of the firm with 'O-theory', in which organizations need only survive, not maximize profits, and participants receive inducements to make contributions.

The general norm throughout the first half of the century was that authors said nothing about their sources of data, and this pattern continued into the late 1940s. For example, the *Journal of Social Issues* devoted one of its first issues to bureaucracy. The contributions to this issue described bureaucracies or their effects (Watson 1945a, b; Brady 1945), but none of these articles described the bases for their observations. Likewise, Bendix (1947: 507) reviewed assorted issues regarding bureaucracy without identifying a specific organization or organizations. He concluded that 'we cannot profit from the efficiency of large-scale organizations unless we succeed in making the initiative of the individual one of the principles of our organization' without adducing any data, even examples, to support his assertions. Also without identifying a specific organization or organizations, Selznick (1948) portrayed organizations' behaviors as specific instances of 'social action' and advocated the use of 'structural-functional analysis' that seeks to explain observed behaviors in terms of 'stable needs and self-defensive mechanisms'. As an example of structural-functional analysis, he discussed organizations' use of cooptation to deal with opposition arising in their environments. Although Selznick's remarks derived in part from his study of the Tennessee Valley Authority, he did not mention this: this omission implies that the norms for sociological research did not require authors to refer to data.

During the late 1940s, some authors began to specify the kinds of data they were using as referents. In some instances, the specifications were quite vague. For example, Turner (1947) reported that navy disbursing officers during World War II did not function as 'ideal-type' bureaucrats insofar as 'rules become of secondary importance' (p. 348). Rules sometimes conflicted with the commands of their superior officers, and the disbursing officers treated their friends differently from others and they engaged in exchanges of favors with officers who controlled other resources. However, Turner did not describe how he observed navy disbursing officers. Similarly, Worthy (1950) described the use of employee surveys in Sears, Roebuck and Co. without presenting data. He said, 'The results of our research suggest that over-complexity of organizational structure is one of the most important and fundamental causes of poor management–employe relationships.... we have found that where jobs are broken down too finely, we are more likely to have both low output and low morale' (p. 174). In a book that he intended to offer advice to restaurant managers, Whyte (1948) used interviews in Chicago restaurants to illustrate sociological concepts such as social status, clique, race relations, and informal organization. Still another example is Stewart's (1951) report on administrative processes in the Selective Service System during World War II.

Selznick (1949) and Jaques (1951) forwarded data-based research by providing book-length case studies. Selznick used his study of the Tennessee Valley Authority (TVA) to illustrate the use of cooptation. While arguing that 'All formal organizations are molded by forces tangential to their rationally ordered structures and stated goals' (p. 251), he interpreted the TVA's behavior as illustrating 'unanticipated consequence in social action'. Unanticipated consequences occur because focusing on specific goals induces people to overlook seemingly irrelevant events and because commitments made earlier limit later options. However, Selznick's theoretical contributions may have been less influential than his methodological contribution of showing an explicit, detailed example. This methodological contribution demonstrated its transitional character in two ways. First, Selznick devoted only three paragraphs in his Preface to describing his research methodology. Second, he did not discuss the potential influence of his prior beliefs on his observations.

Two years later, Jaques (1951) and colleagues exhibited much more methodological sensitivity in their highly visible and influential case study of Glacier Metals Company. Not only did Jaques devote the first chapter to methodology, but the book contains many comments about data-gathering methods, about premises guiding inferences, and about the relations between the researchers and people in the company. In his Introduction to this book, Wilson (1951: p. xv) observed: 'In scientific work of all kinds there has been a growing realization of the part played by the observer himself as one factor determining his observations. Scientific research in relatively new fields of work shows the importance of the observer describing in detail his role, his methods, and his view of the character and limits of his field of observation.' The case study itself affords a good example of why organization theory should not be separated from organizational behavior, for it traced the interdependencies between the firm's origination, formal structural changes, management changes, internal politics, communication patterns, and people's feelings.

5.4 ORGANIZATION THEORY ORGANIZES

By the late 1950s, the writings about organizations were multiplying rapidly. *The Organization Man* and *The Man in the Grey Flannel Suit* had made the public aware of organizations' centrality (Whyte 1956; S. Wilson 1955). *Parkinson's Law* had made organizations a topic for laughter (Parkinson 1957). A number of sociologists went beyond the traditional focus on bureaucracy, with studies of diverse 'complex organizations'. Many sociologists published organizational studies during the late 1950s and those who did so came from the elite of American sociology. Political scientists discussed intraorganizational power relations and decision-making in governmental organizations. Economists, who had exhibited great disinterest in organizational factors, began to consider them for the first time when Marschak (1955) discussed the costs of communication within a 'team' and Penrose (1959) discussed the need for managerial activity to plan and implement expansion. Social psychologists discovered organizations as interesting settings for research, although few of them regarded organizations as coherent social systems. March and Simon (1958) provided a compendium that allowed scholars to explore findings and ideas from diverse fields.

By 1960 organization theorists had become much more numerous and many of them had high social status. Organization theory had arrived, and the following decades have offered it the beneficence of multiplying and expanding degree programs in business. Expansion and affluence have brought pressures to fragment and to become self-absorbed and irrelevant to environmental problems.

Pressures for organization theory to become self-absorbed and irrelevant to its environment have arisen partly from its growing size and rising status and partly from the relevance of its subject matter for degree programs in business. Collegiate business programs have provided steady and rapidly increasing funding after 1950. By 1956, nearly 43,000 Americans per year were graduating from collegiate business programs, and by 1998, this figure had more than quintupled to 233,000 per year. In 1956, just over 3,000 Americans per year were graduating from MBA programs, and by 1998, this figure had rocketed to more than 100,000 per year.

As organization theory has become larger and more respected, it has grown more autonomous from external constraints and more organized. Academics have gained latitude to define what is interesting or important to themselves. Research methodology has received ever more respect, and the most prevalent empiricism has been a stylized type that isolates the observer from the observed and allows the observer to maintain detachment. The subtopics within organization theory have proliferated and derived their popularity from their intellectual attractiveness. Organization theorists have created specialized divisions of professional associations and many specialized journals, including a few that have focused on subtopics within organization theory.

The themes that gave rise to organization theory have received little attention. Few organization theorists have focused on social problems associated with organizations. The old social problems still exist and new ones have appeared, but it is depressing to dwell on what is wrong, and business students are not eager to discuss the disadvantages associated with their future occupations. Few academic organization theorists have sought prescriptions for how organizations can become more productive, efficient, or effective. The frequent management fads—such as Japanese management, downsizing, re-engineering, teamwork, Quality Circles, Six-Sigma quality management, the Learning Organization, outsourcing, knowledge management—have been originated by managers and consultants. Although some academic organization theorists have studied the consequences of such management fads, the most prominent organization theorists have ignored them. The prominent organization theorists have also generally ignored long-run changes in organizations' characteristics that have been stimulated by technological and population changes such as rising educational levels, computerization, telecommunication capacities, or globalization of firms.

Pressures to fragment have originated in the social sciences that organization theory spans. Whereas hostile environments can induce a collective enterprise to coalesce, multiple but friendly environments create ambivalence about participation in collective enterprise. In the case of organization theory, one force toward fragmentation has come from the divide between psychology and sociology. Many social scientists with psychological orientations have defined their focal interest as 'organizational behavior' as distinguished from 'management' or 'organization theory'. 'Organization theory' has consequently been more closely associated with sociology. A second force toward fragmentation has come from teachers and practitioners of 'strategic management', who sought legitimacy by defining a distinctive behavioral domain. However, boundaries between these topics have remained ill-defined, and they have often contributed to strange interpretations of observations when organization theorists ignored issues they perceived to fall into the neighboring domains. Strategic management has itself shown a tendency to split into two domains, one more closely associated with economics and the other more closely associated with sociology or management. A third force toward fragmentation has been dissatisfaction with the effectiveness of existing social theories, which has induced organization theorists to experiment with a wide range of diverse theories. Because it deals with complex phenomena, organization theory has drawn productively from very diverse intellectual domains. However, newer ideas have supplemented older ideas rather than replaced them. For example, population ecology did not replace contingency theory; it added a dynamic perspective that supplemented contingency theory. As a result, contingency theory retained enthusiastic proponents while population ecology gained others. A fourth force toward fragmentation has been culture, as theories and methodologies have evolved differently in different societies.

A few integrating activities have restrained fragmentation and kept boundaries permeable. Foremost among these, have been three prominent academic journals that have bridged the fragments and continued to publish articles on diverse topics—*Administrative Science Quarterly, Academy of Management Journal,* and *Journal of Management Studies.* Likewise, the fragments have not affected the major periodicals for managers—such as *Harvard Business Review, Sloan Management Review, California Management Review,* and *Organization Dynamics.* Also, some researchers have crossed the boundaries between domains. For example, some strategy researchers have studied top-management teams, some organization theorists have applied evolutionary models to strategic changes, and some organizational-behavior researchers have studied managers' perceptions of strategic environments.

Organization theory has developed considerable complexity, so much complexity that doctoral students sometimes complain that it makes no sense to them. The students say they do not understand how the fragments of organization theory relate to each other, how they differ, what each has to offer. In particular, recognition has grown that organizations are quite heterogeneous. Since organizations are diverse and complex, and since they inhabit diverse and complex environments, the complexity of organization theory makes sense. But this complexity poses the classical dilemma of how complicated theories should be. Complex theories capture more aspects of what researchers observe, but they are hard to understand. Simple theories are easy to understand but they overlook phenomena that some people deem important.

References

ALBERTONI, ETTORE A. (1987). *Mosca and the Theory of Elitism,* English trans. Paul Goodrick. Oxford: Basil Blackwell.

ANDERSON, LOUIS F. (1929). *Das Logische, seine Getsetze und Kategorien.* Leipzig: Meiner.

ARGYRIS, CHRIS (1957). *Personality and Organization: The Conflict between System and the Individual.* New York: Harper & Row.

—— (1960). *Understanding Organizational Behavior.* Homewood, Ill.: Dorsey.

ARRIGHI, GIOVANNI, BARR, KENNETH, and HISAEDA, SHUJI (1999). 'The Transformation of Business Enterprise', in Giovanni Arrighi and Beverly J. Silver (eds.), *Chaos and Governance in the Modern World System.* Minneapolis: University of Minnesota Press.

BABBAGE, CHARLES (1832). *On the Economy of Machinery and Manufactures.* London: Charles Knight.

BARNARD, CHESTER I. (1937/1938). *The Functions of the Executive.* Lectures presented at the Lowell Institute, Boston. An expanded version was published as a book in 1938; Cambridge, Mass.: Harvard University Press. The quotation above is taken from the book.

BASKIN, JONATHON BARRON, and MIRANTI, PAUL J., Jr. (1997). *A History of Corporate Finance.* Cambridge: Cambridge University Press.

BENDIX, REINHARD (1947). 'Bureaucracy: The Problem and its Setting'. *American Sociological Review*, 12: 493–507.

BERLE, ADOLF A., Jr., and MEANS, GARDINER C. (1932). *The Modern Corporation and Private Property*. New York: Macmillan.

BIOT, E. (1851). *Le Tcheou-Li*. Paris: L'Imprimerie Nationale.

BOULTON, WILLIAM H. (1931). *The Pageant of Transport through the Ages*. London: Sampson Low, Marston (also New York: Benjamin Blom, 1969).

BOWEN, JAMES (1981). *A History of Western Education*, iii. New York: St. Martin's Press.

BRADY, ROBERT A. (1945). 'Bureaucracy in Business'. *Journal of Social Issues*, 1 Dec.: 32–43.

BRUCE, WILLIAM GEORGE (1920). *Commercial Organizations, Their Function, Operation and Service*. Milwaukee, Wis.: Bruce Publishing Company.

CAMERON, RONDO E. (1993). *Concise Economic History of the World* (2nd edn). New York: Oxford University Press.

CHAN, WELLINGTON K. K. (1998). 'Tradition and Change in the Chinese Business Enterprise: The Family Firm Past and Present'. *Chinese Studies in History*, 31/3–4: 127–44.

CHANDLER, ALFRED D., Jr. (1977). *The Visible Hand: The Managerial Revolution in American Business*. Cambridge, Mass.: Belknap.

—— (1980). 'The United States: Seedbed of Managerial Capitalism', in Alfred D. Chandler, Jr. and Herman Daems (eds.), *Managerial Hierarchies: Comparative Perspectives on the Rise of the Modern Industrial Enterprise*. Cambridge, Mass.: Harvard University Press.

CHEVALIER, JEAN (1928). *La Technique de l'organization des enterprises*. Paris: Langlois.

CHILD, JOHN (1969). *British Management Thought: A Critical Analysis*. London: Allen & Unwin.

CYERT, RICHARD M., and MARCH, JAMES G. (1963). *A Behavioral Theory of the Firm*. Englewood Cliffs, NJ: Prentice-Hall.

DAVIS, RALPH CURRIER (1928). *The Principles of Factory Organization and Management*. New York: Harper.

DENNISON, HENRY STURGIS (1931). *Organization Engineering*. New York: McGraw-Hill.

DOHRN-VAN ROSSUM, GERHARD (1977). *Politischer Körper, Organismus, Organisation: Zur Geschichte naturaler Metaphorik un Begriichkeit in der politischen Sprache*. Dissertation, Universität Bielefeld.

DREEBEN, ROBERT (1968). *On What Is Learned in School*. Reading, Mass.: Addison-Wesley.

EDWARDS, JOHN RICHARD, and NEWELL, EDMUND (1991). 'The Development of Industrial Cost and Management Accounting before 1850: A Survey of the Evidence'. *Business History*, 33: 35–57.

ELBOURNE, EDWARD TREGASKISS (1914). *Factory Administration and Accounts*. London: Longmans, Green.

—— (1934). *Fundamentals of Industrial Administration*. London: MacDonald & Evans.

ENGELS, FREDERICK (1872). 'On Authority'. First published in 1874 in the Italian periodical *Almanacco Repubblicano*. English translation taken from Robert C. Tucker (ed.), *The Marx–Engels Reader* (2nd edn, 1978) (New York: W. W. Norton). Engels's complete writings are on the web site: http://www.marxists.org/archive/marx/works/index.htm.

FAYOL, HENRI (1916). 'Administration industrielle et général'. *Bulletin de la Société de l'Industrie Minérale*, third issue. The 1916 document was a revision of a 1908 document 'Exposé des principes généraux d'administration', which was prepared for the Jubilee Congress of the Société de l'Industrie Minérale. It was published as a book in 1925, *Administration Industrielle et Général* (Paris: Dunod). J. A. Coubrough made an English translation that was first published in 1930: *Industrial and General Administration* (Geneva: International Management Association).

FAYOL, HENRI (1923). *The Administrative Theory in the State.* Address before the Second International Congress of Administrative Science, Brussels. An English translation by Sarah Greer is included in Luther H. Gulick and Lyndall F. Urwick (eds.), *Papers on the Science of Administration* (New York: Institute of Public Administration, Columbia University, 1937). The quotation in this chapter is taken from this 1937 translation.

FISHER, IRVING (1892). 'Mathematical Investigations in the Theory of Value and Prices'. *Transactions of the Connecticut Academy of Arts and Sciences*, 9/1: 1–124.

FLOOD, MERLE M. (1951). *Report of a Seminar on Organization Science.* Santa Monica, Calif.: The Rand Corporation, Research Memorandum RM-709.

FORRESTER, JAY W. (1958). 'Industrial Dynamics—A Major Breakthrough for Decision Makers'. *Harvard Business Review*, 36/4: 37–66.

FOUCAULT, MICHEL (1975). *Surveiller et punir: Naissance de la prison.* Paris: Gallimard. English translation published in 1977 with the title *Discipline and Punish* (London: Allen Lane).

GAUS, JOHN M. (1936). 'A Theory of Organization in Public Administration', in John M. Gaus, Leonard D. White, and Marshall E. Dimock, *The Frontiers of Public Administration.* Chicago: University of Chicago Press.

GEORGE, CLAUDE S., Jr. (1968). *The History of Management Thought.* Englewood Cliffs, NJ: Prentice-Hall.

GIERKE, OTTO FRIEDRICH VON (1868–1913). *Das deutsche Genossenschaftsrecht* (4 vols.). Diverse publishers. Portions of this large work have been translated into English, as follows: Selections from vol. i, trans. Mary Fischer, *Community in Historical Perspective* (New York: Cambridge University Press, 1990). Selections from vol. iii, trans. Frederic W. Maitland, *Political Theories of the Middle Age* (Cambridge: The University Press, 1900 and Bristol, England: Thoemmes Press, 1996). Five sections of vol. iv, trans. Ernest Barker, *Natural Law and the Theory of Society, 1500 to 1800* (Cambridge: The University Press, 1934 and Boston: Beacon Press, 1957).

GINGELL, W. R. (1852). *The Ceremonial Usages of the Chinese, B.C. 1121, as Prescribed in the 'Institutes of the Chow Dynasty Strung as Pearls', or Chow Le Kwan Choo.* London: Elder.

GIOIA, MELCHIORRE (1815). *Nuovo Prospetto delle Scienze Economiche.* Milano: Pirotta e Maspero.

GRAICUNAS, V. A. (1933). 'Relationship in Organization'. *Bulletin of the International Management Institute*, Mar. 1933. Geneva: International Labour Office. Reprinted in Luther H. Gulick and Lyndall F. Urwick (eds.), *Papers on the Science of Administration* (New York: Institute of Public Administration, Columbia University, 1937).

GULICK, LUTHER H. (1937). 'Notes on the Theory of Organization', in Luther H. Gulick, and Lyndall F. Urwick (eds.), *Papers on the Science of Administration.* New York: Institute of Public Administration, Columbia University.

GUTJAHR, EDOUARD (1920). *L'organisation rationelle des enterprises commerciales.* Paris: Dunod.

HALL, R. H. (1963). 'The Concept of Bureaucracy: An Empirical Assessment'. *American Journal of Sociology*, 69: 32–40.

HEYDEBRAND, WOLF (1994). 'Introduction', in *Max Weber: Sociological Writings*, ed. Wolf Heydebrand. New York: Continuum.

HOSKIN, KEITH W., and MACVE, RICHARD H. (1986). 'Accounting and the Examination: A Genealogy of Disciplinary Power'. *Accounting, Organizations, and Society*, 11: 105–36.

JAQUES, ELLIOTT (1951). *The Changing Culture of a Factory*. London: Tavistock.

KALLINIKOS, JANNIS (1996). 'Predictable Worlds: On Writing, Accountability and Other Things'. *Scandinavian Journal of Management Studies*, 12: 7–24.

KILLICK, J. R., and THOMAS, W. A. (1970). 'The Provincial Stock Exchanges, 1830–1870'. *Economic History Review*, 23: 96–111.

KIMBALL, DEXTER SIMPSON (1913). *Principles of Industrial Organization*. New York: McGraw-Hill.

LAMOREAUX, NAOMI R. (2000). 'Partnerships, Corporations and the Problem of Legal Personhood'. Manuscript, UCLA and National Bureau of Economic Research.

LANE, FREDERIC C. (1934). *Venetian Ships and Shipbuilders of the Renaissance*. Baltimore: Johns Hopkins Press.

LASKI, HAROLD J. (1916). 'The Personality of Associations'. *Harvard Law Review*, 29: 404–5.

LAUDON, KENNETH, and STARBUCK, WILLIAM H. (2001). 'Knowledge and Information Work in Organizations', in M. Warner (ed.), *International Encyclopedia of Business and Management* (2nd edn). London: Thompson Learning.

LAW, JOHN (1986). 'On the Methods of Long-Distance Control: Vessels, Navigation and the Portuguese Route to India', in John Law (ed.), *Power, Action and Belief: A New Sociology of Knowledge*, Sociological Review Monograph 32. London: Routledge & Kegan Paul.

LEE, JOHN (1928). *Pitman's Dictionary of Industrial Administration*. London: Pitman.

LEWIS, JOSEPH SLATER (1896). *The Commercial Organization of Factories: A Handbook for the Use of Manufacturers, Directors, Auditors, Engineers, Managers, Secretaries, Accountants, Cashiers, Estimate Clerks, Prime Cost Clerks, Bookkeepers, Draughtsmen, Students, Pupils, etc.* London: Spon.

LITCHFIELD, EDWARD H. (1956). 'Notes on a General Theory of Administration'. *Administrative Science Quarterly*, 1/1: 3–29.

MACHEN, ARTHUR W., Jr. (1911). 'Corporate Personality'. *Harvard Law Review*, 24: 253–67 and 347–65.

MACHLUP, FRITZ (1962). *The Production and Distribution of Knowledge in the United States*. Princeton: Princeton University Press.

MANNHEIM, KARL (1935). *Mensch und Gesellschaft im Zeitalter des Umbaus*. Leiden: A. W. Sijthoff. Mannheim published an expanded English translation of this work in 1940: *Man and Society in an Age of Reconstruction* (New York: Harcourt Brace).

MARCH, JAMES G., and SIMON, HERBERT A. (1958). *Organizations*. New York: Wiley.

MARK, GREGORY A. (1987). 'The Personification of the Business Corporation in American Law'. *University of Chicago Law Review*, 54: 1441–83.

MARSCHAK, JACOB (1955). 'Elements for a Theory of Teams'. *Management Science*, 1: 127–37.

MARSHALL, ALFRED (1892). *Elements of Economics of Industry*. London: Macmillan.

—— (1919). *Industry and Trade: A Study of Industrial Technique and Business Organization*. London: Macmillan.

MARX, KARL (1867). *Das Kapital: Kritik der Politischen Oekonomie*. Hamburg: O. Meissner; New York: L. W. Schmidt. Various parts of *Capital* were published between 1859 and 1883, and vol. i was first published in English in 1887. Marx's complete writings are on the web site: http://www.marxists.org/archive/marx/works/index.htm.

MERKLE, JUDITH A. (1980). *Management and Ideology: The Legacy of the International Scientific Management Movement.* Berkeley: University of California Press.

MERTON, ROBERT K. (1940). 'Bureaucratic Structure and Personality'. *Social Forces,* 18: 561–8.

—— GRAY, A. P., HOCKEY, B., and SELVIN, H. C. (1952). *Reader in Bureaucracy.* Glencoe, Ill.: Free Press.

MICHELS, ROBERT (1911/1999). *Zur Soziologie des Parteiwesens in der Moderne Demokratie.* Eden and Cedar Paul have made an English translation of this work that was first published in 1915: *Political Parties: A Sociological Study of the Oligarchical Tendencies of Modern Democracy* (New York: Hearst's International Library). The quotations in this chapter are taken from a 1999 re-publication of the translation by Eden and Cedar Paul (New Brunswick, NJ: Transaction).

MILL, JOHN STUART (1861). *Consideration on Representative Government.* London: Parker, Son, and Bourn.

MIROWSKI, PHILIP (1994). *Natural Images in Economic Thought: 'Markets Read in Tooth and Claw'.* Cambridge: Cambridge University Press.

MOONEY, JAMES D., and REILEY, ALAN C. (1931). *Onward Industry! The Principles of Organization.* New York: Harper. Reissued as *The Principles of Organization* in 1947.

MOSCA, GAETANO (1884). *Sulla Teorica dei Governi e Sul Governo Parlamentare. Sudii Storici e Sociali.* Turin: Loescher.

ONG, WALTER J. (1982). *Orality and Literacy: The Technologizing of the Word.* London: Methuen.

PARKINSON, C. NORTHCOTE (1957). *Parkinson's Law and Other Studies in Administration.* Boston: Houghton Mifflin.

PEIRCE, CHARLES SANDERS (1887). 'Logical Machines'. *American Journal of Psychology,* 1/1: 165–70.

PENROSE, EDITH T. (1959). *The Theory of the Growth of the Firm.* Oxford: Basil Blackwell.

PETROSKI, HENRY (1996). 'Harnessing Steam'. *American Scientist,* 84/1: 15–19.

POLLARD, SIDNEY (1965). *The Genesis of Modern Management: A Study of the Industrial Revolution in Great Britain.* Cambridge, Mass.: Harvard University Press.

Princeton University (1950–4). *Reports on the Organizational Behavior Project.* New York: Ford Foundation Grant File PA No. 50–269.

RATHENAU, WALTHER (1917). *Von Kommenden Dingen.* Berlin: S. Fischer. Eden and Cedar Paul have made an English translation of this work that was first published in 1921: *In Days to Come* (London: Allen & Unwin).

REINHARD, MARCEL R., ARMENGAUD, ANDRÉ, and DUPAQUIER, JACQUES (1968). *Histoire générale de la population mondiale.* Paris: Éditions Montchrestien.

RINDOVA, VIOLINA P., and STARBUCK, WILLIAM H. (1997*a*). 'Distrust in Dependence: The Ancient Challenge of Superior–Subordinate Relations', in T. A. R. Clark (ed.), *Advancements in Organization Behaviour: Essays in Honour of Derek Pugh.* Aldershot: Ashgate Publishing.

—— —— (1997*b*). 'Ancient Chinese Theories of control'. *Journal of Management Inquiry,* 6: 144–59.

RUBIN, MICHAEL ROGERS, and HUBER, MARY TAYLOR (1986). *The Knowledge Industry in the United States, 1960–1980.* Princeton: Princeton University Press.

SAINT-SIMON, CLAUDE-HENRI DE ROUVROY, comte de (1976). *The Political Thought of Saint-Simon*, ed. by Ghita Ionescu. London: Oxford University Press. Several other books contain the same selections.

SALGADO, SUSAN REILLY, STARBUCK, WILLIAM H., and MEZIAS, JOHN M. (2002). 'The Accuracy of Managers' Perceptions: A Dimension Missing from Theories about Firms', in M. Augier and J. G. March (eds.), *The Economics of Choice, Change, and Organizations: Essays in Memory of Richard M. Cyert* (Cheltenham, UK: Edward Elgar).

SCHMOLLER, GUSTAV FRIEDRICH VON (1898). *Umrisse und Untersuchungen zur Verfassungs-, Verwaltungsund Wirtschaftsgeschichte besonders des Preussischen Staates im 17. und 18. Jahrhundert.* Leipzig: Duncker & Humblet.

SCHUMPETER, JOSEPH A. (1912). *Epochen der Dogmen-und Methodengeschichte.* Tübingen: Mohr. An English translation by R. Aris was published in 1954 as *Economic Doctrine and Method: An Historical Sketch* (New York: Oxford University Press).

SELZNICK, PHILIP (1943). 'An Approach to a Theory of Bureaucracy'. *American Sociological Review*, 8: 47–54.

——(1948). 'Foundations of the Theory of Organization'. *American Sociological Review*, 13: 25–35.

——(1949). *TVA and the Grass Roots: A Study of Politics and Organization.* Berkeley: University of California Press.

SHAFRITZ, JAY M., and OTT, J. STEVEN (1996). 'A Chronology of Organization Theory'. Appendix to the editors' introduction to *Classics of Organization Theory* (4th edn). Belmont, Calif.: Wadsworth.

SHENHAV, YEHOUDA (1995). 'From Chaos to Systems: The Engineering Foundations of Organization Theory, 1879–1932'. *Administrative Science Quarterly*, 40: 557–85.

SIMON, HERBERT A. (1944). 'Decision-Making and Administrative Organization'. *Public Administration Review*, 4: 16–30.

——(1946). 'The Proverbs of Administration'. *Public Administration Review*, 6: 53–67.

——(1947). *Administrative Behavior.* New York: Macmillan.

——(1950). 'Modern Organization Theories'. *Advanced Management*, 15/10: 2–4.

——(1952). 'Comments on the Theory of Organizations'. *American Political Science Review*, 46: 1130–9.

——(1952–3). 'A Comparison of Organisation Theories'. *Review of Economic Studies*, 20: 40–8.

——SMITHBURG, DONALD W., and THOMPSON, VICTOR A. (1950). *Public Administration.* New York: Knopf.

SMITH, ADAM (1776). *An Inquiry into the Nature and Causes of the Wealth of Nations.* London: W. Strahan and T. Cadell.

SPENCER, HERBERT (1862). *First Principles.* London: Williams & Norgate.

——(1876). *The Principles of Sociology*, i. London: Williams & Norgate.

STEWART, DONALD D. (1951). 'The Place of Volunteer Participation in a Bureaucratic Organization'. *Social Forces*, 29: 311–17.

TAYLOR, FREDERICK WINSLOW (1903). *Shop Management.* New York: Harper.

TOULMIN, STEPHEN (1990). *Cosmopolis: The Hidden Agenda of Modernity.* New York: Free Press.

TURNER, RALPH H. (1947). 'The Navy Disbursing Officer as a Bureaucrat'. *American Sociological Review*, 12: 342–8.

United Nations (1998). *World Population Prospects: The 1998 Revision*. New York: United Nations. http://www.popin.org/pop1998/default.htm.

URE, ANDREW (1835). *The Philosophy of Manufactures: Or, an Exposition of the Scientific, Moral, and Commercial Economy of the Factory System of Great Britain*. London: Charles Knight.

URWICK, LYNDALL F. (1933a). *Organization as a Technical Problem*. Paper read to the British Association for the Advancement of Science, in Luther H. Gulick and Lyndall F. Urwick (eds.), *Papers on the Science of Administration* (New York: Institute of Public Administration, Columbia University, 1937).

—— (1933b). *Management of Tomorrow*. London: Nisbet.

—— (1934). 'The Function of Administration', in Luther H. Gulick and Lyndall F. Urwick (eds.), *Papers on the Science of Administration* (New York: Institute of Public Administration, Columbia University, 1937).

—— (ed.) (1956). *The Golden Book of Management: A Historical Record of the Life and Work of Seventy Pioneers*. London: Newman Neame.

VEBLEN, THORSTEN (1904). *The Theory of Business Enterprise*. New York: Scribner's.

VON MISES, LUDWIG (1944). *Bureaucracy*. New Haven: Yale University Press.

WARD, J. K. (1989). 'The Future of an Explosion'. *American Heritage of Invention and Technology*, 5/1: 58–63.

WARNOTTE, DANIEL (1937). 'Bureaucratie et fonctionnarisme'. *Revue de l'Institut de Sociologie*, 17: 245–60.

WATSON, G. (1945a). 'Bureaucracy as Citizens See It'. *Journal of Social Issues*, 1/Dec.: 4–13.

—— (1945b). 'Bureaucracy in the Federal Government'. *Journal of Social Issues*, 1/Dec.: 14–31.

WEBER, MAX (1910–14). *Wirtschaft und Gesellschaft*, Part III, ch. 6. Tübingen: Paul Siebeck, 1922. Although the book was published after Weber's death, references in the text of this chapter indicate that it was written before 1914. The quotation in this chapter is taken from *Max Weber: Sociological Writings*, ed. Wolf Heydebrand (New York: Continuum, 1994).

WHYTE, WILLIAM FOOTE (1948). *Human Relations in the Restaurant Industry*. New York: McGraw-Hill.

WHYTE, WILLIAM H. (1956). *The Organization Man*. New York: Doubleday.

WILSON, A. T. M. (1951). 'Introduction', in Elliott Jaques, *The Changing Culture of a Factory*. London: Tavistock.

WILSON, JOHN F. (1995). *British Business History, 1720–1994*. Manchester: Manchester University Press.

WILSON, SLOAN (1955). *The Man in the Grey Flannel Suit*. New York: Simon and Schuster.

WOLIN, SHELDON S. (1960). *Politics and Vision*. Boston: Little, Brown.

WORTHY, JAMES C. (1950). 'Organizational Structure and Employee Morale'. *American Sociological Review*, 15: 169–79.

WREN, DANIEL A. (1994). *The Evolution of Management Thought* (4th edn). New York: Wiley.

WRIGLEY, EDWARD A. (1969). *Population and History*. New York: McGraw-Hill.

CHAPTER 6

....

THE HISTORICAL AND EPISTEMOLOGICAL FOUNDATIONS OF ORGANIZATION THEORY

FUSING SOCIOLOGICAL THEORY WITH ENGINEERING DISCOURSE

....

YEHOUDA SHENHAV

IN THE 1950s, a new intellectual field, devoted to the study of organizations, came into being. Made up of sociologists, political scientists, psychologists, engineers, management specialists, and economists, it was (and is) known as 'organization studies', 'organization science', or 'organization theory'. At the point of departure,

The author thanks Michal Frenkel, Christian Knudsen, Alexandra Kalev, Dick Scott, and Ely Weitz for useful comments on earlier drafts.

Organization Theory was mainly an American creation.[1] A newly established journal *Administrative Science Quarterly* (which was inaugurated in 1956) and three textbooks—March and Simon (1958), Likert (1961), and Blau and Scott (1962)—signified the crystallization of this body of knowledge into an independent field in the United States (Scott 1998).[2]

Probably more than any other scholar, Richard Scott contributed to the canonization of the field. In his oft quoted book *Organizations: Rational, Natural and Open Systems*, Scott (1987/1998) offers a brief genealogical construction of this interdisciplinary enterprise:

> Within sociology the emergence of the field of organizations may be roughly dated from the translation into English of Weber's (1946, 1947) and to a lesser extent, Michels's (1949) analyses of bureaucracy. Shortly after these classic statements became accessible to American sociologists, Robert K. Merton and his students at Columbia University attempted to outline the boundaries of this new field of inquiry by compiling theoretical and empirical materials dealing with various aspects of organizations (Merton et al. 1952).... For the first time, sociologists were engaged in the development and empirical testing of generalizations dealing with the structure and functioning of organizations viewed as organizations. (Scott 1987: 8; 1998: 9)

It was in this context, according to Scott, that 'more recent forebears, such as Taylor, Barnard and Mayo, were re-discovered and reprinted' (1998: 10). Scott summarizes his description arguing that 'These central and other related efforts gave rise to the identification of a new area of study—organizations'.

My objective in this chapter is to provide an alternative historiography of the field of OT.[3] Whereas I accept Scott's observation about the existence of the two different discourses that form the backbone of Organization Theory (a sociological discourse and a managerial discourse), I challenge his starting point ('degree zero') and his genealogy. Scott's depiction implies that the history of the field starts with Weber's translation into English as if there was no significant study of organizations in the United States prior to that date. In contrast, I argue that Max Weber's work was translated into a context ripe with discourse about organizations, mainly among engineering circles. Furthermore, Weber's work was incorporated into this American engineering discourse and was accommodated to fit its language and epistemology. A historical account of the emergence of the field needs therefore to start with this earlier engineering/managerial discourse, to show its carriers and institutions, and then to focus on the manner by which Weber's work was

---

[1] It was in the United States that a new class of salaried management first emerged in significant numbers (Berle and Means 1932) and set the blueprint for American management theory (Guillen 1994; Shenhav 1995; see also Locke 1996). Organizational discourse was partly an offspring of the American managerial revolution (Shenhav 1999).

[2] Gibson Burrell (1996) coined American OT as NATO: North American Theory of Organizations.

[3] For a discussion of the linkage between historiography and archival data, see Mohr and Ventresca (forthcoming).

incorporated into it. This will provide a more comprehensive analysis of the fusion between the two discourses that were hybridized into one to create the embryo of what we consider today as OT.

I begin the search for an alternative historiography with the assumption that knowledge, any knowledge, tends to grow in chaotic, unorganized, and often hybrid manner. The anarchic nature of knowledge is best characterized by Deleuze and Guattari's metaphor of the rhizome (1987). The rhizome grows in all directions, multiplied in unanticipated directions and diverges at all ends simultaneously. A rhizome ceaselessly establishes connections between semiotic, chains or organizations of power, resulting in interwoven lines, junctions, intersections, and branches which present no definite beginnings or ends. Unlike the tree, the rhizome does not have structure and genealogy, and refuses to be represented or codified. Against the dynamics of the rhizome, science produces axiomatics:

it is the nature of axiomatics to come up against so-called *undecidable propositions*, to confront *necessarily higher powers* that it cannot master... axiomatics does not constitute the cutting edge of science; it is much more a stopping point, a reordering that prevents decoded semiotic flows... from escaping in all directions. The great axiomaticians are the men of State of science, who seal off the lines of flight that are so frequent in mathematics, who would impose a new nexum, if only a temporary one, and who lay down the official policies of science. (Deleuze and Guattari 1987: 461)

It is therefore essential, according to Deleuze and Guattari, to treat every genealogical reconstruction as an administrative task employing axiomatization, which is premissed upon regulation, and requires the 'organizing conjunctions of decoded flows' (Deleuze and Guattari 1987: 451). Scott's historiographical construction signifies an attempt to affirm and canonize the identity of the field and his description is indeed based on two acts of axiomatization.[4] The first refers to the importation of Weber's theory of bureaucracy and rationality into American sociology in the late 1940s. Scott's genealogical description implies an epistemological continuity between Max Weber's theoretical work and the American sociological paradigm prevailing at the time of translation. He describes Weber's 'translation' as merely a linguistic task, while Weber was in fact Americanized—'culturally' translated in the Latourian sense (Latour 1987)—to fit the epistemological rules dominating American sociology during the 1940s and 1950s.

---

[4] Axiomatization is an administrative act, taken by administrators of science, which shunts the development of knowledge into a certain direction. Such administrative acts (not necessarily intentional and not necessarily personal) involve periodization of 'stages', juxtaposition of divergent bodies of knowledge, definition of concepts, codification of enabling language and canonization of previous decisions. Historiographic decisions are acts of axiomatization, since they are not based on 'facts', 'experiments', or 'discoveries', but rather on such administrative procedures. For example, the distinction between the 'New World' and the 'Old World' ('Ancient Regime') in the seventeenth century, which extensively used in the science of history, is an act of axiomatization.

The second act of axiomatization pertains to the juxtaposition of early management discourse with sociological theory. Whereas Scott's account assumed that scattered classical managerial texts (such as Taylor's, Mayo's, and Barnard's) were revived and collected into the sociological paradigm after the translation of Weber' work, I argue that there already existed a systematic discourse about organizations in the United States. This discourse, that was already categorized in 1912 as 'a smaller sister of sociology, as a science of human nature' (*Engineering Magazine*, Jan. 1912: 481; Shenhav 1999: 127), preceded the translation of Weber to English, and was infused into American sociology 'from below' during the first half of the twentieth century. This engineering/managerial discourse invented the 'organization' as a reified epistemological concept[5] and celebrated the idea that it is worthy of intellectual and academic attention.

In this chapter I follow the two discourses—the engineering and the sociological—and their merger, in order to historicize the epistemological assumptions of contemporary OT directly back into the professional project of social engineering around the beginning of the twentieth century.[6]

The chapter is structured as follows. Section 6.1 presents the roots of the engineering-managerial discourse about organizations that dominated industrial America prior to the translation of Weber to English. This discourse was later incorporated into the work of early sociologists and management scholars. Section 6.2 presents Weber's project on rationality, and analyzes the manner in which his work was interpreted by American sociologists. I show how Weber's theory of rationality was translated, in the Latourian sense, according to the peculiar epistemological rules prevailing in US sociology, particularly emphasizing the ahistorical nature of the social science and the hegemony of the Parsonian interpretation. Section 6.3 discusses the epistemological ramifications resulting from the nexus between the two discourses, focusing on two of the key concepts in OT: rationality and uncertainty. These were central concepts in the construction of organizations as rational actors.

---

[5] Just as the courts invented the corporation as a persona ficta roughly at the same time (see Roy 1997).

[6] In Foucault's terms I employ an archeological and genealogical analyses. The archeological analysis focuses on the epistemological regulations and the discursive practices through which statements are generated, formed, shaped, and restricted (see Foucault 1973 and Foucault 1977*a*). The genealogical analysis usually focuses on the relationship between knowledge/power or the interplay between discursive and non-discursive practices (mainly Foucault 1975, 1977*b*, 1977*c*). It is concerned with the manner in which political, economic, and social scientific knowledge came to complement each other and the manner in which experts form their claim to 'objective and positive knowledge'. According to Foucault, these two lines of thought are based on different assumptions. While the archeological analysis explores the more organized and structured aspects of the discourse, the genealogical analysis focuses on dynamic, open-ended, controversial, and conflictual practices.

6.1 THE ENGINEERING/MANAGEMENT PILLAR: THE INVENTION OF AN INDEPENDENT DISCOURSE ABOUT ORGANIZATIONS[7]

As early as the 1880s mechanical engineers, mostly members of the ASME (American Society of Mechanical Engineers), were the leaders of an industry-wide movement that desired to standardize and systematize its technical environment. These individuals attempted to rationalize standards of measurement, nomenclatures, fittings, screws, nuts, bolts, and everything else with which they came in daily contact. Parallel to the attempts to standardize and systematize mechanical matters, the movement spilled over to cover organizational and managerial issues.

Based on their experience, mechanical engineers aspired to enhance their centrality within industrial firms and to extend the boundaries of their expertise to include the design of organizations. As Dunlap, editor of *Engineering Magazine* argued, "The cold logic of a mechanical demonstration may be more effective in industrial reform than any sympathetic appeal of the humanitarian' (*Engineering Magazine*, Nov. 1902: 223–30). Dexter Kimball, Dean of Engineering at Cornell University and later a president of the ASME, suggested 'the extension of the principles of standardization to the human element in production' (Shenhav 1995), assuming that human and non-human entities are interchangeable and can equally be subjected to engineering manipulation.

Individuals such as Alexander Church, John Dunlap, and others—who were labeled by historians as 'systematizers'—applied mechanical engineering methods to the administrative restructuring of firms, to design systems of accountancy, determine wages, and determine selection criteria in employment. They constructed organizations as 'systems' and suggested that 'confusion', 'oversight', and 'neglect' could be eliminated through the use of rational 'systems'. The prominent engineer B. F. Spalding explained the systems ideology behind it: 'The American system is based upon the perfection of the units that are combined in the total which the complete machine represents. It considers the whole as a combination of integers, rather than as the sum of added fractions . . . the excellence of the whole is assured by the attention which the system secures to every part' (*American Machinist*, 6 November 1890: 2–4). 'System, system, system' wrote an enthusiastic visitor to Ford in the *Detroit Journal* at the peak of this craze (Hounshell 1984: 229). The extension of engineering practices and systems ideology to human organizations

---

[7] For a more extensive discussion on the engineering roots of the managerial revolution, see Shenhav 1999.

was an act of 'translation', affirming an underlying unity between elements distinct from one another and creating convergences and homologies by relating things that were previously unrelated (Latour 1987; Callon 1981; Shenhav and Weitz 2000; Weitz and Shenhav 2000).

Despite objections to the systems ideology (e.g. Shenhav 1999: 112–15), the Progressive Era (1900–1917) in the United States was instrumental to the diffusion of this discourse for two important reasons. First, it provided legitimation to the roles for professionals, including engineers, as experts. The Roosevelt administration, for example, maintained close relationships with all engineering societies, and these societies supported Roosevelt's attempts to bring efficiency and rational management into industry and government. Hays (1959) maintains that 'efficiency', 'expertise', and 'system' infused the entire social order of Progressivism. This was congruent with the general trend of 'anti-chaos' reforms labeled by Wiebe as 'the search for order' and was characterized by 'bureaucratic vision' and a desire for 'perfect systematization' (1967).

The professional tools developed by the Progressives were perceived to be objective and rational and therefore above the give and take of political conflict. The struggle of Progressives to find a common ground for society as a 'whole' generated pragmatic culture in which conflicts were diffused and ideological differences ostensibly resolved. At the end of the Progressive period, business philosophy was crystallized around secular engineering ideals rather than around religious, philanthropic, or social Darwinist ones (Barley and Kunda 1992). With the engineering discourse, resorting to politics could be redefined in technical terms. Engineering expertise seemed most appropriate for the resolution of conflictual politics (Shenhav 1999).

Second, the spirit of the Progressive Era was congruent with the promise of systems to promote *progress* and *equality*. Images of progress were often expressed with the logic of efficiency and productivity. Images of equality were often expressed in moral terms and focused on the redistribution of wealth by means of welfare legislation, antitrust laws, and unionism. The development of rational organizational systems seemed to provide a perfect vehicle for reforms. In organizational systems, progress and equality were ostensibly harmonized through the objectivity of the system. Systems were perceived as a safeguard for the morality of organizations, of managers and of employees. They bind individuals in mutual relations of responsibility and accountability, depersonalized these relationships, and thus eliminated favoritism and nepotism. In systems the trajectory of progress can be charted both for individuals and for the organization as a whole, since authority is no longer derived from privileged social positions but is grounded in facts and techniques needed to perform and coordinate interdependent tasks (Miller and O'Leary 1989).

In the emerging organizational discourse during the Progressive Era the concept of system assumed coherence and autonomy and became an object of independent inquiry. As one systematizer wrote 'the important details of factory work are cared for by systems which are homogenous, flexible and efficient; systems which leave nothing to chance, but which care for the smallest and the most important details of factory work alike' (*Engineering Magazine*, Apr. 1902: 15–18). The editors of the *American Machinist*, a major outlet for engineering writings, suggested: 'there is not a man, machine, operation or system in the shop that stands entirely alone. Each one, to be valued rightly, must be viewed as part of a whole' (*American Machinist*, 3 Mar. 1904: 294–6). In 1906 the editors of the *Engineering Magazine* recalled: 'It is almost ten years since the *Engineering Magazine* laid down the first clear definitions of that system of manufacturing which has come to be known as distinctively American' (*Engineering Magazine*, Sept. 1906: 801).[8] Preoccupation with systems was so pervasive that one systematizer put it succinctly: 'You must have a cost system. You can't retain the respect of the manufacturing public if you don't have one.... A cost system is as ncessary to your industrial prestige as a pair of pants to your personal dignity' (*American Machinist*, 3 July 1913: 15). Likewise an editorial in the *Engineering Magazine* announced: 'America ... is God's own country—for any man who has a new system' (*Engineering Magazine*, Aug. 1916: 678).

The efforts to view organizations as systems received public visibility with the work of Frederick Taylor and his followers (Taylor 1911). Taylor's conceptualization of industrial bureaucracy—the extension and codification of mechanical engineering—involved an explicit attempt to systematize the firm. His suggestions were made under the banner of 'social physics', 'a science of production' that was supposed to be 'objective', 'systematic', and 'rational'.

In 1912, the study of organizations was defined in the engineering literature as a separate scientific field, 'a smaller sister of sociology as a science of human nature' (*Engineering Magazine*, Jan. 1912: 481–7). This 'science' invented the concept of rational organization and emphasized the constructive/visible hand of

[8] American creation of management grew out of engineering practices that were different from the European experience. The US engineer-managers were attuned to the economic and organizational constraints of the enterprise and the management of production processes. This was not the case with European engineers, especially with the French, British, and Germans, who were more concerned with technical issues in line with their scientific traditions (Locke 1984; Gispen 1989). Germany's economy was organized around 'rational lines' that were borrowed from the German army and state administration (Guillen 1994). But it did not enjoy the professional discourse that developed in the United States during the Progressive Era. To the extent that managerial and organizational thought developed in Germany or Britain to its current form, it was an American influence. For example, in the mid-1920s Germany's acute economic problems drove engineers, manufacturers, and academics to make pilgrimages to the United States in order to unravel the American romance with modern management (for more details, see Shenhav 1999: ch. 7; Djelic 1998).

management and the universality of its ideals. In 1915, John Dunlap, the editor of *Engineering Magazine* and the most active journalistic sponsor of the management movement, documented what he labeled as 'the historic events in the development of a new science' (*Engineering Magazine*, May 1915: 163–6). This systems discourse, which first entered engineering literature in the 1880s, rose to an average of 26 per cent of the literature on management during the Progressive period. It was a critical period in the history of the field 'the point at which a particular discourse emerged from these techniques and came to be seen as true, the point at which they are linked with the obligation of searching for the truth and telling the truth' (Foucault 1980, cited in Rabinow 1984: 7).

However, as mentioned earlier, the rationalization of organizations as systems was not naturally and universally accepted. Indeed, engineers and managers faced bitter opposition from unions, on the one hand, and objection from capitalists, on the other (Shenhav 1999). To the capitalist mind the idea of 'systems' did not seem to be natural. To many manufacturers, systems appeared costly and superfluous, and seemed to generate red tape, unpredictability, lack of control, conflict, and instability as one explained: 'they had every man in the place running around with a pencil over his ear, and we didn't get the work done' (*American Machinist*, 29 Apr. 1915: 750). Manufacturers viewed systematization as a strategy employed by engineers to expand their professional territory.[9] In their attempts to convince these capitalists that rational systems were necessary, engineers turned to the issue of labor unrest.

The fear of unrest was common to manufacturers, politicians, and the public at large and threatened private property, the state, civil order, and the 'free market' ideology. Building on this fear, mechanical engineers framed[10] labor unrest in technical terms, and suggested that, under a perfectly rational organizational system, unrest would be rendered unnecessary. They sought to position their rationality as impartial and above class prejudice and suggested that management systems could put an end to labor unrest.

According to this systems rhetoric, the properties of the machine-like bureaucratic system were expected to transform chaos into order, ambiguity into certainty, and irrational into rational behavior. They minimized the political significance of unrest and marginalized its ideological foundations, depicting them as 'technical' rather than political issues. Thus, the politics of labor unrest and the rationality of organizations formed a dialectical relationship. Labor unrest was used to justify the rational reconstruction of organization and in turn, the emergent systems perspec-

---

[9] For more detailed empirical description on the objection of manufacturers and capitalists, see Shenhav 1999: ch. 4.

[10] On the issue of framing of social issues, see Gamson 1992.

tive depoliticized labor unrest, translating and describing it in ahistorical and apolitical terms.

During the first half of the twentieth century, the rhetoric and practice of organizational systems have traveled from engineering circles to additional fields and became widely known in American industry and academia. In 1916, John Dunlap the editor of *Engineering Magazine* inaugurated *Industrial Management* which was devoted to issues of organizational systematization and became a professional outlet for organizational thought. Dunlap remained an editor until 1927, when *Industrial Management* merged with *Factory* to form *Factory and Industrial Management* a joint venture of the McGraw-Shaw and the McGraw-Hill publishing companies. In 1933 *Factory and Industrial Management* merged with two additional magazines *Maintenance Engineering* and *Manufacturing Industries*, to form a new periodical titled *Factory Management and Maintenance*. Simultaneously, new schools of managerial thought emerged in the United States, particularly the Human Relations school with its emphasis on industrial psychology (see Trahair 1984). *Industrial Management* established a regular section on personality and employment issues and more specific magazines such as *System: The Magazine of Business* and *Personnel* were established (see Business Periodicals Index and Abrahamson 1997). Many of the subsequent scholars of organizations were readers and writers for these magazines.

The embryonic engineering/management ideas that were published in these magazines were later collected and collated in books, written by individuals such as Harrington Emerson (1909), Henry Gantt (1910), Alexander Hamilton Church (1914), Charles Bedaux (1917), Chester Barnard (1938), Luther Gulick and Lyndall Urwick (1937), James Mooney and Alan Reiley (1939), Fritz Roethlisberger and William Dickson (1941), or George Terry (1953). These books were read by sociologists, psychologists, engineers, political scientists, and became the seedbed from which discourse on rational organizations grew.

The historiography of OT claims that scattered managerial writings were revived after the middle of the twentieth century with the translation of Weber into English. In the following I discuss Weber's theory of rationality and show that this translation was in fact a cultural act of 'Americanization' resonating with the well organized, systematic engineering discourse about rational organizations. At the time of translation American sociology was predisposed to interpret Weber in a peculiar way, that diverged from the original assumptions of his theory. Weber's peculiar translation and its tremendous influence on the emergence of American OT should be understood in this ideological and epistemological context.

6.2 THE SOCIOLOGICAL PILLAR: THE 'TRANSLATION' OF WEBER'S RATIONALITY INTO AMERICAN SOCIOLOGY

Max Weber provided one of the first systematic, secular formulation of rationality and rationalization in sociology.[11] Integrating liberal social theory with Neo-Kantian philosophy and the German institutional school of economics, his work resulted in methodological as well as historical observations about rationality.[12] In his methodological writings, Weber suggested that systems of rationality can be reconstituted as ideal types for the study of social objects (Weber 1949; Bendix 1960). In his historical writings, he examined different aspects of rationality (e.g. action, decision, and systematized world views) and applied rationalization—the cultivation of rationality in western society in particular—to diverse spheres of life such as religion, law, economics, and music (Weber 1921/1968). Weber used the term 'Rationalizierung' ('rationalization') to designate the process by which this historical transformation was brought about.

Weber's impressive legacy on rationality generated, however, unbridgeable contradictions for sociology. Most noticeable are those between the universality of heuristic devices, on the one hand, and the idiosyncrasy of social processes, on the other; between the intentionality of action, on the one hand, and its unintended consequences, on the other; between Kantian-like 'objective' ideal types and the subjective meaning of action. Weber's analysis established well-known contradictions between the peculiar historical aspects of charismatic authority and the ahistorical nature of its routinization; between free choice or moral judgement and the constraints imposed by the iron cage of rationality; between the towering threat posed by mass discipline and domination versus their contribution to stability in an efficient social order; between the impersonal nature of instrumental rationality and the highly personal nature of value-rationality (Bendix 1960). Weber believed that only the coexistence of such negating perspectives—historical and ahistorical, subjective and objective, idiographic and nomological, normative and value neutral—provide sociology with tools to analyze the richness of social action in changing historical patterns.

Weber understood the impossibility of his position, and he reconciled himself to the limits of sociology as a peculiar cultural artifact (e.g. Weber 1921/1968). Sociology, he suggested, should suspend belief in systems of rationality in order to study them in their culturally specific conditions. As Merleau-Ponty pointed out: 'Weber is well aware that history as science is itself a product of history, a moment of

---

[11] For additional early treatments of rationality in sociology by Comte, Tonnies, Simmel, see Coser 1977.

[12] See e.g. Prendergast (1986) on Carl Menger and the Austrian Economic School.

"rationalization" or of the history of capitalism' (Feenberg 1981: 75). This suspen-
sion—a sociological bracketing not unlike Husserl's 'phenomenological reduction'—was introduced by Weber as a constitutive, a priori foundation of
sociology as a science. But Weber, again, did not abandon his incommensurable
dualisms. On the contrary, he foresaw that the strength of sociology as a discipline
lies in maintaining this ambivalence. Grasping the complexity of social life, and
rationality in particular, requires the co-existence of epistemological contradictions.[13]

Many intellectuals were subsequently intrigued with the nature of Weber's
dualistic sociological thought, but often ignored one dimension of his work
or another. For example, Hungarian critic Georg Lukács dissected Weber's methodological writings. In *History and Class Consciousness* (1923), Lukács provided a
cultural critique of reification, arguing that Weber's sociological 'bracketing' of
rationality was incomplete, since he did not include sociology itself in its scope. In
that sense, society, as well as the social sciences that study it, is no more 'rational'
than it is totemistic. Lukács proposed to include the formal rationality of the social
sciences themselves in this bracketing. Rationality should be perceived as a cultural
logic that was reified, and not as a predisposed epistemological condition (Lukács
1923; Feenberg 1981; see also Dobbin 1994). In other words, Lukács (and most
Critical Theorists as well as Berger and Luckmann 1966) preferred the 'reflexive'
dimension of rationality over its reification in a rationalized social structure.

In contrast, a generation of American sociologists refused to accept the Janus-
face features of Weber's formulation and relied on the exact other end. Following
Parsons (1947, 1949, 1951), they perceived Weber's work as a 'generalized theory of
authority' (Gouldner 1954: 18). They borrowed Weber's thesis of the ascendancy of
rationality, and left out his critical views. They subscribed to a reified prescription
that emphasized the consensual and ahistorical nature of rationality, and abandoned the historical and phenomenologial nature of Weber's rationality.

There were at least two reasons for the wide acceptance of this uncritical account
of Weber among American sociologists. First, it was closely linked with the nature
of American social science and the manner in which it developed since the beginning of the century. Ross (1991) attributed much of its spirit to the ideology of
American Exceptionalism that dominated the United States at the turn of the
previous century. According to this ideology, the United States occupies a unique
place in the history of the western world, and has a distinctive mission to perform
which marked it off from the rest of the world. America was perceived as the
only country in the world that was born perfect, since it had no indigenous
feudal institutions. Its 'inherent' political principles of rationality, liberalism, and

---

[13] It should be noted that Weber is sometimes credited for overcoming these contradictions. For the
influence of German Idealist tradition as well as German Historicism on Weber, see Bendix 1960; Coser
1977. Most relevant is the debate regarding the so-called 'Methodenstreit' between Gustav Schmoller
and Carl Menger. Those debates, however, are beyond the scope of this chapter.

democracy—together with affluence and a broad opportunity structure—provided a basis for a society that could escape the miseries of class struggle. As Hawthorn explains, the American Revolution was not a revolution against the ancient regime, as was the case in Europe, but rather an attempt to secure what began in a historical vacuum. In his own words, 'America seemed already to have reached perfection. The past had been consolidated in a future whose integrity lay in remaining as much like the present as possible' (Hawthorn 1987).

Progress was perceived as a quantitative multiplication of its founding institutions, not a process of qualitative change. This rhetoric—which rendered history unnecessary—abounded in popular American culture, media, and the social sciences throughout the nineteenth century. It was 'the discursive frame within which the social sciences worked, the language which set their core problem and shaped the logic of their solutions to it' (Ross 1993: 104). American social sciences lost their historicist orientation and modeled themselves after the natural sciences with an emphasis on the positivist methods of inquiry, and the ahistorical direction embedded in the classical ideology of liberalism. Ross (1991) further explains that given the belief that social classes did not exist and that American society was harmonious and rational, the social and political theory that developed was narrowly defined by the bounds of economic liberalism. Social order was believed to be based on rationality, harmony, and progress (Ross 1991).

To be sure, this view of sociology dates back to August Comte. Comte's progressive/positivist vision was incorporated into American academia as early as the 1890s by the first President of the American Sociological Association, Lester Ward. In Comte's philosophy, the chief dynamic force in history is the advancement of knowledge; scientific rationality, the most advanced form of knowledge, is thus the key to future progress. Comte's positivist project was based on the competency of experts who provide administrative, economic, and social planning. Any knowledge that does not follow the systematization and the generalization of the sciences must be excluded. After all, science is socially defined as a set of objective rules that appear to exist outside any particular social system. Such objective rules seem to be unaffected by power or resource allocations among the group of people that make up the society (Gouldner 1976).

Indeed, the second volume of Ward's *Dynamic Sociology* was devoted to the study of 'sociocracy' (analogous to 'technocracy'—the application of social laws to produce order and progress). Sociocracy was to replace politics as the mechanism for governing society (Ross 1991). In the late 1890s, Edward Ross published several articles in the *American Journal of Sociology*, in which he developed the idea of sociology as a mechanism of 'social control'. To maintain itself, society had to modify individual ideas, feelings, and behavior to conform, and to subordinate, private interests to social interests. Consequently, William Graham Sumner, then the first vice-president of the ASA, stated in his 1906 book, *Folkways*, that sociology 'could lead up to an art of societal administration which should be intelligent, effective, and scientific' (quoted in Ross 1991: 221). Despite his controversial evolutionism and social Darwinism, this statement placed Sumner within the sociological consensus of the time. It was a vision of science that promised prediction and control, tools that gave a technocratic spin to their conception of social roles and positions.

The role of sociologists as agents of social control spilled over also to industrial practice. In 1914, when Henry Ford faced grave organizational problems, he founded a Sociological Department that employed 250 people. Aiming to reduce a daily absentee rate that exceeded 10 percent; a 370 percent yearly turnover rate, requiring nearly $2 million a year to train new workers; and fierce negotiations with one of the most militant unions in the country, Ford designed a new program for loyalty and conformity which paid $5 a day to every 'qualified' employee (Marcus and Segal 1989). The Ford Sociological Department assumed the role of determining who was qualified to receive this remuneration. These agents of social control visited homes, interviewed friends, neighbors, and priests to determine who conformed with the code of conduct stressing family values, community values, thrift, and personal character. They used strict criteria for unsuitability and norms of exclusion: single young men, men who were engaged in divorce, those who did not spend evenings 'wisely', those who used alcohol, or those who did not speak English. They also gave lessons in home management to workers, taught them how to shop, and how to preserve moral values (Marcus and Segal 1989: 236–8). The role of these experts in controlling the worker population was a clear sociological experiment in social design. The Sociological Department served as an agent in the moral bureaucracy of the Ford Motor Company. Sociology as a form of social praxis, sought to establish rational control over human nature and society.

The peculiar interpretation of Weber in the United States is also due to the nuances of Talcott Parsons's translation of Weber to English (Parsons 1947; Cohen *et al.* 1975; Weiss 1983). Parsons's interpretation of Weber was mostly in line with the theoretical perspectives existing in the United States in the 1930s and 1940s. His translation presented Weber as more concerned with value consensus and effective functioning than with the role of conflicting material interests in domination (Weiss 1983).[14] The most well-known difference between Parsons's translation and those of other scholars is over the interpretation of the term *Herrschaft*. Several scholars translated the term as 'domination' (e.g. Gerth and Mills), while Parsons first translated it to be 'imperative coordination' and later as 'leadership' (see also Parsons 1942). Weber did not develop a model for effective functioning as Parsons implied, but rather worked on historical modes of domination. He developed 'a "model" of what "ought" to exist to be carefully distinguished from the analytical construct, which is "ideal" in the strictly logical sense of the term' (Weber 1949: 91–2). Whereas

[14] Recently Kalberg (2001) argued that Parsons's translation of the Protestant Ethic also distorted Weber's text to a great extent. According to Kalberg, Parsons turned Weber 'into a structuralist thinker' which toned down Weber's vocabulary of conflict (2001: 2–4).

the former is a normative concept, the latter is a construct 'which our imagination accepts as plausibly motivated and hence as "objectively possible" and which appear as adequate from the nomological standpoint' (ibid.). It is this sense of possibility that is missing in Parsons's interpretation of Weber.

The crux of Parsons's misrepresentation of Weber is his overweening emphasis on the normative and the nomological dimension which led him to expand what is but a part of Weber's sociology and made it very nearly the whole (Cohen *et al.*, 1975: 240). For example, he interpreted Weber's instrumentally rational action as normative because means and ends are normatively selected (i.e. actors use 'efficient norms'). By so doing, Parsons abandoned a crucial aspect in Weber's dualistic framework, and expanded the normative (which indeed existed in Weber's analysis) to become his entire scheme. Nobody would claim that Parsons was intentionally distorting Weber's meaning. It was the unintended consequences of his attempt to provide American-specific conceptual consistency, not very apparent in the original, since Weber was an observer with ambivalent qualities.

Whereas critical European theorists (e.g. Lukács) promoted critical reflexivity, Parsons—and subsequent American sociologists—mobilized a reified notion of rationality into the foundations of his sociological and theoretical praxis. Weber's ideal type of bureaucracy was treated as prescription for formal organizations and a recipe for corporate managers. Thus, American sociologists, 'translated' Weber— through a 'shuttle' that they wove together entirely of a different set of epistemological assumptions—to create a hybrid of different theoretical cultures (Latour 1993). This 'translation' which converged with the contours of the engineering/ management discourse presented above was based on four strong assumptions about rationality, about history, about epistemology, and about ideology.[15]

Early OT scholars such as Blau (1955, 1956), Gouldner (1954), and Thompson (1967) assumed that Weber equated bureaucratic rationality with efficiency. In the 1987 edition of his book Scott suggested that: 'Max Weber used the term to refer to that form of administrative organization that, in his view, was capable of attaining the highest level of efficiency! (Weber, 1947 trans.: 339)' (Scott 1987: 24).[16] Or as Merton asserted: 'In his discussion, Weber is almost exclusively concerned with what the bureaucratic structure attains: precision, reliability, efficiency. The same structure may be examined from another perspective provided by the ambivalence. What are the limitations of the organizations designed to attain these goals?' (Merton 1949/1957: 198). Weber's bureaucracy was reified and was used as an

[15] As for rationality, the term was used in its constructive, normative, and instrumental sense. As for history, American sociologists attempted to tame it and to incorporate it into the analytic scheme of the sociologist. As for epistemology, they suggested a full-blown identity between rationality in sociology and rationality of its subject matter. As for ideology, they provided little room for conflicts and ideological differences operating under the premisses of the liberal thought (see Shenhav 1999, for more elaborated discussion).

[16] Scott himself was gradually aware of this misinterpretation. He made this point beginning with the 3rd edn of his book (1992: 44–5) and then much more strongly in the 4th edn (1998: 48–9).

ahistorical framework for effective functioning implying a performative intent in his scheme (Lyotard 1984).[17] Fournier and Grey (2000) summarize the point: 'Weberian tradition in US organization theory has been utilized primarily in normative organizational design terms rather than in terms of the critique of rationalization with which it is often associated in the UK' (p. 14). It was the reflexive quality in Weber—which had the ability to look behind those whom he termed 'social actors'—that was missing from the appropriation of his legacy by American sociology. Thus, while admittedly useful for organizational analysis, Robert Merton (1949; Merton et al. 1952) and Peter Blau, among others, incorporated Weber into a functionalist perspective and begun to study empirically the 'dysfunctions of bureaucracy'.

This formulation opened the road for a multiplicity of questions and research problems—such as overconformity, effectiveness, and organizational design—attempting to test the limit of bureaucratic structures and thus endorsing the functional epistemology of rationality. Merton (1949) and Blau (1955) turned to the study of the 'manifest and latent' 'functions' of bureaucracy. Likewise, March and Simon (1958) examined bureaucratic decision-making processes and goal formations, and Gouldner applied what he conceived as a Weberian perspective to the analysis of 'a modern factory administration' (1954: 16). In their frame of reference, rationality was not to be used in the service of social critique, but as an apriori construct in sociological analysis, and an instrument for social management. Put differently, in this version of sociology the logic of rationality has been reversed. Rather than constituting an external object of study, rationality had become the prism through which the (social) world was conceived and understood.[18]

This was apparent in the way early interpreters juxtaposed Weber and the early engineering discourse. It should be recalled that the central objective of Max Weber's essay on bureaucracy was not to provide advice to managers. Rather, he was addressing a theoretical debate carried out by Hegel and Marx concerning the nature of domination in capitalist society. Weber's work sends a strong political and conflictual message to those who study organizations. He perceived bureaucracy first and foremost as a form of domination, an institution that is embedded in the history of conflict in western societies. Weber was intrigued by the strength and power of bureaucracy, one may even say bewitched, yet he alarmed his readers about its unexpected consequences. Ideally 'rational' in the Weberian sense was not concerned with efficient performance, a meaning that was given to

[17] Blau and Scott, for example, represent this confusion arguing that Weber's ideal-type construct of bureaucracy is 'an admixture of a conceptual scheme and a set of hypotheses' (1962: 33). Scott further explained: 'the difficulty being that Weber does not clearly distinguish definitions from propositions in his model' (Scott 1987: 44).

[18] This has been taken to an extreme by the Structural Contingency School in organization theory. It is an imaginary tool-box that is used by theorists to plan and manage organizations. This school reproduces ideological and managerial artifacts that are culturally insensitive, historically ignorant, and politically blind (see Donaldson 1995; Shenhav 1996).

English-language readers by Parsons. The ideal type of bureaucracy was not a managerial manual but rather an analytical tool.

Alexander Hamilton Church and Frederick Winslow Taylor[19]—as representatives of engineering discourse—were enamored with the omnipotence of bureaucracy too but—unlike Weber—they sent a strong apolitical message to those who study organizations. They perceived bureaucracy as an end in and of itself. Rather than alarming one with the unexpected consequences of bureaucracy, they offered it as a solution to ideological cleavages, as a non-political entity responding to the war between the classes. To them, bureaucracy meant steady, efficiently performing, and goal-oriented organization.

Canonical sociology of organizations accepted unquestionably the textual project produced by the systematizers. By hybridizing the two discourses, American organizational theory broke away from the Weberian legacy and fell deep into the trap of reification. Organizational rationality rhetoric conveniently excised the political biography of its own project. It emphasized a social ideology with a strong commitment to engineering standards, scientific doxa, and adherence to the belief that American society was approaching the 'end of ideology'(Bell 1960).

It is therefore not surprising that organization theory says very little about the deceiving role of rationality. It also does not say—probably could not say—that this rationality was different from the rationality expressed by Max Weber or by other political European scholars.

6.3 THE ENGINEERING/MANAGERIAL AND THE SOCIOLOGICAL JUXTAPOSED: THE CANON OF ORGANIZATION THEORY

It was with this spirit that organization theory constructed the image of organizations as systems. The concepts that emerged in the engineering/management discourse were canonized in organization theory, which was now infused with the ideological parameters that were born during the efforts to establish the legitimation of management.[20]

[19] I urge the reader to note that in the historiography of organizations, the conflictual history that preceded Taylor is edited out, and most books on management and organizations begin with Taylor's principles of scientific management (for elaboration, see Shenhav 1999).

[20] This is not to say that some canonical scholars were unaware of politics and conflicts. Scott for example, allows for more irrationality, and struggles in his 'natural systems' or 'open systems' approaches as the title of his book implies.

During the 1950s-1970s, a systems paradigm flourished in the organizations literature and it stimulated the imagination of enthusiastic researchers. It brought together sociological (Yuchtman and Seashore 1967), psychological (Katz and Kahn 1966), engineering (Galbraith 1973), and business school analysts (Lawrence and Lorsch 1967) to create a hybrid discourse. System was used in this literature as a heuristic device, a prescription, an analytic tool, a metaphor, a category of the mind, and an overarching analogy. This paradigm was congruent with the most common and intuitive expectations from functioning organizations.

Organizational scholars juxtaposed early management discourse with the prevailing epistemology in sociology to form a body of knowledge which was then axiomatized as OT. Paramount in this effort were Robert Merton (1957) and Alfred Chandler (1962) (Talcott Parsons's student at Harvard), as well as Alvin Gouldner (1954), and Peter Blau (1955). Their pragmatic and hybrid epistemology entered organizational sociology and shaped its contemporary canon (e.g. Thompson 1967; Scott 1981). The following paragraph which is taken from a contemporary OT textbook represents this deeply hybrid epistemology which is rooted in engineering discourse:

A well-designed machine is an instance of a total organization, that is a series of interrelated means contrived to achieve a single end. The machine consists always of particular parts that have no meaning and no function separate from the organized entity to which they contribute. A machine consists of a coherent bringing together of all parts toward the highest possible efficiency of the functioning whole, or interrelationships marshaled wholly toward a given result. In the ideal machine, there can be no extraneous part, no extraneous movement; all is set, part for part, motion for motion, toward the functioning of the whole. (Ward 1964; quoted in Scott 1998: 33)

Or:

As in a mechanical system, organization systems are designed with a specific goal in mind, their operations are predetermined and their outcomes are rationally controlled. As in machines, organizations are evaluated according to criteria of efficient performance and are perceived as instruments to convert raw materials into final products. (ibid.)

This view is the outcome of the combined discourse produced by engineers and accepted by sociologists. The essence of this epistemology is particularly evident in two key concepts which form the backbone of Organization Theory: rationality and uncertainty.

6.3.1 Rationality

Rationality, though a multi-faceted concept implying values and maxims of thought, as the previous discussion suggests, was reduced in organizational theory to its instrumental-technical dimension defined as complete knowledge of the consequences of choices that are predetermined by structural constraints (Simon

1957).[21] In this literature, rationality can be secured by structures that reduce uncertainty and ambiguity (March and Simon 1958; Thompson 1967). Richard Scott best describes this reductionist approach:

organizations are instruments designed to attain specified goals. . . . How blunt or fine an instrument they are depends on many factors that are summarized by the concept of rationality of structure. The term rationality in this context is used in the narrow sense of technical or functional rationality and refers to the extent to which a series of actions is organized in such a way as to lead to predetermined goals with maximum efficiency. Thus, rationality refers not to the selection of goals but to their implementation. (Scott 1998: 33)

Scholars of organizations decided to set aside substantive rationality, morality, politics, or ideology, and to focus on the search for techniques that link ends and means in the most efficient way. In this view, human action is a subset of 'instrumental rationality' alone, as it is subordinated to unspecified and transient 'external' objectives. According to this definition, instrumental action is rooted in desired outcomes and in beliefs about cause and effect relationships (Thompson 1967). I invoke Weber, who argued that instrumental rationality should also be considered against its non-instrumental consequences and vis-à-vis its political and ideological context. Choosing one side of the equation, as organization theorists have done, elevates instrumental rationality to a supreme position that gainsays attempts at critical assessment.

The troublesome role of instrumental rationality as sole arbiter of reality can be demonstrated by the supreme role assigned to it by Robert McNamara in the Pentagon of the 1960s (Waring 1991). In implementing Operations Research techniques, which were growing in popularity during and after World War II, McNamara fostered the misconception that America was winning the war in Vietnam. Under his influence, and that of his 'whiz kids', American political leaders viewed the conflict in managerial terms, by the use of figures, numbers, charts, and mathematical analyses. They aspired to use resources efficiently and defined their efficiency as kill-ratios. As Gibson suggested: '[The] American defeat in Vietnam was inherent in the managerial thinking that was institutionalized in the Pentagon and American society. Managerial techniques were perfectly applied, but to problems for which they were unsuited, and that was why America lost' (quoted in Waring 1991: 33). The question, of course, is not whether America lost or won. The issue at hand is the omnipresence of managerial activism at the time, and the precedence instrumental rationality was given over other modes of thought. These examples, among many others (see e.g. Bauman 1989), shed light on the dangers of legitimizing unlimited authority to a 'universal' managerial rationality without introducing political, cultural, and moral balances. This is exactly why Weber

---

[21] There are exceptions of course. For example: Selznick (1949). For a critical analysis of the use of rationality in various branches of organization theory, see Dobbin 1994.

decided to keep the epistemological contradictions of 'instrumental' and 'critical' rationality alive together.

6.3.2 Uncertainty

The legitimacy of instrumental rationality was reinforced in OT by contrasting it with the threat associated with uncertainty. Organizations are conceptualized in OT as instruments of uncertainty reduction in their ability to secure stability, predictability, and precision. According to this view, the prevalence of uncertainty creates irregularities and complications in planning, standardization, precision, consistency, and causal linkage between means and ends. James Thompson paradigmatically links 'rationality' and 'uncertainty' as binary opposites (1967: 159):

Uncertainty appears as the fundamental problem for complex organizations, and coping with uncertainty, as the essence of the administrative process. Just as complete uncertainty and randomness is the antithesis of purpose and of organization, complete certainty is a figment of the imagination; but the tighter the norms of rationality, the more energy the organization will devote to moving toward certainty.

The concept of uncertainty assumed almost mythical and magical characteristics for organization theorists. For an organizational narrative constructed around the notion of rationality, uncertainty represented darkness and undesirability. It became a Pandora's box of troubles: opportunism, labor unrest, shortsightedness, competition, and other enemies of the organizational order. The engineer, the manager, and the planner were set to the task of slaying the dragon of uncertainty. Their authority derived from their ability to cope with and reduce uncertainty.

Oliver Williamson, a leading contemporary organizational economist, most explicitly elaborated the theoretical framework that adopted this ideological position. According to Williamson's fourfold framework, uncertainty-reduction and bounded rationality hold crucial importance for the understanding of 'market failures'.[22] His scheme suggests that given 'bounded rationality' (i.e. the limits of the human mind), it is very costly and sometimes impossible to determine all identifiable future contingencies. Transactions and long-term contracts may therefore be supplanted by hierarchies, which Williamson calls 'internal organization' (Williamson 1975: 9):

internal organization permits adaptations to uncertainty to be accomplished by administrative processes in a sequential fashion. Thus, rather than attempt to anticipate all possible contingencies from the outset, the future is permitted to unfold. Internal organization in this way economizes on the bounded rationality attributes of decision makers in circumstances in which prices are not 'sufficient statistics' and uncertainty is substantial.

---

[22] The four concepts are: 'bounded rationality', 'uncertainty', 'opportunism', and 'small numbers'.

'Uncertainty' and 'uncertainty reduction' are used here to legitimize the use of an instrumental definition of rationality (Weitz and Shenhav 2000; Shenhav and Weitz 2000; Weitz 1997). The root metaphor of uncertainty spawned a variety of strategies and frameworks to fight, reduce, or adapt to uncertainty such as 'buffering' and 'bridging' strategies within the 'resource dependence' perspective (Pfeffer and Salancik 1978), or 'information processing' or 'information reduction' strategies within the structural contingency perspective (Galbraith 1973).

Again, I argue that the seeds for the 'uncertainty reduction' and 'bounded rationality' frameworks were sown in late nineteenth-century engineering/management discourse about organizations. For example, the editors of the *American Machinist* maintained that it was the role of engineers to 'serve humanity in the elimination of chance ... [as] there are innumerable uncertainties to be cleared up.' (*American Machinist*, 14, Apr. 1904: 479). They conceptualized the business enterprise as a unified whole that needed to be controlled and coordinated in a systematic, rational fashion, in light of 'the chaotic state of factory practices.' (*Engineering Magazine*, Jan. 1911: 496). They argued that systematization of organizations implies an attempt to transcend dependence upon the capacity of any single individual; it is instead to build a solution into the formal system to achieve 'greater predictability in coordination' and 'forecasting'.

The rationale for systematization was made explicit in connection with the limitations of individual actors. In numerous articles at the turn of the century, the system was portrayed as superior to individuals in handling uncertainty. Harrington Emerson, for example, suggested that 'the object of [organizational] records is to increase the scope and number of warnings, to give us more information than is usually received immediately through our senses.'(*Engineering Magazine*, 1900: 392). Systematizer Horace Arnold argued, 'If all men had absolutely infallible memories, and were incapable of making any statement at variance with those memories, it would be possible, perhaps, to carry on a successful and prosperous manufacturing business without the use of shop books or factory accounts' (Arnold 1901: 9). A related, bounded-rationality argument can be found in the formulations of Alexander Hamilton Church. In Church's view, the justification for systematization in the newly developed factories of the late nineteenth century rested upon the limitation of the human mind faced with exploding complexity. He argued,

The necessity for coordination is an inevitable result of the evolution of the factory, no one mind can grasp and hold all the details. (*Engineering Magazine*, 1900: 392)

And,

It is hardly too much to say that the evolution of a science of management was inevitable as soon as the scale of industrial operations became so great that no single manager, however, naturally gifted, could continue to control personally all the activities of the plant. (*Engineering Magazine*, Apr. 1911: 97)

Canonical organization theory—shaped by the epistemology of American sociology and the engineering discourse—adopted and disseminated the rhetoric, logic, and epistemology that was produced by the agents under its study. Despite the ideological overtones embedded in 'uncertainty' and 'bounded rationality', in organizational theory the concepts were made neutral and universal, without reference to the specific cultural conditions of their origin. The conflict-laden history of management and organizations was edited out of the canon as represented in the reconstruction of the field presented in the outset by Scott (1998).[23]

How can organization theory break away from the incestuous isomorphism with its subject? Berger and Luckmann, who were most concerned with this phenomenon, suggested that 'reification is a modality of consciousness, more precisely, a modality of man's objectification of the human world' (Berger and Luckmann 1966). For phenomena to be taken as objects of social scientific explanation, they must first be stripped of the natural and concrete immediacy in which they appear to everyday consciousness. A reflexive sociology that rejects the reification of rationality—exerted by a growing corps of trained experts and enlightened bureaucracies—seems to hold the answer. Rather than viewing rationality as the ontological basis of society, it should be formulated as a cultural system with explicit reference to its capitalistic, bureaucratic, and scientific sources. This reflexive position undercuts the assumption that instrumental rationality is a universal ontological feature of nature and society.

A growing body of literature has begun to critique management along these lines in recent years. Following intra-paradigmatic (see Locke 1996), neo-Marxist (Marglin 1974; Braverman 1974; Edwards 1979; Clegg and Dunkerley 1980), and postmodern (Burrell 1988; Clegg 1990; Grey 1996) critique, this literature has established an alternative epistemological position for NATO (North American Theory of Organizations). Likewise a new critical outlet *Organization* was established mainly by European entrepreneurs-academics to give voice to heterogeneous views other than that found in the *Administrative Science Quarterly*.

Fournier and Grey (2000) offer a detailed analysis of this new body of literature known as 'Critical Management Studies' (CMS), the title first appearing in Alvesson and Willmott's (1992) edited collection. CMS is mostly a tradition that emerged in the United Kingdom following the non-positivist, non-functional, and postmodernist trends prevalent among sociologists who joined the business schools during the 1980s and 1990s. Business schools, it should be emphasized are new to the United Kingdom, dating roughly to the 1960s (Whitley, Thomas, and Marceau 1981). Unlike the traditional American business schools they allowed for other voices to be heard and a wider range of theoretical options were opened: neo-Marxism, critical theory, post-structuralism, feminism, cultural studies, post-colonial theory,

---

[23] "Labor and Industrial Relations" and "Organization Theory" are two distinct academic research fields as if work is not occurring in organizations.

and deconstructionism (e.g. Czarniawska and Guje 1996; Czarniawska 2000). Fournier and Grey offer three criteria for the demarcation of the critical from the non-critical management studies.

First, they suggest that CMS are not governed by principles that subordinate knowledge to production and efficiency. In other words they do not seek to contribute to the effectiveness of managerial practice and organizations. As they argue: 'the invocation of notions such as power, control and inequality typically betoken some form of critical approach, whilst efficiency, effectiveness, and profitability do not' (p. 17). Furthermore, 'what unites the very disparate contributions within CMS is the attempt to expose and reverse the work of mainstream management theory' (p. 18).

Second, they suggest that CMS are engaged in deconstructing the reality of management and de-essentializing organizational discursive and non-discursive practices. As they argue: 'whilst in mainstream management theories various "imperatives" are invoked ... to legitimize a proposed course of action and to suggest.... That "there is no alternative, CMS is committed to uncovering alternatives that have been effaced by management knowledge and practice"' (p. 18).

Third, Fournier and Grey suggest that CMS employ philosophical and methodological reflexivity with the objectives of unmasking power relations and control structures. This critical endeavor is still in its infancy[24] and its impact is yet to be determined. I regard this chapter as an effort in this direction.

---

[24] Only in 1996 the British Academy of Management and only in 1998 the American Academy of Management established CM sessions for the first time (Fournier and Grey 2000: 28).

References

ABRAHAMSON, ERIC (1997). 'The Emergence and Prevalence of Employee Management Rhetorics: The Effects of Long Waves, Labor Unions, and Turnover, 1875 to 1992'. *Academy of Management Journal*, 40: 491–533.

ALVESSON, M., and WILLMOTT, H. (eds.) (1992). *Critical Management Studies*. London: Sage.

ARNOLD, HORACE L. (1901). *The Complete Cost-Keeper*. New York: Engineering Magazine Press.

BARLEY, STEPHEN R., and KUNDA, GIDEON (1992). 'Design and Devotion: Surges of Rational and Normative Ideologies of Control in Managerial Discourse'. *Administrative Science Quarterly*, 37: 363–99.

BARNARD, CHESTER (1938). *The Functions of the Executive*. Cambridge, Mass.: Harvard University Press.

——(1948). *Organization and Management*. Cambridge, Mass.: Harvard University Press.

BAUMAN, ZYGMUNT (1989). *Modernity and the Holocaust*. Cambridge: Polity Press.

BEDAUX, CHARLES E. (1917). *The Bedaux Efficiency Course for Industrial Application.*

BELL, DANIEL (1960). *The End of Ideology.* Glencoe, Ill.: Free Press.

BENDIX, REINHARD (1960). *Max Weber: An Intellectual Portrait.* New York: Doubleday & Company Inc.

BERGER, PETER L., and LUCKMANN, THOMAS (1966). *The Social Construction of Reality.* Garden City, NY: Doubleday.

BERLE, ADOLPH, Jr, and MEANS, GARDINER (1932). *The Modern Corporation and Private Property.* New York: MacMillan.

BLAU, PETER M. (1955). *The Dynamics of Bureaucracy.* Chicago: University of Chicago Press.

—— (1956). *Bureaucracy in Modern Society.* New York: Random House.

—— and SCOTT, RICHARD W. (1962). *Formal Organizations.* San Francisco: Chandler.

BRAVERMAN, HARRY (1974). *Labor and Monopoly Capital: The Degradation of Work in the Twentieth Century.* New York: Monthly Review Press.

BURRELL, G. (1988). 'Modernism, Post-modernism and Organizational Analysis 2: The Contribution of Michel Foucault'. *Organization Studies*, 9: 221–35.

—— (1996). 'Normal Science, Paradigms, Metaphors, Discourses and Genealogies of Analysis', in S. Clegg, C. Hardy, and W. Nord (eds.), *Handbook of Organization Studies.* London: Sage.

CALLON, MICHELE (1981). 'Struggles and Negotiations to Define What is Problematic and What is Not: The Sociological Translation', in Karin D. Knorr, Roger Krohn, and Richard Whitley (eds.), *The Social Process of Scientific Investigation.* Dordrecht: D. Reidel Publishing.

CHANDLER, ALFRED D., Jr (1962). *Strategy and Structure: Chapters in the History of the American Industrial Enterprise.* Cambridge, Mass.: MIT Press.

—— (1977). *The Visible Hand: The Managerial Revolution in American Business.* Cambridge, Mass.: Harvard University Press.

CHURCH, ALEXANDER HAMILTON (1914). *The Science and Practice of Management.* New York: Engineering Magazine Company.

CLEGG, STEWART (1990). *Modern Organizations: Organizations Studies in the Postmodern World.* London: Sage.

—— and DUNKERLEY, DAVID (1980). *Organization, Class and Control.* London: Routledge & Kegan Paul.

COHEN, J., *et al.* (1975). 'De-Parsonizing Weber: A Critique of Parsons' Interpretation of Weber's Sociology'. *American Sociological Review,* 40: 229–41.

COLEMAN, JAMES S. (1989). 'Rationality and Society'. *Rationality and Society,* 1: 5–9.

—— (1990). *The Foundations of Social Theory.* Cambridge, Mass.: Harvard University Press.

—— (1993). 'Rational Reconstruction of Society'. *American Sociological Review,* 58: 1–15.

COSER, LEWIS A. (1977). *Masters of Sociological Thought* (2nd edn) New York: Harcourt Brace Jovanovich Inc.

CZARNIAWSKA, BARBARA (2000). *Writing Management: Organization Theory as a Literary Genre.* Oxford: Oxford University Press.

—— and SEVON, GUJE (eds.) (1996). *Translating Organizational Change.* Berlin–New York: Walter de Gruyter.

DELEUZE, GIL, and GUATTARI, FELIX (1987). *A Thousand Plateaus: Capitalism and Schizophrenia.* Minneapolis: University of Minnesota Press.

DJELIC, MARIE-LAURE (1998). *Exporting the American Model: The Postwar Transformation of European Business.* Oxford: Oxford University Press.

DOBBIN, FRANK (1994). 'Cultural Models of Organization: The Social Construction of Rational Organizing Principles', in Diana Crane (ed.), *Sociology of Culture: Emerging Theoretical Responsibility.* Oxford: Basil Blackwell.

DONALDSON, LEX (1995). *American Anti-Management Theories of Organization.* Cambridge: Cambridge University Press.

EDWARDS, RICHARD (1979). *Contested Terrain: The Transformation of the Workplace in the Twentieth Century.* New York: Basic Books.

EMERSON, HARRINGTON (1909). *Efficiency as a Basis for Operations and Wages.* New York: Engineering Magazine Company.

FEENBERG, ANDREW (1981). *Lukács, Marx and the Sources of Critical Theory.* Totowa, NJ: Rowman and Littlefield.

FOUCAULT, MICHEL (1973). *The Order of Things.* New York: Vintage.

—— (1975). *The Birth of the Clinic.* New York: Vintage.

—— (1977a). *The Archaeology of Knowledge.* London: Tavistock.

—— (1977b). *Madness and Civilisation.* London: Tavistock.

—— (1977c). *Discipline of Punish.* Harmondsworth: Penguin.

FOURNIER, VALERIE, and GREY, CHRIS (2000). 'At the Critical Moment: Conditions and Prospects for Critical Management Studies'. *Human Relations*, 53: 7–32.

GALBRAITH, JAY (1973). *Designing Complex Organizations.* Reading, Mass.: Addison-Wesley.

GAMSON, WILLIAM A. (1992). *Talking Politics.* Cambridge: Cambridge University Press.

GANTT, HENRY L. (1910). *Work, Wages and Profit.* New York: Engineering Magazine.

GISPEN, KEES (1989). *New Profession, Old Order: Engineers and German Society, 1815–1914.* Cambridge: Cambridge University Press.

GOULDNER, ALVIN W. (1954). *Patterns of Industrial Bureaucracy.* Glencoe, Ill.: The Free Press.

—— (1976). *The Dialectics of Ideology and Technology.* New York: Oxford University Press.

GREY, CHRIS (1996). 'Towards a Critique of Managerialism: The Contribution of Simone Weil'. *Journal of Management Studies*, 33: 591–611.

GUILLEN, MAURO F. (1994). *Models of Management: Work, Authority, and Organization in a Comparative Perspective.* Chicago: University of Chicago Press.

GULICK, LUTHER, and URWICK, LYNDALL (1937). *Papers on the Science of Administration.* New York: Columbia University, Institute of Public Administration.

HACKING, IAN (1983/1992). *Representing and Intervening.* Cambridge: Cambridge University Press.

HAWTHORN, GEOFFREY (1987). *Enlightenment and Despair: A History of Social Theory.* Cambridge: Cambridge University Press.

HAYS, SAMUEL P. (1959). *Conservation and the Gospel of Efficiency: The Progressive Conservation Movement, 1890–1920.* New York: Atheneum.

HEDSTROM, PETER, and SWEDBERG, RICHARD (1996). 'Rational Choice, Empirical Research, and the Sociological Tradition'. *European Sociological Review*, 12: 127–46.

HERNES, G. (1989). 'The Logic of the Protestant Ethic'. *Rationality and Society*, 1: 123–62.

HORKHEIMER, MAX, and ADORNO, THEODORE (1972). *Dialectics of Enlightenment.* New York: Herder & Herder.

HOUNSHELL, DAVID A. (1984). *From the American System to Mass Production 1800–1932: The Development of Manufacturing Technology in the United States.* Baltimore: Johns Hopkins University Press.

KALBERG, STEPHEN (2001). 'The "Spirit" of Capitalism Revisited'. *Perspectives*, 23/1: 2–4.

KATZ, DANIEL, and KAHN, ROBERT L. (1966). *The Social Psychology of Organizations*. New York: John Wiley.

LATOUR, BRUNO (1987). *Science in Action*. Cambridge, Mass.: Harvard University Press.

—— (1993). *We Have Never Been Modern*. Cambridge, Mass.: Harvard University Press.

LAWRENCE, PAUL, and LORSCH, JAY (1967). *Organization and Environment*. Boston: Graduate School of Business, Harvard University.

LIKERT, RENSIS (1961). *New Patterns of Management*. New York: McGraw-Hill.

LOCKE, ROBERT R. (1984). *The End of the Practical Man: Entrepreneurship and Higher Education in Germany, France, and Great Britain, 1880–1940*. London: JAI Press Inc.

—— (1996). *The Collapse of American Management Mystique*. Oxford: Oxford University Press.

LUKÁCS, GEORG (1923/1971). *History and Class Consciousness*. Cambridge, Mass.: MIT Press.

LYOTARD, J. F. (1984). *The Postmodern Condition*. Manchester: Manchester University Press.

MARCH, JAMES G., and SIMON, HERBERT A. (1958). *Organizations*. New York: John Wiley.

MARCUS, ALAN, and SEGAL, HOWARD P. (1989). *Technology in America*. New York: Harcourt Brace Jovanovich.

MARCUS, G. E., and CUSHMAN, D. (1982). 'Ethnographies as Texts'. *Annual Review of Anthropology*, 11: 25–69.

MARGLIN, STEPHEN A. (1974). 'What Do Bosses Do? The Origins and Functions of Hierarchy in Capitalist Production'. *Review of Radical Political Economics*, 6: 60–112.

MERTON, ROBERT K. (1949/1957). 'Bureaucratic Structure and Personality', in id., *Social Theory and Social Structure*. Glencoe, Ill.: Free Press.

—— GRAY, AILSA P., HOCKEY, BARBARA, and SELVIN, HANAN (eds.) (1952). *Reader in Bureaucracy*. Glencoe, Ill.: Free Press.

MOHR, JOHN W., and VENTRESCA, MARC J. (forthcoming). 'Archival Research Methods', in Joel A. C. Baum (ed.), *Companion to Organizations*. Oxford: Blackwell Publishers.

MOONEY, J. D., and REILEY, A. C. (1939). *The Principles of Organization*. New York: Harper.

MILLER, PETER, and O'LEARY, TED (1989). 'Hierarchies and American Ideals, 1900–1940'. *Academy of Management Review*, 14: 250–65.

PARSONS, TALCOTT (1942). 'Max Weber and the Contemporary Political Crisis'. *Review of Politics*, 4: 61–76.

—— (1947). 'Introduction', in *Max Weber: The Theory of Social and Economic Organization*, tr. A. M. Henderson and Talcott Parsons. Glencoe, Ill.: Free Press.

—— (1949). *The Structure of Social Action*. Glencoe, Ill.: Free Press.

—— (1951). *The Social System*. Glencoe, Ill.: Free Press.

PERROW, CHARLES (1986). *Complex Organizations: A Critical Essay*. Glenview, Ill.: Scott, Foresman and Company.

PFEFFER, JEFFREY, and SALANCIK, GERALD R. (1978). *The External Control of Organizations*. New York: Harper & Row.

PRENDERGAST, CHRISTOPHER (1986). 'Alfred Schutz and the Austrian School of Economics'. *American Journal of Sociology*, 92: 1–26.

RABINOW, PAUL (1984). *The Foucault Reader*. New York: Pantheon Books.

ROETHLISBERGER, F. J., and DICKSON, W. J. (1941). *Management and the Worker*. Cambridge, Mass.: Harvard University Press.

Ross, Dorothy (1991). *The Origins of American Social Science*. Cambridge: Cambridge University Press.

—— (1993). 'An Historian's View of American Social Science'. *Journal of the History of the Behavioral Sciences*, 29: 99–112.

Roy, William G. (1997). *Socializing Capital: The Rise of Large Industrial Corporation in America*. Princeton: Princeton University Press.

Scott, W. Richard (1981/1987/1992/1998). *Organizations: Rational, Natural and Open Systems*. Englewood Cliffs, NJ: Prentice-Hall.

Selznick, Philip (1949). *TVA and the Grass Roots*. Berkeley: University of California Press.

Shenhav, Yehouda (1996). 'Lex Donaldson: American Anti-Management Theories of Organization'. *Organization Studies*, 17: 1027–31.

—— (1994). 'Manufacturing Uncertainty and Uncertainty in Manufacturing: Managerial Discourse and the Rhetoric of Organizational Theory'. *Science in Context*, 7: 275–305.

—— (1995). 'From Chaos to Systems'. *Administrative Science Quarterly*, 40: 557–85.

—— (1999). *Manufacturing Rationality: The Engineering Foundations of the Managerial Revolution*. Oxford: Oxford University Press.

—— and Weitz, Ely (2000). 'The Roots of Uncertainty in Organization Theory: A Historical Constructivist Analysis'. *Organization*, 7: 373–401.

Simon, Herbert A. (1957). *Administrative Behavior*. New York: Macmillan.

Taylor, Frederick W. (1911). *Principles of Scientific Management*. New York: Harper.

Terry, George R. (1953). *Principles of Management*. Homewood, Ill.: Irwin.

Thompson, James D. (1967). *Organizations in Action*. New York: McGraw-Hill.

Tilly, Charles (1978). *From Mobilization to Revolution*. Reading, Mass.: Addison-Wesley.

—— (1991). 'Individualism Askew'. *American Journal of Sociology*, 96: 1007–11.

Toulmin, Stephen (1990). *Cosmopolis: The Hidden Agenda of Modernity*. New York: Free Press.

Trahair, Richard C. S. (1984). *The Humanist Temper: The Life and Work of Elton Mayo*. New Brunswick: Transaction Books.

Ward, John William (1964). 'The Ideal of Individualism and the Reality of Organizations', in Earl F. Cheit (ed.), *The Business Establishment*. New York: John Wiley.

Waring, Stephen P. (1991). *Taylorism Transformed: Scientific Management Theory Since 1945*. Chapel Hill, NC: University of North Carolina Press.

Weber, Max (1947). *The Theory of Social and Economic Organization*, trans. M. Henderson and T. Parsons. New York: Oxford.

—— (1949). *On the Methdology of the Social Sciences*. Glencoe, Ill.: The Free Press.

—— (1958). 'The Social Psychology of the World Religions', in H. H. Gerth and C. W. Mills (eds. and trans.), *From Max Weber*. New York: Oxford University Press.

—— (1921/1968). *Economy and Society*, i, ed. Guenther Roth and Claus Wittich. New York: Bedminster Press.

Weiss, Richard M. (1983). 'Weber on Bureaucracy: Management Consultant or Political Theorist?' *Academy of Management Review*, 8: 242–8.

Weitz, Ely (1997). 'The Institutionalization of Uncertainty in Organization Theory'. Ph.D. thesis (Tel-Aviv University).

—— and Shenhav, Yehouda (2000). 'A Longitudinal Analysis of Technical and Organizational Uncertainty in Management Theory'. *Organization Studies*, 21: 243–65.

WHITLEY, R., THOMAS, A., and MARCEAU, J. (1981). *Masters of Business: The Making of a New Elite.* New York: Tavistock.

WIEBE, ROBERT H. (1967). *The Search for Order, 1877–1920.* New York: Hill & Wang.

WILLIAMSON, OLIVER E. (1975). *Markets and Hierarchies: Analysis and Antitrust Implications.* New York: Free Press.

YUCHTMAN, EPHRAIM, and SEASHORE, STANLEY E. (1967). 'A System Resource Approach to Organizational Effectiveness'. *American Sociological Review,* 32: 891–903.

....

CHAPTER 7

FEMINIST THEORY AND ORGANIZATION THEORY

A DIALOGUE ON NEW BASES

....

SILVIA GHERARDI

Is 'GENDER' still an issue in social and organizational sciences? And, if it is, does it concern only bodily difference, discrimination practices, and organizations as reproducing inequality?

Many scholars argue that nowadays 'gender' has lost its importance. A well-known critic of modernity writes: 'As anatomy stops being destiny, sexual identity more and more becomes a life-style issue' (Giddens 1992: 199). The consequences of accepting the definition of sexual identity as gender and gender as a lifestyle are that gender is again relegated to the private, organizations regain innocence, and the micropolitics of organization life are obscured. This representation of gender will be contrasted with the argument that the changing social and historical meaning of 'gender' is destabilizing its interpretative categories, bringing to the fore the plurality of differences (not only those related to gender) and, together with the appearance of multiple voices, the claim to multiple knowledges.

For their encouragement and help, I am very grateful to Attila Bruni, Patricia Yancey Martin, and Barbara Poggio.

Gender has to do not only with bodies, and power, but also with the politics of knowledge, and therefore with organizations as containers of different bodies and sexualities, as arenas of power/knowledge, and with organization theory as a system of knowledge representation.

The contention that the organizational knowledge conventionally called 'organizational theory' (OT) is male gendered is too well known to reiterate. The pun that renders the 'mainstream' as the 'malestream' expresses an awareness that has no need of elaboration. It is less well known, however, that the dialogue that has taken place since the 1970s between critical reflections on gender—what I shall call 'feminist theory' (FT)—and OT has involved numerous voices and has enriched both areas of thought.

In this article I start from the premiss that neither FT nor OT is a homogeneous and unitary body of knowledge, my intention being to illustrate the multiple points of view expressed by those involved in this conversation, and to outline current developments within it. I shall argue that the theoretical interests of OT and FT may converge on a research programme centred on the politics of knowledge. In developing this thesis, I shall briefly survey the main theories in gender studies, showing how they represent the relation between gender and organization and contribute to analysis of organizations and organizational processes. I conclude with a reflection on the politics of knowledge in FT and OT and the—ironic, nomadic, eccentric—knowing subjects.

7.1 Gender as a Situated Category of Analysis

In my experience as a sociologist, teacher, and feminist,[1] when I introduce students to the concepts of 'socially constructed reality', and 'reflexivity', I always use the example of 'gender' as a category invented by feminists at the end of the 1970s. I do so because it is a useful device to illustrate, in a cultural and historical perspective, how social categorization has given form, substance, and visibility to women's experiences. But did not women and their experiences exist before the word 'gender'? And do they not continue to exist outside its semantic domain? Answering these questions is a complex task requiring intricate argument to demonstrate that

---

[1] The use of the first person singular, as well as the personal references, are not accidental. They result from a deliberate rhetorical intent to criticize the 'scientific' style of writing that produces authoritativeness by cancelling the subject and producing dis-embodied texts. On this see, Silverman (1993); Jacques (1997).

the category of gender has given visibility to, and thereby enabled the investigation of, a social reality that was previously 'non-existent' because it was not part of theoretical awareness. The use of the category has given rise to a political subject—a feminist movement—able to conduct autonomous reflection on the conditions of its own existence, and also a critique of what counts as 'knowledge' and how the 'knower' is constructed. Moreover, by generating new knowledge, it has also modified gender relationships. The meaning of the term 'gender' is a social product that changes through the use that a society makes of it and the knowledge that it produces.

In the arbitrary way in which all histories use a point of departure and a founding myth to ground themselves in History, we may follow Piccone Stella and Saraceno (1996) by adopting the convention that the term 'gender' made its first official appearance in scientific discourse in 1975. That was the year when Gayle Rubin, in her book *The Traffic in Women*, used the expression 'sex-gender system' to denote the set of processes, adaptations, patterns of behaviour, and relationships by which every society transforms biological sexuality into products of human activity.

The term 'gender' thus first arose in the academic studies of American feminism (Nicholson 1994). It was then imported into Europe with different outcomes but a shared endeavour in social studies. In fact, the evocative connotation implicit in the term 'gender' arises from the act of classification and the social act of seeing human beings as two, and only two, types of individuals. Gender is therefore a binary concept: men and women constitute gender; or in other words, the ways in which human beings present themselves, self-represent themselves, and are perceived in society constitute gender. In this sense, gender is a relational concept subsumed by a dyadic code that entails constant relation and tension. As a consequence, by exploring the relationships between men and women gender studies modify the concept of gender, defer its historical meaning, and thereby open the way for a plurality of interpretations of what constitutes 'gender'.

Not only should the singular and universal Man give way to the diversity of social experiences in their duality, but scientific categories should change to include this plurality of interpretations. A telling example is provided by Chiara Saraceno (1993) when she points out that if the extension of economic analysis to women's work has uncovered a presence that was previously neglected, this should lead not to sectorial analysis 'of women' but rather to a redefinition of the term 'labour force', and to critical reflection on the measurement of market value. The same example can be set within organizational studies: what is required is not study of participation by women in organizational processes, but rather a redefining of 'organizational categories' so that they explicitly accommodate the experiences of men and women and reveal the ideological consequences of representing an abstract 'labour force' and a de-sexualized and dis-embodied worker in language.

It is an irony of history that it is women who have coined the term 'gender' to denote and give voice to a knowledge grounded in different experiences and situated in possession of a different body, and that many scholars (men and women) have interpreted gender studies as involving the study 'of women', as if only they possessed a body and a gender. The alleged gender neutrality of the term 'labour force' covers its masculinity, and the use of the term 'gender' to refer to women shows that in fact women are not allowed *not* to have a body, and therefore a bodily-situated knowledge. The equations 'sex = gender' and 'gender = women' are not only misunderstandings due to inexperience or to a linguistic operation which attenuates the social embarrassment caused by the word 'sex', replacing it with a more 'polite' one; they are an ideological operation which allows gender studies to continue without calling the gender relation—that is, the relation between the male and female, men and women, masculine and feminine—into question. In this manner, maleness is made invisible, removed from critical reflection and continues to be the prime term, the one in relation to which the other is defined by default.

Formulation of the concept of gender imports two simultaneously evoked differences into OT: sexual differences and power differences. Put briefly, one may say that the concept has affected organizational analysis by prompting study of the extent to which sexual difference is socially and organizationally constructed, and of the extent to which gender relations spring from other than biological differences between men and women. In order to explore whether and to what extent the transformative impact of the category 'gender' has been realized in OT, one must retrace the debate on gender within feminist studies. This will clarify that the concept of gender is not immutable, that it has indeed undergone rapid changes, and that different research programmes in the intersection of gender and organizations are based on different conceptions of gender.

7.2 WHEREIN DOES GENDER DIFFERENCE LIE?

Analysis of sexual difference has identified the subjectivity of a political actor which addresses the question 'What is a woman?' and comes up with three answers, locating the origin of the difference in:

1. *The body*, as the biological basis of both sexuality and the capacity of women to bear children. This is the essentialist position that views the maternal body as defining the qualities of women: nurturance, a capacity for intimacy, and pacifism. The woman/mother relationship also generates the mental mechanisms of early infancy that differentiate a child's first social relationships by gender (Chodorow 1978). However gender may be socially constructed, according to this

approach, it is the body that constitutes the biological material for the differentiation between female or male.

2. *Society, culture, or politics*, this being the position that European debate has
labelled 'culturalist' in order to emphasize the social construction of gender,
and also to stress that the social construction of a person's 'nature' is a social and
organizational process which attributes gender and constructs biology (Lorber
and Farrell 1991). In the Anglo-American debate, the term 'culturalist' is used
to refer not so much to the nature/culture dichotomy as to a 'female culture'
elaborated on biological difference. French and Italian feminism view the body
as the symbolic rather than the physical origin of the subject 'woman' (Irigaray
1974; Cavarero 1990; Muraro 1991). This subject is unable to 'auto-signify herself'
because western philosophical thought has imposed itself as male thought,
devising a universal and neutral subject that defines and represents the world
in its own terms. As a consequence, women have been denied access to the
symbolic.

3. *Language*. According to deconstructionist and post-structuralist analysis,
western logocentric thought has produced individuals shaped by discursive practices. Deconstructionism is therefore a feminist practice that encourages women to
show that the practices which define them are a fiction and are historically situated
in power relations. Post-structuralist feminism and the postmodern debate on
contemporary subjectivity emphasize that the crisis of subjectivity mainly affects
the western male, while 'other' subjectivities are now moving to centre stage (Flax
1987; Hekman 1990).

These three sources of differentiation—body, society, and language—are understood differently according to a plurality of approaches in the conversation between
FT and OT as well. In order to provide a historical overview of feminist approaches,
and of how they have regarded organizational studies, I shall refer to the survey of
the literature conducted by Marta Calás and Linda Smircich (1996).[2] Table 7.1 is an
extreme simplification of their analysis, its sole purpose being to highlight: (i) how
the various conceptions of the sex-gender system translate into different conceptions of the relation between gender and organizational studies, (ii) how epistemological mingling in the social sciences has benefited from the feminist critique, and
(iii) how the latter has completed a cycle of dissemination by moving, so to speak,
from women's studies to gender studies.

---

[2] Calás and Smircich's classification of feminist theories is based on an Anglo-American understanding of political categories and feminist historical movements. These categories partly overlap with
the European understanding of politics and feminist thought, and partly do not represent them. My
reason for not giving an Eurocentric interpretation of feminist theories lays in recognition that there is
an Anglo-American hegemony within OT as well, and keeping the two stories together makes it easier
for the reader to follow the line of argument. In writing for an international audience I adhere to the
fiction of a single (but not universal) body of knowledge called OT, but am well aware of the political
nature of such a representation.

Table 7.1 A summary of feminist approaches

School of thought	Liberal	Radical	Psychoanalytic	Marxist	Socialist	Poststructuralist/ Postmodern	Third World/ Post-colonial
Intellectual roots	Evolved from 18th- and 19th-century political economy	Generated in the women's liberation movements of the late 1960s	Evolved from Freudian and other psychoanalytic theories, in particular object-relations theories	Based on, and a 'correction' of, the Marxist critique of capitalist society since the mid-19th century	Emerged in the 1970s as part of attempts by women's liberation movements to synthesize Marxist, psychoanalytic, and radical feminisms	Located in contemporary French poststructuralist critiques of 'knowledge' and 'identity'	Emerging from intersections of gendered critiques of western feminisms and post-colonial critiques of western epistemologies
Conception of sex/ gender	Sex is part of the essential biological endowment, a binary variable Gender is socialized onto sexed human beings for appropriate behaviour	'Sex class' is the condition of women as an oppressed class Gender is a social construction that ensures women's subordination to men	Individuals become sexually identified as part of their psychosexual development Gender structures a social system of male domination that influences psychosexual development	Gender is part of historical class relations that constitute systems of oppression under capitalism	Gender is processual and is socially constituted through several intersections of sex, race, ideology, and experiences of oppression under patriarchy and capitalism (which are distinct systems)	Sex/gender are discursive practices that constitute specific subjectivities through power and resistance in the materiality of human bodies	Considers the constitution of complex subjectivities beyond western conceptions of sex/ gender, focusing on gendered aspects of globalization processes
Representation of gender/ organization	Organization theory as gender neutral	Alternative feminist organizing practices	Female skills as an organizational advantage	Organizations as sites of reproduction of patriarchy and capitalism	Organizing as gendered processes	Organizing as the discursive mobilization of power/knowledge resources	Globalized economy and worldwide organizing principles

Source: Calás and Smircich 1996 (first and second row), my integration (third row).

Following Calás and Smircich's description of how various feminist approaches intersect with organizational studies, different 'voices' join in a metaphorical conversation (see Table 7.1):

- *Liberal feminist theory.* Following liberal political theorists of the eighteenth and nineteenth centuries, the issue of equal access with men to opportunities in all spheres of life, but without radical transformation of the social and political system, arose in the 1960s, the aim being to achieve equal representation, to fight sex discrimination, and to deny sex differences. Liberal feminists shifted from themes of equality to themes of difference in the 1980s and 1990s, still pursuing the issue of gender justice, while in organizational studies liberal feminist research favoured positivist epistemologies assumed to be gender-neutral. In the same vein organizational theory is based on the assumption of neutrality, and the organizational processes affected by gender stereotypes are viewed as merely 'reflecting' the wider social arrangements between the sexes. In the Anglo-Saxon organizational literature the strand of research which investigates gender equity has been labelled 'women-in-management' and seeks to demonstrate that women are as good as men in fulfilling organizational needs. A representative topic of this scholarship is the concept of 'glass ceiling', which addresses the persistence of sex segregation and tries to elucidate its causes through measurable constructs.

- *Radical feminist theory* takes the subordination of women as its fundamental problematic and has political roots in the new left (in the United States and in the 1968 student movements in Europe). It conceives gender as a system of male domination, a fundamental organizing principle of patriarchal society. Every sphere of life is an arena for sexual politics, because there is no distinction between the 'political' and 'personal' realms. The consciousness raising and separatism that developed as practice-located methods to shed light on women experiences and feminism are thought of as theory and practice of women and among women only. A separatist politics has been theorized in relation to male-dominated organizations in pursuit of alternative organizations that reflect feminist values and are 'leaderless' and 'structureless'. Feminist organizational practices should be informed by equality, community, participation, an integration of form and content (Brown 1991) and should always ask the woman question (Ferree and Martin 1995). Starting from a women-centred theory, some scholars have revised basic organizational concepts such as work, career, and management (Marshall 1984; Tancred 1995).

- *Psychoanalytic feminist theory* denies the biological determinism of traditional psychoanalytic interpretations of gender and sexuality, while considering the patriarchal family engendering distinctions in male/female psychological development and different notions of gendered self and identity. This is not only a problem of socialization but also an epistemological one concerning whose knowledge is valued and whose is devalued (Braidotti 1989). Different psychosexual developments lead to different concepts of justice and morality: male morality is an ethics of justice, while female morality is an ethics of care (Gilligan 1982). By valuing the consequences of different psychosexual developments, organization theory finds explanations for women's fear of success, for female behaviours that are passive, ambivalent towards a career, which fall short in corporate (male) culture and treat women's difference as an advantage for corporate effectiveness: the female resource. Women's ways of knowing and leading, their relational skills, sensitivity, and empathy become skilled resources for global competition.

- *Marxist feminist theory* conceptualizes gender and identity as structural, historical, and material. As with class, gender subsumes women's relation to men under the workers' relation to capital. Marxist feminism analyses how identities are constructed through social practices such as work (and workplace–household intersection) by focusing on relations of inequality, power, patriarchy, and capitalism. It is concerned with the gendered division of labour and women's 'double' oppression by class and sex, capitalism and patriarchy (Hartsock 1983).

- *Socialist feminist theory.* In explaining the persistence of gender segregation and oppression, socialist feminism addresses complex intersections of gender, race, class, and sexuality. 'From equality to differences' was the slogan in Europe that led feminist movements in the 1980s to discover not only differences between men and women but also differences among women and the oppression of women by women. In the United States the influence of other social movements like the black or the sexual liberation movement was more direct and the confrontation more sharp. In both cases the result was deeper awareness that the lines of differentiation are not parallel, but intersect in multiple ways and are expressed in multiple voices. In organization theory, awareness grew that gender assumptions are embedded in societal expectations and that they interact with organizational rules and practices lying 'underneath' macro-social structural arrangements (Acker 1990, 1992). The gendering and racializing of organizations also occurs through symbols, images, ideologies that legitimize gender inequalities and differences. The structuring of organizations along gender lines also involves sexuality (Game and Pringle 1984) and organizational sexuality (Hearn and Parkin 1987).

- *Post-structuralist/postmodern feminist theory.* Postmodernism exhibits a critical distrust concerning 'meta-narratives', transcendental reason, and the possibility of objective knowledge, and with the same attitude post-structuralist feminist theory interrogates the constitution of the 'feminine' within modernity. French feminism (Cixous and Clément 1986) and Anglo-American feminism (Weedon 1987) question the claims of many feminist theories which posit a privileged knowing subject, an essential feminine and universal representation of woman. This approach contains the basis for a broader critique of how 'knowledge' is constructed, in so far as it depends on the possibility of representing a reality that does not exist outside its representation in language. It is through language that researchers constitute the subject of their knowing, their subjectivities as knowers, and what counts as knowledge as distinct from what is 'not knowledge', i.e. the 'other' in the discourse, the silenced term. The precarious position of any claim to knowledge opens spaces for a distinctive feminist politics of knowledge that points to the local operation of power and the crucial role of discourse in sustaining hegemonic power. Using the metaphor of 'rewriting' (as an activity intended to expose the apparently unimpeachable structures of truth and knowledge) the works of Calás and Smircich (1992*a, b*) have been highly influential in focusing on the construction of gender in organizations and the involvement of organization studies as a scientific discipline in the constitution of gendered arrangements.

• *Third World/Post-colonial feminist theory*. Following rediscovery of Frantz Fanon (1952), post-colonial studies and an epistemological critique of western thought have acquired a new voice. The fragility of the category of gender is all the more evident when one considers the specificities of Third World women constituted as 'others' by western knowledges and First World women. In the context of specific First World/Third World relationships, a new subject acquires autonomy in self-signification under the new colonialism represented by globalization. Notions such as hybridization (Bhabha 1988) or *métissage* (Gruzinski 1999) express forms of assimilation and resistance to the dominant culture. In its reading of organizational phenomena such as globalization and transnationalization, the 'women-in-development' literature problematizes the representational space available for Third World women's subjectivities.

Feminism is a discourse on gender, but many different voices exist internally to it. Feminist theories have stressed the constitution of gender, locating it mainly in the body (liberal, radical, and psychoanalytic), in culture and social relations (Marxist, socialist, and post-colonial), and in language (post-structuralist). This brief excursus reveals crucial patterns in feminist thought that are also reflected in research on gender and in OT.

Although the category of gender has been decentralized, and although a web of signification is taking the place of a binary concept, gender is still linked to difference, inequality, and micropolitics of power. In the conversation between different feminisms a new awareness of the category 'gender' emerges in the intersections between bodies, discourses, and practices.

7.3 GENDER IN THE INTERSECTIONS BETWEEN BODIES, DISCOURSES, AND PRACTICES

To continue with the metaphor of science as conversation, I want to stress that some sort of agreement—always partial and unstable—has been reached on certain premises from which the conversation may follow a different course. For example, certain arguments have reached a temporary closure in feminist approaches,[3] and this has also happened in the relationship between FT and OT. In order to delineate how the theoretical interests of OT and FT may converge on a research programme centred on the politics of knowledge, I recall the turning points of several conversations that, in my opinion, have already expressed their potentiality.

The emancipationism which sought to deny gender difference or to posit the substantial extraneousness of women from organizations not based on female thought is a cycle of analysis that has for the moment come to a closure. In organizational studies, it is a cycle represented by the shift from the labelling of the gender/organization relationship as a 'neglected area' (Hearn and Parkin 1983; Mills 1988) to a frenetic endeavour to 'add women in' by both counting them and giving them recipes 'to fit into the organization'.

A second cycle of thought has sought to found a political subjectivity for women. The effect of this project for political action has been to emphasize the homogeneity of women rather than their differences. The latter have been set in relation to the 'other' subject, so that the differences among women and those among men are undervalued. The articulation of gender in relation to class and race has led to the pluralization of subjectivity. In organizational studies, this shift has taken the form of a transition from equality to difference, and it is particularly evident in studies on management and human resources policies. Through the pursuit of equal opportunities and by 'mainstreaming the gender agenda' (defined in the EU as 'feminizing the mainstream'), the claim that OT is gender-neutral has given way to the definition of the female as a 'resource' at the disposal of organizations. The categorization of the female workforce as a newly discovered resource for organizations sustains the discourse on affirmative actions while the valorization of the female becomes an ideological attack on forms of hegemonic masculinity that nowadays are dysfunctional to forms of organization such as 'the flat organization', teamwork, couching leadership, and similar. The apparent valorization of the

---

[3] Pinch and Bijker (1989) use the term 'closure' for the political process of temporary stabilization of an artefact. They distinguish between a rhetorical closure and a closure by problem redefinition. In my opinion, also linguistic artefacts—theories—undergo the same stabilization process.

female as an organizational resource is another ideological device to co-opt white women by means of 'organizational seduction', using women's commitment, pleasure in work, and affirmation desires as means of organizational control.

Equal opportunities programmes and discourses turn the concern for the persistence of inequalities into a normative model that imposes inclusion at all costs on women. The diversity policies now arriving in Europe from the United States have been criticized (Lorbiecki and Jack 2000) as perpetuating rather than combating inequality and as prescribing essentialist categories of difference. The shift from equality to multiple differences is a conversational turn near to closure, but a question is left unanswered: 'Are women a unitary subject or a multiple subject?'

The question illustrates a theoretical stance that privileges both a point of view and a political project of emancipation inscribed in a modernist conception of knowledge. The opposition resides in the debate between a modernist and a postmodernist project, which is not yet near to closure. The questions of who is the female subject and what is a subject revolve around the centrality of language. The use of language by definition involves separation and differentiation, but also power. The relationship between feminism and postmodernism has not been an easy one (Flax 1987; Burman 1990; Hawkesworth 1989) in that the latter has been accused of impeding political action and of leading to relativism in values. Similar difficulties have arisen in OT (Newton 1996: 15) and for similar reasons: 'there is no easy reconciliation between postmodernism and action, whether the action is aimed at changing society or merely one organization.... Action inevitably implies choice, and some basis must be found for that choice.' It is evident that the debate is still open in both FT and OT, and it is within this debate that a convergence of interests may appear. The common ground is provided by the sharing of an epistemic culture (Knorr Cetina 1999).

In order to identify a possible convergence of FT and OT, we may look more carefully at their intersections within a postmodern project. Although the many classifications made of the relation between gender and organization overlap according to the criteria used (Alvesson and Billing 1997), agreement exists on the label of 'post-structuralist feminism'. A reason for this unexpected agreement is forthcoming if one looks at methodology. While discussing the existence or otherwise of a feminist methodology, Harding (1987) distinguishes among three methodological positions: gender as a variable (based on positivist assumptions on reality and methodology); a feminist standpoint perspective (theories for women that begin from the experience and point of view of the dominated and point to their capacities, abilities, and strengths); and post-structuralist feminism (critical reflection on how gender is done, order created, and fragmentation suppressed). I am interested in the third methodological position, since it is a reflexive one and therefore allows a meta-theoretical stance on knowledge production practices at the intersection of gender and organization theories.

Leaving the first methodological position aside, the feature that radically distinguishes the women's standpoint from post-structuralist feminism is the conception of 'action', change, or political project. Whilst a modernist project views action as factual change, a postmodernist project sees the 'political' as residing in the destabilization of the categories used to construct scientificity, objectivity, and neutrality. Within a postmodernist project in OT and in FT lies the possibility of articulating reflexivity in the form of answers to the following questions: what do our writings and sayings *do*? To whom do we speak and are accountable? What other voices do we acknowledge, or silence?

Within FT, I have compared these epistemologies elsewhere (Gherardi 1995: 104), describing them as the woman's standpoint approach versus the positionality approach (Table 7.2). The former represents—also in historical and cultural terms—the position in women's studies which gives priority to a point of view situated in women'experiences, while the latter represents gender studies as they have become institutionalized, since the epistemological turn in social studies that problematizes subjectivity, propounds a more sophisticated politics of knowledge, and focuses the researchers' attention on knowledge-producing practices within their disciplines.

The women's standpoint searched for a common denominator and extolled the condition of sameness. By contrast, positionality presupposes a discursive order where gender relations are the outcome of discourse practices; that is, they derive from the way in which people actively produce social and psychological realities. The scientific and political account that sustains positionality is a postmodern project in the sense that it seeks to problematize knowledge, to delegitimate all beliefs concerning truth, power, the self, language, and everything that is taken for granted. Conversely, the inscribing of a female perspective in knowledge, in power, in the truth system, can be called a modernist project that constructs a definitive subjectivity.

Table 7.2 The 'woman's standpoint' approach compared to the 'positionality' approach

Women's standpoint	versus	Positionality
sees male and female as mutually exclusive		sees male and female as indivisible positions of reciprocal relation
stresses sameness		stresses difference
presupposes a normative order		presupposes a discursive order
recalls a modern project		envisions a postmodern project
emphasizes subjectivity		deconstructs subjectivity

For Davies and Harré (1990) the concept of positioning belongs to social psychology, and their use of the term 'positioning' contrasts with the concept of human agency as role player. It is therefore useful for analysis of the production of self as a linguistic and relational practice within the dynamic occasions of encounters. It is within a particular discourse that a subject (the position of a subject) is constructed as a compound of knowledge and power into a more or less coercive structure that ties it to an identity. A subject position incorporates both a conceptual repertoire and a location for persons within the structure of the rights pertaining to those who use the repertoire. A position is what is created in and through conversations as speakers and hearers construct themselves as persons. A subject position creates a location in which social relations and actions are mediated by symbolic forms and modes of being.

Davies and Harré employ the concept of positioning to illuminate discursive practices at the level of social interactions, Alcoff (1988) uses it to shed light on a politics of identity understood as the choice from among a plurality of selves and as positionality in a social context. Alcoff proposes a positional definition of woman which 'makes her identity relative to a constantly shifting context, to a situation that includes a network of elements involving others, the objective economic conditions, cultural and political institutions and ideologies, and so on' (Alcoff 1988: 433). And part of my conception of positionality (Gherardi 1995) is the production of the positions of women and men as a discursive and material construction of an interpersonal relation in a multi-faceted public process by which gender meanings are progressively and dynamically achieved, performed, transformed, disseminated, and institutionalized. In sum, bodies and activities are constituted in gendered practices, and this conception of gender bypasses the initial location of difference either in the body, in society, or in language. Gender may be defined as a social accomplishment, learnt and enacted on appropriate occasions and organized around shared practical understanding of its performance.

Positioning gender is an approach that does not seek to posit a subjectivity of women or men in oppositional terms. It is instead an approach that reflects the essential indeterminacy of the symbolic order of gender in situated material-semiotic practices, governed as it is by the endless process of difference and deferral[4] of the meaning of male and female. Positioning gender introduces a concept of decentred subjectivity in which the subject is open-ended and indeterminate except when it is fixed in place by culturally constituted gender practices. Women and men

---

[4] 'Every concept is inscribed in a chain or in a system within which it refers to the other, to other concepts, by means of the systematic play of differences' (Derrida 1982: 11). In coining the term *différance* (with an 'a') Derrida combines the two senses of the French *différer*: to differ in space and to defer in time. Therefore there are two ways of conceiving gender difference: as two separate terms—male and female—and as a process of reciprocal deferral where the presence of one term depends on the absence of the other. But the momentarily suppressed term is waiting to return and stands in a supplementary position to the first.

'do gender' in positioning their subjectivities in situated social practices, and gender as a social practice can be seen as the heterogeneous engineering of bodies, artefacts, discourses, institutions, and organizations (Bruni and Gherardi 2001).

Thus understood, gender studies may be the terrain for convergence and alliance between postmodern organizational studies and post-feminism, in that both pursue a politics of knowledge intended to destabilize logocentric and phallocentric thought. To illustrate what may be the point of confluence, I shall refer to the *Handbook of Organization Studies*, given its symbolic value and the fact that every handbook seeks to shape the development of theory. In the Introduction to the book (Clegg, Hardy, and Nord 1996: 3), the authors draw a significant distinction among organizations as empirical objects, organization as a theoretical discourse, and organizing as a social process. With the latter term the authors 'refer to the embeddedness of organizing within distinct local practices, of language, of culture, of ethnicity, of gender'. A parallel may be drawn with gender studies if the focus of analysis is shifted to women and men as empirical objects identifiable on the basis of biological difference, gender as a theoretical discourse informed by local know-ledges, and 'positioning gender' as a social practice which performs gender relations within a network of other social relations and across well-established dichotomies like mind/body, nature/culture, nature/technology, public/private, and many others. Under the umbrella of organizational gender studies three methodological options are present: the study of women and men as empirical referents and gendered individuals, the study of organizational theory as a gendered knowledge practice, and the study of gendering as a reflexive social practice.

Common ground can be found at the intersection of bodies (since knowing is *embodied*), discourses (since language involves power), and practices (as collective accomplishments, materially mediated, of human activities). Looking at the gendering of organization theory and at the organizing of gender practices within organizational settings allows one to reflect on the politics of knowledge that sustain the concepts of 'gender' and 'organization'.

How this convergence has come about can be shown by reviewing the research programmes in organizational gender studies.

7.4 Confluent Research Programmes?

A research programme consists of a set of shared problems arranged around a central theoretical core of puzzles elaborated and re-elaborated over time by groups of scholars (Reed 1992). Some research programmes centre on the relationship between gender and organization, but differ in their identification of core problems.

I have mentioned that an early programme concentrated on the problem of making women visible. I shall not resume discussion of it here because it represents a stage that many scientific disciplines—including OT—necessarily pass through and which I consider to be only the beginning of the conversation. In OT, as in other disciplines like anthropology, history, philosophy, literature, or education—feminist scholarship has undergone the process described by Du Bois *et al.* (1987): feminist challenges were first levelled at prevailing disciplinary traditions; subsequently, a different scholarship developed from those challenges and suggested different analytical and political perspectives in the discipline.

A second research programme centres around the problem of 'gendering organizational analysis' (Mills and Tancred 1983; Mills 1988) and introduces the category of gender as one of the categories of organizational analysis: gendering occurs through symbols, images, ideologies that legitimate the opportunity structure of organizations. In analogy with the theoretical move from 'organization', as the unit of analysis, to 'organizing' as a boundary-less process, the gendering programme crossed significant boundaries: the public/private divide, the economy and the organization, families and work, emotions and work (Acker 1998).

A third research programme centres on a rereading of the discipline's 'classics', both its founding fathers like Weber (Martin and Knopoff 1997), Mayo and Crozier (Acker and Van Houten 1992), and its mothers like Mary Parker Follet (forum in *Organization*, 1996), and Simone de Beauvoir (forum in *Journal of Management Inquiry* 2000). Calás and Smircich (1992*a*) use the metaphor of re-visioning the field in order to produce insights that change the ways we think about classic theories and teach them.

I shall not dwell on these programmes because they complement rather than challenge malestream knowledge production practices in organization theory. I concentrate on the emerging and less well-established programmes that may open both gender studies and organizational studies to what Sandra Harding (1996) calls 'cultural cognitive diversity'.

As Judi Marshall (2000) has pointed out, there is a tendency in organizational scholarship to appreciate gender and diversity and to enclose these issues in separate chapters (the reference is to the *Handbook of Organization Studies*, Clegg. Hardy, and Nord 1996), while there is little discussion of them in other chapters: 'such issues are raised but then marginalized by mainly separate consideration' (Marshall 2000: 170). Mainstream conversation in organizational scholarship reflects a continuing marginalization of gender scholarship, and most mainstream scholarship continues to be presented as if theories and data were gender-neutral (Martin 2000). The main reason for such a marginalization may be found in the 'gender = women' equation. But staying at the margins may represent an advantage as well and a respectable knowing standpoint.

For my part I see no need to integrate gender and organization, or to argue that gender is the fundamental organizing principle. While the proponents of integration maintain that organizational studies should incorporate a gender perspective, I prefer to regard FT and OT as independent of each other, interpreting any convergence between the two strands of theorizing as a confluence of interests or a temporary alliance. Consequently, the alliance of gender studies with organization studies may be only tactical for the time being and it maybe realized at the margins of the disciplines where both FT and OT raise the issue of the politics of knowledge.

In the postmodern bricolage of organizational studies there is a book that can be taken as epitomizing the confluence in postmodernist thought between gender and organization. In *Postmodern Management Theory*, Calás and Smircich (1997) collect twenty-two articles representative of Anglo-American literature, distinguishing between a Foucauldian turn (four articles) and a Derridean turn (eight articles). The latter comprise five articles that assume an explicit gender perspective (Martin 1990; Calás and Smircich 1991; Mumby and Putnam 1992; Calás 1993; Fisher and Bristoc 1994). Without wishing to overstate what may only be the result of an idiosyncratic selection, I nevertheless emphasize that many of the articles that have influenced postmodernist thought in organizations combine the gender and de-constructionist approaches. What these two perspectives share is the methodology of deconstructionism and a critique of the social construction of knowledge rooted in the inseparability of power and knowledge. The confluence of OT and FT may be realized on critical examination or re-examination of the role of organization and management theory in relation to social structure in contemporary society.

In post-structuralism and post-structuralist feminism, writing is the metaphor for knowledge, the mode of constructing the 'general text' of our society in which cultural conditions are inscribed via our modes of signification. Thus a number of texts well-known and affirmed in organization theory are rewritten (by inverting oppositional constructions) to reveal their politics by calling attention to strategies of 'truth-making' while leaving the original text 'under erasure' (Spivak 1974). Once these oppositions have been destabilized, it will be impossible to reinscribe them in their original form.

Deconstructionism is an analytic strategy that exposes the manifold ways in which a text can be interpreted. Martin (1990) offers an example of deconstructive methodology within organization studies. Apparently well-intentioned organizational practices may reify rather than alleviate gender inequalities, Martin argues. She recounts the story of a woman for whom the organization arranged a closed-circuit television so that she could watch the launching of a new product while she was in bed recovering from a Caesarean birth, deliberately timed so she could participate in the launching event.

Martin deconstructs this story in order to reveal the suppressed gender conflicts behind the lines of the text. She lists the following nine deconstruction strategies (1990: 349):

(1) Dismantling a dichotomy, exposing it as a false distinction;
(2) Examining silences—what is not said;
(3) Attending to disruptions and contradictions, places where the text fails to make sense;
(4) Focusing on the element that is most alien to a text or a context as a means of deciphering implicit taboos—the limits to what is conceivable or permissible;
(5) Interpreting metaphors as a rich source of multiple meanings;
(6) Analysing 'double-entendres' that may point to an unconscious subtext, often sexual in content;
(7) Separating group-specific and more general sources of bias by 'reconstructing' the text with iterative substitution of phrases;
(8) Exploring, with careful 'reconstructions', the unexpected ramifications and inherent limitations of minor policy changes;
(9) Using the limitations exposed by 'reconstruction' to explain the persistence of the *status quo* and the need for more ambitious change programmes.

The rationale for deconstructing organizational texts (such as a narrative or 'the classics') is to create marginal textual strategies opening 'transitionary spaces' (Holvino 1996). An example of a transitionary space in Organization Development (OD) is provided by Evangelina Holvino who states that from such a space it is possible to attend to the raced, gendered, and classed subtexts by drawing on the following reading tactics: (1) exploring the symbolic representations of them, (2) identifying the gendered, racialized, and classed identities so created, (3) identifying exclusions of particular subject positions, (4) exploring the rhetorical strategies that inscribe and reproduce current relations of domination in terms of gender, class, racioethnicity. Third World feminism (or post-colonial feminism) not only recognizes differences among women or the intersection of a plurality of differences, but posits the 'issues of *positionality, difference, and subjectivity* as central to theory production by women of colour'. (Holvino 1996: 522, emphasis in original source.) I wish to take her statement further and assume it as central to any theorizing and politics of knowledge.

Deconstruction, post-structuralist, and post-colonial feminisms have helped to shift attention from the subject 'woman' to the gender relation, to how this is positioned in and by language, and to the relationship between discourses and institutional forms which create forms of power backed by knowledge claims. This is not to imply that only these approaches have brought about this shift; nor, even less, that they have become a new orthodoxy, or that the only way to produce knowledge is to deconstruct one text after another. On the contrary, what I find so interesting in the passage from modernity to a postmodern culture is the multiplicity of competing voices that create plurality of perspectives and blur boundaries, so that from an assumption of 'things or persons in themselves' one passes to reconstruction of things and persons as 'achievements' performed in—and through—sociotechnical relations. In my opinion at least three other streams of research may be considered confluent on a similar agenda: the research programme labelled 'to name men as men', cyberfeminism, and 'positioning gender' as performativity.

Of particular importance for organizational studies is the programme that has been labelled 'naming men as men': an expression that prompted Collinson and Hearn (1994, 1996) to study the contents and forms of men/managerialism (Kerfoot and Whitehead 1998; Kerfoot 1999), to conduct a critique of hegemonic masculinity (Connell 1987, 1995; Kimmel 1987) and compulsive heterosexuality. By interweaving men, masculinities, and management, these authors have sought to 'break the silence' (Harlow, Heam, and Parkin 1995) that renders masculinity invisible and removes it from discourse. This silence and expulsion from organizational discourse also concerns organizational sexuality (Hearn and Parkin 1987/1995; Hearn *et al.* 1989) and cathexis (Connell 1995) or sexual desire. In my opinion, the main contribution of these studies to a politics of knowledge in organization theory is the fact that masculinity is also a standpoint claiming to the monopoly of 'objectivity' and within masculinity there are a plurality of voices.

Another contribution to a politics of knowledge is the erosion of the divide between nature/society, science/technology, human/non-human, and text and matter. Donna Haraway (1991)—and cyberfeminism with her—invites reconsideration of the politics of positioning as a new epistemology that conducts a critique of classic humanism and invites us to consider the role of 'high-tech' in changing the meaning of what is 'human' and also of sexual difference. The cyborg metaphor acts on both a material and a textual/mythical level. It is a deconstructive device, proposing a 'materialized reconfiguration' (Haraway 1994: 62); that is, not just to read the webs of knowledge production but to reconfigure what counts as knowledge in the interests of reconstituting the generative forces of embodiment. Cyberfeminism, at the crossroads of science studies, feminist theory, and cultural studies (King 1994), considers technology to be a source of new identities made of rapid connections and dis-connections that transgress the sexual dualism and also the hetero/homosexuality dualism (a queer subject). It posits local but not particularistic, partial but not chaotic, knowledges and resides at the centre of the paradox of postmodern subjectivity in relation to technoscience. The feminist critique of science (and that conducted internally to the sociology of science and technology) has helped to show that even 'universal' knowledge is situated, and that feminist objectivity simply means bodily-situated knowledge. The advantage of a 'partial perspective'—the term is Donna Haraway's taken up by Marilyn Strathern (1991)—is that knowledge always has to do with circumscribed domains, not with transcendence and the subject/object dichotomy. Strathern's (1991) term 'partial connections' links with the European tradition of the notions of relatedness, connectedness-in-action (Cooper and Fox 1990), or 'partially connected' knowledges. Cyberfeminism connects with so-called Actor Network Theory (Law 1999), which basically assumes that technology is society made durable (Latour 1991); identity and social relations should be performed.

A final research programme now consolidating at the confluence between gender and organization centres on the concept of performativity introduced by Judith Butler (1990, 1993, 1999) and subsequently taken up by actor-network theory and by other analyses that problematize professional identities (Dent and Whitehead 2001) or the joint construction of gender and technology within material-semiotics networks. Although this programme has a great deal in common with the previous post-structuralist one, it differs therefrom by not taking the same methodological option and not concentrating principally on discursive practices or text analysis. Instead, it resumes the sociological tradition of symbolic interactionism in the concept of 'doing gender' (West and Zimmerman 1987; Gherardi 1994) and defines gender as situated social practice. Butler (1990: p. xii) proposes 'parodic practices based on a performative theory of gender acts that disrupt the categories of the body, sex, gender and sexuality and occasion their subversive resignification and proliferation beyond the binary frame'. Thus gender (and also organization, as we shall see) is shown to be a performatively enacted signification that 'released from its naturalized interiority and surface can occasion the parodic proliferation and subversive play of gendered meanings' (ibid. 33). Consequently, masculinity, too, can be read as something that men do alone or in the presence of women when they 'mobilize masculinities'. The concept of the masculine subject as a performative accomplishment allows us to see masculinity as a practice and not as an attribute. Patricia Martin (2001) proposes the concept of 'mobilizing masculinities' in inter-pretation of 'the practices wherein two or more men jointly bring to bear, or bring into play, masculinity/ies'. In mobilizing masculinity/ies at work men may mobilize the material and discursive codes of practice of the profession. The ritualistic repetition of these normalized codes gives materiality to belonging to the commu-nity and may explain the persistence of masculinist discourses, jokes, behaviours, styles even in mixed gender practices. The materiality of the social comes into play through the concepts of situated practice and technological artefacts that embody gender concepts. Martin uses the term 'conflation' for the dynamic of fusing masculinities with working processes and she conducts an empirical analysis from the women's standpoint of men's masculinity mobilizing practices. She identifies two substantive categories of masculinities (contesting and affiliating), the audi-ences for men's mobilizing work (for women, for men, or for both), and the dynamic of conflation (work occasions). Martin's analysis can be considered part of the research on 'doing gender' which originated in symbolic interactionism, but the concept of mobilizing is also part of the actor-network literature (Callon 1986a; 1986b).

The notion of mobilization is used in the actor-network literature in its dual political and physical sense: through mobilization (in its political sense) a role and a recognizable identity are conferred on an actor. The theory extends the meaning of the term as applied to social phenomena (a demonstration, an organized movement) to sociotechnical and material systems (a technical drawing, an estimate, a cheque, a scientific report). I borrow both meanings of mobilization in order to describe the mobilization of gender as a social and material practice, since in interpreting something as gendered 'masculine', the silent term is also present in its absence.

Therefore, if gender is a historical and situated social practice, then it can be 'done' (theorized, practised, narrated) differently, since gender is the effect of 'technologies of gender' (De Lauretis 1996). We settle gender relations amongst the subject positions available to us and produced by existing discourses—we are lived embodiments of discourses—but discourses are historically and temporally located and there are limitless other ways of being, thinking, and doing. Foucault (1986: 46) calls *assujetissement* (subjectification) the process by which we come to know about ourselves and to structure the field of our possibilities: there are limitless other ways of subjectification, of knowing, and of producing knowledge.

If an influence of FT on OT is to be discerned, it is situated in the critique of its power/knowledge regime. In other words, a tactical alliance between FT and OT is possible if it takes the form of a politics of knowledge, which reveals that every attempt to label something as 'knowledge' is embedded in a network of power relations that defines both the subject of such knowledge and its object.

7.5 CONCLUSIONS

Organizational theory, as a body of knowledge about organizations and as a theoretical discourse, has adopted the gender perspective somewhat belatedly compared to other academic disciplines such as history or literature. OT has been more tenacious than other disciplines in defending a 'gender-neutral' position that minimizes gender differences. In OT studies, revision of the 'classics' in order to expose the gender bias that has accompanied the institutionalization of the discipline is still in progress (Martin 2000). Finally, in managerial applications of OT, preoccupation with gender discrimination and integration policies has bred an obsession with inclusion of both women and feminist theory at all costs. In sum OT still segregates the gender approach in separate 'chapters' that reproduce its fundamental 'otherness'.

I believe that the principal reason for this is that organizational gender studies are still identified with studies that start from assumptions of biological difference and seeks cultural explanations for it. It is important to highlight biological diversity and emphasize that bodies are part of what individuals bring to play in organizations. But it is restrictive to view the body as the origin or cause of gender. There is no simple or linear cause/effect relationship between body and gender; rather, a network of transfers, translations, inferences, and influences constitute gender relations. With an apt expression Teresa De Lauretis (1999) says that the body is not the cause (of gender relations), but rather a symptom. The body is en-gendered by a social, cultural, and organizational process of gender self-attribution. The latter is not a performative process that mobilizes habits, inclinations, displacements, and phantasms and attaches them to a body already endowed with sexuality and sexual gender. Instead, it is a process that simultaneously produces both a body for the subject and a subject for that body. The significance of the body in relation to practices of organization merits closer attention (Melucci 1996; Hassard, Holliday, and Willmott 2000). The gender approach, therefore, although it starts from the centrality of the body, offers an opportunity for mature reflection on the interrelations among subjects, discourses, and situated social practices. It brings a cultural cognitive diversity into the mainstream agenda.

The body as a symptom and not as a cause is an interpretative key that opens the door to critical reflection on the processes of subjectivation, sexualization, and gender attribution as effects of power/knowledge relations within a social field. The gender approach is an opportunity to interrogate and ground a politics of knowledge that reflects on how social practices shape both the knowing subject and the known objects. It is on this terrain that a confluence may arise between postmodern organizational studies aimed at destabilizing the traditional categories of the discipline, and which therefore conduct critical reflection on the subjects and objects of knowledge, and gender studies.

Numerous conversations are possible and legitimate, but the effects that ensue from them may differ greatly in ethical, political, and aesthetic terms. Faced with this awareness, it is possible either to take up the privileged discursive stance of those who adopt a feminist standpoint or to assume the position of the ironic feminist mindful of both the gender and the language trap. Irony is a strategy in the politics of knowledge as well as a philosophical position (Derrida 1971; Rorty 1989; Ferguson 1991). My concern has been to illustrate the pragmatics of irony; that is, the destabilization in gender arrangements that ironic discourse can produce. Irony insinuates doubt. It suggests that the world can be described in different terms, but it does not propose these other terms as alternative, 'better', 'more correct', or 'truer'. Irony is a processual invitation; an invitation to consider how things (gender relationships and organizational relationship) can be redefined; how common sense can be problematized. Irony does not offer solutions; instead, it calls into question the linguistic games that produce a certain vision of the world.

What I find so interesting in the passage from modernity to a postmodern culture is the multiplicity of competing voices which create plurality of perspectives and blur boundaries, so that from an assumption of 'things or persons in themselves' one passes to reconstruction of things and persons as 'achievements' performed in—and through—sociotechnical relations. The concept of agency situated within a posthumanist social theory recognizes from the beginning that the material world (the non-human) and human agency reciprocally constitute one another. Self-definition and the erosion of self-definition is threatening but it is also challenging: the historical deferral of the meaning of gender does not mean the loss of its heuristic value but the questioning of postmodern subjectivities within power/knowledge relationships and situated practices of gendering the human and the non-human.

At the confluence of FT and OT there is the question of how the subject of knowledge is formed and of what metaphor linguistically represents a decentred subject and a protean subjectivity. The metaphors that problematize the relation among subjects, discourses, and social practices within a politics of knowledge can be provided by irony, nomadism, and eccentricity.

The ironist represents the subjectivity of a knowing subject imprisoned by the language that constitutes his/her 'final vocabulary'. His/her politics of knowledge is redescription rather than inference: 'ironists specialize in redescribing ranges of objects or events in partially neologistic jargon. An ironist hopes that by the time she has finished using old words in new senses, not to mention introducing brand-new words, people will no longer ask questions phrased in the old words' (Rorty 1989: 78).

A second metaphor is that of the nomad subject who seeks to evade the trap of fixed and fixated subjectivity. The subject thus defined traces knowledge itineraries through multiple points of intersection: differences between men and women, differences among women, differences within men. There emerges a strengthened difference that evades hegemonic thought. The politics of knowledge that derives therefrom is, in the words of Rosi Braidotti, a set of conceptual trajectories that constitute a plural and open project: a polyphonous game of multiplicity.

Finally, the metaphor of the eccentric subject (de Lauretis 1999) denotes a subject aware of constituting itself in an ever-becoming history, in an interpretation and rewriting of self based on another cognition of society and culture. This subject is eccentric with respect to the social field, to institutional devices, to the symbolic, to language itself. It is a subject that simultaneously responds to and resists the discourses that interpellate it.

An ironic, nomadic, eccentric knowing subject resists integration into mainstream disciplinary knowledge, but not out of a desire not to isolate but to produce knowledge from the margins and retain a meta-theoretical stance on the practices of knowledge production, both in the mainstream and at its margins. Marginal practices retain the power of undermining local stability and insinuate suspicion in taken-for-granted *habitus*, beliefs, and meanings.

Therefore, a gender perspective within organizational studies that is ironic, nomadic, and eccentric cannot be integrated into the main/malestream, but it can forge tactical alliances with other perspectives critical of the mainstream politics of knowledge and of the social practices sustaining it.

REFERENCES

ACKER, JOAN (1990). 'Hierarchies, Jobs, Bodies: A Theory of Gendered Organizations'. *Gender and Society*, 4: 139–58.

—— (1992). 'Gendering Organization Theory', in A. Mills and P. Tancred (eds.), *Gendering Organizational Analysis*. London: Sage.

—— (1998). 'The Future of "Gender and Organizations": Connections and Boundaries'. *Gender, Work and Organization*, 5/4: 195–206.

—— and VAN HOUTEN, D. (1992). 'Differential Recruitment and Control: The Sex Structuring of Organizations', in A. Mills and P. Tancred (eds.), *Gendering Organizational Analysis*. London: Sage.

ALCOFF, LINDA (1988). 'Cultural Feminism Versus Post-Structuralism: The Identity Crisis in Feminist Theory'. *Signs*, 13/3: 405–36.

ALVESSON, MATS, and BILLING, YVONNE (1997). *Understanding Gender and Organizations*. London: Sage.

BHABHA, HOMI (1988). 'The Commitment to Theory'. *New Formations*, 5: 5–23.

BRAIDOTTI, ROSI (1989). 'The Politics of Ontological Difference', in Teresa Brennan (ed.), *Between Feminism and Psychoanalysis*. London: Routledge.

BROWN, HELEN (1991). *Women Organizing*. London: Routledge.

BRUNI, ATTILA, and GHERARDI, SILVIA (2001). 'Omega's Story: The Heterogeneous Engineering of a Gendered Professional Self', in Mike Dent and Stephen Whitehead (eds.), *Managing Professional Identities: Knowledge, Performativity and the 'New' Professional*. London and New York: Routledge.

BURMAN, E. (1990). 'Differing with Deconstruction: A Feminist Critique', in I. Parker and J. Schotter (eds.), *Deconstructing Social Psychology*. London: Routledge.

BUTLER, JUDITH (1990). *Gender Trouble: Feminism and the Subversion of Identity*. London: Routledge.

—— (1993). *Bodies That Matter*. London: Routledge.

—— (1999). 'Revisiting Bodies and Pleasures'. *Theory, Culture and Society* (special issue), 16/2: 11–20.

CALÁS, MARTA (1993). 'Deconstructing Charismatic Leadership: Re-reading Weber from the Darker Side'. *Leadership Quarterly*, 4: 305–28.

—— and SMIRCICH, LINDA (1991). 'Voicing Seduction to Silence Leadership'. *Organization Studies*, 12/4: 567–602.

—— (1992a). 'Re-writing Gender into Organizational Theorizing: Directions from Feminist Perspectives', in M. Reed and M. Hughes (eds.), *Rethinking Organization: New Directions in Organization Theory and Analysis*. London: Sage.

—— (1992*b*). 'Using the "F" Word: Feminist Theories and the Social Consequences of Organizational Research', in A. Mills and P. Tancred (eds.), *Gendering Organizational Analysis*. London: Sage.

—— (1996). 'From the Women's Point of View: Feminist Approaches to Organization Studies', in S. Clegg, C. Hardy, and W. Nord (eds.), *Handbook of Organization Studies*. London: Sage.

—— (eds.) (1997). *Postmodern Management Theory*. Aldershot: Dartmouth Publishing.

CALLON, M. (1986*a*). 'Some Elements of Sociology of Translation: Domestication of the Scallops and the Fishermen of St. Brieue Bay', in J. Law (ed.), *Power, Action and Belief: A New Sociology of Knowledge?* London: Routledge & Kegan Paul.

—— (1986*b*). 'The Sociology of an Actor-Network', in M. Callon, J. Law, and A. Rip (eds.), *Mapping the Dynamic of Science and Technology*. London: MacMillan.

CAVARERO, ADRIANA (1990). *Nonostante Platone*. Rome: Editori Riuniti.

CHODOROW, NANCY (1978). *The Reproduction of Mothering*. Berkeley: University of California Press.

CIXOUS, HÉLÈNE, and CLÉMENT, CATHERINE (1986). *The Newly Born Woman*. Minneapolis: University of Minnesota Press.

CLEGG, STUART, HARDY CINTHIA, and NORD, WALTER (eds.) (1996). *Handbook of Organization Studies*. London: Sage.

COLLINSON, DAVID, and HEARN, JEFF (1994). 'Naming Men as Men: Implications for Work, Organization and Management'. *Gender, Work and Organization*, 1/1: 2–22.

—— (1996). *Men as Managers, Managers as Men*. London: Sage.

CONNELL, R. W. (1987). *Gender and Power*. Cambridge: Polity Press.

—— (1995). *Masculinities*. Berkeley: University of California Press.

COOPER, ROBERT, and FOX, STEPHEN (1990). 'The Texture of Organizing'. *Journal of Management Studies*, 27/6: 575–82.

DAVIES, BROWNYE, and HARRÉ RON, (1990). 'Positioning: The Discursive Production of Selves'. *Journal of the Theory of Social Behaviour*, 1: 43–63.

DE LAURETIS, TERESA (1996). *Sui Generis*. Milan: Feltrinelli.

—— (1999). *Soggetti Eccentrici*. Milan: Feltrinelli.

DENT, MIKE, and WHITEHEAD STEPHEN, (eds.) (2001) *Managing Professional Identities: Knowledge, Performativity and the 'New' Professional*. London: Routledge.

DERRIDA, JACQUE (1971). *L'Écriture et la difference*. Paris: de Seuil.

DUBOIS, E. C., *et al.* (eds.) (1987). *Feminist Scholarship: Kindling in the Groves of Academe*. Urbana: University of Illinois Press.

FANON, FRANTZ (1952). *Peau noire, masques blancs: L'Expérience vécue du noir*. Paris: École de Paris.

FERGUSON, KATHIE (1991). 'Interpretation and Genealogy in Feminism'. *Signs*, 16/2: 322–39.

FERREE, MYRA MARX, and MARTIN, PATRICIA YANCEY (eds.) (1995). *Feminist Organizations: Harvest of the New Women's Movement*. Philadelphia: Temple University Press.

FISHER, EILEEN, and BRISTOC, JULIA (1994). 'A Feminist Poststructuralist Analysis of the Rhetoric of Marketing Relationship'. *Information Systems Research*, 5: 350–77.

FLAX, JANE (1987). 'Postmodernism and Gender Relations in Feminist Theory'. *Signs*, 12: 621–43.

Forum on Revisiting Simone de Beauvoir (2000). *Journal of Management Inquiry*, 9/2: 165–216.

Forum on the Work of Mary Parker Follet (1996). *Organization*, 3/1: 147–80.

FOUCAULT, MICHEL (1986). *The History of Sexuality*, iii. New York: Pantheon.

GAME, ANN, and PRINGLE, ROSEMARY (1984). *Gender at Work*. London: Pluto.

GHERARDI, SILVIA (1994). 'The Gender We Think, The Gender We Do in Our Everyday Organizational Lives'. *Human Relations*, 47/6: 591–610.

—— (1995). *Gender, Symbolism and Organizational Cultures*. London: Sage.

GIDDENS, ANTONY (1992). *The Transformation of Intimacy*. Cambridge: Polity Press.

GILLIGAN, CAROL (1982). *In a Different Voice*. Cambridge, Mass.: Harvard University Press.

GRUZINSKI, SERGE (1999). *La Pensée métisse*. Paris: Fayard.

HARAWAY, DONNA (1991). 'Situated Knowledges: The Science Question in Feminism and the Privilege of Partial Perspectives', in D. Haraway, *Simians, Cyborgs and Women: The Reinvention of Nature*. London: Free Association Books.

—— (1994). 'A Game of Cat's Cradle: Science Studies, Feminist Theory, Cultural Studies'. *Configurations*, 1: 59–71.

HARDING, SANDRA (1987). 'Introduction: Is There a Feminist Method?', in S. Harding (ed.), *Feminism & Methodology*. Milton Keynes: Open University Press.

—— (1996). 'European Expansion and the Organization of Modern Science'. *Organization*, 3/4: 497–509.

HARLOW, E., HEARN, J., and PARKIN, W. (1995). 'Gendered Noise: Organizations and the Silence and Din of Domination', in C. Itzin and J. Newman (eds.), *Gender, Culture and Organizational Culture*. London: Routledge.

HARTSOCK, NANCY (1983). 'The Feminist Standpoint: Developing the Ground for a Specifically Feminist Historical Materialism', in S. Harding and M. Hintikka (eds.), *Discovering Reality*. Dordrecht: Reidel.

HASSARD, JOHN, HOLLIDAY, RUTH, and WILLMOTT, HUGH (2000). *Body and Organization*. London: Sage.

HAWKESWORTH, MARGARET (1989). 'Knowers, Knowing, Known: Feminist Theory and Claims of Truth'. *Signs*, 14: 533–57.

HEARN, JEFF, and PARKIN, WENDY (1983). 'Gender and Organizations: A Selective Review and a Critique of a Neglected Area'. *Organization Studies*, 4/3: 219–42.

———— (1987/1995). *'Sex' at 'Work': The Power and Paradox of Organization Sexuality*. New York: St. Martin's Press (2nd edn, 1995).

—— SHEPPARD, D., TANCRED-SHERIFF, P., and BURRELL, G. (1989). *The Sexuality of Organization*. London: Sage.

HEKMAN, SUSAN (1990). *Gender and Knowledge: Elements of a Postmodern Feminism*. Cambridge: Polity Press.

HOLVINO, EVANGELINA (1996). 'Reading Organization Development from the Margins: Outsiders Within'. *Organization*, 3/4: 520–34.

IRIGARAY, LUCE (1974). *Speculum: De l'autre femme*. Paris: Les Éditions de Minuit.

JACQUES, ROY (1997). 'The Unbearable Whiteness of Being: Reflections of a Pale, Stale Male', in P. Prasad *et al.* (eds.), *Managing the Organizational Melting Pot: Dilemmas of Workplace Diversity*. Thousand Oaks, Calif.: Sage.

KERFOOT, DEBORAH (1999). 'The Organization of Intimacy: Managerialism, Masculinity, and the Masculine Subject', in S. Whitehead and R. Moodley (eds.), *Transforming Managers: Gendering Change in the Public Sector*. London: Taylor and Francis.

—— and KNIGHTS, DAVID (1993). 'Management, Masculinity and Manipulation: From Paternalism to Corporate Strategy in Financial Services in Britain'. *Journal of Management Studies*, 30/4: 659–79.

—— and WHITEHEAD, STEPHEN (1998). ' "Boys own" Stuff: Masculinity and the Management of Further Education'. *Sociological Review*, 46/3: 437–57.

KIMMEL, M. (ed.) (1987). *Changing Men: New Directions in Research on Men and Masculinity*. Beverly Hill, Calif.: Sage.

KING, KATIE (1994). 'Feminism and Writing Technologies: Teaching Queerish Travels through Maps, Territories, and Pattern'. *Configurations*, 1: 89–106.

KNORR CETINA, K. (1999). *Epistemic Cultures: How the Sciences Make Knowledge*. Cambridge, Mass.: Harvard University Press.

LATOUR, BRUNO (1991). 'Technology Is Society Made Durable', in J. Law (ed.), *A Sociology of Monsters*. London: Routledge & Kegan Paul.

LAW, JOHN (1999). 'After ANT: Complexity, Naming and Topology', in J. Law and J. Hassard, *Actor Network Theory and After*. Oxford: Blackwell.

LORBER, J. (1999). 'Crossing Borders and Erasing Boundaries: Paradoxes of Identity Politics'. *Sociological Focus*, 32/4: 355–70.

—— and FARRELL, S. (1991). *The Social Construction of Gender*. London: Sage.

LORBIECKI, ANNA, and JACK, GAVIN (2000). 'Critical Turns in the Evolution of Diversity Management'. *British Journal of Management*, 11/Special Issue: 17–31.

MARSHALL, JUDI (1984). *Women Managers: Travellers in a Male World*. Chichester: Wiley.

—— (2000). 'Revisiting Simone de Beauvoir: Recognizing Feminist Contribution to Pluralism in Organizational Studies'. *Journal of Management Inquiry*, 9/2: 166–72.

MARTIN, JOANNE (1990). 'Deconstructing Organizational Taboos: The Suppression of Gender Conflict in Organizations'. *Organization and Science* 1/4: 339–59.

—— (2000). 'Hidden Gendered Assumptions in Mainstream Organizational Theory and Research'. *Journal of Management Inquiry*, 9/2: 207–16.

—— and KNOPOFF, K. (1997). 'The Gendered Implications of Apparently Gender-Neutral Theory: Rereading Max Weber', in A. Larson and R. Freeman (eds.), *Women Studies and Business Ethics*. New York: Oxford University Press.

MARTIN, P. Y. (2001). ' "Mobilizing Masculinities": Women's Experience of Men at Work'. *Organization*, 8/4: 587–618.

MELUCCI, ALBERTO (1996). *The Playing Self: Person and Meaning in the Planetary Society*. Cambridge: Cambridge University Press.

MILLS, ALBERT (1988). 'Organization, Gender and Culture'. *Organization Studies*, 9/3: 351–70.

—— and TANCRED, PETA (eds.) (1983). *Gendering Organizational Analysis*. London. Sage.

MUMBY, D., and PUTNAM, LINDA (1992). 'The Politics of Emotion: A Feminist Reading of a Bounded Rationality'. *Academy of Management Review*, 17: 456–86.

MURARO, LUISA (1991). *L'Ordine simbolico della madre*. Rome: Editori Riuniti.

NEWTON, TIM (1996). 'Postmodernism and Action'. *Organization*, 3/1: 7–29.

NICHOLSON, LINDA (1994). 'Interpreting Gender', *Sign*, 20/1: 79–105.

PICCONE STELLA, SIMONETTA, and SARACENO, CHIARA (1996). *Genere: La Costruzione Sociale del Femminile e del Maschile*. Bologna: Il Mulino.

PINCH, T., and BIJKER, W. (1989). 'The Social Construction of Facts and Artifacts: Or How the Sociology of Science and the Sociology of Technology Might Benefit Each Other', in W. Bijker, T. Hughes, and T. Pinch (eds.), *The Social Construction of Technological Systems*. Cambridge, Mass.: MIT Press.

PRASAD, PUSHKALA, MILLS, A., ELMES, M., PRASAD, A. (1997). *Managing the Organizational Melting Pot: Dilemmas of Workplace Diversity*. Thousand Oaks, Calif.: Sage.

REED, M. (1992). *The Sociology of Organizations*. Hemel Hempstead: Harvester.

RORTY, R. (1989). *Contingency, Irony and Solidarity*. Cambridge: Cambridge University Press.

RUBIN, GAYLE (1975). 'The Traffic in Women: Notes on the "Political Economy" of Sex', in R. Reiter (ed.), *Towards an Anthropology of Women*. New York: Monthly Review Press.

SARACENO, CHIARA (1993). 'Elementi per una Analisi delle Trasformazioni di Genere nella Società Contemporanea'. *Rassegna Italiana di Sociologia*, 34/1: 19–57.

SILVERMAN, DAVID (1993). *Interpreting Qualitative Data*. London: Sage.

SPIVAK, GAYATRI (1974). 'Translator's Preface' to J. Derrida, *Of Grammatology*. Baltimore. Johns Hopkins University Press.

STRATHERN, MARILYN (1991). *Partial Connections*. Savage, Md.: Rowman and Littlefield.

TANCRED, PETA (1995). 'Women's Work: A Challenge to the Sociology of Work'. *Gender, Work and Organization*, 2/1: 11–20.

WEEDON, CHRIS (1987). *Feminist Practice and Poststructuralist Theory*. Cambridge: Basil Blackwell.

WEST, C., and ZIMMERMAN, D. (1987). 'Doing Gender'. *Gender and Society*, 1/2: 125–51.

CHAPTER 8

THE STYLES AND THE STYLISTS OF ORGANIZATION THEORY

BARBARA CZARNIAWSKA

> Marshalling one's tropes to go in unconventional ways may be difficult and perhaps lonely, but it is by no means everywhere and always unwelcome.
>
> (Van Maanen 1995*a*: 142 n. 13)

THE quotation above was chosen to replace the standard one from Nietzsche,[1] which by now must be well worn at the edges from overuse. It was also chosen because it expresses a very touching sentiment. It is the last sentence of the last note (the unlucky number 13) in an essay that was to be later described as 'utilizing an emotionally laden, explicitly political, heated-up, purple and provocative language' (Van Maanen 1995*b*). When all the guns are spent, the tired Van Maanen says, lapsing almost into *litotes*,[2] 'write well and you will be rewarded'. But what does it mean 'to write well' in organization theory?

The author thanks Christian Knudsen and Deirdre N. McCloskey for their comments.

[1] The one about truth being a mobile army of metaphors.

[2] Ironical understatement, especially when an affirmative is expressed by the negative of the contrary; see also *meiosis* (Lanham 1991: 95–6).

When Ricca Edmondson wrote her *Rhetoric in Sociology* in 1984, there was little reaction, but when Deirdre N. McCloskey published her *Rhetoric of Economics* in 1985, the uproar was great. Sociologists may well use literary rhetoric but, surely, isn't an economist but a will-less pen in the invisible hand of the market or a similar natural force? But the virus spread, and all disciplines rushed to examine their rhetoric. In 1987 *The Rhetoric of the Human Sciences: Language and Argument in Scholarship and Public Affairs* (edited by Nelson, Megill, and McCloskey) was published, followed by Herbert Simons's (ed.), *Rhetoric in the Human Sciences* (1989) and *The Rhetorical Turn* (1990). By 1988, Robert Solow was pointing out that it was time to move beyond the 'look, Ma, a metaphor' stage and speak about consequences of economic rhetoric (the book under this title has been edited by Klamer, McCloskey, and Solow). One began to speak of 'logic of inquiry', often in a daring plural, and the fact that scientists use a rich repertoire of persuasive instruments was no longer a startling discovery. If anything, the problem in organization theory, postulated Van Maanen, was the disciplinary attempts to put constraints on the use of this repertoire, so that our scholarly discourse has become 'impoverished, stiff, sanitized and humorless' (1995*b*: 687). Much as I agree with John Van Maanen, two things are worth pointing out in this context.

One is related to my favorite analogy between the detective story genre and the genre of organization theory (Czarniawska 1999*a*, *b*). The detective story genre was also judged to have become stale and rigid in the 1920s and the 1930s due to the establishment of canonical rules; these were used by figures such as S. S. Van Dine and Ronald Knox to discipline the new adepts (Hühn 1987). But, as it can be said that Impressionism was produced by the French Academy (which by consistent rejection of paintings not conforming to the rules provoked the opening of the Independent Salon), so one can claim that the rigidification of the rules of the detective genre made transgressions easier. Indeed, the attempts to impose discipline within organization theory seem to coincide with an explosion of textual experimentation in the field (for recent examples, see Harju 1999; Starkey 1999; and Westwood 1999).

The other point is that, although I share Van Maanen's appreciation of Karl Weick's style, organization theory has many excellent stylists, probably due to its much lamented plurality. In what follows, I shall quote several exemplars of such style-as-theory (or perhaps style-as-method, see Latour 1988*a*), to show younger readers that there is a vast repertoire to choose from and to expand. I hasten to add that this is a posteriori judgment: there are no 'styles that persuade', only 'styles that have persuaded'—some readers, at a certain place, at a certain time (Iser 1978). The institutional inertia allows us to extrapolate the audience's reactions, but these can never be taken for granted; institutions are always leaky and under transformation themselves. The grandiloquent style of yesterday is but a ridiculous mannerism today (of which Gabriele D'Annunzio, the Italian writer of the 1920s, is the best example[3]). For this reason, I omit historical examples (they have been closely read by, for example, O'Connor 1996 and Monin, Barry, and Monin 2000).

An explanation is due before I embark on my task: why am I using this old-fashioned term 'style' instead of, for example, 'textual strategy' (Harrari 1979), 'rhetorical repertoire', and the like? I have chosen it simply because the old-fashioned notion of style can encompass all of these. True, it also drags with it some unwanted connotations, as 'old-fashioned' means, among other things, 'used for a long time'. In order to get rid of the most obnoxious ones, I shall try to delimit the way in which I shall understand 'style' in the present text.

Among many definitions offered by the *New Shorter Oxford English Dictionary*, two are especially relevant: III11b 'A particular or characteristic way, form, or technique of making or producing a thing, esp. a work of art; a way of executing a task; a manner of performance' and III13a 'Elegance, refinement, or excellence of manner, expression, form, or performance' (*NS OED* 1993: 3112). Although it is the first meaning that I mostly intend, the second is alluded to—following the example of John Van Maanen's analysis of Weick's style, which was clearly intended to be laudatory. The notion of style points towards a personal character of a text—in a political sense ('style as voice', Megill and McCloskey 1987: 225–8) and in an emotional sense. Indeed, 'style is the man',[4] as literary theorists used to say unchecked for a good while.

The feminist perspective is not the only one expressing a new understanding of style. One clear change in relation to the ancient theory of rhetoric is the inclusion of structure ('Arrangement') into style, obviously due to the impact of structuralist and post-structuralist theory.[5] The second innovation is the collapse of the traditional distinction between the style and the content, or the form and the content, attacked ferociously and with success by Nelson Goodman (1978) in aesthetics and Hayden White (1987) in historiography. This change permitted Van Maanen to speak of 'style as theory'.

Umberto Eco said that style was 'a very personal, unrepeatable, characteristic "way of forming"—the recognizable trace that every artist leaves in his work and which coincides with the way the work is formed. Thus, the artist gives himself form in the work' (1989: 165). This has to do with an idea that a 'Model Author' is a creation in the text, an actant (the subject of sentences that begin with 'I'), and style is her sign of presence. The texts that do not have style build a Model Author out of

---

[3] See e.g. Wills (1999).

[4] A saying attributed to Count Buffon, French aristocrat and biologist, *Le style est l'homme même*. In 1753 Buffon was elected to the Académie Française in recognition of his great bestseller, *Histoire Naturelle* (Lepenies 1985/1988).

[5] However, even in traditional rhetoric, 'a certain slippage in the categories trope and scheme became inevitable, not simply because rhetoricians were inconsistent in their use of terms but because well-constructed discourse reflects a fusion of structure and texture. One is virtually indistinguishable from the other.' *Encyclopædia Britannica Online*, <http://www.eb.com:180/bol/topic?eu=117403&sctn=4>[Accessed 14 October 2000].

an idiolect, 'distinguishing not an individual but a genre, a social group, a historical period' (Eco 1979: 10). The idea of Model Author as a character in a text, originating with Peirce but implied in the entire rhetorical tradition, is in tune with Barthes's (1979) postulates that the work be replaced by a text, and Foucault's (1979) that the author be replaced by a writer. It does not diminish the weight of the individual talent, but it emphasizes the institutional character of social life, where nobody can act in a void, and everybody interacts with a contemporary repertoire of actions, by imitation or by resistance.

Considering all these caveats, I am most comfortable with an unpretentious but informative definition by Lejeune, who says: 'I call here "style", for lack of a better term, everything that disturbs the transparency of written language, ... and makes the work on the words apparent whether we are dealing with parody, plays on meaning, or versification' (1989: 127). The 'transparency of written language' is of course a fantasy figure, a counterfoil: like there is no content without a form, there is no text without a style. Yet we speak of 'texts lacking style' that can be best described as compilations of words and phrases rather than as 'the work on the words'. Style is the writer's awareness of being engaged in writing, incorporated into the text itself (as opposed to lack of such awareness, but also to self-reflective or meta-reflexive texts).

The questions of style, whatever the definition, have been thoroughly discussed in the context of literary theory, aesthetics, and even history. Social sciences had to wait for a 'literary turn' to occur in the 1980s.[6] As usual, the great ancestors are best blamed for this delay:

> Not even his friends regarded Auguste Comte as a great writer.... According to Comte, questions of style were of little importance in the sciences, if only because no two authors have ever been able to agree on what good style was.... The way in which a scientist expressed himself ought not to be determined by artificial rules but must accord with the subjects under discussion.... He employed no artifice but allowed himself to be guided solely by his thoughts—he could do no other than follow his inspiration. (Lepenies 1988: 19)

But even Comte, the enemy of artifice, had to admit that there were different ways of writing, so, in 1851, he set down the rules of style that were appropriate for a scientist.

> No sentence should be longer than two lines of manuscript—which, given his cramped handwriting, amounted to five lines of print. No paragraph should contain more than seven sentences; any hiatus had to be strictly avoided. The same word should not occur twice either in the sentence or in successive sentences—excepting only single-syllable auxiliary verbs. Apart from its introduction and conclusion, every treatise of Comte's would in future comprise seven chapters. Each chapter would be in three parts, each part in seven sections, and each section would consist of a leading paragraph of seven sentences and three further

---

[6] Although there existed harbingers such as Gusfield's 'The Literary Rhetoric of Science: Comedy and Pathos in Drinking Driver Research', 1976.

paragraphs each of five sentences. Rules of this kind would, he maintained, bestow on his prose a strictness of form previously possessed only by poetry. (Lepenies 1988: 20)

Although it is easy to agree with John Stuart Mill's opinion that these rules of composition were a sign of a 'melancholy decline of a great mind' (ibid.), one should point out, in defense of August Comte, that he set those rules for himself. Many contemporary textbooks in scientific writing try to set such rules for other people. Social sciences in general, and organization theory as one of these, tend to oscillate between the idea that thoughts express themselves and the idea that writing can be meticulously prescribed. In between, great styles are born.

Before I attempt to quote and describe some of them, another caveat is necessary. Uncharacteristically, I hope, I shall focus on native English writers, not because they are the only ones to develop a style, but because a rhetorical analysis performed in English on a text written in another language borders on absurdity, and the same analysis applied to a translation from another language raises a host of doubts as to whose style is under description. All analyses are language bound, but a rhetorical one even more so.

8.1 STYLE: SCIENTISTIC

If a genre were represented by one style, the proper style for organization theory would be the scientific one. But what does a scientific style look like? Who has the right to decide, who is the arbiter of the scientific style? There were many attempts to establish a canon (in the sense of a standard of judgment), and there were many aspirants to the role of the arbiter. By the whim of the editors of the present volume, I was temporarily awarded an arbiter function; thus I shall quote an exemplar of my choice. It is James D. Thompson's *Organizations in Action: Social Science Bases of Administrative Theory* (1967). Short and concise, it aims at covering all relevant issues and formulating the proper science of organizations according to scientific ideals, i.e. as a set of formal (at least apparently formal) propositions.

Setting out to be exhaustive and to combine the incompatible (the rational system vs. natural open systems approaches), embracing an impressive range of schools and sources (where Parsons and Goffman sit side by side), it is a striking example of how the conviction that knowledge must accumulate leads to an attempt at a closure of an intellectual field which, if taken seriously, could put an end to the discipline. As I noted before in another context (Czarniawska 1999*b*: 33), if Thompson were to be taken literally, there would be no need for organization theory after him. The mechanical ideal of communication neglects to notice that a perfect communication puts an end to the need to communicate; a perfect language puts an end to creativity, and a perfect knowledge, were such to exist, would put an end to development and innovation.[7] The alternative idea is that knowledge does not accumulate: science is a conversation that, in time, acquires more space and more sophistication, but needs not ever achieve a closure (Oakeshott 1959/1991).

Thompson did not seem to be eager to converse; his aim was to summarize all previous conversations. The rhetorical style he adopted can be best exemplified by an excerpt from his book:

Proposition 4.1: Organizations under norms of rationality seek to place their boundaries around those activities which if left to the task environment would be crucial contingencies.

The implication of this proposition is that we should expect to find organizations including within their domains activities or competencies which, on a technological basis, could be performed by the task environment without damage to the major mission of the organization. For the hotel, for example, provision of rooms and meals would be the major mission, and the operation of a laundry would be excluded; yet we find hotels operating laundries. On the other hand, provision of rooms and meals would not be within the major mission of the hospital, although hospitals commonly include these activities within their domains.

The incorporation of subsidiary competencies along with major missions is commonplace in organizations of all types and is not a major discovery. But our proposition is not an announcement of the fact; rather it attempts to indicate the direction in which domains are expanding. (Thompson 1967: 39–40)

A translation of this organizationalese into English is usually necessary for a novice reader (I admit that I enjoy reading the propositions aloud to graduate students and watching their blank faces). Such translation, innocent as it may seem, already heralds the readings I intend to make next (for translations of economics into English, see McCloskey 1985). Briefly, Thompson says that organizations incorporate those activities that may be crucial to them in order to avoid dependency on their environment.

This is stated in the form of a proposition, i.e. 'a statement expressed in a form requiring consideration of its truth rather than its validity' (*NS OED* 1993: 2382). What is interesting is that the propositions concern not 'things' or 'facts', but tropes, of which the two most important are 'organization' and 'environment'.

'Organization' is clearly a *synecdoche*: that which is organized becomes an entity named after its attribute. The use of organizations in the plural, indicating an entity, appeared as late as the 1960s, with the advent of systems theory in the social sciences (Waldo 1961). In fact, Thompson still spoke of 'administration theory' (administration being the synonym of management, connected by usage with public authority rather than private enterprise). Even more interesting is 'environment': this central concept in organization theory is residual in character, meaning simply 'that

---

[7] These issues are discussed at length by George Steiner (1975/1992) in the context of translation and by Umberto Eco (1995) in the context of the story of search for the perfect language.

which surrounds organizations'. As Meyer (1996) put it succinctly, the environment is the Other to the Actor, as the environment of a modern organization consists increasingly of other organizations (see also Perrow 1991).

Thus Thompson's propositions suggest logical connections between tropes, and as they prompt a consideration of truth rather than validity, they do not have to be tested or proved: they can be illustrated. The illustrations are formulated in a way that resembles and repeats propositions, but the abstract tropes are replaced by generic terms like 'organizations that cross national boundaries', 'general hospitals', 'hotels'. The verbs remain in the gnomic present ('organizations tend to', 'organizations seek to identify'), that is, the tense used to express a general truth without implication of time (*NS OED* 1993: 1107).

In brief, gnomic utterances are the opposite of narrative ones: they are situated neither in place nor in time. Indeed, the land and the epoch of Thompson's stories is called Under Norms of Rationality.

What are the advantages of the use of the gnomic present? As pointed out by McCloskey, it is the tense favored by economists as a way of claiming authority (1985: 11). Partly, it has to do with *ethos*: both Bible and folklore wisdom favor the gnomic present. Partly, it is a matter of special kind of *logos*. There is no base on which to contest a statement in gnomic present. Any sentence situated in a real time and place can be contested as to its validity: there are other witnesses, or at least there are counter-examples from different places and times. Not so with the gnomic present, which is situated no-place in no-time and features abstract protagonists (e.g. 'market rules'). Even utopias are situated, but gnomic statements are not.

'But is this what Thompson intended?' a reader fond of deducing authorial intentions may ask. The text says (to be on a safe side and leave Thompson himself out of it) that 'our [*sic*] proposition is not announcement of the fact: rather it attempts to indicate the direction'. The suggestion seems to be that the proposition contained more than a mere fact; it contained a prediction. Thompson used *prolepsis*: 'the representation of a future act, state, etc., as already done or existing' (*NS OED* 1993: 2373). This strategy can be used to avoid factual statements concerning the past (which can be contested) and to build assurance by displacing them into an (incontestable) future, all with the aid of the gnomic present.

One could thus claim that Thompson's 'scientism' is but a stylization: the entities in question are tropes and could be connected only with one another, the postulated connections are achieved by the use of yet another rhetorical figure, and there are no factual statements that can be tested. It would be wrong, however, to conclude from this that Thompson's text fails to achieve the scientific style; on the contrary, this way of writing is considered 'scientific', nay, 'theoretical', in social sciences. Although Thompson's text is by now relegated to 'courses on classics', the style is by no means extinct. Texts peppered with propositions, speaking with rigor and discipline about abstract entities populating a nowhere in no time, abound. Few of them even try to achieve such a strict stylization as Thompson's.

If this is not a style but a stylization, what are the origins that are being imitated? Theoretical physics is my first guess, or at least a general idea of what such texts look like; the second probable source of inspiration is economics, which, in turn, imitates mathematics (McCloskey 1985).

One can point out, however, that, unlike economics, organization theory did not aspire to the heights of mathematics. The interest in the concrete practices of organizing, combined with influences from sociology and psychology, are probably responsible for visible traces of another natural science: biology. Life cycle theories, organic system theories, and evolutionary metaphors abound in organization theory. The man who used them with greatest skill created a style that hardly can be called scientistic.

8.2 STYLE: POETIC

Karl Weick has played a central role in shaping the discipline of organization theory in the 1980s and 1990s. This role is highly unusual in that he was never a part of the so-called mainstream, and yet his influence was not exerted from the margins of the discipline.

Weick himself was of the opinion that 'theorists often write trivial theories because their process of theory construction is hemmed in by methodological strictures that favor validation rather than usefulness' (Weick 1989: 516). Favoring usefulness, he suggested that theory-making is an organizing process, a sensemaking process that consists of 'disciplined imagination'. A desired result brings out 'a plausible theory, and a theory is judged to be more plausible and of higher quality if it is interesting rather than obvious, irrelevant or absurd, obvious in novel ways, a source of unexpected connections, high in narrative rationality, aesthetically pleasing, or correspondent with presumed realities' (Weick 1989: 517).

This can be taken as a self-description, points out Van Maanen (1995a) who argues that, instead of following methodological strictures, Weick has developed a unique style, which fulfills both the requirement of a high narrative rationality and an aesthetical satisfaction. In other words, one could say that it combines rhetoric with poetics.

Poetics, after some initial scuffles, went hand in hand with rhetoric until the Renaissance (Todorov 1990: 6). In modernity, however, the two have been set in contrast, where poetics stood for ambivalence, and rhetoric for authority (Höpfl 1995: 175). If writers would keep to their genres (as they should, according to modern prescriptions), the two could be easily set apart. The scientific theory would stand for authority, and poetry for ambivalence: the one would repair the damages of the other. But the world does not keep still under categorizations, and the strength of Weick's style is that it blends the two: the ambivalence subverts the authority, while the authority critically examines the ploys of ambivalence.

Van Maanen (1995a) labeled this style 'allegoric breaching'. Perhaps it is worthwhile to dedicate some attention to those two terms. An *allegory* is usually described as an 'extended metaphor', which is correct, but this somewhat reduces its specificity ('*just* an extended metaphor'). A metaphor differs from an analogy[8] in that it creates a similarity that did not exist before (another way of putting it is, in Eco's vocabulary, contrasting *factual judgments* with *semantic judgments*; while the former vie for validity by referring to outside of the language, the latter claim similarity or difference within the language itself). Now, an allegory is an extended metaphor in that it goes further than just stating similarity between two objects—it describes one object under the guise of another. An example that has stuck forever in my mind appeared in an article on leadership (Weick 1978); it involved a Mexican sierra—a fish. Mexican sierra can be a metaphor for leaders, but it is also a metaphor for different approaches—to fish and to leaders, and it is a metaphor borrowed from John Steinbeck.

But Karl Weick needed neither John Van Maanen nor me to tell him what he was doing. He tells it himself: 'This entire book [*Social Psychology of Organizing*] is as much about organizational theorizing as it is about organizational theory.... The book is about ways of talking about organizations, and it is intentionally focused this way in the belief that as ways of talking and believing proliferate, new features of organizations are noticed. That's why the book is more concerned with metaphors and images than it is with findings' (1979: 234). In other words, organizing is an allegory for writing, but it is a reversible allegory: writing is organizing. In that, Weick seems to agree with Ricoeur, who claims a reversible analogy (that is, a much stronger connection) between action and text (Ricoeur 1981).

Breaching, on the other hand, concerns conventional textual practices of the field (Van Maanen 1995a). Weick's style favors an essay form, ambiguity of reasoning, dialectic reconstruction, and a rhetorical strategy of presence, all of which, and especially the last one, go against the textual strategy promoted by the founding fathers of social sciences (see Dorothy Smith on Durkheim 1999: 55 ff.). Much as these traits break with the recommended style of academic writing, the success of Weick's maverick style speaks most eloquently for itself. His influence on both form and context of theorizing organizations is profound. He turned the attention of organization students from structures to processes, from the relevance of academia to the relevance of the field, from mystification to imaginative interpretation. In

---

[8] It is common to equate analogy with metaphor, but I find it much more fruitful to differentiate between them.

brief, if Thompson's rhetoric seemed to aim at ending organization theory, Weick's started it anew.

Weick's frequent use of biological metaphors reveals high sophistication (he refers to 'requisite variety' rather than 'dying organizations'), which permits a seamless combination with cultural metaphors (see also Mangham 1996). As to how this unusual combination came about, one might find a clue in a quotation from Vonnegut inserted into *Social Psychology of Organizing*:

My adviser smiled. 'How would you like to study poetry which pretends to be scientific?' he asked me.
'Is such a thing possible?' I said.
He shook my hand. 'Welcome to the field of social and cultural anthropology,' he said. (Weick 1979: 234)

Vonnegut wrote this in 1975, shortly after Bateson published his *Steps to an Ecology of Mind* and anthropologists had become enchanted with cybernetics (Bateson is much quoted in *Social Psychology*). The more recent history is better known: after all, the rapprochement between organization theory and cultural anthropology that happened under the guise of 'organizational culture' studies was most likely given an impetus by people who wanted to study poetry that pretends to be scientific. But within social science, there are students of poetry who do not wish to pretend they are scientific. The label I put on them is 'revolutionary'.

8.3 STYLE: REVOLUTIONARY

The revolutionary style rejects authority, and yet it is not purely poetic. It promotes ambiguity in the name of an ideology, that is, a potential authority. Revolutionary style often uses a narrative; indeed, Todorov suggests ideological organization as one distinct form of achieving transformation in a narrative, where an abstract rule, an idea, produces the various peripeties (in contrast to mythological and gnoseological transformations, 1990: 36). 'The use of narrative' should be understood very broadly in this context, as the revolutionary use of a narrative can as often as not exploit an anti-narrative.

Such is the case of Gibson Burrell's *Pandemonium* (1997), with a subtitle 'Towards a Retro-Organization Theory'. Linearity kills, is Burrell's main message, on a battlefield and in the field of theory. *Pandemonium* is set against the linear narrative, and against the traditional, that is, modernist, humanist, and progressive organization theory. As a book, it is highly experimental (although not as experimental as

Burrell's foray into video-production, 'Eco and Bunnymen', presented in 1993 at a conference in Keele, a text that I would gladly analyze if the media permitted it). It has two parts running in opposite directions on the same page, bibliography in the middle, gothic-style illustrations, hypertext on certain pages, repeated references to Burrell's family, and, perhaps most revolutionary of all, it 'looks to the peasantry rather than managerial groups or those associated collectivities of blue-collar workers' (Burrell 1997: 5). Retro- though it is, Burrell's interest in the peasantry does not have much in common with the romanticization of the peasant in, for example, Germany, Poland, and Russia at the end of the previous century (Holmgren 1998: 19; Czarniawska 1999*b*: 49). The gothic stylization is as kitschy as it is ironic, and the peasantry is brought in in a somber recognition that it has been forgotten by the enthusiasm of industry-bound modernists. The reaction to this proposal, and to *Pandemonium* as such, will differ from one reader to another, but Burrell's book is important here to mark the difference between an isolated formal experiment and a style, a coherent (if often ambiguous) and reproducible (if often only by the author) approach to the text.

With what right, one may ask, do I put a label of a 'narrative' onto a text that pronounces itself hostile to narrativity? I am not suggesting that the authors do not know what they are doing (much worse, I suggest that the authors are the figments of the reader's imagination or the epiphenomena of the text). I want to point out that the hostility to a (conventional, linear) narrative may find expression in two kinds of forms: texts that ignore the narrative and texts that choose (in the sense of *intentio operis*, Eco 1992) to break the rules of conventional narratology, to bend them, or to play around with them. Burrell's book is one such example (it subverts linearity but it also evokes it, unlike Weick's texts, which ignore linearity); another is Marta Calás and Linda Smircich's use of deconstruction ('Voicing Seduction to Silence Leadership', 1991).

Calás and Smircich, inspired by textual analyses of Derrida and Foucault, reread three classical texts on leadership—Barnard, McGregor, and Mintzberg—in terms of seduction, juxtaposing them to works on sexuality, homosexuality, and narcissism. This particular choice of a reading perspective has been dictated by their standpoint, which is a feminist one. The deconstructive reading of the classics permitted them to disclose the supposed novelty of Peters and Waterman's *In Search of Excellence* as a pastiche of Barnard (where *pastiche* is understood as a parody without humor). They continued with three 'utopias', which were in a sense 'further' readings, moving beyond the edge of what is considered standard organization literature. The utopias took the form of narratives, although the deconstructions obviously did not. In this sense, the utopian narratives can be seen as *reconstructions* (on different ideological premises) of what was deconstructed in the first part of the text. A narrative transformation has taken place by an exchange of the rule that was organizing the narrative. Todorov's example of an ideologically organized narrative is *Les liaisons dangereuses*, and such is, indeed, the title of another of Calás and Smircich's texts ('Dangerous Liaisons: The Feminine in Management Meets Globalization', 1993).

Is the revolutionary style and the ideological organization of the dystopian/ utopian narrative the same as what is often called 'critical management theory' (Alvesson and Wilmott 1992)? Indeed, it is a style belonging to this genre (Burrell is one of Alvesson and Wilmott's authors) although by no means exhaustive of it. I have chosen my examples for several reasons: they are stylistically distinct, that is, the work of shaping the text is visible and appreciable—indeed, it is a style as a method, or rather method as a style, because in the case of both Burrell and of Calás and Smircich the formal proceedings are far from a mechanical following of a prescription. This kind of critical style could be contrasted with the older kind, wherein there were two possible readings—one false and one authentic—and there was but a single utopia. For Calás and Smircich, the readings are endless, and the utopias many; the feminist standpoint is as much a claim to a voice as a humble indication of its limitations.

8.4 STYLE: PHILOSOPHICAL

The present text is yet another victim of linearity: the pages come one after another, and what was before cannot be after. In a 3D-space, however, new proximities could be established. I chose to go from the scientistic to the poetic to the revolutionary style. An alternative route would lead from the poetic to the philosophical style. Unlike the revolutionary, it takes the poetic style not to its extremes but to its fundaments; it tries to be general without being gnomic. The best examples of such a style in organization theory are, to me, the writings of James G. March.

From a myriad of texts that bear March's name on the cover, I have chosen, for obvious reasons, those written by March himself. (Although I think I could guess which parts in co-authored texts were written by March, I would rather not risk such a procedure.) Two articles in particular were oft quoted by young (especially Scandinavian) researchers: 'The Technology of Foolishness' (1971/1988) and 'Bounded Rationality, Ambiguity, and the Engineering of Choice' (1978/1988).

Calling a style 'philosophical' may be seen as a highly problematic enterprise, considering the number of philosophers in western philosophy alone, and the variety of their styles. I hasten to reassure those who might suspect that James March writes like Heidegger that, in fact, he writes like a pragmatist philosopher. In short, James G. March seems to fulfill most of the prescription given by Richard Rorty for 'science as solidarity'.

What do pragmatist philosophers have in common with one another and with James G. March? At least two things: an interest in everyday life with its petty and romantic angles, and an interest in, knowledge of, and skill in literature. They are practical and playful, a combination thought impossible by the venerators of the sublime at the expense of the beautiful.[9] One way in which March acknowledges his proximity to philosophy, poetry, and literature is by making frequent direct references to all three fields.

I shall try to demonstrate that March fulfills the prescription for the new philosophical rhetoric as formulated by Rorty (1987, that is, the prescription is retro-fitting) by doing a March on Rorty's text. One of March's favorite schemes is *enumeration* (called also *distributio*, dividing a subject into components), usually under the rule of one of the magic numbers,[10] such as 3, 5, or 7 (often strengthened by *alliteration*, but my English is not up to such a feat). So this is what Rorty says, sometimes in unison with March, sometimes seemingly explaining and commenting on March:

1. Rationality is one of the central values in our culture (both March and Rorty use 'we' sweepingly but consciously), and is conventionally connected to 'science', 'truth', 'objectivity', and 'method'.

2. An alternative word for 'rational' (a favorite topic of March's) would be 'sane,' 'reasonable', or 'civilized'. 'On this construction, to be rational is simply to discuss any topic—religious, literary or scientific—in a way that eschews dogmatism, defensiveness, and righteous indignation' (Rorty 1987: 40).

3. Truth should be a commendatory term for well-justified belief. And the 'best way to find out what to believe is to listen to as many suggestions and arguments as you can' (p. 46).

4. In a science that so redefined its related terms, there would be 'less talk about rigor and more about originality.... The new rhetoric would draw more on the vocabulary of Romantic poetry and socialist politics, and less on that of Greek metaphysics, religious rationality, or Enlightenment scientism' (p. 51). (These are the vocabularies often invoked by James G. March).

5. A science so redefined will give 'as little reason to be self-conscious about the nature and status of one's discipline as, in the ideal democratic community, about the nature and status of one's race or sex' (p. 52).

While the last is still a utopia, it is a utopia in which James G. March seems to live already. A hybrid product of political science, psychology, engineering, poetry,

---

[9] The modern version of this dichotomy is best known through Edmund Burke's contribution to aesthetic theory, *A Philosophical Enquiry into the Origin of Our Ideas of the Sublime and Beautiful*, 1757.

[10] The usefulness of enumeration has to do with the fact that a numerical structure has a mnemonic function; the preference for certain numbers has most likely to do with mysticism of numbers sedimented in many cultures (Chinese numerology, Jewish Kabbala, etc., Crump 1990).

literature, and philosophy, he seems to think that disciplines are idiolects (Eco 1979), i.e. no more and no less than dialects of different groups. Thus the texts written with Johan P. Olsen (e.g. 1989) resemble political science texts, and those with Guje Sevón (1984) or Zur Shapira (1987) resemble psychology texts. When March writes alone, he writes as a pragmatist philosopher, but also as an extremely accomplished orator. The two texts mentioned above could well serve as illustrations for a textbook in rhetoric.

In 'Technology of Foolishness', the *exordium*[11] 'Choice and Rationality' attracts readers' attention by suggesting, in an understated tone, that beliefs in choice and rationality amount to articles of faith, and that the theory of these topics is comparable to the Scripture (no capital in the original). Such faith is based on three unexamined ideas: pre-existence of purpose, necessity of consistency, and primacy of rationality (where alliterations would be too artificial, March uses *onomatopoeias*[12] and cross-symmetries). 'The Problem of Goals' introduces a *partitio* (division): March separates himself from the traditional theory of choice, pointing out its weaknesses and enumerating its justifications (three). Observe that March seldom uses the *antithesis*, the battlehorse of tired organizational rhetoricians, or black and white figures of speech, that is, *hyperboles* of any kind.[13] The section ends with *asyndeton*:[14] 'Not always. Not usually. But sometimes.' (March 1971/1988: 259), staccato trumpets announcing what comes next. 'Sensible Foolishness' and 'Play and Reason' both combine *probatio* (proof) and *refutatio* in one section; they have parallel structures. In both, refutation precedes proof, an inversion of classical structure. This structural parallelism is accompanied by frequent examples of syntactical parallelism used in enumerations ('Imitation is not necessarily a sign of moral weakness. . . . Coercion is not necessarily an assault on individual autonomy. . . . Rationalization is not necessarily a way of evading morality' (p. 260). *Peroratio*, entitled 'Intelligence and Foolishness', is as a peroration should be: short and rich in images. 'There is little magic in the world, and foolishness in people and organizations is one of the many things that fail to produce miracles' (p. 265).

That March uses classical oratory devices does not mean that his style is mechanical and the rhetoric predictable (with the exception of enumerations and alliterations, which are clearly his favorite toys). 'Technology of Foolishness' does not contain any *narratio* (indeed, it does not contain any reference!), whereas 'Bounded Rationality' contains two: the history of the field of decision theory, and the history of the concept of bounded rationality. Worth emphasizing is his

---

[11] The first part of a classical oration (Lanham 1991: 75).

[12] Use or invention of words that sound like their meaning (Lanham 1991: 105).

[13] This could be because his rhetoric is, in traditional Aristotelian terms, *deliberative* (directed towards the future) rather than *forensic* (judging the past) or *demonstrative* (praising or blaming), Burke 1950/1969: 70.

[14] Omission of conjunctions between words, phrases, clauses (Lanham 1991: 182).

awareness that references constitute narration, and not proof: multiple references are always ordered chronologically. 'Bounded Rationality' is more structurally complex and contains many reiterations of rhetorical schemes. Let me quote only the last sentence of its peroration: 'But though hope for minor progress is a romantic vision, it may not be entirely inappropriate for a theory built on a romantic view of human destiny' (1978/1988: 289).

8.5 STYLE: EDUCATIONAL (IN TWO VARIATIONS)

One could protest that 'educational' is a genre, not a style; I would agree to the point that educational style is obviously a style that produces the best textbooks, but not all, or even most, textbooks can be used as examples of educational style. Most textbooks can be classified under one of two categories: either they faithfully present a state of the art, a history of a topic, a discipline, etc., or else they present an interesting thesis of their author. The former tend to be mundane summaries, the latter, distortions or misrepresentations of other people's work to fit the thesis. The few that combine both purposes and avoid both dangers can be said to be the product of an educational style. Thus my judgment of David Silverman's style as educational does not originate in the fact that he is the author of excellent textbooks (e.g. *Interpreting Qualitative Data*, 1993) but is confirmed by it, and also by Silverman's clear interest in the workings of knowledge (*Reading Castaneda*, 1975). And although Silverman writes more than organization theory, I will limit myself to his writings within our field, most specifically, to his dissertation, which has become one of the most popular textbooks of its time without being intended as such: *The Theory of Organisations: A Sociological Framework*, 1970.

Todorov thus characterized 'a narrative of knowledge', or a *gnoseological* narrative, as exemplified by the story of the quest for the Holy Grail:

The reader's interest is not driven by the question What happens next? which refers us to the logic of succession or to the mythological narrative. We know perfectly well from the start what will happen, who will reach the Grail, who will be punished and why. Our interest arises from a wholly different question which refers instead to the gnoseological organization: What is the Grail? The Grail narrative relates a quest; what is being sought, however, is not an object but a meaning, the meaning of the word Grail. And since the question has to do with being and not with doing, the exploration of the future is less important than that of the past. (1990: 33)

Thompson, Weick, and March rely on mythological narrative, where transformations concern organizing and organization, or writing on organizations. Burrell,

Calás, and Smircich organize their narratives ideologically, with a revolutionary standpoint as a transformative force. In Silverman's text the transformation concerns the status of knowledge, but as it is a quest for knowledge, it is neither the first nor the last transformation, it is one of the transformations that produce the chain of history of social sciences. The quest is for Organization, and Silverman proposes to achieve a new narrative transformation by an adventure consisting of placing the past studies of organizations into a new frame:

The nature of [my] argument may be stated in four propositions: first, that the development of the study of organisations can be shown to have a certain pattern; secondly, that one of the directions in which it now appears to be leading [systems theory] has rather serious limitations; thirdly, that at this stage a statement of an alternative approach making use of certain parts of literature will prove more fruitful than another attempt at synthesis; and, finally, that such an approach may be usefully derived from an emerging sociological frame of reference [social action theory]. (1970: 1–2)

By 'social action theory' Silverman means a frame originating in phenomenology (Schütz, Berger, and Luckmann) and developed, on one hand, by Goffman, and on the other by ethnomethodologists (Garfinkel, Sacks, Cicourel). It is a frame characterized by its problematizing stance towards everyday life—in this case, everyday life in organizations. As in the case of Weick and his insight-engendering metaphors, the utility of this frame is far from exhausted in organizational studies thirty years after Silverman suggested it (Silverman's own example of its use can be found in *Organisational Work*, 1976).

Observe the difference between Silverman's and Thompson's use of 'propositions': in the quotation above, they are statements—suggestions—concerning the relationships between other statements. After all, the co-author of *The Material Word: Some Theories of Language and Its Limits* (Silverman and Torode 1980) knows better than to compare words with things, but also knows better than to perform logical operations on tropes.

A variation on the same educational style can be found in Gareth Morgan (*Images of Organization*, 1986). Instead of immersing past theories of organization in a new bath, Morgan places over them a grid of metaphors (if such an ugly metaphor may be provisionally accepted) which results in a narrative transformation. Note that neither of these two authors uses the time-honored device of educational narratives, which suggests a transformation from the state of ignorance (scholars before us and our enemies) to complete knowledge (we and our friends). Knowledge does not accumulate, the Grail will not be found, and the gnoseological narrative will continue.[15]

[15] However, it will not necessarily be carried on by the same writer. Unlike *Beyond Method* (1983), which was an exercise done before *Images*, later books by Morgan (1988, 1993) switched to a mythological narrative and are concerned with the future, not the past.

There are a great many small differences in the style of the two educators—Silverman's way of writing is terse, almost staccato, while Morgan's is flowing and ornamental, for example—but they share many similarities typical of educational texts: examples, enumerations, summaries, exhibits, etc. The central characteristic, however, is the one that I see as constitutive of the educative style: another step in a never-ending quest for meaning, performed either by setting the old material *into* a new frame, or else putting a new formative grid *onto* it. The first may be called 'framing' in the traditional sense of setting a picture into a frame (on the consequences of such an operation, see Simmel 1907); the second 'framing' in the sense used in photography or film-making (Goffman 1974, although he oscillates uneasily between the two). They are close enough to justify their inclusion into the same style (education by reframing), yet they are distinct enough to warrant separate attention.

8.6 STYLE: ETHNOGRAPHIC (IN TWO PARTS)

'John, go get the goddamn light in the car. If we can see him, he'll come out.'
I run toward the car to get the sturdy multicell flashlight, a copper's tool that gets more service as an effective truncheon than as a source of light. At the car, bumblebee policing—swarming—is in full glory. There are five patrol units plus the K-9 (canine) unit, whose driver arrives saying breathlessly, 'not bad time, eh?'
    I point the men in the general direction of where I'd left David and scramble around in the car to find the flashlight. I find it under the front seat and run back up the driveway to find a half-dozen cops stomping through the bushes, all with guns drawn. I'm standing in civie garb, trembling, and thinking, 'Don't shoot the fieldworker'. (1988: 112)

By and large, however, the people-processing tasks of ride operators pass good naturedly and smoothly, with operators hardly noticing much more than bodies passing in front of view (special bodies, however, merit special attention as when crew members on the subs gather to assist a young lady in a revealing outfit on board and then linger over the hatch to admire the view as she descends the steep steps to take her seat on the boat). Yet, sometimes, more than a body becomes visible, as happens when customers overstep their roles and challenge employee authority, insult an operator, or otherwise disrupt the routines of the job. In the process, guests become 'dufusses', 'ducks', and 'assholes' (just three of many derisive terms used by ride operators to label those customers they believe to have gone beyond the pale). (1991: 71)

Although I neglected to put the name after the quotations, nobody versed in organization studies would hesitate to identify John Van Maanen as the author of both. This is because the specific fieldwork is a part of an ethnographic style: Van

Maanen studied the policemen on the beat, and Van Maanen studied the workers at Disneyland. And yet there is a difference between the two texts, which probably differ by ten years rather by the three indicated by their present quotations. What happened in between? 'An end to innocence', if I may quote Van Maanen on Van Maanen (1995c).

In ethnology and anthropology it would be impossible to speak about one ethnographic style, as there are, and were, a great many such styles. The two disciplines, however, did not spend much time on the analysis of its writing, until hit by the same literary turn as the rest of social sciences. Clifford and Marcus (1986), Geertz (1988), and Van Maanen himself (1988) paid a great deal of attention to how ethnographic texts were crafted. Consequently, they have influenced the very process of crafting, and this is why Van Maanen is speaking about lost innocence.

The first quotation, the Dashiel-Hammett-turned-ethnographer, is a clear-cut example of 'being there' (Geertz 1988) and of 'impressionist writing' (Van Maanen 1988). The second is something between 'the world in a text' and 'I-witnessing' (Geertz 1988). It is not certain whether the author and the observer are the same character; whoever the observer is, she/he is not going native; defamiliarization is clearly at work (Van Maanen 1995c). Dry touches of distancing irony replaced the self-comforting irony of the young (younger?) researcher: an end of innocence is also coming of age.

What remains, and what makes me propose this totalizing move of suggesting 'ethnographic' as a name of a style is a film-like quality of the text. Unlike most other organization texts, ethnographic style produces visual and aural illusions: one can 'see' and 'hear' the Other. In terms of rhetorical analysis, it could be said that ethnographic style favors *hypotyposis*: a rhetorical device 'giving a description so vivid that the reader envisages the event as happening before his or her very eyes' (Edmondson 1984: 24). Thus, the main effect is not so much of the researcher 'being there' but of the reader being 'shifted there' (Latour 1988b). The ethnographic style, as represented here by the writing of John Van Maanen and then in personal variations by Gideon Kunda (1992) and Michael Rosen (2000), has the power to transport the reader to other places, other voices.

8.7 THE STYLES, THE STYLISTS, AND THE *ZEITGEIST*

All of this leads unavoidably to questions such as: is style personal and idiosyncratic or can it be imitated? what does the existence of all these styles mean for the field of organization studies? and what does it mean for how the field is perceived by those outside the field? This brings me to issues debated so fervently between John Van Maanen (1995*a, b*) and Jeffrey Pfeffer (1993, 1995).

It seems to me that in that debate, the two agonists leaned towards slightly different definition of style (in order to improve the debate?). While John Van Maanen was closer to the second *Oxford English Dictionary* definition, style as elegance, Pfeffer was more interested in the first, style as form. This influences the possible answer to a question of whether a style can be imitated: no from the Van Maanen's position, yes from Pfeffer's. Another question returns: if a style can be imitated (style is a text, not a person), can the stylists provide prescriptions on how to do so?

While styles are unrepeatable (in a manner of speaking, as writers form styles by repetition), they are highly imitable. At any rate, style as form can be imitated, although style as elegance cannot; elegance connotes the reception, an effect that a writer cannot foresee. Thus, it is possible to take courses in rhetoric, but nobody can guarantee that the course participants will become orators.

Is it a duty of the stylish writers, then, as one might deduce from Pfeffer's text, to prescribe how to achieve a style similar to theirs? Hardly. They need not know how they are doing what they are doing in order to do it brilliantly. They are, after all, their own figures of speech. It seems much more likely, as history shows, that somebody else can describe their style. Van Maanen's description of Weick's style can be an enormous help to many young readers in appreciating its elegance, so too has Joanne Martin (1990) made Derrida's style transparent to organization re-searchers, more method-like, so to speak. Still, while Calás and Smircich create their own style out of Derrida's model, many others who reach for deconstruction will end with a use of a contemporary idiolect, and I for one cannot see what is wrong with it.

Thus, style as form can become a paradigm (it is in fact paradigmatic by virtue of being repeatedly used by at least one person) and it can be helped by technical analysis and advice. Style as elegance cannot, because uniqueness forms part of what is perceived as elegant. It is a paradox, but unlike Van Maanen and Pfeffer, who wish to resolve it by espousing only one part of it, I would suggest that we maintain it intact. Style is closely related to fashion (certain meanings of the two words are synonymous) and it shares with fashion its paradox of striving for uniqueness *and* conformity, so well explored by Simmel (1907). A widely imitated style *becomes* an idiolect.

So the question becomes rather: how many stylists—and idiolects—can one field carry? Here again one has an impression that while Van Maanen was worried about the possible uniformization within the discipline, Pfeffer was worried about the discipline's image outside of it. To put it bluntly, why is organization theory, with its variety of styles and deep awareness of rhetorical demands, losing to economics, with its one-style-turned-idiolect and its avoidance of self-reflection?

Seen historically, economics has had many powerful stylists and this is perhaps what attracted public attention to the discipline in the first place. With time, one style—scientistic—won over the others and strengthened itself in a self-reinforcing cycle. According to many analysts, among others MacIntyre (1988), a field dominated by one canon is more endangered than a field that has many competing canons. Once that canon becomes delegitimized (as all canons eventually do), the field is in shambles. The weakness of organization theory is also its strength, although this may not be apparent in all those situations when it is confronted with a stronger field and is forced to stand aside. But '[t]o have passed through an epistemological crisis successfully enables the adherents of a tradition of enquiry to rewrite its history in a more insightful way' (MacIntyre 1988: 363). Was not such a crisis happening in the 1970s, and were not texts like Silverman's and later Morgan's and Calás and Smircich's, the 'insightful rewrites' of the field's history?

The issue is not only a matter of one style versus many, but also of what style it is. Style is the message, or form is the content, as White (1987) put it. And it is the *Zeitgeist*, or the spirit of the times, that chooses 'the style whose time has come.' Economics offers the complete (the last?) illusion of modernity, of certainty of the findings and transparency of the method. By carefully avoiding contact with the reality of everyday life, economics can offer the wider public an image of the world as it would be, were we all rational. As one of my Polish colleagues put it, reality is the mess in which we have to live in everyday life, and science should offer us a relief from it, not rub our noses in it even deeper. As long as organization theorists are determined to keep their noses deep in organizational garbage-cans, it is unlikely that they will choose to follow one style, no matter how attractive or elegant. Courses on rhetoric can produce orators, provided that they will always be speaking to the same audience, that is, an audience that never changes, never ages, and never learns. This is surely an even less realistic assumption than that of a profit-maximizing individual.

A small issue of not so small consequence remains. In the text above, I implicitly assumed that the rhetoric of organization theory finds its expression in the form of written texts. This is probably correct as far as the description goes, but the fact remains that, as in the case of Van Maanen and Pfeffer, sometimes people do talk to one another, as in ancient times (although the talk invariably gets inscribed). How do they talk when they do? There is no need to analyze the oratory styles of the two agonists because they have done it themselves. I wish to highlight a certain interesting paradox instead. In his first speech (1995a), Van Maanen praised conversation as a higher form of exchange than a debate: 'The object of debate is . . . to overwhelm or obliterate one's opponent: to prune, pare and discard. The object of conversation is to keep it going: to plant, nurture and cultivate. In the most uncertain domain of organization theory, the latter objective seems preferable' (p. 140).

In his answer, Pfeffer (1995) pointed out that he and Van Maanen agreed more than they disagreed, that many of the supposed antagonisms were the results of Van

Maanen's hyperbolas, not to mention deliberate misunderstandings. In answer, Van Maanen said, 'one always yearns for the last word in the academic blood-sport called debate' (1995b: 687). And he continued in a footnote: 'As a genre of public discourse in an open community, debate is a cornerstone' (p. 691).

My intention is not to gloat over Van Maanen's inconsistency. Far from it—it is an inconsistency that I recognize and share. Like him, I intellectually espouse the ideal of science as conversation, launched in contemporary times by Michael Oakeshott (1959) and warmly spoken for by Deirdre N. McCloskey (1985) and Richard Rorty (1987), among many others. Like him, however, I was brought up in a male-dominated university culture where a duel is the highest form of sport, and a debate is fun. While proclaiming the virtues of a conversation, I turn to a debate at the slightest provocation. Like him, I have the whole western culture behind me, with its idea of agon as the main pattern for a drama. People fight: for freedom, for fun, and for a better world. They fight against enemies and against poverty. They fight for their countries and for their ideals. And while some—mostly intellectuals—choose to thrust and parry—a great many choose to kill. 'We all believe that negation and thus dialectics are the great masters of history, the midwives of our societies. Nothing is achieved, we all admit too quickly, without struggle, and dispute, and wars, and destruction' (Latour 1988c: 91). Yet *agon* was but one convention among many in the highly ritualized Old Greek comedy, and the Old (Aristophanic) comedy only one kind of drama. As genres delimit styles, and styles build genres, they are both important for organization theory. Much as I am for the proliferation and cultivation of styles, I am also for eliminating, or at least minimizing, the use of the genre of debate. There must be better things to do than see who bleeds first or who stays longer on his (yes) feet.

References

ALVESSON, MATS, and WILLMOTT, HUGH (eds.) (1992). *Critical Management Studies*. London: Sage.

BARTHES, ROLAND (1979). 'From Work to Text', in Josué V. Harrari (ed.), *Textual Strategies: Perspectives in Post-Structuralist Criticism*. Ithaca, NY: Methuen.

BATESON, GREGORY W. (1972). *Steps to an Ecology of Mind*. New York: Ballantine.

BURKE, KENNETH (1950/1969). *A Rhetoric of Motives*. Berkeley: University of California Press.

BURRELL, GIBSON (1992). 'The Organization of Pleasure', in Mats Alvesson and Hugh Willmott (eds.), *Critical Management Studies*. London: Sage.

——(1997). *Pandemonium: Towards a Retro-Organization Theory*. London: Sage.

CALÁS, MARTA B., and SMIRCICH, LINDA (1991). 'Voicing Seduction to Silence Leadership'. *Organization Studies*, 12/4: 567–601.

CALÁS, MARTA B., and SMIRCICH, LINDA (1993). 'Dangerous Liaisons: The Feminine in Management Meets Globalization'. *Business Horizons*, Apr.: 73–83.

CLIFFORD, JAMES, and MARCUS, GEORGE E. (eds.) (1986). *Writing Culture: The Poetics and Politics of Ethnography*. Berkeley: University of California Press.

CRUMP, THOMAS (1990). *The Anthropology of Numbers*. Cambridge: Cambridge University Press.

CZARNIAWSKA, BARBARA (1999*a*). 'Management She Wrote: Organization Studies and Detective Stories'. *Studies in Cultures, Organizations and Societies*, 5/1: 13–41.

—— (1999*b*). *Writing Management: Organization Theory as Literary Genre*. Oxford: Oxford University Press.

ECO, UMBERTO (1979/1983). *The Role of the Reader: Explorations in the Semiotics of Texts*. London: Hutchinson.

—— (1989). *The Open Work*. Cambridge, Mass.: Harvard University Press.

—— (1992). *Interpretation and Overinterpretation*. Cambridge: Cambridge University Press.

—— (1995). *In Search for the Perfect Language*. Oxford: Blackwell.

EDMONDSON, RICCA (1984). *Rhetoric in Sociology*. London: Macmillan.

Encyclopaedia Britannica Online, accessed 14 Oct. 2000.

FOUCAULT, MICHEL (1979). 'What Is an Author?', in Josué V. Harrari (ed.), *Textual Strategies: Perspectives in Post-Structuralist Criticism*. Ithaca, NY: Methuen.

GEERTZ, CLIFFORD (1988). *Works and Lives: The Anthropologist as Author*. Stanford, Calif.: Stanford University Press.

GOFFMAN, ERVING (1974). *Frame Analysis: An Essay on the Organization of Experience*. New York: Harper & Row.

GOODMAN, NELSON (1978). *Ways of Worldmaking*. Indianapolis: Hackett Publishing.

GUSFIELD, JOSEPH (1976). 'The Literary Rhetoric of Science: Comedy and Pathos in Drinking Driver Research'. *American Sociological Review*, 41 (Feb.): 16–34.

HARJU, KLAUS (1999). 'Protext: The Morphoses of Identity, Heterogeneity and Synolon'. *Studies in Cultures, Organizations and Societies*, 5/1: 131–50.

HARRARI, JOSUÉ V. (1979). 'Critical Factions/Critical Fictions', in Josué V. Harrari (ed.), *Textual Strategies: Perspectives in Post-Structuralist Criticism*. Ithaca, NY: Methuen.

HARRÉ, ROM, and SECORD, PAUL F. (1972). *The Explanation of Social Behaviour*. Oxford: Basil Blackwell.

HOLMGREN, BETH (1998). *Rewriting Capitalism: Literature and the Market in Late Tsarist Russia and the Kingdom of Poland*. Pittsburgh: University of Pittsburgh Press.

HÖPFL, HEATHER (1995). 'Organisational Rhetoric and the Threat of Ambivalence'. *Studies in Cultures, Organizations and Societies*, 1/2: 175–87.

HÜHN, PETER (1987). 'The Detective as Reader: Narrativity and Reading Concepts in Detective Fiction'. *Modern Fiction Studies*, 33/3: 451–66.

ISER, WOLFGANG (1978). *The Art of Reading: A Theory of Aesthetic Response*. Baltimore: Johns Hopkins University Press.

KLAMER, ARJO, MCCLOSKEY, DEIRDRE N., and SOLOW, ROBERT M. (eds.) (1988). *The Consequences of Economic Rhetoric*. Cambridge: Cambridge University Press.

KUNDA, GIDEON (1992). *Engineering Culture: Control and Commitment in a High-Tech Organization*. Philadelphia: Temple University Press.

LANHAM, RICHARD A. (1992). *A Handlist of Rhetorical Terms*. Berkeley: University of California Press.

LATOUR, BRUNO (1988*a*). 'The Politics of Explanation: An Alternative', in Steve Woolgar (ed.), *Knowledge and Reflexivity*. London: Sage.

—— (1988*b*). 'A Relativistic Account of Einstein's Relativity'. *Social Studies of Science*, 18: 3–44.

—— (1988*c*). 'The Enlightenment Without the Critique: A Word on Michel Serres' Philosophy'. *Contemporary French Philosophy*, 4: 83–98.

LEJEUNE, PHILIPPE (1989). *On Autobiography*. Minneapolis: University of Minnesota Press.

LEPENIES, WOLF (1985/1988). *Between Literature and Science: The Rise of Sociology*. Cambridge: Cambridge University Press.

McCLOSKEY, DEIRDRE N. (1985). *The Rhetoric of Economics*. Madison: University of Wisconsin Press (2nd revised edn 1998).

MACINTYRE, ALASDAIR (1988). *Whose Justice? Which Rationality?* London: Duckworth.

MANGHAM, IAIN L. (1996). 'Some Consequences of Taking Gareth Morgan Seriously', in David Grant and Cliff Oswick (eds.), *Metaphor and Organizations*. London: Sage.

MARCH, JAMES G. (1971/1988). 'The Technology of Foolishness', in James G. March, *Decisions and Organizations*. Oxford: Blackwell.

—— (1978/1988). 'Bounded Rationality, Ambiguity and the Engineering of Choice', in James G. March, *Decisions and Organizations*. Oxford: Blackwell.

—— and SEVÓN, GUJE (1984/1988). 'Gossip, Information and Decision-Making', in James G. March, *Decisions and Organizations*. Oxford: Blackwell.

—— and SHAPIRA, ZUR (1987/1988). 'Managerial Perspectives on Risk and Risk-Taking', in James G. March, *Decisions and Organizations*. Oxford: Blackwell.

—— and OLSEN, JOHAN (1989). *Rediscovering Institutions: The Organizational Basis of Politics*. New York: Free Press.

MARTIN, JOANNE (1990). 'Deconstructing Organizational Taboos: The Suppression of Gender Conflict in Organizations'. *Organization Science*, 1/4: 339–59.

MEGILL, ALLAN, and McCLOSKEY, DEIRDRE N. (1987). 'The Rhetoric of History', in John S. Nelson, Allan Megill, and Deirdre N. McCloskey (eds.), *The Rhetoric of the Human Sciences*. Madison: University of Wisconsin Press.

MEYER, JOHN (1996). 'Otherhood: The Promulgation and Transmission of Ideas in the Modern Organizational Environment', in Barbara Czarniawska and Guje Sevón (eds.), *Translating Organizational Change*. Berlin: de Gruyter.

MONIN, NANETTE, BARRY, DAVID, and MONIN, D. JOHN (2000). *Toggling with Taylor: A Revelational Approach to Reading Management Texts*. A paper presented at the 4th International Conference on Organisational Discourse, King's College, London, 26–28 July.

MORGAN, GARETH (ed.) (1983). *Beyond Method: Strategies for Social Research*. Beverly Hills, Calif.: Sage.

—— (1986). *Images of Organization*. London: Sage.

—— (1988). *Riding the Waves of Change: Developing Managerial Competencies for a Turbulent World*. San Francisco: Jossey-Bass.

—— (1993). *Imaginization: The Art of Creative Management*. London: Sage.

The New Shorter Oxford English Dictionary (1993). Oxford: Oxford University Press.

NELSON, JOHN S., MEGILL, ALLAN, and McCLOSKEY, DEIRDRE N. (eds.) (1987). *The Rhetoric of the Human Sciences*. Madison: University of Wisconsin Press.

OAKESHOTT, MICHAEL (1959/1991). 'The Voice of Poetry in the Conversation of Mankind', in id., *Rationalism in Politics and Other Essays*. Indianapolis: Liberty Press.

O'CONNOR, ELLEN S. (1996). 'Lines of Authority: Readings of Foundational Texts on the Profession of Management'. *Journal of Management History*, 2/3: 26–49.

PERROW, CHARLES (1991). 'A Society of Organizations'. *Theory and Society*, 20: 725–62.

PFEFFER, JEFFREY (1993). 'Barriers to the Advance of Organizational Science: Paradigm Development as a Dependent Variable'. *Academy of Management Review*, 18/4: 599–620.

——(1995). 'Mortality, Reproducibility, and the Persistence of Styles of Theory'. *Organization Science*, 6/6: 681–6.

RICOEUR, PAUL (1981). 'The Model of the Text: Meaningful Action Considered as Text', in John B. Thompson (ed. and trans.), *Hermeneutics and the Human Sciences*. Cambridge: Cambridge University Press.

RORTY, RICHARD (1987). 'Science as Solidarity', in John S. Nelson, Allan Megill, and Deirdre N. McCloskey (eds.), *The Rhetoric of the Human Sciences*. Madison: University of Wisconsin Press.

ROSEN, MICHAEL (2000). *Turning Words, Spinning Worlds*. Reading: Harwood Academic Publishers.

SILVERMAN, DAVID (1970). *The Theory of Organisations*. New York: Basic Books.

——(1975). *Reading Castaneda*. London: Routledge & Kegan Paul.

——(1993). *Interpreting Qualitative Data*. London: Sage.

——and JONES, JILL (1976). *Organisational Work*. London: Collier Macmillan.

——and TORODE, BRIAN (1980). *The Material Word: Some Theories of Language and Its Limits*. London: Routledge & Kegan Paul.

SIMMEL, GEORG (1904/1973). 'Fashion', in George Wills and David Midgley (eds.), *Fashion Marketing*. London: Allen & Unwin.

——(1907/1994). 'The Picture Frame'. *Theory, Culture & Society*, 11: 11–17.

SIMONS, HERBERT (ed.) (1989). *Rhetoric in the Human Sciences*. London: Sage.

——(1990). *The Rhetorical Turn*. Chicago: University of Chicago Press.

SMITH, DOROTHY E. (1999). *Writing the Social: Critique, Theory, and Investigations*. Toronto: University of Toronto Press.

STARKEY, KEN (1999). 'Eleven Characters in Search of an Ethic, or The Spirit of Capitalism Revisited'. *Studies in Cultures, Organizations and Societies*, 5/1: 179–94.

STEINER, GEORGE (1975/1992). *After Babel: Aspects of Language and Translation*. Oxford: Oxford University Press.

THOMPSON, JAMES D. (1967). *Organizations in Action*. New York: McGraw-Hill.

TODOROV, TZVETAN (1990). *Genres in Discourse*. Cambridge: Cambridge University Press.

VAN MAANEN, JOHN (1988). *Tales of the Field*. Chicago: University of Chicago Press.

——(1991). 'The Smile Factory: Work at Disneyland', in Peter J. Frost, Larry F. Moore, Meryl Reis Louis, Craig C. Lundberg, and Joanne Martin (eds.), *Reframing Organizational Culture*. Newbury Park, Calif.: Sage.

——(1995a), 'Style as Theory'. *Organization Science*, 6/1: 133–43.

——(1995b). 'Fear and Loathing in Organization Studies'. *Organization Science*, 6/6: 687–92.

——(1995c). 'An End to Innocence: The Ethnography of Ethnography', in John Van Maanen (ed.), *Representation in Ethnography*. Thousand Oaks, Calif.: Sage.

WALDO, DWIGHT (1961). 'Organization Theory: An Elephantine Problem'. *Public Administration Review*, 21: 210–25.

WEICK, KARL E. (1978). 'The Spines of Leaders', in M. W. McCall and M. M. Lombard (eds.), *Leadership: Where Else Can We Go?* Durham, NC: Duke University Press.

——(1979). *The Social Psychology of Organizing*. Reading: Addison-Wesley.

—— (1989). 'Theory Construction as Disciplined Imagination'. *Academy of Management Review*, 14/4: 516–31.

WESTWOOD, ROBERT (1999). 'A "Sampled" Account of Organisation: Being a De-Authored, Reflexive Parody of Organisation/Writing'. *Studies in Cultures, Organizations and Societies*, 5/1: 195–233.

WHITE, HAYDEN (1987). *The Content of the Form: Narrative Discourse and Historical Representation*. Baltimore: Johns Hopkins University Press.

WILLS, GARRY (1999). 'Fire & Ice'. *New York Review of Books*, 46/4: 6–10.

CHAPTER 9

....

PLURALISM, SCIENTIFIC PROGRESS, AND THE STRUCTURE OF ORGANIZATION THEORY

....

CHRISTIAN KNUDSEN

During the 1980s and 1990s organization scholars have increasingly been debating whether the coexistence of several research programs was a blessing or a curse for the advancement of their field. Two opposing positions have gradually emerged that support either a *unification* or a *pluralist* prescription. Those who support the unification position argue with reference to Thomas Kuhn (1970) and Michael Polanyi (1958) that upholding a scientific consensus is a necessary condition for the accumulation of knowledge. If researchers in a field like organization theory 'were too willing to accept every unorthodox theory, method, or technique, the established consensus would be destroyed, and the intellectual structure of science would become chaotic. Scientists would be faced with a multitude of conflicting and unorganized theories and would lack research guidelines and standards' (Cole 1983: 135). The main advocate of this position in organization theory, Jeffrey Pfeffer

The research has been supported by the Danish Research Council. I would like to thank H. Tsoukas and several anonymous referees for their inputs to earlier versions of this paper.

(1993), argues that scientific fields that are more paradigmatically developed will tend to advance more rapidly, fare better in the contest for resources, have larger and better organized 'invisible colleges', have lower journal rejection rates, have fewer coordination problems and therefore will be more likely to take advantage of the benefits of teamwork than paradigmatically less developed fields. On the other hand, those who support a pluralist position argue that the more research programs are advanced the better for the long-term growth of the field. Several reasons have been given to support this position. One reason is that in order to understand the highly complex reality different theories are required since most theories only highlight one aspect of this world. Another reason is that the existence of many theories promotes competition and increases the chances for scientific advances. One proponent of this pluralist position in organization theory, John Van Maanen (1995*a*, *b*), therefore argues that one of the most important issues related to theory development in organization theory is to answer the following questions. What institutional arrangements are more likely to facilitate tolerance, learning, and conversations? What are the conditions that surround productive scholarly exchanges in the field? However, Van Maanen does not raise the question whether the strategy of 'letting a thousand flowers bloom' actually is a good or bad strategy for organization theory.

The main purpose of this chapter is to define what intellectual structure best promotes the advancement of the field of organization studies. A conceptual framework is proposed to analyze different intellectual structures and appraise how they perform in promoting scientific progress. The term 'intellectual structure' refers to the distribution of activities within a scientific field at a specific point in time. This chapter will especially focus on the distribution between activities aimed at refining existing research programs, on one hand, and activities aimed at searching for new theories, on the other hand. In accordance with studies of adaptive processes, it is argued that in order to make progress over a long period of time a scientific field has to secure a balance between the generation of new theoretical alternatives and the selection and retention of them. As a consequence we may find intellectual fields with a too low as well as a too high degree of theoretical pluralism that each are confronted with a specific set of problems. In fact, it is argued that both the unification strategy and the pluralist strategy may lead to intellectual structures that have suboptimal traits by either having too little or too much pluralism. Fields with too little pluralism run the risk of being caught in a *specialization trap*, while fields with too much pluralism run the risk of being caught in a *fragmentation trap*. Both of these traps emerge as a result of self-reinforcing processes where either the activity of extending an existing research program (normal science) or the activity of searching for new research programs (extraordinary science) get reinforced and sooner or later become dominant in the field.

The *specialization trap*—where the elaboration of a dominant research program completely comes to drive out the search for new and heterodox theories—emerges because the exploitation of an existing research program gives a much faster and safer return than the experimentation with a completely new and uncertain research program. As researchers develop better and better skills at using the problem-solving heuristic of a research program they will be inclined to use this program even more in the future, thus further increasing the strength of its heuristic and the opportunity costs of switching to another research program. The consequence of this trap is a scarcity of exploratory activities that undermines the long-run adaptability of the field to new and unpredictable future situations. This is the main risk of following the unification strategy in organization theory proposed by Pfeffer (1993) and later supported by Donaldson (1995, 1996a).

The second trap is called a *fragmentation* trap. Its main characteristic is that the search for new theories comes to dominate the activity of extending and elaborating a research program. The fragmentation trap will emerge when too many new theories are proposed at a too fast pace in order for the scientific community to be able to evaluate each contribution properly and to integrate them into a reasonable coherent knowledge structure. Three implications follow from this. First, single theories are typically not turned into coherent research programs with their own unified way of solving problems, because there is too little persistence in the community of researchers to 'stick to' one theory in order to investigate its potential for solving other problems as well. Second, there is not enough time to determine the relationship between the different theories, i.e. whether they compete or complement each other. Third, since the relationships between old and new theories are never determined there will be no cumulative growth in the field. New theories will either just succeed—rather than replace—old theories until one or both of them are forgotten. As a consequence the knowledge structure of the field will become more and more fragmented, since new theories are just tacked onto the existing structure in an ad hoc manner rather than being integrated with existing contributions. And with a more fragmented discipline it becomes more and more difficult to use the existing knowledge structure to construct new contributions, which will undermine the chances for scientific progress in the future. This is the risk of following the pluralist strategy proposed by authors like Van Maanen (1995b) and Daft and Lewin (1990) in organization studies itself.

Contrary to both the unification and the pluralist position, this chapter argues for a position of 'limited pluralism' which proposes that upholding a balance between extending existing research programs and searching for new theories is a prerequisite for scientific progress in the field of organization studies. In fact, this 'third' position should not be seen as surprising since it is just an application of organizational learning theory (March 1991; Levinthal and March 1993) to the field of organization studies itself.

But before proceeding any further with the analysis let me shortly describe the perspective from which the field of organization studies is viewed and the methodological position adopted in this chapter. The main argument is that the relationship between pluralism and scientific progress is a contingent rather than an absolute one in the sense that this relationship depends on the 'social structure' of the research community of the field. Consequently, a major part of the chapter will look at the field of organization studies from a 'sociology of science' perspective, with an attempt to establish what 'social structures' have characterized the field at different times. Being a 'non-cognitive' type of sociology of science though, it is closer to the classic sociology of science represented by R. Merton than to the more recent sociology of science of B. Latour (1982). And by studying which effects a higher degree of theoretical pluralism may have on scientific progress, given a specific type of social structure in the field, I assume a *non-relativist* methodological framework in which it is possible to compare different research programs. Contrary to some post-Kuhnian and postmodern views, it is argued that there can be rational debates, communication, and choices between the different theories and paradigms in organization studies.

9.1 A REVIEW OF THE DEBATE ON THE RELATIONSHIP BETWEEN PLURALISM AND SCIENTIFIC PROGRESS IN ORGANIZATION STUDIES

According to several reviewers (e.g. Grandori 1987; Reed 1992) from the late 1950s to the late 1970s organization studies has been characterized by a relatively high degree of consensus with regard to both theoretical and empirical issues mainly due to the hegemony of the structural contingency program. The emergence and later coexistence of several competing research programs in the mid-1970s such as population ecology, neo-institutionalism, resource-dependency theory, and organization economics made it significantly more difficult in organization studies to agree on how to prioritize problems and choose between methods to use in order to solve these problems. As a result, the uncertainty facing the individual organizational researcher in performing his or her research activities has increased significantly. The increase of theoretical pluralism has also produced a field in which the allocation of reputation became more ambiguous and the structure of knowledge became more complex than before.

As one may suspect the high degree of theoretical diversity in organization studies has been appraised very differently. In the period just following the break down of the hegemony of the Structural Contingency Program, many organizational researchers expressed positive feelings regarding the new state of affairs in the field. Not only were organization researchers more receptive and more willing to take on new theoretical and empirical problems, but they were also open to a range of non-positivist methodological frameworks. Burrell and Morgan (1979) were among the first to map the field according to which meta-theoretical positions could potentially be developed within the field. Like many other organization researchers, Burrell and Morgan, regarded this development of the field from a mono-paradigmatic to a multi-paradigmatic state as being very positive. However, looking upon the field from a Kuhnian perspective, they came to the conclusion that the major paradigms in the field were mutually exclusive and incommensurable, since there were no paradigm independent criteria to appraise which of a set of competing paradigms should be preferred. Burrell and Morgan even suggested that the incommensurability thesis could be used by new heterodox paradigms as a way of defending themselves against the mainstream functionalist paradigm through arguing for paradigm closure and *isolationism*.

More subtle statements later replaced the early statements regarding the virtues of theoretical diversity and paradigm closure in organization science. Willmot (1990), Hassard (1993), and Reed (1985) found that Burrell and Morgan's acceptance of the incommensurability thesis and the idea that there can be no communication between paradigms in organization theory was unwarranted. Furthermore, Scott (1998) argued that there exist very different relationships between research programs or 'perspectives' in organization theory. In some cases, the perspectives are 'partially in conflict'; in other cases they 'partially overlap' and in still other cases they 'partially complement one another' (p. 31). Although the different perspectives have emerged at different times, according to Scott, the later perspectives have not been able to completely supplant the earlier ones. Instead, they 'continue to coexist and to claim their share of advocates' (p. 31). This trend of an increasing number of theoretical perspectives in the field may, according to Scott, pose some severe problems. For instance, as more and more new perspectives are introduced into the field, the background knowledge becomes more complex and it is increasingly difficult to uphold a consensus in the field. However, as Scott argues, 'the existence of multiple paradigms may reduce consensus and support, it does not thereby necessarily reduce the power of the ideas and the value of possessing multiple lens through which to observe our world' (118–19).

Recently, a more critical attitude towards theoretical pluralism has emerged. In his early attempt of mapping organization studies by setting up a typology of different research programs, Jeffrey Pfeffer (1982) noticed that due to the proliferation of middle-range theories, the field had become a 'weed patch' rather than a 'well-tended garden'. This tendency towards fragmentation of organization studies due to the proliferation of new research programs could, according to Zammuto and Connolly (1984), be counteracted by teaching new students about the social structure of the field and about strategies for coping with the information overload resulting from the fragmentation. Mone and McKinley (1993) explained the fragmentation of the field as a result of the diffusion of a 'uniqueness value', i.e. a value that emphasized the drive to be novel, original, innovative, etc. rather than a value to conform to and to extend the existing research programs. Furthermore, they argued for the existence of several mechanisms that will further reinforce or promote adherence to the 'uniqueness' value, indicating that the tendency towards fragmentation will, indeed, be very difficult to reverse. Donaldson (1995) took this argument one step further by proposing that the proliferation of paradigms reflects a pathological status contest among individuals who gain a higher reputation by creating new research programs than by expanding and testing existing research programs. Donaldson complained that several of the new research programs reflect an anti-managerial bias among American organization theorists.

The most coherent statement regarding the fragmentation of organization studies so far was published by J. Pfeffer in 1993 with the title: 'Barriers to the Advance of Organization Science: Paradigm Development as a Dependent Variable'. Pfeffer argued that the increased theoretical diversity had several negative implications, including a breakdown of the consensus among scholars that were unable to agree on core issues such as what research should be funded, what articles should be published, etc. This lack of a consensus furthermore weakened the support for the field from the universities and from the state. And if this weakening of the consensus and fragmentation of the field continued, organization studies would, according to Pfeffer, 'remain ripe for either a hostile takeover from within or from outside' (1993: 618). Indeed, the field would come to look more and more like political science, which had been taken over by the 'rational choice' paradigm imported from economics.

It was against this background that Pfeffer argued that organization studies needed to be much more consciously organized and managed, if it wanted to avoid the risk of being taken over by the economists. The community of organizational researchers was therefore urged to invest authority in a small well-published elite that through their control of journals, positions, resources, etc. should be able to enforce a consensus, thereby increasing the reputation, power, and financial support of the profession. However, Pfeffer did not explain in any details how this could be accomplished and towards which paradigm the field should converge. Though Pfeffer was impressed by the way economics as a field had been able to obtain consensus and get plenty of external funding and support, he was very critical towards having the rational choice paradigm as *the* mainstream tradition in organizational research, considering its lack of empirical success.

It was this case for a strategy of unification that Canella and Paetzold (1994) and Van Maanen (1995a, b) all set out to debunk. Since knowledge is socially constructed, according to Canella and Paetzold, organization researchers will be unable to make unambiguous claims on some absolute truth. Trying to enforce a consensus upon the community of organization researchers as argued by Pfeffer will be counterproductive, since it leads to a stagnation rather than scientific progress in the field. While both Canella and Paetzold had followed Pfeffer in taking a formal organizational approach to the advance of the field, Van Maanen focused much more on the rhetoric aspect of organizational research and how the development of good ideas can be facilitated. He argued that Pfeffer's view of organization studies was 'insufferably smug; pious and orthodox; philosophically indefensible; extraordinary naïve as to how science actually works; theoretically foolish, vain and autocratic' (1995: 133). In opposition to Pfeffer, but like Canella and Paetzold, Van Maanen was confident that theoretical pluralism would facilitate the growth of knowledge in the field. Consequently, he was interested in how to increase tolerance between different approaches in order to improve scholarly exchanges and understanding within the field.

It is against the background of these very different descriptions and appraisals of how organization study as a field functions that this chapter will explore the relationship between theoretical pluralism, scientific progress, and the social structure of the scientific community within organization study. Ever since the 'fall' of the contingency program in the mid-to late 1970s and the proliferation of new research programs in the late 1970s and the 1980s, the relationship between pluralism and scientific progress has been a central concern within the community of organization researchers. In accordance with the 'conventional wisdom' of philosophy of science, many organization researchers have taken the position that the increase of theoretical pluralism in organization studies since the mid-1970s was positive, because it facilitated faster growth of knowledge in the field. Lately, however, an increasing number of researchers have raised warnings, questioning the 'conventional wisdom' that more pluralism should lead to faster growth of knowledge. These researchers argue that organization studies may (have) become too fragmented thereby inhibiting, rather than speeding up, scientific progress.

9.2 ON RESEARCH PROGRAMS, SCIENTIFIC PROGRESS, AND THEORETICAL PLURALISM: SOME DEFINITIONS

Osigweh (1989) has suggested that there is a need for greater precision in concept definition. This seems especially true when rather broad concepts such as research program, scientific progress, and theoretical pluralism are debated. Take, for instance, the thesis under debate in this chapter that an increase of theoretical pluralism will lead to faster scientific progress. For many researchers, an increase of pluralism is often simply taken as evidence of scientific progress. Consequently, by not carefully distinguishing between the two concepts, Popper's thesis is hereby turned into a tautology. We may avoid this by carefully defining each concept independently. Let us start with the concept of 'research program'.

Using Imre Lakatos's (1970) Methodology of Scientific Research Programs (MSRP), a research program (such as contingency theory, population ecology, new institutionalism, transaction cost economics, etc.) may be defined as a series of theories $T_1, T_2, \ldots T_n$, that all have a 'family resemblance'. According to Lakatos, there are two reasons for such a family resemblance to exist. First, each of the theories within a research program builds on the same **hard core** propositions (H) that is regarded as non-falsifiable. By gradually exchanging the auxiliary hypotheses in the **protective belt** of the program (B_1 is replaced with B_2 and B_2 is later replaced with B_3, etc.), a series of theories $T_1, T_2, T_3, \ldots T_n$, is constructed in the following way: $T_1 = H \& B_1$, $T_2 = H \& B_2$, etc. In the case of the contingency research program, the hard core is the 'fitness', 'efficiency', or the 'alignment' thesis, while the protective belt consists of the hypotheses describing different types of organizational structures and different types of contingency variables. Second, when researchers construct new theories within a research program by changing some of the auxiliary hypotheses in the protective belt, they rely on the *positive* and *negative heuristic*. That is, they rely on a set of rules defining how problems should or should not be solved for them to be accepted within the program. In the contingency tradition, for instance, the heuristic consists of positive and negative advice on how to develop the protective belt, thereby formulating testable versions of the program.

So far, we have defined what a research program (such as the contingency research program) is and we have described its internal theoretical development or what Kuhn (1970) calls the normal science of such a research program (cf. Donaldson 1996*a*). However, not all theoretical developments have this piecemeal character, where researchers try to solve new problems by taking the 'hard core' and the 'positive' and 'negative heuristic' as given and only make marginal changes in the protective belt. In some cases, researchers do also question the most basic assumptions of their research program and the 'standard' way of solving problems, i.e. they question the hard core and the positive and negative heuristic. This happened in organizational studies during the late 1970s and early 1980s when the contingency research program was partly replaced by newer research programs such as population ecology, organizational economics, new institutionalism, and resource-dependency theory. In this case, both the fitness assumption (the hard core) and the method of solving problems in the contingency program in terms of the variance approach (the positive and negative heuristic) came under attack and were replaced by new hard core propositions and new heuristic rules. While Lakatos describes this kind of development as a 'shift' between research programs, Kuhn talks about either a 'shift' of paradigm or a 'scientific revolution' in order to emphasize the dramatic character of such a change.

The second concept that is used extensively in this chapter and which is in need of a careful definition is the concept of 'scientific progress'. A clarification of this concept can fruitfully take its point of departure in the distinction between the two types of research development defined above. On one hand, the relatively conservative shift between two theories T_1 and T_2 within the same research program and, on the other hand, a much more revolutionary shift between two research programs RP_1 and RP_2.

In this paper 'scientific progress' will be defined as the establishment of a 'correspondence relationship' between two theories or two research programs. Popper has given the following intuitive understanding of this concept: 'I suggest that whenever in the empirical sciences a new theory of a higher level of universality successfully explains some older theory *by correcting it*, then this is a sure sign that the new theory has penetrated deeper than the older ones. The demand that a new theory should contain the old one approximately, for appropriate values of the parameters of the new theory, may be called (following Bohr) the "*principle of correspondence*"' (1972: 202). A 'correspondence' view of scientific progress can also be interpreted as a dialectical view of scientific development. Scientific problems emerge from tensions, contradictions, or anomalies either within a single theory or between two or more theories. According to the correspondence view of scientific progress, tensions, contradictions, or paradoxes emerge because we are trying to use a theory T_1 to solve problems that are in fact lying outside T_1's domain of application D_1. In order to remove the contradiction or tension in a theory T_1, we may try to construct a new and more 'general' theory T_2 that has a wider domain of application D_2. A scientific progress will consist in a new theory T_2 that 'corrects' an older theory T_1 by first clarifying its limited domain of application D_1 and second by making new predictions (or explanations) outside this domain of application ($D_2 - D_1$). We can express this by saying that $T_2 \rightarrow T_1$ in D_1, while $T_2 \rightarrow \sim T_1$ in $D_2 - D_1$. That is, by constructing a new theory T_2, we learn more about the limited domain of T_1 because we are able to explain why the old theory was falsified or could not solve a problem outside its domain D_1. In summary, we say that we have established a correspondence relationship between T_1 and T_2 when:

$$D1 \subset D2, \ V1 \subset V2, \ T2 \Rightarrow T1 \text{ in } D1 \text{ and } T2 \Rightarrow \neg T1 \text{ in } D2 \ - \ D1$$

In the definition of what a research program is, we have distinguished between two types of theoretical developments: a shift between two theories within the same research program (normal science) and a shift between two research programs (a 'scientific revolution'). Our definition of the concept of 'scientific progress' in terms of a relationship of (homogenous) correspondence is mainly linked to the first of these types of theoretical development, i.e. a shift between two theories within the same research program. This is due to the fact that we have been talking about relationships of *homogenous* correspondence where the two theories are basically using the same vocabularies. However, we can extend the relationship of correspondence to also include *heterogeneous* relationships, i.e. relationships between two theories or research programs that are using different vocabularies V1 and V2 like for instance, when researchers belong to two different research programs and build on different hard-core hypotheses, using different heuristics to solve the same problems. A relationship of heterogeneous correspondence between two research programs RP1 and RP2 may be defined in the following way:

$$D1 \subset D2, \quad V1 \Rightarrow V2, \quad RP2 \Rightarrow RP1 \text{ in } D1 \text{ and } RP2 \Rightarrow \neg RP1 \text{ in } D2 \; - \; D1$$

In this case we need to be able to 'translate' the vocabulary V1 of the first research program to the vocabulary V2 of the second research program (otherwise this definition is the same as a relationship of homogeneous correspondence).

The third concept that has a central role in this paper is the concept of *pluralism*. Like so many other popular concepts in organization science, its meaning is often not very clear. To start with, we may note that the notion of pluralism can refer to many different things such as ontological pluralism, methodological pluralism, theoretical pluralism, methodical pluralism, etc. or any combination of these (cf. Mäki 1997). This chapter will mainly be concerned with *theoretical* pluralism.

An argument for theoretical pluralism will have to include an explanation for why it is desirable to have a 'plurality' of research programs. One such justification is that a plurality of research programs will promote scientific progress within the field. Another justification for theoretical pluralism is the argument that since any research program only highlights one or a few aspects of reality, it will be necessary to have a 'plurality' of research programs if our goal is to get a reasonably adequate picture of the complex reality. Researchers that use this argument are often referring to the fable about 'The Blind Man and the Elephant' (cf. Mintzberg, Ahlstrand, and Lampel 1998). This second argument for theoretical pluralism is often used in relation to applied research rather than theory development. Consequently, it may be argued that this literature does not contribute to answer the main question of this chapter.

Since we will primarily be investigating the first of these two arguments for theoretical pluralism, let us shortly explore the modern history of this argument. One of the first philosophers of science to argue in favor of 'theoretical pluralism' was Karl Popper (1945) in his *Open Society and Its Enemies*. Like later falsificationists such as Hans Albert, Imre Lakatos, John Watkins, and the early contributions of Paul Feyerabend, Popper argued that the more 'open' a scientific field is towards new research programs, the tougher the competition and the better the chances for a scientific breakthrough. For the same reason, the scientific community should be very lenient towards new research programs, in order to make sure that they get enough time to mature, before being exposed to the fierce competition of older and maturer research programs. In accordance with this position, Imre Lakatos argued that 'we must not discard a budding research program simply because it has so far failed to overtake a powerful rival. As long as a budding research program can be rationally reconstructed as a progressive problem shift, it should be sheltered for a while from a powerful established rival' (1970: 157). This argument very much resembles the 'infant industry' argument that recommends that new firms should be protected from outside competitors until they have grown strong enough to be exposed to the fierce competition of the world market from older and more mature foreign competitors.

The 'valid domain' of the statement 'that the more pluralistic a field becomes the more competition there will be, and the better will the chances be for a scientific break through', has never been clearly determined. Popper (1945) who was the first philosopher of science to propose this thesis had primarily been interested in physics and other fields with a mono-paradigmatic structure. Due to the lack of variability characterizing the type of fields studied, these philosophers of science never came to question the validity of this thesis. For instance, in less mature and more applied types of scientific fields such as management studies, engineering, etc., the validity of this relationship seems highly questionable. However, before being able to say anything of the restricted domain of the relationship between theoretical pluralism and scientific progress, we need a framework that can inform us about variation between the different scientific fields. The point of departure of this paper is the comparative framework of Richard Whitley that studies how different scientific fields are organized as reputational systems. This framework will be used to describe the recent evolution of organization studies.

9.3 THE STRUCTURE OF ORGANIZATION SCIENCE AS AN INTELLECTUAL FIELD SINCE 1960: PARTITIONED BUREAUCRACY, POLYCENTRIC OLIGARCHY, OR FRAGMENTED ADHOCRACY?

According to Richard Whitley (1984a, b), it is possible to identify some of the most important and distinct features of scientific disciplines by analyzing them as *reputational organizations*. In this type of organization, the members obtain their position in the hierarchy by making contributions to the knowledge structure of their field. The more a scientific community values the contributions of a re-searcher, the higher return in terms of reputation he or she will get. However, fields that are structured on the basis of their member's reputation may have very different structures. Whitley (1984a) argues that it is possible to identify very different modes of how scientific fields are organized based on the following two contingency variables: (1) degree of interdependency and (2) degree of task uncertainty.

The *degree of interdependency* refers to how many researchers in a field are dependent on each other to obtain reputation. The more applied a field is, the more open it will be towards its environment (and its external audiences) and the less interdependency there will be. Conversely, the more basic a science is, the more will researchers have to rely on each other for obtaining their reputation. The *degree of task uncertainty* refers to the degree of uncertainty a researcher may face when trying to solve a specific problem. It is normally claimed that the main function of science is to produce new knowledge. What is accepted as new knowledge depends to a large extent on the background knowledge of the field. The more systematic, exact, and general this knowledge is, the easier it is to determine whether a contribution is new or not and how well this contribution fits into the background knowledge of the field. If the background knowledge is well structured, which is the case of a mono-paradigmatic field, the task uncertainty of an individual researcher will be low. Whitley (1984a) distinguishes between two different aspects of task uncertainties, *technical* and *strategic*. Technical task uncertainty refers to the degree of unpredictability and variability existing in a field with regard to the methods and procedures that is accepted to solve empirical problems. If there exist many different methods and if it is difficult to interpret the (test) results in a field, the degree of technical uncertainty is high. On the other hand, if a certain method has been canonized as being the only legitimate method, the degree of technical task uncertainty is low. Task uncertainty does not only have a technical aspect, but also involves a strategic (theoretical) aspect. In this case, the researchers face a different kind of uncertainty regarding which problems are important, less important, etc. and what goals should govern their research. In fields with a high degree of strategic task uncertainty, researchers are confronted with many different problems, the relevance and importance of which will be appraised very differently by different groups in the field.

According to Whitley, variations in these two contingency variables make it possible to distinguish between at least seven different configurations of scientific field's organizations. These structures include the following types with examples listed in brackets: (1) fragmented adhocracy (management studies), (2) polycentric oligarchy (continental philosophy and classical sociology), (3) partitioned bureaucracy (Anglo-Saxon economics), (4) professional adhocracy (biomedicine, engineering), (5) polycentric profession (experimental physiology), (6) technological integrated bureaucracy (chemistry), and (7) conceptually integrated bureaucracy (physics).

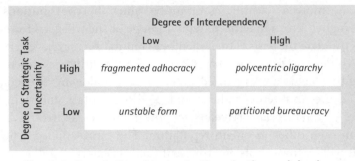

Fig. 9.1 Reputational organizations in the social sciences

Focusing primarily on organization studies, the discussion will be limited to the three configurations found in the social sciences. These are the *partitioned bureaucracy*, the *polycentric oligarchy*, and the *fragmented adhocracy*. An important thesis of this article is that organization studies, since the 1960s, have adopted all these three organizational configurations or at least configurations that are close to them, consecutively. By first giving a description of each of these configurations and second showing how organization studies at a certain point in time or in different areas may fit into these, the stage will be set for the next and main section of this chapter. In this section, it will be analyzed how the structure of organization studies may influence the relationship between theoretical pluralism and scientific progress.

In general, social sciences such as sociology, management studies, anthropology, political science, etc. are less dominated by a single paradigm than the natural sciences are. This implies that we should expect to find less consensus and therefore more task uncertainty in the social sciences than in the natural sciences. The only social science that has diverged from this pattern is economics, which, for a long period, has been dominated by a single paradigm and therefore has a substantially lower degree of strategic task uncertainty and a higher degree of interdependency than the other social sciences. According to Richard Whitley (1983, 1984a), the reputational configuration of economics may be characterized as a *partitioned bureaucracy*.

As a partitioned bureaucracy, economics consists of a core with pure and abstract theorizing (within the optimization paradigm) and a number of peripheral sub-fields of applied research (industrial organization, labour economics, international economics, etc.). Due to the absence of control over the object of research and the ambiguity of empirical testing in the social sciences, any unifying theoretical framework in a social science will be under a permanent threat to be replaced. In economics, however, this problem was solved by partitioning the core of pure theory with formal modeling from the applied and empirical research in the peripheral areas. Compared to other ways of organizing social science fields, economics has a very hierarchical type of reputational organization, since research in the core of the field is viewed as much more prestigious than applied research in the peripheral sub-fields. The term 'partitioned' in partitioned bureaucracy refers to the absence of feedback from the applied research in the periphery to the pure theory in the core, i.e. the abstract models of the optimization paradigm have been 'immunized' from potential 'empirical falsifications' arising in the applied sub-fields.

Though economics is often portrayed (mostly by other social scientists) as having a completely unitary structure, the field includes several heterodox traditions (behavioralism, transaction cost economics, evolutionary theory, institutionalism, etc.) that during the past twenty or thirty years have influenced mainstream economics in profound ways. Take the case of the transaction cost approach of Oliver Williamson that is of interest to organization researchers as well. In the 1970s, when Williamson turned Coase's 1937 article into a research program, most mainstream economists for two reasons viewed the transaction cost approach as heterodox. First, Williamson did not follow the central maxim of not opening up the black box of the firm in orthodox theory. Instead he viewed the firm itself as an important economic institution that was in need of explanation. Second, Williamson based his research program on the hard-core assumption that decision-makers are boundedly rational rather than perfect maximizers. While neither the principle of not opening the black box of the firm nor the principle of bounded rationality were accepted by orthodox theory in the 1970s, both of the principles in transaction cost economics have been adopted by the modern orthodoxy of the 1990s and 2000s.

How did the field of organization study evolve over time? During a relatively short period from the late 1950s to the mid-1970s, a single paradigm has managed to obtain a (near) dominant position within organization studies. By combining an open system view and a structural functionalist frame of explanation, contingency theorists created a paradigm for studying organizations that, for almost fifteen years, united and facilitated coordination within this very young field of study. In fact, the period from the late 1950s to the middle of the 1970s is the only period during its short history where organization studies have had a hierarchical form of reputation organization. Or as stated by Lex Donaldson: 'The normal science that has been pursued within the contingency paradigm is probably the largest single normal science research stream in the study of organizational structure to date' (1996b: 58). However, there are some interesting differences to observe between the way economics and organization studies were organized as fields due to differences between their mainstream paradigms. While the optimization paradigm offered economic theorists a 'coherent' way of doing highly abstract theoretical work, structural contingency theory was more a program for standardizing empirical research and testing empirical structure-contingency relationships than for solving theoretical problems. While the optimization paradigm therefore reduced the *strategic* task uncertainty of economics, structural contingency theory mainly reduced the *technical* task uncertainty of organization studies. Unlike economics, organization studies never managed to separate the theoretical puzzle solving from empirical research by fully adopting a *partitioned* bureaucracy. This may be one of the reasons why economics has experienced a more stable intellectual structure than organization studies over time.

In the early 1970s, the contingency research program came under increasing criticism both internally and externally. The internal criticism was mainly directed towards the inconsistencies and ambiguities in many empirical studies of contingency-structure relationships such as, for instance, the negative relationship between size and administrative intensity (Kimberly 1976 for a review). Indirectly these criticisms were directed towards the positive heuristics of the program that had almost exclusively relied upon a variance approach using cross-sectional data to formulate and test empirical regularities. The external criticism was directed towards the theoretical and philosophical underpinnings of the hard-core assumptions of the contingency approach. It included a critique of its functionalist and deterministic framework that excluded the modeling of strategic choices, power relationships, processes of social change, etc. in organizations.

In the later part of the 1970s, organization studies in the United States experienced a proliferation of new theories such as transaction cost economics (Williamson 1975), population ecology (Hannan and Freeman 1977), institutional theory (Meyer and Rowan 1977), resource dependency theory (Pfeffer and Salancik 1978), etc. As a consequence, the intellectual structure of 'organization studies changed', according to Michael Reed, 'from orthodox consensus to pluralistic diversity' (1992: 248). In the comparative framework of Whitley one may interpret this change as a transition from a bureaucratic type of organization during the hegemony of the structural contingency program to a *polycentric oligarchy*.

A *polycentric oligarchy* is characterized by a high degree of interdependency combined with a high degree of technical and strategic task uncertainty. This type of structure in a field typically emerges when relatively small groups of researchers gain control over critical resources such as positions and journal access. But since the degree of task uncertainty is very high, their control can only be exercised locally and personally, resulting in the establishment of several independent centers. In organization studies these centers were formed around the main theories or research programs that emerged in the late 1970s such as population ecology, transaction cost economics, institutional theory, resource dependency theory, etc. Even though these new theories were all introduced during a period of only three years and organization studies became a fragmented field the innovation rate was subsequently dramatically reduced. During the 1980s no major innovative theories were introduced in the field. However, several of the theories introduced in the mid-1970s such as population ecology, transaction cost economics, and to some extent institutional theory were turned into ongoing research programs. Later during the 1990s several attempts were made to integrate some of the programs like for instance population ecology and institutional theory (Baum and Oliver 1991, 1992). Within each of the research centers formed around these research programs, there was a relatively strong hierarchical reputational organization due to a consensus of what was the basic framework to be used, what were the important problems to be solved, and how reputation should be allocated within the 'specialized' research community. However, there was very little coordination and cooperation between the centers, but rather an intense competition in order to gain control over the field as a whole. The field therefore became balkanized into a set of more or less autonomous centers, each pursuing their own research agenda, with minimal interaction and communication. According to Whitley, examples of polycentric oligarchy include continental philosophy, continental sociology, and organization studies in the period after 1975 in the United States could be added as a third example.

James G. March's description of how organization studies are structured is very much aligned to the polycentric oligarchy concept of Whitley:

As the field has grown and elaborated new perspectives, it has continually been threatened with becoming not so much a new integrated semidiscipline as a set of independent, self-congratulatory cultures of comprehension. This is evident with five of the more lively subfields [research programs] of contemporary studies of organizations.... Although these subfields [research programs] have been particularly successful in augmenting our understanding of organizations... they have exhibited persistent symptoms of isolation, engaging in intermittent internecine worldview cleansing. In the name of technical purity and claims of universality, energized subfields [research programs] have tended to seal themselves off, each seemingly eager to close further the minds of the already converted, without opening the minds of others. There is, to be sure, a certain grim necessity in the process. Exploiting interesting ideas often thrives on commitment more than thoughtfulness, narrowness more than breath, cohesiveness more than openness. (1996: 280, my additions in brackets)

As the structure of polycentric oligarchy gradually developed, it both reinforced and was reinforced by the diffusion of the 'uniqueness value' (Mone and Mckinley 1993). This implied that the separation of the field in different centers was reinforced, making work across the boundaries of the different centers (research programs) less likely. And the insulation of the different theoretical perspectives was reinforced by a rather uncritical acceptance of Kuhn's thesis of incommensurability among the majority of organizational researchers (Scherer 1998).

The shift from a bureaucratic form of intellectual organization in organization studies to a polycentric oligarchy was partly due to the rapid growth of the field during the 1970s itself triggered by the expansion of education in management studies. The growth in positions and resources enabled new approaches to become entrenched in the reputational organizations thereby undermining the hegemony of the contingency research program. With the break-up of contingency theory and the proliferation of new programs in the post-1975 period, the degree of strategic uncertainty and the degree of technical task uncertainty increased. For the individual organization researcher, prioritization of problems to solve and which empirical method to use was no longer as clear as it was during the hegemony of the structural contingency theory.

While the development of organization studies in the United States may be described as a shift from a bureaucratic structure to a structure of polycentric oligarchy, the situation in Europe was rather different. While US organization researchers had constructed a set of new theories or research programs as replacements for the contingency program, European organization researchers reacted mainly by rejecting/replacing the underlying positivistic methodology in the structural contingency program with other methodologies and philosophies. Important contributions were David Silverman (1971), Burrell and Morgan (1979), Morgan (1986), and contributions within the postmodern movement (cf. Alvesson and Deetz 1996). Much of European organization research tended to operate on a meta-theoretical level rather than on a theoretical level by discussing the ontology, epistemology, and methodology of research rather than constructing new theories and research programs as their American collegues did in the late 1970s. The close relationship with philosophy implied, however, that European organization researchers were confronted with even more strategic and technical task uncertainty than their American colleagues. Or as Clegg, Hardy, and Nord state in their introduction to their *Handbook of Organization Studies*: 'Gone is the certainty, if it ever existed, about what organizations are; gone, too is the certainty about how they should be studied, the place of the researcher, the role of methodology, the nature of theory. Defining organization studies today is by no means an easy task' (1996: 3). That is, organization studies in Europe may best be described as being as a fragmented adhocracy.

The *fragmented adhocracy* is characterized by a low degree of interdependency between researchers, which implies a rather 'loose' or flat research organization. Since the researchers are facing very few restrictions in this type of organizational configuration regarding the choice of theoretical framework and the choice of research method, the degree of technical and strategic task uncertainty is very high. This implies a relatively **fragmented** knowledge structure and the existence of much disagreement about the relative importance of different problems to be solved by the field. As a result, the problem-solving activity within the field takes place in a rather arbitrary and ad hoc manner, with limited attempts to integrate new solutions with the existing structure of knowledge. Management studies and contemporary American sociology are mentioned by Whitley (1984*a*) as examples of this type of reputational organizational form.

9.4 TOWARDS A PROCESS PERSPECTIVE ON THE ORGANIZATION OF SCIENTIFIC FIELDS: AVOIDING THE 'SPECIALIZATION' AND THE 'FRAGMENTATION' TRAP

Richard Whitley's (1984a, b) comparative study of how different scientific fields are organized builds on a static type of analysis which is adequate for understanding structural questions such as: How can we describe the structure of a field at a specific time? Why are certain structures observed in specific environments? His framework, however, is less adequate for answering process-oriented questions such as: How did a certain configuration in a scientific field emerge? What forces drive the transformation of a scientific field from one configuration to another configuration? What kinds of processes stabilize or destabilize a configuration?

The strong structural bias of Whitley's framework also makes it less adequate to answer the main (process-oriented) questions of the present chapter: To what extent does the configuration of a scientific field influence the relationship between theoretical pluralism and scientific progress? Is the relationship between increased theoretical pluralism and scientific progress, as implicitly argued by many philosophers of science, valid across all types of scientific fields independently of their social structure? Or is this relationship only valid for fields with some types of configurations (for instance a partitioned bureaucracy) but not for fields with other types of configurations (for instance a fragmented adhocracy) where more pluralism tends to lead to stagnation rather than scientific progress?

To answer these questions, we need a framework that not only describes the structural characteristics of different scientific fields, but also identifies the underlying 'processes' and 'mechanisms' that operate within the different configurations as well as determine the major dilemmas a field is confronted with. By supplementing the structuralist and comparative static framework of Whitley with a process-oriented account, it will be possible to explain how an increase in theoretical pluralism may lead to scientific progress within some configurations, but have the opposite effect within other types of configurations.

A central thesis in this process-approach to the organization of scientific fields is that all disciplines are struggling in order to find a balance between exploitation, i.e. expanding an existing research program (normal science), and exploration, i.e. searching for new research programs (revolutionary science). Or stated in a slightly different way, that all scientific fields are confronted with finding an optimal trade-off between short-run and long-run activities or between continuity and change (cf. McKinley, Mone, and Moon 1999). Most scientific fields are in fact experiencing one of the following two imbalances.

The first imbalance exists when there is too much emphasis on exploiting an already existing research program and too little emphasis on exploring new theories or research programs. In this case, the researchers in the field tend to value short-term more than long-term activities, thereby reducing the adaptability of the field to new situations. The second imbalance exists when there is too much emphasis on exploring new theories in order to establish new research programs and too little emphasis on the exploitation of already existing research programs. In this case, the field is giving too much emphasis to the long-term activities of exploration compared to short-term activities of exploitation.

Finding a balance between exploitation and exploration has also been discussed by the philosopher of science Thomas Kuhn as finding an 'essential tension' between tradition and novelty. New and path-breaking research will, according to Thomas Kuhn (1977), always result from a tension between working within the framework of an existing paradigm while at the same time trying to transcend this paradigm in order to overcome its major weaknesses. Paradigms will always contain the 'seeds' of their own destruction, since scientific revolution would be unthinkable without long periods of normal science that identified the anomalies that triggered the shift from an old to a new paradigm.

Besides having problems with securing a balance between exploiting existing research programs and searching for new research programs, scientific fields are exposed to traps that tend to drive a field into either a self-reinforcing spiral of elaborating existing programs or into a self-reinforcing spiral of search for new research programs. In both cases, the possibilities of keeping the optimal balance between extending existing research programs versus searching for new programs will be upset.

The first trap may be called a '*specialization trap*'. It will be present when normal science drives out revolutionary science and the activity of elaborating and extending an existing research program gradually comes to dominate the search for new research programs. As researchers develop better and better skills in using an existing research program and its problem-solving heuristic, the existing research program will be even more used by them to solve new problems, thus further increasing the strength of the research program's heuristic and the opportunity costs of searching for a new research program. This specialization trap emerges because the exploitation of already existing research programs gives a faster and safer return than the experimentation with completely new and uncertain research programs. The implications of this trap in the long run is a scarcity of exploratory activities that undermines the flexibility of the field by reducing its ability to adapt to new and unpredictable situations. In organization theory a tendency towards such a specialization trap existed during the hegemony of the contingency research program with its strong adherence to a 'variance approach' heuristic. With the elaboration of this program, organization researchers developed more and more refined statistical-empirical methods that made it more and more attractive to refine this heuristic, but less and less attractive to switch to alternative heuristics such as a 'process approach' (cf. Huber and Van de Ven 1995). However, being locked into such a self-reinforcing process of specialization seems to have made the field of organization studies less prepared to switch to studies of organization change when such studies came in high demand due to a more turbulent and changing environment after 1975. It is therefore not surprising that several of the new research programs emerging during the late 1970s had the ambition of viewing organizations from a longitudinal rather than a cross-sectional perspective and to develop a corresponding 'process approach' heuristic. Among the research programs emerging in the late 1970s, population ecology with its 'inertia' assumption seems to have been the most aware of this goal (cf. Freeman and Hannan 1975).

The second trap may be called a *'fragmentation trap'*. It will be present when revolutionary science drives out normal science and the search for new research programs comes to dominate the elaboration of existing research programs. There are several reasons for why a scientific field may end up in a fragmentation trap. First, most new scientific ideas will be worse than the existing pool of ideas. Second, it takes a lot of time and experience before the positive heuristic of a new research program can be developed enough so that it can be successfully exploited by normal scientists. Even the most successful research programs will therefore perform rather badly to start with. Because of a lack of persistency in the scientific community many research programs may therefore never be investigated well enough, before new research programs have been proposed and have replaced them. The 'true' potential of such new research programs will therefore never be discovered. In fact, no mechanisms seem to be in place to secure that progressive programs survive degenerating programs. And when the process that drives revolutionary science to replace normal science takes on a self-reinforcing character, the field ends up in the fragmentation trap where one theory or research program is just replaced by the next theory or research program with minimal accumulation of knowledge.

When no less than four new research programs were introduced into organization studies in the late 1970s to replace the structural contingency program in less than three years, W. R. Scott (1993) issued a warning that may be interpreted as if organization studies was in danger of falling into a fragmentation trap: 'These diverse and conflicting paradigms came tumbling into the placid arena of organizational studies in rapid succession—too rapidly to be properly evaluated or reconciled' (p. 63). Not being able to sort out whether the different research programs were progressive or not and what theoretical relationships existed between them threatened to lead to a fragmentation trap that in the long run would make scientific progress in the field less likely. Observe, however, that it is not the absolute number of research programs but the rate at which new programs are introduced that determines whether a field ends up in a fragmentation trap or not. Since the 1980s may be described as a period of consolidation for US organization studies in the sense that no new programs were introduced and the field escaped falling into a fragmentation trap. Instead, during the 1980s the existing programs were all trying to build a body of empirical data to support their arguments and strengthen their positive heuristics (cf. Van de Ven 1997).

In their attempt to strike a balance between elaborating existing research programs and the search for new research programs, scientific fields may be described as standing on a knife-edge trying to avoid getting locked into either a self-reinforcing specialization trap or a self-reinforcing fragmentation trap. However, there are very complex interactions between activities of exploiting existing research programs and activities of searching for new theories/research programs that tend to undermine any kind of balance that exists between them. Elaborating existing research programs requires the search for new theories and research programs in order to contribute to a scientific field's cumulative growth of knowledge. At the same time each interferes with the other. Elaborating an existing research program tends to undermine revolutionary science by discouraging attempts to find new research programs and problem-solving heuristics that are essential for the long-term survival of a field. Researchers in the field therefore tend to stick to one (currently progressive) program and its problem-solving heuristic to such an extent that there is little exploration of other programs, or in failing to stick to one (underdeveloped and currently degenerating) program long enough to determine its 'true' problem-solving capacity.

In a similar fashion, revolutionary science undermines normal science. Efforts to promote revolutionary science encourage impatience with new research programs and problem-solving heuristics. New research programs are therefore likely to be abandoned before enough time has been devoted to developing the strength of their heuristic, thereby making them progressive. The impatience of revolutionary science results in unelaborated discoveries and a fragmented knowledge structure. As a result of the ways in which normal science and revolutionary science tend to extinguish each other, most scientific fields will be struggling to maintain a healthy balance between the two.

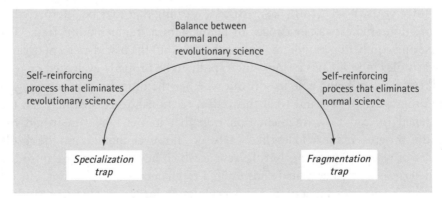

Fig. 9.2 The specialization vs. the fragmentation trap

9.5 Unification, Pluralism, and Avoiding the Specialization Trap and the Fragmentation Trap in Organization Studies

How does this 'process' approach with its discussion of avoiding both the specialization trap and the fragmentation trap fit into the structural approach of Richard Whitley and his discussion of different organizational configurations in scientific fields? There seems to be a very simple answer to this question. The general rule is: if the field is very hierarchical in its research organization, which is the case for the *partitioned bureaucracy* (low degree of strategic task uncertainty and a high degree of interdependency), the field will typically be struggling to avoid a *specialization* trap. If the field, on the other hand, has a more flat organizational configuration such as the *fragmented adhocracy* (high degree of task uncertainty and a low degree of interdependency), the field will typically be struggling to avoid or get out of a *fragmentation* trap. Compared to these two possibilities, fields that are situated in between these two extremes such as the *polycentric oligarchy* will be closer to the ideal of maintaining a healthy balance between elaborating on existing research programs and searching for new research programs.

This clarification may now help us in positioning the process approach vis-à-vis the unification position of Pfeffer, on one hand, and the pluralist position of Van Maanen, on the other hand. From the perspective of the process model, the unification position is a less attractive alternative because it leads to a highly hierarchical structure and a self-reinforcing specialization trap that undermines the field's adaptability to new and unforeseen phenomena. The pluralist position in the form of 'letting a thousand flowers bloom' may, on the other hand, lead to a fragmented adhocracy and get caught in a self-reinforcing fragmentation trap. The process model suggests alternatively that we should look for a healthy balance between the exploitation of already existing research programs and the explorations of new theories and programs, thereby avoiding both the specialization trap of the unification strategy and the fragmentation trap of the pluralist strategy. And the intellectual structure that best supports this kind of balance is the polycentric oligarchy.

The conclusion that a polycentric oligarchy is the most suitable structure for promoting scientific progress in organization studies also find some support in the Schumpeter thesis in industrial organization. According to this thesis, neither perfect competition nor monopoly will be the industrial organization that best promote technological progress. While perfect competition (like the fragmented adhocracy) is too fragmented and monopoly (like the partitioned bureaucracy) is too concentrated, Schumpeter argued that oligopolistic competition (like the polycentric oligarchy) would best promote technological progress by securing an optimal trade-off between static and dynamic efficiency.

To uphold the polycentric oligarchy and secure a reasonable balance between tradition and novelty in organization studies, the research community should try to follow a strategy of creative tension (cf. Poole and Van de Ven 1989). Such a strategy directs the researchers in the field to exploit any opportunity offered by tensions, oppositions, and contradictions between the main research programs in order to construct new and encompassing theories or research programs. By not exploiting such tensions and contradictions between the existing research programs to construct new theories, the field risks falling into a fragmentation trap that will make future progress less likely.

REFERENCES

ALVESSON, M., and DEETZ, S. (1996). 'Critical Theory and Postmodernism Approaches to Organizational Studies', in S. R. Clegg, C. Hardy, and W. R. Nord, (eds.), *Handbook of Organization Studies*. London: Sage.

ASTLEY, W. G., and VAN DE VEN, A. H. (1983). 'Central Perspectives and Debates in Organization Theory'. *Administrative Science Quarterly*, 28: 245–73.

BAUM, J. A. C., and OLIVER, C. (1991). 'Institutional Linkages and Organizational Mortality'. *Administrative Science Quarterly*, 36: 187–218.

—— —— (1992). 'Institutional Embeddedness and the Dynamics of Organizational Populations'. *American Journal of Sociology*, 57: 540–59.

BURRELL, G., and MORGAN, G. (1979). *Sociological Paradigms and Organisational Analysis*. London: Heinemann.

CANELLA, ALBERT A., and PAETZOLD, R. L. (1994). 'Pfeffer's Barriers to the Advance of Organizational Science: A Rejoinder'. *Academy of Management Review*, 19: 331–41.

CLEGG, S. R., HARDY, C., and NORD, W. R. (1996). *Handbook of Organization Studies*, London: Sage.

COASE, R. (1937). 'The Nature of the Firm'. *Economica*, NS, 4: 386–405.

COHEN, W. M., and LEVINTHAL, D. A. (1990). 'Absorptive Capacity: A New Perspective on Learning and Innovation'. *Administrative Science Quarterly*, 35: 128–52.

COLE, S. (1983). 'The Hierarchy of the Sciences?' *American Journal of Sociology*, 89: 111–39.

DAFT, R. L., and LEWIN, A. Y. (1990). 'Can Organization Studies Begin to Break Out of the Normal Science Straitjacket? An Editorial Essay'. *Organization Science*, 1: 1–9.

DONALDSON, L. (1995). *American Anti-management Theories of Organization: A Critique of Paradigm Proliferation*. Cambridge: Cambridge University Press.

—— (1996a). *For Positivist Organization Theory: Proving the Hard Core*. London: Sage.

—— (1996b). 'The Normal Science of Structural Contingency Theory', in S. R. Clegg, C. Hardy, and W. R. Nord (eds.), *Handbook of Organization Studies*. London: Sage.

FREEMAN, J. H., and HANNAN, M. T. (1975). 'Growth and Decline Processes in Organizations'. *American Journal of Sociology*, 40: 215–28.

GRANDORI, A. (1987). *Perspectives on Organization Theory*. Cambridge, Mass.: Ballinger.

HANNAN, M. T., and FREEMAN, J. (1977). 'The Population Ecology of Organizations'. *American Journal of Sociology*, 82: 929–64.

HASSARD, J. (1993). *Sociology and Organization Theory: Positivism, Paradigms and Postmodernity*. Cambridge: Cambridge University Press.

HUBER, G. P., and VAN DE VEN, A. H. (1995). *Longitudinal Field Research Methods: Studying Processes of Organizational Change*. Thousands Oaks, Calif.: Sage.

KIMBERLY, JOHN R. (1976). 'Organization Size and the Structuralist Perspective: A Review, Critique and Proposal'. *Administrative Science Quarterly*, 21/4: 571–97.

KITCHER, P. (1993). 'The Organization of Cognitive Labor', in id., *The Advancement of Science: Science without Legend, Objectivity without Illusions*. New York and Oxford: Oxford University Press.

KRAJEWSKI, W. (1976). *Correspondence Principle and Growth of Science*. Dordrecht: D. Reidel Publishing Company.

KUHN, T. S. (1970). *The Structure of Scientific Revolution*. Chicago: University of Chicago Press.

—— (1977). *The Essential Tension*. Chicago: University of Chicago Press.

LAKATOS, I. (1970). 'Falsification and the Methodology of Research Programmes', in I. Lakatos and A. Musgrave (eds.), *Criticism and the Growth of Knowledge*. Cambridge: Cambridge University Press.

LATOUR, B. (1982). *Science in Action*. Milton Keynes: Open University Press.

LAUDAN, LARRY (1977). *Progress and its Problem*. Berkeley: University of California Press.

LEVINTHAL, D., and MARCH, J. G. (1993). 'The Myopia of Learning'. *Strategic Management Journal*, 14: 95–112.

MCKINLEY, W., MONE, M. A., and MOON, G. (1999). 'Determinants and Developments of Schools in Organization Theory'. *Academy of Management Review*, 24: 634–48.

MÄKI, U. (1997). 'The One World and the Many Theories', in Andreas Salanti and Ernesto Screpanti (eds.), *Pluralism in Economics*, Cheltenham: Edward Elgar.

MARCH, JAMES, G. (1991). 'Exploration and Exploitation in Organizational Learning'. *Organization Science*, 2: 71–87.

—— (1996). 'Continuity and Change in Theories of Organizational Action'. *Administrative Science Quarterly*, 41: 278–87.

—— (1998). *Research on Organizations: Hopes for the Past and Lessons for the Future*. Paper presented at the Scandinavian Consortium for Organizational Research Conference on 'Samples of the Future' Stanford University, 20 Sept. 1998.

MEYER, J. W., and ROWAN, B. (1977). 'Institutionalized Organizations: Formal Structure as Myth and Ceremony'. *American Journal of Sociology*, 83: 340–63.

MINTZBERG, H., AHLSTRAND, B., and LAMPEL, J. (1998). *Strategy Safari: A Guided Tour through the Wilds of Strategic Management*. New York: Free Press.

MONE, M. A., and MCKINLEY, W. (1993). 'The Uniqueness Value and its Consequences for Organization Studies.' *Journal of Management Inquiry*, 2: 284–96.

MORGAN, G. (1986). *Images of Organizations*. Thousands Oaks, Calif.: Sage.

OSIGWEH, C. A. B. (1989). 'Concept Fallibility in Organizational Science'. *Academy of Management Review*, 14: 579–94.

PFEFFER, J. (1982). *Organizations and Organization Theory*. Boston: Pitman.

—— (1993). 'Barriers to the Advance of Organizational Science: Paradigm Development as a Dependent Variable'. *Academy of Management Review*, 18/4: 599–620.

PFEFFER, J. (1995). 'Mortality, Reproducibility, and the Persistence of Styles of Theory'. *Organization Science*, 6/6: 681–6.

—— (1997). *New Directions for Organization Theory: Problems and Prospects*. New York and London: Oxford University Press.

—— and SALANCIK, G. R. (1978). *The External Control of Organizations: A Resource Dependency Perspective*. New York: Harper & Row.

POLYANI, M. (1958). *Personal Knowledge*. London: Routledge & Kegan Paul.

POOLE, M. S., and VAN DE VEN, A. H. (1989). 'Using Paradox to Build Management and Organization Theories'. *Academy of Management Review*, 14: 562–78.

POPPER, K. R. (1945). *The Open Society and Its Enemies*. London: Routledge & Kegan Paul.

—— (1972). *Objective Knowledge*. Oxford: Clarendon Press.

REED, M. (1985). *Redirection in Organizational Analysis*. London: Tavistock.

—— (1992). *The Sociology of Organization: Themes, Perspectives and Prospects*. New York: Harvester Wheatsheaf.

SCHERER, A. G. (1998). 'Pluralism and Incommensurability in Strategic Management and Organization Theory: A Problem in Search of a Solution'. *Organization*, 5/2: 147–68.

SCOTT, W. R. (1987). 'Recent Developments in Organizational Sociology'. *Acta Sociologica*, 36: 63–8.

—— (1993). *Organizations: Rational, Natural, Open Systems*. Englewood Cliffs, NJ: Prentice-Hall.

—— (1998). *Organizations: Rational, Natural and Open Systems* (4th edn). Englewood Cliffs, NJ: Prentice-Hall Inc.

SILVERMAN, D. (1971). *The Theory of Organizations*. London: Heinemann.

VAN DE VEN, A. H. (1997). 'The Buzzing, Blooming, Confusing World of Organization and Management Theory: A View from Lake Wobegon University'. *Journal of Management Inquiry*, 8: 118–25.

VAN MAANEN, J. (1995a). 'Style as Theory' *Organization Science*, 6/1: 132–43.

—— (1995b). 'Fear and Loathing in Organization Studies'. *Organization Science*, 6/6: 687–92.

WEAVER, G. R., and GIOIA, D. A. (1994). 'Paradigm lost: Incommensurability vs. Structurationist Inquiry'. *Organization Studies*, 15/4: 565–90.

WHITLEY, R. (1983). 'The Structure and Context of Economics as a Scientific Field'. *Research of the History of Economic Thought and Methodology*, 4: 179–209.

—— (1984a). *The Intellectual and Social Organization of the Sciences*. Oxford: Clarendon Press.

—— (1984b). 'The Development of Management Studies as a Fragmented Adhocracy'. *Social Science Information*, 23: 125–46.

WILLIAMSON, O. E. (1975). *Markets and Hierarchies: Analysis and Anti-trust Implications*. New York: Free Press.

WILLMOTT, H. (1990). 'Beyond Paradigmatic Closure in Organization Analysis', in J. Hassard and D. Pym (eds.), *The Theory and Philosophy of Organizations*. London: Routledge.

ZAMMUTO, R. F., and CONNOLLY, T. (1984). 'Coping with Disciplinary Fragmentation'. *Organizational Behavior Teaching Review*, 9: 30–7.

PART III

META-THEORETICAL CONTROVERSIES IN ORGANIZATION THEORY

....

CHAPTER 10

THE AGENCY/ STRUCTURE DILEMMA IN ORGANIZATION THEORY

OPEN DOORS AND BRICK WALLS

....

MICHAEL REED

At its best, historical sociology is rational, critical and imaginative. It looks for the mechanisms through which societies change or reproduce themselves. *It seeks the hidden structures which frustrate some human aspirations while making others realisable, whether we appreciate it or not.* This knowledge is well worth searching for. After all, it is useful to know, in any particular case, whether you are pushing against an open door or beating your head against a brick wall. One of historical sociology's objectives should be to distinguish between open doors and brick walls and discover whether, how, and with what consequences, walls may be removed.

(Smith 1991: 1, emphasis added)

WHY is the agency/structure dilemma or debate such a dominant theme in organization theory and analysis? Why does it raise analytical and ethical questions of such a fundamental and controversial nature? Why has it become so important to the conduct of research and the formulation of explanatory theories within the field? Why do we keep returning to it like an old pimple or sore that we can't resist picking? Why not let it alone when we know only too well that further probing will only make matters worse? What is at stake here and why does it matter? If, as Dawe (1979: 363, emphasis added) suggests, 'the idea of social action has been central to sociological thought less as a theory or set of theories in any formal sense than *as a fundamental moral and analytic preoccupation*', then one must ask why the latter has proved to be so enduring?

This chapter reviews and assesses the various ways in which the agency/structure dilemma has been dealt with in organization theory and analysis over the last two decades or so. It identifies three major 'moves' for attempting to clarify, if not resolve, this issue that will not leave us alone and quietly fade into obscurity as a philosophical curiosity properly consigned to the dustbin of intellectual history. First, the *reductionist* move on the agency/structure dilemma that simply reduces structure to agency or vice versa, but usually the former. As a result, each becomes methodologically isolated from the other in such a way as to obliterate—certainly on logical if not contingent grounds—any perceived need for recognizing, much less coping with, the complex interactions between them and the 'emergent order' of interdependencies that they generate (Byrne 1998). Second, the *determinist* approach to the agency/structure problem that starkly dichotomizes the relationship between them in such a way that each, irreparably divided, side of this ontological/methodological dichotomy necessarily results in either behavioural or structural reification, but usually the latter. Third, the *conflationist* interpretation of the agency/structure paradox that directly collapses the latter into the former and consequently treats it as a 'virtualized reality' only traceable in ongoing 'strips' of social interaction. Thus, the conflationist contends, not only are social and organization structures reproduced through social practices but the former only assume any kind of ontological status and explanatory significance as facilitative or mediating processes entirely parasitic on the latter.

Each of these three attempts to resolve—or more appropriately 'dissolve'—the agency/structure dilemma are found wanting in various respects. In response to these perceived deficiencies, a fourth approach to the problem is outlined and supported—that is, a *relationist* conception of the agency/structure link in which they are treated as interrelated but separable components of a 'doubly constituted' interplay between social action and structural constraint. The wider methodological and theoretical implications of this relationist view of the agency/structure dilemma are then briefly discussed.

By providing a detailed review and evaluation of each of these four approaches to the agency/structure dilemma in organization theory and analysis, the chapter aspires to provide some potential answers to the questions that opened it. While aligning itself with the fourth of these approaches, the chapter concludes by recognizing that intellectual consensus around a particular conception is neither achievable nor desirable. Nevertheless, by clarifying the terms of the agency/structure debate and the methodological grounds on which they are founded, it is hoped that the chapter can contribute to more informed, if unavoidably constrained and compromised, choices between alternative theoretical positions in the field of organization studies (Blaikie 1993). In this manner, we can be better placed to discriminate between what Denis Smith (1991) calls 'open doors and brick walls' in organization analysis and its practical implications for the various ways in which we may wish to intervene in the course of social change to realize valued and contested ends. The agency/structure paradox or debate is likely to remain the primary intellectual medium through which these wider questions of institutional order and its ideological and ethical foundations have been articulated and conveyed to an audience beyond the academy (Dawe 1979; Abrams 1982; Reed 1988; Walsh 1998; Ray 1999). As Archer (2000) has recently insisted, the need to develop an analytical framework that coherently links 'structure and agency' is the central theoretical task facing contemporary social and organization theory. How the latter is achieved will also have major ramifications for how we conceive of and attempt to change our embodied organizational practices (Reed 1985). The development of an analytical framework that adequately theorizes the link between structure and agency should provide us with the basis for specifying 'the conditions under which agents have greater degrees of freedom or, conversely, work under a considerable stringency of constraint' (Archer 2000: 6). Analysis of the dynamic interplay between agency and structure over time, *as distinctive and separable aspects of our material and social existence*, can play a vital role in framing the terms on which we proactively attempt to restructure our social and organizational worlds.

10.1 REDUCTIONISM

Recourse to a *reductionist* solution to the agency/structure dilemma in organization theory and analysis is influential to the extent that it resolves ontological, methodological, and analytical complexity through a strategy of extreme simplification and disaggregation. Reductionism offers a conception of organization theory's subject matter and explanatory mission that eradicates ontological diversity and theoretical uncertainty by reducing emergent collective units and properties to their individual constituents in such a way that the former can be treated as aggregated outcomes of the latter. As a consequence of this definitional manoeuvre, social practices and the emergent social structures that they reproduce can now be reformulated as the direct outcomes of individual behavioural dispositions which, in turn, can be explained as being conditioned by certain physiological and biological characteristics that are constitutive of what it means to be a 'human being'. Homans (1973: 59) provides a classic rendition of the reductionist position:

Some theorists have taken the emergence of phenomena like status systems as evidence for Durkheim's contention that sociology was not reducible to psychology. What is important is not the fact of emergence but the question of how the emergence is to be explained. . . . The explanation is provided by psychological propositions . . . the general explanatory principles even of sociology are not sociological, as the functionalists would have them be, but psychological, propositions about the behaviour of men, not about the behaviour of societies.

As Homans also notes, psychological reductionism has underpinned much of the behaviourist ontology on which rational choice theory in economics, sociology, and politics has been developed. Not only does this reduce emergent social structures to standardized universal behavioural dispositions to maximize utilities or rewards for 'the individual' but it also denudes agency of any, even residual, element of what has been called its iterative, projective, and evaluative dimensions (Emirbayer and Mische 1998). Instead, these critical interpretative, temporal, and practical aspects of agency (discussed later), and their strategic role in reproducing, elaborating, and transforming social structures, are simply reduced to the instrumental and calculative procedures necessarily followed by atomized individuals driven by the psychological imperative to maximize their personal utility functions. This decontextualized behaviourist individualism sanctions, in ontological and methodological terms, a conception of agency in which 'subjective' or 'mental' states, as well as their interpretative requirements and processes, are completely expunged from the explanatory agenda (Ions 1977; Hollis 1994). It rests on an ontology that refuses to recognize these subjective/interpretative components of agency in any way whatsoever. The world is deemed to consist of isolated entities whose primary and determining elements are self-interested individuals each of whom are driven to maximize their own utility functions in competition with others. All 'collective' social phenomena, such as institutions, organizations, and groups arise from, and can be methodologically reduced to, the behaviours of individual human beings whose actions are determined by externally driven forces of a material and biological kind rather than chosen and developed through inter-subjective deliberation and intervention.

Within organization theory and analysis, the clearest expression of reductionism and behaviourist individualism are to be found in rational choice theory (Elster 1986; Coleman 1990), decision-making theory (March and Simon 1958), and public choice theory (Downs 1957; Olson 1965; March and Olsen 1984). Individual behaviour is assumed to be driven or programmed by standardized operating procedures based on universalistic rules of rational calculation; collective behaviour is simply an aggregated form of individual selection between predetermined options. Thus, for March and Simon (1958: 169), the basic features of organization structure and process can be directly derived from 'the characteristics of human problem-solving processes and rational human choice'. For Simon (1945: 109), 'social institutions may be viewed as regularisations of the behaviour of individuals through subjection of their behaviour to stimulus-patterns socially imposed on them. It is in these patterns that an understanding of the meaning and function of organisation is to be found.'

Each of the above approaches draws on reductionism/behaviourist individualism in a number of crucial respects. First, they all make the fundamental assumption that 'every individual person is an *independent* centre of rational calculation' (Barnes 2000: 17). Each individual is assumed to possess and act on a fixed set of universal preferences or objectives that determines assessments of utility optimization—at least at a minimally acceptable level of return. Second, this instrumentally driven and continuously calculating individual is abstracted from all time/space relations and the social complexities they necessarily generate. The social location, position, and role of 'the individual' are stripped out of the analytical model on which these approaches to studying organizations theoretically trade in order to identify their explanatory concerns and goals. Organizations are simply regarded as unintended aggregations or consequences of isolated acts of individual calculation relating to a predetermined register of calibrated priorities or ends. Recurrent patterns of social interaction and the structural forms they reproduce, such as organizations, are directly reduced to individual rational decisions mechanically and predictably determined by information-processing devices that directly map on to material and physical imperatives for individual survival and stability (Barnes 2000: 17–33). Third, aggregated patterns of individual behaviour—that is, loosely-speaking, 'structures'—operate as programming mechanisms that remove the need for any concern with the interpretative and interactive work that actors must perform in their attempts to deliberate over the most appropriate way forward in a particular situation. All this 'deliberative or iterative work' is done for them by the registers of predetermined calculations that derive from a universal means-ends or instrumental rationality removed from the, inevitably messy, not to say contradictory, human experience of time, place, space, and others.

Hindess (1988: 29) summarizes the central features of the abstracted, atomized, and universalized model of agency bequeathed by behaviourist individualism in the following terms: 'first, actors are rational and their rationality is understood in strictly utilitarian terms. . . . Secondly, actors are assumed to be narrowly self-interested. Thirdly, they are social atoms. . . . They are human individuals, but they are not regarded as essentially located within a social structure of positions and roles.' In addition to this 'black boxing' of agency, reductionism/behaviourist individualism reduces structure to, at best, a residual analytical category that merely serves as a conceptual shorthand for the aggregated consequences of isolated and atomized acts of individual behaviour (Hollis 1987).

The inherent analytical and methodological limitations of the reductionist programme encouraged by behaviourist individualism and implemented by variants of
rational choice theory in organization analysis have provided the major spur to the
conflationist move on the agency/structure dilemma. However, before proceeding
to a discussion of the latter, we need to examine behaviourist reductionism's alter
ego—that is, determinism and its inherent tendency to degenerate into various
forms of behavioural or, more usually, structural reification.

10.2 DETERMINISM

Reductionism marginalizes, if not erases, the explanatory significance of 'structure',
as referring to recurrent patterns of social interaction that, over time, become
institutionalized as durable forms of social relations that constrain subsequent
phases of collective action. It also promotes a conception of agency in which the
active identification, consideration, and manipulation of 'alternative action
options' are redefined as the mechanical operation of a utilitarian means–ends
calculus that dispenses with the need to engage with history, context, values, and
conflict. Agency is, literally, emptied of any remaining connotations of proactive
deliberation, choice, and intervention, on the part of individuals or groups. Reductionism sees behaviour as being caused by physical and/or biological factors that
condition both the broad parameters and fine detail of its articulation.

Determinism tends to operate with a preferred ontology and logic of explanation
that works in the opposite direction. It works in a direction that considerably raises
the stakes on externalized structural conditions to the point at which agency all but
disappears as an identifiable and recurrent contributor to the structuring of social
life. In this respect, deterministic approaches to the agency/structure problem tend
to favour a social ontology and explanation in which an autonomous and inexorable logic of structural causality or determinism is imposed on social actors,
irrespective of their aspirations, calculations, and interventions. Within a deterministic frame, structure is assumed to dictate to agency in that it programmes,
controls, and directs the circuits along which action travels and the destinations at
which it, however temporarily, terminates. As Walsh puts it (1998: 11), 'the only
agent of social action is structure itself.' Once this becomes accepted as a starting
point for social and organizational analysis, then structure is regarded as an independent, *sui generis* entity completely unaffected by agency, individual or collective,
due to its innate capacity to configure the forms in and through which all human
existence must be organized. Structural forms govern and regulate social life in such
detail and depth that they exercise a determinate hold over both the range of action

choices available to actors and the deliberative modes and techniques through which the latter emerge as viable ways for moving forward in tightly constrained environments. Agency virtually disappears as a distinct and significant generative mechanism in its own right. It is made totally and utterly subservient to the overpowering reality of structural orders and relations that do not simply 'frame' or 'constrain' but *constitute* both the form and content of social action. Not only is agency denuded of its internal powers and resources, but it is also robbed, onto-logically and methodologically, of any remaining capacity to generate emergent organizational systems or to sustain the institutionalization processes through which they become routinized and objectified as social entities (Berger and Luckmann 1966).

Structural Marxism (as opposed to the rational choice Marxism of Elster 1986) and structuralism provide the most dramatic and forceful articulations of the deterministic take on the agency/structure debate within general social theory (Gouldner 1980). Althusser and Balibar (1977: 180, emphasis added) convey the seductive intellectual power of an ontology and a methodology that frees us from any fear or regret over the rather pathetic quality of our puny attempts, *as subjects*, to influence or resist, much less control, structural forms and their underlying developmental logics:

the fact [is] that the structure of the relations of production determines the places and functions occupied and adopted by the agents of production, who are never anything more than the occupants of these places insofar as they are 'supports' (Trager) of these functions. The true 'subjects' (in the sense of constitutive subjects of the process) are therefore not these occupants or functionaries, are not, despite all appearances, the 'obviousness' of the 'given' of naïve anthropology, 'concrete individuals', 'real men'—*but the definition and distribution of these places and functions. The true subjects are these definers and distributors: the relations of production* (and political and ideological social relations). But since these are relations, they cannot be thought within the category *subject*.

This statement (as is the case with reductionism/behavioural individualism) repre-sents 'structuralism' as a distinctive methodology that possesses the necessary characteristics of science. The latter is defined through its focus on relations of cause and effect located within impersonal objective conditions that can be under-stood through the formulation of universalistic principles and/or laws that deter-mine action. Thus, as Runciman (1973: 192) notes, 'this looks in retrospect less like a doctrine than a methodological battle-cry'. But as Bottomore and Nisbet (1979: 591–2) contend,

as a broad movement of thought, structuralism is characterised ... by its anti-humanism or anti-historicism. ... By anti-humanism is meant that the conscious and purposive actions of individuals and social groups ... are excluded from the analysis, and sociological explan-ation is conceived in terms of 'structural causality'...the ultimate reason or basis for transformations that social systems undergo is to be found in the degree of compatibility or incompatibility between structures and in the development of contradictions within structures, especially within the *determining* structure. . . . The anti-historicist orientation of structuralism may be expressed. . . . [in terms of] structural analysis having priority over historical inquiry . . . it is only by defining the inner properties of particular structures and discovering the contradictions inherent in them that we shall be able eventually to establish the causes of historical transformations.

Consequently, structural determinism is not only a methodological strategy for defining the subject matter of the social sciences and the most appropriate way in which entities located within the latter's domain must be explained. It also rests on a powerful set of 'fundamental moral and analytic preoccupations' that categorically convey the determining force of structural causality over human agency and the inescapable ethical and explanatory consequences that flow from this in relation to the futility of human resistance and the unimportance of human intervention. Structures are deemed to operate and change according to a developmental logic that will 'have its way' irrespective of what agents, individual or collective, think or do. Agency is powerless in the face of structural causality.

The determinist/structuralist take on the agency/structure dilemma encompasses some rather odd intellectual bedfellows within the field of organization studies. While their formal theoretical commitments and substantive explanatory content are rather different, they share an ontological grounding and a methodological positioning that identifies them as common members of the structuralist fraternity and its core deterministic proclivities. Thus, determinism can encompass the structural functionalism of Blau (1974; Blau and Schoenherr 1971), the structural contingency theory of Donaldson (1985, 1995, 1996a, b), the evolutionism of Hannan and Freeman (1989) and Aldrich (1979, 1999), the radical structuralism of Burrell and Morgan (1979) and Allen (1975), and the post-structuralism of Clegg (1989). While they may be poles apart in many respects, Blau and Clegg, for example, take not dissimilar positions on the agency/structure issue in that they both assume that agency is subordinated to structure, at least for analytical/explanatory purposes. Also, there is more than a sneaking suspicion that the ontological grounding of both Blau's and Clegg's positions leaves little, if any, room for the possibility that the active interventions of human agents can constitute and configure the structures of social relations through which their identities and strategies are formed. From very different ontological and theoretical starting points, both Blau's structuralism and Clegg's post-structuralism *analytically reconstitute agency as an effect or epiphenomenon of deeper, ineluctable social forces that totally determine the inclinations and capacities of agents*—individually and/or collectively—to reshape the constraining structural conditions under which they act. By treating agency *merely as an effect* of underlying structural relations or imperatives, they deprive it of its distinctive and irreducible properties and capabilities as an emergent entity that has to be accorded due explanatory respect as an equal contributor to the constitution of organization. Even as a form of endemic resistance to power, 'agency' is doomed to reproduce the structural status quo because it, by definition, cannot be afforded its own, inherent properties and powers as *a constitutive generative mechanism shaping the social and organizational forms in and through which we live our lives.*

In these respects, both Blau and Clegg may be able to subscribe to Donaldson's (1996a: 56, emphasis added) view that 'structural decision-making involves human actors such as organisational managers and other persons. However, they are mainly intervening processes between contingencies and the *inevitable structural outcome*'. In all three cases we are left with an overpowering sense of the undeniable fact that social and organizational structures 'work behind people's backs' according to an immanent logic of emergence, elaboration, and change that the latter are unlikely to comprehend much less influence or direct.

There is little or no sense of the *inherently dynamic, creative, and experimental quality of human agency* because of its presumed causal determination by established structures that function in an autonomous manner, completely independent of their contingent grounding in whatever cognitive, interactive, or relational activities human actors may engage in. In this respect, structuralism eradicates the agency/structure dilemma by asserting the *pervasive penetration of structural conditioning on all aspects and levels of social action.* Once this is accepted, then any remaining sense of the inherent contradictions and tensions between structural constraint and social agency—and their complex implications for the form and content of organizational outcomes—is removed as an analytical focus and ontological anchor. Agency disappears as an ontological reality in its own right; at best, it can only be fleetingly glimpsed as a residual element or trace left over from the inexorable operation of structural forces. Structural determinism is the ontological and methodological 'flip side' of behavioural reductionism; they complement and reinforce each other to the extent that they both treat agency and structure as analytical reference points for entities and concepts that occupy bifurcated domains of existence that demand autonomous explanatory logics.

10.3 CONFLATIONISM

The conflationist interpretation of the constitution of agency and structure and the relationship between them has been developed in direct opposition to both the reductionist and determinist approaches. Conflationists, such as Giddens and Bourdieu, reject the ontological and analytical dualism that pervades both reductionism and determinism to the extent that they insist on the mutual and equal co-determination of agency and structure. Thus, they insist that agency and structure are ontologically inseparable and mutually constituting in that they refer to 'active constituting processes or practices' and 'constraining and enabling conditions' that are of equal causal significance in accounting for social action and the structural forms or relations that it generates. Consequently, Giddens (1984) rejects the conceptualization of structure as referring to an externalized set of conditions or frameworks that constrain the 'restructuring potential' inherent in agency. He has consistently maintained that structures, as opposed to systems, only exist as 'time space presences' instantiated in social practices and collective memory traces loosely framing the conduct of knowledgeable and proactive agents (Giddens 1984: 17). As Kaspersen (2000: 42, emphasis added), along with many others, has noted, for Giddens,

> structures have only virtual existence, in that structures exist only as a possibility and have not actively manifested themselves. . . . *structure exists only in practice itself and in our human memory, which is used when we act.* . . . Structures appear only in our memory traces when we reflect discursively over a previously performed act. In other words, *structure does not exist as such*; rather, it is being continually recreated qua the agent, who draws on the same structure (or, more correctly structural properties) whenever action occurs.

By rejecting any conception of structure as constituting and representing external-ized and objectified entities or conditions that independently constrain agency in various ways, Giddens, and conflationists in general, ontologically and analytically collapse structure into agency. This is conceptually legitimated by redefining the former as loosely interrelated configurations of properties, or rules and resources, that are *entirely dependent for their existence and relevance* on their activation through discursive reflection and the human praxis it facilitates. Agency and structure are redefined as inseparable aspects of a flattened social ontology consti-tuted through social practices that reproduce the structural properties on which reflexive social actors routinely draw as a way of 'moving on'.

By insisting on the ontological and analytical inseparability of agency and structure, conflationists tend to 'internalize' the latter in such a way that '*there is no sense in which it can be either emergent or autonomous or pre-existent or causally influential*' (Archer 1995: 97, emphasis in original). Consequently, the complex interplay between agency and structure and its role as an active constituting process that shapes and reshapes organizational forms tends to be lost from view. In ontologically and analytically compacting agency and structure to form a single, radically compressed social reality, conflationism strongly supports the view that *autonomous social practices exclusively constitute* the subject matter dealt with by the social sciences—including the 'sciences of organization'. Giddens's structuration theory transcends the ontological and analytical dualism between agency and structure by conceptually collapsing them both into social practices that are now accorded temporal and relational priority over and above the activities that gener-ated them and the conditions that sustain them as viable interactional patterns or orders (Layder 1994, 1997). The logical implication of this seems to be the denial that institutional order exists as a 'persisting macro-pattern in social activity [that] can be studied from the outside, and characteristics of the pattern unremarked by members themselves can be identified and described using theorists' own categories' (Barnes 2000: 151).

Barley and Tolbert's (1997) recent attempt to develop the notion of 'script' as the key mediating or linking concept between structure and agency provides an instructive illustration of the way in which conflationist thinking has influenced contemporary organization theory and analysis. Their use of the concept of 'script' consistently displays the conflationist tendency to collapse structure into agency by treating the former only as an institutionalization process reflected in the memory traces and interaction patterns of agents rather than a pre-existing and constraining social entity. For them, 'institutions only exist as far as they are instantiated in everyday interaction' (Barley and Tolbert 1997: 99) and enacted through the behavioural regularities that constitute organizational scripts and their discursive formulation. Structures have no ontological status or explanatory significance outside this institutionalization process and the interactional order through which it is reproduced.

In sharp contrast to the conflationists, relationists/realists have insisted that it is only by holding firm to the ontological and analytical separability of agency and structure that we can begin to understand and explain the variable extent to which different social and organizational structures are open to varying degrees of modification and change through social action. For the latter, the interplay between agency and structure provides the explanatory key to how 'we'—as actors and researchers—may be better placed to push on some open doors through some brick walls. Without that key, the relationsts/realists maintain, we are permanently disabled from accessing the temporal and relational complexities of the agency/structure dilemma.

10.4 RELATIONISM

Relationism has been developed as a response to the perceived inadequacies of reductionism, determinism, and conflationism in relation to their ontological bases, analytical frameworks, and explanatory logics. The cumulative effect of the relationist/realist intervention within the agency/structure controversy has been to challenge the conventional assumption that social/organizational science *must choose* between social constructionism/interpretivism and structural determinism/positivism. Instead, relationism/realism offers a radical alternative to this

'Hobson's choice' that, potentially at least, transforms the explanatory goals of social/organizational science and the methodological and analytical means by which they are to be realized (Blaikie 1993). While coming relatively late to organization studies, relationism/realism has become increasingly influential within the field and has begun to promote a very different take on the agency/structure debate than that advanced by the three approaches previously outlined (Tsoukas 1989, 2000; Reed 1997; Clarke 2000; Fleetwood and Ackroyd 2000; Willmott 2000).

Relationism attempts to formulate a conception of agency and structure, and of the complex dynamic interplay between them, which is equipped to deal with the 'double constitution of agency and structure'. The latter demands an ontology and methodology that are sensitive to the fact that 'temporal-relational contexts support particular agentic orientations, which in turn constitute different structuring relationships of actors toward their environments. It is the constitution of such orientations within particular structural contexts that gives form to effort and allows actors to assume greater or lesser degrees of transformative leverage in relation to the structuring contexts of action' (Emirbayer and Mische 1998: 1004). This can only be achieved if the creative and constraining components of both agency and structure are equally recognized. They both have to be incorporated within analytical frameworks that focus on 'how temporal-relational contexts constitute the patterns of response that shape agentic orientations, which go on to constitute different mediating relationships of actors toward those contexts' (Emirbayer and Mische 1998: 1005). Relationists/realists argue that this cannot be realized if either agency or structure are reduced to each other or if they are presumed to determine each other or if they are collapsed within a middle-range concept, such as social practice, that denies structure any kind of distinct ontological identity or independent explanatory power.

In direct opposition to conflationism/constructivism, relationism/realism is based on the fact that the 'ontological subjectivity of the socially constructed reality requires an ontologically objective reality out of which it is constructed.... a socially constructed reality presupposes a non-socially constructed reality' (Searle 1995: 191). Once this ontological presupposition is in place, certain critical methodological and analytical implications and consequences follow for the manner in which the 'double constitution' of agency and structure is approached. Agency depends on actors having practical access to and control over the spatially embedded and temporally located relational positions that structures objectively make available. As Ackroyd (2000: 99–102) puts it, 'organisations are the sites for effective agency.... Organisations are experienced as real—often at the very moment they are being challenged and contested'. Structures depend on the creative and generative powers that agency can develop and exploit, if the conditions and relations in which it is spatially and temporally situated allow them to emerge and flourish. But the changing relationship between agentic creativity and structural constraint cannot be understood if the development of institutional and organizational forms over time is reduced to evolutionary determinism or historical voluntarism (Sztompka 1993). For the relationist/realist, 'actions always presuppose already existing resources and media, many of which have a social dimension that is irreducible to the properties of individuals.... That those resources and social structures are themselves a product of actions (no structures without actions) does not mean that actions and structures can be collapsed into one another' (Sayer 2000: 18). Rather, the relationist/realist insists, creativity and constraint must be equally recognized as constitutive features of social and organizational existence. The critical question is how do we get at—in explanatory terms—the changing relationship between them?

Emirbayer and Mische (1998) suggest that agency must be analytically disaggregated into three interrelated conceptual components: iteration, projectivity, and practical evaluation. Iteration refers to the routine reactivation of *past patterns of thought and action* into contemporary social practices so that they are given a minimum degree of stability and order necessary to sustain identities, interactions, and institutions over time. Projectivity signals the future, rather than past, dimension of social action through the creative generation of possible action options and trajectories that possess the potential to reconfigure existing structures. Practical evaluation conveys the innate capacity of actors to make informed judgements between alternative courses of action in response to the changing situational contingencies that they have to face. Taken together, these necessary analytical elements of agency indicate that agency is a historically and structurally variable phenomenon embedded in changing theoretical and practical conceptions of time and action. As Emirbayer and Mische (1998: 973) argue, their conception of agency 'is intrinsically social and relational since it centres around the engagement (and disengagement) by actors of the different contextual environments that constitute their own structured yet flexible social universe'. By grounding the capacity for human agency in the social structures and relations that unavoidably constrain social action, Emirbayer and Mische simultaneously emphasize the creative and stabilizing potential inherent in the structuring contexts that indelibly shape organizational forms.

Porpora's (1998) reworking of the concept of social structure complements the reconceptualization of agency offered by Emirbayer and Mische. The former suggests that structure is most appropriately thought of as a nexus of social relations within which actors respond in all sorts of creative ways that cannot be predicted in advance. It is only relatively enduring in the sense that it is ultimately dependent on the endemic transformational potential of creative human agency; the potential for change through agency is a necessary feature of structure but is only actualized under the conditions inhering in the latter (Bhaskar 1986; Pratten 2000). Consequently, both agency and structure possess independent causal properties that can exert a powerful influence on the course and consequences of socio-organizational life. But the varying potential for agency causality and structure causality can only be identified and explained in relation to the complex interplay between them as it works its way through in particular institutional contexts that are always pregnant with possibilities for change—of varying scope and impact. However, a relationist/ realist reading of the agency/structure relationship *begins* from the position that *pre-existing* structural conditions and relations establish the institutional and material conditions under which any ongoing sequence of social interaction (in its iterative, projective, and evaluative dimensions) and its organizational outcomes must be located and explained. Thus, social practices, contra-Giddens, are always embedded and located within extant social structures that pre-figure their contingent possibilities for generating creative and innovative restructuring or reassembly (Harris 1980; Reed 1984, 1985). The creative discursive and transformative potentialities inherent in human agency only begin to bite when structural contexts and conditions are generally supportive of those potentialities being actualized in some durable form or another.

Relationism/realism is now beginning to make its influence felt within contemporary organization theory and analysis. As Clarke (2000), drawing on Archer (1995) and Layder (1997), has most recently argued, relationism/realism has major implications for the study and analysis of organizational change. By drawing attention to the critical temporal and structural dimensions of the latter, it allows organizational researchers to distinguish between the reproduction, elaboration, and transformation of social and organizational forms. Once this fundamental ontological and analytical distinction is made, Clarke contends, we are placed in a better position to analyse recurrent action patterns and the determinate material and structural relations within which they are embedded. At the same time, because relationism/realism sensitizes us to the complex interplay between agency and structure, as well as the destabilizing effect that it can have on existing organizational forms, it reminds us of the inherent potential for structural change and transformation entailed in all institutional contexts. However, the activation of this inherent potential for change/transformation is highly dependent on the contingent structural and resource constraints prevailing within any particular context.

It is this dynamic interplay between structure and agency—as referring to separable and autonomous properties and powers of different levels of social organization and analysis—that forms the explanatory focus for relationists/realists. They reject the analytical elision between distinctive and independent properties and powers possessed by agents, on the one hand, and structures, on the other, that is the theoretical and explanatory hallmark of conflationism. It consistently maintains that 'agency' and 'structure' necessarily denote distinctive causal properties and powers that emerge through the social relations that are crystallized as a result of our practical engagement with a material and social world that pre-exists us and will outlast us. As Carter argues (2000: 67–8), 'structure and agency refer to different things, with different sorts of properties (given and emergent), and are therefore not reducible to each other. This is the core principle of a realist approach and insists on an *analytic* separation of structure and agency, or "the parts" and "the people"'. Thus, structure and agency refer to distinct and separable strata of social reality pertaining to different powers and capacities such as institutionalized constraints and enablements (structure) as opposed to collective articulation and mobilization of shared interests (agency). The elaboration, modification, and transformation of social practices and institutions is to be explained as the outcomes of the interplay between these two sets of powers and capabilities over time as it shapes and reshapes the ever-changing balance between structurally embedded constraint and strategically generated choice.

This provides a very different concept of 'organization' to that legitimated by a conflationist interpretation of the agency/structure dilemma. *For relationists/realists, 'organization' is that mechanism which generates and sustains collective or 'corporate agency' as a relatively permanent feature of social reality. It transforms individual action into corporate agency by providing the collective resources and mechanisms that the latter requires to be sustained over time as a viable and effective social entity.* As a transformative mechanism or resource, organization possesses certain causal powers and competencies that may or may not be selectively activated in specific social situations.

As Archer (2000: 11) has recently argued, 'corporate agency transforms itself in pursuing social transformation. Primarily it does this, in the course of its struggles, by inducing the elaboration of the institutional role structure. New roles are created, and these constitute new positions in which more people can willingly invest themselves.' Once these institutional role structures or positions, and the practices that they necessitate, are established, then they inevitably create the conditions under which subsequent phases of collective, and indeed individual, agency must operate. The latter elaborates on existing structural forms and relations, and in doing so opens up the possibility of new ones being created; organizational change is regarded as a series of interrelated sequences or 'cycles' in which modifications of existing forms generate the possibility of more innovative ones emerging later. The extent to which the latter is realized in turn depends upon the structurally specific contingencies prevailing in any particular situation and the relative skill with which they are taken advantage of by the agents operating within that situation.

This approach also suggests a form of organizational analysis that is rather different than that advocated by supporters of the conflationist view. It is the grounding of 'organization' in the material circumstances in which it is (re)produced and the structural context within which it is mobilized that establishes the explanatory focal point for the pursuit of a relationist/realist approach to the agency/structure paradox in organization analysis. The interplay between them—and the distinctive sets of causal powers that they necessarily entail—must be disentangled and then reconstructed before the dynamics and trajectory of 'organizing' in any particular situation can be identified with any degree of confidence.

Only in this way can we get some explanatory leverage on what Archer (2000: 307–8) calls the 'structural inheritance' of different generations of collective or corporate agents and the differential constraints and opportunities that it offers to them in their ongoing struggles to change the conditions under which they act. *It is the 'doing' and 'making' of organization, rather than its 'saying' and 'telling', that is explanatory priority for relationism/realism.* As an objective material and social reality, 'organization' is seen to possess certain causal powers that inevitably constrain collective agency and direct its articulation and mobilization across a range of situations.

10.5 OPENING DOORS
THROUGH BRICK WALLS

What are the implications of the four perspectives on the agency/structure dilemma for the detailed ways in which organization theorists ought to identify and pursue their explanatory goals? In particular, what form of explanatory analysis does relationism/realism recommend as a basis for moving forward? If these recommendations were accepted as a basis for moving forward, what would they entail for the scientific identity and status of organization theory and analysis as a social science?

Reductionism and determinism are located within a behaviourist/positivist conception of scientific research and explanation. Direct observations of empirical events, such as sequences of physical behaviour, are explained by being subsumed within, and hence derived from, universal covering laws specifying the causal relationship between antecedent conditions and the consequences they necessarily produce (Blaikie 1993). Within organization theory and analysis, this translates into a methodological commitment to the search for causal relationships in the form of law-like regularities between environmental, organizational, and behavioural factors that are presumed to exist as entities occupying an ontological domain independent of human agency (Donaldson 1996a). Conflationism rejects this behaviourist/positivist conception of scientific research and analysis. Instead, it is founded on a constructivist ontology and develops an interpretivist methodology that is focused upon the analysis of regularities in social practices as they facilitate the reflexive assembling and ordering of social institutions by social actors (Giddens 1989). This legitimates a model of scientific research and explanation in which a continuous dialogue between social researchers—who are unavoidably part of their own subject matter—and 'knowledgeable' social actors in the wider community over the forms and effects of institutional (re)ordering replaces the search for law-like regularities as its raison d'être. The clearest expression of this perspective on the explanatory priorities that ought to drive organization theory and analysis is articulated within a broad range of approaches sympathetic to the 'post-modernist turn' and its refocusing of research attention around the discursive processes and practices through which social reality is constructed and sustained (Reed 1997, 1998).

Relationism/realism advocates a reformulation of the explanatory aims and methodological strategies that ought to inform contemporary organization theory and analysis in terms of *the creative tension or opposition between agency and structure* as it works its way through 'alternating phases of agential creativeness and structural determination' (Sztompka 1993: 200). This is legitimated by a realist conception of scientific research and explanation in which hypothetical models and theories of real structures and mechanisms are developed in an attempt to identify and confirm their inherent 'generative powers and consequences' within specific sets of historical and contextual contingencies (Bhaskar 1979). These underlying structures and mechanisms are not readily observable or expressible as behavioural regularities, so they must be analytically constructed and reconstructed through hypothetical models or types with anticipated institutional consequences that are amenable to empirical investigation (Layder 1993; Sayer 2000). The explanatory focus for this exercise in 'retroductive analysis' (Blaikie 1993) within organization theory must be upon the '*interface between structures and agents*, operations and actions' because it is here that 'the riddle of social becoming must be traced' (Sztompka 1993: 215, emphasis added). *If this is accepted, then organization theory and analysis is returned to its original Weberian roots, tradition and location as a critical intellectual component of a revitalized historical sociology.* The latter must be focused upon the dialectical interplay between structure and agency as it unfolds over time within changing socio-historical contexts and with varying socio-historical consequences. These consequences cannot be predicted in advance but only understood, retrospectively and retroductively, through in-depth analysis of the underlying structural mechanisms through which they were generated and the action strategies through which they were subsequently sustained in the face of controversy and challenge.

What does relationism/realism do for the 'open doors and brick walls' conundrum that opened this chapter? It redefines and revitalizes organization theory (Wolin 1961; Reed 1985, 1996) as an historical science focused on the explanatory problem of identifying key mechanisms of organizational reproduction, elaboration, and transformation and the wider ethical issues that this exercise in 'structural reconstruction' raises. This can only be attempted if the flattened, 'centreless web' (Sayer 2000: 72) ontology that provides the foundations for so much contemporary organizational theorizing and analysis—in which agency and structure are conceptually conflated within the notion of social practice—is rejected. In its place, relationism/realism offers a stratified social ontology and an analytical dualism that supports 'the view that some structures (mechanisms, objects or whatever we care to call them) are more important than others in shaping *particular* outcomes.... what is central or most important depends on what objects we are dealing with and what we are trying to explain' (Sayer 2000: 74). By attempting to identify the structural and material preconditions for successful practical interventions in the course of socio-historical change and development, relationism/realism can put us in a better position, intellectually and ethically, to open some doors through some brick walls. These will almost certainly close again. But the continuing search to account for, and exploit, the changing balance between agentic possibilities and structural constraints offers organization theory a more realistic basis from which to explore the dynamics of organizational change than either positivist reductionism/determinism or social constructionism and its conflationist ontology.

There are dangers inherent in this quest. As Trigg (2001: 252) warns, realism always 'runs the risk of stressing social structures at the expense of any substantial notion of the self'. Nevertheless, if we are serious about the need to find and prise open some doors through some brick walls we must engage with the complex interplay between agency and structure as the fundamental dynamic that shapes the institutional context and organizational world in which we live. We cannot begin to do this if we continue to believe that we can reduce and/or collapse the distinctive ontological and analytical domains to which these two concepts refer. Only by separating and interrelating the distinctive realities to which these concepts refer can we develop approaches to the study of organizations and organizing that properly attend to the endemic tensions between social action and social structure as they work their way through in our everyday and institutional lives.

REFERENCES

ABRAMS, P. (1982). *Historical Sociology.* Somerset: Open Books.

ACKROYD, S. (2000). 'Connecting Organisations and Societies: A Realist Analysis of Structures', in S. Ackroyd and S. Fleetwood (eds.), *Realist Perspectives on Management and Organisations.* London: Routledge.

ALDRICH, H. (1979). *Organizations and Environments.* Englewood Cliffs, NJ: Prentice-Hall.

—— (1999). *Organizations Evolving.* London: Sage.

ALLEN, V. (1975). *Social Analysis: A Marxist Critique and Alternative.* London: Longman.

ALTHUSSER, L., and BALIBAR, E. (1977). *Reading Capital* (2nd edn). London: New Left Books.

ARCHER, M. (1995). *Realist Social Theory: The Morphogenetic Approach.* Cambridge: Cambridge University Press.

—— (2000). *Being Human: The Problem of Agency.* Cambridge: Cambridge University Press.

BARLEY, S., and TOLBERT, P. (1997). 'Institutionalization and Structuration: Studying the Links between Action and Institution'. *Organization Studies*, 18/1: 93–117.

BARNES, B. (2000). *Understanding Agency: Social Theory and Responsible Action*. London: Sage.

BERGER, P., and LUCKMANN, T. (1966). *The Social Construction of Reality: A Treatise in the Sociology of Knowledge*. New York: Doubleday.

BHASKAR, R. (1979). *The Possibility of Naturalism*. Brighton: Harvester Wheatsheaf.

—— (1986). *Scientific Realism and Human Emancipation*. London: Verso.

BLAIKIE, N. (1993). *Approaches to Social Enquiry*. Cambridge: Polity.

BLAU, P. (1974). *On the Nature of Organisations*. New York: Wiley.

—— and SCHOENHERR, R. (1971). *The Structure of Organisations*. New York: Basic Books.

BOTTOMORE, T., and NISBET, R. (1979). 'Structuralism', in T. Bottomore and R. Nisbet (eds.), *A History of Sociological Analysis*. London: Heinemann Educational.

BOURDIEU, P. (1990). *The Logic of Practice*. Oxford: Polity Press.

BURRELL, G., and MORGAN, G. (1979). *Sociological Paradigms and Organisational Analysis*. London: Heinemann Educational.

BYRNE, D. (1998). *Complexity Theory and the Social Sciences*. London: Routledge.

CARTER, R. (2000). *Realism and Racism*. London: Routledge.

CLARKE, P. (2000). *Organisations in Action: Competition between Contexts*. London: Routledge.

CLEGG, S. (1989). *Frameworks of Power*. London: Sage.

COLEMAN, J. (1990). *Foundations of Social Theory*. Cambridge, Mass.: Harvard University Press.

DAWE, A. (1979). 'Theories of Social Action', in T. Bottomore and R. Nisbet (eds.), *A History of Sociological Analysis*. London: Heinemann Educational.

DONALDSON, L. (1985). *In Defence of Organisation Theory*. Cambridge: Cambridge University Press.

—— (1995). *American Anti-Management Theories of Organization: A Critique of Paradigm Proliferation*. Cambridge: Cambridge University Press.

—— (1996a). *For Positivist Organisation Theory*. London: Sage.

—— (1996b). 'The Normal Science of Structural Contingency Theory', in S. Clegg, C. Hardy, and W. Nord (eds.), *Handbook of Organisation Studies*. London: Sage.

DOWNS, A. (1957). *An Economic Theory of Democracy*. New York: Harper & Row.

ELSTER, J. (1986). *Rational Choice*. Oxford: Blackwell.

EMIRBAYER, M., and MISCHE, A. (1998). 'What is Agency?' *American Journal of Sociology*, 103/4: 962–1023.

FLEETWOOD, S., and ACKROYD, S. (eds.) (2000). *Realist Perspectives on Management and Organisations*. London: Routledge.

GIDDENS, A. (1984). *The Constitution of Society*. Cambridge: Polity Press.

—— (1989). *Sociology*. Cambridge: Polity Press.

GOULDNER, A. (1980). *The Two Marxisms*. London: Macmillan.

HANNAN, J., and Freeman, J. (1989). *Organizational Ecology*. Cambridge, Mass.: Harvard University Press.

HARRIS, C. (1980). *Fundamental Concepts and the Sociological Enterprise*. London: Croom Helm.

HINDESS, B. (1988). *Choice, Rationality and Social Theory*. London: Unwin Hyman.

HOLLIS, M. (1987). *The Cunning of Reason*. Cambridge: Cambridge University Press.

—— (1994). *The Philosophy of Social Science: An Introduction*. Cambridge: Cambridge University Press.

HOMANS, G. (1973). 'Bringing Men Back In', in A. Ryan (ed.), *The Philosophy of Social Explanation*. Oxford: Oxford University Press.

IONS, E. (1977). *Against Behaviouralism: A Critique of Behavioural Science*. Oxford: Blackwell.

KASPERSEN, L. (2000). *Anthony Giddens: An Introduction to a Social Theorist*. Oxford: Blackwell.

LAYDER, D. (1981). *Structure, Interaction and Social Theory*. London: Routledge.

—— (1993). *New Strategies in Social Research*. Cambridge: Polity Press.

—— (1994). *Understanding Social Theory*. London: Sage.

—— (1997). *Modern Social Theory*. London: UCL Press.

MARCH, J., and SIMON, H. (1958). *Organizations*, New York: Wiley.

—— and OLSEN, J. (1984). 'The New Institutionalism: Organizational Factors in Political Life'. *American Political Science Review*, 78: 734–49.

OLSON, M. (1965). *The Logic of Collective Action*. Cambridge, Mass.: Harvard University Press.

PARKER, M. (1999). 'Capitalism, Subjectivity and Ethics: Debating Labour Process Analysis'. *Organization Studies*, 20/1: 25–45.

PORPORA, D. (1998). 'Four Concepts of Social Structure', in M. Archer *et al.* (eds.), *Critical Realism: Essential Readings*. London: Routledge.

PRATTEN, S. (2000). 'Structure, Agency and Marx's Analysis of the Labour Process', in S. Ackroyd and S. Fleetwood (eds.), *Realist Perspectives on Management and Organisations*. London: Routledge.

RAY, L. (1999). *Theorizing Classical Sociology*. Buckingham: Open University Press.

REED, M. (1984). 'Management as a Social Practice'. *Journal of Management Studies*, 21/3: 273–85.

—— (1985). *Redirections in Organizational Analysis*. London: Tavistock.

—— (1988). 'The Problem of Human Agency in Organizational Analysis'. *Organization Studies*, 9/1: 33–46.

—— (1996). 'Expert Power and Control in Late Modernity: An Empirical Review and Theoretical Synthesis'. *Organization Studies*, 17/4: 573–97.

—— (1997). 'In Praise of Duality and Dualism: Rethinking Agency and Structure in Organizational Analysis'. *Organization Studies*, 18/1: 21–42.

—— (1998). 'Organisational Analysis as Discourse Analysis: A Critique', in D. Grant, T. Keenoy, and C. Oswick (eds.), *Discourse and Organisation*. London: Sage.

RUNCIMAN, W. G. (1973). 'What is Structuralism?' in A. Ryan (ed.), *The Philosophy of Social Explanation*. Oxford: Oxford University Press.

SAYER, A. (2000). *Realism and Social Science*. London: Sage.

SEARLE, J. (1995). *The Construction of Social Reality*. London: Penguin.

SIMON, H. (1945). *Administrative Behaviour*. New York: Free Press.

SMITH, D. (1991). *The Rise of Historical Sociology*. Cambridge: Polity Press.

SZTOMPKA, P. (1993). *The Sociology of Social Change*. Oxford: Blackwell.

TRIGG, R. (2001). *Understanding Social Science* (2nd edn). Oxford: Blackwell.

TSOUKAS, H. (1989). 'The Validity of Idiographic Research Explanations'. *Academy of Management Review*, 14: 551–61.

—— (2000). 'What is Management?', in S. Ackroyd and S. Fleetwood (eds.), *Realist Perspectives on Management and Organisations*. London: Routledge.

WALSH, D. (1998). 'Structure/Agency', in C. Jenks (ed.), *Core Sociological Dichotomies.* London: Sage.

WILLMOTT, R. (2000). 'Structure, Culture and Agency: Rejecting the Current Orthodoxy in Organisation Theory', in S. Ackroyd and S. Fleetwood (eds.), *Realist Perspectives on Management and Organisations.* London: Routledge.

WOLIN, S. (1961). *Politics and Vision.* London: Allen & Unwin.

CHAPTER 11

MODES OF EXPLANATION IN ORGANIZATION THEORY

ANDREAS GEORG SCHERER

11.1 THE PURPOSE OF ORGANIZATION THEORY AND THE MULTIPLICITY OF EXPLANATIONS

ORGANIZATION THEORY (OT)[1] is concerned with explaining the genesis, existence, functionality, and the transformation of organizations, and by doing so, it is also concerned, either implicitly or explicitly, with influencing organizational practice. However, in their everyday life individuals already have an intuitive

---

[1] In my chapter I will use the term 'Organization Theory' (OT) (each with capital letters), which in the literature is sometimes referred to as 'Organization Studies', to describe a field of research, i.e. a more or less systematic set of actions (*Handlungszusammenhang*) directed towards the creation of knowledge about organizations. In addition, I will use the phrase 'organization theory' (with small letters) to describe the results (*Handlungsresultate*) of this type of research, i.e. the particular theories generated about organizational phenomena. As we will see there are many organization theories within the field of 'Organization Theory'.

understanding of how organizations work. OT knowledge differs from individuals' lay knowledge by its *systematic and methodic characteristics.*[2] But whoever attends a lecture on OT or consults a textbook will be surprised that 'Organization Theory' is *not* a unified set of knowledge (Pfeffer 1993; Scherer 1998). In fact there are *many* organizational theories in textbooks, scholarly journals, etc., which are entirely different from each other (see e.g. the contributions to Clegg, Hardy, and Nord 1996).

Why are there so many organization theories? Why is it so difficult for organization theorists to converge on a common theory? An answer to this question must consider at least two things: first of all, organizations are highly complex entities where many problems can occur which are worthy of theoretical consideration. The domain of OT is such a wide field that many partial aspects can just not be integrated in one 'super-theory'. For example, scholars consider topics such as interactions between individuals and organizations (e.g. Argyris 1964; Jensen and Meckling 1976; Likert 1961), between groups and organizations (e.g. Hackman and Walton 1986; Janis 1982; Likert 1967; Roethlisberger and Dickson 1939), relationships between organizations and the environment (e.g. Aldrich 1979; Burns and Stalker 1961; Child 1972; Lawrence and Lorsch 1967), or between organizations and society (e.g. Freeman 1984; Freeman and Gilbert 1988), as well as between organizational structures and processes of institutionalization (Meyer and Rowan 1977), relationships between organizing through hierarchy and forms of alternative coordination (such as market processes) (e.g. Williamson 1975), relationships among different organizations (e.g. Alter and Hage 1993; Whetton 1987), the role of power in organizations (Mintzberg 1983; Mumby 1988; Pfeffer 1981; Weber 1947), transformation of organizations (e.g. French and Bell 1978; Huber and Glick 1993; Van de Ven and Poole 1994), etc. To deal with this variety of topics current literature suggests a categorization of themes at different levels of analysis (Hage 1980; Pfeffer 1982; Astley and Van de Ven 1983). Depending on whether theories deal with the behavior of individuals in organizations (and society), with the behavior of a whole organization, or with relationships among organizations, they could be distinguished into micro, meso, and macro theories of organization (Hage 1980). However, the spectrum and variety of topics are not sufficient to understand why integration within a common perspective is not easily possible.

Second, each of those partial aspects could be viewed from different perspectives. Two distinctions are important in this respect: the *research interest* of the researcher and the *methods* used. Following these distinctions, on the one hand, one has to acknowledge that scholars do *not* agree on the purpose of research. Some scholars concentrate on *descriptive* research only. They want simply to 'explain' the existence or the functions of organizations in order to gain knowledge, but are not interested in practical applications. Instead, they want to be rigorous in their scientific

[2] As we will see below, even this characteristic is rejected by proponents of postmodern philosophy.

approach. Some of them explicitly reject a normative approach and argue that science can only answer questions of truth, but cannot rationally decide on norms or values (value-free thesis) (e.g. Hunt 1990, 1992). Others, by contrast, suggest a *prescriptive approach*. They focus on the design of the organization and want to provide relevant knowledge in order to contribute to the improvement of organizational practice (e.g., Daft and Lewin 1993; Hambrick 1994).

On the other hand, organizational researchers do not share a common understanding of what constitutes research and what counts as valid knowledge. This will be surprising for students who believe that science is characterized by *one* special method. Instead, one has to acknowledge that organizational researchers use different methods producing different results, even inconsistent results, and that there is no agreement upon which of the methods is better, i.e. which results are 'more true' (Pfeffer 1993). Supported by different modes of explanation researchers offer different *explanations*, i.e. different answers to the question '*Why* do particular organizational phenomena occur?'. To make sense of the theoretical diversity in OT there have been several attempts to systematize organizational theories according to their underlying *methods* (Astley and Van de Ven 1983; Burrell and Morgan 1979; Gioia and Pitre 1990; Pfeffer 1982) as well as to the *research interests* of the social scientist (Burrell and Morgan 1979; Connell and Nord 1996; Rao and Pasmore 1989; Willmott 1997). These distinctions are important to understand the characteristics of different modes of explanations.

11.2 WHY DO WE NEED PHILOSOPHY OF SCIENCE?

The current status quo of OT with its different theories, schools of thought, and modes of explanation is one of the reasons why fundamental questions are more likely to be discussed in OT than in other fields such as economics, marketing, or accounting, which appear to be more coherent in their terminology, and research objectives and methods. Being a meta-discipline (see Figure 11.1), philosophy of science enables us to engage in critical reflection on the practice of research (Bohman 1991; Hollis 1994; Outhwaite 2000; Rosenberg 1995). Philosophy of science tries to answer the following basic questions (cf. Steinmann and Scherer 1995: 1056 ff.):

(1) What *is* the purpose of research and what *should* be the purpose of research?
(2) Which methodologies and explanatory strategies *are* and *should* be used by researchers for attaining these purposes?

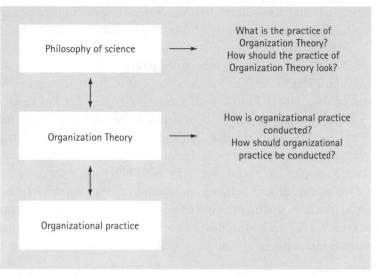

Fig. 11.1 The relationship between philosophy of science, organization theory, and organizational practice (adapted from Scherer 1999: 4)

These questions allow us both to *describe* the current practice of research and *critically prescribe* guidelines for conducting research. The relationship of organizational practice, Organization Theory, and philosophy of science is described in Figure 11.1. OT allows reflecting on organizational practice and outlines how organizational practice *is* conducted and/or how it *should* be conducted. Philosophy of science, in contrast, allows reflection on OT. What *is* the practice of OT and how *should* research efforts be conducted and to what end?

When talking about 'the' philosophy of science, one should not assume that there is one universally accepted concept of philosophy of science. The fact OT scholars use different methods, base their work on different presumptions, and pursue different research interests tells its own tale. Already twenty years ago Burrell and Morgan (1979) examined different schools of sociology and OT and suggested that these schools are based on different modes of explanation, which can be assigned to different 'paradigms' (see critically Deetz 1996). A *paradigm* labels the basic assumptions of a researcher's purpose of activity (research interest), the character of the examined object (ontology), and the suitable methodology for examining (epistemology respectively methodology).

In the following sections we will discuss six different modes of explanation that are commonly found in contemporary OT: Deductive-nomological explanation model, Interpretivism, Critical Theory, Postmodernism, Functionalism, and Rational Choice Theory. I have attempted to organize these different modes in a systematic way as their essential characteristics can be understood better if they are discussed in contrast to each other. I will begin with the so-called 'subject-object model' of research and its underlying *deductive-nomological mode* of explanation (DN explanation), which was adopted from the philosophy of the natural sciences and was the received view of social research for a long period of time (Salmon 1998). Still, hundreds of doctoral students are trained to apply the DN mode as if this were *the* scientific approach without any reservation and without any conceivable alternative. I will contrast the DN mode with alternative conceptions of social scientific research, which were developed in opposition to the subject-object model and highlight its methodological and normative deficits. While *Interpretivism* and *Critical Theory* attempt to propose alternative approaches to the social sciences, *Postmodern Philosophy* questions the very possibility of science as a rational endeavor. Finally, the debate between *Functionalism* and *Rational Choice Theory* focuses not so much on methodological or normative issues, but on the question of social order, i.e. on the embeddedness of social action into society namely on the mutual relationship between action and social institutions.

11.3 THE RECEIVED VIEW OF EXPLANATION IN THE SOCIAL SCIENCES: DN EXPLANATION AND THE SUBJECT-OBJECT MODEL

The question of how to conduct social research has been a matter of debate in the philosophy of social science for ages. The critical issue is whether social science should adopt a natural science approach (*naturalism*) (see e.g. Durkheim 1951, 1895/1965) or whether it has to develop a special social science approach that is more suitable to social phenomena (*anti-naturalism*) (see e.g. Hollis 1994; Outhwaite 2000). In the past century, for a long period of time the majority of philosophers and social researchers argued for the former position. The so-called 'subject-object model' of research is built on this premiss. Along with several philosophical assumptions, which will be presented below, it is based on a *deductive-nomological mode of explanation* (DN explanation) (Hempel and Oppenheim 1948/1998), which is applied to both social and natural phenomena, and was the most influential approach in the twentieth century (Salmon 1998).

Hempel and Oppenheim (1948/1998) proposed a certain understanding of explanation, i.e. a model of deductive explanation, which was already introduced by Mill (1843) and Popper (1935/1959) some time before, but had never been made explicit in sufficient detail. To Hempel and Oppenheim to 'explain' a phenomenon means to answer the question 'Why does a particular phenomenon occur?', which according to the authors should be understood as synonymous to the question 'according to what general laws, and by virtue of what antecedent conditions does the phenomenon occur?' (Hempel and Oppenheim 1948/1998: 207).

At an abstract level the DN model can be described as follows. An explanation consists of statements of two kinds: the explanandum and the explanans. The *explanandum* E is the event-to-be-explained, i.e. the sentence describing the event-to-be-explained, not the event itself. The *explanans* is the class of sentences that account for the explanation of the event, and falls into two subcategories: one contains sentences $C_1, C_2, \ldots, C_k$, which are side conditions, and the other is a set of sentences $L_1, L_2, \ldots, L_r$, which represent general laws. Because the explanation is based on a *logical deduction* of the explanandum from antecedent conditions and general laws (nomological theses) this particular mode of explanation became known as the deductive-nomological mode of explanation. To better understand this distinction both the authors have suggested a figure that became very popular in the philosophy of science (see Figure 11.2).

However, for an explanation to be considered sound, its constituents must comply to several logical and empirical conditions of adequacy (Hempel and Oppenheim 1948/1998: 208 f.): (1) the explanandum must be logically deducible from the antecedent conditions and the general laws; (2) the explanans must contain at least one general law which is actually applied for the derivation of the explanandum; (3) the explanans must have empirical content, i.e. it must be empirically testable; (4) both the antecedent conditions and the general laws must be true.

Originally, Hempel and Oppenheim proposed their approach to explain *particular facts*, both in the natural and in the social sciences. Later, Hempel (1965) developed a more sophisticated model of explanation, which should also account for the explanation of *general regularities*. The explanation of a general regularity should be made by subsuming it under a more comprehensive general law and applying the same DN mode of explanation (cf. Hempel and Oppenheim 1948/1998: 207).

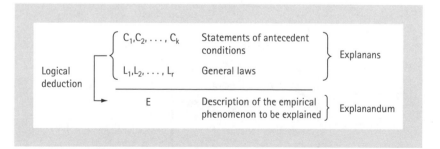

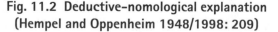

**Fig. 11.2 Deductive–nomological explanation
(Hempel and Oppenheim 1948/1998: 209)**

However, Hempel also realized that not all explanations of empirical events make use of deterministic laws. Instead, both in the natural and in the social sciences researchers have to deal with probabilistic or statistical events that cannot be explained with general laws, but with statistical laws. Hempel (1965) proposed an *inductive-statistical explanation* (IS), which explains particular events by subsuming them under statistical laws, much as DN explanations are derived from general laws. There is, however, an important difference. While in a DN explanation the event to be explained is deductively certain, an IS explanation delivers only an inductive support for the particular event whose expectability depends on the statistical probability of the truth of the constituents of the explanans (cf. Salmon 1998: 243). Just like the IS explanation that covers particular events, Hempel (1965) proposed also a *deductive-statistical explanation* (DS) to explain statistical regularities by deduction from more comprehensive statistical laws. These different modes of explanation proposed by Hempel can be organized into a 2 × 2 matrix. According to Hempel's view, any legitimate scientific explanation should fit into one of the four fields in Figure 11.3.

It is apparent that many textbooks of social research and even those which explicitly emphasize the philosophy of social science often mention the DN mode only. However, as Hempel and Oppenheim (1948/1998: 211) admitted, in the social sciences 'the regularities invoked cannot be stated with the same generality and precision as in physics or chemistry'. Therefore, social scientists usually draw on the IS and DS modes of explanation.

The explanation model proposed by Hempel is embedded in the long tradition of logical empiricism (Carnap, Hahn, and Neurath 1929/1973; Nagel 1961; Neurath 1934/1983) and critical rationalism (Popper 1935/1959), which both contributed to the development of the so-called *subject-object model of research* (SO model). The SO model is the result of the attempt to describe the underlying epistemology of the natural sciences in order to establish a universal philosophy of science ('*Einheitswissenschaft*', Carnap, Hahn, and Neurath 1929/1973) that should be the basis of all sciences. Although the aforementioned philosophers did not agree in all respects, it

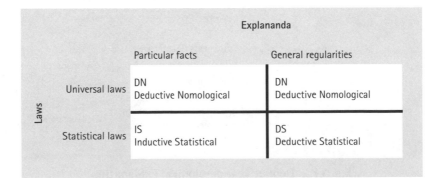

Fig. 11.3. Hempelian models of explanation (from Salmon 1998: 248)

is appropriate here to summarize their basic ideas in such a model. The SO model here qualifies as a more comprehensive philosophical framework in order to understand the essential characteristics of the DN mode better and the critical issues that will be discussed in the subsequent chapter. In core, the SO model can be described as follows (cf. Kunneman 1991: 20; Scherer 1995: 99 ff.).

1. 'Reality' already exists independently of our knowledge of it (realism). Both the natural and the social worlds are made up of general laws, which determine the course of events and the behavior of individuals. In this sense, reality is objectively *given* to the inquirer *(ontological basic assumption)*.

2. Human beings can, in principle, acquire knowledge about reality and its structure. The inquirer attains knowledge about reality by *systematic observations*. On the basis of prior observations, the scientist formulates hypotheses, i.e. general or statistical laws and deductive derivations from these laws, which are subject to further empirical tests. Theories that survive empirical tests can provide for a causal explanation of phenomena of the real world *(epistemological basic assumption)*.

3. The scientific method supplies rules, with whose assistance a learning process can be started up and controlled (Popper 1935/1959, 1969, 1972). In this way a process is started, which constantly increases the available knowledge of nature and culture. This knowledge, formulated in theories about the social and natural worlds, asymptotically approximates reality *(methodological basic assumption)*.

4. The accumulation of knowledge obtained with the help of this learning process not only enables explanation of phenomena, but also predictions that allow for better problem solutions and social progress. What begins as a rationalization process in the sciences, continues in the rationalization of society. Such rationalization, however, refers only to the *technical dimension;* the legitimacy of social norms is independent of scientific activity (value-free thesis) *(philosophical basic assumption)*.

Both the DN model of explanation and the SO model of research as a comprehensive philosophical framework are the bases of *contingency theory*, which is still one of the most favored schools of thought within OT (Donaldson 1996*a,b*). The main argument of contingency theory is that organizational structure is determined by certain contingencies, such as the environment (Burns and Stalker 1961; Lawrence and Lorsch 1967), internal technology (Woodward 1965), size (Blau 1970; Pugh et al. 1969), or strategy (Chandler 1962). Although these initial researches each focused on different factors, the implicit assumption of contingency theorists is that these results can be aggregated to an overall contingency theory with multiple dimensions of organization structure (explanandum), which can be deductively explained by various contingency factors and law-like relationships (explanans). The purpose is to find '[g]eneral causal relationships in the form of law-like regularities ... between contingency and structural factors' (Donaldson 1996*a*: 3).

It is thanks to Lex Donaldson (1996*a*, *b*) that the underlying assumptions of contingency theory have been made explicit so clearly: 'organizations are to be explained by scientific laws in which the shape taken by organizations is determined by material factors.... These laws hold generally across organizations of all types and national cultures. The organization adopts a structure that is required by the imperatives of its situation' (Donaldson 1996*a*: 1). This underlying *theory of structural adaptation* is based on the assumption that the organization must adapt to the contingency factors in order to operate effectively. Seen in this way contingency theory is also a *functionalist theory* (Donaldson 1996*a*), though, as we will see later, based on a narrow conception of functionalism (Gresov and Drazin 1997). Also, the naturalistic character of contingency theory is explicitly stated by Donaldson (1996*a*: 3): 'The theory is scientific in style, with the aim being to produce scientific knowledge of the type achieved in the natural sciences.'

11.4 ALTERNATIVE MODES OF EXPLANATION AND THEIR CONSEQUENCES FOR ORGANIZATION THEORY: INTERPRETIVISM, CRITICAL THEORY, AND POSTMODERNISM

The subject-object model is widely accepted both in the natural and in the social sciences. However, for a long time there has already been an anti-naturalistic tradition in the social sciences which emphasizes methodical and normative deficits of the subject-object model and offers alternative approaches to the study of social phenomena, such as phenomenology (Vaitkus 2000), hermeneutics (Bleicher 1980; Outhwaite 1975), symbolic interactionism (Joas 1987; Plummer 2000), critical theory (Held 1980; Morrow and Brown 1994; Outhwaite 1994), and postmodernism (Smart 2000) (for overviews, see e.g. Giddens 1976; Habermas 1971/1990; Kunnemann 1991: 96 ff.; Steffy and Grimes 1986). These approaches have been picked up by students of Organization Theory who were uncomfortable with the naturalistic approach to the social sciences. In OT these developments led to the increasing adaptation of *interpretive approaches* (cf. e.g. Daft and Weick 1984; Isabella 1990; Osterloh 1993; Smircich and Stubbart 1985), on the one hand, and the attempt to emphasize *normative-ethical questions* (cf. e.g. Alvesson and Willmott 1992, 1995; Deetz 1995; Freeman and Gilbert 1988; Shrivastava 1986; Steffy and Grimes 1986; Steinmann and Löhr 1994; Steinmann and Scherer 2000), on the other. While interpretivism and critical theory each propose a distinct mode of explanation, postmodern philosophy is based on the premiss that this is not an appropriate task. *Postmodern philosophy* questions whether science deserves a prominent status at all and proposes that research, at its best, is just another form of expression of humankind, on the same footing as art, music, or poetry; or, at its worse, scientific research is an unjustified use of power (see e.g. Feyerabend 1987). However, it is very difficult to define a common core of postmodern thinking, since the diversity of approaches under this label made the concept of postmodernism rather vague (Norris 2000).

11.4.1 Interpretivism

An important line of criticism is aimed at the *methodological aspects* of the subject-object model. Here the argument is that a natural science approach is not appropriate for explaining social phenomena. The natural scientist is working with inanimate matter, where (observable) occurrences can be produced under controlled conditions such as experiments. The justification of theories can be based on empirical tests. Their claim to law-like generalizations is ultimately founded on the replication of results. By contrast, anti-naturalists claim that the social sciences are dealing with research 'objects' that are *acting and talking* (Bohman 1991; Hollis 1994; Rosenberg 1995). The 'object' of the social sciences, i.e. any social reality that is to be explained, is constructed by communication and emerges and develops during the research process ('hermeneutic circle'). This process is not fully controllable by the researcher (Giddens 1976; Taylor 1971). Seen this way, the so-called 'object of research' in the social sciences is a reality enacted by human beings. By having created their own history, they demonstrate their *subjectivity*.

Therefore, an objective, neutral approach from the perspective of the outside observer is not feasible, as the *meanings of actions and expressions* cannot be opened up in this way (Beck 1975; Evered and Louis 1981; Habermas 1966, 1968/1971, 1971/1990, 1981/1984–87, 1983/1990b, Taylor 1971). Consequently, *interpretive methods*, which are based on *understanding* ('Verstehen'), are suggested as an alternative mode of explanation for the social sciences (for an overview, cf. Giddens 1976; Habermas 1983/1990b; Osterloh 1993: 76 ff.; Outhwaite 1975). This mode of explanation follows the tradition of hermeneutics, that is the text interpretation in the *Geisteswissenschaften* (human sciences) (Dilthey 1926; Husserl 1936/1970; Schütz 1932/1972; Taylor 1971). Such an approach accounts for the subjectivity of the research 'object' by trying to comprehend the meanings of the actions and communications from the perspective of particular actors.

During the 1970s in the OT literature these ideas became prominent when several doubts were articulated about the DN mode of explanation in general and about contingency theory in particular (cf. e.g. Benson 1977; Clegg and Dunkerly 1980;

Schreyögg 1978; Silverman 1970; Zey-Ferrell 1981). The suggested alternative approaches took account of the above-mentioned philosophical criticism concerning methods and (as we will see below) research interest aspects. In contrast to contingency theory, these approaches treat the organization as an entity that is preserved and changed basically by cultural and political processes. While the contingency approach is looking for objective laws that determine the behavior of individuals, who are unconscious of the driving forces of social behavior, the alternative approaches show that organizations are working according to rules, which are *created and developed* by the actions of the individuals themselves (cf. Benson 1977). From this perspective, the organizational reality is not objectively determined, but it is the result of a *social construction* (cf. Reed 1992: 249).

In such a perspective, the ontological basic assumption of the subject-object model, i.e. realism, is abandoned (cf. Chia 1997; Steffy and Grimes 1986). The entities in the world do not have a meaning on their own, their meaning is rather ascribed by *processes of interpretation*. Organization Theory has to take these issues into account. For the investigation of interpretation processes it is necessary to comprehend the subjective meanings leading the actors in their constructions of organizational reality. However, in his or her investigations, the researcher does not simply understand the reality enacted by the organizational members (first order reality). Instead, he or she also *creates* a reality, i.e. a second order reality, through his/her interpretation of actors' meaningful actions. The problem therefore is how can the research process be directed in such a way that the results at least 'approximate' first order reality, or at least give a reasonable account of first order reality in an anti-realistic sense.

Former contributions to interpretive theory, such as idealism, phenomenology, or hermeneutics (Dilthey 1926; Husserl 1936/1970; Schütz 1932/1972), assumed that the researcher can approach social reality as such and can perceive its true and objective meaning in a monological way, like a divine spectator. By contrast, Heidegger (1927/1996) and Gadamer (1960/1975) reject the idea that meaning can be perceived objectively and directly. Instead, an interpreter uses a frame of reference that is constituted by social practices and traditions in which he/she is embedded (Gadamer 1960/1975). In contemporary interpretive theory monological approaches are abandoned and are now substituted by dialogical approaches where meaning is constituted in a symmetrical communicative process between the researcher and the acting (and speaking) subject (Habermas 1983/1990b; Steffy and Grimes 1986). The objectivity of an interpretation is not based on a comparison between the interpretation and the object of interpretation; rather objectivity is based on the *consensus* between the actor and the interpreter (Habermas 1983/1990b). For such an endeavor the researcher has to adopt a *participating point of view* (Beck 1975; Evered and Louis 1981; Habermas 1983/1990b; Scherer and Dowling 1995).

However, how could the *interpretive mode of explanation* be adequately characterized? It is based on the assumption that social realities are not given as 'hard facts' and cannot be explored accordingly, but rather they have to be constructed and interpreted by the members of a social community. Consequently, social phenomena are not seen as objective entities, but as norms and meanings, which are evolving by the deeds of the actors. The researcher therefore does not adopt the role of the objective observer, as in the SO model, but takes a participating perspective, where he or she tries to come to terms with the subjective meanings of the actors. The investigator thus has to interpret the interpretation of the actors ('double hermeneutics') (cf. Giddens 1976). While the (natural) scientist usually wants to support his or her theories by large samples and quantitative data, the interpretative researcher undertakes one or a few case studies, in which theories should be generated by conducting qualitative in-depth interviews (see e.g. Isabella 1990). The interpretative researcher collects data, which are relevant for the actors involved in the examined case study and tries to receive them as authentically as possible (from first hand) (see Gioia and Pitre 1990). This procedure has a rather inductive character: the researcher tries to be unbiased at the beginning and does not formulate a starting hypothesis at this stage of investigation. Hypotheses should be generated in the process of research interview and then be tested by means of repeated interviews with the (same) respondents. In a prize-winning paper Isabella (1990) gave an excellent example of such an approach. In her paper, she set out to investigate how key managers construe organizational events during change processes and, through case studies, she tried to explain (i.e. understand) why and how certain interpretations had been adopted.

In spite of all these methodological differences with the SO model, the interpretative researcher is still interested in the explanation and thus (at least implicitly) in the *preservation of social order*. No attempt is made to deal with problems of social conflicts and legitimization of social change. Instead, the interpretive researcher deals with questions concerning how actors' subjective meanings and the corresponding processes of interpretation are creating particular social rules and norms (cf. Burrell and Morgan 1979: 31 and 279). Both the interpretive mode of explanation and the DN mode share an orientation toward the status quo of a social order and not at its criticism and possible improvements (cf. Burrell and Morgan 1979; Steffy and Grimes 1986; Willmott 1990: 47).

11.4.2 Critical Theory

While the interpretive approach emphasizes the methodical deficits of the DN mode of explanation, there is also a line of criticism that attacks its underlying normative assumptions. The *normative criticism* questions the social-philosophical basic assumptions of the subject-object model. Here the crucial issue is that social science research based on the SO model, through its results, only reflects the interests of the most powerful interest groups in society, by providing them with the socio-technical means to preserve their power. Other interests are only taken into account as long as they are functional for preserving the status quo of the current distribution of power in society. Within the subject-object model a critical reflection of the status quo of social systems is rejected on grounds of the value-free thesis (Burrell and Morgan 1979). As a result, the social sciences are not open for an explicit discussion of questions which have always been implicitly taken for granted, i.e. the basic assumptions about what is considered 'good' and 'bad' in our social world and, also, the problem of how a social conflict should be resolved and which interests should be heard. The DN mode of explanation, therefore, does not serve neutral ('objective') research interests, but is always implicitly in the service of a specific interest—the interest to make the world *technically controllable*. In contrast, critical theory tries to support an *emancipatory interest*. This means, that scientific work should also be able to criticize the existing social conditions and their present distribution of power (Habermas 1966, 1968/1971; Mumby 1988; Steffy and Grimes 1986; Willmott 1997).

Though critical theory is directed mainly against the positivist model of research, it also considers the deficits of the interpretive approach in the social sciences (Habermas 1971/1990, 1981/1984–1987).[3] In particular, critical theory rejects the conservative, status-quo preserving attitude of both naturalism and interpretivism. The value-free thesis for science cannot be justified. Instead, critical theory claims that any research project is driven by research interests ('knowledge-constructive interests') (Habermas 1968/1971). Social research based on the subject-object model of research ('empirical-analytical sciences') is governed by a *technical interest* in the prediction and control of objectified processes. The historical-hermeneutical sciences are governed by a *practical interest* in intersubjective understanding. Habermas (1968/1971) adds to these knowledge-constructive interests the *emancipatory interest* of critical theory. It is the purpose of critical theory 'to discover which (if any) theoretical statements express unchangeable laws of social action and which, though they express relations of dependence, because they are ideologically fixed, are in principle subject to change' (Habermas 1966: 294).

The socio-critical arguments in philosophy led to a major turn in Organization Theory, in the 1970s. Slowly, the idea was emerging that survival in social systems cannot be explained in the same way as the survival of biological entities. The 'survival of social systems' is rather *culturally defined* than determined by universal social laws (cf. Habermas 1971: 150 f.). As power processes and interests of participating actors play a significant role, this definition has to be seen as a process of

---

[3] For an interesting discussion between proponents of interpretivism and critical theory, see Putnam *et al.* 1993.

political interference (cf. Benson 1977). Following this line of argument, OT scholars began to discuss *who* should be allowed to define survival in social systems and the necessary means for this purpose. This discussion questions the basis of legitimacy of social authority. Hence, the research interest shifts from social orders, their functioning and survival conditions to the *legitimization of the social order* itself (Burrell and Morgan 1979; Clegg and Dunkerly 1980). This means that not only the methodological shortcomings of the ontological assumptions of contingency theorists are discovered, but also the legitimacy of their technical research interest is doubted. While it was generally accepted in the 1960s and early 1970s that an increase in the productivity of an organization automatically leads to an improvement of social conditions, these normative assumptions were more and more questioned by the end of the 1970s (Clegg 1981; Clegg and Dunkerly 1980; Silverman 1970). These early attempts were followed by a stream of research that is now known as 'critical management studies' (e.g. Alvesson 1987; Alvesson and Willmott 1992, 1995, 1996; Alvesson and Deetz 1996, 2000; Deetz 1995), which focuses on the critique of mainstream, i.e. positivist, management, and organization theories.

Is there a particular critical theory mode of explanation?—The answer to this question is 'yes', though this mode itself is not easy to explain (Morrow and Brown 1994; Steffy and Grimes 1986). Critical theory uses much of the interpretive mode of explanation but adds a normative dimension (Habermas 1981/1984–7). As far as the understanding and critique of social actions and institutions is concerned, one has to show the normative basis of critique. Habermas claims that there can be no universal ethical criteria from which one could (monologically) deduce what is right or what is wrong and can objectively measure the ethical rationality of actions or institutions. Rather, truth and legitimation of actions, practices, and institutions can only be determined in an uncoerced discourse by those concerned. However, the social scientist can also take the role of a *critical interpreter* and, at any rate, he/she must give up the position of a neutral (objective) observer, which, as the critique of the subject-object model has shown, is unsustainable. Instead, like in the interpretive approach, the researcher must take a *participatory point of view* instead (Scherer and Dowling 1995): In Habermas's words:

By taking part in communicative action, they [interpreters] accept in principle the same status as those whose utterances they are trying to understand. No longer immune to the affirmative or negative positions by experimental subjects or lay persons, interpreters give themselves over a process of reciprocal critique. Within a process of reaching understanding, actual or potential, it is impossible to decide a priori who has to learn from whom. (Habermas 1983/1990b: 26)

However, unlike in the interpretive approach the critical scientist need not simply accept the propositions of the actor (Scherer and Dowling 1995). Rather, he or she can question its truth and legitimacy through a rational dialogue. Both the researcher and the actor can enter a symmetrical discourse (rational dialogue) in which the *consensus* (as long as it is achieved) will determine what is true or what is right and can be considered ethically sound (Habermas 1973, 1981/1984–7, 1983/1990*a*).

Habermas (1973, 1983/1990*a*) has tried to determine and to justify the special conditions under which such a discourse has to take place. In contemporary philosophy it is at issue what philosophical status his justification has and whether these conditions can count as *universally* valid, or whether they are *culture-bound* (Habermas 1988/1993; Rorty 1985; Steinmann and Scherer 1998).

11.4.3 Postmodernism

Another two lines of methodical criticism of the subject-object model are stated in the light of the so-called '*historical turn*' of the philosophy of science and in the *postmodern movement in philosophy*. Though these two discourses differ in their arguments they share compatible results. The philosopher Thomas Kuhn (1962, 1970) demonstrates in his research that scientific progress cannot be explained by applying a consistent method. In fact, significant progress is often taking place when established methods are abandoned, when mindsets and procedures are employed, which seem to be irrational in the light of the mainstream methods. Kuhn also made popular the notion of 'incommensurability' in the philosophy of science (see also Scherer and Steinmann 1999). His study suggests that there is no measure available to evaluate objectively the methods and findings of competing research paradigms. Instead, what can count as 'true', or as an appropriate methodology, depends on the assumptions of a particular paradigm and is, therefore, historically contingent. This 'historical turn' in the philosophy of science not only gave way to a skepticism in the social sciences where the concept of an objective science is abandoned (Megill 1994; Natter, Schatzki, and Jones 1995), but even questioned the appropriateness of science as a rational endeavor (Feyerabend 1987). Postmodern philosophy draws a similar conclusion.

It is not easy to define the term '*postmodernism*'. On the one hand, the use of this word is not coherent in the literature (Boje et al. 1996; Calás and Smireich 1997; Hassard 1993*a,b*; Kilduff and Mehra 1997; Norris 2000); on the other hand, any fixed definition would contradict one of the basic ideas of postmodern philosophy. However, one could distinguish between 'postmodernism' as an *epoch*, 'postmodernity' as some writers would name it, and 'postmodernism' as a *new form of epistemology* ('postmodern philosophy') (Hassard 1993*a*, *b*; Parker 1992). In order to characterize a postmodern mode of explanation, if possible at all, we need to focus here on the latter use of this concept.

Postmodern philosophy rejects any realist notion of the world and of knowledge about the world. Instead it is argued that the world and any knowledge about the world 'is constituted by our shared language and that we can only "know the world" through the particular forms of discourse our language creates' (Hassard 1993a: 3). This argument is rather similar to that made by interpretivists and critical theorists. It echoes the Wittgensteinian idea that we cannot learn a language and understand any sentences unless we take part in the form of life in which the language is used (Wittgenstein 1953). People participate in different language games that define the rules of how to use words. People learn these rules and become able to 'play' within a language game, i.e. to communicate with and to understand each other.

However, there is a crucial difference. Both, interpretivism and critical theory assume that despite differences in interpretations one can, at least in principle, come to a shared understanding and agreement about organizational reality through an uncoerced discourse that eventually leads to consensus (Habermas 1973, 1981/1984–7). By contrast, postmodernism rejects any attempt for unity and consensus: consensus is thought to be the unjustified suppression of the pluralism of interpretations and forms of life. Instead, for postmodernists, there can only be *local truths*, which depend on the different language games we are playing. These language games each define *different criteria* of what should count as true and just. Modern science tries to establish a meta-discourse in order to define a privileged position for itself—a position over and above all language games (Lyotard 1984). Seen from a postmodern perspective such a position is both not feasible and unjustifiable. Instead of consensus, postmodernism is focused on *differences* and the *preservation of the pluralism of language games*. Postmodernism 'refines our sensitivity to differences and reinforces our ability to tolerate the incommensurable. Its principle is not the expert's homology, but the inventor's paralogy' (Lyotard 1984: p. xxv).

What is the source of and what is the method used by postmodern critique? Postmodernism tries to show how superficial the normative structures of our social world are (Hassard 1993a). To do so, Derrida (1973, 1976) suggests his *deconstructive approach* which can be used to identify implicit and inherent contradictions residing in any text. In addition, he proposes his concept of '*differance*' to reveal that any symbol signifies a certain object but, at the same time, differs from this object. This concept should support more reflexivity and self-critique in research.

Seen in this way, postmodernism is not so much a new mode of explanation in order to generate knowledge, but more of a new form of discourse in order to criticize what counts as established knowledge and a plea for reflexivity. However, as opponents of postmodernism claim, postmodernism lacks a normative theory of social interactions (Habermas 1985/1990; Norris 2000; Thompson 1993; Willmott 1998). According to these scholars postmodernism only attacks established forms of (social) knowledge without offering an alternative.

11.5 SOCIETY, INSTITUTIONS, AND THE EMBEDEDDNESS OF SOCIAL ACTION: FUNCTIONALISM VS. RATIONAL CHOICE THEORY

For OT, both the DN mode and the interpretive mode of explanation are too narrow a concept of explanation. Both focus on methodological issues and suggest different ways of how to explain individual behavior. Neither positivism nor interpretivism develop a theory of social institutions, though they may be linked to a theory of society (Burrell and Morgan 1979). However, for the social sciences in general and for OT in particular it is indispensable to consider the relationships between individual behavior and social institutions more closely. The question here is whether individual behavior is (more or less) determined by social structures (such as, e.g., societies, organizations, cultures, etc.) or whether individual behavior enacts or constitutes social structures (Giddens 1984; Vanberg 1975).

In the social sciences there is an ongoing dispute over which of these assumptions is correct (Giddens 1984; Rosenberg 1995). In this section we will discuss two prominent positions, functionalism (or 'holism') and Rational Choice Theory (RCT), which suggest different modes of explanation for understanding how individual behavior and social institutions are linked together. Both develop distinct assumptions for a theory of society. They provide important foundations for current theories of organization and help to understand how social order is possible at all.

Functionalism and RCT are counterparts in the question of social order. *Functionalism* argues for a *holistic theory of society*. Society has characteristics of its own that cannot be fully explained by individual behavior; rather, individual behavior crucially depends on social characteristics, sustained by supra-individual institutions: 'The members of a society are governed by social forces that exist independent of them. The behavior of individuals is determined by norms of conduct of which we are not aware. These norms are imposed on us by social institutions, which determine the degree of social integration of a society's members' (Rosenberg 1995: 132).

By contrast, proponents of *Rational Choice Theory* favor *methodological individualism*. They argue that there are not 'social facts'. Instead, any social phenomenon can be derived from individual behavior. For a methodological individualist, society is nothing but a collection of atomic individuals. In the following we will describe both of these positions.

11.5.1 Functionalism

The so-called *functional explanation* has been discussed in the social sciences for over a hundred years (e.g. Durkheim 1893/1984, 1895/1965; Spencer 1898). It has to be distinguished from the causal mode of explanation, e.g. the DN model. However, it is at issue whether the functional explanation is simply a special case of the causal explanation or whether the causal explanation is to be regarded as a special case of functional explanation (cf. Luhmann 1962, 1964; Gresov and Drazin 1997).

The concept of the functional explanation was developed mainly by Herbert Spencer (1898) and Emile Durkheim (1895/1965). For both, social systems, such as society, social groups, organizations, etc., have a distinct identity that is different from the parts or individuals that constitute it, i.e. there are 'social facts' (Durkheim 1895/1965) that cannot be fully explained in terms of the behavior of individuals. Instead, social phenomena can be explained by showing their *function* in the constitution and maintenance of social order. To do so, social functional analysis must classify social units or wholes: 'So functionalism is both an analytical strategy for identifying socially significant institutions and an explanatory strategy that accounts for institutions' characteristics by appeal to their effects for society as a whole' (Rosenberg 1995: 144).

Functionalism assumes that there are significant parallels between societies and organisms. For the survival of an organism, its parts have to contribute certain functions that are indispensable. In a similar way, 'functionalist' social sciences try to explain social phenomena by showing that they contribute to the operation of a social system, i.e. that they represent a necessary condition for the existence of a social system. In addition, functionalism shares with biology an evolutionary concept of development. This is based on the premiss that, like in the natural world, in the social world there are external forces that determine which institutions or structural alternatives 'fit' better. These external forces are part of a selection mechanism that will select superior structural alternatives and will lead to a higher evolutionary level. As we have seen above, this assumption is also made by contingency theory and its underlying theory of structural adaptation (Donaldson 1996*a*, *b*; Gresov and Drazin 1997).

These considerations were suggested in different variations of functionalism of which modern systems theory (Luhmann 1984/1995) is the latest one (for an overview, see Burrell and Morgan 1979: 41 ff.; Hollis 1994: 130 ff.; Lechner 2000: 112 ff.; Merton 1957: 19 ff.). Among these, first of all, there is the original functionalist analysis explained by Durkheim (1893/1984, 1895/1965), who is more strongly committed to the methods of the natural sciences than his subsequent functionalist followers. Durkheim assumes that, like in the natural sciences, in the social sciences there are general laws for explaining social phenomena. He considers social functions as effects and infers from functions certain observable social phenomena, e.g. certain organizational structures or institutions, which are regarded as implicit causes. This mode of explanation is based on the assumption that for survival, social systems must meet certain requirements, i.e. they must fulfill societal functions that are completely determined by the environment. Moreover it is based on the premiss that there is only one structural design alternative available for the fulfillment of a function ('postulate of indispensability', cf. critically Merton 1957: 32 ff.; Gresov and Drazin 1997). Therefore, the survival and maintenance of social systems necessarily implies certain structural features, *without* conceivable alternatives. As we have seen, contingency theory is based on this assumption (Donaldson 1996*a*, *b*).

With such a deterministic view, however, social order cannot be explained sufficiently (Rosenberg 1995). At the same time, the postulate of indispensability contradicts with everyday experience where latitude is the rule (Gresov and Drazin 1997). Obviously, there are several problems with this point of view. First, the concept of 'function' is not sufficiently defined (Rosenberg 1995). In many social studies it is linked to the survival of a system. However, it is not clear what is meant by the 'survival of social systems' (Luhmann 1962). Unlike in biology, in the social sciences there is no clear-cut criterion for the 'death' of a social system. Instead, the well-being of society is *normatively defined* and it varies from culture to culture. Functionalists who argue that their theories are value-free, are unable to justify any claim about the normative condition of a particular society (cf. Burrell and Morgan 1979; Habermas 1981/1984–7; Rosenberg 1995: 145). In addition, the definition of a certain function is somehow artificial and arbitrary. It seems that any social occurrences that are observable could finally be explained by a 'function' they allegedly fulfill. This is especially true, when social analysis claims to identify any 'deeper' social functions as is the case in ideological critique of Marxian sociology. Thus, one might argue, functional theories are 'empirically empty': 'Nothing will refute the hypothesis that the institution has some function or another' (Rosenberg 1995: 150).

Second, it is not clear why there should not be alternative institutional solutions ('functional equivalents') available, which are suitable to meet the functional requirements as well. For this reason the proponents of the *new systems theory* want to shift the analysis, in order to better explain the formation of structure (cf. Lechner 2000; Luhmann 1962; Willke 1991: 3 ff.). The deterministic thinking in terms of causality is to be overcome by the *analysis of functional equivalents* (cf. Luhmann 1962; Merton 1957, 1967; Gresov and Drazin 1997). This is possible in two ways: on the one hand, it can illuminate the space of possible causes in view of a fixed effect; on the other hand, it can examine the space of possible (intended and unintended) effects in view of a fixed cause. Thus the newer systems theory tries to examine alternative structural designs in their contribution for the preservation of the boundary between a social system and its environment ('purpose programming'). Alternatively, certain causes can be fixed by 'conditional programming' and be brought up for discussion in their possible effects and side effects (cf. Luhmann 1973).

In such a functional analysis the concept of 'function' is modified. It is not understood as an 'effect' which can be caused, but as 'a regulative interpretative schema', which organizes an aspect of comparison of equivalent performances (Luhmann 1962: 14, translation by the author). Seen from this perspective, the 'causal explanation' of the DN model (e.g. contingency theory) with its one-by-one correspondence between cause (e.g. contingency factor) and effect (e.g. structure) appears to be only a special case of a broader model of functional explanation (cf. Luhmann 1962; Gresov and Drazin 1997).

However, functionalist social science is accused of a conservative attitude (cf. Rosenberg 1995: 145), because it does not take social change sufficiently into consideration (cf. Burrell and Morgan 1979; Dahrendorf 1961) or does not analyze the legitimacy of social structures and the power processes influencing social structures and change processes (Habermas 1971, 1981/1984–7). Here, critical management studies, which is still too much focused on micro issues, could catch up and deliver a distinct, i.e. normative theory of business and society (Habermas 1981/1984–7). However, this would be a brand new endeavor within OT. As far as I have seen, a critical theory of institutions has yet to be developed in Organization Theory (Habermas 1992/1996).

11.5.2 Rational Choice Theory

Rational choice theory (RCT) develops a mode of explanation that can be seen as a counterpart to functionalism or holism (for an overview, see e.g. Bohman 1991: 146 ff.; Hollis 1994: 106 ff.; Rosenberg 1995: 124 ff.; Vanberg 1975). For some scholars are confident in claiming that 'rational choice theory has arguably proven to be the most successful theoretical framework in those social sciences which, like sociology, deal with explanations of macro or system-level phenomena' (Abell 2000: 223).

It is true that rational choice models are very advanced in economics and have become popular in the past decades not only in Organization Theory, but in Sociology and Political Science in general. However, it has to be reconsidered whether this success is based merely on pragmatic grounds, e.g. it is just fashionable to adopt an economic approach, or whether there can be a theoretical argument put forward for the adoption of a rational choice perspective (see critically Kersting 2000; Kondylis 1999: 604 ff.; Scott 2000).

At a very abstract level this mode of explanation can be described as follows (Coleman 1986: 1320 ff.; 1990: 8 ff., see also Abell 2000: 227 ff.). RCT tries to explain social (macro-level) phenomena. To do so, Coleman (1990: 8 ff.) suggests distinguishing four types of relationships: (o) macro- or system-level relationships, for

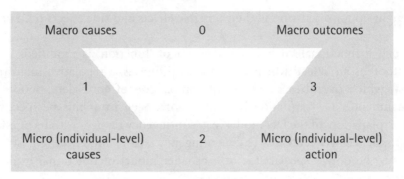

**Fig. 11.4 Macro- and micro-level interrelations (adapted from Coleman 1990: 8
with modifications by Abell 2000: 228 and by the author)**

example, relationships between organizations and society, which however cannot
be sufficiently explained directly; (1) macro-(or system-) level to micro-(or indi-
vidual-) level relationships—these can be relationships between societal structures
and individual preferences of organizational members; (2) micro to micro relationships—these can be, for example, relationships between individual preferences and
individual actions; and (3) micro to macro relationships, for example, between
individual actions and organization structure. Coleman's (1990) framework can be
seen in Figure 11.4.

For RCT, because of its underlying methodological individualism, explanations
of type 0 cannot be made directly, but are derived from a conjunction of the
other three types of explanation (cf. Coleman 1986: 1320 ff.; 1990: 8). Here it
shows that RCT tries to explain macro outcomes not simply by the existence
of 'social facts', but through mechanisms at the individual level. However, many
of the rational choice models proposed until today focus on explanations of type
3, for example, on how individual behavior causes certain institutional arrangements. Explanations of type 1 and 2 are taken into consideration more rarely, at
least the former one, and are combined only in the most advanced forms of RCT.
Type 2, for example, tries to explain how individual values (preferences) cause
individual action (e.g. Vroom 1964), e.g. certain economic behaviors, while
type 1 causally tries to explain the causes of individual values (Fehr and Gächter
2000).

RCT is based on the following three assumptions (Abell 2000: 231):

1. *Methodological individualism:* Unlike Functionalism, rational choice
theory rejects the claim that there are 'social facts', as was suggested by Durkheim
(1895/1965). Instead, it is based on the premiss that social phenomena such as
social institutions or social change can be completely explained by individual
actions, i.e. as the result of individual action and social exchange (Elster 1989;
Homans 1958, 1961).

2. *Optimality:* an individual optimally chooses his or her actions considering his or her preferences and the opportunities he or she faces. Unlike neoclassical economics modern RCT proposes only a weak model of optimality: actors are not completely rational, instead they are 'satisficers' (Simon 1982), i.e. decisions are made under conditions of uncertainty and individuals do the best they can, given the circumstances of their actions as *they* see them.

3. *Self-regard:* the individuals act to satisfy their self-regarding preferences, i.e. they are completely concerned with their own welfare. This means that they intend to maximize their own welfare, though they are usually not able to make entirely rational decisions. While some scholars suggest that the self-regard assumption is an empirical matter, which can be tested (e.g. Abell 2000: 235; Falk 2001; Fehr and Gächter 2000), others insist that it is a methodological assumption without which any economic explanation would collapse into unacceptable tautology.

Unlike in Sociology (Coleman 1986, 1990; Friedman and Hechter 1988) or in the Political Sciences (Downs 1957), in Organization Theory RCT is not very often advocated explicitly, though the theories that are discussed in organizational economics are based on a rational choice mode of explanation. This is true for property rights theory, principal agency theory, transaction cost theory, and game theory, which achieved a prominent status in Organization Theory in the 1990s (see e.g. Barney and Hesterley 1996; Milgrom and Roberts 1992). In the following I will refer to some examples drawn from organizational economics in order to show how a rational choice explanation is developed.

Let us take for example the Alchian-Demsetz approach to *property rights theory* (cf. Barney and Hesterley 1996: 116 f.). Alchian and Demsetz (1972) develop a rational choice type of explanation of why organizations exist. As is well known, classical and neoclassical economic theories point to the pre-eminent ability of markets to coordinate economic behavior via the 'invisible hand' of a decentralized system of prices. Therefore, the puzzling question for economists is why not all exchanges are managed through markets; in other words: why there are firms at all? (Coase 1937). Alchian and Demsetz (1972) explain the existence of institutions such as organizations or firms in terms of the measurement problem there exists to determine the individual contribution of team members in situations of team production. In cases where individuals can produce more efficiently working cooperatively with one another than separately, the individuals on the one hand have an incentive to cooperate, i.e. to produce in teams, in order to achieve production gains. On the other hand, however, the individuals also have an incentive to shirk, i.e. they cheat or pretend to be doing their best, though they are not. In cases where it is difficult or even impossible to determine the contribution of each individual team member, it is rational to assign monitoring roles to certain individuals who monitor the efforts of each team member, so that marginal costs of monitoring equal marginal benefits from reduced shirking. In order to solve the problem of 'monitoring the monitors', it is necessary to create a strong incentive for the monitor for the effective assessment of the efforts of each team member. Alchian and Demsetz suggest that such an incentive can be determined, if the monitor (1) has the right to negotiate the contracts with all team members, (2) has the right to monitor them according to their individual efforts, and (3) finally receives a residual income based on the value created by the team. As monitors are assigned these roles, a hierarchy emerges. With this approach, Alchian and Demsetz (1972) explain structural arrangements at the macro level (the existence of a hierarchical organization or a firm) as a *result* of the rational behavior of economic actors at the micro-(individual-) level. Thus, their approach is a type 3 explanation in Coleman's (1990) terminology.

Another example for a rational choice mode of explanation is *transaction cost theory* (Coase 1937; Williamson 1975, 1985). In contrast to property rights theory, transaction cost theory does not try to explain the existence of a firm per se, but to *explain the choice between different institutional arrangements.* Williamson (1975) asserts that markets and hierarchies are alternative institutional arrangements for coordinating sets of transactions. Ouchi (1979, 1980) adds a third type of arrangement, clans, while more recently others have suggested a variety of intermediate forms (hybrids), such as network organizations, joint ventures, or franchises. Transaction cost theory is based on two assumptions concerning the rationality of economic actors. First, the actors are *boundedly rational* (Simon 1947); and second, actors need to take into consideration the *opportunistic behavior* of others, which includes not only lying, stealing, and cheating, but also misleading, distorting, and disguising in order to confuse the exchange partner and to achieve a personal advantage based on this confusion. Economic actors will choose the institutional arrangement with the lowest costs, taken into consideration, on the one hand, exchange problems created by bounded rationality and, on the other hand, the possibility of opportunism. Both problems lead to *transaction costs*, which can occur as ex-ante or ex-post costs. The former ones are costs of negotiating, drafting, and safeguarding a contract, while latter ones are maladaption costs, haggling costs, and bonding costs (Williamson 1985: 20 f.).

In cases of high levels of *uncertainty* it will be more difficult to use contracts to manage the transactions, i.e. sufficiently to anticipate occurring problems and their solutions in advance. Instead, in hierarchies a third party, i.e. an entrepreneur or a superordinate manager, can decide on the solution of unanticipated problems. Therefore, the creation of hierarchies may be the institutional arrangement that leads to lower transaction costs. The same applies to *transaction specific investments.* If a firm A invests in a specific relationship with another firm B to expedite the exchange, for example by modifying its technology, its policies, or procedures so that it is more suitable to the requirements of B, then firm B may behave opportunistically and threat to suspend business relationships with A if A is not willing to cut prices. Also, in this case, the choice of a hierarchy may effectively reduce this threat and will lead to lower transaction costs. Like the Alchian-Demsetz approach described above, transaction cost theory seeks to explain the existence of a given organizational structure, that is the institutional arrangement at the macro-level, through the rational choice of individual economic actors on the micro-level. Thus, transaction cost economics is also a type 3 explanation of rational choice theory.

Principal agency theory (Eisenhardt 1989; Jensen and Meckling 1976) could also be reconstructed as a rational choice mode of explanation. However, I will here now turn to *game theory* (Luce and Raiffa 1957; Myerson 1991; Neumann and Morgenstern 1948; Raub and Wessie 1992) as it introduces a remarkable difference compared to the economic approaches discussed so far. An important advantage of economic theories is that they take into account the *interdependence of actions*. However, the economic theories described so far only consider *parametric relationships*. This means that the focal actor does not 'calculate what others will do as a consequence of what he or she does or in anticipation of what he or she may do. The actor can take the action, and consequences therefore, of others as given. The action environment of the focal actor is unreactive to what he or she does except insofar as others may subsequently act paradigmatically with respect to the action (or consequences) of the focal actor's action' (Abell 2000: 237). By contrast game theory takes into consideration strategic actions. *Strategic social actions* are actions where the focal actor needs to calculate what others will do *dependent upon* his or her action. This approach, as some scholars will claim, is more suitable to the complexity of micro-macro mechanisms and allows for the explanation of dynamic social relationships (Abell 2000). Here the social environment is not given, but is *reactive* to what the focal actor does or is expected to do.

Game theory tries to model decision situations between two or more 'players' (n-person game theory) where the players mutually take into account the *expected* actions of each other under different side conditions. These side conditions can be characterized by several attributes: (1) by what is or is not known by the players (*complete or incomplete information*), (2) by the ability of the players to communicate with each other and to make binding agreements (*cooperative games*) or the impossibility of forming any coalitions (*non-cooperative games*), (3) and by the frequency of the decision situation (*non-repeated games or repeated games—finite and infinite times*). In cases where an equilibrium solution exists, i.e. a course of action that is advantageous to each individual player, game theory allows the observer to predict the actions which each rational player will take. Game theory tries to explain the emergence of *social norms*, i.e. a macro-level phenomenon, as the result of an exchange between rational players who take into account each others' actions, considering the side conditions described above. In case of repeated games it makes it possible to examine the dynamics of social structures. Therefore, game theory again provides an explanation of type 3, that is how macro outcomes can be explained by micro actions. However, game theory can be extended towards explanations of type 1 and 2. For example, repeated games theory makes it possible to explain the emergence of mutual *trust* and *reputation* (Kreps 1990). Recently, scholars have tried to combine game theory with auxiliary theories, such as evolutionary theory, neo-institutionalism (March and Olsen 1989; Ostrom 1990) or experimental economics (Falk 2001; Fehr and Gächter 2000). These developments at the intellectual frontier set out to explain the emergence of preferences and the possibility of social learning (Ostrom 1990).

Despite its success in the social sciences, rational choice theory has been an object of intense debate (e.g. Elster 1986/1997; Green and Shapiro 1994; Kersting 2000; Kondylis 1999: 604 ff.; Scott 2000; Zey 1998). Critics claim that RCT is unable to explain the cooperation of social actors. In particular, RCT has difficulties in explaining why rational actors form organizations in the first place, in cases where their continuous benefit is *not* guaranteed, or when they can benefit from the outcome of social institutions without any contribution to their constitution (free rider problem) (Hardin 1968; Olson 1971). In addition, the concept of individual rationality based on optimality and self-regard is considered too narrow a concept for the social sciences, since it does not take into account the wide and complex range of factors that influence the decisions of individuals in the social world (Kersting 2000; Kondylis 1999: 604 ff.). A rational choice explanation 'excludes the various meaning-relationships that are the bases of actions and fails to address the fact that actors make decisions to act on a number of complex bases, including group loyalty, trust, cooperation, legitimacy, and authority' (Zey 1998: 52 f.).

While adherents of RCT have tried to counter these issues (e.g. Ostrom 1990), they are, however, principally unable to resolve the *normative deficit* of RCT (e.g. Habermas 1992/1996, 1996/1998, 1998/2001; Kersting 2000). RCT is, at least implicitly, based on a liberal political philosophy that considers individual liberty as its highest value (Dworkin 1982). Social order and the public good are conceived as the aggregation of individual preferences and actions that are *not* subject to further critique. Individual preferences are taken as sacrosanct and are only restricted by the market, which is the medium of exchange not only in economics but also in the political sphere (Downs 1957; Elster 1986/1997). For RCT 'the goal of politics is the optimal compromise between given, and irreducibly opposed, private interests' (Elster 1986/1997: 128). However, such an approach is insufficient for a reasonable political conception that must lay the foundation of social order, i.e. of the state and the economy. To do so it is necessary to open up the *political forum* for a dialogue on how members of society shall live together. In such a dialogue, citizens must transcend their roles as self-regarding private actors ('bourgeois') and become, instead, 'citoyens' who define the public good collectively: 'collective rationality is the result of public and rational dialogue about the common good. In the political realm, a reasonable outcome is more likely when preferences are transformed, not when they are aggregated. The goal of politics should be unanimous and thoughtful consensus, not an optimal compromise between irreducibly opposed interests' (Zey 1998: 18).

RCT is based on the assumption that the proper conditions for market exchange could be determined by political processes that in the end should also be conceived as market exchanges (Downs 1957). However, such an approach would lead into an infinite regress. The market is not a natural state (Simon 1991), but has to be established by political institutions. Proper markets need powerful state institutions (Block 1994), as we have learned from the lessons of transition economies. As there is no clear-cut economic criterion for what counts as legitimate market conditions independently of legitimate forms of (state) regulation,[4] the answer to this question has to be found by a political process that goes beyond market exchange (Block 1994).

11.6 ORGANIZATION THEORY AS REASONABLE PRACTICE: NAVIGATING THROUGH THE PLURALISM OF MODES OF EXPLANATION

For the student of OT the question now is, which of the discussed modes of explanation are acceptable and which should be rejected. Obviously, the problem is how to find a *reasonable orientation* in this *pluralism of modes of explanation*. There are several opinions in current literature to answer that question (for an overview, see Scherer and Steinmann 1999). One position postulates that in comparison to, for example, economics or to the natural sciences, OT is still at a premature stage, which can be overcome in principle (Pfeffer 1993). Therefore, many theories based on different modes of explanation must be produced and subjected to systematical empirical tests. The theories that pass this test can be considered as 'corroborated' and contribute to the core (and advance) of knowledge. The pluralism of theories is not seen as ultimate but as an intermediate state, which is necessary and can be overcome with the help of a universal test procedure adopted from the natural sciences (Albert 1980/1985; Popper 1935/1959, 1969). This view is supported by a mode of explanation, the *deductive-nomological explanation*, which is however, as we have seen, only one possible type of knowledge creation, incompatible with other modes of explanation (e.g. interpretivism, critical theory, postmodernism).

---

[4] See e.g. the problem of child or slave labor which cannot be abandoned on economical grounds alone (Block 1994).

A different point of view sees both, the pluralism of theories *and* modes of explanations, as necessary for pointing out the ambiguous character of organizational phenomena. As Morgan has repeatedly remarked, 'organizations are many things at once' (Morgan 1986: 339). According to this point of view, the pluralism *should not* be overcome in order not to overlook any important aspect. This point of view is supported by authors who believe that there is no objective criterion available for comparing the different points of view, i.e. different modes of explanation (Burrell and Morgan 1979; Jackson and Carter 1991). These authors base their perception on the 'problem of incommensurability', which says that there are no objective criteria that allow for a critical comparison between radically different perspectives (for a critical overview, see Scherer 1998; Scherer and Dowling 1995; Scherer and Steinmann 1999). If those authors are right with their point of view, a critical reflection on organization theories (and philosophy of science) must be abandoned.

However, I do not think that this can and should be the last word. To overcome this problem, one must take a pragmatic approach and conceive 'doing research' as *action*. Based on this idea, the researcher intentionally follows his or her research interest. The selection of a mode of explanation can be considered as a way to pursue one's research objective. According to one's research goal one can determine whether a particular mode of explanation is more or less appropriate. This is, however, only the technical dimension of research. Moreover, one can also open up the normative dimension and critically consider whether a research goal is legitimate or not. To do so, however, one must abandon the value-free thesis, and make researchers accountable for what they do. This, finally, has consequences for the mode of explanation chosen: 'The proper form of explanation in the social sciences is both non-reductionist and non-determinist, treating phenomena that are not only diverse and irregular, but *intentional and complex*' (Bohman 1991: 6 f., emphasis added).

REFERENCES

ABELL, P. (2000). 'Sociological Theory and Rational Choice Theory', B. S. in Turner (ed.), *The Blackwell Companion to Social Theory*. Oxford: Blackwell.

ALBERT, H. (1980/1985). *Treatise on Critical Reason*. Princeton: Princeton University Press.

ALCHIAN, A. A., and DEMSETZ, H. (1972). 'Production, Information Costs, and Economic Organization'. *American Economic Review*, 62: 777–95.

ALDRICH, H. (1979). *Organizations and Environments*. Englewood Cliffs, NJ: Prentice-Hall.

ALTER, C., and HAGE, J. (1993). *Organizations Working Together*. Newbury Park, Calif.: Sage.

ALVESSON, M. (1987). *Organization Theory and Technocratic Consciousness*. Berlin and New York: DeGruyter.

—— and DEETZ, S. (1996). 'Critical Theory and Postmodernism Approaches to Organizational Studies', in S. R. Clegg, C. Hardy, and W. R. Nord, (eds.), *Handbook of Organization Studies*. London: Sage.

—— —— (2000). *Doing Critical Management Research*. London: Sage.

—— and WILLMOTT, H. (1992). 'On the Idea of Emancipation in Management and Organization Studies'. *Academy of Management Review*, 17: 432–64.

—— —— (1995). 'Strategic Management as Domination and Emancipation: From Planning and Process to Communication and Praxis'. *Advances in Strategic Management*, 12A: 85–112.

—— —— (1996). *Making Sense of Management: A Critical Introduction*. London: Sage.

ARGYRIS, C. (1964). *Integrating the Individual and the Organization*. New York: Wiley.

ASTLEY, W. G., and VAN DE VEN, A. H. (1983). 'Critical Perspectives and Debates in Organization Theory'. *Administrative Science Quarterly*, 28: 245–73.

BARNEY, J., and HESTERLEY, W. (1996). 'Organizational Economics: Understanding the Relationship between Organizations and Economic Analysis', in S. R. Clegg, C. Hardy, and W. R. Nord, (eds.), *Handbook of Organization Studies*. London: Sage.

BECK, L. W. (1975). *The Actor and the Spectator*. Clinton, Mass.: Colonial Press.

BENSON, J. K. (1977). 'Organizations: A Dialectical View'. *Administrative Science Quarterly*, 22: 1–21.

BLAU, P. M. (1970). 'A Formal Theory of Differentiation in Organizations'. *American Sociological Review*, 35/2: 201–18.

BLEICHER, J. (1980). *Contemporary Hermeneutics*. London: Routledge & Kegan Paul.

BLOCK, F. (1994). 'The Roles of the State in the Economy', in N. J. Smelser and R. Swedberg, (eds.), *The Handbook of Economic Sociology*. Princeton: Princeton University Press.

BOHMAN, J. (1991). *New Philosophy of Social Science*. Cambridge: Polity Press.

BOJE, D. M., GEPHART, R. P., Jr, and THATCHENKERY, T. J. (eds.) (1996). *Postmodern Management and Organization Theory*. London: Sage.

BURNS, T., and STALKER, G. M. (1961). *The Management of Innovation*. London: Tavistock Publ.

BURRELL, G., and MORGAN, G. (1979). *Sociological Paradigms and Organisational Analysis*. London: Heinemann.

CALÁS, M. B., and SMIRCICH, L. (eds.) (1997). *Postmodern Management Theory*. Aldershot: Dartmouth.

CARNAP, R., HAHN, H., and NEURATH, O. (1929/1973). 'Wissenschaftliche Weltauffassung: Der Wiener Kreis' [The Scientific Conception of the World: The Vienna Circle], M. Neurath and R. S. Cohen (eds.), *Empiricism and Sociology*. Dordrecht: Reidel.

CHANDLER, A. D. Jr (1962). *Strategy and Structure: Chapters in the History of the American Industrial Enterprise*. Cambridge, Mass.: MIT Press.

CHIA, R. (1997). 'Essai: Thirty Years On: From Organizational Structures to the Organization of Thought'. *Organization Studies*, 18: 685–707.

CHILD, J. (1972). 'Organizational Structure, Environment and Performance. The Role of Strategic Choice'. *Sociology*, 6: 1–22.

CLEGG, S. (1981). 'Organization and Control'. *Administrative Science Quarterly*, 26: 545–62.

—— and DUNKERLY, D. (1980). *Organization, Class and Control*. London: Routledge & Kegan Paul.

—— HARDY, C., and NORD, W. R. (eds.) (1996). *Handbook of Organization Studies*. London: Sage.

COASE, R. H. (1937). 'The Nature of the Firm'. *Economica*, 4: 386–405.

COLEMAN, J. S. (1986). 'Social Theory, Social Research, and a Theory of Action'. *American Journal of Sociology*, 91: 1309–35.

—— (1990). *Foundations of Social Theory*. Cambridge, Mass.: Belknap Press.

CONNELL, A. F., and NORD, W. R. (1996). 'The Bloodless Coup: The Infiltration of Organization Science by Uncertainty and Values'. *Journal of Applied Behavioral Science*, 32: 407–27.

DAFT, R. L., and LEWIN, A. Y. (1993). 'Where Are the Theories for the "New" Organizational Forms? An Editorial Essay'. *Organization Science*, 4: i–vi.

—— and WEICK, K. E. (1984). 'Toward a Model of Organizations as Interpretation Systems'. *Academy of Management Review*, 9: 284–95.

DAHRENDORF, R. (1961). *Gesellschaft und Freiheit*. Munich: Piper.

DEETZ, S. (1995). *Transforming Communication, Transforming Business: Building Responsible and Responsive Workplaces*. Cresshill, NJ: Hampton Press.

—— (1996). 'Describing Differences in Approaches to Organization Science: Rethinking Burrell and Morgan and their Legacy'. *Organization Science*, 7: 191–207.

DERRIDA, J. (1973). *Speech and Phenomena*. Evanston, Ill.: Northwestern University Press.

—— (1976). *Of Grammatology*. Baltimore: Johns Hopkins University Press.

DILTHEY, W. (1926). *Gesammelte Werke*. Stuttgart: Teubner.

DONALDSON, L. (1996a). *For Positivist Organization Theory: Proving the Hard Core*. London: Sage.

—— (1996b). 'The Normal Science of Structural Contingency Theory', in S. R. Clegg, C. Hardy, and W. R. Nord (eds.), *Handbook of Organization Studies*. London: Sage.

DOWNS, A. (1957). *An Economic Theory of Democracy*. New York: Harper Collins.

DURKHEIM, E. (1951). *Suicide*. New York: Free Press.

—— (1893/1984). *The Division of Labor in Society*. New York: Free Press.

—— (1895/1965). *The Rules of the Sociological Method*. New York: Free Press.

DWORKIN, R. (1982). 'Liberalism', M. Sandel (ed.), *Liberalism and its Critics*. Oxford: Basil Blackwell.

EISENHARDT, K. (1989). 'Agency Theory: An Assessment and Review'. *Academy of Management Review*, 14: 57–74.

ELSTER, J. (1986/1997). 'The Market and the Forum: Three Varieties of Political Theory', in R. E. Goodin and P. Pettit, (eds.), *Contemporary Political Philosophy: An Anthology*. Oxford: Blackwell.

—— (1989). *The Cement of Society*. Cambridge: Cambridge University Press.

EVERED, R., and LOUIS, M. R. (1981). 'Alternative Perspectives in the Organizational Sciences. "Inquiry from the Inside" and "Inquiry from the Outside"'. *Academy of Management Review*, 6: 385–95.

FALK, A. (2001). 'Homo Oeconomicus vs. Homo Reciprocans: Empirische Evidenz und politische Implikationen'. University of Zurich. Mimeo.

FEHR, E., and Gächter, S. (2000). 'Fairness and Retaliation: The Economics of Reciprocity'. *Journal of Economic Perspectives*, 14: 159–81.

FEYERABEND, P. (1987). *Farewell to Reason*. London: Verso.

FREEMAN, R. E. (1984). *Strategic Management: A Stakeholder Approach*. Boston: Pitman.

—— and Gilbert, D. R., Jr (1988). *Corporate Strategy and the Search for Ethics*. Englewood Cliffs, NJ: Prentice-Hall.

FRENCH, W. L., and BELL, C. H., Jr. (1978). *Organization Development: Behavior Science Interventions for Organization Improvement.* Englewood Cliffs, NJ: Prentice-Hall.

FRIEDMAN, D., and HECHTER, M. (1988). 'The Contribution of Rational Choice Theory to Macrosociological Research'. *Sociological Theory,* 6 (Fall). 201–18.

GADAMER, H.-G. (1960/1975). *Truth and Method.* New York: Seabury Press.

GIDDENS, A. (1976). *New Rules of Sociological Method.* London: Hutchinson.

—— (1984). *The Constitution of Society: Outline of the Theory of Structuration.* Cambridge: Polity Press.

GIOIA, D. A., and PITRE, E. (1990). 'Multiparadigm Perspectives on Theory Building'. *Academy of Management Review,* 15: 584–602.

GREEN, D. P., and SHAPIRO, I. (1994). *Pathologies of Rational Choice Theory: A Critique of Applications in Political Science.* New Haven: Yale University Press.

GRESOV, C., and DRAZIN, R. (1997). 'Equifinality: Functional Equivalence in Organization Design'. *Academy of Management Review,* 22: 403–28.

HABERMAS, J. (1966). 'Knowledge and Interest'. *Inquiry,* 9: 285–300.

—— (1968/1971). *Knowledge and Human Interests.* Boston: Beacon Press.

—— (1971). 'Theorie der Gesellschaft oder Sozialtechnologie? Eine Auseinandersetzung mit Niklas Luhmann', in J. Habermas and N. Luhmann, *Theorie der Gesellschaft oder Sozialtechnologie.* Frankfurt a.M.: Suhrkamp.

—— (1971/1990). *On the Logic of the Social Sciences.* Cambridge, Mass.: MIT Press.

—— (1973). 'Wahrheitstheorien', in H. Fahrenbach (ed.), *Wirklichkeit und Reflexion: Festschrift für Walter Schulz zum 60. Geburtstag.* Pfullingen: Neske.

—— (1981/1984–7). *The Theory of Communicative Action.* 2 vols. Boston: Beacon Press.

—— (1983/1990a). 'Discourse Ethics: Notes on a Program of Philosophical Justification', in J. Habermas, *Moral Consciousness and Communicative Action.* Cambridge, Mass.: MIT Press.

—— (1983/1990b). 'Reconstruction and Interpretation in the Social Sciences', in J. Habermas, *Moral Consciousness and Communicative Action.* Cambridge, Mass.: MIT Press.

—— (1985/1990). *The Philosophical Discourse of Modernity.* Cambridge: Polity Press.

—— (1988/1993). 'The Unity of Reason in the Diversity of its Voices', in J. Habermas, *Postmetaphysical Thinking: Philosophical Essays.* Cambridge, Mass.: MIT Press.

—— (1992/1996). *Between Facts and Norms.* Cambridge: Polity Press.

—— (1996/1998). 'Three Normative Models of Democracy', in J. Habermas, *The Inclusion of the Other.* Cambridge, Mass.: MIT Press.

—— (1998/2001). *The Postnational Constellation: Political Essays.* Cambridge, Mass.: MIT Press.

HACKMAN, J. R., and WALTON, R. E. (1986). 'Leading Groups in Organizations', in P. S. Goodman (ed.), *Designing Effective Work Groups.* San Francisco: Jossey-Bass.

HAGE, J. (1980). *Theories of Organizations: Form, Process, and Transformation.* New York: Wiley.

HAMBRICK, D. C. (1994). 'What If the Academy Actually Mattered?' *Academy of Management Review,* 19: 11–16.

HARDIN, G. (1968). 'The Tragedy of the Commons'. *Science* 162: 1243–8.

HASSARD, J. (1993a). 'Postmodernism and Organizational Analysis: An Overview', in J. Hassard and M. Parker (eds.), *Postmodernism and Organizations.* London: Sage.

—— (1993b). *Sociology and Organization Theory: Positivism, Paradigms and Postmodernity.* Cambridge: Cambridge University Press.

——and PARKER, M. (eds.) (1993). *Postmodernism and Organizations*. London: Sage.

HEIDEGGER, M. (1927/1996). *Being and Time*. Albany: New York State University Press.

HELD, D. (1980). *Introduction to Critical Theory: Horkheimer to Habermas*. London: Hutchinson.

HEMPEL, C. G. (1965). 'Aspects of Scientific Explanation', in C. G. Hempel (ed.), *Aspects of Scientific Explanation and Other Essays in the Philosophy of Science*. New York: Free Press.

——and OPPENHEIM, P. (1948/1998). 'Studies in the Logic of Explanation', *Philosophy of Science*, 15: 135–75. Reprinted in C. G. Hempel (ed.), *Aspects of Scientific Explanation and Other Essays in the Philosophy of Science* (New York: Free Press, 1965). Rev. version reprinted in E. D. Klemke, R. Hollinger, D. Wyss Rudge, with A. D. Kline (eds.), *Introductory Readings in the Philosophy of Science* (3rd edn) (Buffalo NY: Prometheus, 1998).

HOLLIS, M. (1994). *The Philosophy of Social Science*. Cambridge: Cambridge University Press.

HOMANS, G. C. (1958). 'Social Behavior as Exchange'. *American Journal of Sociology*, 63: 597–606.

——(1961). *Social Behavior: Its Elementary Form*. New York: Harcourt, Brace, & World.

HUBER, G. P., and GLICK, W. H. (1993). *Organizational Change and Redesign: Ideas and Insights for Improving Performance*. Oxford: Oxford University Press.

HUNT, S. D. (1990). 'Truth in Marketing Theory and Research'. *Journal of Marketing*, 54 (July): 1–15.

——(1992). 'For Reason and Realism in Marketing'. *Journal of Marketing*, 56 (Apr.): 89–102.

HUSSERL, E. (1936/1970). *The Crisis of European Sciences and Transcendental Phenomenology*. Evanston, Ill.: Northwestern University Press.

ISABELLA, L. A. (1990). 'Evolving Interpretations as a Change Unfolds: How Managers Construe Key Organizational Events'. *Academy of Management Journal*, 33: 7–41.

JACKSON, N., and CARTER, P. (1991). 'In Defence of Paradigm Incommensurability'. *Organization Studies*, 12: 109–27.

JANIS, I. L. (1982). *Groupthink: Psychological Studies of Policy Decisions and Fiascoes*. Boston: Houghton Mifflin.

JENSEN, M. C., and MECKLING, W. H. (1976). 'Theory of the Firm: Managerial Behavior, Agency Costs and Ownership Structure'. *Journal of Financial Economics*, 3: 305–60.

JOAS, H. (1987). 'Symbolic Interactionism', in A. Giddens and J. Turner, (eds.), *Social Theory Today*. Cambridge: Polity Press.

KERSTING, W. (2000). 'Analyse, Konstruktion und Verstehen: Rationalitätskonzeptionen in der politischen Philosophie', in W. Kersting, *Politik und Recht: Abhandlungen zur politischen Philosophie der Gegenwart und zur neuzeitlichen Rechtsphilosophie*. Weilerswist: Velbrück.

KILDUFF, M., and MEHRA, A. (1997). 'Postmodernism and Organizational Research'. *Academy of Management Review*, 22: 453–81.

KONDYLIS, P. (1999). *Das Politische und der Mensch: Grundzüge der Sozialontologie*. Bd. 1. Berlin: Akademie Verlag.

KREPS, D. M. (1990). *Game Theory and Economic Modelling*. Oxford: Clarendon Press.

KUHN, T. S. (1962). *The Structure of Scientific Revolutions*. Chicago: University of Chicago Press.

——(1970). *The Structure of Scientific Revolutions* (2nd edn). Chicago: University of Chicago Press.

KUNNEMAN, H. (1991). *Der Wahrheitstrichter: Habermas und die Postmorderne*. Frankfurt a.M.: Campus.

LAWRENCE, P. R., and LORSCH, J. W. (1967). *Organization and Environment: Managing Differentiation and Integration*. New York: Free Press.

LECHNER, F. J. (2000). 'Systems Theory and Functionalism', in B. S. Turner (ed.), *The Blackwell Companion to Social Theory*. Malden, Mass.: Blackwell.

LIKERT, R. (1961). *New Patterns of Management*. New York: MacGraw-Hill.

—— (1967). *The Human Organization*. New York: MacGraw-Hill.

LUCE, D., and RAIFFA, H. (1957). *Games and Decisions*. New York: Wiley.

LUHMANN, N. (1962). 'Funktion und Kausalität'. *Kölner Zeitschrift für Soziologie und Sozialpsychologie*, 14: 617–44. Cited after: N. Luhmann, *Soziologische Aufklärung* (Opladen: Westdeutscher Verlag, 1991).

—— (1964). 'Funktionale Methode und Systemtheorie'. *Soziale Welt*, 15: 1–25.

—— (1973). *Zweckbegriff und Systemrationalität*. Frankfurt a.M.: Suhrkamp.

—— (1982). *Differentiation of Society*. New York: Columbia University Press.

—— (1984/1995). *Social Systems*. Stanford, Calif.: Stanford University Press.

LYOTARD, J. -F. (1984). *The Postmodern Condition*. Manchester: Manchester University Press.

MARCH, J. G., and OLSEN, J. P. (1989). *Rediscovering Institutions: The Organizational Basis of Politics*. New York: Free Press.

MEGILL, A. (ed.) (1994). *Rethinking Objectivity*. Durham, NC: Duke University Press.

MERTON, R. K. (1957). *Social Theory and Social Structure* (rev. edn). New York: Free Press.

—— (1967). *On Theoretical Sociology*. New York: Free Press.

MEYER, J., and ROWAN, B. (1977). 'Institutionalized Organizations: Formal Structure as Myth and Ceremony'. *American Journal of Sociology*, 83: 340–63.

MILGROM, P., and ROBERTS, J. (1992). *Economics, Organization, and Management*. Englewood Cliffs, NJ: Prentice-Hall.

MILL, J. S. (1843). *A System of Logic*. London: John W. Parker.

MINTZBERG, H. (1983). *Power In and Around Organizations*. Englewood Cliffs, NJ: Prentice-Hall.

MORGAN, G. (1986). *Images of Organization*. Newbury Park, Calif.: Sage.

MORROW, R.A., with BROWN, D. D. (1994). *Critical Theory and Methodology*. London: Sage.

MUMBY, D. K. (1988). *Communication and Power in Organizations: Discourse, Ideology and Domination*. Norwood, NJ: Ablex.

MYERSON, R. B. (1991). *Game Theory: Analysis of Conflict*. Cambridge, Mass.: Harvard University Press.

NAGEL, E. (1961). *The Structure of Science: Problems in the Logic of Scientific Explanation*. New York: Harcourt, Brace, and World.

NATTER, W., SCHATZKI, T. R., and JONES, J. P., III (eds.) (1995). *Objectivity and its Other*. New York: Guildford Press.

NEUMANN, J. V., and MORGENSTERN, O. (1948). *Theory of Games and Economic Behavior*. Princeton: Princeton University Press.

NEURATH, O. (1934/1983). 'Radical Physicalism and the "Real World"', in O. Neurath, *Philosophical Papers 1913–1946*. Dordrecht: Reidel.

NORRIS, C. (2000). 'Post-modernism: A Guide for the Perplexed', in G. Browning, A. Halcli, and F. Webster, (eds.), *Understanding Contemporary Society: Theories of the Present*. London: Sage.

OLSON, M. (1971). *The Logic of Collective Action: Public Goods and the Theory of Groups.* Cambridge, Mass.: Harvard University Press.

OSTERLOH, M. (1993). *Interpretative Organisations- und Mitbestimmungsforschung.* Stuttgart: Poeschel.

OSTROM, E. (1990). *Governing the Commons: The Evolution of Institutions for Collective Action.* Cambridge: Cambridge University Press.

OUCHI, W. G. (1979). 'A Conceptual Framework for the Design of Organizational Control Mechanisms'. *Management Science*, 25: 838–48.

—— (1980). 'Markets, Bureaucracies, and Clans'. *Administrative Science Quarterly*, 25: 129–41.

OUTHWAITE, W. (1975). *Understanding Social Life: The Method Called Verstehen.* Lewes: Jean Stroud.

—— (1994). *Habermas: A Critical Introduction.* Stanford, Calif.: Stanford University Press.

—— (2000). 'The Philosophy of Social Science', in B. S. Turner (ed.), *The Blackwell Companion to Social Theory.* Malden, Mass.: Blackwell.

PARKER, M. (1992). 'Postmodern Organizations or Postmodern Organization Theory?' *Organization Studies*, 13: 1–17.

PFEFFER, J. (1981). *Power in Organizations.* Marshfield, Mass.: Pitman.

—— (1982). *Organizations and Organization Theory.* Marshfield, Mass.: Pitman.

—— (1993). 'Barriers to the Advance of Organizational Science: Paradigm Development as a Dependent Variable'. *Academy of Management Review*, 18: 599–620.

PLUMMER, K. (2000). 'Symbolic Interactionism in the Twentieth Century', in B. S. Turner (ed.), *The Blackwell Companion to Social Theory* (2nd edn). Maldon, Mass.: Blackwell.

POPPER, K. R. (1935/1959). *The Logic of Scientific Discovery.* London: Hutchinson.

—— (1969). *Conjectures and Refutations: The Growth of Scientific Knowledge.* London: Routledge & Kegan Paul.

—— (1972). *Objective Knowledge.* Oxford: Oxford University Press.

PUGH, D. S., HICKSON, D. J., HININGS, C. R., and TURNER, C. (1969). 'The Context of Organization Structures'. *Administrative Science Quarterly*, 14: 91–114.

PUTNAM, L. L., BANTZ, Ch., DEETZ, St., MUMBY, D., and VAN MAANEN, J. (1993). 'Ethnography Versus Critical Theory: Debating Organizational Research', *Journal of Management Inquiry*, 2: 221–35.

RAO, M. V. H., and PASMORE, W. A. (1989). 'Knowledge and Interests in Organization Studies'. *Organization Studies*, 10: 225–39.

RAUB, W., and WESSIE, J. (1992). 'Sociological Applications to Game Theory'. ISCORE Part 4. Utrecht University.

REED, M. I. (1992). *The Sociology of Organizations: Themes, Perspectives and Prospects.* New York: Harvester Wheatsheaf.

ROETHLISBERGER, F. J., and DICKSON, W. J. (1939). *Management and the Worker.* Cambridge, Mass.: Harvard University Press.

RORTY, R. (1985). 'Solidarity or Objectivity?', in J. Rajchman and C. West, (eds.), *Post-analytic Philosophy.* New York: Columbia University Press.

ROSENBERG, A. (1995). *Philosophy of Social Science* (2nd edn). Boulder, Col.: Westview.

SALMON, W. (1998). 'Scientific Explanation: How We Got from There to Here', in E. D. Klemke, R. Hollinger, D. Wyss Rudge, with A. D. Kline (eds.), *Introductory Readings in the Philosophy of Science* (3rd edn). Buffalo, NY: Prometheus.

SCHERER, A. G. (1995). *Pluralismus im Strategischen Management: Der Beitrag der Teilneh-merperspektive zur Lösung von Inkommensurabilitätsproblemen in Theorie und Praxis.* Wiesbaden: Gabler/DUV.

—— (ed.) (1998). 'Thematic Issue on Pluralism and Incommensurability in Strategic Management and Organization Theory: Consequences for Theory and Practice'. *Organization*, 5/2: 147–68.

—— (1999). 'Kritik der Organisation oder Organisation der Kritik? Wissenschaftstheore-tische Bemerkungen zum kritischen Umgang mit Organisationstheorien', in A. Kieser (ed.), *Organisationstheorien* (3rd edn). Stuttgart: Kohlhammer.

—— and DOWLING, M. (1995). 'Towards a Reconciliation of the Theory-Pluralism in Strategic Management—Incommensurabiliy and the Constructivist Approach of the Erlangen School'. *Advances in Strategic Management*, 12A: 195–247.

—— and STEINMANN, H. (1999). 'Some Remarks on the Problem of Incommensurability in Organization Studies'. *Organization Studies*, 20: 519–44.

SCHREYÖGG, G. (1978). *Umwelt, Technologie und Organisationsstruktur: Eine Analyse des kontingenztheoretischen Ansatzes.* Bern and Stuttgart: Haupt.

SCHÜTZ, A. (1932/1972). *The Phenomenology of the Social World.* London: Heinemann.

SCOTT, J. (2000). 'Rational Choice Theory', in G. Browning, A. Halcli, and F. Webster (eds.), *Understanding Contemporary Society: Theories of the Present.* London: Sage.

SHRIVASTAVA, P. (1986). 'Is Strategic Management Ideological?' *Journal of Management*, 12: 363–77.

SILVERMAN, D. (1970). *The Theory of Organizations.* London: Heinemann.

SIMON, H. A. (1947). *Administrative Behavior.* New York: Free Press.

—— (1982). *Models of Bounded Rationality.* Cambridge, Mass.: MIT Press.

—— (1991). 'Organizations and Markets'. *Journal of Economic Perspectives*, 5/2: 25–44.

SMART, B. (2000). 'Postmodern Social Theory', in B. S. Turner (ed.), *The Blackwell Companion to Social Theory* (2nd edn). Maldon, Mass.: Blackwell.

SMIRCICH, L., and STUBBART, Ch. (1985). 'Strategic Management in an Enacted World'. *Academy of Management Review*, 10: 724–36.

SPENCER, H. (1898). *The Principles of Sociology.* New York: D. Appleton.

STEFFY, B. D., and GRIMES, A. J. (1986). 'A Critical Theory of Organization Science'. *Academy of Management Review*, 11: 322–36.

STEINMANN, H., and LÖHR, A. (1994). *Grundlagen der Unternehmensethik* (2nd edn). Stuttgart: Poeschel.

—— and SCHERER A. G. (1995). 'Wissenschaftstheorie', in H. Corsten (ed.), *Lexikon der Betriebswirtschaftslehre* (3rd edn). Munich and Vienna: Oldenbourg.

—— —— (1998). 'Corporate Ethics and Global Business: Philosophical Considerations on Intercultural Management', in B. N. Kumar and H. Steinmann (eds.), *Ethics in International Management.* New York: Walter de Gruyter.

—— —— (2000). 'Corporate Ethics and Management Theory', in P. Koslowski (ed.), *Contemporary Economic Ethics and Business Ethics.* New York: Springer.

TAYLOR, C. (1971). 'Interpretation and the Sciences of Man', in E. D. Klemke, R. Hollinger, D. Wyss Rudge, with A. D. Kline (eds.), *Introductory Readings in the Philosophy of Science* (3rd edn, 1998). Buffalo, NY: Prometheus.

THOMPSON, P. (1993). 'Postmodernism: Fatal Distraction', in J. Hassard and M. Parker (eds.), *Postmodernism and Organizations.* London: Sage.

VAITKUS, S. (2000). 'Phenomenology and Sociology', in B. S. Turner (ed.), *The Blackwell Companion to Social Theory* (2nd edn). Maldon, Mass.: Blackwell.

VANBERG, V. (1975). *Die zwei Soziologien: Individualismus und Kollektivismus in der Sozialtheorie.* Tübingen: Mohr.

VAN DE VEN, A. H., and POOLE, M. S. (1994). *Explaining Development and Change in Organizations.* Strategic Management Research Center. Discussion Paper No. 189. Minneapolis: University of Minnesota.

VROOM, V (1964). *Work and Motivation.* New York: Wiley.

WEBER, M. (1947). *The Theory of Social and Economic Organization.* New York: Free Press.

WHETTON, D. A. (1987). 'Interorganizational Relations', in J. Lorsch (ed.), *Handbook of Organizational Behavior.* Englewood Cliffs, NJ: Prentice-Hall.

WILLIAMSON, O. E. (1975). *Markets and Hierarchies.* New York: Free Press.

—— (1985). *The Economic Institutions of Capitalism.* New York: Free Press.

WILLKE, H. (1991). *Systemtheorie* (3rd edn) New York: Gustav Fischer.

WILLMOTT, H. (1990). 'Beyond Paradigmatic Closure in Organizational Enquiry', in J. Hassard and D. Pym (eds.), *The Theory and Philosophy of Organizations: Critical Issues and New Perspectives.* London: Routledge.

—— (1997). 'Management and Organization Studies as Science?' *Organization,* 4: 309–44.

—— (1998). 'Towards a New Ethics? The Contributions of Poststructuralism and Posthumanism', in M. Parker (ed.), *Ethics and Organizations.* London: Sage.

WITTGENSTEIN, L. (1953). *Philosophical Investigations.* Oxford: Blackwell.

WOODWARD, J. (1965). *Industrial Organization: Theory and Practice.* London: Oxford University Press.

ZEY, M. (1998). *Rational Choice Theory and Organizational Theory: A Critique.* London: Sage.

ZEY-FERRELL, M. (1981). 'Criticisms of the Dominant Perspective on Organizations'. *Sociological Quarterly,* 22: 181–205.

CHAPTER 12

MICRO AND MACRO PERSPECTIVES IN ORGANIZATION THEORY

A TALE OF INCOMMENSURABILITY

WILLIAM MCKINLEY

MARK A. MONE

ALMOST forty years have passed since the initial development of the structuralist perspective in organization theory (Hickson, Pugh, and Pheysey 1969; Pugh, Hickson, Hinings, Macdonald, Turner, and Lupton 1963; Pugh, Hickson, Hinings, and Turner 1968). During this period, a complex array of new approaches and schools of thought has arisen in organization theory, and these schools have largely supplanted the discipline's original focus on the structural dimensions of organizations. Several commentators have discussed the emergence and development of these newer schools, which include neo-contingency theory, resource dependence theory, transaction costs theory, the population ecology approach, agency theory, and neo-institutional theory (see e.g. Astley and Van de Ven 1983; Davis and Powell 1992; Donaldson 1995; Pfeffer 1997). In addition, scholars such as McKinley, Mone,

We thank Hari Tsoukas for his many helpful comments during the development of this chapter.

and Moon (1999) have presented a theory of 'schooling', identifying factors that encourage the development of new schools of thought in organization theory and their establishment as legitimate intellectual frameworks.

Despite these attempts to make sense of the array of organization theory schools of thought, the broad sweep of sometimes inconsistent perspectives remains confusing. One way to inject some order into the current structure of the discipline is to categorize existing schools of thought by level of analysis. Performing such a categorization is the first goal of this chapter, and we distinguish specifically between micro and macro levels of analysis. We follow Astley and Van de Ven (1983) and Davis and Powell (1992) in defining the micro level as single organizations adapting to their individual task environments. The macro level, on the other hand, refers to populations of organizations and to multi-organizational fields or sectors (DiMaggio and Powell 1983; Hannan and Freeman 1977; Scott and Meyer 1983). Thus organization theory schools of thought at the micro level capture the way that single organizations modify their structures to take account of contingencies originating in their individual task environments. Schools of thought at the macro level focus on the evolution of aggregates of organizations and the characteristics of organizational collectivities such as fields. The former group of schools contains such perspectives as Donaldson's (1995, 1999) neo-contingency theory, as well as resource dependence theory and transaction costs theory. The latter group—the macro group—includes population ecology theory and neo-institutional theory (Davis and Powell 1992). The classification of these five schools into micro and macro levels of analysis may be viewed as a tentative heuristic that helps make sense of organization theory's current complexity, rather than a final 'truth' about the way the field is structured.

We focus on the five schools of thought enumerated above because they are among the most prominent schools in contemporary organization theory, and because they are responsible for much of the empirical research on organizations being conducted today. We review each of these schools, specifying in more detail why each is categorized as a micro or macro perspective, and what the underlying logic and theoretical propositions of the school are. We also offer a critique of each school, pointing out weaknesses and issues that require resolution in future empirical research. In particular, we argue that all these schools are founded on ambiguous theoretical constructs. While ambiguous constructs foster creativity in empirical research (McKinley, Mone, and Moon 1999), they also preclude conclusive empirical testing of the schools that are organized around them (Astley and Zammuto 1992) and make the schools incommensurable with one another. By 'incommensurable', we mean that there are no widely accepted standards by which the relative empirical validity of different schools with competing claims can be judged (McKinley and Mone 1998; Scherer 1998; Scherer and Steinmann 1999). The role of ambiguous constructs in producing incommensurability is elaborated below. Such incommensurability makes it difficult for contemporary organization theory to claim the status of a science, at least if a science is an endeavor character-ized by the ability to conclusively evaluate the relative accuracy of different theoret-ical perspectives.

12.1 MICRO PERSPECTIVES

12.1.1 Neo-Contingency Theory

Neo-contingency theory has been developed most completely by Donaldson (1995, 1999), though important contributions have also been made by Alexander and Randolph (1985), Drazin and Van de Ven (1985), Gresov (1989), and others. Neo-contingency theory is the latest in a long line of reinterpretations of structural contingency theory that have occurred over the last few decades in organization theory (see e.g. Lawrence and Lorsch 1967; Schoonhoven 1981; Thompson 1967; Woodward 1958, 1965). We concentrate here on Donaldson's version of neo-contingency theory because it is a recent perspective and because Donaldson (1995) has made a strong claim that it should constitute the foundation of a new, integrated organization theory paradigm. Neo-contingency theory qualifies as a micro perspective in our classification scheme because it focuses on conformity of individual organizations to the environmental and technological 'contingencies' they face.

In the neo-contingency model, individual organizations adapt to contingencies, and being in a state of adaptation means that the organization's structure 'fits' the contingency or contingencies that the organization is confronted with at a given point in time. A contingency could be a particular environmental state, a manufac-turing technology, or a given level of organizational size. Donaldson (1999; see also Alexander and Randolph 1985; Drazin and Van de Ven 1985; Gresov 1989) envisions a line of 'fit' that defines a series of matches between levels of a contingency variable and levels of a structural variable. To be on the 'fit' line is to maximize organiza-tional performance, and high organizational performance produces slack resources that are usually reinvested in the organization (Donaldson 1999). Such reinvestment leads to increases in the contingency variable in question; for example, if the contingency variable were organization size, investment of slack resources would result in the expansion of the workforce. The increase in the contingency variable in turn moves the organization away from the 'fit' line and into a state of misfit and poor performance. With the resulting decline in organizational performance comes pressure for structural adaptation, and that adaptation moves the organization back to the line of 'fit' at a higher level of structural complexity. When fit is attained again, organizational performance is renewed, and the cycle of slack generation, investment, change in the contingency variable, misfit and decline, and structural adaptation back to renewed fit begins all over again. Thus Donaldson's (1995, 1999) model posits a self-correcting loop (Masuch 1985) in which fit and resulting high performance create the seeds of their own disruption and eventual renewal.

Donaldson's neo-contingency model is appealing because it helps explain why organizations often fluctuate through repeated cycles of performance growth and decline. However, there are a number of criticisms that can be leveled at the model. The first, and perhaps most important, is the ambiguity of the construct 'fit'. Donaldson (1995, 1999) never provides a specific definition of fit that attaches a unique meaning to the construct and differentiates 'fit' from the construct 'organizational performance'. Equally critical, Donaldson never specifies the exact combination of values on a contingency variable and an associated structural variable that would constitute a 'fit'. For example, given an organizational size level of 10,000 employees, exactly what level of formalization or structural differentiation is required for the organization to be in 'fit'? Exactly what level of product diversification (Chandler 1962) constitutes a 'fit' with a product divisionalized structure? Assuming a transition from a mass to a process production system (Woodward 1965), exactly how much change in organization structure is required to keep the organization in 'fit'? While such questions are difficult to answer with current theoretical resources, unless some answers can be provided, there seems to be little to substantiate the existence of 'fit' as a phenomenon independent of organizational performance. Barring a clearer definition of 'fit' in future neo-contingency work, plus the development of some scholarly consensus around that definition, the construct of 'fit' may be subject to the same type of deconstruction that has overtaken constructs like 'effectiveness' (Hirsch and Levin 1999).

As a result of the ambiguity surrounding the meaning of 'fit', many of Donaldson's (1999) propositions are not currently open to the possibility of conclusive empirical testing. Given this lack of falsifiability (Bacharach 1989), the propositions would appear not to meet basic standards for adequate theory building. We doubt that theorists such as Donaldson seek construct ambiguity intentionally, but nevertheless we believe there is a disincentive for them to eliminate it, because as Astley and Zammuto (1992) suggested, it allows them to explain away findings that do not support their theoretical positions. Donaldson (1995: 34) provides an example of this when he explains one study's null relationship between fit and performance (which contradicts his theory) by questioning the measure of 'fit' that was used. Donaldson's ability to do this can be attributed to the ambiguity of the 'fit' construct itself. While construct ambiguity and attendant lack of falsifiability may be convenient for the individual theorist, McKinley and Mone (1998) have argued that construct ambiguity represents a problem for the discipline of organization theory, because (as highlighted in the next section) it promotes incommensurability and makes it difficult to adjudicate between conflicting theoretical positions.

Yet another problem with Donaldsonian neo-contingency theory is its apparent assumption that structural adaptation following a performance decline will always take the organization back to the line of 'fit'. This suggests a degree of managerial rationality that is hard to accept in view of acknowledged limits on the ability of humans to sift through options and predict the outcomes of those options (Simon 1997). How do managers know exactly what types of structural change to undertake to return their organizations to the line of 'fit', and how do those managers know exactly when to stop changing structure so as not to move beyond the 'fit' line into an overadapted hinterland? Donaldson does not answer these questions, and barring specification of the exact contingency-structure combinations that constitute 'fits', it is hard to see how managers could answer them either.

Finally, Donaldson's neo-contingency model deals only with *increases* in contingency variables like organizational size, technological complexity, or environmental uncertainty. Donaldson is silent about what happens when those contingency variables *decrease*, as is true for example in the popular management strategies of downsizing (Freeman and Cameron 1993; McKinley, Zhao, and Rust 2000) or downscoping the level of diversification (Hoskisson and Hitt 1994). Based on Donaldson's (1999: 19) diagram showing cycles of incremental growth and adaptive structural change, one would infer that if a contingency variable decreased, the change in structure would be the exact reverse of what would follow an equivalent increase in the same contingency variable. In other words, a condition of causal symmetry would apply (Lieberson 1985). The validity of such causal symmetry has been questioned in the case of the organizational size / organizational structure relationship, and empirical research has suggested that reductions in organizational size may not produce structural consolidations that are the mirror image of the structural expansions that occur during growth in size (see McKinley 1992 for a review of this research). Donaldson's neo-contingency theory would benefit from a more complete articulation of what can be expected when contingency variables decrease as well as increase, because continual increase in these variables is not always the pattern that applies in the real world.

12.1.2 Resource Dependence Theory

Like Donaldson's neo-contingency theory, resource dependence theory operates at the micro level of analysis. That is, resource dependence theory focuses on the adaptations of single organizations to the contexts that confront them. In contrast to neo-contingency theory, however, the adaptations highlighted by resource dependence theory are not confined to changes in the focal organization's internal structure. Instead, the adaptations can include initiatives that bridge the boundaries of the organization, managing interdependence with other organizations in the task environment (Pfeffer and Salancik 1978). In pursuit of that goal, organizations often build alliances, merge with one another, or co-opt other organizations they are dependent on (Thompson 1967). In describing the management of interdependence with other organizations, the resource dependence perspective envisions a more proactive role for the focal organization than the neo-contingency perspective does.

One of the most important foundations of resource dependence theory was established with the publication of Hickson, Hinings, Lee, Schneck, and Pennings's (1971) strategic contingencies theory of intra-organizational power (see also Hinings, Hickson, Pennings, and Schneck 1974). Hickson *et al.*'s (1971) theory focused on the role of power in the internal functioning of organizations, and expanded the construct of power beyond the hierarchical conceptualization that had dominated discussions previously. Hickson *et al.* (1971) argued that power accrues to those organizational subunits that are successful in coping with 'strategic contingencies' that affect other subunits, with 'strategic contingencies' broadly conceptualized as sources of uncertainty. In other words, the power of unit X over unit Y is determined by X's ability to cope with uncertainty that impinges on Y. Strategic contingencies can include such factors as a lack of resources, missing information, or any other condition that makes it difficult for Y to perform its function reliably. Creation of subunit power through coping with strategic contingencies for others is often an explicit concern of organizational subunits, as illustrated by the activities of maintenance workers in Crozier's (1964) well-known study of French tobacco factories. In addition, Hickson *et al.* (1971) pointed out that dependence by others on X's coping activity, and therefore the magnitude of X's power, is enhanced if X is a non-substitutable source of that coping activity. This emphasis on non-substitutability is interesting because it links the strategic contingencies theory of power to the concept of monopoly in economic theory.

Like the construct of 'fit' in neo-contingency theory, the construct of 'strategic contingencies' is broadly conceptualized and open to a number of interpretations. While this renders the construct difficult to falsify (Bacharach 1989), it also means that the strategic contingencies theory of power has been a stimulus for extensive theorizing and research. One outcome of this work is Pfeffer and Salancik's (1974; Salancik and Pfeffer 1974) departmental version of resource dependence theory. Salancik and Pfeffer (1974) noted that an important strategic contingency faced by all organizational units is acquisition of resources. Thus the strategic contingencies theory of power implies that units that acquire resources valuable to other units will also obtain power over them. If subunit X can gain resources that are critical for the operation of other subunits, X buffers them from uncertainty, makes them dependent, and gains power over them. If the other subunits also have access to resources that are critical for X, the dependency is reciprocal, and there is a balancing of the power relationship between X and the other units. The net ability of X to influence Y will thus depend on the relative magnitude and criticality of the resources X provides for Y versus those Y provides for X.

Salancik and Pfeffer (1974; Pfeffer and Salancik 1974) tested their departmental version of resource dependence theory in a study of academic departments in a major research university. They found that academic departments that provided resources critical to the university acquired power as a result. Furthermore, Salancik and Pfeffer (1974) emphasized that the relationship between resource acquisition and power was self-reinforcing (Masuch 1985). Departments that acquired critical resources gained power, and that power then influenced internal resource allocation such that a disproportionate share of the internal budget was allocated back to the most powerful departments. The disproportionate share of the budget that powerful departments obtained was then available for investment in the acquisition of more resources, leading to more power, and a continuation of the 'rich get richer' cycle.

Hickson et al.'s (1971) strategic contingencies theory of power and Salancik and Pfeffer's departmental version of resource dependence theory have several interesting implications. First, these perspectives can be used to understand changes in power distributions within organizations over time. Since the strategic contingencies that generate uncertainty for an organization or the resources that are critical for it are likely to shift as time passes, power will flow to those internal subunits or individuals who can provide the coping capacity demanded by the strategic contingency or the resource need of the moment. Power structures are therefore malleable, mutual dependencies get reconfigured, and specialists rise to dominance only to lose it later as conditions change.

Second, if one combines the resource dependence school of thought with the enactment perspective (e.g. Smircich and Stubbart 1985; Weick 1979, 1995), it becomes evident that individuals or subunits may compete to define what the strategic contingencies are, rather than just accepting them as given by the environment. If one can persuade one's bosses that a particular contingency is really the critical one, or that a particular resource is what's needed by the organization, one's expertise in dealing with that contingency or providing that resource can be converted into a source of power. At the same time, political players may downgrade the importance of rivals' resource acquisition skills or coping capacities by arguing that the contingencies those capacities are targeted toward are unimportant or even illusory. This argument is based on the assumption that organizational reality is not objectively fixed, but emerges from the mutual constructions of organizational participants (e.g. Berger and Luckmann 1966). Thus there may be a contest between political players to construct organizational reality in a manner consistent with their own political interests.

Finally, the theories of Hickson et al. (1971) and Salancik and Pfeffer (1974; Pfeffer and Salancik 1974) highlight how important the creation and preservation of non-substitutability is for those who wish to build power. Individuals or subunits that have attained non-substitutability in coping or resource provision can be expected to resist changes that would erode that non-substitutability, and this may help explain much of the skepticism that often surfaces during planned organizational change efforts. Threats to non-substitutability can come from many sources, including routinization and standardization of business processes (Hickson *et al.* 1971). One would thus anticipate attempts to block routinization and standardization initiatives in many organizations, as illustrated for example by the resistance of physicians to standardization of medical care procedures by health maintenance organizations.

Pfeffer and Salancik (1978) have extended the basic principles of resource dependence theory to the relationships between focal organizations and other organizations in their task environments. According to Pfeffer and Salancik (1978), a dominant goal of most organizations is to preserve autonomy by buffering themselves from dependence on other organizations. Pfeffer and Salancik (1978) described a number of different types of inter-organizational dependence to which organizations are subject, including 'symbiotic interdependence' (dependence related to acquisition of inputs and disposal of outputs) and 'commensalistic interdependence' (stemming from competitive interaction). Symbiotic interdependence can be reduced by vertical integration, which buffers the focal organization from dependence on an independently owned supplier or distributor. Commensalistic interdependence, on the other hand, is reduced by horizontal merger, and the implication of the theory is that mergers are motivated largely by the desire to eliminate competitors and moderate competitive uncertainty. These arguments echo Thompson's (1967: 39) assertion that organizations under norms of rationality seek to place their boundaries around those activities that if left to the task environment would be crucial contingencies. Thus there is a theoretical link from Pfeffer and Salancik's (1978) inter-organizational dependence theory back to Thompson's (1967) earlier theoretical framework, demonstrating a continuing interest among organizational scholars in the problem of dependence and its resolution.

Donaldson (1995) has offered a number of criticisms of resource dependence theory, the most fundamental of which is its departure from explanations based on managerial rationality. Donaldson (1995) believes that resource dependence theory puts too much emphasis on politics and too little emphasis on the attainment of instrumental objectives by organizations that are dedicated to performing specific tasks. According to Donaldson (1995), organizations are not contexts for the acquisition of power and the avoidance of dependence so much as instruments for accomplishing tasks efficiently.

As was true in the case of neo-contingency theory, our concern with resource dependence theory revolves around the ambiguity of its key constructs and the role of that ambiguity in promoting incommensurability. To see the part played by ambiguity in fostering incommensurability, imagine attempting a critical empirical test to determine whether avoidance of inter-organizational dependence or enhancement of contingency-structure fit is the more important determinant of the adoption of vertical integration by organizations. The former argument would be consistent with resource dependence theory while the latter would be consistent with neo-contingency theory. In order to conduct such a test and invest the results with discipline-wide credibility, one would first have to resolve the ambiguity about the meaning and measurement of constructs such as 'inter-organizational dependence', 'fit', and 'vertical integration'. Without such a resolution, one could report empirical results, but they would almost certainly be subject to reinterpretation by those theorists whose theoretical position was not supported by the findings (Astley and Zammuto 1992). In other words, there is no widely accepted definitional standard by which the relative empirical validity of resource dependence theory and neo-contingency theory can be assessed, so the two schools of thought are incommensurable. McKinley and Mone (1998) proposed the creation of a standard, democratically built construct dictionary to deal with this problem, but at this stage of the development of our discipline, there appears to be little enthusiasm for such a project.

12.1.3 Transaction Costs Theory

The third micro-level perspective that we discuss here is transaction costs theory (Williamson 1981, 1991; Williamson and Ouchi 1981). Like neo-contingency theory and resource dependence theory, transaction costs theory is relevant to the behavior of the individual organization. Unlike neo-contingency theory and resource dependence theory, however, transaction costs theory considers the 'transaction' the primary focus of analysis; the need to manage transactions is the major determinant of structural configurations in organizations (Williamson 1981). A transaction occurs 'when a good or service is transferred across a technologically separable interface' (Williamson 1981: 552).

Transaction costs theory is concerned with the way transactions are governed, and the theory distinguishes three governance mechanisms that are available for this task: markets, hierarchies, and hybrid structures. Williamson (1981, 1991) adopts the traditional neo-classical conceptualization of markets as regularized exchanges of goods between autonomous economic actors, while the term 'hierarchies' is used as a synonym for formal organizations. Examples of hybrid governance structures, which combine features of markets and hierarchies, include long-term contracts and franchising (Williamson 1991). Williamson (1981, 1991) argues that governance structures are (or should be) matched to transactions in such a way as to minimize the costs of managing the transactions (the 'transaction costs'). Thus the attributes of transactions become the determinants of variance in governance structures, and one needs to understand the dimensions along which transactions differ in order to understand structural differences in the organizational world.

For Williamson (1981; see also Williamson and Ouchi 1981), the most important dimensions along which transactions differ are recurrence, uncertainty, and asset specificity. Recurrence refers to the frequency with which a transaction takes place, with high recurrence signifying that the transaction is repeated frequently in a routine manner. Uncertainty refers to the degree of predictability of transaction outcomes: the higher the uncertainty, the more difficult it is to forecast those outcomes. Finally, asset specificity is the degree to which transaction-specific investments are required to realize least-cost supply (Williamson 1981). In transactions with high asset specificity, one or both of the parties involved in the transaction make specialized investments intended to satisfy the idiosyncratic demands of that transaction. These investments cannot be diverted easily to other uses. Thus asset specificity locks transaction partners into the transaction, creating exit barriers that make it difficult to move flexibly into exchanges with other partners.

In addition to the dimensions discussed above, transaction costs theory rests on two fundamental assumptions about human behavior. The first is that human beings are boundedly rational (Simon 1997; Williamson and Ouchi 1981). This means that humans, while seeking to make rational decisions, lack the time and the information processing capacity to fully achieve that standard. In particular, humans generally do not have the cognitive capacity and the leisure to engage in the comprehensive assessment of alternatives and their consequences that would be necessary to maximize utility along one or more predefined utility functions.

Second, transaction costs theory assumes that agents engaging in transactions are potential opportunists. That is, they have incentives to engage in self-interest seeking with guile, which might involve lying, hiding information, or other forms of prevarication. While not all economic agents actually behave opportunistically, the potential is always there, and therefore opportunism is an important 'hazard' threatening the reliable conduct of transactions. As is true for bounded rationality, Williamson (1981) points out that the assumption of opportunism departs from assumptions about human behavior in neo-classical economic theory.

Under most conditions, Williamson (1981, 1991) suggests, markets are a satisfactory governance mechanism to regulate transactions between economic agents. Markets maximize the economic incentives that come into play in the behavior of the agents, and the price mechanism operative in markets guarantees an 'efficient' allocation of assets to productive uses. The central problem for market governance occurs when asset specificity is high, because in that circumstance exchange partners experience bilateral dependency (Williamson 1981). Given transaction-specific investments, any opportunistic behavior that disrupts the transaction means that the agents are forced to engage in a difficult reallocation of their assets to other exchanges in which those assets have much lower value. In that case transaction costs theory argues that markets 'fail' as a governance mechanism, and there is a need to replace market governance with hierarchies or hybrid structures such as franchises. Hierarchies and hybrids offer better monitoring, control, and continuity properties than markets do, and potential disputes arising from opportunistic behavior by one or more exchange partners can be resolved by administrative fiat.

Transaction costs theorists have used the general theoretical framework summarized above to explain a number of different structural features of organizations. One of these features is the placement of an organization's boundaries. Which transactions will be conducted within the boundaries of an organization and which will be outsourced to the market? Williamson (1981) argued that organizations will position their boundaries around transactions in an 'efficient' way, one that minimizes transaction costs. This basically means that transactions with higher asset specificity will tend to be internalized (Williamson 1981). For example, internalization of component sourcing will be preferred by a manufacturer when use of the component in manufacturing requires investments that are highly specific and idiosyncratic. External component sourcing (buying components on the market) will be preferable when the components are standard and easily available from a number of alternate suppliers. Walker and Weber (1984) tested this argument in a study of make or buy decisions in a division of a US automobile manufacturing company, and concluded that 'the results show mixed support for Williamson's theory' (p. 387).

As an extension of the 'efficient boundaries' problem, transaction costs theorists have also devoted considerable attention to the phenomenon of vertical integration. In fact, Barney and Hesterly (1996: 120) characterized vertical integration as the 'most researched application of TCT [transaction costs theory]'. As suggested above, the logic of transaction costs theory would predict internalization of upstream or downstream transactions through vertical integration when those transactions are high in asset specificity and thus entail a situation of bilateral dependence between the focal organization and a particular upstream supplier or downstream customer. Transaction-specific investments along the chain of transactions ranging from raw materials extraction through processing to manufacturing, wholesaling, and retail distribution provide the incentive for managers to bring transactions in-house, monitoring and controlling them through an integrated administrative hierarchy. An example offered by Williamson (1981) to illustrate this process is the acquisition of Fisher Body by General Motors as the asset specificity of the transactions between the two companies increased in the 1920s.

Transaction costs theory has attracted its fair share of criticism, including an interesting set of commentaries developed in a three-way debate between Williamson and Ouchi, Perrow, and Chandler. Perrow (1981), responding to Williamson and Ouchi's (1981) presentation of transaction costs theory, criticized the theory for its overemphasis on efficiency and its neglect of power. Perrow's (1981) preferred explanation for vertical integration lay in the desire of managers to gain hegemonic market power rather than their urge to manage transactions efficiently. Vertical integration is an effective means of dominating upstream or downstream markets, restricting access by competitors to raw materials or distribution channels. Chandler's (1981) position, elaborated in response to Perrow (1981), mirrored the theoretical framework Chandler developed in his 1977 opus, *The Visible Hand*. According to Chandler (1977, 1981), vertical integration owes its existence to the productivity advantages integrated hierarchies achieve in certain industries, rather than to the need for efficient governance of asset-specific transactions or the search for market power. Chandler (1981) argued that vertically integrated hierarchies appeared in those industries where the speed and flow of goods across stages in the production and distribution processes made administrative coordination of those flows more efficient than market coordination.

A second set of critiques has come from Ghoshal and Moran (1996), who argued that transaction costs theory is too preoccupied with the issue of opportunism. Ghoshal and Moran (1996) admitted that opportunism exists, but they pointed out, as have others, that it is moderated by a social context that 'embeds' (Granovetter 1985) economic transactions. Furthermore, Ghoshal and Moran (1996) noted that the assumption of opportunism has the potential to generate a self-fulfilling prophecy. The expectation that employees or exchange partners will be opportunistic leads to the creation of surveillance mechanisms and controls to govern transactions with those individuals. But the very imposition of controls sends a message to the targets that they are not considered trustworthy, and that can evoke opportunistic behavior from them. Thus the prophecy of opportunism is fulfilled through the regimes of control that are designed to reduce it. The outcome of more opportunism represents a classic case of an unanticipated consequence of purposive social action (Merton 1936, 1968). This explains Ghoshal and Moran's (1996) conclusion that transaction costs theory is bad for practice.

Our own critique revolves around the same concern we expressed above with respect to neo-contingency theory and resource dependence theory: the ambiguity of many of the key constructs at the core of the transaction costs perspective. Constructs such as 'transaction' and 'efficiency' are formulated at such an abstract level in transaction costs theory that their meaning is unclear, and multiple interpretations are possible. This situation could be considered good for transaction costs theory in the sense that no individual empirical study, or even a body of studies, is likely to constitute a conclusive falsification of the theory (Astley and Zammuto 1992). However, it is not evident that the situation is good for organization theory as a whole, because construct ambiguity makes it difficult to assess the validity of transaction costs theory relative to other schools.

As an example of this incommensurability problem, consider an empirical test designed to compare the validity of neo-contingency theory, resource dependence theory, and transaction costs theory as explanations for the popular contemporary management strategy of outsourcing. Neo-contingency theory would likely explain outsourcing as a structural adaptation to changes in the levels of specific contingency variables. Donaldson (1995, 1999) might argue, for example, that changes in information technology now allow closer coordination between a customer and independent suppliers, reducing the need to internalize supply relationships. Thus outsourcing is a structural adaptation that brings the structure of supply relationships into 'fit' with current information technology levels. Resource dependence theory, on the other hand, would likely explain outsourcing by reference to power imbalances between suppliers and customers. If a purchasing firm is large and accounts for a large percentage of a supplying firm's revenue, for example, the purchaser's market power allows it to control the behavior of the supplier even if the supplier is independently owned. Thus the power imbalance acts as a kind of governance mechanism that regulates the behavior of independent contractors and allows supply relationships to be outsourced. Finally, transaction costs theorists would likely explain outsourcing as an efficient governance mechanism under conditions of low asset specificity. For example, increasing standardization of the parts or services provided by suppliers might reduce the need for asset-specific investments in transacting business with them, making the market (outsourcing) the efficient way to manage buyer–supplier relationships.

We submit that any efforts to assess the relative validity of these three explanations for outsourcing would be problematic, due to construct ambiguity. Because the constructs underlying the different explanations—constructs like 'asset specificity', 'information technology', 'efficiency', 'fit', and 'power'—are ambiguous, any measures purporting to tap those constructs would be open to dispute. Barring discipline-wide consensus on the meaning of the constructs and the nature of the indicators that measure them validly, empirical results would always be subject to contention by the school(s) whose explanations were not favored by the results. Thus we reiterate the conclusion we arrived at above: construct ambiguity and incommensurability are major problems in any effort to compare organization theory schools of thought empirically.

12.2 MACRO PERSPECTIVES

12.2.1 Population Ecology

Neo-contingency theory, resource dependence theory, and transaction costs theory all focus on adaptations individual organizations make to local contingencies and task environments. In contrast, the two perspectives we review now focus on the macro attributes of organizational populations or the characteristics of supra-organizational entities such as sectors or fields (DiMaggio and Powell 1983; Scott and Meyer 1983). The first of these macro perspectives is the population ecology school. Population ecology (Aldrich 1979; Hannan and Freeman 1977, 1984; Baum

1996) borrows from models of population biology to study the demographics of organizational populations and the rates of organizational birth and death that drive those demographics.

One of the most salient theoretical features of the population ecology perspective is its emphasis on selection rather than adaptation to explain organizational change. In an early formulation of the theory, Hannan and Freeman (1977) pointed out a number of factors (e.g. sunk costs in plant and equipment, institutionalized routines, and political coalitions) that create structural inertia and limit the capacity of individual organizations to adapt freely to the conditions they face. Accordingly, Hannan and Freeman (1977) suggested that organizational change be explained as a product of selection rather than adaptation. New organizations entering a population exhibit a range of structural features, some of which match environmental demands and give the organization a competitive advantage in resource acquisition, and some of which do not. When 'matches' occur, they are not necessarily the product of intentional design by an organization's founders, but usually occur as a result of random variation. Those organizations with features that match environmental requirements have a competitive advantage and are therefore selected for survival, while those organizations with features that do not match die out. As the attributes of the environments encompassing populations of organizations shift over time, the dominant attributes of the organizations in the populations also shift, but through a process of selection and culling rather than a process of individual organizational adaptation.

While Hannan and Freeman (1977) used structural inertia to justify their claim that selection should be studied in preference to adaptation, Hannan and Freeman (1984) modified this logic by arguing that structural inertia is a by-product of selection. Selection in organizational populations, Hannan and Freeman (1984) stated, favors those organizations that can deliver a product or service reliably. Selection also favors organizations that can account rationally for their actions, because the expectation of rational organizational action is deeply embedded in western culture (Thompson 1967). Reliability and accountability depend on daily reproducibility of organizational structure, and the price of reproducibility is high structural inertia. Thus selection processes in organizational populations winnow those populations in favor of organizations with high structural inertia. Given the thrust of most business press rhetoric and (arguably) the beliefs of most managers, which are that only the nimble survive, Hannan and Freeman's (1984) thesis is provocative. Hannan and Freeman (1984) also advanced the controversial proposition that attempts at reorganization increase the hazard of organizational death, because such attempts disrupt reliability and accountability.

Population ecology in the 1990s and the new millennium appears to have converged on a narrower model, called density dependence theory. This model arguably forms the dominant paradigm for the current population ecology school (see Baum 1996 for a thorough review of empirical research in the area of density dependence). As articulated by Hannan and Carroll (1992), the density dependence model holds that birth and death rates in organizational populations are a function of population density: the number of organizations existing in a population at any given point in time. As population density increases, the legitimacy of the organizational form constituting that population also increases, at least when legitimacy is defined as taken-for-grantedness (Hannan and Carroll 1992). The increasing legitimacy of the form encourages organizational foundings while reducing the hazard of organizational death. Thus birth rates rise with increasing density while death rates fall. But at a certain point, increasing density sets into motion processes of inter-organizational competition that begin to overwhelm the effects of increasing legitimacy. As these competitive pressures build, the trajectories of birth rates and death rates reverse, so that birth rates peak and begin to fall, while death rates begin to rise. The overall result of this pattern of population dynamics is an inverted-U function for population density graphed against time: as an organizational population ages, population density first increases and then falls. Hannan and Carroll (1992) documented this empirical regularity for a wide variety of organizational populations, including populations of labor unions, newspapers, brewers, life insurance companies, and banks.

Consistent with Kuhn's (1970) description of 'normal science', much empirical research has been devoted to elaborating the details of the density dependence model (e.g. Barnett and Amburgey 1990; Baum and Oliver 1992; Budros 1994; Carroll and Hannan 1989; Schultz 1998). While these elaborations are interesting, they remain focused on the issue of organizational birth and death rates and how those rates are related to the number of organizations in a population. None of this research illuminates the mechanisms through which selection operates, since most population ecology studies seem content with an indirect measurement of selection through rates of organizational death. Is selection primarily the result of active environments operating on passive, inert organizations, the product of an interaction between active environments and active, but misdirected organizational adaptation efforts, or some other combination of events? Population ecology seems to be largely silent on this question.

The inattention to direct measurement of selection is also duplicated with other key constructs in the population ecology school. For example, Zucker (1989) has taken ecologists to task for failing to directly operationalize the institutional processes (e.g. legitimation) that are a major explanatory resource in the density dependence model. Similarly, Young (1988) has critiqued population ecology for definitional and operational ambiguities. The problem with reliance on density, birth rates, and death rates as indirect proxies for underlying sociological and economic processes is that it separates empirical research in population ecology from the theoretical models that are supposedly being tested by the research. Population ecology is not alone in exhibiting this gap between theory and empirical research, but the fact remains that the gap does not promote confidence in the validity of the perspective.

In addition to the measurement issues raised by Zucker (1989) and Young (1988), population ecology can be critiqued for its reliance on an excessively reified (Berger and Luckmann 1966) notion of the environment. In most of population ecology theory and research, the 'environment' is a hard reality completely external to organizations, implacable and impermeable to influence by them. There is little acknowledgement that organizations sometimes penetrate and even enact their environments, rather than being selected for death or survival by them (see e.g. Smircich and Stubbart 1985; McKinley and Scherer 2000).

Donaldson (1995) has also critiqued population ecology for its neglect of the internal structures of organizations. Other than the research on liabilities of new-ness and smallness (see Baum 1996), there has been little attention in population ecology to structural characteristics of organizations as predictors of vital rates. In particular, Donaldson (1995) points out that there has been little emphasis on determining why one organization dies while another in the same environment does not. These organization-level issues are masked by the preoccupation with birth and death *rates* and their environmental determinants, such as population density. This brings us back to the micro–macro distinction that anchors this chapter, and re-emphasizes the fact that population ecology is primarily couched at a macro level of analysis, in contrast to the organization-level phenomena that concern the micro organization theories.

While population ecology may have attained more of a paradigmatic status than the other contemporary schools of thought in organization theory (Pfeffer 1993), this does not mean that the key constructs that form the foundation of the school are any more precisely specified, or that incommensurability between population ecology and other schools is any less of a problem. Consider, for example, the task that would face researchers who wished to empirically compare the predictions of population ecology and neo-contingency theory with regard to the effects of adaptation on organizational performance and survival. As noted above, popula-tion ecology suggests that structural adaptation increases the risk of unreliable performance and consequently of organizational death (Hannan and Freeman 1984). Neo-contingency theory, on the other hand, advocates a different perspec-tive: structural adaptation returns organizations to the line of 'fit' and therefore increases performance and (implicitly) lowers the hazard of death (Donaldson 1999). A researcher seeking to test these inconsistent assertions would need to measure 'structural adaptation', 'performance', and 'death'. Due to the ambiguity that surrounds these key constructs and the lack of discipline-wide consensus about their definitions (see McKinley and Mone 1998), any measures of the constructs would be open to challenge if results based on the measures were inconsistent with the theoretical position of the challenger. The ambiguity and lack of consensus that permits such challenges effectively preserves a state of incommensurability between population ecology and neo-contingency theory that is similar to the cases of incommensurability described earlier.

12.2.2 Neo-Institutional Theory

The final organization theory school of thought we review is neo-institutional theory. Like the population ecology school, neo-institutional theory is articulated primarily at the macro level of analysis, concerning itself with such phenomena as social institutions, organizational fields, institutional environments, and societal sectors (DiMaggio and Powell 1983; Meyer, Boli, and Thomas 1994; Scott and Meyer 1983). While neo-institutional theory pays more attention to organizational structure than population ecology does, the determinants of structure are for the most part abstract sociological phenomena and processes that reside at a higher level of analysis than the task environments of individual organizations.

An early statement of neo-institutional theory was the seminal article by Meyer and Rowan (1977) in which they drew attention to the ways in which organizational structure is molded by 'institutional rules'. Institutional rules are taken for granted templates that define the appropriate ways to manage organizations and to structure internal or extra-organizational relations. These rules are components of 'institutional environments' that vary across different cultures, organizational fields (DiMaggio and Powell 1983) or societal sectors (Scott and Meyer 1983). While institutional rules furnish prescriptions about the right way to manage, those prescriptions are not necessarily based on concrete evidence that the prescribed practices increase technical or financial performance. Instead, institutional rules are 'rationalized myths' that give the appearance of rationality without necessarily achieving the substance of it. At the extreme of high institutionalization, institutional rules exhibit the quality of displacement of ends: following the rule becomes the end, and the connection between the rule and technical or financial performance fades in importance.

An example of an institutional rule that arguably exhibits this quality of displacement is organizational downsizing. McKinley, Sanchez, and Schick (1995) have argued that organizational downsizing has become institutionalized as a taken for granted management technique, despite the internal disruption it causes and the lack of concrete evidence that it actually improves financial performance (McKinley, Zhao, and Rust 2000; Mentzer 1996). In many announcements of corporate layoffs, little information is given about the performance goals of the layoff; instead, emphasis is placed on metaphors ('leanness', 'flexibility', and 'competitiveness') that naturalize the layoff and make it seem an external, objective phenomenon rather than a management decision (see Dunford and Palmer 1996 for a discussion of the role of metaphors in corporate restructuring).

In Meyer and Rowan's (1977) framework, conformity to institutional rules is rewarded with increased legitimacy and reduction of uncertainty. Organizations that embrace institutionalized organizing templates are perceived by external constituents as reliable and accountable, and thus institutional conformity forestalls skepticism about an organization's claim on societal resources (Meyer and Rowan 1977). In linking their framework to the constructs of reliability and accountability, Meyer and Rowan (1977) provide a point of convergence with the population ecology school (Hannan and Freeman 1984).

DiMaggio and Powell (1983) built on Meyer and Rowan's (1977) initial formulation of the neo-institutional perspective by focusing on the problem of 'institutional isomorphism' in organizational fields. By 'institutional isomorphism', they meant the tendency of organizations in a field to become more similar over time. By an organizational field, 'we mean those organizations that, in the aggregate, constitute a recognized area of institutional life: key suppliers, resource and product consumers, regulatory agencies, and other organizations that produce similar services or products' (DiMaggio and Powell 1983: 148). In explicit contrast to population ecology, whose orienting question was 'Why are there so many different types of organizations?' DiMaggio and Powell (1983) sought to answer the question, 'Why are organizations so similar?' This question distinguished DiMaggio and Powell's assumption of homogeneity of organizational form from the niche-based differentiation that was assumed in population ecology. DiMaggio and Powell (1983) tended to conceptualize isomorphism as a field-level construct, a phenomenon that affects aggregates of organizations, rather than an adaptation of individual organizations to their particular task environments.

DiMaggio and Powell (1983) located the sources of institutional isomorphism in three distinct social processes. The first process was labeled coercive isomorphism: the pressure to conform to institutionalized organizing templates such as those described by Meyer and Rowan (1977). The second source of institutional isomorphism was mimetic isomorphism, a tendency to imitate the practices of other organizations as a response to uncertainty. Finally, the third process was normative isomorphism, originating in the development of the professions and associated professional networks. DiMaggio and Powell (1983) also specified several conditions under which they expected institutional isomorphism to be especially strong. For example, they argued that resource dependence exacerbates coercive isomorphism—organizations that are dependent on a focal organization for resources experience pressure to conform to the organizing models advocated by that organization. The relationship between corporations and the Wall Street financial institutions on which the corporations are dependent for assistance in marketing their securities illustrates the role of resource dependence in promoting coercive isomorphism. Arguably, today's corporations have been influenced, even coerced, to adopt shareholder friendly policies and governance structures by their dependence on Wall Street. Correspondingly, DiMaggio and Powell (1983) stated that uncertainty about the relationship between means and ends in an organization's core technology creates a fertile context for mimetic isomorphism, leading organizations to model themselves after other organizations they perceive to be successful. Goal ambiguity also has a similar effect, enhancing the tendency of organizations to clone the management practices of other organizations. By introducing such variables as resource dependence, technological uncertainty, and goal ambiguity into their model, DiMaggio and Powell strengthened the continuity (McKinley, Mone, and Moon 1999) between their theory and other organizational schools of thought. These continuity linkages have probably made the DiMaggio and Powell framework more meaningful for organizational scholars than it would otherwise have been (McKinley, Mone, and Moon 1999), and may help explain the widespread use of the framework in subsequent theory and research (e.g. Haveman 1993; Haunschild 1993; McKinley, Sanchez, and Schick 1995; Mizruchi and Fein 1999).

While neo-institutional theory has been classified as a macro perspective in this chapter, there is one important issue in this school of thought that spans micro and macro levels of analysis. This is the question of how institutions (or 'institutional rules' in Meyer and Rowan's (1977) terminology) come into being. Berger and Luckmann (1966; see also DiMaggio and Powell 1991) addressed this issue, describing how social reality gets constructed through the development of habitual action and the abstraction of that action into 'reciprocal typifications'. These typifications are constructs that are shared by members of a social group, and they specify how a particular activity is to be performed. Examples might include the method of building a fire for ceremonial purposes, the processes to be followed in governing a social group, the techniques of trading financial securities, and so on. At some point these typifications assume an objective quality, being perceived by members of the social group as objective phenomena external to themselves and their actions. This is the process that Berger and Luckmann (1966) call 'reification' or 'objectivation'. In this way such social institutions as firemaking, government, financial markets, and of course, organizations, are born. Once these social institutions have been reified, they act as an external constraint on the behavior of individuals and are continually re-enacted by those individuals in the course of everyday life.

Consistent with this cognitively and behaviorally oriented approach, Zucker (1977) conducted experiments to demonstrate the effects of institutionalization on the persistence of behavior, and Suchman (1995) described the institutionalization of contract norms in venture capital finance. Tolbert and Zucker (1996) added depth to the processes described by Berger and Luckmann (1966), presenting a model that specified the stages in the institutionalization process. Tolbert and Zucker (1996) labeled these stages innovation, habitualization, objectification, and sedimentation. The sedimentation stage is particularly interesting because it is equivalent to Berger and Luckmann's reification, where reciprocal typifications acquire the attribute of objectivity and emerge as full-blown institutions. Based on this earlier work, McKinley, Zhao, and Rust (2000) developed a sociocognitive model of organizational downsizing, describing the institutionalization of downsizing as a process in which alternate schemas about the effectiveness and morality of downsizing were winnowed, and one schema was elevated into an external institution. In this way institutionalization is presented as a movement toward greater cognitive simplicity, which is reinforced by the cognitive order it generates for participants in the process (McKinley, Zhao, and Rust 2000).

As is true for the other theories we review, there are several criticisms of neo-institutional theory. One of these concerns the school's ambivalent position on the issue of rationality. On the one hand, early proponents of neo-institutional theory (Meyer and Rowan 1977; DiMaggio and Powell 1983) suggested that the motive for conforming to institutionalized practices is acquisition of legitimacy and reduction of uncertainty, rather than improvement of technical or financial performance. In this way neo-institutional theory is differentiated from other perspectives, such as neo-contingency theory, that make assumptions of managerial rationality. On the other hand, legitimacy was argued by the same neo-institutional theorists to be necessary for organizational survival (Meyer and Rowan 1977); and empirical evidence has been presented (e.g. Singh, Tucker, and House 1986) that is consistent with that position. One could therefore argue that conformity to institutionalized practices and the legitimacy it provides are effectively rational actions, whether or not they are intended as such (Donaldson 1995), because they improve the chances of organizational survival.

Donaldson (1995) also notes that the constructs of neo-institutional theory are prone to loose conceptualization, and we concur with this assessment. As is true for the other schools of thought we have discussed, this state of affairs is both a strength and a weakness. On the one hand, loose conceptualization and resulting construct ambiguity expand the boundaries of a school of thought, making it easier to explain a variety of empirical phenomena by invoking the school's constructs and theories (Astley 1985; Astley and Zammuto 1992). Neo-institutional theory certainly fits this characterization, for example in its ability to explain the diffusion of almost any organizational form or attribute as a process of institutional isomorphism. On the other hand, as pointed out already, construct ambiguity promotes incommensurability between different schools of thought and makes it difficult to conclusively test their relative validity.

For neo-institutional theory, this is illustrated by a hypothetical case that McKinley and Mone (1998) discussed. McKinley and Mone (1998) asked their readers to imagine an empirical comparison between neo-institutional theory and the theory of competitive strategy (Porter 1980, 1985) with regard to their explanations of organizational performance. The two perspectives are at least partially inconsistent in the way they account for performance: neo-institutional theory suggests that organizations need to become like other organizations in order to be perceived as legitimate and therefore to perform well, while the theory of competitive strategy suggests that organizations need to be different from other organizations to attain the same goal. In competitive strategy theory (Porter 1980, 1985), organizations must establish a unique position along parameters of cost, product differentiation, or service in order to attain a sustainable competitive advantage and survive over time. Which school of thought is correct about the way to attain high performance? Is being isomorphic with other organizations or being different from them the key? We believe that at this point in the development of organization studies, no empirical test can answer these questions because of the ambiguity of such constructs as 'organizational performance', 'isomorphism', and so on. Barring consensual, field-wide definitions that would anchor widely acknowledged measures of these constructs and provide a standard for empirical comparison, the neo-institutional and competitive strategy perspectives will remain incommensurable.

12.3 CONCLUSION: THE FUTURE OF ORGANIZATION THEORY

We have discussed five contemporary organization theory schools of thought, three at the micro level of individual organizations and their task environments, and two at the macro level of populations and fields. The development of these schools in the 1970s, 1980s, and 1990s expanded the domain of organization theory far beyond the dimensions of organization structure that were the primary concern of organizational scholars in the 1960s. This expansion introduced many interesting new research questions into the discipline, particularly questions concerning the relationships between organizations and their task environments and concerning the attributes of organizational populations. At the same time, the expansion has produced a fragmented discipline (McKinley, Mone, and Moon 1999; Pfeffer 1997; Whitley 2000) whose schools of thought are largely incommensurable due to the lack of consensus on how basic constructs should be defined and measured.

In this concluding section, we speculate briefly on the future of organization theory. Of course, there are many possible futures for this discipline, and each of these futures is currently available for enactment by organization theorists. However, we will concentrate on two possible futures that we regard as particularly interesting. The first of these involves a scenario of competition, in which the current schools of thought would be pitted against one another in a contest for validation. In that future, organization theorists would focus on the empirical domains in which different schools of thought make conflicting predictions or offer competing explanations for an organizational phenomenon. For example, does transaction costs theory, resource dependence theory, or neo-contingency theory provide the better explanation for the phenomenon of vertical integration? Are restructuring and organizational change beneficial for organizational perform- ance and survival chances, as suggested by neo-contingency theory, or do they threaten survival chances, as suggested by population ecology (Hannan and Freeman 1984)? Is being the same as other organizations or being different from them the key to competitive advantage and organizational effectiveness? These are the kinds of research questions that would occupy organization theorists in a future scenario of competition for validity.

Enacting this future would require a concentrated effort, not only to identify the empirical domains in which competing predictions and claims are present, but also to pose research questions in such a way that those competing predictions become evident. Organization theorists would also have to agree on the definitions and measures of the key constructs included in the research questions. Most import- antly, organization theorists would have to agree to be bound by those definitions and measures in their collective evaluation of empirical results, regardless of whether the results were favorable or unfavorable to any individual scholar's theoretical allegiances. Given that kind of consensus, a conclusive empirical assess- ment of competing theoretical claims could unfold, and the results of the empirical tests would have the kind of field-wide credibility that is rarely achieved in contem- porary organization theory research. The likely outcome of this assessment process would be a 'downscoping' of current organization theory schools to narrower empirical domains in which their claims had resisted disconfirmation.

In our opinion such a scenario, while appealing to some scholars, would face major obstacles. The level of focus and consensus required from members of the organization theory discipline would be one principal barrier. A case can be made that in recent decades, organization theory has been dominated by a 'uniqueness value', which dictates that unique work is good and constrains scholars toward the production of intellectual novelty (Astley 1985; Mone and McKinley 1993). The scenario envisioned above conflicts sharply with the uniqueness value, since it would require scholars to give up their idiosyncratic conceptualizations and meas- ures of constructs and come to field-wide agreement about how constructs are to be defined and measured. Furthermore, the narrowing of schools' empirical domains that would likely ensue from the scenario of competition would not necessarily be welcomed by the prominent organization theorists who have spearheaded the founding and development of the schools.

In our view, a second scenario, involving the dampening of competition, is more likely. Indeed, there is some evidence that this scenario is already beginning to unfold. For example, Meyer and Rowan's (1977) original presentation of neo- institutional theory contrasted that perspective with models that explain organiza- tion structure as a means for coordinating work efficiently. More recently, however, theorists have sought an accommodation between neo-institutional theory and such efficiency-based perspectives as transaction costs theory (Roberts and

Greenwood 1997) or economic theory (Dacin 1997). This kind of accommodation reduces the motivation of scholars to pit neo-institutional and efficiency-based perspectives directly against one another.

Other evidence of the tendency to reduce competition lies in the potential synthesis of the population ecology and neo-institutional perspectives (Baum 1996). In addition to the use of legitimation in the density dependence model, neo-institutional constructs have been invoked to explain birth and death rates in many population ecology studies. For example, Singh, Tucker, and House (1986) found that legitimacy—as measured by such factors as the possession of a charitable registration number and a community directory listing—moderated the liability of newness in Canadian social service organizations. Thus legitimacy offered these organizations some protection from the hazard of death. If population ecology and neo-institutional theory were to combine based on results like these, the combination would be the dominant player in the macro intellectual 'space' of organization theory. The merged entity would probably lose some of the conceptual flexibility that presently characterizes neo-institutional theory, but it might further solidify the quasi-paradigm status (Pfeffer 1993) maintained by population ecology's narrow focus on the issue of vital rates. Quasi-paradigm or paradigm status would, in turn, facilitate a consensus-based approach to answering a worthwhile, albeit limited, set of research questions.

What appears to be happening in these accommodations and incipient merger movements is a softening of the between-perspective differences that were highlighted (or constructed) in the initial formulations by the founders of the organization theory schools. Highlighting differences between perspectives early in the evolution of a school serves to underline the school's 'opportunity for contribution' (Locke and Golden-Biddle 1997) and to position the school as novel and worthy of notice (McKinley, Mone, and Moon 1999). But once a school is well established and has its own disciples and its own stream of empirical research, the need to stress differences between it and other perspectives may become less urgent.

The moderation of inter-school competition through integration and reinterpretation of the initial formulations of school founders could conceivably lead to the creation of a unified paradigm for organization theory. For example, Donaldson (1995) has attempted to develop such a framework, combining theoretical elements from neo-contingency theory, population ecology theory, resource dependence theory, and neo-institutional theory. In our view a unified paradigm would be a positive development, but it would not necessarily guarantee consensus on the definitions of the key constructs that would form the building blocks of the paradigm. One of the virtues of the first scenario described above—the scenario of competition for validation—is that it would force the establishment of at least provisional agreement on definitions and measures of constructs. It is possible that a unified organization theory paradigm emerging from the second scenario would remain as resistant to conclusive empirical testing as the separate organization theory schools are today. For better or worse, that would reduce organization theory's claim to the label of 'science'.

Which of these two scenarios—or any of the other possible futures for organization theory—will actually occur? The answer to that question is, of course, dependent on the collective action of organization theory scholars. In the end, it's up to us.

REFERENCES

ALDRICH, H. E. (1979). *Organizations and Environments*. Englewood Cliffs, NJ: Prentice-Hall.

ALEXANDER, J. W., and RANDOLPH, W. A. (1985). 'The Fit between Technology and Structure as a Predictor of Performance in Nursing Subunits'. *Academy of Management Journal*, 28: 844–59.

ASTLEY, W. G. (1985). 'Administrative Science as Socially Constructed Truth'. *Administrative Science Quarterly*, 30: 497–513.

—— and VAN DE VEN, A. H. (1983). 'Central Perspectives and Debates in Organization Theory'. *Administrative Science Quarterly*, 28: 245–73.

—— and ZAMMUTO, R. F. (1992). 'Organization Science, Managers, and Language Games'. *Organization Science*, 3: 443–60.

BACHARACH, S. B. (1989). 'Organizational Theories: Some Criteria for Evaluation'. *Academy of Management Review*, 14: 496–515.

BARNETT, W. P., and AMBURGEY, T. L. (1990). 'Do Larger Organizations Generate Stronger Competition?', in J. V. Singh (ed.), *Organizational Evolution: New Directions*. Newbury Park, Calif.: Sage.

BARNEY, J. B., and HESTERLY, W. (1996). 'Organizational Economics: Understanding the Relationship between Organizations and Economic Analysis', in S. R. Clegg, C. Hardy, and W. R. Nord (eds.), *Handbook of Organization Studies*. London: Sage.

BAUM, J. A. C. (1996). 'Organizational Ecology', in S. R. Clegg, C. Hardy, and W. R. Nord (eds.), *Handbook of Organization Studies*. London: Sage.

—— and OLIVER, C. (1992). 'Institutional Embeddedness and the Dynamics of Organizational Populations'. *American Sociological Review*, 57: 540–59.

BERGER, P. L., and LUCKMANN, T. (1966). *The Social Construction of Reality: A Treatise in the Sociology of Knowledge*. New York: Doubleday.

BUDROS, A. (1994). 'Analyzing Unexpected Density Dependence Effects on Organizational Births in New York's Life Insurance Industry, 1842–1904'. *Organization Science*, 5: 541–53.

CARROLL, G. R., and HANNAN, M. T. (1989). 'Density Delay in the Evolution of Organizational Populations: A Model and Five Empirical Tests'. *Administrative Science Quarterly*, 34: 411–30.

CHANDLER, A. D. (1962). *Strategy and Structure: Chapters in the History of the American Industrial Enterprise*. Cambridge, Mass.: MIT Press.

—— (1977). *The Visible Hand: The Managerial Revolution in American Business*. Cambridge, Mass.: Harvard University Press.

—— (1981). 'Historical Determinants of Managerial Hierarchies: A Response to Perrow', in A. H. Van de Ven and W. F. Joyce (eds.), *Perspectives on Organization Design and Behavior*. New York: John Wiley and Sons.

CROZIER, M. (1964). *The Bureaucratic Phenomenon*. London: Tavistock.

DACIN, M. T. (1997). 'Isomorphism in Context: The Power and Prescription of Institutional Norms'. *Academy of Management Journal*, 40: 46–81.

DAVIS, G. F., and POWELL, W. W. (1992). 'Organization–Environment Relations', in M. Dunnette and L. M. Hough (eds.), *Handbook of Industrial and Organizational Psychology* (2nd edn). Palo Alto, Calif.: Consulting Psychologists Press.

DIMAGGIO, P. J., and POWELL, W. W. (1983). 'The Iron Cage Revisited: Institutional Isomorphism and Collective Rationality in Organizational Fields'. *American Sociological Review*, 48: 147–60.

————(1991). 'Introduction', in W. W. Powell and P. J. DiMaggio (eds.), *The New Institutionalism in Organizational Analysis*. Chicago: University of Chicago Press.

DONALDSON, L. (1995). *American Anti-Management Theories of Organization: A Critique of Paradigm Proliferation*. Cambridge: Cambridge University Press.

—— (1999). *Performance-Driven Organizational Change: The Organizational Portfolio*. Thousand Oaks, Calif.: Sage.

DRAZIN, R., and VAN DE VEN, A. H. (1985). 'Alternative Forms of Fit in Contingency Theory'. *Administrative Science Quarterly*, 30: 514–39.

DUNFORD, R., and PALMER, I. (1996). 'Metaphors in Popular Management Discourse: The Case of Corporate Restructuring', in D. Grant and C. Oswick (eds.), *Metaphor and Organizations*. London: Sage.

FREEMAN, S. J., and CAMERON, K. S. (1993). 'Organizational Downsizing: A Convergence and Reorientation Framework'. *Organization Science*, 4: 10–29.

GHOSHAL, S., and MORAN, P. (1996). 'Bad for Practice: A Critique of the Transaction Cost Theory'. *Academy of Management Review*, 21: 13–47.

GRANOVETTER, M. (1985). 'Economic Action and Social Structure: The Problem of Embeddedness'. *American Journal of Sociology*, 91: 481–510.

GRESOV, C. (1989). 'Exploring Fit and Misfit with Multiple Contingencies'. *Administrative Science Quarterly*, 34: 431–53.

HANNAN, M. T., and CARROLL, G. R. (1992). *Dynamics of Organizational Populations: Density, Legitimation, and Competition*. New York: Oxford University Press.

—— and FREEMAN, J. (1977). 'The Population Ecology of Organizations'. *American Journal of Sociology*, 82: 929–64.

————(1984). 'Structural Inertia and Organizational Change'. *American Sociological Review*, 49: 149–64.

HAUNSCHILD, P. R. (1993). 'Interorganizational Imitation: The Impact of Interlocks on Corporate Acquisition Activity'. *Administrative Science Quarterly*, 38: 564–92.

HAVEMAN, H. A. (1993). 'Follow the Leader: Mimetic Isomorphism and Entry into New Markets'. *Administrative Science Quarterly*, 38: 593–627.

HICKSON, D. J., HININGS, C. R., LEE, C. A., SCHNECK, R. E., and PENNINGS, J. M. (1971). 'A Strategic Contingencies' Theory of Intraorganizational Power'. *Administrative Science Quarterly*, 16: 216–29.

—— PUGH, D. S., and PHEYSEY, D. G. (1969). 'Operations Technology and Organization Structure: An Empirical Reappraisal'. *Administrative Science Quarterly*, 14: 378–97.

HININGS, C. R., HICKSON, D. J., PENNINGS, J. M., and SCHNECK, R. E. (1974). 'Structural Conditions of Intraorganizational Power'. *Administrative Science Quarterly*, 19: 22–44.

HIRSCH, P. M., and LEVIN, D. Z. (1999). 'Umbrella Advocates Versus Validity Police: A Life-Cycle Model'. *Organization Science*, 10: 199–212.

HOSKISSON, R. E., and HITT, M. A. (1994). *Downscoping: How to Tame the Diversified Firm*. New York: Oxford University Press.

KUHN, T. S. (1970). *The Structure of Scientific Revolutions* (2nd edn.). Chicago: University of Chicago Press.

LAWRENCE, P. R., and LORSCH, J. W. (1967). *Organization and Environment: Managing Differentiation and Integration*. Boston: Harvard Business School Press.

LIEBERSON, S. (1985). *Making it Count: The Improvement of Social Research and Theory*. Berkeley: University of California Press.

LOCKE, K., and GOLDEN-BIDDLE, K. (1997). 'Constructing Opportunities for Contribution: Structuring Intertextual Coherence and "Problematizing" in Organization Studies'. *Academy of Management Journal*, 40: 1023–62.

MASUCH, M. (1985). 'Vicious Circles in Organizations'. *Administrative Science Quarterly*, 30: 14–33.

MCKINLEY, W. (1992). 'Decreasing Organizational Size: To Untangle or not to Untangle?' *Academy of Management Review*, 17: 112–23.

—— and MONE, M. A. (1998). 'The Re-construction of Organization Studies: Wrestling with Incommensurability'. *Organization*, 5: 169–89.

—— —— and MOON, G. (1999). 'Determinants and Development of Schools in Organization Theory'. *Academy of Management Review*, 24: 634–48.

—— SANCHEZ, C. M., and SCHICK, A. G. (1995). 'Organizational Downsizing: Constraining, Cloning, Learning'. *Academy of Management Executive*, 9/3: 32–44.

—— and SCHERER, A. G. (2000). 'Some Unanticipated Consequences of Organizational Restructuring'. *Academy of Management Review*, 25: 735–52.

—— ZHAO, J., and RUST, K. G. (2000). 'A Sociocognitive Interpretation of Organizational Downsizing'. *Academy of Management Review*, 25: 227–43.

MENTZER, M. S. (1996). 'Corporate Downsizing and Profitability in Canada'. *Canadian Journal of Administrative Sciences*, 13: 237–50.

MERTON, R. K. (1936). 'The Unanticipated Consequences of Purposive Social Action'. *American Sociological Review*, 1: 894–904.

—— (1968). *Social Theory and Social Structure*. New York: Free Press.

MEYER, J. W., BOLI, J., and THOMAS, G. M. (1994). 'Ontology and Rationalization in the Western Cultural Account', in W. R. Scott, J. W. Meyer, and Associates, *Institutional Environments and Organizations: Structural Complexity and Individualism*. Thousand Oaks, Calif.: Sage.

—— and ROWAN, B. (1977). 'Institutionalized Organizations: Formal Structure as Myth and Ceremony'. *American Journal of Sociology*, 83: 340–63.

MIZRUCHI, M. S., and FEIN, L. C. (1999). 'The Social Construction of Organizational Knowledge: A Study of the Uses of Coercive, Mimetic, and Normative Isomorphism'. *Administrative Science Quarterly*, 44: 653–83.

MONE, M. A., and MCKINLEY, W. (1993). 'The Uniqueness Value and its Consequences for Organization Studies'. *Journal of Management Inquiry*, 2: 284–96.

PERROW, C. (1981). 'Markets, Hierarchies, and Hegemony', in A. H. Van de Ven and W. F. Joyce (eds.), *Perspectives on Organization Design and Behavior*. New York: John Wiley and Sons.

PFEFFER, J. (1993). 'Barriers to the Advance of Organizational Science: Paradigm Development as a Dependent Variable'. *Academy of Management Review*, 18: 599–620.

—— (1997). *New Directions for Organization Theory: Problems and Prospects*. New York: Oxford University Press.

—— and SALANCIK, G. R. (1974). 'Organizational Decision-Making as a Political Process: The Case of a University Budget'. *Administrative Science Quarterly*, 19: 135–51.

—— —— (1978). *The External Control of Organizations: A Resource Dependence Perspective*. New York: Harper & Row.

PORTER, M. E. (1980). *Competitive Strategy*. New York: Free Press.

—— (1985). *Competitive Advantage*. New York: Free Press.

PUGH, D. S., HICKSON, D. J., HININGS, C. R., MACDONALD, K. M., TURNER, C., and LUPTON, T. (1963). 'A Conceptual Scheme for Organizational Analysis'. *Administrative Science Quarterly*, 8: 289–315.

—— —— —— and TURNER, C. (1968). 'Dimensions of Organization Structure'. *Administrative Science Quarterly*, 13: 65–105.

ROBERTS, P. W., and GREENWOOD, R. (1997). 'Integrating Transaction Cost and Institutional Theories: Toward a Constrained-Efficiency Framework for Understanding Organizational Design Adoption'. *Academy of Management Review*, 22: 346–73.

SALANCIK, G. R., and PFEFFER, J. (1974). 'The Bases and Use of Power in Organizational Decision-Making: The Case of a University'. *Administrative Science Quarterly*, 19: 453–73.

SCHERER, A. G. (1998). 'Pluralism and Incommensurability in Strategic Management and Organization Theory: A Problem in Search of a Solution'. *Organization*, 5: 147–68.

—— and STEINMANN, H. (1999). 'Some Remarks on the Problem of Incommensurability in Organization Studies'. *Organization Studies*, 20: 519–44.

SCHOONHOVEN, C. B. (1981). 'Problems with Contingency Theory: Testing Assumptions Hidden within the Language of Contingency "Theory"'. *Administrative Science Quarterly*, 26: 349–77.

SCHULTZ, M. (1998). 'Limits to Bureaucratic Growth: The Density Dependence of Organizational Rule Births'. *Administrative Science Quarterly*, 43: 845–76.

SCOTT, W. R., and MEYER, J. W. (1983). 'The Organization of Societal Sectors', in J. W. Meyer and W. R. Scott (eds.), *Organizational Environments: Ritual and Rationality*. Beverly Hills, Calif.: Sage.

SIMON, H. A. (1997). *Administrative Behavior: A Study of Decision-Making Processes in Administrative Organizations* (4th edn). New York: Free Press.

SINGH, J. V., TUCKER, D. J., and HOUSE, R. J. (1986). 'Organizational Legitimacy and the Liability of Newness'. *Administrative Science Quarterly*, 31: 171–93.

SMIRCICH, L., and STUBBART, C. (1985). 'Strategic Management in an Enacted World'. *Academy of Management Review*, 10: 724–36.

SUCHMAN, M. C. (1995). 'Localism and Globalism in Institutional Analysis: The Emergence of Contractual Norms in Venture Finance', in W. R. Scott and S. Christensen (eds.), *The Institutional Construction of Organizations: International and Longitudinal Studies*. Thousand Oaks, Calif.: Sage.

THOMPSON, J. D. (1967). *Organizations in Action: Social Science Bases of Administrative Theory.* New York: McGraw-Hill.

TOLBERT, P. S., and ZUCKER, L. G. (1996). 'The Institutionalization of Institutional Theory', in S. R. Clegg, C. Hardy, and W. R. Nord (eds.), *Handbook of Organization Studies.* London: Sage.

WALKER, G., and WEBER, D. (1984). 'A Transaction Cost Approach to Make-or-Buy Decisions'. *Administrative Science Quarterly*, 29: 373–91.

WEICK, K. E. (1979). *The Social Psychology of Organizing* (2nd edn). Reading, Mass.: Addison-Wesley.

—— (1995). *Sensemaking in Organizations.* Thousand Oaks, Calif.: Sage.

WHITLEY, R. (2000). *The Intellectual and Social Organization of the Sciences* (2nd edn). Oxford: Oxford University Press.

WILLIAMSON, O. E. (1981). 'The Economics of Organization: The Transaction Cost Approach'. *American Journal of Sociology*, 87: 548–77.

—— (1991). 'Comparative Economic Organization: The Analysis of Discrete Structural Alternatives'. *Administrative Science Quarterly*, 36: 269–96.

—— and OUCHI, W. G. (1981). 'The Markets and Hierarchies Program of Research: Origins, Implications, Prospects', in A. H. Van de Ven and W. F. Joyce (eds.), *Perspectives on Organization Design and Behavior.* New York: John Wiley and Sons.

WOODWARD, J. (1958). *Management and Technology.* London: Her Majesty's Stationery Office.

—— (1965). *Industrial Organization: Theory and Practice.* New York: Oxford University Press.

YOUNG, R. C. (1988). 'Is Population Ecology a Useful Paradigm for the Study of Organizations?' *American Journal of Sociology*, 94: 1–24.

ZUCKER, L. G. (1977). 'The Role of Institutionalization in Cultural Persistence'. *American Sociological Review*, 42: 726–43.

—— (1989). 'Combining Institutional Theory and Population Ecology: No Legitimacy, No History'. *American Sociological Review*, 54: 542–5.

CHAPTER 13

ECONOMIC VERSUS SOCIOLOGICAL APPROACHES TO ORGANIZATION THEORY

RICHARD SWEDBERG

ORGANIZATION THEORY has displayed a remarkable creativity during its roughly one hundred years of existence and there are a number of reasons for this. One of these has clearly to do with the fact that organizations have increasingly come to occupy an ever more important role in modern society. Another is that contributions to organization theory have been made not only by academics, as is the norm in the social sciences, but also by practitioners such as Frederick W. Taylor and Chester Barnard. A third reason for the remarkable creativity of organization theory is that this field does not belong to one single social science discipline, but is interdisciplinary in character.

But even if organization theory is interdisciplinary, it remains a stubborn fact that most research on organizations is carried out within distinct disciplines and according to disciplinary traditions. This means that questions of the following type need to be addressed: On what points do the different social science analyses of organizations differ? Given that each social science has its own vantage point, can they nonetheless be said to complement each other? There also exist some disturbing questions: What do you do when two types of analyses contradict one another? Is it true that one type of social science analysis is so superior that it should take precedence over all other types of analyses? And was Schumpeter right when he warned that 'cross-fertilization [between two social sciences] might easily result in cross-sterilization' (Schumpeter 1954: 27)?

In this chapter I shall first present organizational economics (Section 13.1), mainly focussing on transaction cost analysis, agency analysis, and what I call evolutionary, game theoretical and property rights perspectives. This will be followed by a presentation of the way that firms have been studied in economic sociology, and here I discuss the Weberian heritage in organizational sociology, the focus on firms (as opposed to the firm) in this type of sociology and the role that culture and meaning plays in it (Section 13.2). I will conclude with a brief discussion of the antagonism between organizational economics and the sociology of organizations, and how this antagonism perhaps can be overcome (Section 13.3).

13.1 ORGANIZATIONAL ECONOMICS

13.1.1 The View of the Firm in Organizational Economics

With 'organizational economics' is meant a kind of analysis that has come to predominate in the analysis of the firm in contemporary economics (e.g. Barnes and Ouchi 1986; cf. Douma and Schreuder 1998). Included are first and foremost agency theory and transaction cost economics but also evolutionary approaches, game theoretical approaches, and approaches inspired by the property rights literature. With the exception of Coase's well-known article on the nature of the firm from 1937, references to works before 1970 are rare. This means among other things that in order to give a full picture of the way that economics looks at organizations, a few words need to be said about pre-1970 attempts to analyze the firm.

While one can find a few comments on business firms already in *The Wealth of Nations* (1776), the theory of the firm is traditionally seen as originating in the work of Cournot from 1838 (e.g. Blaug 1980: 175). Cournot saw the firm as maximizing profit, subject to the constraints of technology and demand. A particularly useful tool for analyzing the economic role of the firm in the twentieth century has been the so-called production function, typically defined in the following manner: 'The production function is the technical relationship telling the maximum amount of output capable of being produced by each and every set of specified inputs (or factors of production); it is defined for a given set of technical knowledge' (Samuelson 1970: 516). While helpful in constructing the cost curves of individual firms as well as their demand curves for factors of production, it is also clear that the organizational structure of the firm cannot be captured through the production function. During the last few decades this has led to a number of harsh criticisms. One author writes, for example, that 'in standard price theory, the firm is itself a primitive atom of the economy, an unindividuated, single-minded agent interacting with similarly unindividuated consumers and factor suppliers in the market economy' (Putterman 1986: 5).

But even if mainstream economics for most of the twentieth century has ignored the organizational structure of the firm, there exist a few outstanding exceptions. One is Alfred Marshall, whose work contains a wealth of innovative ideas about the firm, some of which have been further developed in evolutionary theories and in research on industrial districts (e.g. Archibald 1987: 358–9). A special mention should also be made of Marshall's suggestion that 'organizations' be seen as the fourth production factor (Marshall 1920/1961: 138–9, 240–313). Marshall's strength comes mainly from his great capacity to combine analytical thinking with empirical knowledge of the economy.

This combination of analytical thought and empirical insights can also be found in the work on the behavioral theory of the firm, as created by Herbert Simon, James March, and Richard Cyert (e.g. March and Simon 1958; Cyert and March 1963). Also a number of innovative ideas can be found here, including the notion of the firm as 'a political coalition'. Instead of making the assumption that the firm is a unit which has a single uncontested objective, March suggests that it can be seen as coalition consisting of various groups, such as employees, investors, suppliers, and so on (e.g. March 1962). Finally, some important ideas in this context can be found in the works of Frank Knight on 'the economic organization' and by Jacob Marschak on 'teams' (Knight 1933/1967; Marschak and Radner 1972).

13.1.2 Transaction Cost Analysis

The foundation for transaction cost analysis was laid through a very famous article. This is 'The Nature of the Firm' (1937), written by R. H. Coase when he was in his twenties and hardly knew any economics. Coase later noted that it was not till the 1970s that his article started to have a real impact on the economics profession and that Oliver Williamson's work had done much to prepare the ground for its reception. When Coase in 1991 received the Nobel Prize, his article from 1937 was singled out, together with 'The Problem of Social Cost' (1960).

The fact that 'The Nature of the Firm' was not much read till the 1970s indicates that its main idea was ahead of its time. And this idea was that economics could not only be used to explain the market but also the firm. Coase, in other words, had found a way to extend the reach of economics. By the 1970s, it should be noted, this way of thinking went very well with the efforts to apply the economic way of analysis to non-economic topics which had been initiated in the 1950s and 1960s by people such as Gary Becker, James Buchanan, and Anthony Downs (e.g. Udehn 1991).

In 'The Nature of the Firm' Coase starts out by noting that even though economists argue that everything that happens in the economic sphere is voluntary, there also exist parts of the economy where orders are given and people have to obey. The firm is an example of the latter; and Coase concludes from this that there are *two* ways of getting things done in capitalist economies. The firm and the market can consequently be seen as 'alternative methods of co-ordinating production' (Coase 1937/1993: 19).

But if there exist two ways of getting things done in the economy, when is one rather than the other used? Why, in particular, do firms exist if there are markets? Coase's answer to this question is that there is a cost for using the market, and if this cost exceeds the cost for using a firm, a firm will in principle be created. 'The main reason why it is profitable to establish a firm would seem to be that there is a cost of using the price mechanism', to cite the single most important sentence in 'The Nature of the Firm' (Coase 1937/1993: 21). Coase does not use the term 'transaction cost' in his article, but the idea is clearly there. The cost of using the market, he says, covers such items as the cost to acquire information, to draw up a contract, and so on. Coase concludes that his theory of the firm is both '[*analytically*] *manageable*' and '*realistic*' (Coase 1937/1993: 30; emphasis added).

If Coase was the person who invented the idea of transaction cost, it was Oliver Williamson who popularized it and made it known in economics as well as in neighboring sciences. This was done through a steady stream of books and articles in the 1970s and 1980s, the most important of which is *Markets and Hierarchies* (see also Williamson 1985, 1986). The key idea of *Markets and Hierarchies* (1975) is neatly captured by its title and dramatizes Coase's insight from 1937, namely that markets and firms constitute alternative methods of coordinating production or, in Williamson's terminology, different 'governance structures'.

Even though Williamson had received his main intuition to his transaction cost analysis from Coase, he also added his own ideas and eliminated some of Coase's concerns. The term 'transaction cost', for example, was invented by Williamson who defines it in the following way:

The *ex ante* costs of drafting, negotiating and *safeguarding* an agreement and, more especially, the *ex post* costs of maladaptation and adjustment that arise when contract execution is misaligned as a result of gaps, errors, omissions, and unanticipated disturbances; the costs of running the economic system. (Williamson 1991: 103)

While Coase had only spoken of two governance structures—markets and firms—Williamson, under the pressure of criticism, soon added a third: a 'hybrid' or an autonomous form of organization, based on long-term contractual relations (Williamson 1991: 102). Economic actors, in Williamson's version of transaction cost analysis, are opportunistic and make their choices with the help of bounded rationality. Very importantly, Williamson also attempted to operationalize Coase's insights and to state under which circumstances the market rather than a firm was likely to be used. The tendency, he argued, is that a firm will be used when transactions are frequent, uncertain, and demand special investments ('asset specificity'). The market, on the other hand, will typically be used when no asset specificity is involved, when transactions are straightforward, and only occur once.

According to the Social Science Citation Index, Williamson's work is cited more often than any other author in organization theory, and Williamson himself has stated that transaction cost analysis is 'an empirical success story' (David and Han 1998; Williamson 1996: 53). According to a survey of various attempts to test Williamson's theories empirically, however, only half of these have been successful (David and Han 1998). Part of the reason for this poor result, one suspects, has to do with the fact that in taking over Coase's ideas, Williamson failed to pay attention to Coase's argument that economic theories should not only be analytical but also 'realistic'. While in Coase's work there has always existed a certain tension in relation to mainstream economics because it is too far removed from empirical reality, this is not the case with Williamson.

13.1.3 Agency Theory

The concept of agency comes from legal thought and has its origin in medieval church law and in British legal thought (e.g. Müller-Freienfels 1978). The legal problem that this concept is used to handle has to do with the situation in which a person needs to be represented vis-à-vis a third person; and its solution is centered around the two concepts of 'principal' and 'agent'. When economics started to adopt this view of looking at things in the 1970s, a third actor was quickly added to the analysis: 'the monitor' or the person who checks the agent, on behalf of the principal (e.g. Alchian and Demsetz 1972/1986).

Agency theory has mainly been used to analyze a central problem in finance, namely how do you safeguard the interests of the owner when she does not manage the company herself? As an example of this type of research one can mention what is probably the most cited article in the agency literature, namely Michael Jensen and William Meckling's 'Theory of the Firm: Managerial Behavior, Agency Costs, and Ownership Structure' (1976/1986). The main purpose of this article is to develop a theory of what kind of owner structure a firm ought to have; and as part of this purpose, a number of situations are discussed in which ownership and management are in different hands (see also Fama and Jensen 1983/1986).

Jensen and Meckling also note that if the manager does not own 100 percent of the firm she will have an incentive to behave in an opportunistic manner and set her own interests ahead of those of the owner. She may be interested in perquisites or in some other way of satisfying her own interests at the cost of the firm. In order to counter behavior of this type, agency theory teaches, the owner can try to control the manager in various ways; she may also try to steer the behavior of the manager through some kind of award (agency bonding). All of this costs money—but in a perfectly competitive capital market, Jensen and Meckling argue, it will ultimately be the manager who pays for the so-called agency costs (cf. Smith 1987). It is consequently in the interest of the manager, the authors conclude, to introduce a capital structure into the firm where agency costs are minimized.

The basic structure of agency theory is as follows: the analysis begins with a principal who wants something done, and an agent who is paid to carry out the task but who also has her own interests. The interests of the principal and the agent can be aligned, but this may be hard to accomplish, especially if the agent is opportunistic. There do exist a few ways, however, in which the principal can safeguard her interests. One is to introduce a monitor who watches over the agent and sees to it that the task is done. This naturally costs money—the monitor has to be paid—but it also means that the problem is simply transferred elsewhere since the monitor herself has to be controlled. Another way to proceed in this situation is to give the agent an incentive to do what the principal wants; and in this situation no monitor is needed. Work against commission represents a well-known example of this type of safeguarding the interests of the principal.

While there exist a number of studies that have tried to test transaction cost analysis against empirical reality, this is much less true for agency theory. Here you only find impressionistic statements, such as Kenneth Arrow's argument that in many situations where agency theory argues that rewards should have a very complex structure, this is not the case in reality (Arrow 1985: 48–9). Arrow has also pointed out that in several cases, where agency theory states that it is the principal who will decide the price of a service, this is not what actually takes place. As an example he cites the doctor–patient relationship, where in theory it should be the patient who decides the price. In brief, while agency theory has made a number of important theoretical contributions, it needs to be better checked against reality.

13.1.4 Evolutionary, Game Theoretical, and Property Rights Perspectives

Besides agency theory and transaction cost theory, organizational economics also includes attempts to analyze organizational behavior by drawing on evolutionary, game theoretical, and property rights perspectives. Though all of these approaches have made valuable contributions to organizational economics, none has developed a full-fledged theory of the firm. It should also be emphasized that it is very common to find elements from different strands of organizational economics in one and the same analysis. To some extent, one could say that the future of organizational economics rests more on the successful accumulation of ideas from several perspectives, than on the further development of one specific theoretical approach.

As to contributions to organizational economics from evolutionary economics, a special mention must be made of Richard Nelson and Sidney Winter's *An Evolutionary Theory of the Firm* (1982). What is novel about this study is its focus on 'routines' and how these under certain circumstances may evolve in novel directions (for a critique, see however Mirowski 1988). Evolutionary perspectives are also very common in recent game theory, where organizations are often seen as the solution to reiterated games (e.g. Axelrod 1984; cf. Schotter 1981). But game theory can naturally also be used in other ways to conceptualize organizations, as already von Neumann and Morgenstern illustrate through their analyses of 'coalitions' (von Neumann and Morgenstern 1944/1980). Judging from the enormous success of game theory in industrial organization, one is probably justified in having high hopes that game theory will one day develop a successful theory of organizations (e.g. Tirole 1988). Up till now, however, game theory has mainly been used to elucidate various aspects of the behavior of firms (e.g. Baron and Kreps 1999). Finally, the perspective of property rights can throw an interesting light on many issues in organization theory. The idea of separation between the ownership and the management of a firm is, for example, easily conceptualized in property rights terms. Also the position that workers and other employees have in a firm can be elucidated through a property rights perspective.

13.2 ECONOMIC SOCIOLOGY

13.2.1 The View of the Firm in Economic Sociology

The great majority of studies in organizational economics are devoted to the firm, as opposed to non-economic organizations such as political organizations, religious organizations, and so on (e.g. Marshak 1987: 757). In this sense economic theories of organizations differ from the sociology of organizations since the latter attempts to cover the whole spectrum of organizations and also to develop general theories of organizations (for overviews of the different schools in the sociology of organizations, see Perrow 1986 and Scott 1997). Only a minority of the studies carried out by sociologists are actually devoted to the firm, and little attempt has been made to develop a distinct sociological theory of firms (for an exception, see e.g. Bernoux 1995). Nonetheless, firms *do* differ on several accounts from other organizations: the institution of the firm has its own history, which differs from those of religious, political, and other organizations; the legal status of firms is covered in special legislation; firms, as opposed to other organizations, have as their goal to make a profit; and firms also control most economic resources in modern society, which raises the issue of economic power. To make the comparison in this chapter between economic and sociological theories of organizations more meaningful, I shall therefore say something about the way that the firm has been analyzed in economic sociology. With economic sociology, it can be added, is in all brevity simply meant the sociological approach applied to economic topics (e.g. Smelser and Swedberg 1994).

13.2.2 The Weberian Heritage in Organizational Sociology

Max Weber's contribution to the study of organizations has been enormous, and something needs to be said both about Weber's own views and the way in which his ideas have been assimilated by other sociologists. Economists, it may be noted in passing, have shown practically no interest in Weber's analysis of organizations. As to Weber's own contribution, the main point to stress is that sociologists of organization have often had a restricted view of Weber's work. More precisely, they have limited their reading of Weber to some excerpts from his analysis of bureaucracy and missed his general sociology of organizations as well as his analysis of economic organizations.

Weber's general sociology of organizations will not be discussed here, as opposed to his analysis of the firm. Weber's three main contributions to the latter topic are, in brief, the following. First, Weber tried to map out the evolution of the firm throughout history (e.g. Weber 1922/1978, 1924/1981). Second, Weber opened the door to an interesting cultural-sociological analysis of the firm by emphasizing the role that 'spirit' plays in it (Weber 1904–5/1958). And third, Weber introduced the figure of the entrepreneur directly into his analysis of the capitalist firm, thereby endowing it with considerable dynamic (e.g. Swedberg 2000).

The secondary literature on Weber's theory of organizations has mainly been centered on his theory of bureaucracy. On the whole one can say that Weber's ideas on this topic have been found wanting on a number of points—but have also inspired some outstanding studies of economic organizations (e.g. Gouldner 1954; Crozier 1964; for critiques, see e.g. Albrow 1970: 50–66). As an example of a creative attempt to both criticize and further develop Weber's ideas one can mention Stinchcombe's well-known analysis of the construction industry, in which the author argues that there exist other ways of getting things done in a firm than through bureaucracy (Stinchcombe 1959). Besides telling people what to do, one can also let certain units of production possess relevant knowledge ('bureaucratic' versus 'craft administration of production'). Paul Hirsch has later added to Stinchcombe's insights by showing that not only construction but also various cultural items, such as books and records, cannot be produced by a bureaucracy but only by small and independent units of one or a couple of persons (Hirsch 1972). A special mention should also be made of Gary Hamilton's attempt to draw attention to the fact that capitalist firms do not only operate through bureaucracy but also through domination or *Herrschaft* (e.g. Hamilton and Biggart 1988).

13.2.3 The Focus on Firms—as Opposed to the Firm— in Organizational Sociology

While economists have had a tendency to focus on the single firm, contemporary sociologists typically study a number of firms. This shift from the individual firm to a collective of firms, Granovetter says, represents just as much a qualitative leap in social science analysis as the shift from the individual to the firm (Granovetter 1994: 453). Sociologists often refer to 'the organizational field'; they analyze how an organization is dependent on other organizations ('resource dependence'); they look at whole series of organizations ('population ecology'); and they have recently developed the concept of 'business groups' to study certain groups of firms. Sociologists have also pioneered 'networks' as a way of analyzing organizations.

The idea of a field has been independently developed by sociologists in the United States and in Europe, and it has been given its most elaborate theoretical expression by Pierre Bourdieu (e.g. DiMaggio 1986; DiMaggio and Powell 1991: 64–5; Bourdieu and Wacquant 1992). 'In analytical terms', Bourdieu states, 'a field may be defined as a network, or a configuration, of objective relations between positions' (Bourdieu and Wacquant 1992: 97). A field is also characterized by the fact that it has a distinct history and that the behavior of the actors is partly shaped by their past behavior ('*habitus*'). There is a constant struggle in a field and the actors have various forms of capital at their disposal (financial capital, social capital, symbolic capital, and so on). The economy constitutes a special kind of field, and so does the individual corporation (Bourdieu 2000). Actors in economic fields have distinct dispositions ('*economic habitus*'); the composition of capital is of a special kind; and the struggle between the actors follows its own logic. Bourdieu also points out that Scherer's type of industrial organization was much more empirical in nature than that of Tirole and other game theoreticians (Bourdieu 2000: 243–4).

The concept of resource dependence emerged in the 1970s in organizational sociology and basically states that in order to survive an organization needs resources from its environment—that is, from other organizations (e.g. Pfeffer and Salancik 1978). One effect of this is that an organization will be dependent on its environment; another that its management will develop a strategy for how to cope with external constraints. The idea of resource dependence is for obvious reasons congenial to the analysis of economic organizations and has been used for this purpose especially by Ronald Burt (e.g. 1983). A firm has 'structural autonomy', Burt argues, when it has many suppliers and customers but there are few who produce the same item; and the reason for this is that more competitors in principle means less autonomy and less profit.

In population ecology the relevant unit of study is not the individual firm but the number or population of firms of the same type (Hannan and Freeman 1989; Hannan and Carroll 1992). These populations typically go through a process of initial slow growth, explosive growth, and finally stabilization into an equilibrium. Factors that help to explain this process include the degree of competition and the process of legitimation that a new form of organization goes through. A well-known unit of study in economic life is the industry, and population ecology has made a number of contributions to the understanding of various industries, including brewing, investment banking, and biotechnology (e.g. Carroll and Hannan 1995, 2000). Some critique has, however, also been directed at population ecology. In particular, the question has been raised how much further one can go by drawing on this perspective (e.g. Hedström 1992; Haveman 2000: 477).

The concept of 'business group' was given prominence in the early 1990s by Mark Granovetter, who defines this type of organization as 'a collection of firms bound together in some formal and/or informal ways' (Granovetter 1994: 454; cf. Granovetter 1995). According to Granovetter (forthcoming), it is important for sociologists to begin to study the kind of organizational figurations that can be found midway between the individual firm and macroeconomic phenomena. Business groups, he continues, are characterized by variations along the following six dimensions: ownership relations, principles of solidarity, authority structure, moral economy, finance, and relations to the state. Concrete examples include *keiretsu* in Japan, *chaebol* in South Korea, and *grupos economicos* in Latin America.

Sociologists have also made a key contribution to the study of organizations, including firms, by drawing on network theory (for an overview, see e.g. Powell and Smith-Doerr 1994). As an analytical method, the networks approach is very flexible and can be used to trace relations between as well as within firms (e.g. Uzzi 1996). There also exists a school of thought which argues that artifacts, not only individuals and organizations, should be seen as nodes in networks (e.g. Callon 1997). A common network exercise has been to investigate the patterns caused by the fact that one and the same individual can be a member of several boards (e.g. Mizruchi 1996). The idea of networks has also been used to analyze the structure of different forms of economic organizations, such as industrial districts, inter-organizational forms of cooperation and 'network organizations' (e.g. Saxenian 1994; Ebers 1997; Baker 1992). It has also been suggested that networks are characteristic of the post-Fordist economy; while others rather see the emphasis on flexible production as part of a new capitalist ideology (e.g. Piore and Sabel 1984; Castells 1996; Boltanski and Ciapello 1999).

13.2.4 The Role of Culture and Meaning in Organizational Sociology

Certain branches of recent sociological work on organizations have been very interested in culture and meaning, something that is much less true for organizational economics (see, however, Kreps 1990). One important reason for this development, besides the heritage of interpretive sociology from Weber, has been the recent emergence of cultural sociology as a distinct subfield in sociology (e.g. DiMaggio 1994; Berezin 1997). Of fundamental importance to the so-called new institutionalism in sociology is an article from 1977 by John Meyer and Brian Rowan, in which it is suggested that modern organizations cannot be adequately understood in terms of efficiency and instrumental action (Meyer and Rowen 1977). There rather exist two contradictory claims on the modern organization, according to this view: to get things done and to incorporate features from its surroundings which will endow it with legitimacy—but which will make it harder to get things done. One way of solving this problem, John Meyer and his co-author argue, is for the organization to adopt a formal structure that is legitimate, while you have a practice that is relatively independent of the formal structure ('decoupling'). The idea that organizations snugly fit their environments for structural reasons ('contingency theory') is consequently challenged. Meyer and his co-author propose that organizational and institutional features can essentially be understood as 'social constructions' and that modern society is filled with rational myths about the way things should be done.

Since the 1980s the ideas of John Meyer have been developed in a number of directions by students and followers (e.g. DiMaggio and Powell 1991). In a well-known article by DiMaggio and Powell, entitled 'The Iron Cage Revisited: Institutional Isomorphism and Collective Rationality in Organizational Fields' (1983), it is emphasized that what needs to be explained is not so much why there exist so many different types of organizations, as why there exist so few. What often happens, according to new institutionalists, is that distinct models for what organizations should look like are developed and then diffused throughout society.

The perspective of new institutionalism emerged to some extent as a reaction against the idea that organizations can be adequately explained through economic and technological variables; and this may also account for some of its reluctance to study economic organizations as opposed to public organizations, such as schools and universities. Nonetheless, some interesting studies of economic organizations have also emerged, such as Neil Fligstein's *The Transformation of Corporate Control* (1990) and Frank Dobbin's *Forging Industrial Policy* (1994). Fligstein's study can be characterized as an attempt to explain the evolution of the huge American corporation since 1880, which challenges Alfred Chandler's standard account (cf. Freeland 1996 for another sociological critique of Chandler). While Chandler sees the modern huge corporation as a natural response to the emergence of a national market around the turn of the century, Fligstein highlights several other factors, including the role of the state, how managers think about strategy ('conceptions of control'), and the role of isomorphism in the diffusion of the huge corporation (e.g. Fligstein 1985). Dobbin similarly rejects the rational choice approach in *Forging Industrial Policy*, which can be described as a study of industrial policy vis-à-vis the railroads in France, England, and the United States during the period 1825–1900. Modern western culture is instrumental in character, Dobbin argues, but this is something that needs to be explained and must not be taken for granted, as economists have a tendency to do. A close look at the kind of industrial policies concerning railroads that can be found in France, England, and the United States also indicates that actors often regard their own economic behavior as perfectly objective and lawlike, while in reality it can better be characterized as a form of social construction (cf. Berger and Luckmann 1967). 'A cultural approach to modern economic institutions', as Dobbin phrases it, 'would not merely follow the lead of the natives, but would show the natives a new way to see their own world' (Dobbin 2001: 421).

13.3 CONCLUDING REMARKS AND DISCUSSION

Even in a brief chapter of this type, it quickly becomes clear that economists and sociologists view organizations, including firms, in very different ways (see Table 13.1 for a summary). This naturally raises the question which analysis is to be preferred; and as far as I can see there exist two basic options. Either economics or sociology is judged superior, and the other approach is given up; or some way is found to mix economics and sociology without leading to the 'cross-sterilization' that Schumpeter warned about.

There are several facts that speak in favor of *sociology replacing economics* when it comes to analyzing organizations; and it is naturally the case that most sociologists would argue for this solution (for a critique of organizational economics by sociologists, see e.g. Granovetter 1985; Perrow 1986; Zey 1998). Sociology, it is often said, has a much more healthy attitude to empirical reality than economics,

Table 13.1 The economic vs. the sociological view of organizations

	Mainstream sociology	Mainstream economics
1. Basic view of organizations	Organizations are seen as special types of groups or institutions (sociology of organizations)	*Earlier*: The firm was included in the production function. *Today*: the firm is conceptualized as a hierarchy, constructed according to the principles of microeconomics (organizational economics)
2. Different approaches within the basic view of organizations	Weberian analysis, population ecology, resource dependence, new institutionalism, and other approaches	Agency theory, transaction cost analysis, property rights analysis, evolutionary and game theoretical approaches
3. Relation of organizations to their environment	Organizations are seen as part of several larger contexts, such as 'organizational fields' and society at large	The single organization interacts with other organizations through instrumental contacts
4. Internal structure of the organizations	Organizations have formal and informal structures; there is a multitude of empirical actors	Firms are seen as hierarchies with a few stylized actors
5. Origin of the organization	Organizations have had a slow historical emergence, as part of the modernization process	Organizations represent profitable solutions to problems
6. Basic approach in the analysis of organizations	Mainly description and historically based explanations; rationality is seen as a variable	Explanation and prediction through modeling; rationality is an assumption
7. Key figures in each tradition	Max Weber, Arthur Stinchcombe, John Meyer, and others	Alfred Marshall, R. H. Coase, Oliver Williamson, and others

and is ready to change its theories when these are contradicted by empirical reality. Furthermore, sociology is not dogmatically wedded to the assumption of rationality, be it in the form of bounded rationality or the maximization of utility. Finally, sociology has a tradition of taking the subjective views of the actors into account, something that makes it easier for sociology (it is often argued) to handle such issues as cognition and meaning structures.

But there also exist several good reasons to let *economics replace sociology* when it comes to analyzing organizations; and these, no doubt, will be cited by most economists. Economics, as opposed to sociology, has supposedly a perfectly clear understanding of the role that analytical thinking should play in the analysis. Economics typically tries to produce full explanations and does not simply let the analysis stop after a description has been made, as often happens in sociology. Finally, and of great importance when it comes to analyzing economic organizations, economists have a very sharp understanding of the role of economic interests in human affairs. Sociologists, on the other hand, often avoid the issue of interests and try to cast everything in terms of social structures or 'social constructions'.

Does there exist some way that one could possibly reconcile the approaches of economics and sociology to organizations? In my opinion the answer is probably 'no'—but there may exist a thin ray of hope for a unified theory of firms, and the reason for this is as follows. During the last few years there has been a general resurgence in the economy of innovative behavior. Especially in the business school community an attempt has been made to respond to this development by teaching entrepreneurship on a mass scale, that is, to do for entrepreneurship what the business schools did for 'management' a few decades ago—analyze it, reformulate its basic principles, and teach it to the students.

In contrast, mainstream economics and mainstream sociology have failed to respond to the multitude of new innovations in the economy. Mainstream economics is, for example, unable to deal with increasing returns to scale and entrepreneurship. The sociology of organizations has also ignored entrepreneurship; and whatever theories of entrepreneurship have developed, have done so on its margins or outside its confines. The sociology of organizations and the emerging sociology of entrepreneurship belong to two essentially different bodies of work, and these have failed to come together.

But a small number of people from both economics and sociology have attempted to deal with the ideas that a new entrepreneurial economy—and a new entrepreneurial firm—may be out there. In economics there is first and foremost the work by Brian Arthur and the economists at Santa Fe; and in sociology there has recently been a renewal in what is called the sociology of entrepreneurship (e.g. Waldrup 1992; Arthur 1994; Thornton 1999; Swedberg 2000). Both of these efforts attempt to get a handle on what is going on in the entrepreneurial parts of the economy in an open-minded manner, without bothering too much with boundaries and traditions. The idea of path dependency has come out of this research as well as important new insights about entrepreneurship.

Where these attempts will end up is still much too early to say—but it is from these efforts, in my opinion, that a unified theory of the firm will emerge, if at all. What such a theory will look like in detail is naturally hard to know. All that can be said today, I think, is that this new theory of firms will have to unite, in one single theory, the two key ideas in economics and sociology respectively: *economic interests* and *social structures*. These two elements will have to be woven together in some novel 'molecular' fashion (to speak with Harrison White), in the attempt to theorize what happens inside and outside the firms—especially to capture the novel structures that firms will have to develop in order to survive in an entrepreneurial economy.

REFERENCES

ALBROW, MARTIN (1970). *Bureaucracy*. London: Macmillan.

ALCHIAN, ARMEN, and DEMSETZ, HAROLD (1972/1986). 'Production Information Costs and Economic Organization', in Jay Barnes and William Ouchi (eds.), *Organizational Economics*. San Francisco: Jossey-Bass Publishers.

ARCHIBALD, G. C. (1987). 'Firm, Theory of the', in John Eatwell *et al.* (eds.), *The New Palgrave: A Dictionary of Economics*, ii. London: Macmillan.

ARROW, KENNETH (1985). 'The Economics of Agency', in John Pratt and Richard Zeckhauser (eds.), *Principals and Agents: The Structure of Business*. Boston: Harvard Business School Press.

ARTHUR, BRIAN (1994). *Increasing Returns and Path Dependence in the Economy*. Ann Arbor: University of Michigan Press.

AXELROD, ROBERT (1984). *The Evolution of Cooperation*. New York: Basic Books.

BAKER, WAYNE (1992). 'The Network Organization in Theory and Practice', in Nitin Nohria and Robert Eccles (eds.), *Networks and Organizations*. Boston: Harvard Business School Press.

BARNES, JAY, and OUCHI, WILLIAM, (eds.) (1986). *Organizational Economics*. San Francisco: Jossey-Bass Publishers.

BARON, JAMES, and KREPS, DAVID (1999). *Strategic Human Resources: Frameworks for General Managers*. New York: John Wiley & Sons.

BEREZIN, MABEL (1997). 'Politics and Culture: A Less Fissured Terrain'. *Annual Review of Sociology*, 23: 361–83.

BERGER, PETER, and LUCKMANN, THOMAS (1967). *The Social Construction of Reality: A Treatise in the Sociology of Knowledge*. New York: Doubleday.

BERNOUX, PHILIPPE (1995). *Sociologie des entreprises*. Paris: Points-Seuil.

BOURDIEU, PIERRE (2000). *Les Structures sociales de l'économie*. Paris: Seuil.

—— and WACQUANT, LOÏC (1992). 'The Logic of Fields', in eid., *An Invitation to Reflexive Sociology*. Chicago: University of Chicago Press.

BLAUG, MARK (1980). 'The Theory of the Firm', in id., *The Methodology of Economics*. Cambridge: Cambridge University Press.

BURT, RONALD (1983). *Corporate Profits and Cooptation*. New York: Academic Press.

CALLON, MICHEL (1997). 'Society in the Making: The Study of Technology as a Tool for Sociological Analysis', in Wiebe Bijker *et al.* (eds.), *The Social Construction of Technological Systems*. Cambridge,: Mass. MIT Press.

CARROLL, GLENN, and HANNAN, MICHAEL (eds.) (1995). *Organizations in Industry*. New York: Oxford University Press.

————(2000). *The Demography of Corporations and Industries*. Princeton: Princeton University Press.

CASTELLS, MANUEL (1996). *The Information Age i. The Rise of the Network Society*, Oxford: Blackwell.

COASE, R. H. (1937/1993). 'The Nature of the Firm', in Oliver Williamson and Sidney Winter (eds.), *The Nature of the Firm: Origin, Evolution, and Development*. New York: Oxford University Press.

———— (1991). 'The Nature of the Firm: Origin, Meaning, Influence', in Oliver Williamson and Sidney Winter (eds.), *The Nature of the Firm: Origin, Evolution, and Development*. New York: Oxford University Press.

CROZIER, MICHEL (1964). *The Bureaucratic Phenomenon*. Chicago: University of Chicago Press.

CYERT, RICHARD, and MARCH, JAMES (1963). *A Behavioral Theory of the Firm*. Englewood Cliffs, NJ: Prentice-Hall.

DAVID, ROBERT, and HAN, SHIN-KAP (1998). 'Assessing Empirical Evidence of Transaction Cost Economics: A Meta-Analysis'. Cornell University, Unpublished paper.

DIMAGGIO, PAUL (1986). 'Structural Analysis of Organizational Fields: A Blockmodel Approach', in Barry Staw and L. L. Cummings (eds.), *Research in Organizational Behavior*, viii. Greenwich, Conn.: JAI Press.

———— (1994). 'Economy and Culture', in Neil Smelser and Richard Swedberg (eds.), *The Handbook of Economic Sociology*. New York and Princeton: Russell Sage Foundation and Princeton University Press.

———— and POWELL, WALTER (1983). 'The Iron Cage Revisited: Institutional Isomorphism and Collective Rationality in Organizational Fields'. *American Sociological Review*, 48: 147–60.

————————(eds.) (1991). *The New Institutionalism in Organizational Analysis*. Chicago: University of Chicago Press.

DOBBIN, FRANK (1994). *Forging Industrial Policy: The United States, Britain, and France in the Railway Age*. Cambridge: Cambridge University Press.

———— (2001). 'Why the Economy Reflects the Polity: Early Rail Policy in Britain, France, and the United States', in Mark Granovetter and Richard Swedberg (eds.), *The Sociology of Economic Life* (2nd rev. edn). Boulder, Colo.:Westview.

DOUMA, SYTSE, and SCHREUDER, HEIN (1998). *Economic Approaches to Organizations* (2nd edn). London: Prentice-Hall.

EBERS, MARK (ed.) (1997). *The Formation of Inter-Organizational Networks*. Oxford: Oxford University Press.

FAMA, EUGENE, and JENSEN, MICHAEL (1983/1986). 'The Separation of Ownership and Control', in Jay Barnes and William Ouchi (eds.), *Organizational Economics*. San Francisco: Jossey-Bass Publishers.

FLIGSTEIN, NEIL (1985). 'The Spread of the Multinational Form among Large Firms, 1919–79'. *American Sociological Review*, 50: 377–91.

———— (1990). *The Transformation of Corporate Control*. Cambridge, Mass.: Harvard University Press.

FREELAND, ROBERT (1996). 'The Myth of the M-Form? Governance, Consent and Organizational Change'. *American Journal of Sociology*, 102: 483–526.

GOULDNER, ALVIN (1954). *Patterns of Industrial Bureaucracy*. New York: Free Press.

GRANOVETTER, MARK (1985). 'Economic Action and Social Structure: The Problem of Embeddedness'. *American Journal of Sociology* 85:481–510.

—— (1994). 'Business Groups', in Neil Smelser and Richard Swedberg (eds.), *The Handbook of Economic Sociology*. New York and Princeton: Russell Sage Foundation and Princeton University Press.

—— (1995). 'Coase Revisited: Business Groups in the Modern Economy'. *Industrial and Corporate Change*, 4: 93–130.

—— (forthcoming). 'Business Groups and Social Organization', in Neil Smelser and Richard Swedberg (eds.), *The Handbook of Economic Sociology* (2nd edn). New York and Princeton: Russell Sage Foundation and Princeton University Press.

HAMILTON, GARY, and WOOLSEY BIGGART, NICOLE (1988). 'Market, Culture and Authority: A Comparative Analysis of Management and Organization in the Far East'. *American Journal of Sociology*, 94: S52–S94.

HANNAN, MICHAEL, and CARROLL, GLENN (1992). *Dynamics of Organizational Populations*. Oxford: Oxford University Press.

—— and FREEMAN, JOHN (1989). *Organizational Ecology*. Cambridge, Mass.: Harvard University Press.

HAVEMAN, HEATHER (2000). 'The Future of Organizational Sociology'. *Contemporary Sociology*, 29: 476–86.

HEDSTRÖM, PETER (1992). 'Is Organizational Ecology at an Impasse?' *Contemporary Sociology*, 21: 751–3.

HIRSCH, PAUL (1972). 'Processing Fads and Fashion: An Organization-Set Analysis of Cultural Industry Systems'. *American Journal of Sociology*, 77: 639–59.

JENSEN, MICHAEL, and MECKLING, WILLIAM (1976/1986). 'Theory of the Firm: Managerial Behavior, Agency Costs and Ownership Structure', in Jay Barnes and William Ouchi (eds.), *Organizational Economics*. San Francisco: Jossey-Bass Publishers.

KNIGHT, FRANK (1933/1967). *The Economic Organization*. New York: Augustus M. Kelley.

KREPS, DAVID (1990). 'Corporate Culture and Economic Theory', in James Alt and Kenneth Shepsle (eds.), *Perspectives on Positive Political Economy*. Cambridge: Cambridge University Press.

MANSKI, CHARLES (2000). 'Economic Analysis of Social Interactions'. *Journal of Economic Perspectives*, 14/3 (Summer): 115–36.

MARCH, JAMES (1962). 'The Business Firm as a Political Coalition'. *Journal of Politics*, 24: 662–78.

—— and SIMON HERBERT, (1958). *Organizations*. New York: Wiley & Sons.

MARSCHAK, JACOB, and RADNER ROY, (1972). *The Economic Theory of Teams*. New York: Yale University Press.

MARSHAK, THOMAS (1987). 'Organization Theory', in John Eatwell *et al.* (eds.), *The New Palgrave: A Dictionary of Economics*, iii. London: Macmillan.

MARSHALL, ALFRED (1920/1961). *Principles of Economics* (9th, Variorum Edition). 2 vols. London: Macmillan and Co. Limited.

MEYER, JOHN, and ROWEN BRIAN, (1977). 'Institutionalized Organizations: Formal Structure as Myth and Ceremony'. *American Journal of Sociology*, 83: 340–63.

MEYER, MARSHALL (1990). 'The Weberian Tradition in Organizational Research', in Craig Calhoun *et al.* (eds.), *Structures of Power and Constraint*. Cambridge: Cambridge University Press.

MIROWSKI, PHILIP (1988). 'Nelson and Winter's *Evolutionary Theory of Economic Change*', in id., *Against Mechanism*. Boston: Rowman & Littlefield.

MIZRUCHI, MARK (1996). 'What Do Interlocks Do? An Analysis, Critique, and Assessment of Research on Interlocking Directorates'. *Annual Review of Sociology*, 22: 271–98.

MÜLLER-FREIENFELS, WOLFRAM (1978). 'Agency, Law of', in *Encyclopaedia Britannica (Macropaedia)*, i. Chicago: Encyclopaedia Britannica.

NELSON, RICHARD, and WINTER SIDNEY, (1982). *An Evolutionary Theory of Economic Change*. Cambridge, Mass.: Harvard University Press.

NEUMANN, JOHN VON, and MORGENSTERN OSKAR, (1944/1980). *Theory of Games and Economic Behavior*. Princeton: Princeton University Press.

PERROW, CHARLES (1986). *Complex Organizations: A Critical Essay* (3rd edn). New York: Random House.

PFEFFER, JEFFREY, and SALANCIK GERALD, (1978). *The External Control of Organizations*. New York: Harper & Row.

PIORE, MICHAEL, and SABEL CHARLES, (1984). *The Second Industrial Divide*. New York: Basic Books.

POWELL, WALTER, and SMITH-DOERR LAUREL, (1994). 'Networks and Economic Life', in Neil Smelser and Richard Swedberg (eds.), *The Handbook of Economic Sociology*. New York and Princeton: Russell Sage Foundation and Princeton University Press.

PUTTERMAN, LOUIS (1986). 'The Economic Nature of the Firm: Overview', in Louis Putterman (ed.), *The Economic Nature of the Firm: A Reader*. Cambridge: Cambridge University Press.

SAMUELSON, PAUL (1970). *Economics* (8th edn). New York: McGraw-Hill.

SAXENIAN, ANNALEE (1994). *Regional Advantage: Culture and Competition in Silicon Valley and Route 128*. Cambridge, Mass.: Harvard University Press.

SCHOTTER, ANDREW (1981). *The Economic Theory of Social Institutions*. New York: Cambridge University Press.

SCHUMPETER, JOSEPH A. (1954). *History of Economic Analysis*. London: Allen & Unwin.

SCOTT, RICHARD (1997). *Organizations: Rational, Natural, and Open Systems* (3rd edn). Englewood Cliffs, NJ: Prentice-Hall.

SMELSER, NEIL, and SWEDBERG RICHARD, (1994). 'The Sociological Perspective on the Economy', in Neil Smelser and Richard Swedberg (eds.), *The Handbook of Economic Sociology*. New York and Princeton: Russell Sage Foundation and Princeton University Press.

SMITH, CLIFFORD (1987). 'Agency Costs', in John Eatwell *et al.* (eds.), *The New Palgrave: A Dictionary of Economics*, i. London: Macmillan.

STINCHCOMBE, ARTHUR (1959). 'Bureaucratic and Craft Administration of Production'. *Social Science Quarterly*, 4: 168–87.

—— (1960). 'The Sociology of Organization and the Theory of the Firm', *Pacific Sociological Review*, Fall: 75–82.

—— (1986). 'Rationality and Social Structure', in id., *Stratification and Organization*. Cambridge: Cambridge University Press.

SWEDBERG, RICHARD (1998). *Max Weber and the Idea of Economic Sociology*. Princeton: Princeton University Press.

—— (2000). 'The Social Science View of Entrepreneurship', in Richard Swedberg (ed.), *Entrepreneurship: The Social Science View*. Oxford: Oxford University Press.

THORNTON, PATRICIA (1999). 'The Sociology of Entrepreneurship'. *Annual Review of Sociology*, 25: 19–46.

TIROLE, JEAN (1988). *The Theory of Industrial Organization*. Cambridge, Mass.: MIT Press.

UDEHN, LARS (1991). 'The Limits of Economic Imperialism', in Ulf Himmelstrand (ed.), *Interfaces in Economic and Social Sciences*. London: Routledge.

—— (1996). *The Limits of Public Choice: A Sociological Critique of the Economic Theory of Politics*. London: Routledge.

UZZI, BRIAN (1996). 'The Sources and Consequences of Embeddedness for the Economic Performance of Firms: The Network Effect'. *American Sociological Review*, 61: 674–98.

WALDROP, M. MITCHELL (1992). *Complexity: The Emerging Science at the Edge of Order and Chaos*. New York: Simon and Schuster.

WEBER, MAX. (1904–5/1958). *The Protestant Ethic and the Spirit of Capitalism*. New York: Scribner's.

—— (1922/1978). *Economy and Society*. 2 vols. Berkeley: University of California Press.

—— (1924/1981). *General Economic History*. New Brunswick: Transaction Books.

—— (1949). *Essays in the Methodology of the Social Sciences*. New York: Free Press.

WHITE, HARRISON C. (1992). *Identity and Control: A Structural Theory of Social Action*. Princeton: Princeton University Press.

WILLIAMSON, OLIVER (1975). *Markets and Hierarchies: Analysis and Antitrust Implications*. New York: Free Press.

—— (1985). *The Economic Institutions of Capitalism*. New York: Free Press.

—— (1986). *Economic Organization*. New York: New York University Press.

—— (1991). 'Transaction Cost Economics', in Neil Smelser and Richard Swedberg (eds.), *The Handbook of Economic Sociology*. New York and Princeton: Russell Sage Foundation and Princeton University Press.

—— (1996). 'Economic Organization: The Case for Candor'. *Academy of Management Review*, 21: 48–57.

ZEY, MARY (1998). *Rational Choice Theory and Organizational Theory: A Critique*. London: Sage.

CHAPTER 14

META-THEORETICAL CONTROVERSIES IN STUDYING ORGANIZATIONAL CULTURE

JOANNE MARTIN

> To see a world in a grain of sand,
> And a heaven in a wild flower,
> Hold infinity in the palm of your hand,
> And eternity in an hour.
>
> (Blake, *Auguries of Innocence I*, 2000: 285)

To UNDERSTAND the contemporary state of organizational culture theory and research, it is necessary to grapple with some of the major intellectual disputes that have swept through the humanities and social sciences in recent years. Some researchers choose to study a single cultural context, in great detail and depth. In effect, these researchers heed Blake's advice and see the world in a grain of sand; they

This chapter is a revised version of Chapter 2, in J. Martin, *Organizational Culture: Mapping the Terrain* (Foundations of Organizational Science Series; Newbury Park, Calif.: Sage Publications, 2002). It is revised and reprinted here with the permission of Sage Publications. I wish to thank H. Tsoukas for helping me sharpen some of the philosophical material in this chapter.

study culture with a sample size of one context. Other researchers react with disdain to such case studies, and prefer to study many cultures, even if that means understanding less about each one. Such differences in research strategies occur because cultural researchers make radically different assumptions regarding fundamental issues.

Often these disagreements are framed as methodological disputes about the relative merits of quantitative and qualitative methods for studying cultures in organizations (e.g. Rousseau 1990a; Martin and Frost 1996). Others prefer to frame the disagreements in terms of theoretical differences (Frost *et al.* 1991; Martin 1992). Still others frame the conflicts as reflecting managerial interests or the views of critical theorists (Alvesson and Melin 1987; Barley, Meyer, and Gash 1988; Calás and Smircich 1987; Stablein and Nord 1985; Martin, forthcoming). However underlying these important sources of disagreement are other, meta-theoretical controversies that merit discussion.

Five of these controversies are the focus of the present chapter. These controversies include: objectivity and subjectivity; etic (outsider) and emic (insider) research; generalizable and context-specific research; focus and breadth; and level of depth. These issues are introduced in terms relevant to all of organizational studies and their particular application to cultural studies is then discussed. These disputes are usually framed as struggles between opposing terms—dichotomies, such as 'objectivity and subjectivity' or 'etic and emic'. I use the word 'and' between these opposing terms to signal that these dichotomies are overdrawn, exaggerating differences at the expense of understanding ways these oppositions blur and merge.

14.1 ONTOLOGY AND EPISTEMOLOGY: A BIT OF BACKGROUND

As a prelude to discussing objective and subjective approaches to studying culture, a few words about ontology and epistemology may be useful.[1] Here I draw heavily on the work of Chia (1996), because his framing is of particular relevance for cultural research. Chia usefully distinguishes two kinds of ontology, which he calls being-realism, and becoming-realism.

[1] Ontology is a set of assumptions about the nature of reality, how things are. In contrast, epistemology concerns theories about how we *know* about the nature of reality, that is, how we *know* about how things are. Of course, epistemology entails some assumptions about the nature of reality itself, making it difficult to disentangle it from ontology.

14.1.1 Being-Realism

Chia (1996: 36) argues that in being-realism:

there is a fundamental split between the *word* and the *world* (Harre 1986) and that the world
is made up of discrete and identifiable material and social entities (Whitehead 1926/1985: 58)
which can be faithfully documented using precise literal concepts and categories... to *know*
means to be able to represent accurately in our minds using linguistic or visual forms what
the world 'out there' is really like... combinations of words, from which theories are built,
somehow match up with pieces of the 'real' world. (author's emphasis)

According to being-realism, reality 'pre-exists independently of observation' (Chia
1996: 33). This approach enables organizational scientists to treat ideas, such as
'organizations' or 'cultures' as unproblematic objects of analysis, as if 'their ontological status were not a critical issue in its own right'.

Unlike some other researchers to be discussed below, Chia believes that ontology
and epistemology are tightly coupled. He argues that being-realism is congruent
with representational epistemologies, presuming that language can be used, unproblematically, to represent reality, accurately communicating what is 'out there'.
Chia (1996: 39) explains it this way:

The grammatical structures of language organize our consciousness and thought processes,
making it then possible for us to think about our experiences retrospectively in a discrete,
differentiated, linear and sequential manner. As an epistemological posture, therefore,
representationalism entails the systematic filtration of our concrete experiences into the
precast moulding of the grammatical logic of language. In this abstractive manner, we
selectively reduce and make more comprehensively manageable our lived experiences in
the very act of recounting them.

Representational epistemology is invoked, implicitly, when a critic observes that
a particular study 'reifies culture'. Reification means writing about culture as if it
could be accurately known and as if that knowledge could be represented in
language, unproblematically. To use my own work as an example, I have (fortunately, rarely) described the three theoretical perspectives that have dominated
most organizational culture research in being-realism terms (Martin 2002): 'Although there is little that these three theoretical perspectives agree about, each has
generated an impressive body of empirical support, suggesting (to those of a neo-
positivist persuasion) that none of these three perspectives can be easily dismissed.'
If (and only if) one disregards the parenthetical remark alluding to neo-positivism,
this 'being realism' language treats the three theoretical perspectives as if they were
reified things 'out there', whose existence could not be challenged because of the
volume of empirical evidence that supports their existence. In contrast, as described
below, a becoming-realism ontology would ask how these concepts came to be
created as categories, perhaps drawing attention to what other conceptual approaches represent 'paths not taken', that could have been utilized.

14.1.2 Becoming-Realism

Becoming-realism focuses on the process of becoming, so that how things come to be, defines what they are. Becoming-realism directs the attention of organizational researchers, according to Chia (1996: 34), to processes: how we order, codify, frame, and classify our perceptions, our data, and our theoretical abstractions. These processes create *apparently* stable and reified ideas, such as truth claims about what is known about abstractions such as 'individuals', 'organizations', and 'cultures'. Thus, processes of ordering and classifying, etc. are intimately intertwined with the ways we use language in our texts to summarize data and build theories about how reality is socially structured. Chia is an advocate of becoming-realism. He argues that the problem with being-realism ontology and representational epistemologies is that they gloss over important shortcomings in our knowledge base, shortcomings that are inescapably tied to the inherent limitations of language, and the ways those limitations shape our perceptions and conceptualizations. As Chia (1996: 39) explains:

As an academic ideology for directing research and inquiry, [representationalism] suppresses the problematical nature of its own truth claims by unreflexively concentrating attention onto the 'outcomes' of research, thereby ignoring the philosophical problems underpinning its own epistemological stance. In so doing it conveniently ignores the paradoxes and contradictions surrounding its knowledge claims.

Chia argues that we can know only what we can put into language, but if we use representational writing strategies, we are not expressing awareness of the ways language is shaping what we can think. Thus, whether we want to or not, when researchers write or speak about culture, we use words, categories, and concepts to alter meanings, hide ambiguities, and circumvent problematic contradictions and uncertainties. There are ways to write about culture, in accord with becoming-realism, to highlight the inevitable uncertainties of the conceptualization and writing processes. These writing strategies attempt to reflect the ambiguities inherent in the study and representation of cultural material (Clifford and Marcus 1986; Van Maanen 1988; Martin 2002).

14.1.3 Relationships between Epistemologies and Methods

One assumption, underlying Chia's arguments, merits discussion here. Chia views ontology, epistemology, methods choices, and writing strategies as tightly coupled (see also Burrell and Morgan 1979). Others view methods and epistemology as being much more loosely coupled, taking the position that the problem for research lies not in being-realism, but in representational epistemologies. From this point of view, one can accept the being-realism view, yet endorse epistemologies that eschew representationalism. For example, assuming we are all limitedly rational knowers, we may construct knowledge within the constraints of language, and do so in a way that captures elements of differing viewpoints. Cultural descriptions, written in this manner, can refrain, to a limited extent, from using representational epistemologies. In spite of these differences of opinion, Chia's ideas, particularly regarding representational epistemology, will be useful background for the material that follows below.

14.2 OBJECTIVITY AND SUBJECTIVITY

Much of the organizational literature, like most fields of social science, reads as if scholars could discover and accurately represent the objectively 'true' nature of the empirical world, in accord with being-realism and representational epistemology. This is the dominant view in the United States, particularly in most mainstream organizational journals. In contrast, European scholarship often remains open to other viewpoints. In accord with this emphasis on objectivity, in the United States most doctoral students are taught to do organizational research according to the scientific method, using deduction and induction to prove or falsify hypotheses. However, most researchers, when pressed, would agree that purist claims of objectivity (sometimes labeled 'naïve realism') are overblown (e.g. Bogdan and Taylor 1975; Cook and Reichardt 1979; Gephart 1988; Van Maanen 1979). As H. Markus (personal communication, 2000) puts it, 'Counting pond scum or stars requires categorization, and is therefore subjective and problematic.'

This modesty about objectivity is appropriate. Philosophers of science have repeatedly undermined claims of objectivity, challenging the logical foundations of the fundamentals of the scientific method, such as induction, deduction, and falsification (e.g. Chalmers 1982; Nord and Connell 1998). Even 'hard' scientists such as physicists struggle with the implications of data suggesting that the act of perceiving or measuring transforms whatever is being assessed. In addition, what may seem objectively true at one time is subject to revision as it changes and as apparent understandings change. What may seem to be objective fact, such as an experience or a body of data, is subjectively perceived by humans and processed by human sensemaking (e.g. Rorty 1991; Tsoukas, 1998).

Research in a variety of disciplines lends support to this contention. Even an apparently objective stimulus, such as the set of sounds in a language, may be heard differently by speakers of different languages, as their preconceptions influence the sound distinctions they can perceive (Boas 1901). In a psychological experiment, subjects identified slides of ordinary playing cards; when anomalous cards, such as red spades or black hearts, were added to the deck of cards, study participants misperceived the anomalous cards, in accord with their preconceptions (Bruner, Goodnow, and Austin 1956). For similar reasons, eyewitness testimony is notoriously unreliable, as different people observing the same event recall it differently (e.g. Yarmey and Yarmey 1997).

This brief and simplified discussion of objectivity and subjectivity has implications for cultural research. As discussed above, some cultural researchers treat culture as a reified object, a 'thing' 'out there' that can be objectively perceived and measured, the same way, by anyone who views it. This is, in part, what is meant by the criticism that a study 'reifies' culture, in according with being-realism and representational epistemologies. In contrast, most cultural researchers argue, in accord with becoming-realism, that researchers and cultural members subjectively interpret and represent what they observe, rather than perceiving an objective reality. For example, the taste of some foods, like dog meat, is not objectively determined. There is considerable variation in people's subjective reactions: Americans deem dogs inedible and esteem beef, while some Indians refuse to eat beef and some Africans consider dog meat a delicacy (Sahlins 1995). As these examples indicate, the same material conditions can produce a variety of perceived and enacted cultural 'realities'. Sahlins (1995) supports a subjective position, arguing that the cultural cannot be derived directly from experience or event, because experiences occur in a world already symbolized, and so meanings are always somewhat arbitrary in relation to the object being signified.

Many cultural researchers adopt a modified version of a subjectivist approach, viewing perceptions as constrained by what is being perceived. As Stablein (1996) argues, subjectivity does not mean 'anything goes'. Subjectivity is constrained by aspects of the stimulus being perceived, and this process of perception, memory, and interpretation is not just an individual phenomenon. Observation occurs in a collective, social context where the social construction of reality (Berger and Luckmann 1967) constrains and influences judgments. If reality is subjectively constructed even in this limited way, then a cultural researcher must focus some attention on the subjective frameworks of cultural members, in addition to the apparently objective 'facts' and material conditions of their lives.

Although some of organizational culture studies take a purely objectivist or subjectivist approach, many researchers view culture as both objectively and subjectively constrained. This approach implies that cultural descriptions should include physical manifestations of a culture, such as dress norms, the noise and dirt, or the quiet and luxury of a workplace, as well as observable formal practices and structures, such as the amounts of money different employees earn or who they report to. Subjective meanings associated with observable cultural manifestations must also be gathered and interpreted. Material and ideational aspects of culture cannot be easily distinguished and both must be studied.[2]

It is important to note that subjectivity does not imply consensus. Interpretations need not be consensual, as the same cultural manifestation may carry different meanings for different perceivers (e.g. Martin 1992). For example, if an oil company gives women managers a 9 percent pay raise, the management may believe that this pay increase is quite generous, while the women managers may be discontent because comparable male managers still earn considerably more (Martin, Brickman, and Murray 1984). A ritualized event, such as an award banquet, a training program, or a planned change intervention may be perceived differently by different participants, who may react variously, with skepticism, ambivalence, or enthusiastic endorsement (e.g. Bartunek and Moch 1991; Rosen 1991; Van Maanen and Kunda 1989). When cultural studies include meanings and interpretations of material cultural manifestations, their authors are tacitly or explicitly assuming that the social meanings of an object, event, or experience are subjectively experienced and interpreted and cannot be inferred directly from its material or physical characteristics.

14.3 ETIC (OUTSIDER) AND EMIC (INSIDER) RESEARCH

The distinction between objective and subjective approaches to the study of culture is reflected and refined in the distinction between etic and emic research (e.g. Agar 1986; Morris *et al.* 1999). Most organizational research outside the cultural arena takes an etic stance, assuming that a researcher can adequately, and perhaps even accurately, decide what categories and questions are appropriate for investigating a particular context or set of theoretical questions. Usually, in etic research, categories are deduced from prior theory and research, not from material gathered during a study.

To give a quantitative example of an etic approach used in cultural studies, a researcher might decide (drawing on prior research) which dimensions are import-

---

[2] Rorty (1991) offers an explanation for the difficulties encountered when a researcher attempts to distinguish objective and subjective, or material and ideational approaches to studying culture. Perceptions of the material aspects of culture are inevitably mediated by language. They enter discourse as already-contextualized objects. In Rorty's terminology, the world causes us to have beliefs but it cannot tell us what to believe in. Only other people can help us with that, hence the significance of language, discourse, and the acknowledgement of subjectivity (Tsoukas 1998).

ant aspects of culture in organizations. This researcher might then construct a questionnaire, asking respondents to report cultural norms along these dimensions. For example, members might be asked to rate, on a nine-point Likert scale, whether their group is cooperative or competitive, individualist or collective, or autocratic or participative. These kinds of self-report data are etic, in that the researcher who chooses the dimension categories does so while maintaining an outsider position with regard to the cultures being studied. Responses to these kinds of questionnaires can be factor analyzed. Here too the researcher etically determines the labels assigned to those factors, naming the relevant dimensions of cultural comparison. An example of this kind of research is Hofstede's multi-dimensional classification of national cultures (1980, 1991) in terms of power distance, masculinity–femininity, individualism–collectivism, etc. (see also dimensional studies of organizational culture by Kilmann, Saxton, Serpa, and Associates 1985; Denison 1990; Rousseau 1990b). Etic cultural research includes any study, quantitative or qualitative, where the conceptual categories are imposed by the researcher, rather than initiated by the cultural member who is being studied. The key, for an etic study, is to explain cogently why these particular concepts and operationalizations were chosen, usually with reference to both reliability and validity.

In contrast, most organizational studies of culture follow the lead of those socio-cultural anthropologists who have argued that it is essential that a researcher learn, as far as is humanly possible, to see things from an emic or insider point of view. One of the first to articulate this approach was Malinowski (1922/1961: 25) who claimed (although he also kept scandalous, racist research diaries) that he sought to 'grasp the native's point of view, his relation to life, to realize his vision of his world'. Geertz (1983: 58) described the emic approach in more colloquial language, 'The trick is to figure out what the devil they think they are up to.' The emic approach is particularly useful when a researcher is trying to understand cultural practices, such as headhunting or mass layoffs, that may be quite unfamiliar to the researcher. For example, Evans-Pritchard (1937: 69 ff.) studied Azande beliefs in witchcraft, 'a group of people were sitting beneath a granary which, unknown to them, had been weakened by termites. The granary collapsed, causing injury, and witchcraft was blamed.' As Hatch rephrases Evans-Pritchard's observations (1973: 249), 'The Azande were aware that the natural cause of the granary's collapse was the action of termites, but to the people this merely explained how, and not why, the structure fell. Why was it *this* granary which happened to collapse, and why did it do so precisely when these persons were beneath it?'

To reach the level of understanding required to phrase the question in this way, especially when trying to understand an unfamiliar or distasteful cultural practice, a researcher needs to learn enough about a culture to get inside the minds of cultural members, to 'think like a native'. Among anthropologists, Boas is sometimes given credit for being among the first to pack his bag, pitch his tent in the middle of a village, and attempt to get 'behind the veil' that stood between him and the thoughts of the people he wished to understand. How does a researcher achieve this kind of empathetic understanding? (Boas 1901: 1) advised:

the student must endeavor to divest himself entirely of opinions and emotions based on the peculiar social environment into which he is born. He [*sic*] must adapt his own mind, so far as it is feasible, to that of the people whom he is studying. The more successful he is in freeing himself from the bias based on the group of ideas that constitute the civilization in which he lives, the more successful he will be in interpreting the beliefs and actions of man [*sic*].

This is an idealized description, implying that a cultural researcher must have a corner on the empathy market, 'some sort of extraordinary sensitivity, an almost preternatural capacity to think, feel, and perceive like a native ... some unique form of psychological closeness, a sort of transcultural identification' (Geertz 1983: 56). Instead, Geertz offers a more attainable vision of the process of developing emic understanding, 'understanding the form and pressure of ... natives' inner lives is more like grasping a proverb, catching an allusion, seeing a joke—or ... reading a poem—than it is like achieving communion.' Geertz (1983: 10) describes the anthropologists' task as that of a translator (rather than being an empathizer) from the native's emic into the translator's community's etic, blurring boundaries between emic and etic:

'Translation,' here, is not a simple recasting of others' ways of putting things in terms of our own ways of putting them (that is the kind in which things get lost), but displaying the logic of their ways of putting them in the locutions of ours; a conception which again brings it rather close to what a critic does to illumine a poem than what an astronomer does to account for a star.

Implicitly, Geertz's description of research as a translation task draws attention to the difficulty of making a clear distinction between the etic and emic approaches, a point explored in more depth in critiques of social science research (e.g. Clifford and Marcus 1986). Emic analysis inevitably incorporates the etic (and vice versa), at least in so far as the researcher's emic perspective is etic to the situation being studied. Geertz (1973: 9) describes this problem in simpler terms: 'What we call our data are really our own constructions of other people's constructions of what they and their compatriots are up to'. For example, Boas refers, in the quotation above, to the researcher as 'he' and the subject of study as 'man'. This language choice prefigures the criticisms of feminist anthropologists, who have found that male anthropologists mostly study men, in part because it is easier for male anthropologists to establish close relationships and build emic understandings of members of their own sex. To the extent that male and female experiences of a culture differ, such studies are incomplete (e.g. Rosaldo and Lamphere 1974).

There are many different versions of what it means to adopt an emic perspective, but most acknowledge that the identity of the ethnographer inevitably creates an objectifying distance between researcher and informants. In contrast, reflexive ethnography seeks to characterize the relationship between the ethnographer and the informant in more equal terms (Bruni and Gherardi 2001):

a relation of reciprocal implication and participation: while the researcher observes, s/he is observed, so that ethnography can be viewed as the result of a textual collaboration, as the outcome of this dual hermeneutic process. The ethnographer is considered to be engaged in a symmetrical reflective exercise (Linstead 1993) and, far from being an 'alien', the ethnographer conveys cultural assumptions and preconceptions, and enjoys an active presence which makes his/her role different from that of the 'professional stranger' (Agar 1980) as an 'uncontaminated expert' (Van Maanen 1988; Tedlock 1991).

Acknowledging the difficulty of attaining an emic position uncontaminated by etic distancing, Geertz suggests a more modest goal (1973: 57)—that the researcher's task is to find a balance between emic and etic vantage points:

so as to produce an interpretation of the way a people lives which is neither imprisoned within their own mental horizons, an ethnography of witchcraft written by a witch, nor systematically deaf to the distinctive tonalities of their existence, an ethnography of witchcraft written by a geometer.[3]

Organizational researchers who seek an emic–etic balance have an extremely difficult task to perform, because we do not study tribes living on isolated Pacific islands or deep in the jungles of Brazil. In most cases, the cultures we study are microcosms of the cultures we live in, or if not, they are at least more familiar to us than the witches of Azande were to Evans-Pritchard. The difficult of finding an etic–emic balance is exacerbated for those of us who do 'halfie research,' that is 'research conducted by a researcher who comes from the culture she studies, but who, during the work, is a member of another culture, that "commissioned" the research project' (Czarniawska 1998: 4). This kind of study is becoming more common, as anthropologists return home from exotic islands to study their own cultures, as those 'exotic' cultures are penetrated by influences from the industrialized world, as immigrants study the cultures of their origins, and as cultural scholars study organizations in their own societies. In such circumstances, as Czarniawska (1998: 5) points out, researchers and actors in the field keep alternating between 'She is like us/I am like them' and 'She is . . ./I am different,' making misunderstandings multiply.

For many organizational researchers, whether or not we are 'halfies', it is as difficult to maintain sufficient distance from what we observe, to free ourselves from strong preconceptions, as it is to translate 'what the devil they think they are up to' with sufficient empathy. The illusion that we may have attained an emic view may come too easily to us, unless we deliberately select organizations that seem, at first glance, to be odd, distasteful, or simply unusual. And if the sites we study are outliers in some way, then how can we think about moving from our data to some

---

[3] A geometer practices geometry.

kind of generalizable theory? Of course, as outlined in the next section, many cultural researchers do not seek to build generalizable theory—a stance that is inconceivable to many organizational researchers trained in the neo-positivist tradition.

14.4 GENERALIZABLE AND CONTEXT-SPECIFIC KNOWLEDGE

Geertz's words, quoted immediately above, reveal an important assumption: the task of an anthropologist is to produce '*an* interpretation of the way *a* people lives'. Geertz is assuming that the task of a cultural researcher is to study a singular way of life, not to produce abstractions that can be used to generalize across cultures. He seeks to describe a single culture, richly and deeply (e.g. 1973), and/or to contrast a very small number of cultures, mostly in order to highlight their differences (e.g. 1983). Many ethnographers and other researchers share Geertz's focus on the concrete details of particular contexts. For example, Van Maanen and Barley (1985: 35) state their distrust of theoretical abstractions quite openly:

Theorists of the social world deal with the most ephemeral, delicate, and elusive of matters. It is easy to slip away and start granting theoretical entities (like culture, rules, deviants, organizations, etc.) status as iconic significations. They are always metaphoric. From my perspective, the only effective antidote for the air sickness caused by theoretical flight is periodic returns to the field.

One reason given for preferring to avoid generalization is the assumption that every culture is unique. Boas explained this viewpoint by arguing that historical accidents, such as a hostile attack from a neighboring tribe, produce a singular cultural configuration, much as a boulder tumbling down a mountainside produces an erosion pattern unmatched anywhere else. Particularly if people place great value on individual distinctiveness (less often the case in collectivist societies such as China, e.g. Markus and Kitayama 1991, 1994; Morris and Peng 1994), it may be socially desirable to belong to a collectivity which is (objectively) or which sees itself (subjectively) as unique.

Organizations often seek to define themselves as unique, in order to have a distinctive niche in a market or in order to attract and retain employees. Some— but by no means all—organizational studies of culture assume cultural uniqueness. Others make a softer claim: that specific kinds of cultural knowledge may be context-specific, as when copier repair technicians give advice in the form of context-specific recommendations rather than general, abstract rules (e.g. Brown and Duguid 1991). It is likely that organizational cultures, being a microcosm of the societies in which they are embedded, contain some elements that are unique, some that are falsely believed to be unique, and still others that are not unique at all (Martin *et al.* 1983; Martin 1992).

Another way to justify the study of a single culture is to argue that any one culture is not the only one conceivable in a particular context. The same circumstances could have led to a multiplicity of possible outcomes (e.g. Sahlins 1985; Sebag 1964: 166–7). From this point of view, the study of a single case is possible; the study of generalizable principles—a dead end road. The objective of a single case study, then, is an appreciation of contextually specific knowledge, rather than an understanding that emerges from the process of abstraction and generalization across cases. Geertz (1983: 232) admits that this approach is 'rather entranced with the diversity of things'. He concludes (1973: 43) that 'the notion that the essence of what it means to be human is most clearly revealed in those features of human culture that are universal, rather than those that are distinctive to this people or that, is a prejudice that we are not necessarily obligated to share.'

For other researchers, trained to appreciate large sample sizes, random sampling procedures, reliability and validity measures, and statistical tests, a disdain for generalization is hard to comprehend: isn't building theory, they ask, the goal of empirical research? What use is a study unless the goal is to understand what causes a phenomenon and to use that knowledge to predict, under appropriate conditions, what effects will occur? At the very least, shouldn't one seek multiple, systematic comparisons to build generalizations within and across case studies of culture? Such concerns for generalization, for example, led Hodson (1998) to code organizational and workplace characteristics (rough indicators of culture) in 108 English-language ethnographic case studies, seeking generalizations. There is some tendency for a concern with generalizability to be congruent with an objectivist approach to representation, which in turn has some congruence with being-realism and a search for causal laws.

In contrast, other social scientists adopt a different explanatory strategy. They search for reasons, rather than causes. Reasons make actions rationally intelligible, show how a given action is appropriate, efficient, and/or correct (Rosenberg 1988: 28–30). For example, ethnographic accounts often do not focus on generalizability concerns, for they are often not trying to provide knowledge for instrumental application, for which a presumably 'accurate' representation of 'reality' is desired. Instead, they often are (in accord with being-realism) offering practitioners and scholars a way to reflect on experience in novel ways, in order to construct new forms of action.

For all these reasons, ethnographers' goals are to understand a context deeply, provide reasons that explain social phenomena, and offer an interpretative frame for understanding. They do not usually seek to make predictions, discover generalizable laws, or build theories of causality:

A characteristic of scientific explanation is that it allows predictions, since it attempts to supply the causal factors behind a phenomenon so that when appropriate conditions exist, the phenomenon can be expected. By contrast, [ethnography] attempts to make a phenomenon intelligible, and the issue of prediction does not arise. (Hatch 1973: 336)

Conceptualization [in ethnography] is directed toward the task of generating interpretations of matters already in hand, not toward projecting outcomes of experimental manipulations or deducing future states of a determined system. (Geertz 1973: 26)

This disagreement, regarding contextually specific versus generalizable knowledge, underlies a conflict in the cultural literature. Studies that treat culture as a variable, and seek to predict outcomes (such as commitment or profitability) usually are trying to build generalizations, while studies that define culture as a metaphor, a way of looking at life within a collectivity, usually focus on context-specific knowledge (Smircich 1983b) and eschew most generalizations.

If ethnographies do not seek to build generalizable theories, what then is the purpose of ethnography? Is there any role for abstraction or for theory in context-specific cultural research? Geertz (1973: 25–6) addresses this issue:

The major theoretical contributions not only lie in specific studies—that is true in any field—but they are very difficult to abstract from and integrate into anything one might call 'culture theory' as such. Theoretical formulations hover so low over the interpretations they govern that they don't make much sense or hold much interest apart from them... the essential task of theory building here is not to codify abstract regularities but to make thick description, not to generalize across cases but to generalize within them....

[Cultural theory is] inseparable from the immediacies thick description presents.... What generality it contrives to achieve grows out of the delicacy of its distinctions, not the sweep of its abstractions.

'Thick descriptions' are richly detailed accounts of single cultures. Echoing the quotation from the poet Blake, with which this chapter began, such case descriptions give readers an ability to 'see the world in a grain of sand', that is, to see an entire culture in a single, sharply focused description. Such a description is based on information from multiple informants and other sources of information, such as conversational analysis (e.g. Tulin 1997). The objective of such accounts is not to build generalizations from a sample size of one (context).

From this point of view, an abhorrence of generalization or abstraction is more comprehensible, because these conceptual activities gloss over the richly textured detail that is the content and the goal of ethnographies. For example, Alvesson (1998) challenges Hofstede's classification of national cultures according to power distance, drawing on ethnographic evidence that suggests such categories are misleading. Alvesson concludes (1998: 15):

The rich interpretive capacities of culture can only be utilized if the study is open-minded, careful, locally oriented and close to social practices and meanings in organizations. This is then the opposite from questionnaire-based, generalization-oriented research, which cannot go beyond 'thin description' (to reverse Geertz' concept of thick description).

This debate about the desirability of generalizability echoes the old dispute between ideographic research (interpretation of a single case) and nomothetic research (developing generalizable laws from the study of many cases) (e.g. Morrill and Fine 1997). Nomothetic researchers, such as experimental psychologists and quantitative sociologists, often disdain the ideographic approaches of their case-study-oriented forebears, echoing the old Talmudic saying, 'For example is no proof.' In contrast, ideographic researchers, such as those who do ethnographic case studies, are also sometimes disdainful of abstraction, being especially critical of those who would develop an abstract theory from a single case study. For example, Geertz (1973: 21) is dismissive of the 'Jonesville-is-the-USA microcosmic model' and 'the Easter-Island-is-a-testing-case "natural experiment" model.'

Such expressions of disdain for opposing points of view regarding generalization should be regarded with some skepticism. It is a rare ethnographer who does not fall into some kind of generalizing language. Even Geertz (1983) argued that he did not study the culture *of* a village; he studied the culture of a larger collectivity *in* a village. His claim can be seen as a variant of the whole/part fallacy; generalizing about a whole culture from the study of a smaller unit within it is a fallacy because one cannot assume cultural homogeneity (e.g. Martin 1992). Indeed, some ethnographic accounts, rather than being disdainful of generalization, use ethnographic detail as an occasion for sharpening abstract analysis (Tsoukas 1989). Thus, the dichotomies evident in any discussion of generalizability tend to mask a more complex reality (Weick 1999). In any discussion of methodology, rhetoric is often more dichotomous than what people actually do, at least when they study cultures.

14.5 FOCUS AND BREADTH

Cultural research shows great variation in what is studied, when researchers claim to be studying culture. Some studies focus narrowly, on one or more cultural manifestations. Thus, for example, O'Reilly, Chatman, and Caldwell (1991) asked study participants, in what is called a Q sort task, to sort cards, each card containing an adjective, into piles of words that did and did not describe the cultures of the organizations where they worked. Kilmann *et al.* (1985) and Rousseau (1990*b*) used questionnaires, much like those described above as etic research, to get study participants to report the behavioral norms of their organizational cultures. These are narrowly focused, or specialist studies of culture. They use one kind of cultural manifestation, such as self-reports of behavioral norms, to operationally define a culture. Implicitly, narrowly focused studies assume that it is sufficient to study a single cultural manifestation or a very few manifestations, because if a wider range of manifestations were studied, the results would be largely the same. Implicitly, then, such studies assume that study participants' answers would be consistent across manifestations, another version of the whole/part fallacy.

In contrast, other cultural studies emphasize breadth by examining a variety of cultural manifestations. In these studies, researchers need not assume that interpretations of these manifestations are consistent with each other. For example, Botti's (1995) study of a Japanese-Italian effort at collaboration in a manufacturing plant, Kondo's (1990) examination of a family-owned food processing company in Japan, and Kunda's ethnography of a US engineering company (1992) all include interpretations of formal policies, structures, informal practices, rituals, and organizational stories, as well as extensive descriptions of the physical environments in which people worked. In Geertz's terms, these are thick descriptions.

This breadth, in the range of cultural manifestations studied, is characteristic of ethnographic research, and is more difficult to achieve when quantitative measures are used. Because it takes time to build a rich understanding of the relationships among a wide variety of cultural manifestations, breadth is achieved at the cost of being able to study only one or a very few cultural contexts, thus making generalization across contexts, even if it were desired, very difficult to attain. Tradeoffs, then, between focus and breadth, constrain the kinds of theoretical conclusions that can be drawn from a study. It is important to acknowledge that this dichotomy between focus and breadth, like many of the other dichotomies discussed in this chapter, is overdrawn. Deciding how much breadth is enough requires a judgment call, and any research project requires compromises regarding the breadth of cultural manifestations studied.

14.6 LEVEL OF DEPTH

14.6.1 An Argument for Depth of Cultural Understanding

Socio-cultural anthropologists advocate that researchers learn the language of cultural members, and then spend one or two years as a participant-observer, living and working with the people being studied. Eventually, hopefully, the researcher will come to be accepted as a cultural member. Under ideal circumstances, the researcher might even be invited to undergo a formal, ritualized initiation into membership status. This is a first step toward emic understanding, which is predicated on the researcher being able to 'penetrate the front' of public, polite behavior and gain the insights that come when people relax the constraints expected in interactions with outsiders. Psychologists make similar points when they argue that social desirability concerns affect how people behave, for example, when they try to control the impression they make on others. Only when facades are penetrated can a researcher hope to gain depth of understanding.

More recent ethnographic accounts are often skeptical about the difficulties of a researcher ever being accepted as an insider or ever being able to see a culture from an emic perspective. On the cover of Clifford and Marcus's (1986) book, which critiques such claims of privileged cultural acceptance, the cover photograph shows an ethnographer. He is pictured bent over his notes, with a cloth over his head shielding him from the sun and blinding him to his surroundings. 'Natives' stand in the shadows watching with various indecipherable expressions. Granted, this ethnographer's notes may contain deeply empathetic, emic understanding of the 'natives', but the photograph suggests otherwise. However, even skeptical views regarding the ability of ethnographers to develop emic understandings, like those in Clifford and Marcus's book, retain the conviction that the insights available from a long-term participant observation study offer greater depth of understanding than other, more superficial approaches to understanding, such as the use of quantitative survey instruments.

Schein (1985, 1996, 1999) and Rousseau (1990a) also stress the theoretical importance of depth of understanding. Schein (1985) distinguished three levels of depth in cultures, beginning with the most superficial: artifacts, such as stories, rituals, dress, décor, etc.; values (attitudes which can be articulated with relative ease); and basic assumptions (which are usually tacit, hard to see because they are taken for granted). According to Schein (1987), the best method for gaining an in-depth understanding of the assumptions underlying a culture is to enter a discussion with cultural members, using the interview goals and techniques of a clinical psychologist to tap unconscious and preconscious preconceptions. Schein argued that within a collectivity such as an organization, if a researcher attains in-depth understanding, he or she can ascertain if most members of the collectivity share the same basic assumptions. According to Schein, these assumptions tend to be quite abstract, such as whether people can be trusted or whether concerns about an organization's well-being should focus on short- or long-term considerations. This emphasis on depth in cultural studies has been crucially important, in part because the methods most easily able to create in-depth understanding, such as ethnography and clinical interviews, had become unfashionable wherever and whenever quantitative methods gained dominance in organizational studies.

14.6.2 An Example of Depth Analysis

Perhaps an extended example will clarify this depth argument. When Ouchi (1981) studied a particular electronics company, employees told a 'second chance' story about an employee who made a disastrous mistake. When the culprit was called to his boss's office, he feared he would be fired. Instead, his boss expressed faith that the employee would never make another such mistake, and gave him a very tough assignment. This assignment was a testimony of the boss's faith that the employee could redeem himself, as a second mistake would have done the company grievous harm. This story ended happily; the employee succeeded beyond his boss's fondest dreams, and was thereafter one of the company's most loyal employees.

A second, and superficially unrelated manifestation of the culture at this firm was the company's promotion policy, sometimes labeled the spiral staircase. Before being promoted up a level, employees were usually moved laterally to another functional area. In this way, the high-level employees of the firm had extensive exposure to the problems of marketing, engineering, finance, human resources, etc., giving them a broad perspective on the firm as a whole. Although these two manifestations, the story and the spiral staircase promotion policy, may seem unrelated, Schein might argue that they appear unrelated because this analysis, so far, has been relatively superficial, focusing on the level of artifacts. If the interpretation were to go deeper, as Schein argues it should, the researcher might conclude that both manifestations illustrate a tacit, basic assumption about the benefits—to individual employees and to the company as a whole—of taking a long-term perspective.

14.6.3 Another Approach to Depth of Understanding

Others (including myself) argue that artifacts and values are not necessarily superficial. A cultural artifact, such as a story or a ritual, is important because of how people interpret its meanings. Those meanings need not be superficial; they may reflect deep assumptions. In this way, artifacts, values, and assumptions do not necessarily reflect separable, varying levels of depth. A cultural researcher should, I would argue, seek deep meanings associated with each type of cultural manifestation. For example, in a superficial cultural study, interpretations and meanings can reflect formulaic expressions of espoused values in a 'Corporate Values' statement. Alternatively, interpretations may reflect deeply held personal values that take the form of basic assumptions, sometimes so taken for granted that they are hard to articulate. Such basic assumptions may include 'walking the talk'—values inferred from, and congruent with, behavior. Other kinds of interpretations of events and artifacts are less value-laden, and more like cognitive conclusions, or beliefs, about 'how things are'. Some of these beliefs may have the characteristics of basic assumptions.

In each of these examples, what is important is not the cultural manifestation itself, but how people interpret it. The depth of a researcher's analysis of these interpretations, that is, the patterns of meaning underlying a collection of cultural manifestations, can approach the depth of understanding that Schein terms 'basic assumptions'. However, it is important to note that even at the level of deep assumptions, collectivity-wide consensus may not emerge. In a single context, some assumptions might generate collectivity-wide consensus. Other assumptions might be common to some subcultures but not others. And, finally, some assumptions might be so ambiguous that clear agreement or disagreement among substantial numbers of people would be unlikely (Meyerson and Martin 1987; Martin and Meyerson 1988; Martin 1992).

14.6.4 The Costs of In-Depth Study: Pragmatic Considerations

Depth of understanding clearly has its advantages, but it is purchased at a cost: the time it takes to gain in-depth understanding. Although this is a pragmatic concern, rather than a theoretical issue, it merits consideration. An anthropologist, for example, may invest years in learning a language, traveling to a distant land, enduring physical discomfort, emotional isolation, and other forms of hardship. He or she may spend a year or two doing participant-observation, then another year or two deciphering and interpreting field notes. The final product of all this effort is (usually) a book-length ethnography, because the complexity of this kind of data is difficult to carve up in journal-length articles. This is a large time investment, particularly in universities where tenure decisions are usually made after the first seven years of employment.

Ethnographers studying organizational culture share some, but not all of these problems of time investment. As long as an ethnographer studies an organization within a familiar culture, the problems of physical and emotional hardship, travel, and language differences are minimized. The etic–emic dimension, however, is difficult to manage in a relatively familiar organizational culture, and many of the other difficulties of ethnographic research remain. Some obstacles to ethnographic research are intensified in organizational studies. In the academic departments where many organizational researchers work, there is not much understanding of the assumptions underlying ethnographic methods and even less sympathy with putting 'all one's eggs in a single basket'—a book—rather than publishing numerous refereed journal articles. An organizational ethnographer pays these costs and deals with worrisome publication decisions, in part, because of a conviction that depth of understanding is crucial. Imagine, then, an ethnographer's reaction to a study claiming to understand a culture on the basis of a questionnaire or a short-term qualitative study, involving a few months of observation and/or interviewing. Appreciation seems unlikely.

Given all this emphasis on depth, who would advocate a 'superficial' approach to studying culture? There are pragmatic reasons for doing so. Doing a good ethnography is difficult and very time-consuming. And when it is finished, it is still only a study with a sample size of one. Although several publications can come out of a single ethnographic study, sooner or later a researcher may want to go back to the field to study a different context. However, given the realities of modern academic and family life, most researchers do only one long-term ethnography—the dissertation.

These pragmatic considerations have theoretical implications. The time involved in each study means that an ethnographic researcher is unlikely to be able to use his or her own data to make comparisons among significant numbers of cultures, or to build empirically-based, theoretical generalizations about culture. Some culture researchers may not want to do so, but for those who want to build empirically based theoretical generalizations, less time-consuming methods for studying cultures are essential. Depth must be sacrificed, in these instances, if generalization is the goal.

However, this struggle regarding depth, like the other dichotomies discussed above, is overdrawn; it is important not to regard the issue as a dichotomous choice between depth or superficiality. There are many ways to gain a multi-faceted, moderately unsuperficial understanding of a culture, even using short-term qualitative methods or innovative survey measures. All methods can be designed and applied in slap-dash or probing ways, making some degree of depth a possibility worth striving for, even in a study that seeks to generalize across a number of cultures.

14.7 Effects of these Intellectual Disputes on Organizational Studies: The Paradigm Proliferation Debates

These disputes about objectivity and subjectivity, etic and emic research, generalizability and context-specific knowledge, focus and breadth, and level of depth are of particular relevance to cultural research, but they also have surfaced, to varying degrees, in organizational studies as a whole. Scholars have engaged in a fierce debate about whether these disputes have had favorable or unfavorable effects on the development of organizational theory and research.

Within organizational studies in the United States, disputes about these issues have been framed as the 'paradigm proliferation problem'. In the 1960s and 1970s, a single paradigm (focused on neo-positivism and quantitative methods) held sway among most US organizational scholars. In the early 1980s, the renaissance of interest in cultural studies and, more broadly, qualitative methods, activated many of the intellectual disputes described above. As a result of these and other intellectual influences, now there is some lack of consensus within the international domain of organizational studies about what theories are worth studying, what methods are valid, what values and interests should be pursued, and what epistemological assumptions are merited (e.g. Burrell and Morgan 1979; Clegg and Dunkerly 1977; Nord and Connell 1998; Donaldson 1985; Silverman 1970; Smircich, Calás, and Morgan 1992). Thus, the intense disputes within organizational culture studies are mirrored in the organizational field as a whole.

Concern about these issues within organizational studies in the United States came to a head with the paradigm proliferation debates at the Academy of Management annual award ceremonies. As always when discussing paradigms, it is useful to begin by noting how this disputed term is being defined. A paradigm offers a way of approaching scientific work, as Van de Ven (1997: 2) explains:

A paradigm is a worldview, a general perspective, a way of breaking down the complexity of the real world. As such, paradigms are deeply embedded in the socialization of adherents and practitioners, telling them what is important, what is legitimate, what is reasonable. Paradigms are normative; they tell us what to do without the necessity of long existential considerations.

I would argue, in accord with Donaldson (1985), that the concept of a paradigm has been over-utilized; the various intellectual disputes discussed above do not fall easily together, into well-defined, competing paradigms. However, among cultural researchers, positions in these various disputes do tend to cluster. For example, some scholars favor being-realism, representational epistemologies, etic research, the search for empirically based, generalizable theory; this cluster of researchers generally prefer a relatively narrow focus on a few cultural manifestations, with relatively less concern about issues of depth. This cluster of approaches, usually hovering around being-realism assumptions, has dominated organizational research and, more specifically organizational culture research in the United States, because it promises control over a complex and ambiguous reality (attractive to management) and it justifies avoiding the costs (time investments, etc.) of ethnographic field studies.

Other cultural scholars prefer becoming-realism, post-representational epistemologies, and emic research, in order to affirm the advantages of a broader and deeper contextual understanding. Of course, there are exceptions to these clusters—different ways to mix and match preferences regarding these issues. Organizational researchers outside the cultural domain also tend to fall in these two clusters. Whether these clusters represent different paradigms, or simply a cacophony of different opinions about fundamental issues, is less important than the dialogues that have ensued.

Three recent recipients of an annual major award from the Academy of Management used their acceptance speeches to articulate quite different reactions to the developing discord within the field. In his speech, Pfeffer (1993) argued that the proliferation of research paradigms in the field of organizational studies had eroded the field's prestige in the rest of academia, making it difficult for us to garner resources, and impeding the cumulative development of knowledge. Pfeffer argued that, for the advancement of the field and the enhancement of knowledge, a board of elite researchers should select a small number of research topics, on which all organizational researchers would have to work.

The next year's award recipient, Van Maanen (1995), took umbrage at Pfeffer's call for the dominance of a few elite-approved research topics, which Van Maanen labeled 'Pfefferdigms'. Van Maanen argued that any elitist determination of what topics were worth studying was 'insufferably smug; pious and orthodox; philosophically indefensible; extraordinarily naïve as to how science actually works; theoretically foolish, vain, and autocratic'. Van Maanen saw the proliferation of paradigms as a sign of the moral and intellectual health of the field, and called for 'letting a thousand flowers bloom' as an effective means of encouraging innovative research.

Subsequently, a third award recipient, Van de Ven (1997) spoke vehemently against the ways advocates of particular paradigms had demeaned and devalued research conducted from other paradigmatic orientations. Van de Ven (1997: 9) used neo-positivist language to argue that empirical evidence could resolve the competing claims of paradigms, 'Valid empirical evidence is the ultimate external arbitrator for sifting and winnowing among our paradigms and for advancing those that provide empirically better explanations than others.' In these remarks, Van de Ven was making assumptions about the objectivity of data, and its determinant value in a theoretical dispute. The assumption that theoretical (and possible paradigmatic) differences of opinion can be empirically resolved is a basic tenet of neo-positivism (e.g. Campbell and Stanley 1966).

Many other scholars, working from different (not neo-positivist) epistemological or methodological positions, would challenge Van de Ven's assumptions in this regard. Burrell and Morgan (1979) made a strong and influential argument for 'paradigm incommensurability',[4] that is, evaluating contributions by the standards

---

[4] To address these issues, I will put aside for the moment differences of opinion about whether or not these are truly paradigmatic disputes (Donaldson 1985).

of their own paradigm, not the standards of others. These authors carried 'paradigm incommensurability' a step farther, arguing that research within paradigms should be kept separate, so that less known paradigms could develop without outside interference. Soon Hassard and Pym (1990) and Weaver and Gioia (1994) called for an end to this 'smug protectionism'. As calls for paradigm incommensurability became less accepted, uncertainty increased (Fleming and Stablein 1999): 'Now paradigm differences must be taken seriously, not ignored or granted "separate but equal" status (Reed 1996). Today, we are left with the uncertainties that characterize the 1990's regarding definitions, meaning, method, the nature of theory and the role of the theorist (Clegg and Hardy 1996).' The disputes among cultural researchers, that have been the focus of this chapter, can therefore be seen as part of a larger struggle—the paradigm proliferation debates in the field of organizational studies.

14.8 THE CULTURE WARS

The uncertainties that spread throughout the field of organizational studies at the turn of the century, giving rise to the paradigm proliferation debates, are particularly intense within the domain of organizational culture studies. In addition to the five issues discussed in this chapter, cultural researchers are deeply divided on the question of whose interests and values merit representation and advocacy, which theoretical perspectives should be used, and whether quantitative or qualitative methods are preferable. When cultural studies come to contradictory, empirically based conclusions, these fundamental disagreements make it difficult to adjudicate conflicting conclusions, perhaps with further empirical research. For these reasons, intellectual disputes have made it nearly impossible to write a cumulative review of 'what we have learned' so far, about cultures in organizations.

For example, when Peter Frost and I were asked to contribute a handbook chapter reviewing the accomplishments of culture research to date, we found it impossible to write the usual enlightenment tale of knowledge advancement. Instead, we (Martin and Frost 1996) described cultural theory and research using a 'culture wars' metaphor.[5] We described culture research as a series of ongoing battles between opposing viewpoints. We began with the 'revolutionary vanguard' who spearheaded the renaissance of interest in cultural studies in the 1980s. Next,

[5] In contrast to the usage in this chapter, the term 'culture wars', in popular usage, refers to multicultural conflicts among representatives of different groups, defined usually by race, gender, ethnicity, class, or ideology.

we described attacks and counter-attacks by armies representing opposing theoretical viewpoints, a skirmish between quantitative and qualitative methodologists, a meta-theoretical move to alter 'the battle lines', and a postmodern[6] attempt to rout all armies from the field of battle.

Although we had fun using the culture wars metaphor to review the cultural literature, these intellectual disputes (a local version of the paradigm proliferation debate) have had serious consequences. Because it is difficult to present a cumulative picture of what has been learned from culture research, as Pfeffer predicted in his speech, the perceived worth of this area of inquiry has been difficult to explain and understand, making it easier for critics to marginalize and devalue work in this area. When a theoretical domain, such as cultural research, challenges neo-positivist assumptions about the empirical resolution of theoretical differences, it runs the risk of being dismissed, by some, as unverifiable, and therefore empty rhetoric. For example, to continue with extracts from Van de Ven's award acceptance speech (1997: 5), 'Then there are the endless rhetorical diatribes of neo-modernists—culture theorists, critical theorists, post-positivists, feminists, Saussurean linguists. They are taking the discursive turn to deconstruct one another, and particularly the schools in Pfefferdigm. They lay bare the belly of the positivists.' Although critical, feminist, postmodern, and linguistic theoreticians offer cultural researchers fine intellectual company, this remark could be interpreted as an attempt to marginalize and devalue cultural research. Even if Van de Ven did not intend this, he may have influenced others to do so.

If cultural researchers are to counter attempts to marginalize and devalue cultural research, we need to make ourselves understood, build on each other's work, and begin to explain, to the rest of the field, why what we are doing is important. This is difficult, in part because cultural researchers do not have commonly accepted, unproblematic resolutions to offer, to the debates that are the focus of this chapter.

Cultural researchers have several options at this point. We could prolong the culture wars by continuing to take sides in these battles. Following Pfeffer's advice, we could enforce conformity to elite preferences (here I would agree with Van Maanen about the undesirability of this alternative). We could try to build consensus about the 'right' answers (an unlikely outcome, given the depth of conviction on these disputed issues). Or, we could, whatever our positions on these issues, learn about viewpoints other than our own, read research conducted in accord with these viewpoints, and see, open-mindedly, how these divergent ideas could enrich our own. Given that paradigms have proliferated in the cultural domain, and more broadly speaking in the field of organizational studies, this last alternative seems to

---

[6] For a deeper discussion of postmodern approaches to culture, see Alvesson and Willmott (1996); Berg (1989); Calás and Smircich (1991); Czarniawska-Joerges (1988); Grafton-Small and Linstead (1987); Jeffcut (1991); and Letiche (1991).

be elusive and desirable, as it would leave an important role, as teacher, for those who prefer to advocate particular resolutions to these debates.

REFERENCES

AGAR, M. (1980). *An Informal Introduction to Ethnography.* New York: Academic Press.

—— (1986). *Speaking of Ethnography.* Beverly Hills, Calif.: Sage.

ALVESSON, M. (1998). 'The Local and the Grandiose: Method, Micro and Macro in Comparative Studies of Culture and Organizations'. Unpublished manuscript, Lund University, Sweden.

—— and MELIN, L. (1987). 'Major Discrepancies and Contradictions in Organizational Culture: Both in the Phenomenon of Culture Itself and in Cultural Studies'. Paper presented at the International Conference on Organizational Symbolism and Corporate Culture. Milan, Italy.

—— and WILLMOTT, H. (1996). *Making Sense of Management: A Critical Analysis.* London: Sage.

BARLEY, S., MEYER, G., and GASH, D. (1988). 'Cultures of Culture: Academics, Practitioners, and the Pragmatics of Normative Control'. *Administrative Science Quarterly,* 33: 24–61.

BARTUNEK, J., and MOCH, M. (1991). 'Multiple Constituencies and the Quality of Working Life Intervention at FoodCom', in P. Frost, L. Moore, M. Louis, C. Lundberg, and J. Martin (eds.), *Reframing Organizational Culture.* Newbury Park, Calif.: Sage.

BERG, P. (1989). 'Postmodern Management? From Facts to Fiction in Theory and Practice'. *Scandinavian Journal of Management,* 5: 201–17.

BERGER, P., and LUCKMANN, T. (1967). *The Social Construction of Reality.* Garden City, NY: Doubleday.

BLAKE, W. (2000). *Selected Poetry and Prose.* Harlow, England: Longman.

BOAS, F. (1901). 'The Eskimo of Balin Land and Hudson Bay'. *Bulletin of the American Museum of Natural History,* 15/Part 1.

BOGDAN, R., and TAYLOR, S. (1975). *Introduction to Qualitative Research Methods.* New York: Wiley.

BOTTI, H. (1995). 'Misunderstandings: A Japanese Transplant in Italy Strives for Lean Production'. *Organization,* 2: 55–86.

BROWN, J., and DUGUID, P. (1991). 'Organizational Learning and Communities-of-Practice: Toward a Unified View of Working, Learning, and Innovation'. *Organizational Science,* 2: 40–57.

BRUNER, J., GOODNOW, J., and AUSTIN, G. (1956). *A Study of Thinking.* New York: John Wiley and Sons.

BRUNI, A., and GHERARDI, S. (2001). 'Omega's Story: The Heterogeneous Engineering of a Gendered Professional Self', in M. Dent and S. Whitehead (eds.), *Managing Processional Identities.* London and New York: Routledge.

BURRELL, G., and MORGAN, G. (1979). *Sociological Paradigms and Organizational Analysis.* London: Heinemann.

CALÁS, M., and SMIRCICH, L. (1987). 'Post-culture: Is the Organizational Culture Literature Dominant but Dead?' Paper presented at the International Conference on Organizational Symbolism and Corporate Culture, Milan, Italy.

CALÁS, M., and SMIRCICH, L. (1991). 'Voicing Seduction to Silence Leadership'. *Organization Studies*, 12: 567–602.

CAMPBELL, D., and STANLEY, J. (1966). *Experimental and Quasi-experimental Designs for Research*. Chicago: Rand McNally.

CHALMERS, A. (1982). *What Is This Thing Called Science?* (2nd edn). Brisbane: University of Queensland Press.

CHIA, R. (1996). 'The Problem of Reflexivity in Organizational Research: Towards a Postmodern Science of Organization'. *Organization*, 3: 31–59.

CLEGG, S., and DUNKERLEY, D. (eds.) (1977). *Critical Issues in Organizations*. New York: Routledge & Kegan Paul.

——and HARDY, C. (1996). 'Organizations, Organization and Organizing', in S. Clegg, C. Hardy, and W. Nord (eds.), *Handbook of Organization Studies*. London: Sage.

CLIFFORD, J., and MARCUS, G. (1986). *Writing Culture: The Poetics and Politics of Ethnography*. Berkeley: University of California Press.

COOK, T., and REICHARDT, C. (1979). 'Beyond Qualitative Versus Quantitative Methods', in T. Cook and C. Reichardt (eds.), *Qualitative and Quantitative Methods in Evaluation Research*. Beverly Hills, Calif.: Sage.

CZARNIAWSKA, B. (1998). *A Narrative Approach to Organization Studies*. Qualitative Research Methods Series. Thousand Oaks, Calif.: Sage.

CZARNIAWSKA-JOERGES, B. (1988). *Ideological Control in Non-ideological Organizations*. New York: Praeger.

DENISON, D. (1990). *Corporate Culture and Organizational Effectiveness*. New York: Wiley.

DONALDSON, L. (1985). *In Defense of Organization Theory: A Reply to the Critics*. New York: Cambridge University Press.

EVANS-PRITCHARD, E. (1937). *Witchcraft, Oracles and Magic among the Azande*. Oxford: Clarendon Press.

FLEMING, P., and STABLEIN, R. (1999). 'Normative Control: A Review'. Massey University, New Zealand. Manuscript in preparation.

FROST, P., MOORE, L., LOUIS, M., LUNDBERG, C., and MARTIN, J. (eds.) (1991). *Reframing Organizational Culture*. Newbury Park, Calif.: Sage.

GEERTZ, C. (1973). *The Interpretation of Cultures*. New York: Basic Books.

——(1983). *Local Knowledge: Further Essays in Interpretive Anthropology*. New York: Basic Books.

GEPHART, R. (1988). *Ethnostatistics: Qualitative Foundations for Quantitative Research*. Newbury Park, Calif.: Sage.

GRAFTON-SMALL, R., and LINSTEAD, S. (1987). 'Theory as Artifact'. Paper presented at the International Conference on Organizational Symbolism and Corporate Culture, Milan, Italy.

HARRÉ, R. (1986). *Varieties of Realism: A Rationale for the Natural Sciences*. Oxford: Blackwell.

HASSARD, J., and PYM, D. (eds.) (1990). *The Theory and Philosophy of Organizations: Critical Issues and New Perspectives*. London: Routledge.

HATCH, E. (1973). *Theories of Man and Culture*. New York: Columbia University Press.

HODSON, R. (1998). 'Organizational Ethnographies: An Underutilized Resource in the Sociology of Work'. *Social Forces*, 76: 1173–1208.

HOFSTEDE, G. (1980). *Culture's Consequences: International Differences in Work-Related Values*. Beverly Hills, Calif.: Sage.

—— (1991). *Cultures and Organizations: Software of the Mind*. New York: McGraw-Hill.

JEFFCUTT, P. (1991). 'Styles of Representation in Organizational Analysis: Heroism, Happy Endings and the Carnivalesque in the Organizational Symbolism Literature'. Paper presented at the International Conference on Organizational Symbolism and Corporate Culture, Copenhagen, Denmark.

KILMANN, R., SAXTON, M., SERPA, R., and Associates (1985). *Gaining Control of the Corporate Culture*. San Francisco: Jossey-Bass.

KONDO, D. (1990). *Crafting Selves: Power, Gender, and Discourses of Identity in a Japanese Workplace*. Chicago: University of Chicago Press.

KUNDA, G. (1992). *Engineering Culture: Control and Commitment in a High-Tech Corporation*. Philadelphia: Temple University Press.

LETICHE, H. (1991). 'Postmodernism Goes Practical'. Paper presented at the International Conference on Organizational Symbolism and Corporate Culture, Copenhagen, Denmark.

LINSTEAD, S. (1993). 'From Postmodern Anthropology to Deconstructive Ethnography'. *Human Relations*, 46: 97–120.

MALINOWSKI, B. (1922/1961). *Argonauts of the Western Pacific*. New York: E. P. Dutton and Company.

MARKUS, H., and KITAYAMA, S. (1991). 'Culture and the Self: Implications for Cognition, Emotion, and Motivation'. *Psychological Review*, 98: 224–53.

—— —— (1994). 'A Collective Fear of the Collective: Implications for the Selves and Theories of Selves'. *Personality and Social Psychology Bulletin*, 20: 568–79.

MARTIN, J. (1992). *Cultures in Organizations*: Three Perspectives New York: Oxford University Press.

—— (2002). *Organizational Culture: Mapping the Terrain* (Newbury Park, Calif.: Sage Publications).

—— (forthcoming). 'Feminist Theory and Critical Theory: Unexplored Synergies', in M. Alvesson and H. Willmott (eds.), *Critical Management Studies*. London: Sage.

—— BRICKMAN, P., and MURRAY, A. (1984). 'Moral Outrage and Pragmatism: Explanations for Collective Action'. *Journal of Experimental Social Psychology*, 20: 484–96.

—— FELDMAN, M., HATCH, M., and SITKIN, S. (1983). 'The Uniqueness Paradox in Organizational Stories'. *Administrative Science Quarterly*, 28: 438–53.

—— and FROST, P. (1996). 'The Organizational Culture War Games: A Struggle for Intellectual Dominance', in S. Clegg, C. Hardy, and W. Nord (eds.), *Handbook of Organization Studies*. London: Sage.

—— and MEYERSON, D. (1988). 'Organizational Culture and the Denial, Channeling and Acknowledgment of Ambiguity', in L. Pondy, R. Boland, Jr., and H. Thomas (eds.), *Managing Ambiguity and Change*. New York: Wiley.

MEYERSON, D., and MARTIN, J. (1987). 'Cultural Change: An Integration of Three Different Views'. *Journal of Management Studies*, 24: 623–47.

MORRILL, C., and FINE, G. (1997). 'Ethnographic Contributions to Organizational Sociology'. *Sociological Methods and Research*, 25: 424–51.

MORRIS, M., LEUNG, K., AMES, D., and LICKEL, B. (1999). 'Views from Inside and Outside: Integrating Emic and Etic Insights about Culture and Justice Judgment'. *Academy of Management Review*, 24: 781–96.

—— and PENG, K. (1994). 'Culture and Cause: American and Chinese Attributions for Social Physical Events'. *Journal of Personality and Social Psychology*, 7: 949–71.

NORD, W., and CONNELL, A. (1998). 'Criteria for Good Theory in Organization Studies 2000 A.D.' Unpublished manuscript, University of South Florida, Tampa.

O'REILLY, C., CHATMAN, J., and CALDWELL, D. (1991). 'People and Organizational Culture: A Profile Comparison Approach to Assessing Person–Organization Fit'. *Academy of Management Journal*, 34: 487–516.

OUCHI, W. (1981). *Theory Z: How American Business Can Meet the Japanese Challenge.* Reading, Mass.: Addison-Wesley.

PFEFFER, J. (1993). 'Barriers to the Advance of Organizational Science: Paradigm Development as a Dependent Variable'. *Academy of Management Review*, 17: 599–620.

REED, M. (1996). 'Organizational Theorizing: A Historically Contested Terrain', in S. Clegg, C. Hardy, and W. Nord (eds.), *Handbook of Organization Studies.* London: Sage.

RORTY, R. (1991). *Objectivity, Relativism, and Truth: Philosophical Papers,* 1. Cambridge: Cambridge University Press.

ROSALDO, M., and LAMPHERE, L. (eds.) (1974). *Woman, Culture, and Society.* Stanford, Calif.: Stanford University Press.

ROSEN, M. (1991). 'Breakfast at Spiro's: Dramaturgy and Dominance', in P. Frost, L. Moore, M. Louis, C. Lundberg, and J. Martin (eds.), *Reframing Organizational Culture.* Newbury Park, Calif.: Sage.

ROSENBERG, A. (1988). 'Reasons and Causes', *Philosophy of Social Science.* Boulder, Colo.: Westview Press.

ROUSSEAU, D. (1990a). 'Assessing Organizational Culture: The Case for Multiple Methods', in B. Schneider (ed.), *Frontiers of Industrial and Organizational Psychology,* 3. San Francisco: Jossey-Bass.

—— (1990b). 'Normative Beliefs in High and Low Fund Raising Organizations'. *Group and Organization Studies,* 15: 448–60.

SAHLINS, M. (1985). *Islands of History.* Chicago: University of Chicago Press.

—— (1995). *How 'Natives' Think about Captain Cook, for example.* Chicago: University of Chicago Press.

SCHEIN, E. (1985). *Organizational Culture and Leadership.* San Francisco: Jossey-Bass.

—— (1987). *The Clinical Perspective in Field Work.* Newbury Park, Calif.: Sage.

—— (1996). 'Three Cultures of Management: The Key to Organizational Learning'. *Sloan Management Review,* 38: 9–21.

—— (1999). *The Corporate Culture Survival Guide: Sense and Nonsense about Culture Change.* San Francisco: Jossey-Bass.

SEBAG, L. (1964). *Marxisme et structuralisme.* Paris: Payot.

SILVERMAN, D. (1970). *The Theory of Organizations.* New York: Basic Books.

SMIRCICH, L. (1983a). 'Concepts of Culture and Organizational Analysis'. *Administrative Science Quarterly,* 28: 339–58.

—— (1983b). 'Organizations as Shared Meanings', in L. Pondy, P. Frost, G. Morgan, and T. Dandridge (eds.), *Organizational Symbolism.* Greenwich, Conn.: JAI Press.

—— Calás, M., and MORGAN, G. (eds.) (1992). 'Theory Development Forum [Special Issue]'. *Academy of Management Review,* 17.

STABLEIN, R. (1996). 'Data in Organization Studies', in S. Clegg, C. Hardy, and W. Nord (eds.), *Handbook of Organization Studies.* London: Sage.

—— and NORD, W. (1985). 'Practical and Emancipatory Interests in Organizational Symbolism: A Review and Evaluation'. *Journal of Management,* 11: 13–28.

TEDLOCK, B. (1991). 'From Participation Observation to Observation of Participation: The Emergence of Narrative Ethnography'. *Journal of Anthropological Research*, 47.

TSOUKAS, H. (1989). 'The Validity of Idiographic Research Explanations'. *Academy of Management Review*, 14: 551–61.

—— (1998). 'The Word and the World: A Critique of Representationalism in Management Research'. *International Journal of Public Administration*, 21: 781–817.

TULIN, M. (1997). 'Talking Organization: Possibilities for Conversation Analysis in Organizational Behavior Research'. *Journal of Management Inquiry*, 6: 101–19.

VAN DE VEN, A. (1997). 'The Buzzing, Blooming, Confusing World of Organization and Management Theory: A View from Lake Wobegon University'. Paper presented at Academy of Management Conference, Boston.

VAN MAANEN, J. (ed.) (1979). *Qualitative Methodology*. Beverly Hills, Calif.: Sage.

—— (1988). *Tales of the Field: On Writing Ethnography*. Chicago: University of Chicago Press.

VAN MAANEN, J. (1995). 'Style as Theory'. *Organizational Science*, 1: 133–43.

—— and BARLEY, S. (1985). 'Cultural Organization: Fragments of a Theory', in P. Frost, L. Moore, M. Louis, C. Lundberg, and J. Martin (eds.), *Reframing Organizational Culture*. Beverly Hills, Calif.: Sage.

—— and KUNDA, G. (1989). ' "Real Feelings": Emotional Expression and Organizational Culture', in L. Cummings and B. Staw (eds.), *Research in Organizational Behavior, 11*. Greenwich, Conn.: JAI Press.

WEAVER, G., and GIOIA, D. (1994). 'Paradigms Lost: Incommensurability vs. Structurationist Inquiry'. *Organization Studies*, 15: 565–89.

WEICK, K. (1999). 'Theory Construction as Disciplined Reflexivity: Tradeoffs in the 90s'. *Academy of Management Review*, 24: 797–806.

WHITEHEAD, A. (1926/1985). *Science and the Modern World*. London: Free Association Books.

YARMEY, A., and YARMEY, M. (1997). 'Eyewitness Recall and Duration Estimates in Field Settings'. *Journal of Applied Social Psychology*, 27: 330–44.

PART IV

ORGANIZATION THEORY AS A POLICY SCIENCE

CHAPTER 15

ACTIONABLE KNOWLEDGE

CHRIS ARGYRIS

THE focus of this chapter is upon producing actionable knowledge. Propositions that are actionable are those that actors can use to implement effectively their intentions. Effective implementation occurs when (a) a match is produced between the intentions of the actors and the actual outcomes, (b) in such a way that the outcomes persevere, and (c) without deteriorating the existing level of problem-solving effectiveness.

15.1 THE IMPORTANCE OF ACTIONABLE KNOWLEDGE

Why should social scientists focus upon actionable knowledge?

1. Most social scientists claim that producing knowledge that can assist in enhancing human effectiveness is an important objective for scholars. (Read, for example, in my country, the charters of the American Psychological, Sociological, and Anthropological Associations.) Many researchers who support actionable

knowledge also say that in order to produce actionable knowledge we may have to wait until the descriptive knowledge cumulates to the point that it can be used to produce actionable knowledge. In an analysis of the literature I concluded that, in the field of organizational studies, there is little additivity of knowledge that leads to the promises made by scholars (Argyris 1980).

Since then, I have suggested another reason why the additivity required to produce actionable knowledge is not likely to occur. The reason is that the ideas in good currency about rigorous research inveigh against the production of actionable knowledge. This is especially true if the knowledge is about changing the status quo and creating what some scholars call 'liberating alternatives'. More about this below.

2. The most powerful empirical tests for theories are provided when predictions are made about changing the universe, not simply describing it. Lewin made this point when he said that if we wished to truly understand the universe, try changing it. When we describe the universe, there is some wiggle-room for our claims. As we shall see when we strive to change the universe, we require knowledge that can be used to create something new and rare. In order to do so, we must specify causal propositions about how to create change. Moreover, as we shall see, these causal propositions must be crafted in the form that the human mind can store, retrieve, and implement in an on-line manner.

3. Most theories and much empirical research often contain gaps, inconsistencies, and inner contradictions. Some of these arise because of incompleteness of our knowledge. The expectation is that with further empirical research, they will be discovered. The expectation is often not fulfilled.

But, what if these gaps, inconsistencies, and inner contradictions occur because we are following correctly the rules of normal science research? What if these rules and the norms that they create in the scholarly community help to keep us unaware of the gaps and inconsistencies and unaware that we are unaware?

I suggest that the most powerful way to surface these issues is to attempt to intervene; to state predictions about *creating* phenomena that do not exist presently.

4. Actionable knowledge is the knowledge that is most likely to be of help to human beings because it prescribes how they should act. The basis for the sense of competence, self-esteem, and self-efficacy is effective action (White 1959; Bandura 1986). Action is therefore at the heart of what it means to be human.

Actionable knowledge also empowers the users. It provides them with powerful reasons to accept or reject the claims of applicability made by researchers. The users are empowered because they can see that they have been helped or because they have good evidence to reject the claim of the validity of the knowledge.

15.2 Norms and Rules about Producing 'Scientific' Knowledge

There are four fundamental norms and rules about producing scientific knowledge that, when implemented correctly, will limit and inhibit the production of valid actionable knowledge. They are (1) describe the universe as is, (2) be pluralistic in outlook, (3) focus on internal and external validity, all of which combine to create, (4) unintentional gaps and inconsistencies.

15.2.1 The Importance of Describing the Universe as Completely and Validly as Possible

One of the most fundamental norms of the social science community is that the task of scholars is to describe their chosen universe as completely and validly as possible. The test for completeness and validity is the derivation of falsifiable hypotheses that are tested empirically.

One rule that flows from this norm is that scholars should remain descriptive and avoid being normative and especially prescriptive. The latter emphases are delegated to 'applied researchers' who are not conducting basic research.

For example, Cronbach and Suppes (1969) separate 'conclusion-oriented research' (basic) from 'decision-oriented research' (applied). Coleman (1972) continued and expanded the distinction by calling the former 'discipline research' and the latter 'policy research'. Many scholars accept this distinction. An excellent compilation of their positions can be found in Stringer (1982). Basic research is designed to test theories and to produce generalizations, is open to scrutiny by the scholarly community, and does not begin with an intention to be of help or to produce implementable knowledge (Coleman 1972).

Action or applied research, on the other hand, seeks to solve client problems and to produce workable solutions that are usually not abstract (in order to be relevant to the concrete problems of practice), are rarely subject to scholarly scrutiny, and are intended for implementation. Some would go as far as saying that it might not be necessary or useful for such researchers to be concerned about truth. Indeed, they might find that being helpful requires ignoring truth (Ellis 1982).

McGrath and Brinberg (1984) have developed a model that attempts to show why many of these differences between basic and applied research may be symptomatic of researchers' defenses. Using the validity network schema, they are able to show that basic and applied research may have different pathways but that both are centrally concerned with the validity and generalizability of propositions. They suggest that both camps show an interest in each other's biases but that they tend to deal with that interest by mentioning it last. I believe that there is much wisdom in McGrath and Brinberg's perspective. However, I hesitate to agree with their proposition that basic researchers are primarily concerned with the conceptual domain and applied researchers with the substantive domain.

Peters and Robinson (1984) conclude that both versions of applied research espouse involvement-in-change and organic research processes heavily influenced by collaboration between researchers and subjects. They also conclude that the researchers who advocate the strong version tend to place a heavier emphasis upon constructivist / interactionist epistemology. The latter stresses that our understanding of the world is partially constitutive of it, and that social actors create their own histories and are capable of reflection-in-action in order to change the world as it is. The strong version, they conclude, is emancipatory.

I believe further that research to produce actionable knowledge can and should be exposed to self-correcting procedures. It may be, as Coleman (1972) suggests, that much of the self-correcting activity in present policy research is best conducted by independent studies. I am recommending that self-correcting procedures should be designed into studies because these procedures protect the human subjects, as well as foster the production of valid basic knowledge.

15.2.2 Unintended Cover-up of Gaps and Inconsistencies

The second problem with separating descriptive from normative and prescriptive research is that it inhibits the most robust testing that is possible of a theory; it unintentionally covers up the gaps and inconsistencies of a theory, and finally it places social science in the role of being the servant of the status quo. I should like to illustrate these claims by inquiring into the Behavioral Theory of the Firm (BTF). Cyert and March (1963) define four relational concepts at the core of their perspective. They are: (1) quasi-resolution of conflict, (2) uncertainty avoidance, (3) problemistic search, and (4) limited organizational learning. Twenty-five years later, in an introduction to a collection of his essays, March (1988) identified four key concepts of BTF, which he now described as 'heresies' in the eyes of many economists and students of traditional decision-making. They are: (1) the importance of allocating attention, (2) the omnipresence of conflict, politics, and coalition groups, (3) the conception that action involves rules that adapt to experience, rather than anticipatory choices, and (4) the importance of ambiguity, preferences, technology, and history.

March takes on concepts such as routines, control, loyalty, and trust. March (1981: 221) states that it is the standard operating procedures and routines that are causally responsible for much of the behavior that is observed in organizations.

Mundane rules are at the heart of organizational activity. Rules, in turn, are based upon previous experience and history (p. 224). If change is to occur, it must be clearly linked to mundane rules (p. 222).

What is the meaning of 'linked'? One reading is that all changes, if they are to persevere, have to be linked to routines and procedures. I agree.

There could be another reading of the term 'linked'. This reading could lead researchers to focus so heavily upon routines that they pay little attention to research that is aimed at non-trivial changes in the routines themselves. The focus on routines leads to reinforcing the status quo. For example, if it works, don't fix it or question it. The routines are taken for granted. One of the most difficult learning problems organizations may face is to learn that they are not able to learn, and that the cause of this inability is the focus on what is taken for granted namely, routines. If one claims that limited learning, quasi-resolution of conflict, and competitive coalition groups are omnipresent and routine, it is not difficult to conclude that they are to be taken for granted and therefore not likely to be altered.

I turn next to the concept of control. March states that control is a fundamental process in most organizations. I agree. Then, March links control and conflict in the following way. He suggests that control systems drive conflict systems because once measures are developed to evaluate performance and compliance they invite manipulation. Once the rules of evaluation are set, conflict of interest between the rule setters and their followers assures that there will be some incentives for the latter to maximize the difference between the rule setters and the rule followers. It assures that there will be some incentives for the latter to maximize the difference between their score and their effort. 'Any system of accounts is a road map to cheating on them' (March 1981: 220).

The reasoning appears to be as follows. Control processes are fundamental to organization; controls require the evaluation of performance. People cope with such evaluations by manipulation and cheating. They create coalition groups to bring about and to protect these self-protective processes. If this self-interest is not consistent with the organization's, then more manipulation and cheating will occur. This, in turn, results in more control. The processes can become self-reinforcing.

March uses similar logic in discussing trust and loyalty. Trust and loyalty, he asserts are hard to find. The problem of trust is exacerbated by organizational politics. Organizational politics is a central feature of most organizations. '[T]he first principle of politics is that everyone is rational and no one can be trusted.' There may be a few who can be trusted, but they are to be characterized as innocent and naive (March 1981: 219).

The consequence is that the organizations are composed of winners and losers. The players will try to look trustworthy even though they are not, in order to be trusted by those people who might become winners. It is therefore, a palpable feature of organizational life, 'that organizations may be validly characterized as individuals and groups pursuing their own interests by the manipulation of information' (March 1988: 6). It is not surprising that March concludes changes in the domains of conflict and trust... 'through the confrontation and resolution of conflict are not likely to be effective' (March 1988: 8). In effect, March paints a valid (I believe) picture of dysfunctionalities around issues of control, loyalty, trust, cheating. He then argues that these are not likely to be alterable. Not surprisingly, he and others have not conducted empirical research to test the claim.

There is a theme running throughout this reaction that also occurs throughout the chapter. The theme is illustrated by Lewin's advice that if we wish to understand the universe fully we should strive to change it. The discussion above provides several reasons why this advice is sound.

First, as we have seen, describing the universe, tells us little about the actions that the members of that universe used to create the universe in the first place. Thus, the 'relational' concepts represent, in my view, valid descriptions of organizations. However, stopping at this description tells us very little about how these variables were produced in the first place.

Second, if the universe is described as being composed of relatively stable patterns, it is necessary for us to explain the causal mechanism by which the patterns maintain their stability. These causal mechanisms are not likely to be discovered until there is an intervention intended to change them fundamentally. Under these conditions, the causal mechanisms that create the stability will be activated.

It follows, I suggest, that making description the ultimate goal risks placing organization theory in the role of being the servant of the status quo. The risk related to the world of practice is that such knowledge will not help practitioners who seek to change the status quo. The risk to science is that the goal of seeking as complete descriptions of the universe is limited by design because little attention is paid to understanding how to make fundamental changes in the patterns.

15.2.3 The Importance of Pluralism

A basic norm of normal science is that researchers should focus on describing the universe of their choice. The researchers should craft their findings in the form that they are generalizable and empirically testable. One result of this is the development of a variety of frameworks and methodologies. The norm is that scholars are free to pursue their interests in describing their chosen universe. For example, Bolman and Deal 1991; Burrell and Morgan 1979; Gill and Johnson 1991; McGrath, Martin, and Kukla 1982; Morgan 1983; Scott 1981; Van Maanen 1982; advocate a pluralistic approach as an effective strategy for seeking truth.

There are, at least, two difficulties with this approach. The first is that since valid description and testable propositions are the two main qualifiers for valid scholarship, most scholars focus primarily on developing their own perspectives and on being critical of competing perspectives. The result is intergroup rivalries where the critiques provide little insight into how to close gaps and inconsistencies, and even less as to how to produce actionable knowledge. For example, the humanistic-interpretive scholars assert, I believe correctly, that positivists strive to be objective. In doing so, they tend to ignore the meanings held by human beings because a consideration of those meanings would require an intuitive, subjective, and empathic grasp of the subjects' consciousness (Giddens 1976). They also tend to ignore the processes by which their subjects construct their realities (Rosen 1991).

This results in positivistic researchers' distancing themselves from their subjects. Humanistic-interpretive researchers get close to their subjects, according to Van Maanen (1982), because they live among their subjects. I agree with this conclusion up to a point. The point can be defined by asking, how close is close?

Van Maanen certainly had close relationships with his subjects. Witness the rich dialogue that he reports, including candid comments by some policemen about their behavior toward the citizens they arrest. I think it is fair to say that Van Maanen documents that police expressed a nontrivial amount of hostility and prejudice toward the citizens they serve. He also documents how this hostility can become internalized by individuals (appearing, for example, as constant swearing) and can be the basis for a police culture that protects such individual defenses.

Van Maanen does not, as far as I can tell, conduct research to explore the causes of these individual and cultural defenses in more depth. This could be done, for example, by developing an intervention program, intended to surface and reduce the defenses. I believe Van Maanen would not disagree with this possibility but would maintain that intervention to change taken-for-granted behavior is not part of his research practice. The point that I am making is not that he must change. The point is that he and other ethnographers ought to specify the distancing that they create, just as they specify the distancing the positivists create.

Another position often taken by field researchers who focus on naturalistic observations is that such research goes deeper than does research that is designed to be distant in order to be objective. Again, this position seems plausible. However, there are gaps and inconsistencies to be found, which are illustrated by Dyer and Wilkins's (1991) critique of Eisenhardt's (1989) position on how to conduct research.

Dyer and Wilkins favor using stories to generate theory. They believe that single case stories can deliver deep insights, while those developed from comparative case studies are likely to be 'thin'. The difficulty is that they craft their position so that it is not disconfirmable; indeed, it is not producible. For example, what are the properties of an effective story? What are the properties of 'thin' insights? Dyers and Wilkins state: 'Although it is difficult to determine how deep a researcher must go to generate good theory, the classic case study researchers certainly went deeper into the dynamics of a single case than Eisenhardt advocates' (p. 616). But the authors do not define what an appropriate depth is. Until this is done, how can we judge Eisenhardt's position to be wanting?

Dyer and Wilkins assert that in multi-case studies the focus is on the construct to the detriment of the context. I am in favor of focusing on the context. But those of us who support contextual research are, I suggest, responsible for defining context in a way that is not self-referential, which makes testing features of it difficult. Dyer and Wilkins approvingly cite several classic case studies that tell a story (for example, Whyte 1991). Yet, as Eisenhardt shows in her reply, those studies had features that were consistent with her view of context as much if not more than with Dyer and Wilkins's view.

Finally, Rosen (1991) also suggests that ethnographers do not allow any theoretical preoccupations to decide whether some facts are more important than others. I agree that competent ethnographers focus on the relatively directly observable data. It is difficult to agree, however, that ethnographers do not allow any theoretical preconceptions to decide whether some facts are more important than others. As I see it, by eschewing interventions to change the constructed world they describe, they ignore, or do not permit to surface, the data that would arise if anyone tried to change that world. They may not let their preconceptions decide which facts are and are not important. But they allow their preconceptions to create conditions under which crucial facts will never arise.

Kunda is quoted by Rosen (p. 21) as saying that 'ethnography is the only human activity in the social sciences . . . [that] is not divorced from the modes of experience that I consider human.' I do not question that Kunda considers ethnography to be connected to what it means to be human, but the validity of the assertion is, in my judgment, doubtful. Kunda's study, which in my opinion is an excellent example of ethnography, misses the core of what it means to be human, according to *his* standards. Being human means to act, to construct a world, and to engage the world in ways that engage the actors.

Kunda observed human beings 'being human', but he never became human in the sense of taking action to help his subjects in the struggle of being human. It was possible for Kunda to become as human as his subjects by developing interventions. Interventions are human experiments that have the intention of constructing different virtual worlds. Engström (2000) suggests that ethnographers consider seriously to become more interventionist in approach if they are to fulfill the claims that they espouse.

Another example of counterproductive rivalries is illustrated by a review of invited papers to a conference on applied communications. The papers were selected by applied communications experts as representing some of the best and current empirical research representing the naturalistic, humanistic, interpretive (NHI) approaches. An analysis of these papers indicated that the writers were critical of the objectivist positive approach. Yet, the papers represented some puzzles. For example, the proponents of NHI speak of wholeness, choice, meaning, flexibility, open texts, and dialogue. Yet much of the research that I reviewed was in the service of compliance, closed dialogue, and closed texts. Many of the scholars questioned the normal science concepts of causality. Yet, my analysis suggests that the reports rely upon a tacit concept of causality. The NHI scholars were critical of the distancing produced by positivism yet, they produced their own distancing and seemed unaware that they did so (Argyris 1995).

Finally a problem arises ironically by attempts made by scholars to reduce the counterproductive consequences of academics by integrating various approaches. The result of these approaches is to integrate through the use of approaches that amount to a live-and-let-live approach where the strengths of each approach is emphasized and the weaknesses are de-emphasized.

For example, Morgan and Smircich (1980) suggest a way to integrate the various paradigms. They present an analytical model that describes each paradigm's assumptions about ontology, human nature, epistemology, metaphors, and research methods. The resulting thirty-box table is organized around the concepts of interpretivist and functionalist paradigms, which, in turn, are conceptualized along a continuum ranging from subjectivist (for the former) to objectivist (for the latter).

A first reaction to the table is that it makes good sense. There are indeed paradigms that are primarily subjectivist and others that are primarily objectivist. However, a second reaction is that the table does not accurately characterize the assumptions regarding ontology, human nature, epistemology, metaphors, and research methods if intervention and implementation are to be taken seriously. Those who conduct such research find that almost all the categories are relevant. For example, in an organizational study, it is shown that the pattern of the director group's defensive routines represents reality as a social construct. It is implemented in a realm of symbolic discourse. It is a contextual field of information. It is a representation of concrete processes and structures in the sense that these processes and structures exist 'out there'. It coerces different directors to behave in similar manners (Argyris 1993).

The assumptions about human nature illustrated in this research also range from the extremes of subjectivism to those of objectivism. For example, the participants were symbol creators, symbol users, and actors using symbols. The intervention research depended heavily on understanding them as information processors with limited capacity to deal with environmental complexity. Many examples were described where the same individuals were primarily adapters and responders before and after the interventions.

Finally, the research methods ranged from explorations of pure subjectivity, to script and symbolic analysis, to contextual analysis, to historical analysis of the director group, and to the design and execution of many experiments. Moreover, the entire research project occurred over a period of five years before publication and it continues. History became increasingly important as the interventions became cumulative, but so did the testing and experimenting used to assess the extent to which the new pattern contained processes and structures that 'coerced' action in the service of learning and of reducing defensive routines at all levels.

When individuals, groups, intergroups, or organizations are studied under conditions where interventions are an integral part of the activity, I suggest that both subjectivist and objectivist assumptions will always be relevant. For example, the interventionists had to help the directors become aware of how they constructed reality (subjectivist). They then helped them see how these constructions led to a pattern that was 'out there' because they had placed it out there, through actions designed to inhibit. This, in turn, required that they map contexts and study systems and processes. Finally, this led the interventionists to help the directors see how they had created a world where a positivist stance was both necessary and counterproductive.

When the 'subjects' were helped to learn a new pattern, it was done by using metaphors and to keep side-by-side the metaphors of theater and culture and the metaphors of cybernetics and organisms. The directors were also helped to design and implement many experiments in order to create over time a new pattern that was 'out there' and that 'coerced' the new behavior.

When the objective is to produce actionable knowledge, the strategy is not consistent with the pluralistic strategy of using several different perspectives relatively independently of each other. For example, Hassard (1991) has described a study in which four different paradigms (functionalist, interpretive, radical structuralist, and radical humanist) were used to study features of an organization. Each study was conducted consistently with each perspective's assumptions regarding ontology, epistemology, human nature, and methodology. Each produced different descriptions of different features of the organization.

Moreover, there was no attempt reported to produce actionable knowledge relevant to changing the status quo. The exercise met the needs of the researchers, who wanted to see what the different perspectives would produce, and the subjects' interests were subordinated to the researchers' interests. The same is true of the analysis made by Allison (1971) of the Cuban missile crisis.

The researchers also produced, by design, defensive routines in their relationships with the subjects. They withheld their interest in conducting the research with four different paradigms, because they feared that they might not gain access if they revealed their intentions fully. In my view, they bypassed embarrassment and threat and covered up the bypass.

Donaldson (1985) suggests that integrative research, which allows paradigms to be used conjointly, is necessary because integration can lead to increasingly comprehensive theories, a consequence favored by science. Those in the pluralistic camp disagree. They claim that such approaches are, in, effect, a succumbing to the dominant paradigms, such as the functionalist-positivistic. Jackson and Carter (1991) defend paradigm incommensurability because doing so expands 'dramatically the scope of organization studies, the interests represented, and those empowered to speak' (p. 111). I support the expansion. My argument is that when guided by pluralism, it does not go far enough or deep enough because the necessity for implementable knowledge is reduced. Therefore, the plea for incommensurability, which is intended to avoid domination by any one approach or combination of approaches, may have the unintended consequence of becoming a plea for merely a different kind of scientistic authoritarianism.

15.2.4 The Importance of Internal and External Validity

Another fundamental rule is that the empirical research should pass the tests of internal and external validities. The former stipulates that the research is designed to minimize unrecognized contaminations and distortions. The latter stipulates that the empirical results can be shown to be relevant in contexts other than those in which the research was conducted.

Elsewhere, I have tried to show the unintended consequences for producing valid actionable knowledge when we focus our criteria upon internal and external validity.[1] For example, in order to produce internal validity the experimenter keeps the true objectives of the research secret; controls the choices the subjects can make; makes undiscussable the design and purpose of the experiment, makes the undiscussability undiscussable, as well as the modes of analysis to be used. All these conditions are consistent with the top-down relationship between superiors and subordinates in traditional hierarchical organizations (Argyris 1980, 1990, 1993).

If this is true, then the results of experiments should be crafted so that they read that the propositions produced are valid when the conditions used to produce them are consistent with traditional hierarchical arrangements. To my knowledge, such statements are rarely included. They are, I suggest, crucial if one has implementability in mind.

For example, Barker, Dembo, Lewin (1941), in a carefully designed experiment reported a curvilinear relationship between creativity and frustration. Let us assume that a leader of a group wishes to produce mild degrees of frustration in order to mobilize a desired degree of creativity. How will she do it? The research studies suggest that she should block the group's action. How will she block action? How will she know when the frustration is mild? How will she know when frustration becomes counterproductive? The researchers can specify how she could find out, because the researchers faced the same challenge. They developed several different types of measuring instruments that they used behind a one-way vision screen. But how will the group leader introduce the use of these instruments?

---

[1] Because of space limitations, I refer to my book *The Inner Contradictions of Rigorous Research* for many more examples.

Should she tell the group members about her intentions and about the measuring instruments? How would she interrupt the flow without confounding her problem? Could not the very mention of her plans increase the frustration?

If there were a way to cover up her strategy, then she would have to cover up the cover-up. What are the ethical issues of researchers' producing knowledge that requires creating such undiscussable tactics? What would happen to the sense of trust between the leader and her group if they ever found out? Indeed, what would happen to the credibility of the researchers in the eyes of society?

15.3 CRITICAL THEORY AND IMPLEMENTATION

Similar problems arise with scholars who place action and change high on their agenda yet their propositions are not crafted to be implementable. The first example is critical theorists, especially Habermas, and his claims about authentic communication. Scholars associated with critical theory raise questions about normal science views on causality and the methods used to generate knowledge. Moreover, many of them espouse a view that inquiry and research should go beyond focusing on the status quo and to generate 'liberating alternatives'.

Geuss (1981:76) proposes that a critical theory is composed of three main constituent parts:

- A part which shows that a transition from the present state of society... to some proposed final state is... possible...
- A part which shows that the transition... is 'practically necessary,' i.e. that
  1. ... the present social arrangements cause pain, suffering, and frustration... agents ... only accept the present arrangements... because they hold a particular world picture... one they acquired only because they were in conditions of coercion;
  2. the proposed final state will be one which will lack the illusions and unnecessary coercion and frustration... which... will be easier for the agents to realize their true interests;
- A part which asserts that the transition from the present state to the proposed final state can come about only if the agents adopt the critical theory as their 'self-conscious' and act on it.

In order to satisfy the several claims Geuss describes, a critical theory must make many empirical assertions. On the one hand, for example, it must identify the causal links between present social arrangements and their negative consequences, and show that alternative arrangements would not create these same consequences. On the other hand, it is not clear that the claim that agents would reject their current world view if they were in a position to know better is empirical. Assuming this claim is not simply a tautology (if they had different wants, they would want different things), what is its status? And related to this, what are we to make of the reference to agents' 'true interests'? Assuming agents do not now 'know better' and are unaware of their 'true interests', how are these to be determined? Geuss identifies the point at issue when he observes that a critical theory 'doesn't merely give information about how it would be rational for agents to act if they had certain interests; it claims to inform them about what interests it is rational for them to have' (1981: 58).

Critical theory justifies advocacy of a normative position by adhering to the principle of internal criticism. The ultimate criterion of validity is free assent in a discussion, in which the test of truth is that investigators who begin with different views converge on one opinion in the course of inquiry.

Habermas, for example, argues that human interaction presumes what he calls an 'ideal' speech situation. He argues that all linguistic communication involves four kinds of validity claims: that what is uttered is comprehensible, that the content of what is said is true, that the speaker is being truthful (the utterance is congruent with the speaker's intentions), and that the speech acts being performed are legitimate (Habermas 1979: 2, 28; Bernstein 1976: 211). Now, if any of these validity claims are questioned, speakers resort to what Habermas calls a 'discourse' in which the claims are examined and tested. The criteria for good discourse, that is, for the rationality of the consensus that may be achieved through discourse, are that it approximates the ideal speech situation. That is, 'what it means for a statement to be true is that it would be the one on which all agents would agree if they were to discuss all of human experience in absolutely free and uncoerced circumstances for an indefinite period of time' (Geuss 1981: 65). Habermas argues that the ideal speech situation is the grounding for the ideas of rationality, freedom, and justice, as well as the idea of truth.

Habermas has argued that acceptability in the ideal speech situation is a 'transcendental' criterion of truth, by which he means that all human beings everywhere at all times are committed to recognizing it by virtue of the nature of linguistic communication. This may be a valid claim of how individuals should act. But, as will be illustrated below, we find that most individuals espouse such commitments but do not act consistently with them. Moreover, they are systematically unaware of the discrepancies and, unaware that they are unaware.

In this connection, I participated in a lengthy seminar at Harvard led by Habermas. The audience was composed primarily of doctoral students, many of whom, including myself, were admirers of Habermas's contributions. Whenever questions were asked to clarify and inform Habermas acted consistently with the requirements of the ideal speech situation. However, when the audience raised critical questions neither Habermas nor the students acted consistently with the requirements of authentic communication. Nor was this discussable. To my knowledge, Habermas has not conducted inquiries into the problems of implementing the ideal speech situation: how can human beings be educated to diagnose their respective positive or negative contributions to producing ideal speech situations?

15.4 Psychoanalysis and Implementation

Another example of systematic discrepancies may be found in the use of psychoanalysis in studying organizations. This example is especially important because central to the psychoanalytic clinical perspective is implementation. Recently (Gabriel 1999) and his collaborators published an excellent analysis of the use of psychoanalytic theory and method in the study of organizations. The authors emphasize that one of the key features of the psychoanalytic approach is that it focuses on the features of 'depth' in organizations.

For example, the NASA Challenger disaster is described and psychoanalytic 'depth' explanations are provided. The psychoanalytic explanation concludes that NASA officials deceived themselves because it was too painful for them to acknowledge that the organization they loved and cared for was fallible. The blindness of NASA officials, we are told, was caused by repression and narcissism, which led top management to place loyalty above reality in order to sustain America's narcissistic delusion of itself. These defensive actions were shaped by feelings of pride, anxiety, pain, that, in turn, were connected to their experiences in their early lives. All these causal explanations may be valid but the interpretative processes are not defined explicitly so that readers, and more important, potential users, can make up their own mind as to its validity and implementability.

How implementable are recommendations based upon the above psychoanalytic explanations? Let us assume that highly skilled psychoanalytic scholars can implement the recommendations. But, how about, for example, the executives whose ways of managing would be greatly affected. It is doubtful that they could become as skillful as the professionals. It is even more doubtful that they could create an organizational setting where the psychoanalytic concepts can be used by the participants at all levels of the organization. The psychoanalytic professionals may respond that they do not claim that their perspective is implementable by non-professionals. They recognize that implementable validity for non-professionals may be low.

There are, at least, two problems with this response. First, it makes the practitioners dependent upon the professionals precisely in the area of managing where their sense of competence is highly involved. The resulting sense of unilateral control over the executives, according to the psychoanalytic theory, should lead to inner conflicts and anxieties, which, in turn, activates defenses on the part of the client. The psychoanalytic professionals may be creating the same top-down management action that NASA officials were accused of using and that was diagnosed by the psychoanalytic professionals as dysfunctional.

The second problem is related to managers developing the requisite skills and using them in the task of managing employees at all levels. All too many years ago, I interviewed British executives on organizational issues. They asked me about advice that might emanate from research about intergroups and interdepartmental conflicts conducted in the United States. I was surprised because one reason I was visiting England was to study the Tavistock approach to these problems. I asked the executives why they were not looking to Tavistock for help. As I recall, at least six executives, had attended Tavistock workshops. They found them to be interesting. They felt however that British, or any executives, were not likely to develop the requisite skills nor was it clear how managers or employees could be educated so that legitimate claims of the implementability of the Tavistock concepts could be given a fair test. The value of psychoanalytic theory, as exemplified by Tavistock, an organization that Gabriel describes as a pioneering one (a claim that I believe is justified) had decreased in the eyes of the managers.

The reader might ask if it is not a fundamental assumption of psychoanalytic theory that if awareness is enhanced, it will help individuals become more effective in designing their actions. The answer is yes. Such an answer, however, raises a deeper question. How do we know when we have understood something? I suggest that our claim that we know something is most rigorously tested if we can produce what we claim we know.

If we claim that through the use of such concepts as neurosis, narcissism, and repression we can explain the Challenger tragedy, a test of this claim would be for us to produce ways to help NASA learn not to repeat the organizational defensive routines that were documented. In other words, awareness should be in the service of action. Action then becomes the criterion for the validity of our awareness.

This suggests that if other theories exist that provide a causal theory of the Challenger tragedy that is more closely connected to action; to re-education of the executives, and to organizational change, they should be compared with the psychoanalytic position.

One candidate is the theory of action described in this chapter. An analysis was made of the Challenger disaster using similar reports (Argyris 1990). The analysis suggested that an explanation can be achieved by focusing on the theories of action used by the participants, the organizational defensive mechanisms and barriers to effective communication. The analysis also suggested that these problems are not unique to NASA. Indeed many organizations (private and public) exhibit the same features. Finally, it was shown that this theory has been used to design intervention programs to correct many of the individual group, and organizational errors described above. Let us now turn to describing the theory of action approach.

I should now like to close with a very brief description of how a theory of action approach deals with many of the problems identified above.[1]

15.5 A Theory of Action Approach

15.5.1 Designs for Action: Model I

Human beings hold two types of theories of action. There is the one that they espouse, which is usually expressed in the form of stated beliefs and values. Then there is the theory that they actually use; this can only be inferred from observing their actions, that is, their actual behavior. To date, most human beings studied have the same theory-in-use. There is diversity in espoused theories, but not in theories-in-use. A model of the theory-in-use (that we call Model I) follows. Model I theory-in-use is the design we found throughout the world. It has four governing values. They are: (1) achieve your intended purpose, (2) maximize winning and minimize losing, (3) suppress negative feelings, and (4) behave according to what you consider rational.

The most prevalent action strategies that arise from Model I are the following: (1) advocate your position, (2) evaluate the thoughts and actions of others (and your own thoughts and actions), and (3) attribute causes for whatever you are trying to understand (Argyris 1982, 1990, 1993; Argyris and Schön 1996).

These actions must be performed in such a way that satisfies the actors' governing values—that is, they achieve at least their minimum acceptable level of being in control, winning, or bringing about any other result. In other words, Model I tells individuals to craft their positions, evaluations, and attributions in ways that inhibit inquiries into and tests of them with the use of independent logic. The consequences of these Model I strategies are likely to be defensiveness, misunderstanding, and self-fulfilling and self-sealing processes (Argyris 1982).

---

[1] Because of space limitations I am able to select an example that deals with individual and group phenomena. Illustration of organizational phenomena may be found in Argyris 1982, 1990, 1993, Argyris and Schön 1996.

Model I theory-in-use requires defensive reasoning. Individuals keep their premisses and inferences tacit, lest they lose control. They create tests of their claims that are self-serving and self-sealing. The likelihood of misunderstanding and mistrust increases. The use of defensive reasoning prohibits questioning the defensive reasoning. We now have self-fueling processes that maintain the status quo, inhibit genuine learning, and reinforce the deception. (Figure 15.1)

Human beings learn their theories-in-use early in life, to use them constantly, and therefore the actions that they produce are highly skilled. Little conscious attention is paid to producing skilled actions. Indeed, conscious attention could inhibit producing them effectively. This creates unawareness of what we are doing when we act skillfully. The unawareness due to skill and the unawareness caused by our unilaterally controlling theories-in-use produce a deeper unawareness; namely, we become unaware of the programs in our heads that keep us unaware. The results are skilled unawareness and skilled incompetence (Argyris 1980). For example, when individuals have to say something negative to others (e.g. 'Your performance is poor') they often ease-in, in order not to upset the other. Two of the most frequent easing-in actions that we observe are (a) non-directive questioning and (b) face-saving approaches. In order for these to work, the individuals must cover up that they are acting as they are, in order not to upset the other. In order for a cover-up to work, the cover-up itself must be covered up.

Under these conditions, we find that the recipients are wary of what is happening. They sense that there may be a cover-up. Because they hold the same theory-in-use, they too cover up their private doubts. The result is counterproductive consequences for genuine problem-solving. All of this occurs with the use of skillful behavior; hence, the term *skilled incompetence.*

When organizational worlds become dominated by these consequences, human beings become cynical about changing the self-fueling counterproductive process.

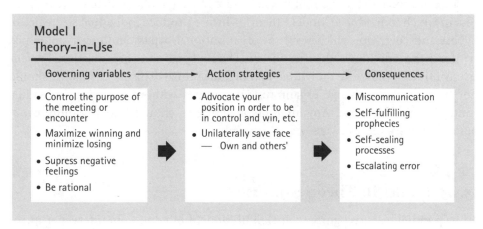

Fig. 15.1 Model I theory-in-use

Not surprisingly, they learn to distance themselves from taking responsibility, losing, and suppressing negative feelings, especially those associated with embarrassment or threat. Individuals use behavioral strategies consistent with these governing values. For example, they advocate their views, making evaluations and attributions in such a way as to ensure their being in control, winning, and suppressing negative feelings.

In short, individuals learn theories-in-use that are consistent with producing unilateral control. It is true that organizations are hierarchical and based on unilateral control. It is equally true that individuals are even more so. Place individuals in organizations whose structures are designed to be more egalitarian, and individuals will eventually make them more unilateral and authoritarian. The most massive examples of such situations of which I am aware are the 'alternative schools' and communes of the 1970s. Most have failed and slowly have faded away (Argyris 1974).

15.5.2 Organizational Defensive Routines

Organizational defensive routines are any action, policy, or practice that prevents organizational participants from experiencing embarrassment or threat and, at the same time, prevents them from discovering the causes of the embarrassment or threat. Organizational defensive routines, like Model I theories-in-use, inhibit genuine learning and overprotect the individuals and the organization (Argyris 1990).

There is a fundamental logic underlying all organizational defensive routines. It can be illustrated by one of the most frequently observed defenses, namely, sending mixed messages, such as, 'Mary, you run the department, but check with Bill,' or 'John, be innovative but be careful.' The logic is: (1) send a message that is inconsistent, (2) act as if it is not inconsistent, (3) make Steps 1 and 2 undiscussable, and (4) make the undiscussability undiscussable.

Organizational defensive routines are caused by a circular, self-reinforcing process in which individuals' Model I theories-in-use produce individual strategies of bypass and cover-up, which result in organizational bypass and cover-up, which reinforce the individuals' theories-in-use. The explanation of organizational defensive routines is therefore individual *and* organizational. This means that it should not be possible to change organizational routines without changing individual routines, and vice versa. Any attempts at doing so should lead to failure or, at best, temporary success.

15.5.3 Model II: Theories-in-use

To help individuals recognize their skillful Model I blindness, an intervener introduces Model II theories-in-use. Model II theories are, at the outset, espoused theories. The challenge is to help individuals transform their espoused theories into theories-in-use by learning a 'new' set of skills and a 'new' set of governing values. Because many individuals espouse Model II values and skills, these traits are not totally new to them. However, the empirical fact to date is that very few individuals can routinely act on their espoused values, and they are often unaware of this limitation.

The governing values of Model II are valid information, informed choice, and vigilant monitoring of the implementation of the choice in order to detect and correct error. (Figure 15.2) As in the case of Model I, the three most prominent behaviors are advocate, evaluate, and attribute. However, unlike Model I behaviors, Model II behaviors are crafted into action strategies that openly illustrate how the actors reached their evaluations or attributions, and how they crafted them to encourage inquiry and testing by others. Productive reasoning is required to produce such consequences. Productive reasoning means that the premises are explicit, the inferences from the premises are also made explicit, and finally conclusions are crafted in ways that can be tested by logic that is independent of the actor. Unlike the defensive reasoning, the logic used is not self-referenced. As a consequence, defensive routines that are anti-learning are minimized, and genuine learning is facilitated. Embarrassment and threat are not bypassed and covered up; they are engaged (Argyris 1982; Argyris and Schön 1974).

To the extent that individuals use Model II theory instead of merely espousing it, they will begin to interrupt organizational defensive routines and begin to create organizational learning processes and systems that encourage double-loop learning in ways that persist. These are called *Model II learning systems* (Argyris and Schön 1996).

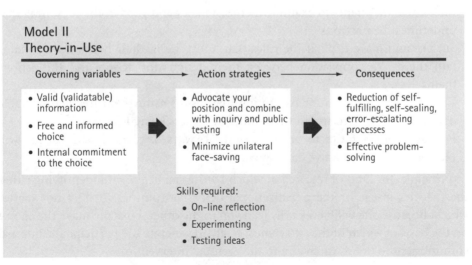

Fig. 15.2 Model II theory-in-use

15.5.4 Design of the Research-Intervention Activities

There are design rules that follow from the theoretical framework described above that can be used to design the research and the intervention activities:

- Discover the degree to which the clients' theories-in-use are consistent with Model I.
- Discover the degree to which the clients use defensive reasoning whenever they deal with embarrassing or threatening issues.
- Discover the designs (rules) the clients have in their heads that keep them unaware of the discrepancies among their espoused values, their actions, and their theories-in-use.
- Discover the degree to which the clients discourage valid reflection on their actions while they are acting. To put this another way: discover how the clients create designs for action that they do not follow but that they believe they do follow, while they are also being systematically unaware of this discrepancy and are behaving in ways that prevent them from discovering the discrepancy and the causes of their unawareness.
- Discover the defensive routines that exist in the organization and limit learning. Develop maps of these organizational defensive routines, specifying the actions that lead to limited-learning consequences and cause them to persist even though the directors wish to be free of them.

In order to reach these goals, re-education and change programs begin by producing relatively directly observable data about these clients' reasoning and actions. The clients must accept responsibility for creating these data, and these data must be in a form from which the clients' theories-in-use can be inferred (e.g. recorded conversations):

- Encourage the clients to examine inconsistencies and gaps in the reasoning that underlines their actions.
- Surface and make explicit the rules that 'must' be in their heads if they maintain there is a connection between their designs for action and the actions themselves.
- View any bewilderment or frustration that results as further directly observable data that can be used to test the validity of what is being learned.
- Produce opportunities to practice Model II ways of crafting actions that will reduce counterproductive consequences.

In principle, the kind of research of which I write can begin with identifying either the theories-in-use or the organizational defensive routines. It does not matter which, because one will necessarily lead you to the other. I usually make the choice on the basis of which of the two is most likely to generate the participants' internal commitment to the research and to the eventual intervention.

15.5.5 The Left- and Right-hand Column Case Method

The case method described next is one of several instruments used in our action science research (Argyris, Putnam, and Smith 1985; Argyris and Schön 1996). The key features of all the research methods and this case method in particular are:

1. It produces relatively directly observable data such as conversation. Such data are the actual productions of action, and therefore can become the basis for inferring theories-in-use.

2. It produces data in ways that make clear the actors' responsibility for the meanings produced. When used properly, the respondents cannot make the research instrument causally responsible for the data that they produced (e.g. 'I didn't really mean that'; or 'I didn't understand the meaning of that term').

3. It produces data about the respondents' causal theories, especially those that are tacit because they are taken for granted.

4. It provides opportunities for the respondents to change their responses without hindering the validity of the inferences being made. Indeed, the actions around 'changing their minds' should also provide data about their causal reasoning processes. It provides opportunities to change their actions as well as actions of groups, intergroups, and organizations over which they have some influence. It provides such knowledge in ways that are economical and do not harm the respondents or the context in which they are working.

The directions to write a case are given to each individual. The directions request:

1. In one paragraph, describe a key organizational problem as you see it.

2. Assume you could talk to whomever you wish in order to begin to solve the problem. Describe, in a paragraph or so, the strategy that you would use in this meeting.

3. Next, split your page into two columns. On the right-hand side write how you would begin the meeting—what you would actually say. Then write what you believe the other(s) would say. Then write your response to their response. Continue writing this scenario for two or so double-spaced typewritten pages.

4. In the left-hand column, write any idea or feeling that you would have that you would not communicate for whatever reason.

In short, the case includes a statement of the problem, the intended strategy to begin to solve the problem, the actual conversation that did or would occur as envisioned by the writer, the information that the writer would not communicate for whatever reason.

15.5.6 Reflecting on the Cases

In analyzing their left-hand columns, to cite one example, the executives found that each side blamed the other side for the difficulties, and they used the same reasons. For example, each side said about the other side: 'You do not *really* understand the issues'. 'If you insist on your position, you will harm the morale that I have built.' 'Don't hand me that line. You know what I am talking about.' 'Why don't you take off your blinders and wear a company hat?'

These results illustrate once more the features of skilled incompetence. It requires skill to craft the cases with the intention not to upset others while trying to change their minds. Yet, as we have seen, the skilled behavior used in the cases had the opposite effect. The others in the case became upset and dug in their heels about changing their minds.

15.5.7 Redesigning their Actions

The next step is to begin to redesign their actions. The executives turned to their cases. Each executive selected an episode that he wished to redesign so that it would not have the negative consequences. As an aid in their redesign, the executives were given some handouts that described Model II set of behaviors. The first thing they realized was that they would have to slow things down. They could not produce a new conversation in the milliseconds that they were accustomed. This troubled them a bit, because they were impatient to learn. They kept reminding themselves that learning new skills does require that they slow down.

One technique they used was that each individual crafted, by himself, a new conversation to help the writer of the episode. After taking five or so minutes, the individuals shared their designs with the writer. In the process of discussing these, the writer learned much about how to redesign his words. However, the designers also learned much as they discovered the gaps in their suggestions and the ways in which they made them.

Practice is important. Most people require as much practice to learn Model II as is required to play a not-so-decent game of tennis. However, the practice does not need to occur all at once; it can occur in actual business meetings where people set aside some time to make it possible to reflect on their actions and correct them. An outside facilitator could help them examine and redesign their actions, just as a tennis coach might do. But, as in the case of a good tennis coach, the facilitator should be replaced eventually by the group. The facilitator might be brought in for periodic 'boosters' or to help when the problem is of a degree of difficulty and intensity not experienced before.

There are several consequences of this type of change program. First, the executives begin to experience each other as more supportive and constructive. People still work very hard during meetings, but their conversation begins to become additive; it flows to conclusions that they all can own and implement. Crises begin to be reduced. Soon, the behavioral change leads to new values, and then to new structures and policies to mirror the new values (Argyris 1984, 1993; Argyris and Schön 1996).

This, in turn, leads to more effective problem-solving and decision-making. In the case of this group, they were able to define the questions related to strategy, to conduct their own inquiries, to have staff people conduct some relevant research, and to have three individuals organize it into a presentation that was ultimately approved and owned by the top group. The top group also built in a process of involving their immediate reports so that they too could develop a sense of ownership, thereby increasing the probability that all involved will work at making it successful.

15.5.8 Basic Criteria for Success in Diagnosing and Changing at any Level of the Organization

There are four criteria that are central to design diagnostic instruments *and* interventions in organizations. They are:

1. The criterion for ultimate success should not be change in behavior or attitudes. The criterion should be changes in defensive reasoning and the theories-in-use that produce skilled unawareness and skilled incompetence and the resulting organizational defensive routines.

2. The changes just described should unambiguously lead to reductions in the self-fulfilling counterproductive activities, at all levels of the organization.

3. It is not possible to achieve Criteria 1 and 2 without focusing on the actual behavior of the participants. The trouble with the old criteria is that they began and ended with behaviors. The new criteria begin with behavior in order to get a window into the mental maps and type of reasoning that the individuals use and the organizational culture that they create.

4. The success of programs is not assessed by measuring insight gained or learning reported by the participants. Individuals often report high scores on insight and learning, yet have not changed their defensive reasoning, their theories-in-use, their skilled unawareness and incompetence, and the organizational defensive routines.

15.5.9 Summary

1. Actionable knowledge requires propositions that make explicit the causal processes required to produce action. Causality is key in implementation. Shoham

(1990) writes, 'If causal reasoning is common in scientific thinking, it is downright dominant in every day sense making' (p. 214).

2. One of the most powerful inhibitors of effective action is inner contradictions. Inner contradictions exist when the propositions to act are implemented correctly, the result is the effective consequence predicted and *necessarily* counterproductive consequences that were not predicted.

3. One cause of inner contradiction is the methodologies used by most normal social scientists to discover problems and to invent solutions. The design of these methodologies is dominated by the requirements of internal and external validity.

4. The features above cause the degree of seamlessness and the validity of the implementation to be reduced. Moreover, the actors tend not to be aware of these problems while they are producing them. If they become aware, the tendency is to blame factors for which they claim they are not responsible.

5. The focus on describing reality in ways that satisfies the requirements of internal and external validity makes it less likely that attention is paid to the implementable validity of the propositions. This, in turn, leads to propositions that are abstract (in order to be generalizable) and disconnected from implementable action. This is a major problem because much of the advice about effective leadership, organizational learning and transformational change promises Model II consequences but they are formulated in Model I concepts. This results in major inconsistencies, which, in turn, results in the advice losing its credibility, and is often relegated the status of fads (Argyris 2000).

15.6 IMPLICATIONS FOR FUTURE RESEARCH

1. It is not news for social scientists that they must master the current ideas about producing valid knowledge. For example, the concepts of internal and external validity are well known and respected. What may be news is that following the rules for producing internal and external validity will tend to create gaps, inconsistencies, and inner contradictions, especially when the intent is to produce actionable knowledge that questions the status quo and to create rare emancipatory events. Moreover, as we have seen the same rules for conducting rigorous empirical research will tend to produce unawareness of the gaps, inconsistencies, and inner contradictions.

The reason is that actionable knowledge about effective action must be formulated in the form of causal propositions that are storable, retrievable, and implementable by the executive function of the mind/brain. In order for this to be accomplished the propositions must be normative (because the criteria for effectiveness are based on subjective or personal choices). They must also be formulated in the form of prescriptions for action that the executive function can implement. These are the very features that social scientists are told to downplay.

Both positivists and humanists exhibit the same problem. For example, positivists may specify an empirical relationship between two variables. This is accomplished by developing systematic observable patterns and then describing these quantitatively. But such propositions do not specify the causal designs required by the executive function to produce this relationship. The humanists who focus on crafting stories, seeking authenticity in communication, exhibiting empathy with the 'subjects' and emphasizing wholeness have not to my knowledge, specified the causal designs that the executive function requires if it is to implement these features.

2. Policies, plans, strategies are not actionable knowledge. The gaps and inconsistencies identified above also exist at a more macro level. I refer to those who craft policies, plans, and strategies. Such plans are inventions for effective action but not designs for effective implementation of the invention. In order to explain the reasoning behind this claim, I should like to present a model (largely based on the work of Dewey and Lewin).

In order to produce effective action, human beings implement four phases of a cycle for designing and executing action. The phases are to *discover* a problem, to *invent* a solution, to *produce* the invented solution, and to *evaluate* the production (Figure 15.3).

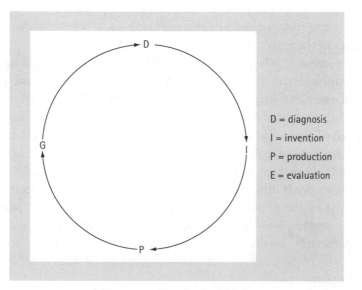

D = diagnosis
I = invention
P = production
E = evaluation

Fig. 15.3 The Action Cycle

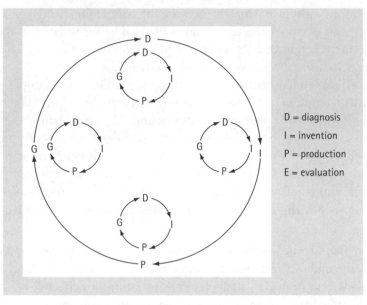

Fig. 15.4 The action and sub-routine cycle

Figure 15.1 does not adequately describe what is going on in order to produce action. The reason is that action is required in order to implement each of the phases. For example, the phase 'discovery', if it is to be produced, requires actions that include discover how to discover, invent ways to discover, produce the inventions, and evaluate the effectiveness of the production. This is true for invention, production, and evaluation. If they are to be implemented each requires action and therefore each requires sub-cycles to produce their respective phases. We have therefore, a model similar to a hologram where each part (sub-cycle) of the whole contains the same features of the whole (Figure 15.4).

Actionable knowledge is produced when all four phases and their respective sub-cycles are implemented. It is important not to view the knowledge required to produce discovery and invention as actionable. These actions are in the service of producing discovery and inventions and not in producing the intended consequences derived from the inventions. The moment that attempts are made to implement the plans or policies, those actions are about actionable knowledge.

For example, two recent and well-known examples, in the United States, are the Clintons' health programs and the policy recommendations for securing nuclear secrets defined by the Secretary of Energy, Mr Richardson. Both plans failed the criterion of being implemented. The creators of the health policy assumed that if their plans were first rate they would be implemented. The Secretary acknowledged that the security plans were not implemented because of what he described as the culture of the laboratories.

3. Researchers will have to become more concerned about their credibility with the society at large that funds and wishes to use their research. For example, in the United States, a congressman who was a strong supporter for giving social scientists freedom to choose their research, reluctantly concluded, after twenty years, that he was systematically lied to by social scientists who promised that user-friendly actionable knowledge was a primary concern (Johnson 1993). In the early days, the Ford Foundation had a similar policy of encouraging the freedom of social scientists to choose their research. After several decades, the officials decided if the Foundation were to help mankind then they would have to define the research to be done. Indeed many now support various experiments designed and produced by non-social scientists.

4. Social psychologists, sociologists, and anthropologists have produced an enormous literature about the impact that situations, roles, and culture have upon the way human beings think and act; upon their sense of competence, self-efficacy, self-confidence, and upon their fundamental values. May I suggest that we will take seriously these findings to examine our actions and our respective scientific communities. I suggest that we create for ourselves, what Thorstein Veblen called 'trained incapacity' (1919).

Imagine, for example, what would happen if social scientists dealt in the way they deal with those seeking to benefit from their research. They might say to the child facing conflict or bewilderment, in effect, that they focus on describing the universe. For example, my focus is describing phenomena, and I cannot offer any suggestions to you. Finally imagine a child pleading for prescriptions and being told by the parents that the existing descriptive data are inadequate to formulate prescriptions.

This is precisely what happens when adults called clients, seek help from those scholarly-consultants, who adhere to the rules described above. In a study that I have just begun, I have interviewed and observed world-class consultants who are also world-class scientists. They all hold, with various degrees of explicitness, a framework to understand and explain as well as rigorous empirical methods to conduct inquiry. I ask them if they have been in a situation where they felt their analysis was sound and the clients expressed doubts. All responded affirmatively. Next, I ask what do they do. In effect they repeat the presentation to assure the client of its validity. They often ask the clients to present the reasoning behind their doubts. When they do, the scholar-consultants identify gaps and inconsistencies in the clients' reasoning processes by using the framework that got them into trouble in the first place. They appear to hold the rule: if the client doubts the validity of the presentation, repeat the presentation. If the client continues to have doubts, encourage them to express the doubts and, by using the original framework, help them to see where they are wrong. If repetition of this strategy does not work, find polite ways to exit the relationship. By the way, the clients also produce their version of defense. The two versions clash and the result is little learning and self-sealing processes.

Holding a position that makes the production of normative and prescriptive knowledge as central makes social scientists vulnerable. It is one thing to be challenged about actionability and be able to respond that one is focused on being descriptive. It is quite another to be challenged when the social scientists' prescriptions do not work as predicted. Perhaps the defense of this 'trained incapacity' is an additional cause for the down play of actionable knowledge.

References

ALLISON, G. (1971). *Essence of Decision: Explaining the Cuban Missile Crisis.* Boston: Little, Brown.

ARGYRIS, C. (1980). *Inner Contradictions of Rigorous Research.* San Diego: Academic Press.

—— (1982). *Reasoning, Learning and Action: Individual and Organizational.* San Francisco: Jossey-Bass.

—— (1990). *Overcoming Organizational Defenses: Facilitating Organizational Learning.* Needham, Mass.: Allyn & Bacon.

—— (1993). *Knowledge for Action.* San Francisco: Jossey-Bass.

—— (1995). 'Knowledge When Used in Practice to Test Theory: The Case of Applied Communication Research', in Kenneth N. Cissna (ed.), *Applied Communications in the 21st Century.* Mahwah, NJ: Lawrence Erlbaum.

—— (1997). 'Field Theory as a Basis for Scholarly Consulting'. *Journal of Social Issues,* 53/4: 809–24.

—— (2000). *Flawed Advice and the Management Trap.* New York: Academic Press.

—— and KAPLAN, R. S. (1994). 'Implementing New Knowledge: The Case of Activity-Based Costing'. *Accounting Horizons,* 8/3: 83–105.

—— and SCHÖN, D. (1974). *Theory in Practice.* San Francisco: Jossey-Bass.

—— —— (1996). *Organizational Learning II.* Reading, Mass.: Addison Wesley.

—— PUTNAM, R., and SMITH, D. (1985). *Action Science: Concepts, Methods, and Skills for Research and Intervention.* San Francisco: Jossey-Bass.

BANDURA, A. (1986). *Social Foundations of Thought and Action: A Social Cognitive Theory.* Englewood Cliffs, NJ: Prentice-Hall.

BARKER, R. G., DEMBO, T., and LEWIN, K. (1941). *Frustration and Regression.* University of Iowa Studies in Child Welfare 1. Ames: University of Iowa Press.

BERNSTEIN, R. J. (1976). *The Restructuring of Social and Political Theory.* Philadelphia: University of Pennsylvania Press.

BOLMAN, L. G., and DEAL, T. E. (1991). *Reframing Organizations: Artistry, Choice and Leadership.* San Francisco: Jossey-Bass.

BURRELL, G., and MORGAN, G. (1979). *Sociological Paradigms and Organizational Analyses.* London: Heinemann.

COLEMAN, J. S. (1972). *Policy Research in the Social Sciences.* Morristown, NJ: General Learning Press.

CRONBACH, L. J., and SUPPES, P. (eds.) (1969). *Research for Tomorrow's Schools*. London: Macmillan.

CYERT, RICHARD M., and MARCH, JAMES G. (1963). *A Behavioral Theory of the Firm*. Englewood Cliffs, NJ: Prentice-Hall.

DONALDSON, L. (1985). *In Defense of Organizational Theory*. Cambridge: Cambridge University Press.

DYER, G. W., Jr, and WILKINS, A. L. (1991). 'Better Stories, not Better Constructs, to Generate Better Theory: A Rejoinder to Eisenhardt'. *Academy of Management Review*, 16/3: 613–19.

EISENHARDT, K. M. (1989). 'Building Theories from Case Study Research'. *Academy of Management Review*, 14/4: 532–50.

ELLIS, P. (1982). 'The Phenomenology of Defensible Space', in P. Stringer (ed.), *Confronting Social Issues*. San Diego: Academic Press.

ENGSTRÖM, YRJÖ (2000). 'From Individual Action to Collective Activity and Back: Developmental Work Research as an Interventionist Methodology', in Paul Luff, John Hindmarsh, and Christian Heath (eds.), *Workplace Studies*. Cambridge: Cambridge University Press.

GABRIEL, YIANNIS, *et al.* (1999). *Organizations in Depth: The Psychoanalysis of Organizations*. London: Sage Publications.

GEUSS, R. (1981). *The Idea of a Critical Theory*. Cambridge: Cambridge University Press.

GIDDENS, A. (1976). *New Rules of Sociological Method*. London: Hutchinson.

GILL, J., and JOHNSON, P. (1991). *Research Methods for Managers*. London: Chapman.

HABERMAS, J. (1979). *Communication and the Evolution of Society*. Boston: Beacon Press.

HASSARD, J. (1991). 'Multiple Paradigms and Organizational Analysis: A Case Study'. *Organization Studies*, 12/2: 275–99.

JACKSON, N., and CARTER, P. (1991). 'In Defense of Paradigm Incommensurability'. *Organization Studies*, 12/1: 109–27.

JOHNSON, D. (1993). 'Psychology in Washington. Measurement to Improve Scientific Productivity: A Reflection on the Brown Report'. *Psychological Science*, 4/2: 67–9.

LEWIN, K. (1935). *A Dynamic Theory of Personality*. New York: McGraw-Hill.

—— (1948). *Resolving Social Conflicts*, ed. G. W. Lewin New York: HarperCollins.

—— (1951). *Field Theory in Social Science*, ed. D. Cartwright. New York: HarperCollins.

McGRATH, J. E., and BRINBERG, D. (1984). 'Alternative Paths for Research'. *Applied Social Psychology Annual*, 5: 109–20.

—— MARTIN, J., and KUKLA, R. A. (1982). *Judgment Calls in Research*. Newbury Park, Calif.: Sage.

MARCH, JAMES G. (1981). 'Decision-Making Perspective', in Andrew H. Van De Ven and William F. Joyce (eds.), *Perspectives on Organizational Design and Behavior*. New York: John Wiley & Sons.

—— (1988). *Decisions and Organizations*. Oxford: Basil Blackwell.

MORGAN, G. (1983). *Beyond Method*. Newbury Park, Calif.: Sage.

—— and SMIRCICH, L. (1980). 'The Case for Qualitative Research'. *Academy of Management Review*, 5/4: 491–500.

PETERS, M., and ROBINSON, V. (1984). 'The Origins and Status of Action Research'. *Journal of Applied Behavioral Science*, 20/2: 113–24.

ROSEN, M. (1991). 'Coming to Terms with the Field: Understanding and Doing Organizational Ethnography'. *Journal of Management Studies*, 28/1: 1–24.

SCOTT, W. R. (1981). *Organizations: Rational, Natural and Open Systems.* Englewood Cliffs, NJ: Prentice-Hall.

SEASHORE, S. E. (1985). 'Institutional and Organizational Issues in Doing Useful Research', in E. E. Lawler III, A. M. Mohrman, Jr., S. A. Mohrman, G. E. Ledford, Jr., T. G. Cummings, and Associates (eds.), *Doing Research that is Useful for Theory and Practice.* San Francisco: Jossey-Bass.

SHOHAM, Y. (1990). 'Nonmonotonic Reasoning and Causation'. *Cognitive Science*, 14: 213–302.

SIMON, H. A. (ed.) (1976), *Administrative Behavior: A Study of Decision-Making Processes in Administrative Organization.* New York: Free Press.

—— (1990). 'Invariants of Human Behavior'. *Annual Review of Psychology*, 41: 1–20.

STRINGER, P. (ed.) (1982). *Confronting Social Issues*, ii. San Diego: Academic Press.

VAN MAANEN, J. (1982). 'Introduction', in J. Van Maanen, J. M. Dabbs, Jr, and R. R. Faulkner (eds.), *Varieties of Qualitative Research.* Newbury Park, Calif.: Sage.

VEBLEN, THORSTEIN (1919). *The Theory of the Leisure Class.* New York: B. W. Hurbach.

WHEELAN, S. A., PEPITONE, E. A., and ABT, V. (1990). *Advances in Field Theory.* Newbury Park, Calif.: Sage.

WHITE, R. W. (1959). 'Motivation Reconsidered: The Concept of Competence'. *Psychological Review*, 66: 297–333.

WHYTE, W. F. (1991). *Social Theory for Action: How Individuals and Organizations Learn to Change.* Newbury Park, Calif.: Sage.

CHAPTER 16

....

THEORY AND PRACTICE IN THE REAL WORLD

....

KARL E. WEICK

You have to figure out how to manage this enterprise in a space that is not defined by things that you learn in simplistic case studies. You are out in the real world. You are out in the world where, as a director, you have to recognize that the management of the company is going to be slow to come to grips with the problem for a lot of human reasons.

(John Reed (2000: 60) former co-CEO, Citigroup)

WHEN practitioners refer to the 'real world' they often do so when theorists comment on practice but elide context, overlook constraints, take the wrong things for granted, overestimate control, presume unattainable ideals, underestimate dynamism, or translate comprehensible events into incomprehensible variables. When practitioners complain that no one is addressing the real world, these are not so much complaints about a place as they are complaints about situated activity and the inability of people to conceptualize it. The complaints reflect unhappiness with the way scholars have addressed a problem identified by Kierkegaard. 'It is perfectly

I acknowledge with deep appreciation the thoughtful comments of Lance Sandelands and Haridimos Tsoukas on earlier drafts of this chapter.

true, as philosophers say, that life must be understood backwards. But they forget the other proposition, that it must be lived forwards' (Gardiner 1988: 90).

The dominant tension that lies at the heart of this chapter is captured in Kierkegaard's words. Life is understood backward when detached theorists deploy analysis, abstraction, and simplification after the fact in order to impose order and patterns on previous activities that were lived forward by involved practitioners. The living forward itself, however, is an altogether different form of activity. When practitioners live forward they tend to mix together false starts, routines, automatic thinking, unanticipated consequences, recoveries, trade-offs, improvisation, and trial and error. Their living is both less orderly and of a different order than it appears in hindsight. This difference is so striking in fact that Heidegger describes living forward as a condition of 'thrownness'. Thrownness makes it hard to use stable representations of cause–effect linkages, which are the primary theory products of hindsight. Living forward does have its moments of hindsight (e.g. the reflective practitioner, Schon 1987) just as understanding backward has its moments of foresight (e.g. Frank 1992; Gioia 1992). But in both cases these shorter moments typically are incidental to the larger tasks of theory construction or everyday action. As a result, moments of theory-driven foresight or practice-driven hindsight furnish relatively minor inputs to theory and practice.

All of this suggests that theory and practice are qualitatively different. Theory is often equated with thinking, abstractness, explanation, knowing that, and dissection into parts. Practice, by contrast, is equated with doing, concreteness, understanding, know how, and wholes. These contrasts are sufficiently strong that the persistent question is, how can they be reconciled, if at all? That is the question addressed in this chapter.

We first examine the terminology used in discussions of theory–practice and discover that the word 'understanding' is a major source of trouble. We then review eight different ways in which people have tried to reconcile theory and practice. These include the suggestions that the relationship between theory and practice is correspondent (Lewin), complementary (Roethlisberger), incommensurable (Sandelands), coordinate (Dutton and Starbuck), parallel (Thomas and Tymon), reciprocal (Craig), conceptually equivalent (Argyris), and methodologically equivalent (Kilduff and Mehra). It will then be argued that theory and practice can be partly reconciled if living forward is differentiated into ready-to-hand living and unready-to-hand living, a distinction first proposed by Heidegger. If theorists and practitioners alike focus on the interruptions of unready-to-hand, then the theorist is forced to sense more of the world as it is experienced by the practitioner and the practitioner is forced to detach from the flow of events, objectify portions of what normally is a flow, and adopt a mindset toward barriers similar to that of the theorist. The chapter concludes with an example of unready-to-hand theorizing.

16.1 TERMINOLOGY IN DISCUSSIONS OF THEORY AND THE REAL WORLD

There are at least four key words whose meanings matter in discussions of theory and the real world: theory, explanation, understanding, and practice.

16.1.1 Theory

The word *theory* refers to a dimension rather than a category (Runkel and Runkel 1984: 129–30). This means that when theory is defined as 'a collection of assertions, both verbal and symbolic, that identifies what variables are important for what reasons, specifies how they are interrelated and why, and identifies the conditions under which they should be related or not' (Campbell 1990: 65) or as 'an inference from data that is offered as formula to explain the abstract and general principle that lies behind them as their cause, their method of operation, or their relation to other phenomena' (Weick 1987: 102), the force of these definitions is to identify dimensions along which ideas can vary. As ideas become elaborated more fully into abstract variables, underlying principles, interrelations, and conditions for related-ness, their resulting content moves away from mere speculations and becomes more deserving of the label theory. As the ideas become more abstract they also move away from the phenomenology of practice.

16.1.2 Explanation

Theories are often treated as synonymous with *explanation*. This is where the trouble starts in theory–practice debates (e.g. Craig 1996). The trouble comes because, depending on how you portray explanation, you make it easier or harder to link explaining with acting. Traditionally, an explanation is viewed as a general-ization that offers reasons for or causes of an event, and thereby simplifies the context of the event. Explanations are a form of knowledge that essentially asserts that certain things follow from other things (Sandelands 1990: 237). They constitute *knowledge that* interconnections exist, but not *knowledge of how* to make those connections happen.

A deeper understanding of theory and explanation is made possible by Fritz Roethlisberger's (1977), reflections on a lifetime of research on action. He found that theorizing and abstract systems tended to be associated with a completely different mindset called simply 'B relations' than was true for action and concrete systems called 'A relations'. A sample of these differences is listed in Table 16.1.

Table 16.1 Mindsets associated with concrete and abstract systems

A relations	B relations
Concrete	Abstracted
Nonlogical	Logical
Subjective	Objective
Internal	External
Here-and-now	There-and-then
Mutually dependent	Simple cause and effect
Exchange	Unilateral
Reflexive	Irreflexive
Intransitive	Transitive
Symmetrical	Asymmetric
Cyclical	Linear
Intrinsic	Extrinsic
Satisfying, rewarding	Optimal
Process	Structural
Emergent	Planned, designed
Diffuse	Specific
Existential	Probabilistic
Etc.	Etc.

Source: Roethlisberger 1977: 439.

Theory and explanations, both of them B list activities, embody a distinctive orientation in Roethlisberger's view. Theorists intent on constructing an explanation talk about classes or variables rather than concrete phenomena, relations that can be treated apart from the entities, reactive actors, artificial systems, maps of phenomena rather than the phenomena themselves, linear relations rather than polarities, distinctions between knower and known, and they make efforts to objectify the subjects of knowledge. These B list orientations differ from those associated with understanding and practice. Again, judgments of the magnitude and kind of these differences influence the degree of one's optimism toward the establishment of meaningful theory–practice linkages.

16.1.3 Understanding

Understanding, the third key term in theory–practice debates, is about know-how rather than the know-that of explanation. Thus, understanding is to practice as explanation is to theory. To understand is to make sense of, to be conversant with, to apprehend, and to know thoroughly by close contact and long experience. Understanding is developed gradually rather than imparted suddenly. Understanding is as much about particulars as explanation is about generalities. Understanding tends to come in wholes and patterns whereas explanation tends to come in parts and assemblies.

This all seems quite tidy until you recall Kierkegaard's statement that we started with. 'It is perfectly true, as philosophers say, that life must be *understood* backwards. But they forget the other proposition, that it must be lived forwards' (Gardiner 1988: 90). If he had said life is explained backwards and understood forward, then this would have been consistent with the alignments of terminology already proposed. But he did not. If we stick with Kierkegaard's idea that life can be understood backward, then this means that it is possible for theorists to apprehend phenomena intimately and encode what they learn into know-how. And if they can do that, then there would be no theory–practice disjunction. But there also might be no theory as we traditionally envision that tool (Freeman 2000). For the moment, it is sufficient to note that Kierkegaard keeps the term 'understanding' in play. His usage keeps understanding from becoming the sole possession of either theorists or practitioners. As we will see later, it is that very fluidity that may be crucial for improved dialogue on theory–practice issues.

16.1.4 Practice

We are left then with *practice* as the final term to unpack. Practice is the world of Roethlisberger's List A. To work within the A list is to focus on concrete persons, relations that are intrinsic to the entities, proactive actors, natural systems, relationships of polarity (p. 450) in which there can be either too much or too little (e.g. there can be too much conformity or too little conformity so there is a tendency toward equilibrium seeking), the indistinguishability of knower and known, and structures that are subinstitutional and therefore unable to develop without larger institutions (p. 442).

Practice is also a state of 'thrownness' as we said earlier. If we look more closely at the nature of 'thrownness', it becomes clearer that this condition has an affinity for many of the conditions in List A. Thrownness is a mixture of unknowability, unpredictability, and enactment, as Winograd and Flores (1986: 34–6) make clear in their summary of what thrownness feels like:

1. You cannot avoid acting: Your actions affect the situation and yourself, often against your will.
2. You cannot step back and reflect on your actions. You are thrown on your intuitions and have to deal with whatever comes up as it comes up.
3. The effects of action cannot be predicted: The dynamic nature of social conduct precludes accurate prediction.
4. You do not have a stable representation of the situation: Patterns may be evident after the fact, but at the time the flow unfolds there is nothing but arbitrary fragments capable of being organized into a host of different patterns or possibly no pattern whatsoever.
5. Every representation is an interpretation: There is no way to settle that any interpretation is right or wrong, which means an 'objective analysis' of that into which one was thrown is impossible.
6. Language is action: Whenever people say something, they create rather than describe a situation, which means it is impossible to stay detached from whatever emerges unless you say nothing, which is such a strange way to react that the situation is deflected anyway.

Quantum theory and chaos theory suggest that the experience of thrownness should not surprise us. The world is less like a machine and more like patterns of relationships. These patterns are unknowable, since to measure something is to change it. These patterns are also unpredictable, since very small differences in initial conditions can lead very quickly to very large differences in the future state of a system (McDaniel 1997). In an unknowable, unpredictable world, sensemaking is all we have. In a private communication to the author Reuben McDaniel put the point this way:

Because the nature of the world is unknowable (chaos theory and quantum theory) we are left with only sensemaking. Even if we had the capacity to do more, doing more would not help. Quantum theory helps us to understand that the present state of the world is, at best, a probability distribution. As we learn from chaos theory, the next state of the world is unknowable. And so we must pay attention to the world as it unfolds. Therefore, it is a good thing that we can't do more than sensemaking...because then we would only be frustrated by our inability to know. But believing enables actions which leads to more sense (sometimes) and taking action leads to more sense (sometimes) and sensemaking connects actions to beliefs (sometimes).

To portray practice as thrownness is not to equate it with chaotic, short-sighted bumbling. When technicians are thrown into the middle of an incomprehensible problem of repairing a copying machine, they are not without resources or actions. It is just that it is intuitions, improvisations, prototypes, and talk that help them, not manuals, training, and lists (Brown and Duguid 2000; Orr 1996). Thrownness is about the holistic character of practice, the character of losing oneself in the world, that theorists sometimes strip out when they resort to detached hindsight (Starbuck and Milliken 1988). Thrownness 'contradicts the traditional assumption that one can always know something best by gaining a reflective and detached clarity about it' (Dreyfuss 1995: 173). Knowing something best, instead, comes from direct access to the world through practical involvement and unreflective action. 'Detached contemplation can be illuminating, but it also obscures the phenomena themselves by isolating and categorizing them.... [thrownness is] the condition of under-standing in which our actions find some resonance or effectiveness in the world' (Winograd and Flores 1986: 32–3). Thrownness highlights the possibility that practitioners act their way into meaning and that their main tools for doing so are acting thinkingly (Weick 1983). Most of all, thrownness reminds analysts that practice is unfolding, fluid, ongoing, shifting, wholistic, and dynamic, which means that static structural explanations such as those associated with institutional theor-ies may widen the theory–practice gap rather than bridge it.

To summarize, the terminology of explanation and theory suggest that comprehen-sion lies in the direction of detachment, separable elements causally connected, and abstraction, whereas understanding and practice suggest that comprehension lies in the direction of involvement, wholes, and concreteness. All four terms represent dimensions rather than categories meaning that there are variations in the extent to which they conflict or complement in discussions of theory and practice. We turn now to a brief examination of some relationships that have been proposed.

16.2 FORMS OF RELATIONSHIP BETWEEN THEORY AND PRACTICE

Scholars have mixed together theory, explanation, understanding, and practice in quite different ways. These relationships have been described as correspondent (Lewin), complementary (Roethlisberger), incommensurable (Sandelands), coord-inate (Dutton and Starbuck), parallel (Thomas and Tymon), reciprocal (Craig), conceptually equivalent (Argyris), and methodologically equivalent (Kilduff and Mehra).

16.2.1 Correspondent Theory and Practice

Undoubtedly the best-known assertion in theory–practice discussion is Kurt Lewin's soothing mantra, 'there is nothing so practical as a good theory.' This statement suggests that the relationship between theory and practice is one of harmony where each part is correlative to the other. Theorists take refuge in the assertion that there is *nothing* so practical as the theories they are creating. Practitioners take refuge in the implication that when they fail, it is probably because no one gave them a *good* theory. Lewin's statement itself is the object of repeated glossing. For example, Sandelands (1990) tweaks us by asking, just what other vehicles of understanding does Lewin have in mind when he says 'nothing' compares to theory in its practicality? Does Lewin mean alternatives to theory such as visual art, performance art, poetry, essays, great literature, and music, or does he mean more prosaic alternatives such as common sense, maxims, pre-scientific inquiry, and pragmatic action? Even more tricky, does Lewin even mean what we think he means? This possibility arises because of Shelley Taylor's (1998: 87) discovery that what Lewin actually said was, 'A business man once stated that there is nothing so practical as a good theory' (Lewin 1943: 118). It makes a big difference whether the practicality of theory is attributed to a skeptical business practitioner or a self-interested academic theorist.

16.2.2 Complementary Theory and Practice

Roethlisberger (1977), who crafted the contrast between A relations and B relations introduced earlier, argued that neither list can be reduced to the other, and that they each preserved different truths about organizing (p. 465). Thus, each completes the other and they are complementary. Both forms of relations appear in social reality, in knowledge, and in action. But, in Roethlisberger's view, the B relations tended to dominate. The most serious consequences of this dominance was that investigators objectified active subjects, and in doing so, 'lost the quality of activity' (p. 441). Furthermore, he felt that B relations were cultivated by managers and people in power even though they mostly encounter A relations on a daily basis (p. 450). Roethlisberger's lifelong quest was to improve the skill and knowledge with which people handled A relations. His rationale for this focus is itself a fascinating statement that reflects both A and B relations.

In trying to understand the polarized forms of too much or too little in which A-relations expressed themselves, I discovered the equilibrium seeking properties of these relations. They seemed to be seeking states of practical equilibrium, which from the point of view of the participants in them—not that of an external observer—were rewarding and just. Furthermore, if someone paid attention to these relations instead of ignoring them, sometimes they also became efficient in an external sense. . . . By listening to A-relations in their efforts to find states of equilibrium—rather than states of polarity composed of either too much or too little—I could both understand and take action in regard to them at the same time. And I would not be prescribing what I thought A-relations should do: I would be facilitating what they wanted to do. This for me was the lesson of 'the Hawthorne effect' (p. 452).

In this short observation we see a B-relation rationale (equilibrium seeking) for an A-relation intervention (active listening) derived from B-relation research

(Hawthorne study) that uncovered A relations in the workplace (the informal system), the intervention culminating in a potential increase in B-relation efficiency through the removal of obstructions to A-relation interactions.

While Roethlisberger felt that A relations and B relations were incommensurable, he also felt they were complementary. Knowledge developed through A relations alone is mere self-knowledge that remains at the level of acquaintance with separate events and leads to self-centered uncoordinated action. Knowledge developed through B relations alone leads to attempted rationality and control that is subverted by the ignored A relations. The challenge is to specify the conditions under which each list is of greater use.

16.2.3 Incommensurable Theory and Practice

Lance Sandelands (1990) framed the theory–practice contrast as an opposition between explanation and understanding, and argued that the two could not be compared, since they are incompatible. Like Roethlisberger, he argued that knowledge presupposes understanding and that understanding precedes explanation. 'Understanding furnishes explanation its basic concepts and logic, and moreover the background necessary to make sense of what it says. Explanation presents formally and incompletely what is already understood' (p. 247). Sandelands argued that explanation and understanding are logically incommensurable and therefore not 'intertranslatable' (p. 258), which means that practice and theory may occur coincident with one another, but one cannot causally affect the other. Craig (1996) took issue with this position and argued that it was based on unusually narrow definitions of explanation and understanding.

Sandelands's argument does not preclude the possibility that practice may develop differently in the presence of theory. And it is on this point that Sandelands adds considerable richness to our grasp of how to work between theory and the real world (pp. 253–9). He suggests, for example, that theory often calls to mind action or action tendencies that would have gone unnoticed.

Here, theory enters into practice in something like the way art enters into experience. Just as art consists of an arrangement of materials (e.g. colors, shapes, sounds) which can (but need not) call to mind certain impulses and feelings in beholders, so too theory consists of an arrangement of ideas (e.g. concepts, propositions) which can (but need not) call to mind certain actions and feelings in practitioners. And, just as contact with art may bring out new ways of seeing or feeling, so too contact with theory may bring out new ways of practice. (p. 254)

As if on cue John Reed, former co-CEO of Citigroup, concurred when he said, 'All that research can do is inform us. It certainly does not give us answers. It informs us with regard to what an appropriate behavioral response might be' (Reed 2000: 60).

Consistent with his earlier arguments, Sandelands claims that theories cannot teach us anything we do not already know (p. 256). This has the interesting implication that it is the expert, not the novice, who is more likely to be moved by theory. Thus, while theory cannot affect practice directly, it can call attention to ideas, which may call attention to certain actions, which people may then enact. Theory does not cause practice. Instead, people acted differently in light of those ideas. Freud introduced the idea of unconscious motives, and people who resonated to this idea, acted differently when issues of trust came up in relationships.

16.2.4 Coordinate Theory and Practice

Dutton and Starbuck (1963) acknowledge that managers use theories, but they argue that the ones managers use are specific and implicit and have limitations that can be offset with general-explicit theories that have a different set of limitations. The two forms of theory are of equal importance, hence coordinate, yet their differences suggest the wisdom of hybrids. Specific-implicit theories tend to be used only once, they are more like a consumption good than an investment, they tend to be overly influenced by cultural theory, they are difficult to communicate, their logic is unclear, their assumptions are invisible, they cannot be torn apart and rebuilt, they are based on limited experience, and they have an unreflective generally solitary origin. If these theories are transformed into general-explicit theories, or if they are blended with general-explicit theories, then many of the problems just listed disappear. A general-explicit theory is a theory that can be used more than once, is not constrained by cultural theory, is communicable, abstract, its logic is clear, its assumptions are visible, it has a social origin, it can be torn apart, it is based on extensive experience, and it has a reflective origin.

The idea that managerial theories originate and persist as specific-implicit formulations is not as straightforward as it seems. For example, it makes a big difference whether a general-explicit theory is plucked out of thin air or evolved from specific personal experience. If people start with specific-implicit theories that work, and evolve them toward generality and explicitness, then the resulting theories should be powerful, since they are grounded in understanding before they are converted into explanation. Aside from the issue of evolution there is the issue of implied epistemology. To describe managerial theories as specific-implicit and limited is to impose List B imagery on List A ready-to-hand living. If practitioners are basically lay scientists, then indeed, their inferior specific-implicit theories could be costly and misleading. But if their ready-to-hand functioning is also nonlogical, subjective, reflexive, emergent, and existential, then whether their theories meet the standards of normal science or not is irrelevant, since their living is not theory-driven anyway. This is not to say that theories are trivial in practice.

Rather, it is to suggest that the dimensions of specificity and explicitness may be less crucial for practitioners than for theorists, and other dimensions such as narrativity (Czarniawska 1998) may be more important.

16.2.5 Parallel Theory and Practice

Thomas and Tymon (1982) approach the theory–real world relationship by proposing five 'necessary properties of relevant research'. They suggest analogous aspects of theory and practice. By identifying comparable parts they suggest important parallels. Their argument is that those who specialize in B relations and theory can generate directly useful ideas if they meet practitioner needs for descriptive relevance, goal relevance, operational validity, nonobviousness, and timeliness. These five properties can be phrased as questions:

(1) Do the concepts and findings describe phenomena you actually experience?
(2) Do the variables in the theory correspond to outcomes you want to influence?
(3) Can you manipulate the independent variables in the theory we hand you?
(4) Does our theory meet or exceed the complexity of the common sense theories you already use?
(5) Will the theory be available in time to deal with your problems?

If Roethlisberger and Heidegger are right, then this language of variables, concepts, findings, independent variables will be a weak basis on which to connect theory with practice, since practice tends not to be punctuated with that kind of language (see also Abbott 1992). That, however, does not seem like an insurmountable problem. Practitioners can translate the above questions into their own terms. There are other implied issues that are trickier. For example, academics may like nonobvious theories, but practitioners tend to find them unsettling. Practitioners who are already swamped with uncertainty often prefer theories that affirm rather than disconfirm their understanding. Operational validity, question 3 above, requires tough calls regarding what is controllable. Practitioners are notorious for their expansive needs to control, their flawed estimates of what they control (e.g. the fallacy of centrality, Westrum 1982), and their eagerness to disown control when outcomes turn bad. Given the strong emotions that surround issues of control, practitioner descriptions of what they do and do not control tend to be shifting, unreliable, and contested. This means that 'controllability' can be a precarious bridge by which one can move from theory to practice. Part of this precariousness may also stem from the possibility that levers posited by theorists are an artifact of detached present-at-hand viewing, and 'disappear' in engaged coping.

An important sidelight on Thomas and Tymon is furnished by John Miner's (1984) empirical work to see how useful and valid the 32 theories in organizational science available at that time were perceived to be. The four theories judged most useful and most valid were all motivational and included theories of job characteristics (Hackman), goal-setting (Locke), achievement (McClelland), and role motivation (Miner). These four theories are psychological and, interestingly, are also the four theories out of the 32 that most closely resemble the theories that Lewin developed, the same Lewin who touted the practicality of good theory. Again, as if on cue, John Reed would second these findings. Reed says,

We go nuts in this business world trying to incent behavior. Frankly, we do not know as much about how to do that as we would like.... We need the opportunity to stand back from our immediate concerns to get some sense of what the research community has learned about incentives.... The willingness of people to change is limited, and what you pay them seems to be inversely correlated with their willingness to change. I used to believe that once you paid people some of these astronomical salaries that we currently pay, you would have mature, self-sufficient, self-confident individuals on your team. Let me assure you, it is not the case. (2000: 59, 61)

If we go back to Miner's other findings, of equal interest is the combination, high validity, low usefulness because this combination runs contrary to Lewin's maxim. The work of March and Simon, George Graen, Stacy Adams, and Arnold Tannenbaum fit this combination (Miner 1984: 301). It would be interesting to see if any of the several ways of relating theory to the real world reviewed here would make these latter four theories more useful.

16.2.6 Reciprocal Theory and Practice

Near the end of Dutton and Starbuck's (1963) essay mentioned above, they argue that application is a circular process. 'Specific models are generalized because general models can be more effective. But in individual applications it is advantageous to make general models specific again. The first is a social process; the second depends on individual imagination' (p. 10). This is an informal way of pointing to a much more robust relation between theory and the real world, joint reciprocal interpretation modeled after a hermeneutic circle. There is an 'interplay between evolving general conception and the rich perception of the particular' (Nussbaum 1990: 96). The hallmark of this relation is that application is not viewed as a linear translation of theory into practice. Instead,

the application of a theoretical principle to a particular context of practical action involves both the theoretical principle and the practical situation in a hermeneutic circle of interpretation that adjusts each to the other until a unified understanding of both is achieved. Application is intrinsic to interpretation because the meaning of a universal principle is always uniquely disclosed within the particular practical situation of the interpreter. The meaning of a theoretical principle changes with every act of application.... (T)he meaning of theory evolves in reciprocal interaction with practice. (Craig 1996: 76)

What seems crucial in relating theory to practice is the mutual adjustment. Adjusting need not compromise accuracy. Instead, practice is seen accurately as nuanced action just as theory is seen as rich in connotations. We learn what the theory means by using it, we learn what the concrete situation means by labeling it. For example, the Tenerife air disaster (Weick 1990) in which two 747 aircraft collided on the ground in the Canary Islands, killing 583 people, takes on distinct form as theories impose a clearer figure on the ground of the calamity. And particulars make clearer how a theory is doing its work of explaining and what it assumes.

As a starting point, one can begin with the speculation that, because of delays and interruptions, airline personnel at Tenerife were agitated, frustrated, and operating at higher than normal levels of arousal. That in turn suggests the possibility that tunnel vision may be unfolding along with regressing to more habitual ways of acting and the withholding of more and more information. Those features now stand out in the particular event but they cycle back to the theory in the form of questions such as what is being excluded from narrowing perception, which habits terminate the regressing, is arousal affected by level of expertise? The theory is adjusted to suggest answers, and in the adjusting, is itself redrafted in closer alignment with at least one real world. Likewise, the relevancies in the real world are adjusted in line with features that the theory singles out as pivotal.

Mutual adjustment may compound the problems of cumulating theories within a discipline, since the theory is not frozen long enough to determine stable paths of future development. But mutual adjustment simplifies the problems of real world application and meaningful theoretical abstraction by grounding the abstraction in a single common referent. If done successfully, this form of relation resembles the systematic move from specific-implicit to general-explicit that is suggested by Dutton and Starbuck. What we are depicting here is also not all that different from Sandelands use of theory as an evocative text for practice, except that, in a hermeneutic circle, theory and the real world are more tightly coupled, more open to mutual influence, more provisional in their substance, and less wedded to causal logic.

16.2.7 Conceptually Equivalent Theory and Practice

Conceptual equivalence occurs when similar concepts are used in both theory and practice and retain similar meanings. This form of relationship can be illustrated by means of the concepts of paradigm and theory of action.

The concept of paradigm is often used to blend the real world with theory (e.g. Bresser and Bishop 1983; R. H. Brown 1978; Weick 1995: 118–21). By paradigm we refer to 'those sets of assumptions, usually implicit, about what sorts of things make up the world, how they act, how they hang together, and how they may be known. In actual practice, such paradigms function as a means of imposing control as well as a resource that dissidents may use in organizing their awareness and action' (R. H. Brown 1978: 373). Pfeffer (1982: 227–8) describes a paradigm in a way that fits equally well with theory and practice. A paradigm is a 'technology, including beliefs about cause–effect relations and standards of practice and behavior, as well as specific examples of these, that constitutes how an organization goes about doing things'. He further observes that

the level of paradigm development is a concept analytically similar to that of technological uncertainty, an equivalence made also by Lodahl and Gordon [1972]. To have consensus on methodology, curriculum, and principal research issues is to share a common understanding concerning the technical requirements for research and teaching in a field. This is similar to sharing beliefs about connections between operating strategies, marketing strategies, and profits in a business firm. (1981: 76)

If theorists and practitioners alike work by means of paradigms, then both the mode of working and the products have mutual relevance.

A similar equivalence is found in Argyris's (2000) theory of action perspective. He argues that practitioners and scientists alike produce actions using designs that are causal, intentional, value-infused, actionable, testable, and may differ between their espoused content and their achieved outcomes. These similar designs employed by theorists and practitioners theoretically make for easy transfer of knowledge from one realm to the other. Theories of actionable knowledge, defensive reasoning, self-fulfilling prophecies, self-sealing processes, and routine learning that are created by theorists and applied to their own activities are found in and applied within practitioner activities as well. This straightforward equivalence, which normally would aid dialogue between theory and practice, sometimes has the opposite effect because it is embedded in a prescription of one best way to learn. This tends to seal off the theory of actionable knowledge from revision despite growing attention to A relations, thrownness, and ready-to-hand absorbed coping.

16.2.8 Methodologically Equivalent Theory and Practice

Methodological equivalence between theory and practice is implied by findings from studies of the sociology of scientific knowledge (e.g. Ashmore 1989; Woolgar 1988) and postmodern interpretations of the conduct of science (e.g. Kilduff and Mehra 1997). The basic argument is that scientific inquiry and practical inquiry (e.g. Polkinghorne 2000) are basically indistinguishable. If they are indistinguishable, then A relations and B relations may be acted into meaning in a similar manner, which means their products should be mutually relevant. The image of contested entrepreneurial science driven by ambition, selective perception, and preoccupation with competitors is virtually interchangeable with the image of other forms of entrepreneurial commerce with the same dynamics. Likewise, if postmodernism is interpreted as 'a rejection of overarching propositions, an acceptance of pluralism and fragmentation, an emphasis on difference and heterogeneity, and an ironic admission of the ephemerality of things' (Kilduff and Mehra 1997: 456), then it becomes virtually synonymous with A relations. If this equivalence holds up, then postmodern science has considerable overlap with the contemporary situation of organizational members. The boundaries of two formerly separate real worlds of theory and practice become blurred, and each has more to say directly to the other.

Science is not dismissed in postmodern theory. Instead, it is recast. The goal of science is to 'challenge the content and form of dominant models of knowledge and also to produce new forms of knowledge through breaking down disciplinary boundaries and giving voice to those not represented in dominant discourses' (Kilduff and Mehra 1997: 458). The postmodern emphasis on paradox, irony, eclecticism, and plurality is found in the classic work of Erving Goffman and Leon Festinger, the latter being noteworthy because he was a student of Lewin's (Kilduff and Mehra 1997: 461). The several strands of postmodernism tend to converge on the idea that the aim of social science is not generalizability (B relations), but instead to put ideas into practice, to shape policies, to pose new questions, and 'to progress toward ever greater knowledge of our own ignorance' (p. 466).

16.3 Theory and the Real World as Modes of Being

The gap between living forward through A relations and understanding backward through B relations can be made tangible if we follow the lead of a growing number of investigators (e.g. Dreyfuss 1997; Packer 1985; Stenner 1998; Thachankary 1992) and adopt the language of Heidegger's (1962) three modes of engagement to describe it. The basic idea is this. The starting point in any investigation should not be the assumption that people are detached, contemplative, and theoretical, but rather that they are involved, concerned, and practical (Stenner 1998: 61). People engaged in practical activity are concerned with projects and action in context and their concerns shift as their needs shift. What practical activity does NOT consist of is a separation between subject and object. Instead, it consists of 'absorbed coping' which Heidegger describes as a *ready-to-hand* mode of engagement. When people act in this engaged mode, they are aware of the world holistically as a network of interrelated projects, possible tasks, and 'thwarted potentialities' (Packer 1985: 1083) rather than as an arrangement of discrete physical objects such as tools. Equipment is known by its uses and the way it fits into the world (e.g. there is hammering, not a hammer). Measurable qualities of equipment recede unnoticed into the background. Thus, a glass may measure 15 centimeters high, but its usability cannot be established simply by detached looking. What is decisive about the glass is that it is a 'piece of equipment for maintaining a body of otherwise disobedient liquid in order that we might drink' (Stenner 1998: 70), although it might also be worshipped as a relic, displayed in a gallery, or used as a receptacle to hold flowers. Its meaning lies in a wider network of use.

If an ongoing project is interrupted, then experience changes into an *unready-to-hand* mode. Problematic aspects of the situation that produced the interruption stand out in the manner of a figure–ground organization, but people still do not become aware of context-free objects. For example, if one is delayed leaving the house to catch a scheduled train, then time and the train station become salient as do shorter routes, one-way streets, anticipated parking problems, timetables, back up departure times, etc. 'Particular aspects of the whole situation stand out but only against a background provided by the project we are engaged in and the interests and involvements guiding it' (Packer 1985: 1084). In the case of Heidegger's favorite example of hammering, as the project proceeds the hammer may prove to be too heavy for the task. When this happens, its weightiness 'becomes salient whereas before it was transparent; but I am not aware of the objective "weight" of the hammer (so many pounds), only that it is "too heavy" to do its appointed job successfully' (Packer 1985: 1084).

The third mode of engagement, which again involves a shift of experience, is *present-at-hand*. This mode occurs when people step back from their involvement in a project and reflect on it using analyses that are general and abstract and context-free. It is not until this stage that tools, artifacts, and objects emerge as independent entities, removed from tasks, endowed with distinct measurable properties of mass and weight, that are manipulated by distinct subjects. This is the mode of theoretical reflection, which is important in the present context because of Heidegger's (1962: 99) claim that 'the ready-to-hand is not grasped theoretically at all.' It is that disturbing possibility that lies at the core of this chapter.

If we tie Heidegger's distinctions back to Kierkegaard's concern over living forward and understanding backward, then Kierkegaard's concern could be restated thusly: philosophers may be right that life is explained using present-to-hand images, but what they forget is that these images simplify the prior understandings embedded in ready-to-hand living. The crucial point is that the potential for better theorizing lies in closer scrutiny of those moments where backward and forward views meet, namely, unready-to-hand moments. These are moments when practitioners are interrupted and discover relevancies that had been invisible up to that point. And these same unready-to-hand moments are opportunities for theorists to get a richer glimpse of what those ongoing practitioner projects were and what their relevancies looked like to engaged people. Theorists may produce better theories if they focus on such events as interruptions (Mandler 1984), breaches (Garfinkel 1963), shocks (Schroeder, Van de Ven, Scudder, and Polley 1989), disconfirmed expectations (Staw 1980), breakdowns and situations of irresolution (Winograd and Flores 1986: 147), experiments at the edge (Rasmussen 2000), or shifts from automatic to controlled information processing (Louis and Sutton 1991).

Early on, organizational theory embraced interruptions when Mintzberg (1973) documented the fragmented world of management in which an interruption occurred every nine minutes. A moment of interruption is a moment during which a forward going project remains largely intact but becomes more visible when part of its breaks down. And a moment of interruption is also a moment in which there is partial detachment from the project and a more deliberate, visible effort to look backward in search of abstractions and labels that make sense of the breakdown. During situated detachment we see both engaged under-standing and disengaged explanation. If people act their way into meaning, then an interruption is a period during which acting and meaning-making occur simultaneously. Acting concurrent with interruption is the closest glimpse that a theorist is likely to get of what really matters when living forward proceeds undeterred. And meaning-making concurrent with interruption is the most relevant glimpse that a practitioner is likely to get of abstractions that tie the world together in a sensible way that facilitates resumption of the interrupted activity. Practitioners are best able to spot the theories that matter in their world of practice when that world is interrupted. And theorists are best able to spot the situated action they should be puzzling over in their world of theory, in the presence of those same interruptions. During an interruption, forward living reaches less far ahead and backward explanation lags less far behind. It is in the moment of interruption that theory relates most clearly to practice and practice most readily accommodates the abstract categories of theory. Whatever concepts fit best to foster resumption of the interrupted interval, presumably continue to remain valid during more opaque moments when unimpeded living and unimpeded theorizing proceed.

Theories built around what people notice when they are interrupted and how they cope with interruptions (e.g. Berscheid 1983; Levy 1962; Mandler 1982) are not just commentaries on how people react to irritants and hassles. Instead, those theories point to fundamental properties of ongoing, involved, practical activity. In this sense those who study problem-solving, a prominent research topic in professional schools, have direct access to unready-to-hand engagement and indir-ect though meaningful access to ready-to-hand engagement. Regrettably, because of institutional pressures, business school researchers usually reach automatically for the explanation of bounded rationality and fail to see how little it covers. Problems are a common meeting ground for theory and practice because of their nearness to ready-to-hand engagement. When everyday projects suffer a breakdown of action, theorists and practitioners alike share a common vantage point from which they can glimpse thwarted potentialities embedded in networks of projects. This is not just warmed over action research. Instead, it is basic research where the workings of ready-to-hand engagement become equally visible to people with quite different interests. Furthermore, attempts to describe the common referent in a meaningful way encourage continuing dialogue dedicated to getting the account 'right'.

16.4 Theory and the Unready-to-Hand: The Case of Friendly Fire[1]

We turn now to a brief illustration of the illumination made possible when real world activity is interrupted, and A relations and B relations become mutually informative. In the no-fly zone of Iraq on 14 April 1994, twenty-six people riding in two US Army helicopters died instantly when two US Air Force F-15 fighter planes misidentified the helicopters as Russian Hind aircraft and shot them down (Snook 2000). That incident of 'friendly fire' occurred despite the fact that all four aircraft were under the air traffic control of a nineteen-person AWACs crew flying above them and they were the only four aircraft being tracked by the crew.

Here, in slightly more detail, is what happened. Two army helicopters (UH-60s), based in Turkey, had been assigned to land at a village just inside the Iraqi border, pick up high-ranking UN personnel, and ferry them deeper into the Iraqi secure zone to meet with Kurdish leaders. The helicopters were visible only intermittently on the Air Force AWACs radars because their signals would fade in and out as they landed or flew behind mountains. Radios in the Army helicopters were incompatible with those in the Air Force fighters. Furthermore, the helicopters did not use a different electronic identification code when they flew in Iraq from the one they used in Turkey even though all other friendly aircraft did. This discrepancy had continued for almost three years of the peacekeeping operation. On the morning of the shootdown, two Air Force F-15 fighter planes, accustomed to air-to-air combat at high altitudes, were assigned to sweep the secure zone at all altitudes for enemy aircraft. They believed that they were the first aircraft into the secure zone that morning and when they spotted the two helicopters on their own radar screens, they tried unsuccessfully to identify whether they were friend or foe. The AWACs crew, flying their first mission together, was of no help. The fighters then decided to

[1] Portions of this discussion are adapted from my book review of Scott Snook, *Friendly Fire* (Princeton University Press, 2000), that was prepared for *Administrative Science Quarterly*. I am grateful to Captain Jennel Eickhoff for her help in understanding this incident.

attempt a visual identification. The lead pilot flew above and to the left of the low-flying US helicopters and misidentified them as Russian 'Hind' helicopters. This misidentification was confirmed by the second fighter pilot, and both fighters circled around behind the helicopters, turned on their missiles, and informed the AWACs crew that they had 'engaged two Hinds'. This meant they were ready to fire on the targets. All the AWACs said back was, 'Roger, engaged'. The pilots assumed this meant that it was permissible to fire the missiles and triggered their release. All twenty-six people on board the helicopters were killed instantly. The pilots did not learn of the error until five hours later when they heard about the shootdown on CNN.

Theory relates to this real world incident in several different ways. For example, a detached, present-at-hand view suggests that different levels of analysis can be imposed on this incident, and each level adds new insights. The shootdown resulted from a misidentification by fighter pilots, but also from non-intervention by an AWACs crew and non-integration of Air Force and the Army activities that supposedly were a joint operation. These three errors lend themselves to analysis at the individual, group, and organizational level of analysis. To illustrate, at the individual level of analysis, the misidentification was attributed in part to ambiguous stimuli and to a powerful set of expectations. The distinguishing features of Hinds helicopters that are taught to fighter pilots who are being schooled in aircraft recognition, look just like the features of a US UH-60 helicopter when that aircraft is viewed from above. Pictures of the UH-60 that are used in training are all photographed from ground level looking up at the helicopter. This means that trainees never see the overhead view that confronted the F-15 pilots the morning of 14 April. Furthermore, F-15 pilots have no incentive to learn about aircraft that fly below 500 feet, since all of their work consists of air-to-air combat at high altitudes. The orders for the day on 14 April listed no takeoff times for the helicopters and listed the two fighters as the first aircraft that were to enter the secure zone that day. In the pilots' words, 'If it's not there on the tasking orders, then it shouldn't be happening.' The lead pilot was junior in rank to the second pilot who was his commander. And in this 'inverted hierarchy' the lead person wanted to impress his commander and also assumed that, if he had made a mistake, surely his superior officer would catch it.

The shootdown also engages traditional theory. Thompson's (1967) theory of interdependence fits this incident beautifully. He argued that different types of interdependence necessitate different coordinating mechanisms: pooled interdependence requires standardization, sequential interdependence requires plans, and reciprocal interdependence requires mutual adjustment. All three forms of interdependence were present in the shootdown, but in every case, the appropriate coordinating mechanism was missing (Snook 2000: 152–73).

Newly developed theory also finds its way into this analysis. Scott Snook, an Army Lt./Colonel and a Ph.D. in Organizational Behavior who authored the friendly fire book, was himself a victim of friendly fire in 1983 on Grenada. He was wounded by machine-gun fire from a 'friendly' Air Force A-7 and by a bomb dropped from a 'friendly' Navy A-6 aircraft. Snook took these experiences and his specific-implicit theories of what happened, paid close attention to other specific-implicit theories presumably at work in Iraq, and developed a general-explicit theory of practical drift (pp. 186–201).

Practical drift is the 'slow uncoupling of local practice from written procedure' (p. 225). When a global system such as a peacekeeping operation is first designed, it is treated as a tightly coupled system with safeguards built in to prevent worst case scenarios. When these designs are implemented, they often prove unworkable locally. Units adopt their own local variations which get perpetuated when new crews rotate into units, and are briefed by leaders who themselves have little historical perspective of why things are done the way they are. With each new cycle of briefing, the entire system becomes more loosely coupled and the logic of the local task becomes more compelling. People become less and less familiar with the original, tightly coupled logic of the entire operation. The conditions for practical drift include senior leader actions, formal organizational rules, inter-group isolation, intra-group norms, and individual sensemaking.

What is crucial in this ongoing loosening of coordination is that each unit that is following its own unique path assumes that all other groups are behaving in accord with the *original* set of established rules (p. 198). If a system that has drifted into locally acceptable procedures suddenly becomes tightly coupled with other units, the local adaptations no longer mesh and this produces an incomprehensible, often catastrophic moment. Practical drift explains how a high reliability system—there had been 50,000 hours of safe flight operations up to this point—can still have a normal accident (Perrow 1984). This possibility had been presumed highly improbable until Snook's investigation.

So, Snook's analysis stands out as a good example of how to zero in on an unready-to-hand moment of interruption, and come away with a deepened understanding of ready-at-hand coping and with a present-to-hand theory that is general and generative. This blending of the concrete with the abstract was made possible because the theorist focused on a breached project, in this case the interruption of an air defense activity.

16.5 Conclusion

People in the real world are thrown into a world where context, holistic awareness, emotion, interruption, reflection through action, situated artifacts, knowledge creation through activity, time constraints, reciprocal ties between appraisal and action, and involvement, matter. These labels for their A relations represent a B-relation rendition. But the rendition maintains its relevance for theory and practice because it is grounded in analysis of unready-to-hand episodes. Theorists who focus on the unready-to-hand treat the real world, not as a place, but as a distinct form of activity. That form most closely resembles 'thrownness' and includes activity embedded in projects, activity that restores interrupted projects, and activity that is resilient in the face of threatened interruptions. These activities involve more than mere information processing and problem-solving. They involve understanding that is complex in its confusions, but potentially profound in the simplifications toward which it is moving.

REFERENCES

ARGYRIS, CHRIS (2000). 'The Relevance of Actionable Knowledge for Breaking the Code', in M. Beer and N. Nohria (eds.), *Breaking the Code of Change*. Boston: Harvard Business School Press.

ASHMORE, M. (1989). *The Reflexive Thesis*. Chicago: University of Chicago.

BERSCHEID, E. (1983). 'Emotion', in H. H. Kelley, E. Berscheid, A. Christensen, J. Harvey, T. Huston, G. Levinger, A. Pelau, and D. R. Peterson (eds.), *Close Relationships*. San Francisco: Freeman.

BRESSER, R. K., and BISHOP, R. C. (1983). 'Dysfunctional Effects of Formal Planning: Two Theoretical Explorations'. *Academy of Management Review*, 8: 588–99.

BROWN, J. S., and DUGUID, P. (2000). *The Social Life of Information*. Boston.: Harvard Business School Press.

BROWN, R. H. (1978). 'Bureaucracy as Praxis: Toward a Political Phenomenology of Formal Organizations'. *Administrative Science Quarterly*, 23: 365–82.

CAMPBELL, J. P. (1990). 'The Role of Theory in Industrial and Organizational Psychology', in M. D. Dunnette and L. M. Hough (eds.), *Handbook of Industrial and Organizational Psychology*,: (2nd edn). Palo Alto, Calif.: Consulting Psychologists.

CRAIG, R. T. (1996). 'Practical Theory: A Reply to Sandelands'. *Journal for the Theory of Social Behaviour*, 26/1: 65–79.

CZARNIAWSKA, B. (1998). *A Narrative Approach to Organization Studies*. Thousand Oaks, Calif.: Sage.

DAVIS, M. S. (1971). 'That's Interesting'. *Philosophy of the Social Sciences*, 1: 309–44.

DREYFUSS, H. L. (1995). *Being-in-the-World*. Cambridge, Mass.: MIT Press.

——(1997). 'Intuitive, Deliberative, and Calculative Models of Expert Performance', in C. E. Zsambok and G. Klein (eds.), *Naturalistic Decision-Making*. Mahwah, NJ: Erlbaum.

DUTTON, J. M., and STARBUCK, W. H. (1963). 'On Managers and Theories'. *Management International*, 6: 1–11.

FRANK, A. W. (1992). 'The Pedagogy of Suffering'. *Theory and Psychology*, 2/4: 467–85.

FREEMAN, M. (2000). 'Theory Beyond Theory'. *Theory and Psychology*, 10/1: 71–7.

FREESE, L. (1980). 'The Problem of Cumulative Knowledge', in L. Freese (ed.), *Theoretical Methods in Sociology: Seven Essays*. Pittsburgh: University of Pittsburgh.

GARDINER, P. (1988). *Kierkegaard*. Oxford: Oxford University Press.

GARFINKEL, H. (1963). 'A Conception of, and Experiments with, "Trust" as a Condition of Stable Connected Actions', in O. J. Harvey (ed.), *Motivation and Interaction*. New York: Ronald.

GIOIA, D. A. (1992). 'Pinto Fires and Personal Ethics: A Script Analysis of Missed Opportunities'. *Journal of Business Ethics*, 11: 379–89.

HEIDEGGER, M. (1962). *Being and Time*. New York: Harper & Row.

KILDUFF, M., and MEHRA, A. (1997). 'Postmodernism and Organizational Research'. *Academy of Management Review*, 22/2: 453–81.

LEVY, D. M. (1962). 'The Act as a Unit'. *Psychiatry*, 25: 295–314.

LEWIN, K. (1943). 'Psychology and the Process of Group Living'. *Journal of Social Psychology, SPSSI Bulletin*, 17: 113–31.

LODAHL, J., and GORDON, G. (1972). 'The Structure of Scientific Fields and the Functioning of University Departments'. *American Sociological Review*, 37: 57–72.

LOUIS, M. R., and SUTTON, R. I. (1991). 'Switching Cognitive Gears: From Habits of Mind to Active Thinking'. *Human Relations*, 44: 55–76.

MCDANIEL, R. R. Jr (1997). 'Strategic Leadership: A View from Quantum and Chaos Theories'. *Health Care Management Review*, 21–37.

MANDLER, G. (1982). 'Stress and Thought Processes', in L. Goldenberger and S. Breznitz (eds.), *Handbook of Stress*. New York: Free Press.

—— (1984). *Mind and Body*. New York: Free Press.

MINER, J. B. (1984). 'The Validity and Usefulness of Theories in an Emerging Organizational Science'. *Academy of Management Review*, 9: 296–306.

MINTZBERG, H. (1973). *The Nature of Managerial Work*. New York: Harper & Row.

NUSSBAUM, M. C. (1990). *Love's Knowledge*. New York: Oxford University Press.

ORR, J. (1996). *Talking about Machines: An Ethnography about a Modern Job*. Ithaca, NY: ILR Press.

PACKER, M. J. (1985). 'Hermeneutic Inquiry in the Study of Human Conduct'. *American Psychologist*, 40: 1081–93.

PERROW, C. (1984). *Normal Accidents*. New York: Basic Books.

PFEFFER, J. (1982). *Organizations and Organization Theory*. Boston: Pitman.

POLKINGHORNE, D. E. (2000). 'Psychological Inquiry and the Pragmatic and Hermeneutic Traditions'. *Theory and Psychology*, 10/4: 453–79.

RASMUSSEN, J. (2000). 'The Concept of Human Error: Is It Useful for the Design of Safe Systems in Healthcare?', in C. Vincent and B. De Mol (eds.), *Safety in Medicine*. Amsterdam: Pergamon Press.

REED, J. (2000). 'A Practitioner's View of Management'. *Academy of Management Executive*, 14/1: 56–62.

ROETHLISBERGER, F. J. (1977). *The Elusive Phenomena*. Cambridge, Mass.: Harvard University Press.

RUNKEL, P. J., and RUNKEL, M. (1984). *A Guide to Usage for Writers and Students in the Social Sciences*. Totowa, NJ: Rowman & Allanheld.

SANDELANDS, L. E. (1990). 'What Is So Practical about Theory? Lewin Revisited'. *Journal for the Theory of Social Behaviour*, 20: 235–62.

SCHON, D. A. (1987). *Educating the Reflective Practitioner*. San Francisco: Jossey-Bass.

SCHROEDER, R. G., VAN DE VEN, A. H., SCUDDER, G. D., and POLLEY, D. (1989). 'The Development of Innovation Ideas', in A. H. Van de Ven, H. L. Angle, and M. S. Poole (eds.), *Research in the Management of Innovation: The Minnesota Studies*. New York: Ballinger.

SNOOK, S. (2000). *Friendly Fire*. Princeton: Princeton University Press.

STARBUCK, W. H., and MILLIKEN, F. J. (1988). 'Executives' Perceptual Filters: What They Notice and How They Make Sense', in D. C. Hambrick (ed.), *The Executive Effect: Concepts and Methods for Studying Top Managers*. Greenwich, Conn.: JAI.

STAW, B. M. (1980). 'Rationality and Justification in Organizational Life', in B. M. Staw and L. L. Cummings (eds.), *Research in Organizational Behavior*, vii. Greenwich, Conn.: JAI.

STENNER, P. (1998). 'Heidegger and the Subject: Questioning Concerning Psychology'. *Theory and Psychology*, 8: 59–77.

TAYLOR, S. E. (1998). 'The Social Being in Social Psychology', in D. T. Gilbert, S. T. Fiske, and G. Lindzey (eds.), *The Handbook of Social Psychology,*: (4th edn). Boston: McGraw-Hill.

THACHANKARY, T. (1992). 'Organizations as "Texts": Hermeneutics as a Model for Understanding Organizational Change'. *Research in Organizational Change and Development*, 6: 197–233.

THOMAS, K. W., and TYMON, W. G., Jr (1982). 'Necessary Properties of Relevant Research: Lessons from Recent Criticisms of the Organizational Sciences'. *Academy of Management Review*, 7: 345–52.

THOMPSON, J. D. (1967). *Organizations in Action*. New York: McGraw-Hill.

WEICK, K. E. (1983). 'Managerial Thought in the Context of Action', in S. Srivastava (ed.), *The Executive Mind*. San Francisco: Jossey-Bass.

—— (1987). 'Theorizing about Organizational Communication', in L. M. Porter, L. J. Putnam, K. H. Roberts, and F. M. Jablin (eds.), *Handbook of Organizational Communication*. Beverly Hills, Calif.: Sage.

—— (1990). 'The Vulnerable System: Analysis of the Tenerife Air Disaster'. *Journal of Management*, 16: 571–93.

—— (1995). *Sensemaking in Organizations*. Thousand Oaks, Calif.: Sage.

WESTRUM, R. (1982). 'Social Intelligence about Hidden Events'. *Knowledge*, 3/3: 381–400.

WINOGRAD, T., and FLORES, F. (1986). *Understanding Computers and Cognition*. Norwood, NJ: Ablex.

WOOLGAR, S. (1988). *Knowledge and Reflexivity*. London: Sage.

CHAPTER 17

....

ORGANIZATION THEORY AND ETHICS

VARIETIES AND DYNAMICS OF CONSTRAINED OPTIMIZATION

....

RICHARD P. NIELSEN

ORGANIZATIONAL THEORY and ethics are not only mutually informing and entangled historically, they may also be codependent. That is, it may not be possible to have an operational organization theory without an at least implicit ethical or normative foundation for that organizational form. Simultaneously, it may not be possible to actualize social ethics without organizational form.

A key foundational principle in both organization studies and ethics is 'constrained optimization'. The operating and at least implicit primary purpose or reason for being of an organization is what is optimized. Optimization is both a normative idea and a descriptive idea. That is, something is optimized and there is

The author would like to thank Professor Haridimos Tsoukas for his very insightful and substantive editorial help and contributions to this chapter.

often some contention and motivation about what should be optimized (Simon, 1945: 38–41, 240–4; Cyert and March 1963: 26–43). Simultaneously, in order to achieve social ethics in a bureaucratic and institutional society, organizational form is necessary.

For example, in the business organizational form of 'investor capitalism', which is currently the dominant form of business organization in the United States, shareholder wealth is optimized (Useem 1996). In some contrast and in many emerging markets, the traditional large family-owned form of business organization is the dominant form of business organization. In this latter type of organization, what is often optimized is family wealth and influence rather than either shareholder wealth or economic efficiency.

What are constrained are often the needs and desires of constituencies such as employees or local community neighbors that can help and/or block what an organization is trying to optimize. For example, the optimization of shareholder wealth criterion can be in some conflict with employee pensions and community environmental needs. Such conflicts can have important ethical implications both with respect to process and outcomes.

Sometimes, what is optimized and what are constrained are aligned or can be aligned without much conflict or difficulty. At other times and structures, ethics issues and conflicts arise in the spaces between what is optimized and what is constrained. For example, an ethics issue and conflict can arise when shareholder wealth is optimized at the expense of retired employee pensioners who are denied cost of living adjustments in their pensions as has recently occurred at General Electric (Birger 2000). In another example where a traditional large family-owned business is primarily concerned with family political power in a domestic setting, an ethics issue can arise when a person who is loyal to the family might be given preference in a hiring or promotion decision relative to a person who might be more objectively and more technically or economically qualified.

This chapter focuses on various types of business organization. What is constrained and optimized for government and nonprofit organizations can be very different. It proceeds as follows. First, the chapter analyzes and compares how key theorists from the time of Adam Smith, who analyze both ethics and business organizational forms, consider varieties of constrained optimization.

Six different types of constrained optimization are considered in more or less historical order. However, different regions of the world have adopted different forms of organization and constrained optimization at different times.

The six forms of constrained optimization considered here are:

(1) Smith's (1720–1790) small family business;
(2) Hegel's (1770–1831) and Marx's (1818–1883) oppressive large family-controlled business;
(3) Weber's (1906) large family-owned business 'ascetic reformers';

(4) Weber's (1920), Simon's (1945), and Chandler's (1977) professional, scientific, 'Managerial Capitalist' business;

(5) Friedman's (1962) and Jensen and Meckling's (1976) 'Investor Capitalist' business; and

(6) Postmodern simultaneous cooperative and competitive diversity.

Second, change processes through which varieties of constrained optimization evolve are analyzed.

Third, the epistemological question of how 'normative' organizational ethics questions and knowledge can be considered together with social and behavioral 'science' based organizational phenomena and knowledge is examined.

See Table 17.1 for a summary of the different perspectives, optimization criteria, epistemologies, and change processes.

Table 17.1 Perspectives on organization theory and ethics

Perspectives	Optimization criterion	Epistemology	Change process
Smith's small family business	family income	pragmatic experience and religious-spiritual	emergent micro competition
Hegel's and Marx's macro oppressive large family-controlled business	family wealth and power	emergent, joined community-based ethical efficiency	dialectic political-economic emergence
Large family-controlled business 'ascetic' reformers	organizational community development	pragmatic experience and religious-spiritual	micro, developmental social construction
Weber's, Simon's competitive Chandler's large, professional, scientific, 'managerial capitalist' business	rational, efficient social contract	modernist social science	rational efficiency
Friedman's and Jensen's 'investor capitalist' business	shareholder wealth	modernist economic science	competitive rational efficiency
Perhaps—emergent postmodern, cooperative, and competitive diversity	contested contingent, separate, diversity	kaleidoscopic	emergent and temporary power-based competition

17.1 Smith's (1720–1790) Small Family Business

17.1.1 Constrained Optimization

As referred to above, at least as far back as Adam Smith (1720–1790), ethics has been a key part of theories about organizational phenomena. Smith's two books, *Theory of Moral Sentiments* (1759) and *An Inquiry into the Nature and Causes of the Wealth of Nations* (1776), are very much concerned with ethics and organizations.

Smith (1776: 81) was primarily concerned with small family businesses that characterized the business economy of eighteenth-century England. Smith was quite skeptical about the large state-chartered colonial trading organizations that were given local colonial monopolies by the British governments, shared revenues with the British governments, and claimed to be operating in the public interest.

For Smith, a small family business owner-manager should optimize 'self-interest' as constrained by a 'self-interest that does not hurt my neighbor'. Within Smith's framework, what is optimized and what is constrained? For Smith, there is, for the most part, no agency issue between owner and manager, since the owner is in most cases the manager and his own agent. Smith did recognize that the agency problem does exist when the owner and master are different.

Relevant constituencies for Smith include competitors, customers, employees, and the general society. What is optimized is the owner-manager's self-interest. What is constrained is a 'self-interest that does not hurt my neighbor.'

James and Rassekh (2000) and Viner (1968 1991) interpret this part of Smith's organizational ethics as a 'negative virtue' in the sense that it is about not hurting others. That is, for Smith it is appropriate for the owner-manager to optimize his self-interest as long as it does not unfairly hurt one's competitors, customers, employees, or the general society. For Smith using an athletic competition analogy, it is appropriate to win with respect to one's competition by providing better and/or more efficient goods and services, but not to violate current ethical norms in the way one competes with one's competitors.

17.1.2 Epistemology

With respect to epistemology, how does Smith know whether his conclusions about ethics and organizations are true? In part, Smith's approach is inductive and philosophically pragmatic. That is, he observes that the business owner-managers who behave as 'self-interest that does not hurt my neighbor' and in the absence of non-market government preferences to competitors, are empirically more economically successful and benefit society more than those owner-managers who either claim to be acting in the public interest or who do 'hurt my neighbor'. In a sense, Smith takes a philosophically pragmatist approach to organizations and ethics. He interprets principle–behavior links by their effects. Since the effects are good, the principle of 'self-interest that does not hurt my neighbor' is both good and empirically true with respect to its good effects.

However, Smith also seems to think this principle is true for religious reasons. For example, Baumol (1978: 117) suggests that for Smith the 'invisible hand' of the market is 'an instrument of Deity designed to curb the frailty of humanity. It is a devise adopted by a very practical Providence to deal with the unfortunate but very common weakness of human character.' That is and if Baumol's interpretation of Smith is correct, Smith also knows that his principle is true from some form of almost mystical religious insight. Smith's epistemology appears to be both empirically and philosophically pragmatic and religious.

17.1.3 Change Processes

Within Smith's framework, change occurs in at least two ways. Those family-owned business organizations that operate according to a 'self-interest that does not hurt my neighbor' will succeed in market competition. Customers will prefer such organizations relative to organizations that do 'hurt my neighbor'. In addition, suppliers and other business organizations will prefer to do business with organizations that do not hurt them. In more modern terminology, business organizations will prefer to do business with organizations that engage in win–win practices and relationships relative to organizations that hurt them by engaging in win–lose practices.

Smith also recognized that government through political preferences can interfere with a market place that favors organizations that operate according to an efficient 'self-interest that does not hurt my neighbor'. Governments can give such preferences either because they are misguided in their thinking about 'public interest' independent of a 'self-interest that does not hurt my neighbor'. Smith also recognized that governments can give such preferences for corruption reasons.

17.2 HEGEL'S (1770–1831) AND MARX'S (1818–1883) OPPRESSIVE LARGE FAMILY-CONTROLLED BUSINESS

17.2.1 Constrained Optimization

Hegel, Marx, Josephson, and current observers of 'crony capitalism' perceived and perceive a different world than the one Adam Smith saw or hoped for. The latter observers saw much more a feudal-like systematic exploitation by large family-owned businesses, particularly large family-owned banks, allied with powerful feudal-like large landowner, military, and church interests, what Weber termed 'notables'.

Where Smith saw small family businesses and the English economy prospering because of small businesses that acted in their own self-interest, but constrained by a 'self-interest that does not hurt my neighbor', Hegel saw a culture and political-economy of repression and oppression, of 'lordship and bondage'. In the world that Hegel observed most closely in the Germanic states such as Prussia and Austria, he did not see much of a small business based market with an 'invisible hand'. For Hegel, the 'hand' was very visible, brutal, and oppressive. The large landowners, the military, and the church in economic, cultural, and political alliance with large family businesses, particularly large family-owned banks, dominated the political-economy and both the middle and lower socio-economic classes.

Marx essentially agrees with Hegel's observations to this point. According to Bernstein (1971: 33), 'It is as if Marx were saying to Hegel, "Yes, you are right . . . but with your System, that task is now completed. . . . Now the point is to change the world."'

Marx (1887) saw the industrial conditions of 1860 as even worse than the terrible conditions that Smith portrayed in 1776. While Smith believed and hoped that industrial conditions would greatly improve after his 1776 portrait, Marx found that, instead, conditions had gotten worse.

For Hegel and Marx, in the historical moment of oppression, there was very little constraint to the optimization of the self-interest of capitalists in feudal alliance with large landowners, the military, and the church in their joint oppression of the lower and middle socio-economic classes. Josephson (1934) and current observers of 'crony capitalism' make similar observations about the oppression of the lower and middle socio-economic classes by feudal-like alliances among dominant polit-ical party controlled corruption networks, militaries, and large family-owned businesses who cooperate with the corruption networks. However, as discussed in the next section, there have been and are very important large family-owned business reformers who have been and are very effective in changing these feudal-like 'crony capitalist' corruption networks.

With respect to the 'crony capitalism' that the reformers are trying to change, in many emerging markets, the political economies are in a sense more 'feudal', corruption network controlled and 'crony capitalist' than either socialist, social democratic, 'managerial capitalist', or 'investor capitalist' (Myrdal 1968; Lindblom 1977; Oppenheimer 1996; Nielsen 1996, 2000; Biggart 1998; *The Economist* 2002; Bellman 1999). That is, there are relatively few families within and with links to the major political parties, the military, the major family-owned businesses, the media, and the government that control the country's political economy. These families are immensely wealthy and powerful oligarchies.

17.2.2 Epistemology

Marx was very much concerned about the epistemological issue of the relationship between 'normative' ethics and social 'scientific' theory. As a young man at the age of 19 writing to his father, Marx wrote, 'I was greatly disturbed by the conflict between what is and what ought to be.' According to Bernstein (1971: 72), 'What Marx found in Hegel is an attempt, indeed the most ambitious attempt in post-Kantian philosophy, to overcome the dichotomy of the "is" and the "ought."'

Marx also moves through three evolving periods with respect to his view of this issue. In the first period of Marx's youth, he seems to believe that ethics and social science are separate and different, but that normative ethics can and should guide how we scientifically and socially construct a better and more ethical world. In a second period that might be characterized by the view expressed in the 'Communist Manifesto', ethics is referred to as ideological illusion and irrelevant to social scientific construction. In Marx's third period as seen in the 'German Ideology' and 'The Critique of the Gotha Program', Marx appears to think that there can be a transcendence beyond the distinction between 'normative ethics' and social 'science'.

Kain (1998: 179) compares the latter Marx's ethics with that of Aristotle. 'When Aristotle says that between friends justice is unnecessary, he is talking, I think, about transcending justice without rejecting it.... He holds that friendship is a truer and higher form of justice, and that friendship is more important than ordinary justice in holding a community together.' That is, if a real organizational or political-economic community were to emerge from the dialectic transformation of the feudal-like, large family-owned business based capitalist society, it would be a community of friends where need-based ethical behavior would be as natural as it sometimes is among real friends.

17.2.3 Change Processes

Hegel and Marx used the language and metaphors of 'lordship and bondage' and 'master and servant' to describe relationships within organizations between owner-manager and worker and within society between upper classes and lower classes. In Hegel's 'Lordship and Bondage', the lord or master tries to optimize himself by dominating the bondsman or servant-worker (Bernstein 1971: 25).

For both Hegel and Marx, these 'lordship and bondage' relationships are unethical, destructive, internally contradictory, and unstable. In addition and potentially, the internal contradictions may be able to stimulate transformation to more ethical organizational and social communities.

How does this dialectic change and transformation occur? Bernstein (1971: 20) explains:

There has been a lot of loose talk about Hegel's dialectic being a movement from thesis to antithesis to synthesis. Not only do these concepts play an insignificant role in Hegel's philosophy, they are essentially static concepts and completely misrepresent what Hegel means by 'dialectic.' The dialectic...is essentially a dynamic and organic process. One 'moment' of a dialectical process, when it is fully developed or understood gives rise to its own negation; it is not mechanically confronted by an antithesis. The process here is more like that of a tragedy where the 'fall' of the tragic hero emerges from the dynamics of the development of his own character.

According to Bernstein (1971: 27). 'This is the dialectical movement by which the master's project ends in failure.... Ironically (or dialectically) it is precisely out of and because of his labor which initially was labor for another (the master) that the slave comes to the realization of his own self-existence and freedom... this abstract freedom is the seed out of which concrete freedom will emerge.'

This is a key moment where Marx tries to build upon Hegel's dialectic change process. That is, Marx views the role of the change agent as helping the 'bondsman' understand this moment in Hegel's dialectic. Bernstein (1971: 49) explains:

We recall that in Hegel's dialectic of master and slave, there is a moment when the slave sees his reality and essential nature as being a slave for a master. This is one of the major reasons why Marx is sharply critical of those who think that amelioration of the basic frustrations of the working class gets at the political and economic roots of alienation. On the contrary, the chief task of revolutionary leaders, 'the educators who must be educated,' is to foster and develop the consciousness of the basic alienated condition of the exploited.

How and where will this technology facilitated, dialectic change process end? According to Kain (1998: 188), 'Much as for Aristotle and the ancient world, the highest end, for Marx, is the full realization of individuals as ends in themselves. In *Capital*, Marx speaks of creating the material conditions.... He also speaks of shortening the work day so as to create a realm of leisure time in which "begins the development of human energy which is an end in itself, the true realm of freedom."' Marx is somewhat specific about some elements that he hopes and expects will emerge from this dialectic change process. For example, Marx anticipates emergent organizational and social communities of friendship, technology boosted productivity that permits ample leisure and needs satisfaction, and, common control of production. Nonetheless, Marx is more concerned with emergent dialectic action and learning processes. Marx is more sure that change occurs through dialectic action-learning than he is about the specific times that these changes will emerge and even the specific historical stages through which they will progress.

17.3 LARGE FAMILY-CONTROLLED BUSINESS 'ASCETIC REFORMERS'

17.3.1 Constrained Optimization

Many of the owners of large family businesses in the eighteenth, nineteenth, and early twentieth centuries and today in emerging market countries saw and see many of the same unethical, abusive, oppressive, and destructive business conditions and practices that Smith and Marx wrote and theorized about. Some of these large family business owners were and are important reformers.

Today, the potential reformer role of large family business owners in emerging markets can be particularly important. In developed, mature market countries, large family-owned businesses were for the most part replaced by 'managerial capitalist' corporations where the organizations are managed by professional managers, ownership of the corporation is spread among thousands of individual investors and institutional investors, and family members have for the most part withdrawn from the management of the business.

Unlike Marx, many of these eighteenth-, nineteenth-, and early twentieth-century large family-owned business reformers did think that 'amelioration' and reform of the basic frustrations of industrial society could get at the fundamental roots of problems. Unlike Smith, the reformers thought that it would take the visible hand of the large family business owner-manager to help solve the fundamental ethical and social problems of industrial society.

Often motivated by ascetic religious and ethical reasons (Weber 1906), these ascetic reformers believed that they could optimize community welfare by reasonably satisfying the needs of multiple constituencies such as owners, employees, customers, suppliers, competitors, and community. They saw relatively little conflict between optimizing their own welfare with the welfare of their various constituencies. In a sense, these reformers were precursors of the 'win–win social contract' of 'managerial capitalism' and 'welfare capitalism' that optimized organizational efficiency and development as constrained by the needs of organizational constituencies.

Edward Cadbury, a company personnel managing director in 1912 and a family owner, summarized this view as follows. 'The supreme principle has been the belief that business efficiency and the welfare of the employees are but different sides of the same problem.... The test of any scheme of factory organization is the extent to which it creates and fosters the atmosphere and spirit of cooperation and good will, without in any sense lessening the loyalty of the worker to his own class and organizations' (1912: p. xvii).

For such large family-owned business reformers, this is different than Adam Smith's 'self-interest that does not harm my neighbor'. It is more a positive than a negative virtue approach. What is optimized is the organization's efficiency and competitive edge. However, the reason for maintaining the efficiency and competitive edge is both ascetic and to positively satisfy the needs of the organization's various constituencies.

This is not quite the same as 'welfare capitalism' (Cochran and Miller 1942) or Drucker's managerial capitalist (1980) 'enlightened self-interest' and 'optimal satisficing'. That is, it is not quite the view of this type of reformer that the way to optimize one's self-interest is to reasonably satisfy the needs of constituencies. Instead, from the perspective of this type of reformer, the way to optimize our common and community interest is to maintain the economic viability of the organization while simultaneously reasonably satisfying the needs of all constituencies, but not at the expense of the economic viability of the organization, since the organization makes it possible to satisfy our common good.

17.3.2 Epistemology

How did the large family-owned business reformers know that acting ethically to try to reform the problems of industrial civilization would also improve the competitive edge of their businesses and derivatively improve the needs satisfaction of all constituencies?

In Europe and the Americas, a large part of this type of business reformer's epistemology was religious and ascetic, but also combined with something of a philosophically pragmatist perspective. Examples of combined religiously and pragmatically informed large family-owned business reformers from this early nineteenth century time are Barclays, Cadburys, Hersey, Johnson, Lever Brothers, Lloyds, Palmers, Price-Waterhouse, Roundtree, Wharton, etc.

On the pragmatist side, George Cadbury explains that, 'I never looked at the small people who had failed. I fixed my eye on those who had won the greatest success. It was no use studying failure. I wanted to know how men succeeded and it was their methods I examined and, if I thought them good, applied, (Gardiner 1923: 24). By 'good' he meant simultaneously efficient and ethical or at least not unethical.

On the ascetic religious side, Gardiner (1923: 24) describes the perspective of George Cadbury in 1850.

His ideas … were simple but fundamental. Work, and again work, and always work; to pay his way as he went; to contract no liability he could not meet; to win a reputation for honest dealing which should make the name a hallmark; to take care of the detail and let the total take care of itself; to gather round him happy, contented workpeople; to bring his faith into his affairs – these were the springs of his action.

Gardiner (1923: p. vi) further contrasts the perspective of George Cadbury with that of Andrew Carnegie.

In George Cadbury the two motives (religious and economic) were so interwoven as to form a single strand of purpose. It was a superficial view which saw in him a remarkable example of dual personality, such as that, for instance of Andrew Carnegie. The ruthless ironmaster (Carnegie) and the Friend of Man (Cadbury) lived concurrent lives, but they live them on different planes. … To him … the only true wealth of a nation was in the life of its people, and if that life was perishing in sunless slums and fetid hovels the country was doomed even though forests of mill chimneys spread up above every valley and plain.

17.3.3 Change Processes

As referred to above, the large family-owned business reformers while they believed in 'the invisible hand', the efficiency of markets, and negative virtue of Adam Smith, they also believed that visible hands did and could operate for better and/or for worse. That is, they believed in owner-manager discretion and power to maintain and make worse the problems of industrial society and/or to make things better and more ethical and more socially just. They believed that they could influence social conditions both within their own organizations and within markets.

Their methods combined efficiency with social welfare. That is, they simultaneously adopted more efficient methods to improve productivity while simultaneously improving working and social conditions.

In addition to working individually within their own organizations and society, many of these reformers also established networks of political consciousness raising, institution building, and lobbying for social reforms. For example, in England, the 'Conference of Employers', a group of family-owned business reformers, developed dialogs and lobbying efforts on behalf of minimum wages, participate decision-making works councils, working conditions, security of employment, and even what to do with 'surplus profits' (Hodgkin 1918).

17.4 WEBER'S (1920), SIMON'S (1945), AND CHANDLER'S (1977) PROFESSIONAL, SCIENTIFIC, 'MANAGERIAL CAPITALIST' BUSINESS

17.4.1 Constrained Optimization

While Weber was certainly a critic of the 'Iron Cage' of bureaucratic rationality, he also recognized it as an improvement over the feudal-like industrial abuses that Smith, Marx, and the large family-owned business reformers observed and objected to. In Weber's Germany, bureaucracy that was more or less independent of who Weber termed 'the notables', that is, the arbitrary power of the royalty, the military, the large landowners, and the large family-owned banking and industrial businesses aligned with the older power groups, emerged relatively recently.

In modernist bureaucracy, efficient rationality is optimized as constrained by the reasonable, and win–win, satisfaction of legitimate constituencies' needs. Rationality has to do with the efficient optimization of the reason for being of an organization rather than subservience to the arbitrary power of such groups as the royalty, the military, the large landowners, and the wealthy business families.

Three key elements characterized Weber's 'ideal-type' bureaucracy: (1) professional, trained, and expert managers and administrators make decisions rather than ('the notables'), i.e. the wealthy families, the military, or political party officials; (2) these professional managers optimize the rational functionality of the reason for being of the organization, e.g. efficient transportation; (3) these professional managers are constrained by rational rules concerning both efficient optimization and rational treatment of employees, customers, citizens, and owners.

With respect to business organizations, the shareholder wealth of owners is not optimized, it is reasonably satisfied. Financial return to owners is considered more of a constraint than something to be optimized.

Part of expert based, industrial engineering rationality meant treating employees as well as machines. That is, if it made sense to keep machines in good health and not burn them out, it also made sense to keep employees in good health-maintenance. In addition, expertness and skill were considered valuable and were rewarded. Both professional managers and skilled employees were rewarded for their knowledge-based work. Professional managers optimized the rational efficiency of the functional reason for being of the organization as constrained by the reasonable needs of the public-customers, employees, and owners.

As referred to above, Weber was troubled when bureaucracy was corrupted by powerful special interests, but he was also troubled when bureaucracy operated in its ideal rational, efficient sense. Weber (1906/1958: 181) recognized that there was an 'iron cage' of bureaucratic rationality. That is, Weber saw that the voluntary ascetic efficiency of the religion-based, large family-owned business reformers, when and if it was required by a 'machine' bureaucracy, could and would have some very negative effects.

Weber (1906/1958: 154, 179, 181–2) explains, 'This rationalization of conduct within this world...was the consequence of the concept of calling of ascetic Protestantism.... *The Puritan wanted to work in a calling; we are forced to do so*....the case for external goods should only lie on the shoulders of the "saint like a light cloak, which can be thrown aside at any moment." But fate decreed that the cloak should become an *iron cage*.'

For Weber, administrative efficiency as method became what he referred to as an 'iron cage'. That is, ascetic, efficient method was to a large extent separated from the reason for being of organizations. Ascetic, efficient method became an end in itself.

Herbert Simon in his foundational for organization studies, 1945 book, *Administrative Behavior*, in a sense, defends this separation of ends and means. Simon (1945/1976: 48) explains: 'Hence, there is one sense in which the correctness of his [the administrator's] decision can be judged: it is a purely factual question whether the measures he takes in order to accomplish his aim are appropriate measures. It is not a factual question whether the aim itself is correct or not, except in so far as this aim is connected, by an "in order," to further aims.' For Simon, the subject of administrative science and organization studies was much more focused on the efficiency of 'in order' utilitarian, instrumental means than the ethical appropriateness of ends. That is, the subject of administrative and organizational rationality is essentially separate from the ethical consideration of ends.

Simon recognizes that this is a significant departure from the Aristotelian practical wisdom that considers 'phronesis', practical wisdom, a necessary combination of effective and efficient method with ethical ends. For Aristotle, means and ends are different moments of one process that need to be considered together.

Simon disagrees. According to Simon (1945/1976: 470), it may be possible 'to derive the conclusion that people will be happier under one set of circumstances than under another, but this does not prove that they ought to be happier. The Aristotelian definition – that something is good for man which makes him correspond more closely with his essential nature as a rational animal – suffers from the same limitation.'

Tsoukas and Cummings (1997) further extend this Aristotelian criticism of the separation of ethical organizational ends from instrumental means. Tsoukas and Cummings (1997: 668) explain:

Simon (1976, p. 250) has persistently argued that, in administrative science, unless we keep facts uncontaminated by values we risk not being scientific.... Within such a dualistic way of thinking we have to choose: either we follow the canons of the scientific discourse and thus accumulate factual statements but stay mute on important questions concerning end purposes and values; or we comprehend ourselves as moral creatures only and, thus, become unwilling to be concerned with the empirical regularities of the world. This is certainly a problematic situation to be in.

The economic and business historian, Alfred Chandler (1977), observed phenomena similar to Weber's expert administered, rational bureaucracy which Chandler referred to as 'The Visible Hand' of 'Managerial Capitalism'. Chandler (1977: 1) explains:

The theme propounded here is that modern business enterprise took the place of market mechanisms in coordinating the activities of the economy and allocating its resources. In many sectors of the economy the visible hand of management replaced what Adam Smith referred to as the invisible hand of market forces.... The rise of modern business enterprise in the United States, therefore, brought with it managerial capitalism.

As in Weber's professional bureaucratic organization, in Chandler's managerial capitalist organization, the rational functionality of the organization is optimized. That is, instead of optimizing profitability for owners, the rational development of the organization is optimized. Financial return to owners and other constituencies such as employees is constrained and reasonably satisfied. Professional managers optimized the long-term development of the organization as constrained by the reasonable needs satisfaction of its constituencies. Conflict with shareholders over this optimization of organizational development instead of shareholder wealth led to another form of constrained optimization and capitalism that is discussed in the next section, 'investor capitalism'.

17.4.2 Epistemology

The origins of Weber's bureaucratic ethics epistemology came from the religious asceticism of large family-owned business reformers. Weber observed that relatively soon thereafter, such efficiency-seeking ascetic ethics became competitively very successful, secularized, and inexorably linked to the nature of efficient, competitive, machine bureaucracy. That is, the ascetic ethics of efficiency, deferred gratification, meritocracy, and social security came to dominate bureaucratic organization and society. This type of ascetic, efficiency ethics was considered in a pragmatist sense to be experimentally valid. That is, those organizations that practised this type of ascetic, efficiency ethics were more successful than those that did not, thus justifying the ethics.

This ethics was a form of utilitarianism. The benefits of rational, efficient, meritocracy were considered to outweigh its costs. The utilitarian benefits included treating, for example, workers as well as machines with respect to rest, health, safety, and adequate income.

The meritocracy called for sharing the rewards of efficiency with those who helped produce it. What was once voluntary social contract sharing of profitability by the large family-owned business reformers with respect to pensions, health care, education, rising incomes, job security, etc. became characteristic of ascetic, machine bureaucracy.

Part of the extension from the voluntary to the required social contract was based on a religious sense of sharing the rewards from efficiency. Another part of the extension to such required social contract was the industrial engineering view that it was also efficient and productive to do so. That is, the social contract benefits were considered as conducive to further economic efficiency. Social security and performance-based rewards were considered efficient and productive.

Nonetheless, Weber was very concerned with the costs in this dominant utilitarian calculation. Weber (1906/1958: 182) characterized this system of required ascetic rationality as inexorably producing 'Specialists without spirit, sensualists without heart; this nullity imagines that it has attained a level of civilization never before achieved.'

17.4.3 Change Processes

For both Weber and Chandler, rational, efficient bureaucracy and efficient managerial capitalism emerged because they were competitively more efficient than their predecessor types of organization. For Weber, the origin of this type of organization was perhaps both accidental and experimental. As a result of or at least concomitant with the rise and relative success of the ascetic, large family business reformers who succeeded against their less efficient competitors, there emerged efficient, rational bureaucratic organizations. For Weber, once these new types of organizations emerged, they took on something of a life of their own. This system of organization was more competitive than the former alternatives. They grew to dominate in spite of the political opposition of the old oligarchies but not without some accommodation to those oligarchies.

Similarly for Chandler, managerial capitalist organizations emerged and essentially replaced the older forms of business organization because they were more efficient than the older forms. For example, the experiment of the managerial capitalist General Motors proved more efficient than the large family-owned and managed Ford Motors. General Motors gained market share and Ford had to imitate the efficiency of General Motors in order to survive.

While both Weber and Chandler recognized the political processes involved in this change, Drucker (1980) emphasized the more or less win–win, political process of this change. Weber and Chandler concentrated more on the rational, efficiency aspect of the change.

Drucker (1980: 211–13), interpreting Herbert Simon's (1945/1976) concept of 'optimal satisficing' explains, 'When it comes to the performance of the primary task of an institution . . . the rule is to optimize. . . . But in dealing with the constituencies outside and beyond this narrow definition of the primary task, managers have to think politically—in terms of the minimum needed to placate and appease and keep quiet constituent groups that otherwise might use their power of veto.'

17.5 FRIEDMAN'S (1962), JENSEN AND MECKLING'S (1976), AND USEEM'S (1996) 'INVESTOR CAPITALIST' BUSINESS

17.5.1 Constrained Optimization

The dominant form of capitalism and business organization in the United States today is 'Investor Capitalism'. It is also spreading rapidly around the world. What is investor capitalism? Useem (1998: 1–11) explains,

If the principles of family capitalism dominated industrialization at the turn of the century, and if the concepts of managerial capitalism rose to dominance by mid-century, the new rules of investor capitalism are coming to prevail by century's end. . . . Managerial capitalism tolerated a host of company objectives besides shareholder value. Investor capitalism does not. . . . The developing relationships between investors and managers resemble neither markets nor organizations. Rather, they are emerging as enduring networks, a lattice of informal ties that come to guide a continuous two-way exchange of information and exercise of influence. . . . Now, when a large investor is dissatisfied with a company's top management, it often retains much of the holding but presses for improved performance. If results are not forthcoming, it lobbies the directors, votes against management, or even seeks new management—as the executives of the Bank of Boston, Kmart, Morrison Knudsen, Philip Morris, and W. R. Grace learned to their dismay.

One of the first to recognize the seriousness of this structural conflict between shareholders and professional managers was the Nobel Prize winning economist Milton Friedman (1962). Friedman addressed the issues in terms of the conflict between optimizing shareholder value vs. managerial discretion with respect to satisfying the needs of other constituencies. Friedman, who is often considered a rather direct ideological descendant of Smith, shares much of Smith's perspective (James and Rassekh 2000), makes extensions with respect to modern economic contexts, but with at least two exceptions.

For example, in an extension of Smith's negative virtue of 'not harming my neighbor', Friedman extends the concept of 'nor harming my neighbor' to environmental issues. Friedman (1962: 30) explains that 'the man who pollutes a stream is in effect forcing others to exchange good water for bad.'

With respect to some key differences between Smith and Friedman, unlike Smith and since the modern economic conditions are different from the small family business environment of Smith's time, Friedman is very concerned with the ethics and agency issue and potential conflict of interest between shareholders and managers which emerged with the development of large family businesses and large public equity financed corporations.

With respect to the ethics and agency issue and potential conflict of interest between owners and managers and the potential conflict of interest between owners, managers, and other constituencies, Friedman (1970: 33) explains that: 'the corporate executive would be spending someone else's money for a general social interest. Insofar as his action in accord with his 'social responsibility' reduces returns to stockholders, he is spending their money. Insofar as his actions raise the price to customers, he is spending the customer's money. Insofar as his action lower the wages of some employees, he is spending their money.' However, if the 'insofar' were, for example, to benefit owners indirectly through some positive public relations effect, presumably, Friedman would perceive at least a reduced conflict of interest. In addition, Friedman does not indicate that he shares Smith's religious interpretations of a 'visible hand' in relation to a 'deity' or a 'divine providence'.

Within the field of corporate finance, Jensen and Meckling (1976) extend Friedman's criticism and suggest that the theory of the firm had to be restructured from a managerial capitalist perspective to an agency costs based, shareholder wealth optimization theory of the firm.

Jensen and Meckling argue that the objective function of the firm has been improperly restructured under managerial capitalism. That is, Jensen and Meckling argue that in the objective function of the firm, shareholder wealth should be the primary, optimizing criterion variable rather than managerial welfare, organizational welfare, or constituencies' welfare. In their analysis, managers are the agents of the shareholders and they should act in the interest of optimizing shareholder wealth.

This type of investor capitalist organization appears to be spreading rapidly around the world. Even after the 1998 European elections, which for the most part elected social democratic governments, the growth of investor capitalism proceeds. Similarly, in Japan, East Asia, and Latin America, the growth of the investor capitalist form of organization is increasing (Useem 1996; Tagliabue 1998; Baker and Smith 1999; *The Economist* 2000).

17.5.2 Epistemology

Ethics in the investor capitalist form of business organization appears to be focused relatively narrowly on the contract theory of property rights (Alchian 1968; Ross 1973; Jensen and Meckling 1976). For example, Jensen and Meckling explain (1976: 307–8),

We focus...on the...property rights specified in the contracts between the owners and managers of the firm.... Since the relationship between the stockholders and manager of a corporation fit the definition of a pure agency relationship it should be no surprise to discover that the issues associated with the 'separation of ownership and control' in the modern diffuse ownership corporation are intimately associated with the general problem of agency.... The problem of inducing an 'agent' to behave as if he were maximizing the 'principal's' welfare is quite general. It exists in all organizations and in all cooperative efforts—at every level of management in firms.

17.5.3 Change Processes

The interest of the shareholder group is relatively narrowly defined as shareholder wealth. It is normally measured in pecuniary, monetary terms. Similarly, the solution to the agency cost problem between shareholders and managers is usually considered in terms of tightly aligning shareholder financial interests with the financial interests of managers. That is, managerial compensation is tightly aligned with stock market performance and profitability. The primary change process is financial alignment of the interests of owners and managers.

As a result of investor capitalism, there have also been changes in emphasis among the various parts of the human resources management and organizational development mixes within organizations. For example, within managerial capitalism there was a relative balance among recruiting, training and development, employee relations, career development, compensation and benefit strategies.

Within investor capitalist organizations, the primary change method is compensation rewards and penalties (Ulrich 1997). For example, if managers meet their financial objectives they are very well compensated in bonuses and stock options. However, if they do not meet their numbers one year, they may be given a second year, but if the financial objectives are not then met, either the manager or the strategic business unit has to go.

Concurrent with this relatively dramatic shift to compensation as the primary strategy for motivating change and performance of upper and middle level managers, it is generally true that average income levels are rising across income groups. It is nonetheless also true that the income distribution of employees within investor capitalist organizations and investor capitalist societies such as the United States has become much more unequal (*The Economist* 1999a; *Business Week* 2000).

17.6 POSTMODERN SIMULTANEOUS COOPERATIVE AND COMPETITIVE DIVERSITY

17.6.1 Constrained Optimization

A criticism of the agency costs contract approach to the ethics of investor capitalism from the modernist ethics perspective of managerial capitalism is that even if investor capitalism is very successful in optimizing the wealth of shareholders and fulfilling a contractual agency cost relationship, there are other important relationships that need to be balanced. That is, from the modernist, managerial capitalist perspective, it is ethically better to balance the needs of multiple constituencies than it is to optimize the wealth of one constituency, shareholders (Bowie and Freeman 1992).

From a postmodern perspective, investor capitalism with its primary and optimizing concern for the shareholder wealth criterion for the most part ignores the legitimate needs of multiplicity and diversity of groups and their interests in the service of optimizing the need satisfaction of one priority group, shareholders. In a sense, this narrow focus on the interests of the shareholder group may provide a source of energy and motivation for the postmodern multiplicity perspective.

That is, since 'they', the powerful supporters of investor capitalism care only or primarily about shareholder interests, then 'we' and 'our' multiplicity groups are justified in not caring about 'their' interests and may express overtly or clandestinely primary loyalty not to the organization, but instead to my personal career, my portfolio, my ethic group, my gender group, my sexual preference group, etc. Perhaps it is no accident that both investor capitalism and postmodern perspectives may be reinforcing one another.

17.6.2 Epistemology

Postmodern perspective extends the criticism that both modernist managerial capitalism and investor capitalism artificially separate ends from means and values from facts. For example, the postmodern ethicist Bauman (1993) disagrees with Simon (1945/1976) and extends Weber's criticism that there are important problems with separating the study and practice of efficient method from ethical ends. Bauman (1993: 193) explains: 'As Max Weber told us, the world as conjured up by technology is a "dis-enchanted" world: a world without meaning of its own, without "intent", "purpose", "destination".... Modern science, in tune with the spirit of technological revolution, promptly produced the operative definition of being which forbade the use of value-related terms.' If only efficiency can be discussed in the relevant real world or modern organization and not ethical values, then efficiency becomes an end in itself without ethical content but nonetheless having unexamined ethical and unethical effects.

Tsoukas and Cummings (1997: 663) explain the postmodern Foucault's epistemology as follows:

Foucault (1966) approached the past as if it were a kaleidoscope containing a number of discrete fragments, not a collective and cumulative learning process: it reveals a pattern, but one largely shaped by contingencies. To move from one episteme (Foucault's neologism for, roughly, a particular period's matrix of thought-cum-practice) to another was to 'twist the kaleidoscope', and create a new pattern.... It is this tension between relevance and difference that enables us, late-modern (or post-modern) individuals, to creatively appropriate the insights of great thinkers from the distant past.

With respect to epistemology among diverse groups within an organization, this might mean that, at one moment, constituency and stakeholder groups can cooperate with the separated ends-means, efficiency-based epistemology of shareholder wealth optimization. Simultaneously and/or at another moment, diverse groups may competitively understand and do sensemaking through a lens of power-based biases and competition with shareholders and their aligned managerial agents.

Postmodernism may even be in some sort of codependent relationship with investor capitalism. Postmodern ethics emphasizes that there are multiple principals that need to be able to express agency for themselves. Further, postmodernists perceive that rules and contracts tend to have biases that favor more powerful groups relative to less powerful groups. Constituency and stakeholder groups are in some competition with one another. In addition, when new powerful groups replace old powerful groups, the biases are often changed rather than eliminated. That is, when the shareholder wealth group replaces the managerial capitalist group as the more powerful corporate governance group, biases are changed rather than eliminated.

Also as has been referred to above and perhaps paradoxically, as the emphasis on the priority shareholder wealth criterion has increased, it appears that identity consciousness of multiplicity and diversity has increased relative to identify with the work organization. That is, as financial alignment as the primary change motivation process within the investor capitalist organization has increased, so also has consciousness of one's identity separate from the organization increased. There appears to be simultaneously changes with respect to tighter alignment with the financial goals of organizations and greater separation of one's identity from the investor capitalist organization.

As one manager in a shareholder wealth optimization, driven downsizing at Procter & Gamble explains (Fraser 2001; Greenhouse 2001: 7), 'Employees feel less loyal to a company, companies feel less loyal to an employee. Attitudes have changed. I don't know anyone who feels anymore, "I love this place. I'm always going to be here." Before, it used to be, "I'm a Procter & Gamble person." Now, it's "I'm a Paul person," or whatever your name is.'

The old long-term social contract of bureaucratic and managerial capitalism appears to have changed. As referred to above, perhaps there is some codependency between investor capitalism and postmodern multiplicity. Perhaps the postmodern business organization will emerge as some combination of unenthusiastic cooperation with the financial shareholder wealth criterion, but with little loyalty or identity or long-lasting sense of relationship with the business organization.

17.7 CONCLUSION

There appears to have been both mutual informing and continuity among ethics and organization theory over the various periods and types of organization. Some things seem to have remained the same and some things seem to have changed. What seems to have remained more or less the same is that there is a continuing principle of constrained optimization operating across time periods and types of organization. What has changed is that what is optimized and what is constrained have differed greatly.

The different types of constrained optimization appear to be: Smith's small business based 'self-interest that does not harm my neighbor'; Hegel's, Marx's, and Josephson's large family-owned business that optimizes self-interest with relatively little constraint or concern for our neighbors; the ascetic, large family-owned business reformers who voluntarily optimized organizational efficiency and community welfare and derivatively the needs of the various shareholder, employee, community interests; Weber's bureaucracy, Simon's administrative science, and Chandler's managerial capitalism that found such functional efficiency competitively so very successful that it was systematized and institutionalized; the current 'investor capitalist' form of organization that is perhaps both a reversion to the self-interest of Smith's owner-manager without much of the concern for our neighbors; and, perhaps the codependent and emergent postmodern business organization that is simultaneously tightly coupled to the financial interests of shareholders and loosely coupled to the loyalty and identify of other organizational constituencies such as employees.

What has also changed are the epistemological foundations for organization ethics with respect to relationships between 'scientific' and 'normative' knowledge. For Smith, the ethics foundation appears to be both normatively religious and pragmatic with respect to tested competitive effectiveness.

For Hegel and Marx, the dialectic of 'lordship and bondage' was both scientifically accurate, self-contradictory, and unstable as well as normatively unethical. Marx resolves the distinction between the scientific and the normative through the expected and hoped for emergence of a communitarian society of Aristotelian friendship where it would be scientifically natural to allocate resources geometrically 'from each according to his ability to each according to his needs'.

The large family-owned ascetic business reformers based their ethics simultaneously on a scientific observation that ascetic functional efficiency was more competitive than exploitation and oppression. In addition, such organizational optimization with derivative concern for constituencies was also religiously normative.

Weber observed that such ascetic business reformers were politically effective in getting the state to protect the interests of efficiency from the self-interest of the 'notables' and the oligarchs. Weber also observed that such ascetic, functional rationality took on a life of its own in the sense that it competitively absorbed more and more of the political economy, but also became an involuntary 'iron cage' that was very narrowly focused relative to the wider range of humanistic interests. For Weber, his ethics epistemology appears to be primarily pragmatic. That is, he observed that acetic, functional rationality had religious origins, but apparently did not share those religious views. His perspective seems to be pragmatic in the sense that functional rationality, iron cage or no, operated more efficiently and less oppressively than oligarchy.

Similarly in Simon's (1945) 'administrative science' and Chandler's (1976) 'Invisible Hand' of 'Managerial Capitalism', there is a utilitarian calculus that the benefits of professional management that optimizes organizational development and derivatively the needs of multiple constituencies including owners, was more efficient than previous forms of business organization. Since 'managerial capitalism' was more efficient, it was both 'scientifically valid' and 'normatively' efficient. Since managerial capitalism derivatively also better satisfied the needs of multiple constituencies than other forms of business organization, that was a normatively good side-effect, but the primary and implicit ethical criterion was administrative and competitive efficiency.

In 'Investor Capitalism' we have something of a reversion to Smith's self-interest criterion but without much articulation of either the negative virtue of not harming one's neighbors or the positive virtues of caring for one's neighbors. Instead, there is the relatively narrow, property rights perspective of financial contract between shareholder owners and managers. In its origin in the literature, this optimization of shareholder wealth appears to be primarily normative in its theoretically articulated links to property rights and contracts. However, the argument is also made that is it 'scientifically' and pragmatically more efficient and productive than 'managerial capitalism'.

Concurrent with investor capitalism is the postmodern, pragmatic observation, if not 'scientific', perspective that rules and laws are based at least as much on power and the self-interest of powerful groups as they are on ethics. Nonetheless, there are group-specific, valid ethical concerns that emerge and are socially constructed from the discourse within diverse groups that are valid for those groups. The primacy of optimizing shareholder wealth as the reason for being of business organization is both in contradiction to the postmodern perspective of multiplicity, but is also at least partial justification for primary concern for ones 'base' group instead of the narrowly focused 'investor capitalist' organization.

Organizational theory and ethics are not only mutually informing and entangled historically, they may be codependent. That is, it may not be possible to have an operational organization theory without an at least implicit ethical understanding of that organizational form. Simultaneously, it may not be possible to actualize social ethics without organizational form.

REFERENCES

ALCHIAN, A. A. (1968). 'Corporate Management and Property Rights', in id., *Economic Policy and the Regulation of Securities*. Washington, DC: American Enterprise Institute.

BAKER, GEORGE, and SMITH, GEORGE (1999). *The New Financial Capitalists*. Cambridge: Cambridge University Press.

BAUMAN, ZYGMUNT (1993). *Postmodern Ethics*. Oxford: Blackwell Publishers.

BAUMOL, W. J. (1978). 'Smith versus Marx on Business Morality and the Social Interest,' in E. Glahe (ed.), *Adam Smith and the Wealth of Nations, 1776–1996 Bicentennial Essay*. Boulder, Colo.: Colorado Associated University Press.

BELLMAN, ERIC (1999). 'Asian Companies Find Value in Disclosure'. *Wall Street Journal*, Dec. 27: C14–C15.

BERNSTEIN, RICHARD J. (1971). *Praxis and Action*. Philadelphia: University of Pennsylvania Press.

BIGGART, NICOLE WOOLSEY (1998). 'Deep Finance: The Organizational Bases of South Korea's Financial Collapse'. *Journal of Management Inquiry*, 7/4: 311–20.

BIRGER, JON (2000). 'Glowing Numbers'. *Money*, Nov.: 112–22.

BOWIE, NORMAN E., and FREEMAN, R. EDWARD (1992). *Ethics and Agency Theory*. New York: Oxford University Press.

Business Week (2000). 'How Prosperity is Reshaping the American Economy', Feb. 14: 100–9.

CADBURY, E. (1912). *Experiments in Industrial Organization*. London: Longman, Green.

CHANDLER, ALFRED D. (1977). *The Visible Hand: The Managerial Revolution in American Business*. Cambridge, Mass.: Harvard University Press.

COCHRAN, THOMAS C., and MILLER, WILLIAM (1942/1961). *The Age of Enterprise*. New York: Harper.

Conference of Employers (1918). *Report*. Darlington: North of England Newspaper Co.

CYERT, RICHARD M., and MARCH, JAMES G. (1963). *A Behavioral Theory of the Firm*. Englewood Cliffs, NJ: Prentice-Hall, Inc.

DRUCKER, PETER F. (1980). *Managing in Turbulent Times*. New York: Harper & Row.

The Economist (1998). 'Frozen Miracle: A Survey of East Asian Economies', Mar. 7: 1–18.

—— (1999*a*). 'Cutting the Cookie, and the Rich Get Richer'. Sept. 11: 26.

—— (1999*b*). 'Scourge of the Chaebol'. Mar. 27: 68.

—— (2000). 'The End of Tycoons: A New Generation, a New Economy, and a New Capitalism are Changing the Way in which Business is Done in East Asia'. Apr. 29: 67–9.

—— (2002). 'The Lessons from Enron'. Feb. 9: 9–10.

FRASER, JILL ANDRESKY (2001). *White-Collar Sweatshop: The Deterioration of Work and Its Rewards in Corporate America*. New York: Norton.

FRIEDMAN, M. (1962). *Capitalism and Freedom*. Chicago: University of Chicago Press.

—— (1970). 'The Social Responsibility of Business is to Increase its Profits'. *New York Times Magazine*, Sept. 13.

GARDINER, A. G. (1923). *Life of George Cadbury*. London: Cassell and Co.

GARDNER, HOWARD (1995). *Leading Minds*. New York: Basic Books.

GREENHOUSE, STEVEN (2001). 'After the Downswing, a Downward Spiral'. *New York Times*, Apr. 8: BU7.

HEGEL, GEORG W. F. (1949). *The Phenomenology of Mind*. London: George Allen & Unwin.

—— (1953). *Reason in History: A General Introduction to the Philosophy of History*. New York: Liberal Arts Press.

HODGKIN, J. E. (1918). *Quakerism and Industry*. Darlington: North of England Newspaper Co., Ltd., Priestgate.

JAMES, HARVEY S., and RASSEKH, FARHAD (2000). 'Smith, Friedman, and Self-Interest in Ethical Society'. *Business Ethics Quarterly*, 10/3: 659–74.

JENSEN, M. C., and MECKLING, W. H. (1976). 'Theory of the Firm: Managerial Behavior, Agency Costs and Ownership Structure'. *Journal of Financial Economics*, 3: 305–60.

JOSEPHSON, MATTHEW (1934). *The Robber Barons*. New York: Harcourt, Brace & Co.

KAIN, PHILIP J. (1998). *Marx and Ethics*. Oxford: Clarendon Press.

KANE, E. J. (1993). 'What Lessons Should Japan Learn from the U.S. Deposit-Insurance Mess?' *Journal of the Japanese and International Economies,* 7: 329–55.

KLITGAARD, R. (1983). *Corruption in Mexico.* Cambridge, Mass.: Kennedy School of Government, Harvard University.

—— (1985). *Choosing Elites.* New York: Basic Books.

—— (1988). *Controlling Corruption.* Berkeley: University of California Press.

LINDBLOM, C. E. (1977). *Politics and Markets: The World's Political Economic Systems.* New York: Basic Books.

McGREGOR, DOUGLAS (1960/1985). *The Human Side of Enterprise.* New York: McGraw-Hill.

MARX, K. (1887). *Capital: A Critical Analysis of Capitalist Production.* Moscow: Foreign Languages Publishing House.

—— (1978). 'Critique of the Gotha Program', in *The Marx–Engels Reader,* ed. Lewis S. Feuer. New York: Norton.

MAYO, ELTON (1938). *The Human Problems of an Industrial Civilization.* New York: Macmillan Company.

MYRDAL, GUNNAR (1968). *Asian Drama: An Inquiry into the Poverty of Nations.* New York: Pantheon.

NIELSEN, RICHARD P. (1996). *The Politics of Ethics: Methods for Acting, Learning, and Sometimes Fighting, with Others in Addressing Ethics Problems in Organizational Life.* New York: Oxford University Press, The Ruffin Series in Business Ethics.

—— (2000). 'The Politics of Long Term Corruption Reform: A Combined Social Movement and Action-Learning Perspective'. *Business Ethics Quarterly,* 10/1: 305–18.

—— and BARTUNEK, JEAN B. (1996). 'Opening Narrow, Routinized Schemata to Ethical Stakeholder Consciousness and Action'. *Business and Society,* 35/4: Dec. 483–519.

NOONAN, J. T. (1984). *Bribes.* New York: Macmillan.

OPPENHEIMER, A. (1996). *Bordering on Chaos: Guerrillas, Stockbrokers, Politicians, and Mexico's Road to Prosperity.* Boston: Little Brown.

POWELL, WALTER W., and DiMAGGIO, PAUL J. (eds.) (1991). *The New Institutionalism in Organizational Analysis.* Chicago: University of Chicago Press.

PRESTON, J. (1995). 'Mexican Plot: Salinas Family, Swiss Bank and $84 Million'. *New York Times,* Nov. 25: 4.

—— (1998). 'Mexico's Elite Caught in Scandal's Harsh Glare'. *New York Times,* July 13: 3.

RACANELLI, VITO J. (2000). 'Germany's Tax Reform Has a Downside for Investors'. *Barron's,* Jan. 24: MW6.

ROSE-ACKERMAN, SUSAN (1999). *Corruption and Government: Causes, Consequences, and Reform.* Cambridge: Cambridge University Press.

ROSS, S. A. (1973). 'The Economic Theory of Agency: The Principals Problems'. *American Economic Review,* 62/May: 134–9.

SIMON, HERBERT A. (1945/1976). *Administrative Behavior.* New York: Free Press.

SMITH, A. (1776). *An Inquiry into the Nature and Causes of the Wealth of Nations.* Indianapolis: Liberty Classics.

SOLOMON, JAY (2000). 'A Tycoon Nearly Sunk by Indonesia's Straits Lands on Solid Ground'. *Wall Street Journal,* Jan. 12: 1, 8.

TAGLIABUE, JOHN (1998). 'New Activism Shakes Europe's Markets'. *New York Times,* Mar. 25: D2–D3.

Tsoukas, Hardimos, and Cummings, Stephen (1997). 'Marginalization and Recovery: The Emergence of Aristotelian Themes in Organization Studies'. *Organization Studies*, 18/4: 655–83.

Ulrich, Dave (1997). *Human Resource Champions*. Boston: Harvard Business School Press.

Useem, Michael (1996). *Investor Capitalism*. New York: Basic Books.

Viner, J. (1968/1991). 'Adam Smith', reprinted in id., *Essays on the Intellectual History of Economics*. Princeton: Princeton University Press.

Waldman, Peter (1998). 'Hand in Glove, How Suharto's Circle and a Mining Firm Did So Well Together'. *Wall Street Journal*, Sept. 29: 1, 10.

Weber, Max (1906/1958). *The Protestant Ethic and the Spirit of Capitalism*. New York: Schribner.

—— (1920/1978). *Economy and Society*, ed. Guenther Roth and Claus Wittich. Berkeley: University of California Press.

Welling, Kathryn M. (1998). 'Crony Capitalism?' *Barron's*, Sept. 28: 3.

Williamson, Oliver E. (1996). *The Mechanisms of Governance*. New York: Oxford University Press.

CHAPTER 18

CHARACTER AND VIRTUE IN AN ERA OF TURBULENT CAPITALISM

IAIN MANGHAM

IN recent years there has been an upsurge in anti-capitalist protest in the form of articles, books, and direct action. Three aspects of capitalism appear to give rise to particular concern: its influence on the environment, on inequality, and on cultural hegemony.[1] Thanks to the efforts of these writers and the actions of people brave enough to take to the streets, many more of us have become sensitive to the impact that capitalism—particularly in its more recent forms—has had upon our physical, political, and cultural surroundings. Perhaps a significant minority of people in the developed world are now aware that we depend upon these environments, that they are fragile, and that what we do may change them irrevocably, thereby threatening our own quality of life and that of the generations that will follow. However perhaps

I am grateful for the advice and patience of Haridimos Tsoukas in the preparation of this essay, and for the support of my colleagues at King's College, Tim Clark, Tom Keenoy, and Cliff Oswick.

[1] There is indeed a massive literature. Books that I have found useful and stimulating include: Bauman 1998, 2000; Bronk 1998; Frank 2001; Greider 1997; Haslett 1994; Hirschhorn 1998; Klein 2001; Lane 1991; Rosenberg 2000.

fewer of us are conscious of the effect that capitalism has had and is having upon the ethical environment in which we operate. This is the surrounding climate of ideas about how to live our lives (Blackburn 2001). Modern societies appear to be marked by intractable disagreements over what it is to lead a good life in the company of others. Some commentators hold that the market, particularly in its more liberal or untrammelled form, is destructive of community-based notions of the good life. It cultivates the vice of personal acquisitiveness and in doing so breaks the bands of affection that hold communities together (MacIntyre 1981; Buchan 1997). Others think such views are mistaken (Ferguson 2001).

In this chapter I wish to examine aspects of this argument. I will focus in particular upon two concepts: character and virtue. And I will consider the ways that these terms have been deployed in discussions of the impact of capitalism on the ethical climate both within and beyond organizations. The chapter was stimulated by Richard Sennett's widely acclaimed book *The Corrosion of Character: The Personal Consequences of Work in the New Capitalism* (Sennett 1998). For those unfamiliar with the book I offer a synopsis of some of his ideas and look at what support there is elsewhere for the general thrust of his argument. I go on to challenge the use that he and others make of *character* and *virtue* as explanatory concepts. My position is that while both concepts have a long and distinguished history neither is of much value in understanding the impact of contemporary forms of capitalism upon ethical climate and behaviour. Hearkening back to a deferential and largely patriarchal era when moral stances were taken to be more absolute than they are now, the terms may be seen as both nostalgic and perhaps even reactionary. I begin however with Aristotle. Many of us writing and thinking about character use his ideas matter-of-factly, as if they were self-evident truths. It may be as well to remember what he actually thought and said. [2]

18.1 ARISTOTLE

For Aristotle *character* has to do with a person's enduring traits, which are, generally, dispositions to have thoughts and feelings of a certain sort, and thus to act in certain ways. As relatively permanent features of the individual's make-up, these dispositions will explain not merely why he acted in the way that he did, but why he can be counted on to act in a similar way in the future (Sherman 1989).

[2] My exposition of Aristotle's ideas has been particularly influenced by Sherman 1989, 1997; Gottlieb 2000; Loptson 1995; Rachels 1978; Solomon 1993. The edition of Aristotle that I quote from is the Cambridge Text edited by Crisp.

Character is the community's ideals seen through the medium of the individual's dispositions. It is an exemplary way of 'manifesting in one's thoughts, feelings and actions the ideals and aims of the entire community' (Solomon 1993). Aristotle refers to those traits or dispositions that meet his approval as *virtues*: 'states worthy of praise we call virtues' (Aristotle 2000). Since Aristotle famously considered man to be a social animal, it is not surprising to find that the Aristotelian virtues comprise just and decent ways of living as a social being.[3] His views on character repeatedly stress this collaborative dimension. Virtuous agents conceive of their own well-being and thriving as including the well-being and thriving of others (Loptson 1995).

From an Aristotelian point of view, the relative stability of character is explained by the fact that it is acquired through teaching and habituation and is reinforced on a daily basis through interaction with like-minded individuals. The role of the family—and particularly of the mother—is to model and to inculcate the virtues that are considered to be beneficial both to the full flourishing of the growing infant and to the well-being of the community into which he has been born. Additionally the family—and particularly the mother—bear the major responsibility for education in the emotions. In the Aristotelian scheme of things, education in the emotions has an important part to play in the development of character. It is the inculcation of sensitivity to people, objects, and events. For Aristotle emotion is more than a way of responding. It is a way also of perceiving, of being affected, a way of noticing and then acting or reacting (Sherman 1989). Emotions are to be cultivated or habituated so that they will become reliable resources for the many roles they play in the individual's moral and social life. As a result emotions become socialized modes of response and an important aspect of virtue. To act rightly is to act rightly in affect and in conduct. Development takes place within the context of important relations to others, whereby children and young adults come to feel emotions in increasingly more differentiated and selective ways. Maturity is marked by the stable condition of feeling 'specific emotions finely—in the right way, in the right circumstances' (Sherman 1997).

Social relations beyond the family figure prominently in Aristotle's ideas. The significance of *philia*, friendship, within his account of the development of character is unmistakable. As with everything associated with the development of character, friendship requires time and familiarity. Friends have fun together and talk to each other about matters of importance in their lives. But there is more to friendship than simple association however pleasurable that may be. Friendship is

---

[3] Aristotle considered women to be rationally defective. According to him they are unable to assess questions from all sides, or to bring to bear the sort of empirical knowledge that good decision-making requires. They are however, also, directly and largely responsible for the inculcation of practical reasoning in the young. Nowhere does Aristotle face up to this contradiction (Sherman 1989: 154–5). I do not share his prejudice but I have made no attempt to alter the tone or tenor of his thoughts by substituting she for he, her for him, etc.

instrumental. It is fundamental to the development of character. 'Just as when we want to see our own faces, we see them by looking in a mirror, similarly when we wish to know our own characters, we can know them by looking up a friend.' In effect the friend is taken to be another self. If a friend has a specific virtue to a greater degree than the individual has it, then the individual can strive to perfect that virtue to a greater degree himself. Character is the acquisition of dispositions through habituation. The process of habituation involves practice and repetition and is life-long. We acquire virtues

by first exercising them. The same is true with skills, since we need to learn before doing: for example, we become builders by building and lyre players by playing the lyre. So too we become just by doing just actions, temperate by temperate actions, and courageous by courageous actions... So it is not unimportant how we are habituated from our early days; indeed it makes a huge difference—or rather all the difference. (Aristotle 2000)[4]

18.2 THE CORROSION OF CHARACTER

Much of Aristotle's thinking has been absorbed into Sennett's vocabulary. He deploys both character and virtue to argue that in the new era of what he terms 'flexible capitalism' where workers are expected to 'behave nimbly, be open to change on short notice, [and] to take risks continually', character is likely to be 'corroded'. He defines character—*inter alia*—as that which focuses 'on the long-term aspect of our emotional experience' and which 'concerns the personal traits, which we value in ourselves and for which we seek to be valued by others'. The traits that he sees as being under particular attack are those qualities of character 'which bind human beings to one another and furnishes each with a sense of sustainable self'. He ranges widely over a variety of topics, but the main thread of his argument appears to be that the decades spanning the mid-twentieth century were the golden age when 'strong unions, guarantees of the welfare state, and large-scale corporations combined to produce an era of relative stability'. During these good years family, friends, peers, the community, the form of capitalism that prevailed and the culture of the workplace supported the development and sustaining of an individual's character. There was little or no conflict between the virtues that the individual embraced beyond the workplace and those that prevailed within it. Sennett does not spell out a full list of these virtues, but he does offer loyalty, trustworthiness, and commitment as representative of the virtues that found

---

[4] For those interested in an alternative perspective on character, see Kupperman 1991. Goldie 2000 offers some corroboration of trait theory and emotions.

widespread support. These years, however, were an interlude between what he sees as the destructive force of the early forms of capitalism and the corrosive impact of the newer forms and they soon passed. The newer forms demand very different virtues, very different ways of being and working. The 'traits of character which appear among people truly at home in the new capitalism' are those that 'signal a capacity to let go one's past, a confidence to accept fragmentation and to dwell in disorder'. Nowadays corporations break up or join together; jobs appear and disappear as events lacking connections. Instability and uncertainty are 'woven into the everyday practices of vigorous capitalism'. In circumstances where an organization operates as flexible and loose network structure rather than by rigid command from the top, social bonds are often seriously weakened. Furthermore the short-termism that Sennett sees as the hallmark of 'impatient capitalism' erodes trust and commitment. Social bonds take time to develop. In one of his many felicitous phrases, he characterizes social bonds as: 'slowly rooting in the cracks and crevices of institutions'. The short time frame of modern institutions limits the ripening of informal trust and demands instead detachment and superficial co-operativeness. As a consequence the action an employee needs to take and the way he has to live in order to survive at work sets 'his emotional, inner life adrift'. Furthermore behaviour that earns success in the organization offers little to the employee at home or in his community. Frequent job changes and consequent relocation means that friends no longer serve as support and communities— although not entirely devoid of neighbourliness—offer no long-term support or witness to another person's life. Families too lose their role as inculcators of character. As Sennett sees it, the employee's deepest worry is that he cannot offer the substance of his work life as an example to his children of 'how to conduct themselves ethically'. He concludes that flexible behaviour may bring success at work, but it weakens character in ways for which 'there is no practical remedy'.

18.3 THE LITERATURE

This tale of declension and loss is, of course, usually in a less specific form a familiar version of recent American history. It is a staple of conservative political rhetoric and of the publications of right-wing intellectuals and think tanks. In its crudest form the argument cleaves to the notion that there was once a golden age when society organized itself around a cluster of powerful and widely shared values with an emphasis upon loyalty, trustworthiness, and commitment. Somewhere around the middle part of the twentieth century—opinions vary but the sixties are usually taken to be responsible—the old values were replaced by a more relativistic approach to social ethics. Given the popularity of this version of recent American history it is not difficult to find support for some of Sennett's views in the conservative literature. Gertrude Himmelfarb, for example, in a powerful and erudite piece of work argues at some considerable length that character and virtue are under attack as sources of morality in society. Like Sennett she regrets the loss of trust, the decline of the family, of neighbourhoods and communities as moralizing forces for both the individual and society. She has little to say about the impact of the market and nothing about specific forms of capitalism, but in citing Schumpeter's argument that the very entrepreneurial spirit that would ensure the success of capitalism would undermine the institutions that sustained it, she appears to travel a long way along the path taken by Sennett. For her, capitalism as an all too successful process of creative destruction has taken its toll on the moral life of society (Himmelfarb 1999). James Davison Hunter goes further than Sennett (whom he appears not to have read) does when he traces the death of character to the disintegration of the moral and social conditions that make character possible in the first place. He assembles an impressive array of evidence to suggest that it is difficult to think of another time where the individual has been so disconnected, 'both socially and metaphysically', from stable communities. Where one has been so 'spectacularly free to determine one's own fate to be sure, yet at the same time, restless with few if any fixed bearings for the journey' (Hunter 2000). In a passage that appears to echo some of Sennett's thoughts, he asserts that the 'demands of multinational capitalism' have created conditions that make a 'coherent self that unites history, community and subjectivity all but impossible'. And he attributes the changes in the ethical requirements placed upon individuals in the early decades of the twentieth century to the rise of the market economy, but that is as far as he goes in support of Sennett.

Elsewhere there is widespread support for many of Sennett's comments on trust. Indeed it is possible to argue that questions of how social trust is produced and what kinds of social trust enhance economic performance are fast becoming a central set of theoretical issues in social science (Levi 1993). A large number of commentators have noticed that we live in confused, uncertain and—as the old Chinese saying goes—interesting times. Many of the issues raised by Sennett are those that have been repeatedly raised over the past twenty years or so in some of the many valiant attempts that have been made to theorize more concrete and meaningful criteria of trust in modern, turbulent, highly differentiated societies.[5]

The empirical support for Sennett's ideas, however, is somewhat sparse. Robert Putnam in his massive study *Bowling Alone: The Collapse and Revival of American Community* confirms that the social fabric of American society is in a bad state, but he attributes only 10 per cent of the decline to what he terms 'the intensification of

[5] See e.g. Hart 1988; Giddens 1994; Gambetta 1998; Wolfe 1991; Fukuyama 1996; Misztal 1996.

work' (Putnam 1998). And his statistics have been questioned. At first glance Robert Jackall's very detailed piece of work, *Moral Mazes: The World of Corporate Managers*, appears to be concerned with the issues that Sennett raises. Jackall studied how a particular form of capitalism—in this case bureaucracy—shapes moral consciousness amongst managers. But his focus was upon how the form shaped consciousness and behaviour *within* the workplace not beyond it. He concluded that 'the enduring genius of the organizational form is that it allows individuals to retain bewilderingly diverse private motives and meanings for their actions'. He found that 'bureaucratic work causes people to bracket, while at work the moralities that they might hold outside the workplace or that they might adhere to privately and to follow instead the prevailing morality of their particular organ-isational situation' (Jackall 1988). He did not offer any comment on the impact of bureaucratic values upon the wider community.

The problem of Sennett's book is that it is rather long on philosophical reflection and somewhat short on data.[6] Recently however a series of small serendipities led me to a couple of books that deal with the financial services industry, specifically with the history and development of the City of London institutions. Both provide some considerable data in support of aspects of Sennett's argument: that the form of capitalism may impact upon the ethical environment that prevails at a particular time. The first to appear was *The Death of Gentlemanly Capitalism* by Philip Augur, a sometime top broker who offers a perspective on the City from the point of view of a player (Augur 2000). The second, *The City of London: A Club No More*, by David Kynaston, a professional historian, who has written extensively on the City was published a year later (Kynaston 2001). Together the books contain some twelve hundred pages of data documenting the day-to-day life of those who worked in the City as it moved from one form of capitalism, *gentlemanly capitalism*, to another that Sennett would probably recognize as *flexible* or *impatient capitalism*.[7] Seren-dipitous indeed. What the books offer us is a chance to look at almost pure cases of both of these forms in an industry that lies at the heart of capitalism. Thus we are able to add to Sennett's findings in two settings: before and after *Big Bang*. This is the dramatic term used to encapsulate the deregulation of the operations of the City that was implemented on 27 October 1986. It is important to note that neither author sets out to demonstrate the impact of a particular form of capitalism upon the ethical climate of the times. Neither focuses explicitly on the notions of character and virtues. The data that they provide constitutes a kind of naive grounded theory in that they offer many comments of interest to us, some of

---

[6] Sennett is somewhat coy about the number and identity of those from whom he derived his views. He states that he has conflated some of the voices, but it is not evident in the text where this has and has not occurred.

[7] Kynaston's text is based around the notion of the City as a club, but club capitalism does not have quite the same ring as Augur's gentlemanly capitalism—a phrase that he borrowed from Hutton (1995) who in turn borrowed it from someone else.

which they filter through a frame that is largely—and presumably unwittingly—
Aristotelian.

18.4 GENTLEMANLY CAPITALISM

Character does not exist without particular content. Aristotelian virtues were
rooted in a specific community, grounded in concrete circumstances, situated
within a distinct system of social relations. Pre–Big Bang the City of London was
such a particularity. Kynaston offers a very detailed analysis of the structural
features of gentlemanly capitalism. There is not the space to go into that here
suffice it to say that up until the late 1970s there were two quite distinct Cities—one
centring on the still largely UK oriented stock market, the other focusing mainly on
the much more international Euromarket. The former was the natural terrain of the
City establishment and it is this part of the City that we will be talking about below.
For these people London was still a little island. One of Kynaston's respondents
sums it up rather graphically: 'It was very narrow in those days, we might just have
known what American interest rates were doing but no one looked at sterling-
deutschmarks or had any idea when the Bundesbank was meeting' (Kynaston 2001).
In many respects the City remained self-policing and self-regulating even though
there had been a number of scandals that threatened its independence. In important
respects, however, the City benefited from controls. During most of the second half
of the 1970s strict exchange controls were still operating. British institutions were
not allowed to invest capital abroad except by special Treasury permission, based on
the specific returns that they would make on their capital. Not only was the City a
little island, it was a strongly defended little island. Gentlemanly capitalism thrived
within an insulated market.

   The natural terrain of little Englanders had remained largely the same for a
couple of hundred years. Individual firms rarely comprised more than a couple of
hundred people and most of these were situated within an area one-mile square.
Aristotle's theory of human development is centred upon and celebrates the
benefits of a small urban community. The City as reflected in the work of Augur
and Kynaston is such a community. Augur notes the result of this modest scale and
single-site location was that most of the people in a firm knew each other personally
and quite a large proportion of the broking and jobbing community were able to
recognize each other by name, face, or reputation. The personal relationships that
were possible in such a small community were reinforced by the intimacy of a
dealing system in which people dealt face to face rather than over the phone or via

screens. Augur believes that the size and the daily contact fostered the notion that those working together were not only part of a team, they were part of a family. Kynaston, whose tone throughout is somewhat more sceptical than that adopted by Augur, offers a quote from one of those he interviewed that initially appears to contradict this picture. 'The partners for the most part were not agreeable. They were the sort of people who were charming to clients or potential clients but treated us lower order like the minions that we were.' However overall Kynaston agrees with Augur by asserting that the typical firm was 'an intimate, family-like working environment, knit together by seemingly inalienable ties of mutual trust and loyalty. Most firms were still small enough for that roseate ambience to be possible, if far from inevitable.'

Size, location, and ownership patterns also tended to reinforce patterns of behaviour. One joined a firm, learned the ropes from one's colleagues, worked one's way up the hierarchy, became a partner and amassed a moderate amount of wealth before retiring. Redundancies and sackings were rare events and occurred only in the direst of circumstances. Such loyalty to staff was generally reciprocated. As late as the 1970s it was rare for people to change firms. Those who attempted to came under considerable pressure from their colleagues. They were accused of 'letting down their colleagues, letting down the firm, and behaving in an ungentle-manly manner'. If they succumbed to the pressure to stay all was forgiven. If they insisted on leaving, they were 'made to feel ashamed'. This shaming took the form of 'quite subtle body language and a rather distant courtesy' (Augur 2000). This shaming was part of the informal code of behaviour that governed how one should behave for the good of oneself and for the good of the community. Word spread quickly when individuals or firms were misbehaving and such parties were 'ostra-cized' 'and found it very hard to get liquidity or to be shown business'. Before Big Bang the predominant virtues (a term used by both Augur and Kynaston) were those inculcated by families many of whom had a tradition of working in the City, by the public schools, and, to a lesser extent, by the Oxbridge colleges. As late as 1990 thirteen of the fifteen most senior figures in the City had been to public school, seven of them to Eton.[8] Augur quotes Michael Verey and how Eton set the standards for the City. 'During my time in the City, those who hadn't been to Eton were striving for Eton standards and the Eton ethos dominated from Kim Cobbold, Governor of the Bank of England, downwards. Good Etonian standards means a total trust—if you say something, you'll do it.'

Much of what Augur and Kynaston have to say is directly concerned with how those who worked in the City in the era of gentlemanly capitalism saw the good life. It was a life where one worked and was supported by colleagues of similar back-ground and aspiration whom one probably knew socially as well as commercially.

---

[8] A public school in England is, of course, one that is private.

Those party to the good life conducted themselves so as to enhance their own opportunities whilst simultaneously enhancing the life of the community. By doing so they affirmed the virtues by which they lived. And they did it willingly. Like Aristotle's good men, the men in the City did not need to reflect upon their decisions, did not need to look up some code or other. They knew what was expected of them and they made their decisions freely. Character enacts judgement and does so freely. One learned the moral order and worked within it. Trust, honesty, loyalty, decency, civility, generosity, and fairness were expected, were enacted, and were rewarded. The City was a circumstance, a particularity, within which one acted as a virtuous citizen and where's one's employment was compatible with being a whole man. For those towards the top end of this particularity, being a whole man meant that one did not work very hard. And certainly not obsessively. One started around nine in the morning, enjoyed a lunch break that was often accompanied by fine wine, and one finished around four in the afternoon before taking the train home. On Fridays one finished earlier and in many cases one went to one's house in the country. Occasionally one socialized with one's peers at one's club or in a restaurant. One's hobbies comprised hunting, shooting, and fishing. In winter one followed rugby, in summer cricket was a unifying influence, played or watched.

The important thing to remember here is that both of the authors are talking about a particularity. They are not talking about British industry as a whole nor even about the activities of everyone in the City. Most of the comments offered in the last couple of paragraphs refer to that part of the City that was not internationalist in its orientation. Admittedly this was a large part of the City, but it was only part. What Kynaston and Augur succeed in doing, albeit unintentionally, is to remind us that character and virtue are rooted in specific historical situations, they flourish in discrete concrete circumstances and are manifestations of particular social relations. Thus their material takes us a step beyond Sennett's ideas since he provides us with little or no particularity in which we can ground his comments. Augur and Kynaston provide us with numerous examples of the ethical climate within the square mile. They provide major support for the idea that the notions of character and virtue can be useful in looking at how a particular form of capitalism impacts upon the ethical climate of a particular industry at a particular time. Unfortunately their analyses of gentlemanly capitalism provide no data on the ethical climate beyond the City other than the observation that the City appeared to be out of step with the broader community. During the post-war period leading up to Big Bang, the City was the target for industrialists, politicians, and economists who believed that its attitudes and practices were holding back the performance of British manufacturing companies. The City was seen to be an anachronism. No doubt a little devilling could reveal the impact of its dispositions upon others, since there appears to be a great deal of data upon which one could draw.

18.5 Impatient Capitalism

Within a few years of Big Bang the City has changed radically. In the eyes of some it now was nothing more than 'raw capitalism'. All but two of the top ten merchant banks in 1983 have been taken over and all ten of the top firms of brokers have been through so many changes that they are unrecognizable as the firms that they once were. Many functions have been changed and many specialized tasks are now put together in large international departments. Firms that formerly employed a couple of hundred people now employ thousands spread across the world, and are often themselves part of even bigger enterprises. The barriers between the world's capital and money markets have come tumbling down; nation states are increasingly engaged in competitive deregulation of the financial markets with exchange controls, tax barriers, and impediments to foreign access going down like ninepins. It is no exaggeration that the City is now part of a global, seamless market in all things financial (Kynaston 2001). The personnel are different. The City has thrown off its reputation as a haven for 'well-dressed gents of often modest intellectual means'. The Americans are everywhere treating the square mile as if it were Wall Street and importing their values. Pay has rocketed—million pound salaries plus bonuses are now common—and work has become an obsession for those who wish to succeed. Evenings off, as one commentator wryly puts it, 'have become an endangered species'. It is not only the Americans who have stormed the citadel. Post–Big Bang women have gained a foothold in the City— perhaps a toehold would be a more accurate description—but at last they are in a position to compete for top jobs with men. Previously the idea of a woman occupying any role in the City beyond that of waitress, clerk, or typist was 'inconceivable'. Self-made men have made it to the top of some of the organizations without the benefit of a public school or university education. Many of the dealers on the London International Financial Futures and Options Exchange come from working-class homes in the East End and worked on commission. 'We find the barrow-boy type is best at this game,' one senior figure is said to have remarked (Kynaston 2001). The brave new world belongs to the ambitious, thrusting young. Forty-year-olds working in the City are worried about keeping their jobs. People are rewarded for being 'brutal, combative, and relentless'. The prevailing atmosphere in the City is reported to be 'aggressive, macho, and generally in-your-face'. More than one commentator offers the view that it is 'dog eat dog' in the City in the 1990s. Augur notes that frequent changes of ownership and the imposition of regular redundancies, on the one side, and the 'lure of the head-hunters' gold, on the other, have eroded the bonds that obtained in the old partnerships. As he sees it, in the era of impatient capitalism money has replaced honour and the search for short-term reward has pushed out the idea of long-term commitment.

Some are worried about how the values of the City are affecting their lives. Kynaston writes of a young woman who had spent several years in the City who claimed that it created an imbalance in her life in her outlook. She argued that while it is possible to make a lot of money in the City the price to be paid is a 'tremendous amount of stress' and probably 'a ragged social and home life'. Colleagues whom she saw as having the potential to make a great deal more out of other sides of their personalities became so totally focused on making money, that other 'elements of their capabilities just withered and died'. Kynaston reports on the suicide of a senior figure that is widely thought to have been brought about by the changes in the ethos of the City.

Beyond the City the new values have had a clear impact. Impatient capitalism fuels the engines of hyperactive management consultants and is the driving force behind many company mission statements. 'Shareholder value' has become the rallying cry of thousands of small investors. City values have not only impacted on much of industry they have now infiltrated areas such as education, the National Health Service, and public service organizations. Many of these organizations now audit the performance of individuals and groups, reward staff differentially, offer bonuses for meeting short-term performance targets and stress the importance of giving value to their 'stakeholders' or 'clients'.

18.6 Discussion

What is immediately striking in the descriptions that are offered of the post–Big Bang City neither author has recourse to the notions of character or virtue other than in moments of nostalgia. Perhaps this is not surprising. It must be remembered that although Aristotle himself was part of a large Macedonian kingdom grown, under his pupil Alexander the Great, into a huge, pluralistic, imperial order, he chose not to write about it (Loptson 1995). He chose instead to write about a small urban city-state where slaves did most of the work, where women and foreigners were considered incapable of advanced forms of reasoning, and where relatively wealthy and middle-aged men had the leisure to sit around in the sun talking about philosophy. His ideal society was paternalistic, hierarchical, and deferential. As of course was the City at the time of gentlemanly capitalism. Throughout both Augur's and Kynaston's descriptions of the pre–Big Bang City, one has the strong impression that the traditional figures of authority, the partners, were seen as a legitimate elite.[9] Father figures within what was still pervasively

---

[9] In the *Republic* Plato held up character as the defining qualification of the ruling class. See Hunter (2000).

considered to be a pre-ordained and patriarchal hierarchy. A conviction reinforced by the absence of women other than in the role of handmaidens to the men, and the frequent representations of the status hierarchy as an extended family, implicitly seen as the most inherently natural formation.

Much of both texts is taken up with descriptions of settings and costumes. During the era of gentlemanly capitalism the offices were panelled and thick with carpet and dressed as if they were country houses. Some partnerships even had uniformed butlers to greet clients and in nearly all of them waitresses dressed in traditional black and white served lunch to partners and their guests. Clothing appeared to be important throughout the City. Messengers wore a special costume and everyone else conformed to clothing deemed appropriate to their status. Augur notes that the only colours permitted were blue or grey and the only variation acceptable was in the 'width and thickness of the pin stripe'. Brown suits were simply not worn 'except by clerks'. Shirts were plain or striped, never check and the button down variety was seen only on Americans. Ties were silk, plain or patterned, but polyester 'was for the back office, the clearing bankers or the insurance companies' (Augur 2000).

The delicate balance between the various groupings within the firm and the City appears to have been maintained through the enactment of ritualized social exchanges during which roles and their appropriate attitudes were both produced and dramatically represented. For example the presentation of turkeys to the staff at Christmas as documented by Augur may be seen as pure theatre. On the morning of Christmas Eve lorries could be seen queuing up outside many of the broking firms. Porters were unloading hundreds of turkeys, the traditional gift from the partners to the staff. Now this can be seen as an example of the generosity of the partners and/or as an action that reinforces role and status. Reminds everyone of his place (Augur 2000).

This theatricality is crucial to the maintenance of deference hierarchies. By the term 'theatrical' I especially intend to emphasize the visible, public, and performative quality of these physical interactions (Hadley 1995). From an Aristotelian perspective, of course, it is crucial. Aristotle argues that the virtues are neither innate nor natural. They are best regarded as acquired dispositions that are reinforced by repeated use. One learns how to act by acting and one first learns what is appropriate action in everyday situations by observing how things are done (Alderman 1997: 148). It is a theory that at every turn depends upon emulation. Effectively one's character is simultaneously created and represented by theatrical exchanges. What is more the virtues and feelings that one manifests are socially constructed, they do not exist independently of the social exchanges in which one participates. Character is not idiosyncratic. It is irreducibly social and emerges from theatricalized public exchange. The kind of exchanges documented in the pages of both Kynaston and Augur highlight the conversation of setting, dress, gesture, and speech that reveals each person's place in the community. Such exchanges operate at their best in a culture where people are bound together by common economic interests, where people stay in one place most of their lives, and where face to face exchange is customary and frequent. The senior partner recognizes and acknowledges those who work for him, the small manufacturer knows the names and something about each of the individuals who work in his factory. The social actors inhabit a relatively stable setting and share a common script. Each knows and dramatizes his obligations to the other.

The advent of impatient capitalism changes everything. It embraces both structural changes as well as the behavioural and perceptual changes among those who work in the City. The numbers employed becomes much larger, the management of the enterprise becomes more distant, and the notion of competition within and between various parts of the industry becomes very important. Very quickly those involved become less likely to see themselves as sharing in a common enterprise and—as a consequence—there are fewer opportunities to participate in the enactment of communal ties. Individualism replaces the notion of the family, the firm, or the extended community as the source of moral authority. Virtues—the cultivation and expressions of those dispositions that are good for the individual *and* good for the community—are replaced by *values*, a term which has no such connotations. This is an important change. Himmelfarb argues that the shift in language is more than important—it is 'momentous'. For her it is the great philosophical revolution of modernity and it occurred almost without comment. Towards the latter part of the nineteenth century, Friedrich Nietzsche launched an attack on the notion of virtues. He argued that the 'death of god' would mean the death of the truth of any morality. There could be no good and no evil, no virtue and no vice. Only values (Himmelfarb 1993). The new term brought with it the assumption that how one ought to conduct oneself was a matter for oneself. Values were not the expressions of universal truth; nor were they the commanding manifestations of a community's ideals. They are to be seen as customs and conventions that have a purely instrumental purpose that can be picked up and put down as the individual wishes.

So long as how one should live one's life was couched in the language of character and virtue it had a firm ring to it. For a particular group of people at a particular time the notions of character and virtue have weight and authority. They are not simply matters to be taken up or put down lightly. One cannot say of virtues as one can of values, that anyone's virtues are as good as anyone else's virtues. Nor can one sensibly declare that everyone has a right to his own virtues.

The character made manifest and the virtues that lay behind the perceptions, feelings, thoughts, and actions of people in the City during the era of gentlemanly capitalism (or during Sennett's golden years), were fixed and certain. Not in the sense of governing the actual behaviour of all of the people all of the time (or even most of the people most of the time). They were, however, probably taken to be the standards against which behaviour could and should be measured. The standards were firm even if the individuals did not always measure up to them. And when conduct was particularly unbecoming, it was judged in moral terms as bad or wrong, something for which you should be ostracized or shamed. In committing the offence you had brought disrepute on yourself and on the community of which you were a part. Those who worked in the City pre–Big Bang were—as were all people of character—people who displayed moral attachment. They affirmed their commitment to a community beyond themselves. They were also people of moral discipline. In their perceptions, feelings, thoughts, and actions they did not let the side down (Hunter 2000).

The era of gentlemanly capitalism has a Victorian feel to it. One can imagine that its heroes would be carbon copies of Tom Brown possibly the most famous schoolboy of them all. In *Tom Brown's Schooldays*—a novel written in 1857 but still in print today—we see how the hero, Tom the commonest type of English boy with an explicitly common name, is shaped by the atmosphere of his public school. The book written by Thomas Hughes, is a dramatization of the methods of the famous Dr Thomas Arnold who was credited with altering the whole atmosphere of Public School life. His great contribution was to introduce morals into his scheme of education. His own hierarchy of educational desiderata was clear. 'What we must look for here is, first, religious and moral principles; secondly gentlemanly conduct; thirdly, intellectual ability.' *Tom Brown's Schooldays* is fired by Arnold's moral principles (Sanders 1999). It illustrates his belief that the responsible adult can be developed out of the irresponsible boy. We follow Tom's adventures as he progresses through the school. In splendid Aristotelian/Arnoldian fashion he benefits from the spirituality and seriousness of his friendship with George Arthur and learns much about himself from his relationship with Harry East. After many adventures he triumphs over the villain of the piece—Flashman—and leaves the school as a Victorian hero, an average boy who matures through a series of challenging circumstances and moral dilemmas prepared to go into the world and take on his moral and social responsibilities.[10] No doubt he went on to work in the City where he met dozens of other Tom Browns.

Those who work in the City post–Big Bang appear to lack any notion of moral or social responsibility. Impatient capitalism appears to have freed them from all constraint. The doctrine that business has no concerns beyond shareholder value appears to have given them licence to do whatever they are not actually prevented from doing as long as it makes money for them and for their shareholders. It is as if they are hard-wired to be selfish, greedy, and competitive (Nicholson 2000). The term 'character' is redundant in such a setting. Those who operate within the contemporary City appear to scorn notions of the common good. They appear to

---

[10] Central to Hughes's novel is the desire 'to infuse into a society of boys such elements as, without being too dissimilar to coalesce thoroughly with the rest, shall yet be so superior as to raise the character of the whole.' As earnestly as his mentor, Dr Arnold, Hughes sought to extend the ambience of a well-run school to society as a whole.

subscribe to a cult of individualism that directly or indirectly may have been inspired by Nietzsche's writings filtered no doubt through the minds of many others (Shapiro 1989; Thiele 1990; Richardson and Leiter 2001). For Nietzsche, the individual is a law unto himself, unpredictable and unmanageable. For Nietzsche, virtue, no less than duty, must be an individual invention: 'And so should each in his own manner do his best for himself—that is my moral:—the only one that still remains for me' (Thiele 1990). To be an individual is to consider oneself supra-moral. It follows that society cannot be composed of individuals. Society requires *members*. To be a member—to control and be controlled by others—requires that one must be made 'uniform' and that one's behaviour must be rendered predictable. For this purpose morality and the 'social straitjacket' are employed. We can see this in the description of the City during the era of gentlemanly capitalism that required that one should be of a modest, obedient, and self-effacing disposition. The form itself rested on a rigid and undemocratic class system; protected existing hierarchies on the basis not of merit but tradition and influence; imposed upon many members standards of behaviour and belief that some may have found oppressive and rigid; and thwarted the aspirations of generations of women. Nietzsche sees 'morality as the herd instinct in the individual, but claims that the price of membership of any society is the forfeiture of self-rule'. According to this view, society holds the individual to be its greatest threat and morality serves as its none too secret weapon (Thiele 1990). The followers of Nietzsche welcome up-heaval and the upsetting of social relations as 'the harbingers of individualism' (Thiele 1990). The resultant ripping apart of the social straitjacket liberates the individual from the morality of custom and renders him sovereign. He or she no longer has to follow the script written by others, but is free to improvise.

In some of the descriptions of individual actions in the post–Big Bang one can discern something of this order. One particular example quoted by Kynaston, stands out. Michael Lewis an American trader working for Salomon Brothers, an American firm, talks of his big moment, which came when he managed to unload $86 million worth of unwanted bonds on an overtrusting French client:

For two days messages of congratulations arrived from distant points in the Salomon Brothers' system. . . . The sweetness of the moment dulled the pain of knowing I had just placed my most cherished customer in jeopardy. The most important call of all came. It was from the Human Piranha. 'I heard you sold a few bonds', he said. I tried to sound calm about the whole thing. He didn't. He shouted into the phone, '*That* is fuckin' awesome. I mean *fuckin'* awesome. I *fuckin'* mean *fucking* awesome. You are one Big Swinging Dick, and don't let anybody ever tell you different.' It brought tears to my eyes to hear it.

Contemplating the aggressive and egregious behaviour that appears to be occasioned by impatient capitalism, reminds me that Tom Brown's story has been much derided in the latter part of the twentieth century, but the one participant in his destiny who has been vigorously resurrected is Harry Flashman (MacDonald Fraser

1969). He who was the opposite of Tom in virtually all respects and was by his own admission, 'a scoundrel, a liar, a cheat, a thief and a coward', has become a supramoral hero for our times. And it appears that he could well have friends in the City.

18.7 Conclusion

In this essay I have attempted to put together some thoughts on character and virtue prompted by Sennett's portrait of the American workplace in the age of flexible capitalism. I have suggested that there is strong support for the idea that forms of capitalism impact upon ethics—the moral climate in which we live. Capitalism that is under strict control appears to produce a climate different to that which obtains when capitalism is freed from control. I question, however, whether particular forms of organization impact directly upon ethical climate. The changes wrought in the City were the result of the deregulation of the markets, the consequence of capitalism being freed from control. I have shown that the concepts of character and virtue are more than adequate in describing what occurred in the era of gentlemanly capitalism, but both terms lack purchase in the modern era, as some of those who promoted the idea three hundred years forecast that they would. Albert Hirschman in another splendid book—positively the last that I will be drawing to your attention in this chapter—makes the case for capitalism rest on the belief that 'it would activate some benign human proclivities at the expense of some malignant ones' (Hirschman 1997). In brief he argues that capitalism was stimulated by a number of independent thinkers who argued that avarice should be promoted rather than despised. That self-interest should be given its head. Eminent lay figures such as the redoubtable Dr Johnson were in favour of it and, albeit in a slightly different form and with some reservations, the great philosopher Adam Smith gave it his blessing. Adam Ferguson argued against it and noted the negative effects of the division of labour and commerce on the personality and social bonds of the individual citizen. In the process he contrasts the solidarity characteristic of closely knit tribes with the 'spirit which reigns in a commercial state where man is sometimes found a detached and solitary being, where 'he deals with his fellow creatures as he does with his cattle and his soil, for the sake of the profits they bring', and where 'the bands of affection are broken' (Hirschman 1997).

In the modern era the bands of affection have been well and truly shattered. Aristotelians put their faith in virtue ethics, heroically arguing for the social life and asserting that the good life is a life lived according to reason and the practice of virtue. They appear to believe that men will see sense and voluntarily submit themselves to a new moral order. (Crisp 1996; Hurka 1993, 2001). Sennett, on the other hand, has looked into the eyes of some of the supermen and believes that they know that they have 'left behind' the vast majority of the people and they are frightened. Their promotion of impatient flexibility does not give and cannot give any guidance to conduct of an ordinary life. He is pessimistic but concludes that if change is to come it will happen on the ground, between persons speaking 'out of inner need, rather than through mass uprisings' (Sennett 1998). I trust that he does not want to return to the iron cage of character and virtue though I can detect clear notes of nostalgia in what he has to say. Simon Blackburn is guardedly optimistic (Blackburn 2000). If we reflect on the increased sensitivity to the environment, to gender, to the disadvantaged, and to people different from ourselves that has occurred in the midst of the turmoil created by rampant capitalism we can, he claims, see small victories. Hard-won and fragile victories to be sure, but if events or people can stimulate sensitivity to the damage done to our ethical climate by unbridled capitalism, change could well occur.

REFERENCES

ALDERMAN, H. (1997). 'By Virtue of Virtue', in D. Statman (ed.), *Virtue Ethics: A Critical Reader*. Edinburgh: Edinburgh University Press.

ARISTOTLE (2000). *Nicomachean Ethics*. Cambridge: Cambridge University Press.

AUGUR, P. (2000). *The Death of Gentlemanly Capitalism*. London: Penguin Books.

BAUMAN, Z. (1998). *Globalization: The Human Consequences*. Cambridge: Polity Press.

—— (2000). *Liquid Modernity*. Cambridge: Polity Press.

BLACKBURN, S. (2001). *Being Good: A Short Introduction to Ethics*. Oxford: Oxford University Press.

BRONK, R. (1998). *Progress and the Invisible Hand: The Philosophy and Economics of Human Advance*. London: Little, Brown and Company (UK).

BUCHAN, J. (1997). *Frozen Desire: An Inquiry on the Meaning of Money*. London: Heineman.

CRISP, R. (ed.) (1996). *How Should One Live*. Oxford: Clarendon Press.

FERGUSON, N. (2001). *The Cash Nexus: Money and Power in the Modern World 1700–2000*. London: Penguin Press.

FRANK, T. (2001). *One Market under God: Extreme Capitalism, Market Populism and the End of Economic Democracy*. London: Secker and Warburg.

FUKUYAMA, F. (1996). *Trust: The Social Virtues and the Creation of Prosperity*. New York: Free Press.

GAMBETTA, D. (ed.) (1998). *Trust: Making and Breaking Cooperative Relations*. Oxford: Basil Blackwell.

GIDDENS, A. (1991). *Modernity and Self-Identity*. Cambridge: Polity Press.

—— (1994). 'Risk, Trust and Reflexivity', in U. Beck, S. Lash, and A. Giddens (eds.), *Reflexive Modernization*. Cambridge: Polity Press.

GIDDENS, A. (1999). *Runaway World: How Globalisation is Reshaping our Lives*. London: Penguin.

GOLDIE, P. (2000). *The Emotions: A Philosophical Exploration*. Oxford: Clarendon Press.

GOTTLIEB, A. (2000). *The Dream of Reason: A History of Philosophy from the Greeks to the Renaissance*. London: Penguin.

GREIDER, W. (1997). *One World, Ready or Not: The Manic Logic of Global Capitalism*. London: Penguin Press.

HADLEY, E. (1995). *Melodramatic Tactics: Theatricalized Dissent in the English Market Place 1800–1885*. Stanford, Calif.: Stanford University Press.

HART, K. (1988). 'Kinship: Contract as Trust', in D. Gambetta (ed.), *Trust: Making and Breaking Cooperative Relations*. Oxford: Blackwell.

HASLETT, D. W. (1994). *Capitalism with Morality*. Oxford: Clarendon Press.

HIMMELFARB, G. (1995). *The De-moralization of Society: From Victorian Virtues to Modern Values*. London: IEA Health and Welfare Unit.

——(1999). *One Nation, Two Cultures*. New York: Alfred A. Knopf.

HIRSCHHORN, L. (1998). *Reworking Authority: Leading and Following in the Post-Modern Organization*. Cambridge, Mass.: MIT Press.

HIRSCHMAN, A. O. (1997). *The Passions and the Interests: Political Arguments for Capitalism before its Triumph*. Princeton: Princeton University Press.

HUGHES, T. (2000). *Tom Brown's Schooldays*. Oxford: Oxford University Press.

HUNTER, J. DAVISON (2000). *The Death of Character: Moral Education in an Age Without Good or Evil*. New York: Basic Books.

HURKA, T. (1933). *Perfectionism*. New York: Oxford University Press.

——(2001). *Virtue, Vice and Value*. New York: Oxford University Press.

HUTTON, W. (1995). *The State We're In*. London: Jonathan Cape.

JACKALL, R. (1988). *Moral Mazes: The World of Corporate Managers*. New York: Oxford University Press.

KLEIN, N. (2001). *No Logo*. London: Harper Collins.

KUPPERMAN, J. (1991). *Character*. New York: Oxford University Press.

KYNASTON, D. (2001). *The City of London: A Club No More 1945–2000*. London: Chatto and Windus.

LANE, R. E. (1991). *The Market Experience*. Cambridge: Cambridge University Press.

LEVI, M. (1993). Review of D. Putnam, et al. *Making Democracy Work*. *Comparative Political Studies*, 26: 375–87.

LOPTSON, P. (1995). *Theories of Human Nature*. Peterborough, Ontario: Broadview Press.

MAC DONALD, FRASER (1969). *The Flashman Papers*, i. *Flashman*. London: Harper Collins.

MACINTYRE, A. (1981). *After Virtue: A Study in Moral Theory*. London: Duckworth.

MISZTAL, B. A. (1996). *Trust in Modern Societies*. Cambridge: Polity Press.

NICHOLSON, N. (2000). *Managing the Human Animal*. London: Texere.

PUTNAM, R. (1998). *Bowling Alone: The Collapse and Revival of American Community*. New York: Simon and Schuster.

RACHELS, J. (1978). *Elements of Moral Philosophy*. New York: McGraw-Hill.

RICHARDSON, J., and LEITER, B. (eds.) (2001). *Nietzsche*. Oxford: Oxford University Press.

ROSENBERG, J. (2000). *The Follies of Globalisation Theory*. London: Verso.

SANDERS, A. (1999). Introduction to Thomas Hughes, *Tom Brown's Schooldays*. Oxford: Oxford University Press.

SENNETT, R. (1998). *The Corrosion of Character: The Personal Consequences of Work in the New Capitalism.* New York: W. W. Norton and Company.

SHAPIRO, G. (1989). *Nietzschean Narratives.* Bloomington: Indiana University Press.

SHERMAN, N. (1989). *The Fabric of Character: Aristotle's Theory of Virtue.* Oxford: Clarendon Press.

——(1997). *Making a Necessity of Virtue: Aristotle and Kant on Virtue.* Cambridge: Cambridge University Press.

SOLOMON, R. (1993). *Ethics and Excellence: Cooperation and Integrity in Business.* New York: Oxford University Press.

THIELE, L. P. (1990). *Friedrich Nietzsche and the Politics of the Soul.* Princeton: Princeton University Press.

WOLFE, A. (1991). *America at Century's End.* Berkeley: University of California Press.

PART V

THE FUTURE OF ORGANIZATION THEORY

CHAPTER 19

THE FUTURE OF ORGANIZATION THEORY

PROSPECTS AND LIMITATIONS

GIBSON BURRELL

IT IS difficult in 4,000 words to say much with or of any subtlety. The 'new' question that needs to be addressed, perhaps, is 'For whom do we write?' Notice that the verb chosen relates to writing and not to speech nor consulting nor teaching. Immediately, then, I am emplacing the organization theorist as a research-orientated, publishing scholar above anything else. Put simply (not for the last time in this piece), there are four possible socio-economic groupings for whom we may wish to write. These are, namely, Board members or their equivalent, middle management, the subordinate employee, or, of course, other academics. Much of 'strategic management' seeks explicitly or implicitly to gain the ear of those who inhabit the most senior levels of the organizational world. The language here is of the relevance of what we say for the widespread process of 'strategizing' but the research is typically done with and on senior executive levels of the corporation, or its equivalent in the public or voluntary sectors. This seems to reflect a view that, like medics, our status comes from what or with whom we usually interact. Our raw material designates our status (Ackroyd and Crowdy 1992). Thus, just as the brain surgeon and the pedicurist gain cultural capital to differing degrees on the basis of which particular piece of human flesh they incise, it seems to me that strategic management only seeks, wholeheartedly, to learn about what the corporately powerful think and do. This, of course, can be exceptionally valuable as an aid to our understanding of organizational life but the issue is whether we write FOR and in the interest of these elite groups or not.

Middle management, for me, is the grouping about which much of organization theory is written. The growth in the Warfare and Welfare states across most of the developed world before and after World War II created huge swathes of bureaucratized landscapes which Max Weber's work was translated (both linguistically and spatially) in order to understand. The theory of bureaucracy, built upon Weber's huge historical understanding (but also, it must be recognized erected upon his own personal pursuit of what 'greatness' meant: Bologh 1990), identified the bureaucrat in a middle management position as a key figure of the twentieth century. Thus much of the post-war work on the dysfunctions of bureaucracy and the (often misguided) attacks upon the 'ideal type' had the swelling ranks of middle management as its theoretical and political object. We should note here that while management was the *explanandum* of the research on bureaucracy it was *not* the category that the early organization theorists wished to support and foster in its professional project. For example, it might be interesting to research the associated politics of the early organization theorists and investigate how the Harvard 'Pareto Circle' with its extraordinary but largely unsung impact upon the growth of organization theory may well have been motivated by deep concerns for the protection of the owners of capital and their elite positioning and not for their administrative arm. In the face of the growth of the State and provincial bureaucrat, the Pareto Circle seems to have been much more 'pro' the Board and its concerns (personified by Chester Barnard) rather than the groups it researched. Given the presence of Barnard (an owner of large amounts of capital) and A. N. Whitehead (a minor British 'aristocrat') amongst their number, it would be surprising had class-based interests been totally avoided!

I think it would be foolish, however, to believe that the MBA audience that many of us teach will escape from their middle rankings of the organizational bureaucracy into the Board level. And it is the typical MBA group (with its associated class position) which many staff within Business Schools see as the social grouping whose interests they wish to reflect and see prosper. If strategic management, then, targets the Board for research sites and sponsorship, organization theory targets the middle-ranking manager for precisely the same reason. Perhaps, therefore, it is better to think of the Pareto Circle as early strategic management consultants rather than organization theorists. And, of course, this would ease into an explanation of why the Harvard Business School is strong today in precisely this type of work. Interestingly, and as an aside, it is precisely here where Oxford and Cambridge Universities are seeking to place their new twenty-first century intellectual effort in the 'management' academic field: at Board level.

In general, the subordinate in paid employment or within the voluntary sector remains the subject of industrial or organizational sociology. She or he is researched about and very rarely researched for. Within Industrial Relations there is still a tradition of work being carried out for the Trade Unions, which may appear to contradict the previous sentence. However, it must be recognized that many a trade union is a corporate hierarchy like the businesses they deal with and so the individual worker, in whatever sector, has little done for them in terms of their research needs. Of course, to look at management is to also look at subordinates. The supervisory relationship definitionally is key to what it means to 'manage'.

The academics, of course, are the social grouping for whom we usually write. Whilst many outside, but also inside the profession, regard this orientation to the community of scholars as an introverted irrelevance, it seems to me that this is what remains at the core of our professional identity and is the *sine qua non* of university life. This is despite the existence of deep internal epistemological and methodological divisions and the obvious cloistering of our writing within disciplinary boundaries, a topic on which I will comment below.

Thus, we have at least four social groupings, (there is a fifth identified in the last paragraph of the piece) for whom we might write. My view is that organization theory is largely about management in many of its guises and how this intermediate group relates to both its hierarchical superiors and its subordinates. So my position is that organization theory is (and not necessarily 'ought to be') concentrated around the 'knowledge/management' dyad. But the precise links between knowledge and management needs to be thought through too. Is organization theory about knowledge for management, knowledge by management, or knowledge of management? The first of these leads to responsiveness to demands for approaches which are deemed relevant and interesting by MBA audiences and their sponsors. The task we face becomes one of producing material that is thought to be fit for consumption by managerial audiences. I reject this as a knowledge in which I should be interested. The knowledge that managers possess through and in their daily organizational lives is of some interest to me but not if it were seen as a form of superior understanding which comes from experiential learning. It is a form of knowledge in which one has an 'anthropological' interest. The third form of knowledge is knowledge about management. This is the stuff of the community of scholars, since it is based on research and theorizing, not on common sense understandings.

Thus organization theory for me is the careful investigation and critique of knowledge about management developed by the community of scholars (Tsoukas 2000), where management is seen as a middle-ranking social grouping within organizational contexts and is only understood in terms of its relations to its superiors and subordinates. It is a discourse designed explicitly for those within academia.

Next question; what methodological and epistemological orientations need to be adopted? Before answering this question, I think it important to turn our back on one overwhelmingly predominant orientation. Dale (2001) has shown that under-lying much of organization theory is the *anatomizing urge*. This hugely successful approach draws upon the techniques and language of anatomy and autopsy with-out us recognizing that a form of butchering is going on in our work which produces theoretical and methodological frameworks in which we have de-natured (i.e. killed) that which we seek to understand. The understanding of the human body upon which much of western medicine relies is drawn from analysis of the dissection of the dead cadaver upon the anatomist's table. The object of the anatomizing urge has to be deathly still in order for it to be rendered useful to analyse. But we are not only talking of medicine here. The more incisive one can be, so much the better; to penetrate down to the depths of the subject matter one needs sharpness and insight. Tissues are pinned down, de-natured, fixed, stained, put in wax, and sliced by the scalpel into smaller and smaller samples. They are analysed by using the 'objective' lens of the microscope. The privileging in science, whether organizational science or not, of these anatomizing terms reveals, for Dale, how dependent we are on the techniques of the anatomist. First, procure your freshly killed body and then proceed to eviscerate it. First, treat the organization as a fixed structure in time and space so that one can write about it. If we find something alive, vibrant, and difficult to pin down, we are so tempted to 'de-nature' it in order to proceed to gain insight of its 'underlying' mechanisms. Because of the unsung superiority of the role of the autopsist in the social sciences as well as the natural sciences, I would suggest that we must be very wary of the anatomizing urge and its role in organization theory. The language and metaphors we use within the community of scholars, says Dale (2001), are often drawn from such a deathful and violent context. This does not leave us methodologically or ethically unscathed.

On a different front, there has been a revival in the fortunes of a realist perspec-tive to epistemology within the United Kingdom. The paradoxical thing is that this may be better seen as the *ontological turn* (Brigham 2000) rather than something exclusively epistemological, for it deals with the supposed nature of reality. The ontological turn attempts to return debate to issues of the 'real' from what are seen as the excesses of the postmodern turn in organization theory where the question of what is real and non-real cannot be answered for 'there is nothing outside of the text' (Derrida 1977). The debate has valorized the work of Harré (Harré and Secord 1973; Harré and Madden 1975), Bhaskar (1978, 1989), Outhwaite(1987), and Archer (1995; Archer *et al.* 1998) and places the emphasis on the way in which the 'real' may be constructed and analysed and used (Keat and Urry 1975) These writings have begun to find their way into organization theory through Ackroyd and Fleetwood's collection (2000) but in forms which are not easily digestible philosophy. I will attempt to put the case for understanding what is going on in this arena, albeit crudely, because it is an interesting site of investigation.

In brief, realists might typically (for example Archer *et al.* 1998: 3–10) adopt the following assumptions and value positions:

1. Inter-subjective and rational scientific knowledge of the real world is possible. The real world is made up of essences or has an inner constitution (of forces, structures, processes, entities, etc.), which are not amenable to human observation. Essences or deep structures are knowable but are not observable. What *is* observable is the domain of the empirical. Between the real and the empirical lies the domain of the actual.

2. Since deep structures are not observable, they are not available for experimental technique, measurement, or operationalizability. The penetrative metaphors of incisiveness and revelation are not much in evidence. Bhaskar speaks of realism as 'clearing the ground' and 'removing the rubbish' that stands in the way of knowledge (Marsden 1999: 43). Quantification of the world of essences is not possible nor is prediction of future events or happenings, since these emanate from the 'essential'. In order for the human being to understand non-empirical causal mechanisms within the real, she/he is required to develop thought-objects. The unavoidable use of such of 'thought-objects' always intervenes between the experience of the theorist and the real. These devices perhaps are akin to natural science technologies of 'visualization'.

3. Structures are real things and are not to be confused with models. Whilst it is difficult to avoid analogy and metaphor in realist thinking it is important that the realist is aware of the constraining nature that our thought-objects (i.e. conceptualizations or technologies of visualization) have on our view of real objects.

4. Observable reality—the level of appearance and how it is experienced—cannot be explained in terms of empirically based 'facts'. One cannot reduce events or phenomena on the level of appearance to explanation on that same superficial level. This is what empiricists are seen as having done throughout the course of the Scientific Age. Explanation must be in terms of essences or deep structures without necessary recourse to the observables of the world. Here an obvious geological metaphor is often invoked whereby the 'surface' is differentiated from the 'deep' and both from the level of the actual. Thus there is the invocation of the need to study the 'generative mechanisms' (Harré and Secord 1973) of surface phenomena and these mechanisms are seen as having arisen from the 'deep' via the intermediate level of events. At each level within this stratified world, new properties may emerge in contingent ways.

5. Realists tend to see causality in a different way to empirically based science. For the empiricist, the Newtonian imagery of billiard ball causality usually suffices. Here, three elements are crucial in a view often associated with the philosopher, David Hume. First, cause and effect must be identifiably separate, second there must be constant conjunction (i.e. the same effect will always follow the same cause), and the cause must be necessary and sufficient to explain the effect. For the realist, on

the other hand, there is the possibility of embracing metonymic causality rather than Humean causality. Within this Althusserian structuralist stance, it is possible for cause and effect to occur together in place and time. Thus causality might be seen as being synchronous. Moreover, the relationship may not be one of constant conjunction in that structural forces may precipitate surface events on some occasions but not others. Predictability is thus a false hope. But outcomes can be explained *post facto*.

Obviously, space does not permit the portrayal of these views in anything but skeletal form but for those of an empiricist or phenomenological bent there should be enough to get their teeth into. My task here is to paint a very broad brush picture of one future for organization theory so let me put these assumptions of realism alongside models of science and see what possibilities exist. Unsurprisingly, things become very complicated indeed.

Three '*logics of science*' may be identified which are relevant to any discussion of realism and, it may be noted, to any epistemological differences between us. The first logic is the Logic of Discovery. Here the real world is seen as possessing regularities and behaves according to law-like rules which scientists can discover through detailed observation and experimentation. Theories lie within the real world awaiting discovery. Hence Pope could famously claim in 1730:

> 'Nature and Nature's laws lay hid in night;
> God said "Let Newton be!" and all was light'

The second logic is the Logic of Conjecture. In this perspective, theories do not lie there waiting to be discovered but are the creations of geniuses. Great thinkers produce conjectures that must be tested against the real world to see how they match up. Theories and reality then, are different but correspond with each other to varying degrees. The third logic is the Logic of Invention. Within this framework, the real world is seen as only knowable through our theories. Theories actually create the world for us in a process whereby our epistemology determines our ontology. Theories are inventions therefore, but so is the real world. Correspondence between the two is no test of a theory's validity.

Let me try to assess the possibilities for organization theory using the following elements that the preceding paragraphs have mentioned. There is the distinction between the *surface* world of observable appearances, the intermediate world of events, and the domain of hidden *deep* structures, which we have to bear in mind. There are three different *logics of science* and two different approaches to *causality*. Put these together and the epistemological and methodological possibilities for the discipline are not insignificant. The approaches identified as possibilities using this framework for looking at the ontological turn are:

1. *Naive empiricism.* Here the approach is to see surface phenomena as connected to other surface phenomena through the mechanism of some Humean causality. There is no or very little sense of depth. All relationships are 'horizontal' and the approach possesses no ontic depth. Much of our field can be seen as eschewing any notion that does rest on naive empiricism because it will be deemed non-scientific or even downright metaphysical. Everything is governed by the Logic of Discovery.

2. *Analytical empiricism.* In this development out of naive empiricism, the logic of discovery is still in force for those phenomena at the surface level but the approach recognizes that deep structures may come into play to explain certain superficial events and occurrences. These deep structures are graspable through the logic of conjecture in which the Great Scientist reveals what is masked for the rest of us. Humean causality is in operation within and between both levels.

3. *Conventionalism.* This perspective sees only reasons and not causes as connecting phenomena. In other words, it is a human attribution of interconnectedness that relates one thing to another. Were we to label it differently, then the mechanisms of connection would also change. Here the logic of invention reigns supreme and there is no room for any ontic depth, since the surface and the deep are simple metaphorical devices to explain the world to ourselves.

4. *Orthodox realism.* As we have seen in earlier paragraphs, there is a recognition of the distinction between the surface and the depths. The logic of discovery plays its part at the surface but the logic of invention is necessary to understand the deep. What and how we theorize is crucially important to the ways in which we understand how generative mechanisms come to work. There is some acceptance of Humean causality at and within the three ontic levels but synchronous causality is often seen as important too.

My own starting point is more subjectivist than that of orthodox realism and is dependent entirely on the logic of invention. No scientific endeavour can do without empirical grounding, but this is not to say that we should valorize empirical research, as usually understood. As Clegg (1975: 82) says, 'We have no need to produce data because they surround us at every turn.' Since we are always and forever producing material inscribed by the anatomizing lesions of our conceptualizations upon the real world, we can do nothing other than invent, through the scalpel of language, that which we treat as the researched (the explanandum) and that which we use to do the research (the explanans). How then is the scientist to avoid seduction into solipsistic ramblings or escape the charge that reality is merely a personal product of the language game inhabited by the theoretician? At this point we come back to the question of why and for whom do we research? If we work for the community of scholars, it is this body that assesses what constitutes knowledge and what represents good theory. The most one can hope for is that this group, or subgroups within it most likely, will see one's theory as both plausible and informative. It is for this reason that the language game we collectively play as academics is worth defending, for it makes us the constructors of *explanans* and *explanandum* and not some other tendentious social grouping. The issue of why we do not research with and for subordinate social groupings but merely ourselves is addressed later.

Realism. I see it both as important and as gaining devotees. Possibly because it offers an 'ontological turn' in the face of the epistemological interests of the ageing postmodernists, it has been resurrected very recently from the cryogenic chamber in which it was placed in the early 1980s (Reed 2000: 61). So long as what we have learnt from postmodernism is not completely forgotten, then something different allows temporary escape from philosophical boredom. So realism is diverting. But realism also stands in places as a proxy for the reintroduction of Marxism and this is entirely healthy. What I see as positive is the politicization of academic discourse and colleagues behaving once again as if things mattered.

The third question on the future of organization theory concerns the *interrelationships* that may emerge between existing research traditions. I have no wish to add to the gravitational pull exerted by the powerful within our discipline. Convergence and alliance reduces the polymorphic flow of ideas and the variety of positions possible. It coalesces them into increasingly sclerotic structures of domination. Here instead I would wish to focus on the possibilities of neo-disciplinarity (Burrell *et al.* 1994). Now by this term the following is meant.

1. Notwithstanding the consensual view of knowledge applied above as the litmus test of knowledge development and enhancement, it would be a foolish member of the academy who thought that all was well within our present disciplinary arrangements. Foucault has told us that the disciplinary technologies currently available in the present epoch contain dressage, the confession, the panopticon, and the judges of normality. Each, in detail, can be seen as part of the panoply of constraints that surround us within the discipline. Here again language is suggestive for we do profess 'discipline' and we do 'submit' our papers for scrutiny. So, whilst I have no wish to dispense with the centrality of the aggregation of academics as the grouping to whom I wish to appeal, I do wish to escape from the shackles of much of the disciplinary field. One way to do this is to create a more robust but less disciplined community of scholars.

2. This community should be much more democratically organized than at present. The Academy is full of the paraphernalia of power. The long march from research fellowship to full chair is a nightmare road for many, containing the pitfalls of academic politics and fear of offending the powerful. We require, might I suggest, journals and organs of publication that are controlled less by the gerontocracy and more by the younger generation. The issues of quality control, of course, would be seen as central but one lesson we might take from Kuhn (1963) is that defunct paradigms die out and allow revolutionary developments only when the paradigm

disciplinarians actually (rather than metaphorically) die out. Given this, and since I am editor of a journal, it might strike the reader that the best thing that might happen then, is for yours truly to shuffle off this mortal coil. Less threatening personally, perhaps, is the possibility that it should be feasible to see editorial teams of Ph.D.s editing leading journals (on at least an occasional basis, if you so wish) and to see what impact this has on the inventiveness, quality, and impact of the material published. Would it improve?

3. The community does not have to be the one as presently constituted. In my view there is much going on in Geography and Accounting and Cultural Studies with which we should be familiar and which would make much better correspondence with organization theory than some approaches which are obviously calling themselves by that label. So 'neo-disciplinarity' is about widening the field of our interest to learn from others. Widening the field is not in any way, shape, or form a military metaphor when used here, for the idea is not to forage and plunder in someone else's intellectual territory but to sit and listen to what they have to say and see if we can gain illumination. Neo-disciplinarity then is short of the disciplinary technologies outlined by Foucault but long on listening sympathetically to work in cognate areas. Neo-disciplines in brief do not have to look (as some twenty-first century universities still do) like they are a product of the German university system at the time of Humboldt. They could be exciting communities of scholars, more democratically organized than we are used to, where graduate students ran journals and where gerontocracy was less well established.

4. The predominance of North Atlantic Theories of Organization (NATO) also needs to be addressed within any neo-disciplinary move. Globalization was creatively and usefully analysed by a group of researchers (Waters 1995) at one possible location of what we might call *Ultima Thule*. This particular 'end of the world' was on the island of Tasmania. It appears to me as if insight may well come from one's marginal position vis-à-vis the world economy or whatever other types of centre of power are significant. The location of the marginal in relation to what passes for the global in organization theory may well be an expedition that we could take part in and otherwise encourage.

In summary, I would hope to see the concept of neo-disciplinarity as outlined above take a concrete form and develop over the next decade.

The final issue to address then is the question of what are the most *important problems* to be solved. The whole question, of course, relies upon the notion that solutions to intellectual problems really exist and that the questions raised in Ancient Athens were solved some time ago. Research questions that have answers are what doctoral candidates are expected to ask. The important problems of ethics, aesthetics, power, and control remain ever with us. I have argued elsewhere (Burrell 1997) that the peasantry remains one key social grouping in whom, demonstrably, we have absolutely no interest. A key question to ask ourselves is why? Might it be that the relevance of our understandings for the lives and thoughts of over half the world's population is absolutely zero. Organization theory is a product of the twin processes of industrialization and bureaucratization. It might be asserted that all societies on the face of this small planet might eventually embrace both processes to the full. Hence organization theory may await the entry of every human being as part of its explanandum. Meanwhile, however, are we supposed to see the glaring absence of the peasantry from our theories and methods as natural or even defensible? The southern border of the United States with Mexico may be thought to represent in some small way this division between an organization theory which is exclusionary and a society in which the concept of peasant has not yet lost its total significance. If American colleagues feel that this is not relevant as a concept to them, then one must accept it perhaps. But in Europe where bureaucratization and industrialization may be thought to have run their course for decades, we neverthe-less must realize that the peasantariat are alive and well in Spain, Italy, Portugal, Greece, and France, to say nothing of the post-communist nations. Yet they are outside of our logic of invention, our logic of conjecture, and our logic of discovery.

What has been attempted here is to provide a very personal account of what other contributors have been asked to consider. What might organization theory see as a 'new' question? My answer: who do we write for? My take on new epistemological and methodological positions is to argue for a rejection of the 'anatomizing urge' which haunts much of science without us being aware of its baleful influence and to think again (not necessarily positively) about some form of 'realism' within the 'ontological turn' now evident in some arenas of organization theory. My view of realism, however, is that it is still an epistemological stance rather than a question of 'reality' and it will always rely on a logic of invention rather than of discovery or of conjecture. The question of what interrelationships we might encourage within organization theory needs to be rephrased (it seems to me) to include the encour-agement of neo-disciplinarity, the involvement of the young in the dissemination and creation of newly published material and closer connections of a non-exploitative kind with other social science disciplines. Finally, what we need to look at, and have not yet done so, is the three billion people on the planet who remain outside conventional western notions of organization and even outside of our conventional notions of the subordinate. This is the peasantry.

REFERENCES

ACKROYD, S., and CROWDY, P. (1992). 'Can Culture be Managed? The Case of the English Slaughtermen'. *Personnel Review*, 19/5: 3–13.
——— and FLEETWOOD, S. (eds.) (2000). *Realist Perspectives on Management and Organiza-tions*. London: Routledge.

ALTHUSSER, L. (1969). *For Marx*. Harmondsworth: Penguin.

ARCHER, M. (1995). *Realist Social Theory: The Morphogenetic Approach*. Cambridge: Cambridge University Press.

——BHASKAR, R., COLLIER, A., LAWSON, T., and NORRIE, A. (eds.) (1998). *Critical Realism: Essential Readings*. London: Routledge.

BHASKAR, R. (1975). *A Realist Theory of Science*. Brighton: Harvester.

——(1989). *The Possibility of Naturalism*. Hemel Hempstead: Harvester Wheatsheaf.

BOLOGH, R. (1990). *Love or Greatness*. London: Unwin Hyman.

BRIGHAM, M. (2000). 'Technology, Organization and Actor-Network Theory'. Unpublished manuscript, University of Warwick.

BURRELL, G. (1997). *Pandemonium: Towards a Retro-organization Theory*. London: Sage.

——CALÁS, M., REED, M., SMIRCICH, L., and WHITAKER, A. (1994). 'Why Organization? Why now?' *Organization*, 1/1: 3–9.

CLEGG, S. (1975). *Power, Rule and Domination*. London: Routledge & Kegan Paul.

DALE, K. (2001). *Anatomising Embodiment and Organization Theory*. Basingstoke: Palgrave.

DERRIDA, J. (1977). *Of Grammatology*, trans. G. Spivak. Baltimore: Johns Hopkins University Press.

HARRÉ, R., and MADDEN, E. H. (1975). *Causal Powers*. Oxford: Blackwell.

——and SECORD, P. (1973). *The Explanation of Social Behaviour*. Oxford: Blackwell.

KEAT, R., and URRY, J. (1975). *Social Theory as Science*. London: RKP.

KUHN, T. S. (1963). *The Structure of Scientific Revolutions*. Chicago: University of Chicago Press.

MARSDEN, R. (1999). *The Nature of Capital*. London: Routledge.

OUTHWAITE, W. (1987). *New Philosophies of Social Science*. London: Macmillan.

POPE, A. (1730). Epitaph intended for Sir Isaac Newton.

REED, M. (2000). 'In Praise of Duality and Dualism', republished in S. Ackroyd and S. Fleetwood (eds.), *Realist Perspectives on Management and Organizations*. London: Routledge.

RUSSETT, C. (1966). *The Concept of Equilibrium in American Social Thought*. New Haven: Yale University Press.

TSOUKAS, H. (2000). 'What is Management? An Outline of a Metatheory', republished in S. Ackroyd and S. Fleetwood (eds.), *Realist Perspectives on Management and Organizations*. London: Routledge.

WATERS, M. (1995). *Globalization*. London: Routledge.

CHAPTER 20

MANAGING ORGANIZATION FUTURES IN A CHANGING WORLD OF POWER/KNOWLEDGE

STEWART CLEGG

AT THE core of management is the legitimation, extension, and normalization of dominant property rights, the practical disciplining of the everyday organizational life of members, and the framing of knowledge that can be ascribed a key role in extending, limiting, and otherwise shaping these rights. I call this the discourse of power/knowledge—a discourse that, in academic terms, functions as a surrogate for discussion of sovereignty.

It is a schizoid discourse. On the one hand, the issues of sovereignty are largely evaded or avoided—even where one might expect to find them—such as in

I would like to acknowledge the helpful comments made on an earlier version of this chapter by John Garrick, Alfred Kieser, Dexter Dunphy, and Ray Gordon, although none of them are responsible for the views that are elaborated here. Elements of this argument were developed from earlier joint work with Thomas Clarke and Eduardo Ibarra, although it is correct to say that the ideas expressed here are my own. No one else is responsible for them.

discussions of power by significant theorists, including Pfeffer (1981, 1992) and Mintzberg (1983). These deal with power merely as a matter of, respectively, strategic resource control or illegitimate moves in the legitimate organization game. Neither of them addresses the already deeply embedded and power-saturated context within which any specific episodes of power might occur as, itself, a constitutive part of power. In fact, the organization theory debate is marked most significantly in many areas by its absences and silences, its ellipses and prevarications. Thus, Cynthia Hardy and I once ironically termed a piece that we wrote on the topic, 'Some Dare Call it Power'—because most did not dare address it at all. On the other hand, the broader debates in social science theory, as they have developed from Lukes (1974) and Foucault (1979), where the issues are more adequately addressed, remain barely acknowledged. Look in vain in the bibliographies of almost all the standard OT texts and you will find no awareness of a debate that dominated late twentieth-century social theory and social science. Looking at the standard Business Studies degree curriculum, it would seem that most organization and management theory seems to have effectively inoculated itself against being a broader part of the academy of social sciences. While power may have a central role to play in areas such as political theory, sociology, political science, public administration, and macroeconomics, it rarely seems to feature much in the standard organizations curriculum—at least if one looks as the usual textbooks.

What might be meant by power? In brief: all forms of organization are forms of organization of social relations. All social relations involve power relations. Power is evident in these relations as relations not only of ownership and control but also of structuration and design. These relations may take many forms. They may be embodied as financial capital, intellectual capital, or social capital, for instance. Such relations are likely to be both differentially distributed and socially constructed as well as exist in differential demand in differentiated markets. Power is also evident in the various forms of knowledge that constitute, structure, and shape these markets and organizations[1].

It is these power/knowledge relations that I wish to address—especially as they are likely to shape the future of our practice. Our practice, I take it, is to address analytically the methods of managing and organizing that members of various organizational bodies and communities find conventional to use and to detail something more to members accounts than they might be able to tell us themselves.

I shall begin by addressing 'Managing'.

[1] The following are relevant but not complete references to my evolving views on power: Clegg (2000; 1997a; 1997c; 1995; 1990; 1992; 1989a; 1989b; 1987; 1983; 1981; 1979; 1977; 1975), Clegg and Wilson (1992) and Hardy and Clegg (1999). *Frameworks of Power* (1989b) is the most complete statement, one I would not wish to revise significantly.

20.1 Managing

Managers, above all, are practical people who have to manage extremely difficult and challenging tasks: they are beset by many contingencies on a daily basis, some routine, others not. If Mintzberg (1973) is a reliable guide, they need to find solutions to new problems every ten minutes or so. Not surprisingly, they have little time for other than the most local, contextual, and bounded working knowledge.

From an academic point of view, managing involves creating an ordered ensemble of relations between past histories and future actions as strategies that construct the present. Managing means creating nexi of peoples, materials, and technologies that can act semi-autonomously in pursuit of these strategies. Managing enables people, materials, and technologies—bound together through ideas about their interrelation—to traverse spaces and times. Managing makes knowledge work to constitute specific spaces and times into patterned locales and arenas in which people make sense of and transform materials and technologies.

Sending ideas out into the wide world, to traverse space and time, has always been destructive of local cultures. Weber (1976) recognized this explicitly at the outset of modern organization studies when he represented the battle that the 'Protestant ethic' fought with other rationalities. These involved the replacement of the rhythms of a rural and Catholic past of holy days, saints days, name days, with a more disciplined regime of rational management of time (see also Thompson 1968). The *Protestant Ethic* overlaid and rationalized the traditions of the past.

Modern managing still involves the creative destruction of existing recipes and practices in order to reinvent the world of organizations. Such managing means disorganizing and deconstructing the routines of the past, retaining some while changing others, melding them to new technologies, devices which the workforce experience as new rhythms of work. Management has always pursued this project: little has changed today other than the tempo, and the global reach, of the reorganization that contemporary management knowledge requires.

Knowledge always has a provenance, or, as one might say, exists within a discursive realm. The bulk of management theory originates in the United States. Consequently, in many other places, spaces, and cultures, managers will struggle to make sense of organizations and politics through theories overwhelmingly produced and reproduced elsewhere, under different assumptions, from different realities. For non-English speakers, language and culture are a large part of the problem: outside of the English language, what one regards as familiar attributes of managing and organizing, such as a shared sense of time, turn out to be quite unfamiliar. For instance, there are still many locales where concepts of time have not been institutionalized by the factory; where the rhythms of religion, agriculture, family, community, or political obligation are much more powerful (Child and Rodrigues 1996).

In practice, how do managers make sense of the experience of managing? It is not quite as rational a process as management academics would prefer to think. Let me begin with some famous high-profile managers. The ex-President of the United States, Ronald Reagan, consulted the scripts of films that he knew, such as 'Star Wars': his First Lady, Mrs Nancy Reagan consulted her astrologer. Don't mock: the predictions of astrologers, or *feng shui* practitioners, for example, are at least as important as those of econometricians or management consultants for many significant economic actors in some highly successful economies, such as Hong Kong. (It should be noted that, while one finds the rituals of *feng shui* more charming than those of econometricians, one leaves it to others to judge their relative reliability.) Some other managers, trained in Business Schools, may seek to apply some models that they dimly remember from their MBA. Still others will think of the most recent columns they read in the press or that last book they bought at the airport on a business trip, or how their mother or father brought them up, or how a winning football team is managed. Managers in various contexts will have different relevancies guiding their managing. Thus, we may say that, in historical and comparative practice, managers have drawn on many forms of knowledge.

Consequently, there are many sources from which orientations to practice might develop: not only from university courses but also from popular books, training sessions, magazines, websites, the popular press, as well as the usual friendship networks. In practical terms, university academics enjoy neither an exclusive nor a privileged role: they are not legislators of management knowledge but are simply among its many interpreters (Bauman 1987). Thus, our power is very limited and our knowledge is in no way legislatively mandated. However, many university academics continue to practice their craft *as if* they were powerful legislators rather than particular interpreters. It is, of course, largely a myth. The institutionalized norms of journal production support this myth.

How do the various sources of management knowledge relate to the work that management academics do? There is a range of views on this central question. For some colleagues, such as Donaldson (1992: 464), a clear relation exists. It should be 'the moral project advocated by Popper (1945) for social science: by use of the critical method of theory construction and testing to dispense with bogus ideologies and thereby to ground social discourse in actualities so that policy choices could be made in a clearer light.' Well, moral projects are all very well but are not necessarily descriptive of what ordinarily occurs. If they were, they would hardly be considered necessary. Moreover, as Latour (1993) suggested, Popper did not even capture what scientists actually did when they did science so one should not easily assume that his representations will prescribe the relation between the hard-pressed ten-minute managers and a body of evidence taught and published elsewhere in rather abstracted conditions.

Astley and Zammuto (1992) saw the relation between managers and academics as metaphorical: sometimes managers and academicians play coincidental metaphorical language games; sometimes they do not. If utility is a criterion then it is managers who should set the terms of trade, they suggested. Beyer (1992) struck a mid-point: it is the operationalization of metaphors and testing them against empirical reality that is important. If academicians are serious about trade with managers, then they should commit resources to mechanisms designed to maximize the trade, on the model of the successful diffusion of innovation by the US agricultural extension service (Rogers 1995). What may be required is a cadre of academics who specialize in translation into field settings: knowledge out-workers refabricating scientific knowledge by shaping it to applied purposes.

Each of these accounts seems to characterize managers as what Garfinkel (1967) once referred to as 'cultural dopes': actors unable to write or mouth their own scripts but subject only to those foisted on to them by analytic outsiders—in this case organization scholars. What is clear is that while Donaldson (1992) and Beyer (1992) see the role of organization science as something that should be the source of management practice, Astley and Zammuto (1992) saw the possibility of management practice as an autonomous sphere. For the former, organization science stands as a causal grammar underlying what managers do or should do; for the latter, the accounts of managing that managers have available are not causal springs of their actions. Instead, Astley and Zammuto (1992) tend to see practical management actions as something that may be discursively legitimated by abstract management knowledge, in another version of 'elective affinity', where practitioners choose the affinities. No necessary relation exists between the words and the deeds: managing means being discursively creative in justifying situational actions.

For managers, the craft of academia, at best, provides a set of popular recipes and tools. These can be useful in trying to find solutions to the problems of managing modern organizations; with such guidelines and tools, managers are able to create order out of potential chaos, are able to be seen to be managing rather than merely coping. In fact, most of what is borrowed lacks scientific proof and is often used retrospectively to legitimate decisions made and actions taken on grounds that are more personal or political.

Thus far I have assumed, on the one hand, an autonomous and coherent sphere of management practice and, on the other hand, a coherent and autonomous sphere of management knowledge. In neither case is coherence or autonomy necessarily the case, as I shall explore next. Thus, I address the status of 'paradigms'.

20.2 PARADIGMS

One knows the term 'paradigm' in the social sciences principally from Thomas Kuhn (1962), the historian of science. Applying his ideas about the constitutive truth-framing role of paradigms, one may note that paradigms define the key terms of their own discourse. Thus, in science they define what motion is, what gravity is; in social science they may define differently, and at various times, what efficiency is, what property is, what excellence is, and so on. The social science concepts are clearly 'constructs in use' for the primary actors—managers—as well as for those secondary actors—social scientists—who observe them. And therein lies the rub. What is critical to the legitimacy of such second-order constructs is either that managers see themselves within and thus act in terms of these paradigmatically constitutive definitions and images, or that what managers might think and do is irrelevant for academic practice.

Clegg and Hardy (1996) have described the 'paradigm wars' of Organization Studies. But the concept of paradigm at issue in these wars to this point has been applied only to academic social scientists not to managers as actors. In Organization Studies, the paradigm wars sparked off by Burrell and Morgan (1979) were a debate almost entirely confined to academics, the community within which the Astley and Zammuto/Donaldson/Beyer interchange occurred.

Elsewhere, however, consultants were getting in on the act and in the process the 'meaning in use' of the term 'paradigm' changed (Barker 1992). While the concept of managers using different organizations studies paradigms to think with has been translated into the paradigms idea of 'frames' or images' (Bolman and Deal 1991; Morgan 1986), these academic concerns with paradigms still remain separate from the concerns of practitioners. Meanwhile, practitioner concerns had gained support in a more general literature (see the overview by Clarke and Clegg 1998), in a conception of 'business paradigms'. These were not the models that academicians used to make sense of organizational reality but those that the organizational sensemakers themselves use. In the academic sense, they would be first-order meta-constructs. Such constructs are clearly not only of rhetorical significance but also of practical relevance in the way that businesses are run, relating not to academics meta-frameworks for understanding organizational life but to the frameworks that managers use in their ordinary understandings of what they do.

Business paradigms, as the sensemaking methods in use of everyday business people, may be seen as an example of what Foucault (1979) termed the pastoral guidance of each epoch; they represent the changes in the 'imaginary' of managers between one epoch and another. These imaginaries define who one is by showing one how to construct reality, what place one has is in it, as well as the place of others and other things. Through such imaginaries one is able not only to normalize particular constructions of reality in and around organizations but also to stigmatize and marginalize those who do not accept the reality of the epoch that one is in the business of creating.

Business paradigms synthesize ideas that represent the world from the point of view of managers and businesspeople, responding to their perceptions of the changing business environment, often as interpreted by popular writers and consultants. They provide systems of value, with which managers can interpret reality, act on it, and place ethical limits upon behaviour. The meaning given to concepts such as work, property, management, efficiency, performance, quality, excellence, innovation, and knowledge, not only orient social practices but also provide the means deemed adequate for those purposes. They provide a set of images that orient the conduct of individual organizations, considering specific materials, relations, and procedures. These paradigms are developed and achieve ascendancy only to reveal their limitations and be subsumed within former business paradigms, as a new paradigm is constructed to deal with the next business dilemma.

At the core of these paradigmatic representations, in fluid, innovative, and competitive market economies, as de Gaudemar (1991) suggested, the problem of work for management becomes not that it be obligatory but attractive.[2] This is particularly necessary in periods of economic expansion when skilled labour is hard to attract and also in knowledge-based organizations where management has to rely on the inner motivation of the workers. For the majority of employees without alternatives to the sale of their wage-labour, what determines the terms of their effort bargain is the attractiveness and interest of their work, not its necessity. For the majority, necessity is a priori. Employee attitudes will be transformed less through punishment and more through the foundation of a new mode of life that creates the conditions for voluntary and productive work. The constitution of discipline in organizations and the transformation of employees thus rest on the progressive invention of recipes that aid the constitution of the working self as one who is somewhat creative, reasonably obedient, and fairly satisfied. With these main ideas, de Gaudemar stresses the link between the images of the manager and discipline at work: if this image changes, as the manager's paradigm changes, then the discipline changes. Thus, during this century one can appreciate that business paradigms are the tip of an iceberg of deeper material changes that have occurred inside enterprises.

In the management literature the assumption has often been that management and organization theories are 'culture free' (Hickson *et al.* 1974). That is, they posit, represent and predict a stable and universal reality. Yet, of course, theories are both

---

[2] Thanks to Eduardo Ibarra for the reference and translation of the key point.

culturally contingent (Maier 1975) in their adaptation and simultaneously recursive and reflexive in their relation to the realities that they purport to posit, represent, and predict. It is not so much that they depict a universal essence but rather that they are continually reconstituting a moving target, with shifting boundaries of changing practice. The moral philosophy of science is one of universalism. What it takes to be true here and now, should, in all probability be true there and then, providing its protocols are observed. How have these contradictions been reconciled or challenged?

Reconciliation is achieved largely through institutional separation—the classic strategy of institutionalization. On the one hand, there are the institutions of science as it is translated from research into publication in the top-tier journals which proudly deploy their armouries of scientificity to produce artefacts that can be valued as best research practice. Such work is exemplary and there is much to be learnt from it (Frost and Stablein 1992). On the other hand, however, it leaves the relation between institutional spheres begging. The institution of science does not address the issue of translatability beyond the research journals and into the recursive and reflexive realm of practice or the profound differences between the social and the natural sciences. At the nub of these differences is that while the subject matter of the natural sciences may be presumed to have no working knowledge, those in the social sciences do. Moreover, these subjects not only enjoy their own working knowledge; they are increasingly reluctant to submit themselves to the imperious authority of institutions of science that treat their knowledge as irrelevant, wrong, or just plain uninteresting. That the mundane knowledge of management should be seen as such is the standard response of the expert scientist, when faced with practices that they do not support (Hilmer and Donaldson 1996). Mundane management ideas are presumed, on the whole, to be ignorant of the deeper structural or causal currents that lie beyond the ken of managers and which are explicable only in the realm of science. The imperiousness of institutions that would insist on such a profound disregard for what their subjects might think is as evident as its provenance is clear: it derives from a moral model in which the sentiments of ordinary people are unimportant because ordinary people are not its subjects. In fact, ideally, the subject realm should be wholly a world of objects, and if it is not, it should be treated as if it were. Some of our colleagues do a great job creating such reification.

Somewhat surprisingly, the major challenge to the presumed universalism of paradigms has not come from a critique of the institutional weakness of management knowledge conceived as a universal scientific enterprise. Instead it has arisen from the economic success of organizations whose local realities seemed starkly at odds with those assumed by universalism. One thinks, for example, of Whitley's (1992) accounts of East Asian business systems, of Redding's (1990) account of the 'Spirit of Chinese Capitalism', of Clegg's (1990) account of 'French Bread, Italian Fashions, and East Asian Enterprise'. In more practical and less academic terms the currency turbulence of 1997–8, and the IMF response to it, threatened the assumption that there might be organizational scope for local realities, local rationalities, that ran counter to the trend of universalization. Such events, irrespective of any moral argument about the efficacy of the different regimes of truth at issue, are instances, precisely, of normalization, marginalization, and stigmatization. Any recourse to a universalizing vision of order and equilibrium, where everything has its place, is weakened by accounts that suggest alternative realities. Whatever interpretation one might make of the market's judgement of the East Asian economies, it is evident that much changed organizationally. Initially, organizational changes were experienced locally; liquidity tightened; credit became more expensive; firms went bankrupt; workers were laid off; currencies devalued. But the effects were not just local: these experiences result in part from the international connectedness of worldwide markets such that no market is an island.

Information technology (IT) connects local rationalities, with their local peculiarities, to the expressive essence of universal rationality constructed as the effects of buy or sell decisions made on a few thousand terminals around the world on a 24-hour basis. Speculation translates the rationality of the market into life and death judgements that impact most adversely on those business systems and organizations that do not correspond to universally accepted economic prescriptions for excellence, as interpreted through the electronic global market. Information technology capacities and the decision-making that they support have a universal dimension. Thus, the technological advances associated with information technology transform the nature of managing.

IT has other effects. Managing is also being transformed by the re-engineering of established occupations; new occupations have been born on the back of the new technologies, which, to a considerable extent, have also made the boundaries of organizations extremely permeable. IT also creates new opportunities for market transactions in areas where insufficient availability of information had in the past made it difficult to construct them. One consequence is that the market has penetrated many of the most bureaucratic areas of organizational life. However, at the same time, learning has penetrated many of the most market-oriented areas, such that even the specificity of that last redoubt of bureaucracy, universities, is under challenge. Social organizations, such as universities, are becoming more like business firms, while business firms (as learning or intelligent organizations) are becoming more like universities used to be thought to be (see Gibbons *et al.* 1994; Ezkowitz and Leydesdorff 1997). The old orders seem to be melting away, however contingently solid they once might have seemed, under the pressures of reflexive knowledge working.

20.3 REFLEXIVE KNOWLEDGE WORKING

Working knowledge, typically, involves 'a fluid mix of framed experience, values, contextual information and expert insights that provides a framework for evaluating and incorporating new experiences and information' (Davenport and Prusack 1998: 4). Such knowledge, as Davenport and Prusack immediately go on to point out, 'often becomes embedded not only in documents or repositories but also in organizational routines, processes, practices and norms'. Most of the embedded knowledge that students learn in Management and Organization Studies tends to be functionalist, positivist, and universal in its aspirations. Yet, given the many local realities and diversities one has to navigate as a manager, what role do these universal theories, grand narratives, as Lyotard (1985) called them, play in the constitution of such locales? Or, to put it slightly differently: how, in the past, had the symbolic function of universalism justified imperious—not to say imperialist— ambitions and practices? How did it reintegrate diverse worlds? How did it perform the odd trick of being a particular universalism that denied its provenance as it simultaneously sought to hold sway over all domains, all places, all times?

The institutional spaces within which organizational and management knowledge flourish are dominated by an ethnocentric vision that assumes the *a priori* of modernity already installed. It is only within this modernity that one can think in terms of its presumed universalism. Local differences are to be managed from within a logic of development in which everything that does not respect the rule of the grand narrative can only be considered as deviant, as an example of the type of error for which the universal theory serves as a corrective. As Morin (1982) suggests, one needs a theory of error rather than of order.[3] Universal theory requires local error; without it truth would not be transparent. For this reason, the unique problem for universalism resides in the determination of ways in which problems of organization are constituted as problems outside of the norm, outside of the rule, outside of that which would be universal. Thus, rationally, those organizations chastened in order to render them modern exemplars of the one reality that is universal, rather than of the many realities that are local, from this perspective have to be in error. Such error defines the core reality, representing the imperial hope either of integrating or containing everything that exists within the logic of its rationalization. That which cannot be integrated or contained must be destroyed; what remains appears to be a universal logic, especially for those subjected to its dictates.

Any universal gaze of the cultural world must, by definition, be ethnocentric. A universal gaze, surveying all it can see from its pinnacle, will see everything only in

---

[3] Thanks to Eduardo Ibarra for the reference and translation of the key point.

terms of that which is normatively close to it, despite that its viewpoint may appear encompassing. Culturally, others who do not fit into the normatively close-at-hand appear as a space with no real substantive existence in the face of such an overriding presence. The other only becomes recognizable in as much as its presence is subordinated to the universal gaze; that is, when it attains a subjected position.

A universalizing gaze will range across cultural terrains that only assume their distinctive contours in ways of seeing that are more local, temporally contingent, and less universalistic. These terrains—those that would be reclaimed by the postmodern, post-industrial, post-Fordist, post-bureaucratic world—become flattened by the parameters of universalism. From within these terrains, especially where less universally inclined and more locally oriented academics constitute differences, post-(or pre-) universal rationalities will be at play. These other realities, often *past* (not post) *societies* that are not advanced, not economically rational, not white, and not western, when seen from the universal peak provide only an occasion for the market to correct.

In reality the problem is complex because a diverse world coexists simultaneously with an organizational logic that presumes and assumes a universal character, one, however, that can only ever find its specific forms in the institutional and cultural contexts of every local reality. As already indicated, the contrast between the fashionable recipes and the results of their translation to these diverse locales, establishes the terms of this ambivalence.

Practices always have to be implemented through local regimes. Local regimes thus function as the crucial point of reference in the construction of universal paradigms. These 'other' realities act as a demonstration of the 'truth' of the universal in two ways. First, they serve as good examples of local experiences that do not function 'properly' to contrast with current business paradigms. If local realities do not function in the way the theory establishes, they simply need to be improved and modernized with the help of the business paradigms: in Weberian terms they must be made Protestant. Second, if these local realities provide successful experiences, they will be used to support the advent of new business paradigms (which, in reality, will be only modifications of the prevailing paradigm with sufficient difference as to provide a consulting and career edge).

Local realities thus have two faces: local success and/or local failure prove the truth of universal business paradigms; if they function they support a shift in paradigms; if they fail, they prove the validity of the current ones. An example is Japanese management: the cycle of 1960s criticism of Japanese management by the late 1970s had receded in favour of some practices that previously had been demeaned as Japanese. Subsequently, some of these practices, after the reinterpretation of the work of Deming (1982), were themselves reinterpreted as American lessons that the Japanese had remembered while they had been forgotten at home. By the 1980s they became the basis for the new 'lean' paradigm that Womack, Jones, and Roos (1990) captured in their studies of Toyota. Japanese experiences thus became best practice in the world because they represented the new 'how to...' in management. It was from Japan, for instance, that scholars drew the necessary support for the importance of culture as the strategic key to managing successfully (Kono and Clegg 1999). Now, with the recent crisis, another crop of management theorists can demonstrate that culture should be seen as only one of the elements in the complex flux of organizing: tight fiscal controls and managing by the numbers are now seen to have their place, after all.

Organizations and their management are always inscribed in a tension between attempts at universalism, as business paradigms are taken up and institutionalized in local knowledge, and the pull of situational particularism, those locales, places, spaces, and times, in which are inscribed specific substantive values. Sometimes these are the stuff that makes the new forms of organization possible; on other occasions they may be deeply destructive and disorganizing of projects for managing locally. Increasingly, they are deeply destructive of academic paradigms for Management and Organization Theory being used as a basis for understanding; the shift is to 'knowledge [being] understood as a matter of what one can do' (Barnett 2000: 16) rather than what academics can publish. Barnett goes on to say that increasingly modern 'knowledge is generated *in action*. Characteristically, the knowledge-in-action that is most highly prized in the modern world is that which is produced in situ in the domain of work: that is, in settings that are systematic, collective, often large-scale, and oriented towards production, profit and growth' (Barnett 2000: 16). Hence, the universalism of the traditional academicians' conception of a paradigm is under attack from new definitions of working knowledge. Perversely, it seems to be both the postmodernists and the new materialists who want to privilege the local and the contextual. For the latter, the authenticity of knowledge comes from its ability to be put to work; work is a source of knowledge and work offers a means of testing knowledge (Barnett 2000: 17). For the former, the authenticity of local knowledge comes from the rebukes it offers to universalizing claims. The effect is the same: the universal and normal science paradigms of the academicians are under duress, of diminishing value in an applied sense, and subject to increasingly contested claims.

These new trends in knowledge are particularly problematic for the knowledge of work contained in twentieth-century organizational and management representations for these were invariably cast in terms of universal themes. After all, universalism, in its eclipse of particularism, was the very hallmark of modernity, according to influential theorists such as Talcott Parsons. Yet, if paradigms normally ascribed a universal imaginary, how would it be possible for them to change?

20.4 WHY DO PARADIGMS CHANGE?

Kuhn (1962) stressed the importance of punctuated equilibrium. Normal science comprises long periods of relative stability. The equilibrium of this stability is punctuated by extreme flux when anomalies accrue as puzzles develop that the existing paradigm cannot solve, or does not even address.

What creates the flux? Kuhn (1962) stressed the political nature of paradigms in scientific life, but did not really tell us why the adherents of subordinated paradigms suddenly triumphed when they did, other than to say that the anomalies were becoming an embarrassment for the powerful adherents of the existing paradigm. In organization studies, influential purveyors of the paradigm concept, such as Burrell and Morgan (1979), never really answer this question of change, either. For them the paradigms never really change: they serve simply as spaces for the creation of new intellectual capital whose struggles with existing paradigms is how the politics of careers play out. As the existing dominant paradigm becomes over-crowded a few pioneers will build intellectual capital in other paradigms. Interest-ingly, the whole paradigm debate in organization studies is producer driven. It is a debate generated by academics, about academic texts, for other academics, one that started with the framework offered by Burrell and Morgan (1979) in *Sociological Paradigms and Organizational Analysis*. The Burrell and Morgan (1979) approach provided a sensemaking device to account for and locate new approaches, as well as carving out legitimate spaces in which they could flourish. The idea that organiza-tion studies should comprise a parallel set of unrelated options, different menus, and disconnected conversations, became part of an extremely influential debate during the 1980s. The framework, which classified research on organizations according to functionalist, interpretative, radical humanist, and radical structuralist paradigms, may have seemed just a relatively straightforward way to catalogue a limited number of available options for the study of organizations. But *Paradigms* was not proposed merely as a theory of knowledge. It was a means to carve out a protected niche where alternative researchers could do their thing, protected from the criticisms of functionalists, free from what they saw as the necessity of having to try to explain their work to them. The key to this defensive strategy lay in the incommensurability of the paradigms and the language differences that precluded communication among them.

Burrell and Morgan (1979) argued that most existing organization and manage-ment theory worked within the assumption that *only* objective knowledge could be valid, and that, typically, a regular social order characterized society, which fluctu-ated around a normative equilibrium. The interpretive space found people *making* social order, as they *made sense* of various other frames of references. The more radical version, known as radical humanism, where more powerful, elite, or hege-monic groups dominate sensemaking, was used far less frequently, as was the radical structuralist frame. Like the radical humanist frame this shared the same stress on domination, although the emphasis was less on its subjective mechanisms (such as consciousness) and more on objective aspects such as the class structure of particular modes of production. (For instance, one might stress that relations of property produce two basic classes in capitalist societies: those who own the means of production and those who do not.) Typically, while individuals might change paradigms on rare occasions, the paradigms themselves were unchanging in their form: only the content that was formulated within and through them would differ. There is no substantial difference between paradigms that appear at first glance different. Management paradigms may differ in their form, but they share the same imaginary base.

One can easily identify Burrell and Morgan's approach as a theory of essential forms, as Platonist, after the view of the ancient Greek philosopher. Plato argued that reality presents itself to us as a series of unchanging forms. Some management educators revel in this Platonist view, and use it to relativize paradigms. The liberatory potential emerges, especially, when management educators can point out that most theorists only employ conceptual resources from one or other of the possible forms; usually the most conservative functionalist frame in the bottom right-hand corner of Burrell and Morgan's scheme. Knowing this, the task of the management educator is to spread enlightenment through surfacing the assumptions that managers routinely use. Having done so, the odds are that they normally will be functionalist in some way. These managers can then be exposed to the way that the world looks from other forms. Different paradigms (sometimes termed metaphors or frames) reveal different facets of our understanding of management (Morgan 1985; Bolman and Deal 1991).

Many MBA and Executive Management programs now use a method of switching frames as a learning device. Using new frames or seeing through different assumptions means that the managerial and organizational world not only looks different; it becomes different, because *it is* the way that we see it. With the exception of the metaphors (Morgan 1985) and framing (Bolman and Deal 1991) takes on paradigms, the arguments move in an academically tight hermeneutic circle. What they do not do is address lay or practitioner conceptions of paradigms and changes to them. Thus, on this occasion, our interest is more oriented to the changing paradigms that business commentators, pundits, and authorities focus on. For many such people, the notion of changing paradigms captures the flux of recent and projected organizational, management, and business experiences. One would argue that if Organization Studies were unable to bring these practitioner concerns with paradigms into its loop, the concept of paradigm would diminish in value, for the simple reason that it addresses only a restricted audience of paradigm warriors. The implementation of new paradigms in practice will be under-theorized, thought of merely as fads and fashions, rather than as extraordinarily powerful material practices.

A cynical answer to the question 'Why do paradigms change?' suggests that it is all a question of fashionable knowledge. Consulting organizations seek to become the Versace and Armani of the business world, purveyors of expensive designs tailored to the needs of wealthy clients. Knowledge, in this sense would most certainly be viewed as a child of its time: adaptable, flexible, pragmatic, focused on key questions such as 'does it work?' It is a knowledge form suited to our materialist era. Some theorists propose that management theories consist predominantly of recipe knowledge: a mixture of inexact science, artful appreciation, and pragmatic taste. Some reviewers are sceptical about the novelty of the latest paradigms. While there may be a plethora of fashionable paradigms they propose that few offer genuinely new recipes. A good example is the pioneer work of Richard A. Feiss (1910–1925) who early introduced industrial democracy and recognized the importance of corporate culture (see Wrege and Greenwood 1991: 161–71). For instance, Peter Drucker introduced the term 'post-modern world' as early as 1957, before Touraine (1971) and Bell (1973) had built the post-industrial concept. It is clear that 'the new' is not so new as one always believed. In this sense paradigms could be interpreted as the introjection of some representations and values that were sleeping for a long period of time, giving place to a new social imaginary that orients practices and discourses in a new way.

Some theorists suggest that, because management writing is afflicted by fads and fashion, all the important questions, and most of the important answers, have already been asked from within the confines of one existing paradigm of appropriate scientific practice (Donaldson 1995; Hilmer and Donaldson 1996). The dedicated proliferation of new paradigms is quite unnecessary because existing paradigms already answer all the questions that the new paradigms propose and sensible managers would be better off following advice from scientific experts rather than responding to the vagaries of the market in ideas.

Kieser (1997: 50) offered the strongest version of the view that paradigms are merely fads and fashions when he suggested that the recipes for managing that are offered in the popular market are somewhat similar to the recipes of ancient apothecary in the use of bold promises, bustling consultants, magic, and sporadic reference to strict academic science. Ancient apothecary may be an appropriate analogy for the more outlandish consulting quick-fixes but, on the whole, one may say simply that management is an uncertain art; a type of cookbook knowledge, where each recipe uses similar ingredients in conjuring up dishes. However, these ingredients can be combined in many different ways (contingent upon the aptitude of those who use the recipe books and the techniques, implements, ingredients, and utensils available to them), sometimes as new recipes. It is realization of this that is behind Gibbons *et al.*'s (1994) increased emphasis on 'world 2', as applied paradigms of working knowledge in action, for management. What such application provides are paradigmatic recipes.

If the metaphor of recipes captures a part of the reality of management, it is a metaphor that requires extending into the market in which recipe knowledge circulates. Cookbooks, whether of management or food, are best sellers. They jostle together on the non-fiction lists as fashionable and profitable commodities. (There may be some market segmentation, inasmuch as management and cookery books may command slightly separate audiences.) Management knowledge, like any other fashionable commodity, sells in a marketplace where variations and innovations compete with each other for acceptance and normalization, where it is difficult to predict what will emerge dominant at the time that one is seeking to design, retail, or wholesale something new. But, when the fashion trend is discernible, some styles will rapidly be abandoned and others as easily accepted as they become normalized around the victorious themes (Kieser 1997: 51).

Why do some variations and innovations succeed where others fail? Kieser offers basically three separate explanations. First, there is *trickle-down theory* that suggests that norms govern the widespread adoption of organization recipes. New forms of organization, like multidivisional structures in the United States in the 1930s, become widely accepted because they become identified with successful companies. Being adopted by organizations held in high regard, they diffuse widely. Note that the argument is not that they diffuse because they are more efficient, but more fashionable. Certain ideas attain high cultural capital, or distinctiveness. Perhaps, as well as being adopted by powerful organizations, they are advanced by prestigious professors or consultants. Others then emulate the practices because they seem powerful. Sometimes they seem powerful because they display a showy web site, one that legitimates itself as truth because of the space technology provides them with. Thus, such web sites function in the same way that books functioned in the past, as 'truth' because they were printed. Good examples are the web sites of Tom Peters and Stephen Covey.[4]

Second, *collective selection theory* stresses the functions that fashionable recipes fulfil for audiences. Fashion tells us what to wear or what to read and practice and thus creates order from the chaos of choice. Achieving detachment from the past fashions propels us forward persuading us to leave the past behind in the embrace of the new. Orderly innovation occurs through the gauntlet of competition and collective selection from fashionable recipes. In this way, the range of variation recedes as people attend to more limited variation than the environment presents, registering only those trends that appear already to be gaining recognition, thus seeking to avoid the role of fashion victim.

Third, *marionette theory* regards fashions as the natural outcome of competitive capitalism in its blind pursuit of profit. A constant supply of new recipes feeds the fires of commerce. Fashions are merely fetishistic recipes collectively consumed. Consumers dance to the strings that the fashion-producing industry pulls. In the

---

[4] Thanks to Eduardo Ibarra for this suggestion.

case of management the puppet masters are academics and consultants. Consulting houses have to have new and different recipes to sell, discontinuous from those that they previously sold, in order to maintain profits. A good example is Peters, who seems always to be 'searching' for new recipes to sell. Compare, for example, the classic 'excellence' research of Peters and Waterman (1982) with Peters's (1987) *Thriving on Chaos* and *The Circle of Innovation* (1997). Many managers become marionettes for consultants. Others know that the latest management recipe, whatever it is, can be functional: using the rhetoric of downsizing, for instance, they can achieve goals long held for other reasons: perhaps to rid themselves of that troublesome HRM Department or some of those creative R&D types. Out with the old recipe; out with the old enemies. Sometimes, the fashionable recipe simply seems overwhelming. Just as, in an era of wide ties no male executive who wanted to be thought fashionable would be seen in a narrow tie, so no manager would want to be seen espousing yesterdays theories and practices.

Kieser follows the nub of institutional theory in suggesting that when new fashions have been embraced by the rich and famous, the powerful, big end of town players, others will flock to them, as a matter of fashionable and unfashionable rhetoric. Fashionable rhetoric promotes recipes that emphasize one best factor as the sole principle of the new way of doing things and stresses the inevitability and necessity of the new principle. (Resistance is futile, as the Daleks used to say: obviously, they did not know their Foucault [1979].) Only fools who do not respect the icons of the age could or would resist, for who can be against recipes that promote progress, efficiency, effectiveness, and so on? Successful fashions will connect their legitimacy to their founding and use by people of great genius, rather than academic theorists. Thus, empirical research should be regarded cavalierly: enlightenment need not be researched but it may be revealed. Above all, the recipes should read well: they are not academic documents but timely texts for busy practitioners. As such, they should flow from experience: practical men (rarely women) command considerably more respect in the business community than do professors from universities, irrespective of their gender. Anyway, new recipes require simple metaphors, not complex empirical proofs. New recipes replace not rubbish but previously sound recipes whose day is now done. Such simple metaphors are best when highly ambiguous in meaning: one should be able to read many possibilities in them. Such metaphors should promise great challenges, as well as great rewards, if their mastery is achieved, even though the risks may be high. Above all, they must not close off imagination (or 'imaginization' as one guru [Morgan 1991] has it).

The cynical view of paradigm rhetoric advanced by Kieser (1997) is limited. It fails to attend to the real bunching of innovation that some writers such as Eccles and Nohria (1992), and Ezzamel and Willmot (1993) have observed. Different notions of business paradigm develop as a way of attending to changing realities rather than to rhetoric that leaves reality unchanged. For entrepreneurs and managers, located within the creative destruction of market forces rather than the more sheltered groves of academia, the experience of change is somewhat more compelling than the preservation of any existing intellectual capital whose investment they might presently attend to. For practitioners, preservation spells extinction. Firms that display arrogance in the face of innovation do not usually survive to tell the tale. In the contemporary world of business books, magazines, and consulting, new business paradigms are everywhere, while the paradigm debates in organization studies resolutely fail to address these concerns.

Recall that the 'fashion' perspective on paradigms and rhetoric does not suggest why innovation occurs in the first place. Other organization theory can come to the rescue. Some theorists, such as Ramsay (1996), use a 'long-wave' narrative to structure their argument.[5] Long-wave theories entered management initially in the work of an industrial relations writer, Harvie Ramsay (1977). Ramsay was an early and influential British proponent of this connection of waves and rhetoric in his 'cycles of control' hypothesis (which was influential in the development of Clegg 1979 and Clegg and Dunkerley 1980). More recently they have been taken up by US theorists of management such as Barley and Kunda (1992), DeGreene (1988), and Gill and Whittle (1993). The most recent and empirically sophisticated proponent is Eric Abrahamson (1997). He agrees with Kieser (1997) that the paradigms consist of a change of rhetoric. While Abrahamson confines his survey to personnel management, I have extended it to incorporate some of the major management fads of the past century, which I prefer to think of, in Gibbons *et al.*'s (1994) terms, as world 2 paradigms.

These applied management paradigms, as world 2 models in practice, constitute grand narratives of working knowledge that exploit myths associated with signs of

[5] It was a Soviet economist called Kondratieff (1935) who first pioneered long-wave theory, but it has gained many adherents. Long-wave theory proposes that the world economy will display a rhythmical pattern, as rapid expansion and stagnation alternate with a periodicity of around about fifty years. A single long wave is estimated to have about a fifty-year cycle through initial growth to decline. Some theorists emphasize, as did Kondratieff, that the causes of the seismic changes that long waves represent are the result of massive investments in, and the subsequent depreciation of, major aspects of infrastructure such as canals, railways, and roads. Others follow Schumpeter (1934) and think that it is less the decline in infra-structure that is responsible and more the fact that clusters of innovation bunch together, creating new and discontinuous leading edge sectors in the world economy, driving macroeconomic growth. Eventually further innovation restarts the whole cycle around further discontinuous innovation-bunches. Pérez (1985) writes about long waves and the techno-economic subsystem. Innovations precipitate system changes across firms, industries, and countries. New eras are ushered in by innovations like the steam engine, automobile, and computer. Each innovation-lead system change, and their key factors, steel, oil, and electronics, crystallize a new rational technological paradigm in the upstream and a normative paradigm, designed to extract diminishing returns through additional motivational zeal in the downswing, with each phase accompanied by substantial economic restructuring and organizational redesign. The advent of mass production bureaucracy contingent upon the dawn of the automobile era would be one example; today, the corollary would be the impact of the digital revolution that has accompanied the growth and importance in computers. The impact is variable across countries, industries, and organizations, and each of these adds their own level of indetermination to the picture, producing a highly contingent outcome.

success in different epochs.[6] Such paradigms are a way not only of interpreting reality, of constructing it, and giving it definitive sense but also of constituting different realities. Such knowledgeable realities can always outlast their epochs, or can migrate and colonize new spaces, far from sophisticated centres of trade and commerce in ideas. It does not matter then, if the reality does not correspond to the paradigm representing it: the point is that managers will act with reference to the reality that their paradigm constructs.

In a brief overview of dominant twentieth-century narratives one may begin with scientific management—the harbinger of the twentieth century as the age of managerialism. The one best way of scientific management represents a set of images and meanings to reinforce control and discipline behaviour at work. Though yielding productivity this was at the expense of meaningful work and the commitment of workers to the labour process. In a pattern that was to be repeated throughout the twentieth century, contradictions inherent in one business paradigm sowed the seeds of innovation for the next, as Clegg and Dunkerley argued (1980). Thus, by the early 1940s the paradigm of human relations had increasingly overlain scientific management in the United States, especially during World War II. The human relations paradigm represented a set of images and means to complete the Taylorist dream, proposing a rhetoric for inventing a new identity at work, allowing management to try to take control of the soul of 'happy workers'. Though ameliorative in many circumstances, this did not in itself provide the competitive efficiency required. It was a rational innovation, the continuous production line, placing workers under the discipline of Fordism, which permitted the successive gains in productivity necessary in modern competitive conditions. Economies of scale under mass production allowed the mental and physical injuries of work to be compensated for by the pleasures of consumption. However, as the post-war era showed, improvements in the quantity of goods produced were not matched by improvements in their quality. Thus, by the 1980s, in rapidly changing and increasingly global markets, dominated by Japanese consumer goods, in which customers had become more discerning, the quality paradigm became an essential adjunct to Fordism (even though total quality management involved dismantling some elements of Taylorism and Fordism). The quality movement provided commitment to improving products but not identification with the enterprise.

The post-1982 emphasis upon corporate culture and the pursuit of excellence was an elaborate and subtle development of the quality paradigm (Peters and Waterman 1982). Images and meanings reinforced the conduct of individuals, as they see themselves as autonomous practical subjects, responsible for their own actions, success, and failure in the service of the enterprise. However changing markets and tastes quickly made redundant businesses and products that, briefly, had appeared

---

[6] Of course, there is an irony in using a 'long-wave' account to organize narratives: a kind of double, double hermeneutic, of grand narratives!

excellent. Thus, the rhetoric of flexible specialization added technical innovation and flexibility to the drive for quality and excellence. Highly skilled technical operatives employing flexible technologies could respond to market shifts and identify market niches. The rhetoric of the learning organization took the lessons of the quality movement, the pursuit of excellence, and flexible specialization, and built them into a philosophy of management adapted to the knowledge economy and information workers. While scholars such as Weick and Westley (1999) and consultants such as Peters (1992) urged no strict rules as organizationally appropriate from this paradigm, employees were to be set free intellectually to pursue goals within institutional parameters that were generally pre-established. Most recently, in world-class organizations, the Taylorist scientific management paradigm returns anew to inspire organizations not only to achieve the highest international standards of quality, price, and performance but also to benchmark continually with customers, employees, and competitors. If they do so, they are assured, it will ensure the organization remains at the forefront, superseding its own products and services before a competitor does. A cycle of ever-shortening neurosis sets in, about an organization's ability to meet markets, avoid the exhaustion of intense competition, and, if US-based, avoid US anti-trust laws and, internationally, World Trade Organization (WTO) censure of labour hire, safety and related work practices in retaining world leadership. Such management paradigms should not be seen as 'merely rhetorical', says Abrahamson: they comprise working knowledge whose rhetoric has important functions: it provides vocabularies of meaning and motive that managers use to provide legitimate accounts of how they manage their employees, as de Gaudemar (1991) also suggested. New rhetoric may trigger the diffusion of new management techniques, and the persistence of rhetoric may aid the continued use of these techniques. Rhetoric also aids managers to better grasp the changing environmental realities that confront them in their organizations and businesses (Abrahamson 1997: 492).

Why does rhetoric innovate and proliferate? Two hypotheses suggest themselves: performance gaps and pendulum swings. Performance gaps open up when the targets that managers wish to meet, and their performance in meeting them, do not coincide; when the targets are out of reach. Consequently, managers become interested in rhetoric that holds promise that they can bridge the gap; should management or environmental changes narrow these gaps, then interest will shift to other rhetoric that seems better able to address other gaps that have been ignored or have opened up more recently.

The pendulum swings thesis has three parts: rhetoric is either rational or normative. Rational rhetoric stresses technical aspects of work organization while normative rhetoric stresses the orientations of the employees. Rational and normative rhetoric are irreconcilable; hence they never emerge simultaneously but in a pendulum or cyclical alternation. New rhetoric emerges around the onset of each expansionary upswing of the long wave, a wave of economic activity that takes approximately twenty-five years to crest and twenty-five years to recede. Thus each long wave has about a fifty-year duration.

Rational rhetoric is associated with upswings; normative rhetoric with downswings. As one shall see, an explanation exists for this difference in emphasis. Rational rhetoric stresses the formalization and rationalization of management and organizations, such as Taylor's (1947) 'scientific management'. It takes a mechanistic view of the organization and uses engineering-type analogies and metaphors to make the rhetorical point. While this clearly characterized scientific management, it also characterized the systems rationalism of the 1950s and 1960s, although now the mechanistic analogy was less with a machine and more with the organization as a type of cybernetic system.

Normative rhetoric stresses that it is the orientation and attitude of employees that is most important. The stress is on the needs of the employees and their satisfaction in the firm, modelled as a community. Managers must meet employee needs (Human Relations) and simultaneously unleash their creative energies (Corporate Culture). While the rational rhetoric is stronger in the upswing and the normative rhetoric is stronger in the downswing, neither is ever wholly dominant. They coexist with greater or lesser emphasis. While the digital revolution is rationalist in some of its implications, the impact that it is presumed to have for organization design is highly normative. In fact, it is less easy to separate out these 'moments' than Abrahamson (1997) presumes. For example, it is a bit problematic to place only 'organization culture and quality' into the period 1971–96, as he does: lean production, downsizing, and re-engineering also fall into this period.

Empirically, it is the pendulum thesis that explains the emergence of new rhetoric and the performance-gap thesis that explains their prevalence after their emergence. Moreover, the pendulum effect of rhetoric may not only be an effect of the underlying long waves. It may also be midwife to them: it may ease their transition from embryo's to emergent forms in their own right as periodic 'gales of creative destruction' in macroeconomics wipe out pre-existing innovations and the regimes of rhetoric associated with their dissemination through organizations.

20.5 FUTURE PARADIGMS FOR WORKING KNOWLEDGE

The present era is one in which world 2 type working knowledge is increasingly being promoted as an appropriate model for Faculties such as Business. In part, at least in Australia, this is connected to substantial cuts in government funding of tertiary education. Associated with this budgetary pressure has been a shift to a renewed emphasis on university entrepreneurship and a 'user-pays' principle in funding—fertile conditions for an increased emphasis on 'working knowledge' on world 2 lines because it creates conditions in which a degree of de-institutionalization of tertiary knowledge occurs. No longer funded as a matter of right or principle and faced with diminishing support from government spending of tax dollars this knowledge needs to find new clients, sponsors, and patrons. And there is only one set of probable patrons with resources. These are the top managers of corporate organizations. These, however, are those very people whose knowledge has been routinely spurned by leading scientific researchers in Faculties of Business as either uninteresting (the paradigm warriors) or misguided (the normal scientists), when it does not align with their expertise. Any bridge must lie between the affinities that might link the two fields as well as across the resource chasm that divides them.

Presently, Sibbet (1997) characterizes the key issues in the current environment of management education as globalization, knowledge workers, digitalization, and sustainability. Clarke and Clegg (1998) argue that there are more contenders. They do so after considering a substantial management literature on business paradigms. Additionally, they assess significant corporate responses to paradigm shifts (such as Shell's 'triple bottom line') and major private and public sector reports (such as the 1995 'Enterprising Nation' Report in Australia, chaired by Karpin and the 'Tomorrow's Company Report of 1994 in the United Kingdom). While each of these is likely to be important, given the logic of the earlier argument concerning fashions, one is unable to calibrate their relations at this point. What one can do is to suggest the implications of each for the present universe of Organization Studies as a type of world 1 knowledge that is particularly exposed to world 2 pressures on its corpus. Hence, the chapter concludes with an account of the implications of this changing reality for Organization Studies. Several directions present themselves, as one surveys the present scene. In what follows, the disparate threads of our previous argument are brought together in some possible scenarios; the argument starts from those I favour least to those I find most appealing and challenging.

20.5.1 Globalization

Once the certainties were known: one knew competitors, customers, and suppliers personally, because they were local: now, with the internationalization and globalization of business, these significant others may be worldwide. The globalization of the world economy presents a new business environment in which competition is international in a growing number of industries, and where it is only world-class standards that will satisfy customers. Thus, the story goes, local paradigms will disappear as one paradigm of best practice becomes universal. While such a view seems to neglect the academic capacity for spinning out difference, it may point to the increasing irrelevance of such, from a business point of view, trivial pursuits. From this perspective, those disciplines in the Business Schools that are unable to present a unified front (as Pfeffer [1993] suggests), are likely to wither. New entrants to the academic market, consulting companies in alliance with global software and communications companies, will package glossy and up-to-the-minute versions of functionalism for mass consumption and training. In such a global market, there may be room for niche players offering non-standardized paradigmatic solutions from non-conventional paradigm positions, but they will be, literally, marginalized. From this perspective one sees the bleakest future for Organization Studies: withering on the vine of increasing irrelevancy.

20.5.2 Flexibilization and the Emergence of a Different Form of Organization

The emphasis is on a shift from older, more imperative methods of managerial fiat, based on prescription, command, and control, to empowerment, teamwork, and networked relations. These, it is argued, are more suited to the postmodern world as one of instability and fragmentation, where both product and service markets, as well as the systems that sustain them, change at a bewildering rate compared to the old certainties of mass-production and mass-marketing. Traditional command and control forms of organization that predominated in twentieth-century industry failed to respond quickly and creatively enough to the developing demands of consumers and to emerging market opportunities. Organizations today have to be intelligent, have to have learning capacity built-in, to take full advantage of the opportunities that changing realities afford. Here the paradigm options are determined by practice setting the agenda and theory responding accordingly: a handmaiden or applied conception of the role of business academics who have become market agents in the universities. Organization Studies will do as it is told as local research strategies shaped by powerful corporate players determine the structures of its knowledge.

20.5.3 From Planning to Strategy

Stable markets and long production runs are disappearing to be replaced by niche markets and shortening product life cycles. Consequently, earlier methods of strategic planning based on rational modes of analysis become too rigid and are replaced by more creative strategic thinking. Rational modes of analysis mean using mathematical models to build the future right now, as a simulacrum, as Baudrillard (1984) would say. Here the representation must be the real, giving the real no place to survive. Such simulations can respond more sensitively to rapid shifts in demand. Once organizations sought to plan, constructing scenarios on the basis of what they knew and what was past. What businesses know today is an unreliable guide to what they need to envision tomorrow. Recognizing this, in many companies, planning has melded into strategizing. Here, the concern with paradigms becomes a tool of the corporate planner, constructing scenarios. From this perspective, Organization Studies will continue to have a role in so far as it is associated with questions of strategy; otherwise its options look limited for further development.

20.5.4 Multiple Management Paradigms as a Solution Rather than a Problem

Donaldson, Kieser, and Beyer, who were surveyed earlier, together with Pfeffer (1993), all regard the plurality of management paradigms as a problem: it is a source of potential customer confusion, bad marketing, rather than an opportunity for managers to learn to think systematically differently. Yet, the latter point—that alternate images of organizations opens the doors of perception—is one of the key contributions that writers such as Morgan (1986) have made. On this reckoning, as Organization Studies practitioners our task is to become metaphorical innovators, poets of organization practice, in search of ever more telling juxtapositions: the humanists on the trading-floors of finance, accounting, economics, and so on. Astley and Zammuto (1992) support this prognosis. At risk is a positivist and legislative conception of organization studies as a science: however, lacking institutional mechanisms to outlaw those whom one defines as charlatans, it is hard to see how the legislative model might actually govern practice outside of the policies of specific journal editors. There are no bodies with equivalent functions to a national professional association of Doctors, or Dentists, for instance, limiting professional practice only to those who satisfy its criteria. Growing demand for applied working knowledge may place pressure on the social organization of knowledge relations in peer-reviewed journals, with their emphasis on the transparent attempt to construct universal knowledge under the sway of dominant paradigms. What then of academic Organization Studies careers? Under the pressure of funding-needs, industry-linkages, and relevance, will the traditional universalism, with its long mean times for article development (see Frost and Stablein 1992—where the 'exemplars' almost all took several years—in one case eight—to make it from conception to publication), still hold sway? Who will have the time when the lengthy wait for news from yesterday of the normal science model can no longer be justified for a world already transformed beyond that which is being reported on?

20.5.5 New Stakeholders

Companies that succeed in this increasingly competitive business environment will need to build better business relationships with all their stakeholders. While improving relationships with investors is part of this effort, companies will have to manage a much wider array of strategic relations with other constituencies who claim a stake holding in the company. Thus, today businesses have to account for many, and to, many more stakeholders. Included among these might be the ecology (and green groups who claim to represent it), ethnic or sub-national groups who live where ones firm works, various rights based advocacy groups, all clamouring for a representation that reflects more broad-based performance measures than do quarterly accounting representations of the bottom line. Thus, in this conception, paradigm innovation becomes a way of legitimating new players in the corporate scene. Organization Studies, on this criterion, will increasingly become part of the struggle to establish new norms of diversity in practice. It will be increasingly tied to radicalized definitions of local working knowledge, struggling to determine what is global, and therefore universal (for now, at least), and what is local and different, as it tries to work both agendas.

20.5.6 Digitalization

As a result of digitalization and the creation of intelligent networked organizations, one may rarely, if ever, see those with whom one does business on a face-to-face basis. Interaction occurs in cyberspace, through the worldwide web and the Internet. The old world, based on manual operations, hard copy, and analogue processes has been replaced. The convergence of computing power and telecommunications reach is providing new technological and information resources with which to pursue business opportunities, but this is only achievable if the management and organization of enterprises is transformed to capture the potential of new technologies. The two disparate concerns with the notion of paradigm, those of the practitioner and the academic, thus fuse in a practice of organization design, that draws on the postmodern, the virtual, in creating new networked worlds of organizations of working knowledge. In many ways such a fusion is the most exciting and challenging of the options for Organization Studies. If in the past, theorists of structural contingency theory likened themselves to engineers designing the best fit for organizations with their contingencies, this option opens the possibilities of imaginative architectural practice, where one envisions structures and designs that exploit new technologies, theories, and feelings.

20.5.7 Sustainability

How long will today's businesses last and what impact will they leave on the planet? Arie de Geus (1997) addressed the first question when he was part of a team asked to consider how many of today's major firms have been around for at least 100 years. They could only find 40, worldwide, including firms like Mitsui, Sumitomo, and DuPont. If one were to narrow down that list to firms that have not only sustained themselves, but also the communities and ecologies with which they interact, it becomes smaller still. Yet, these will be the criteria for sustainability in the future. Here, the concern with paradigms becomes a call to moral awakening: creating new paradigms can call to attention neglected and potentially destructive aspects of present practice. New paradigms add moral, as well as long-term bottom line superiority. From this perspective, one would anticipate either that the ethical implications of Organization Studies would become uppermost or that Organization Studies will only continue to exist if it helps forge the new paradigm and becomes a key player in an alliance with those managers working out that paradigm in practice.

20.6 CONCLUSION

Despite the rhetoric of globalization there is no more reason today to think that there will be universal solutions to organizational issues than there was in the past, despite the universal one best way implications of some of the present digital approaches in the market. How issues of sustainability, new stakeholders, strategy, flexibilization, and globalization are defined, addressed, and resolved, will, as ever, depend on how they are embedded and constructed locally. Even in an era of globalization and digitalization, universalizing tendencies if ever there were any, one has no reason to expect common stakeholder, strategic, and flexible responses. The critical research question remains the local impact of global changes on particular organizations, in distinct locales, and the impact of these on working knowledge: will it become universalized, in the normal science paradigm, or will one witness the emergence of more plural local knowledge?

Academic conceptions of Organization Studies paradigms relate to an era when theorists had a far greater capacity to determine agendas. Even Peters and Waterman (1982), despite its McKinsey provenance, also had Stanford Graduate School of Business origins, yet, as Barley *et al.* (1988) demonstrate, it reversed the terms of academic/practitioner trade. Markets change not just as an effect of marketing but also as a consequence of product innovations. The major post-1982 innovations in the field of business paradigms have been slighted and disdained by Organization Studies gurus. Moreover, not only are its paradigms out of tune with those of practitioners but also the field seems ill-equipped to deal with local situations increasingly dominated by practical conceptions of working knowledge.

A range of options exists for different forms of engagement, withdrawal, or defeat by academic practitioners confronted with the world of practice with(in) which one struggles to make sense. In addressing a universalizing reality recursively, rather than pluralizing texts discursively, the concept of paradigm has nothing to lose but its irrelevance. Moreover, we have everything to gain by way of a future. To remain within the old paradigms, intellectually, as well as practically, is to spin out careers of declining intellectual capital and diminishing returns. It could, in short, be a blueprint for redundant knowledge, prefiguring a loss of utility of whatever intellectual property rights we still aspire to and a future of declining power and influence. Of course, to the extent that this happens, then the power/knowledge relations that do configure organizational life will be even further from critical scrutiny. Perhaps, after all, this would be only appropriate? Having resolutely avoided issues concerning its own sovereignty for so long, having produced increasingly practically useless knowledge, like an intellectual lap-dog, it might well be kinder not to maintain the illusion of its own yapping so far from the corridors of power. Knowledge barely theorizing power is not likely to be really useful knowledge to power: once its silence about *realpolitik* has been appreciated its irrelevance will be overwhelmingly evident.

REFERENCES

ABRAHAMSON, E. (1997). 'The Emergence and Prevalence of Employee Management Rhetorics: The Effects of Long Waves, Labour Unions, and Turnover, 1875 to 1992'. *Academy of Management Journal*, 40/3: 491–533.

ASTLEY, W. G., and ZAMMUTO, R. F. (1992). 'Organization Science, Managers and Language Games'. *Organization Science*, 3/3: 443–60.

BARKER, J. A. (1992). *Paradigms: Understand the Future in Business and Life*. Melbourne: Business Library.

BARLEY, S. R., and KUNDA, G. (1992). 'Design and Devotion: Surges of Rational and Normative Ideologies of Control in Managerial Discourse'. *Administrative Science Quarterly*, 37: 363–99.

—— *et al.* (1988). 'Cultures of Culture: Academics, Practitioners and the Pragmatics of Normative Control'. *Administrative Science Quarterly*, 33: 24–60.

BARNETT, R. (2000). 'Working Knowledge', in J. Garrick and C. Rhodes (eds.), *Research and Knowledge at Work: Perspectives, Case-Studies and Innovative Strategies*. London: Routledge.

BAUDRILLARD, J. (1984). *Simulations*, trans. P. Foss, P. Patton, and P. Beitchman. *Simulacres et simulation: English*. New York: Semiotext(e).

BAUMAN, Z. (1987). *Legislators and Interpreters: On Modernity, Post-modernity and Intellectuals*. Cambridge: Polity Press.

BELL, D. (1973). *The Coming of Post-Industrial Society: A Venture in Social Forecasting*. New York: Basic Books.

BEYER, J. M. (1992). 'Metaphors, Misunderstandings and Mischief: A Commentary'. *Organization Science*, 3/3: 467–500.

BOLMAN, L. G., and DEAL, T. E. (1991). *Reframing Organizations: Artistry, Choice and Leadership*. San Francisco: Jossey-Bass.

BURRELL, G., and MORGAN, G. (1979). *Sociological Paradigms and Organizational Analysis*, London: Heinemann.

CHILD, J., and RODRIGUES, S. (1996). 'The Role of Social Identity in the International Transfer of Knowledge through Joint Ventures', in S. R. Clegg and G. Palmer (eds.), *The Politics of Management Knowledge*. London: Sage.

CLARKE, T., and CLEGG, S. (1998). *Changing Paradigms: The Transformation of Management Knowledge for the 21st Century*. London: Harper Collins Business.

CLEGG, S. R. (1975). *Power, Rule and Domination: A Critical and Empirical Understanding of Power in Sociological Theory and Organizational Life*. London and Boston: Routledge & Kegan Paul, The International Library of Sociology.

—— (1977). 'Power, Organization Theory, Marx and Critique', in S. Clegg and D. Dunkerley (eds.), *Critical Issues in Organizations*. London and Boston: Routledge & Kegan Paul.

—— (1979). *The Theory of Power and Organization*. London and Boston: Routledge & Kegan Paul.

—— (1981). 'Organization and Control'. *Administrative Science Quarterly*, 26: 545–62.

—— (1983). 'Organizational Democracy, Power and Participation', in C. Crouch and F. Heller (eds.), *The International Yearbook of Organizational Democracy*. London: John Wiley.

—— (1987). 'The Language of Power and the Power of Language'. *Organization Studies*, 8/1: 61–70.

—— (1989a). *Frameworks of Power*. London: Sage.

—— (1989b). 'Radical Revisions: Power, Discipline and Organizations'. *Organization Studies*, 10/1: 101–19.

—— (1990). *Modern Organizations: Organization Studies in the Postmodern World*. London: Sage.

—— (1992). 'Poder, Linguagem e Açao nas Organizações', in J.-F. Chanlat (ed.), *O Indivíduo na Organização: Dimensões Esquecidas*. São Paulo: Editora Atlas.

—— (1993). 'Narrative, Power and Social Theory', in Dennis K. Mumby (ed.), *Narrative and Social Control*, Volume 21 in Sage Annual Reviews of Communication Research. Beverley Hills: Sage Inc.

CLEGG, S. R. (1995a). 'Power and the Resistant Subject', in John Jermier, Walter Nord, and David Knights (eds.), *Resistance and Power in Organizations: Agency, Subjectivity and the Labor Process*. London: Routledge.

—— (1995b). 'Weber and Foucault: Social Theory for the Study of Organizations'. *Organization*, 1/1: 149–78.

—— (1997a). 'Foucault, Power and Organizations', in A. McKinlay and K. Starkey (eds.), *Foucault, Management and Organization Theory: From Panopticon to Technologies of Self*. London: Sage.

—— (1997b). 'Foucault, Power, Social Theory and the Study of Organisations', in Clare O'Farrell (ed.), *Foucault: The Legacy*. Brisbane: Queensland University of Technology.

—— (1997c). 'Power', in Malcolm Warner (ed.), *Concise International Encyclopedia of Business and Management*. London: Thomson.

—— (2000). 'Power and Authority, Resistance and Legitimacy', in H. Goverde, P. G. Cerny, M. Haugaard, and H. Lentner (eds.), *Power in Contemporary Politics: Theories, Practices, Globalizations*. London: Sage.

—— and DUNKERLEY, D. (1980). *Organization, Class and Control*. London: Routledge & Kegan Paul.

—— and HARDY, C. (1996). 'Representations', in S. R. Clegg, C. Hardy, and W. R. Nord (eds.), *Handbook of Organization Studies*. London: Sage.

—— and WILSON, F. (1992). 'Power, Technology and Flexibility in Organizations', in J. Law (ed.), *A Sociology of Monsters: Essays on Power, Technology and Domination*, Sociological Review Monograph, No. 38. London: Routledge.

DAVENPORT, T. H., and PRUSACK, L. (1998). *Working Knowledge: How Organizations Manage What They Know*. Boston: Harvard University Press.

DE GAUDEMAR, J.-P. (1991). *El Orden Y La Producción*. Madrid: Trotta.

DEGREENE, K. B. (1988). 'Long Wave Cycles of Sociotechnical Change and Innovation: A Macro-Psychological Perspective'. *Journal of Occupational Psychology*, 61: 7–23.

DEMING, W. E. (1982). *Quality, Productivity and Competitive Position*. Cambridge: MIT.

DE GEUS, A. (1997). *The Living Company*. Boston: Harvard Business School Press.

DIMAGGIO, P., and POWELL, W. (1983). 'The Iron Cage Revisited: Institutional Isomorphism and Collective Rationality in Organizational Fields'. *American Sociological Review*, 48/2: 147–60.

DONALDSON, L. (1992). 'The Weick Stuff: Managing Beyond Games'. *Organization Science*, 3/3: 461–6.

—— (1995). *American Anti-Management Theories of Organization: A Critique of Paradigm Proliferation*. Cambridge: Cambridge University Press.

DU GAY, P. (1996). *Consumption and Identity at Work*. London: Sage.

ECCLES, R. G., and NOHRIA, N. (with James D. Berkely) (1992). *Beyond the Hype: Rediscovering the Essence of Management*. Boston: Harvard Business School Press.

ETZKOWITZ, H., and LEYDESDORFF, L. A. (eds.) (1997). *Universities and the Global Knowledge Economy: A Triple Helix of University-Industry-Government Relations*. London: Pinter.

EZZAMEL, M., and WILLMOTT, H. (1993). 'New Management Thinking'. *European Management Journal*, 12: 454–61.

FOUCAULT, M. (1979). *Discipline and Punish: The Birth of the Prison*, trans. A. Sheridan. Harmondsworth: Penguin.

—— (1997). 'The Birth of Biopolitics', in M. Foucault, *Ethics, Subjectivity and Truth*, ed. P. Rabinow. New York: New York Press.

FROST, P., and STABLEIN, R. (eds.) (1992). *Doing Exemplary Research*. London: Sage.

GAGLIARDI, P. (ed.) (1990). *Symbols and Artifacts: Views of the Corporate Landscape*. Berlin: Walter de Gruyter.

GARFINKEL, H. (1967). *Studies in Ethnomethodology*. Englewood Cliffs, NJ: Prentice-Hall.

GEUS, DE A. (1997). *The Living Company: Growth, Learning and Longevity in Business*. London: Nicholas Brealey.

GIBBONS, M., LIMOGES, C., NOWOTNY, H., SCHWARTZMANN, S., SCOTT, P., and TROW, M. (1994). *The New Production of Knowledge*. London: Sage.

GILL, J., and WHITTLE, S. (1993). 'Management by Panacea: Accounting for Transience'. *Journal of Management Studies*, 30: 281–95.

HARDY, C., and CLEGG, S. R. (1999). 'Some Dare Call It Power', in Stewart Clegg and Cynthia Hardy (eds.), *Studying Organizations*. London: Sage.

HICKSON, D. J., MACMILLAN, C. J., HININGS, C. R., and SCHWITTER, J. (1974). 'The Culture-free Context of Organization Structure: A Tri-National Comparison'. *Sociology*, 8/1: 59–80.

HILMER, F. G., and DONALDSON, L. (1996). *Management Redeemed: Debunking the Fads that Undermine Corporate Performance*. New York: Free Press.

IBARRA, E. (1995). 'Strategic Analysis of Organizations: A Model from the Complexity Paradigm'. *Human Systems Management*, 14/1: 51–70.

KIESER, A. (1997). 'Rhetoric and Myth in Management Fashion'. *Organization*, 4/1: 49–74.

KONDRATIEFF, N. D. (1935). 'The Longwaves in Economic Life'. *Review of Economics and Statistics*, 17: 105–15.

KONO, T., and CLEGG, S. R. (1999). *Transformation of Corporate Culture: Experiences of Japanese Companies*. Berlin: de Gruyter.

KUHN, T. S. (1962). *The Structure of Scientific Revolutions*. Chicago: University of Chicago Press.

LATOUR, B. (1993). *We Have Never Been Modern*. London: Sage.

LUKES, S. (1974). *Power: A Radical View*. London: Macmillan.

LYOTARD, J.-F. (1985). *The Postmodern Condition: A Report on Knowledge*. Minneapolis: University of Minnesota Press.

MAIER, C. S. (1975). *Recasting Bourgeois Europe: Stabilization in France, Germany, and Italy in the Decade after World War I*. Englewood Cliffs, NJ: Prentice-Hall.

MARSDEN, R., and TOWNLEY, B. (1996). 'The Owl of Minerva: Reflections on Theory in Practice', in S. R. Clegg, C. Hardy, and W. R. Nord (eds.), *Handbook of Organization Studies*. London: Sage.

MINTZBERG, H. (1973). *The Nature of Managerial Work*. New York: Harper & Row.

—— (1983). *Power In and Around Organizations*. Englewood Cliffs, NJ: Prentice-Hall.

MORGAN, G. (1985). *Images of Organizations*. Thousand Oaks, Calif.: Sage.

—— (1986). *Images of Organization*. Beverly Hills: Sage.

—— (1991). *Imaginization*. Thousand Oaks, Calif.: Sage.

MORIN, E. (1982). 'El error de subestimar el error', in E. Morin, *Ciencia con Consciencia*. Barcelona: Anthropos.

NELSON, D. (1979). *Managers and Workers: Origins of the New Factory System in the United States, 1880–1920*. Madison: University of Wisconsin Press.

PÉREZ, C. (1985). 'Microelectronics, Long Waves and World Structural Change: New Perspectives for Developing Countries'. *World Development*, 13/3: 441–63.

PETERS, TOM (1987). *Thriving on Chaos: Handbook for a Management Revolution*. New York: Knopf.

——(1992). *Liberation Management: Necessary Disorganization for the Nanosecond Nineties*. London: Macmillan.

——(1997). *The Circle of Innovation: You Can't Shrink Your Way to Greatness*. London: Hodder & Stoughton.

——and WATERMAN, R. (1982). *In Search of Excellence*. New York: Harper & Row.

PFEFFER, J. (1981). *Power in Organizations*. Boston: Pittman.

——(1992). *Managing with Power*. Boston: Harvard Business Press.

——(1993). 'Barriers to the Advance of Organizational Science: Paradigm Development as a Dependent Variable'. *Academy of Management Review*, 18/4: 599–620.

POPPER, K. (1945). *The Open Society and its Enemies*. London: Routledge & Kegan Paul.

RAMSAY, H. (1977). 'Cycles of Control: Workers Participation in Sociological and Historical Perspective'. *Sociology* 11/3: 481–506.

——(1996). 'Managing Sceptically: A Critique of Organizational Fashion', in S. R. Clegg and G. Palmer (eds.), *The Politics of Management Knowledge*. London: Sage.

REDDING, S. G. (1990). *The Spirit of Chinese Capitalism*. Berlin: Walter de Gruyter.

ROGERS, E. (1995). *Diffusion of Innovations* (4th edn.) New York: Free Press.

SANDKULL, B. (1996). 'Lean Production: The Myth which Changes the World?', in S. R. Clegg and G. Palmer (eds.), *The Politics of Management Knowledge*. London: Sage.

SCHUMPETER, J. A. (1934). *The Theory of Economic Development: An Enquiry into Profits, Capital, Credit, Interest and the Business Cycle*, trans. from German by Redvers Opie. Cambridge, Mass.: Harvard University Press.

——(1942). *Capitalism, Socialism & Democracy*. New York: Harper & Row.

SIBBET, D. (1997). '75 Years of Management Ideas and Practice 1922–1977'. *Harvard Business Review Reprint 975000*. Cambridge, Mass.: Harvard Business Review Press.

TAYLOR, F. W. (1947). *The Principles of Scientific Management*, New York: Norton.

THOMPSON, E. P. (1968). *The Making of the English Working Class*. Harmondsworth: Penguin.

TOURAINE, A. (1971). *The Post-Industrial Society. Tomorrow's Social History: Classes, Conflicts, and Culture in the Programmed Society*, trans. Leonard F. X. Mayhew. New York: Random House.

WEBER, M. (1976). *The Protestant Ethic and the Spirit of Capitalism*. London: Allen & Unwin.

——(1978). *Economy and Society: An Outline of Interpretive Sociology*, 2 vols., ed. G. Roth and C. Wittich. Berkeley: University of California Press.

WEICK, K., and WESTLEY, F. (1999). 'Organizational Learning: Affirming an Oxymoron', in S. Clegg, C. Hardy, and W. Nord (eds.), *Managing Organizations: Current Issues*. London: Sage.

WHITLEY, R. (1992). *Business Systems in East Asia: Firms, Markets and Societies*. London: Sage.

WILLIAMS, K., HASLAM, C., and WILLIAMS, J. (1992). 'Ford Versus "Fordism": The Beginning of Mass Production?' *Work, Employment & Society*, 6: 517–55.

WITTGENSTEIN, L. (1968). *Philosophical Investigations.* Oxford: Blackwell.

WOMACK, J. P., JONES, D. T., and ROOS, D. (1990). *The Machine That Changed the World.* New York: Rawson.

WREGE, C. D., and GREENWOOD, R. G. (1991). *Frederick W. Taylor, The Father of Scientific Management: Myth and Reality.* Burr Ridge, Ill.: Irwin.

CHAPTER 21

THE FUTURE OF ORGANIZATION STUDIES

BEYOND THE SELECTION– ADAPTATION DEBATE

ARIE Y. LEWIN

HENK W. VOLBERDA

DECADES of research in strategy and organization science and in branches of economics and decision sciences have not resolved the adaptation–selection debate (Baum 1996; Lewin, Weigelt, and Kim, forthcoming). This debate persists in the face of a concerted research effort and vast growth in the stock of knowledge in this area. The proliferation of research and persistence of this debate reflect the many different theoretical lenses and empirical methods employed in advancing knowledge and understanding of the role of intentionality in the adaptation process of organizations. In reality the theoretical and empirical literature is much more comprehensive and detailed about the sources and causes of structural inertia than about the role of intentionality, strategic choice, or about self-renewing organizational forms that counteract structural inertia (Lewin and Volberda 1999). A comparison of strategic management and organizational ecology theories highlights the nature and source of the debate. While organizational ecology theories focus on selection, variation, and retention processes for explicating the evolution of populations of organizations, strategic management theories focus on firm-level adaptation as a function of strategy and organization design. Organizational ecology research is based on longitudinal data and shares essential variable definitions and measurements across studies. Strategic choice empirical research has employed mostly cross-sectional designs or studies of short-term adaptation events or single case studies. Moreover, the weak comparability of empirical findings across strategic management studies is a direct consequence from the many competing theoretical formulations, proliferation of model specifications, and the absence of shared definitions for variables and measures. Organizational ecology research, however, is disconnected from micro strategic and organizational adaptation events at the level of the individual organizational unit and therefore cannot directly contribute to explicating firm-level adaptation. Thus the adaptation–selection debate rages on.

Research on the emergence or evolution of new organizations has been attracting increasing attention (Tushman and Romanelli 1985; Romanelli 1991; Lewin, Long, and Carroll 1999). Most research on evolution of organizations involves studies of short-term adaptations under various contingencies, or retrospective case studies (Pettigrew 1985; Baden-Fuller and Stopford 1992), and panel studies (e.g. Whittington *et al.* 1999). Such studies, however, focus on restructuring and transformations within the prevalent M-Form and are not specifically concerned with emergence of new organizational forms. Several theories propose that new organizational forms emerge from entrepreneurial activities of new entrants (Aldrich and Mueller 1982; Aldrich and Zimmer 1986) or from creative technology-destroying competencies of industries (Schumpeter 1950; Tushman and Anderson 1986). In all of these studies, the new form of interest is the population or industry not the organization.

Contemporaneously, many popular and academic writers speculate on the features or characteristics of new organizational forms (cf. Lewin and Stephens 1993; Volberda 1996, 1998). Management futurologists conceptualize the new organization landscape as virtual corporation (Davidow and Malone 1992); hollow corporation; dynamic network form (Miles and Snow 1986); cellular organization (Miles *et al.* 1997); hypertext organization (Nonaka and Takeuchi 1995); platform organization (Ciborra 1996); and shamrock organization (Handy 1995). Most of these studies, however, represent retrospective accounts of single case examples of a successful adaptive organizational form at a cross-section of time (e.g. Sun Microsystems' virtual organization; Dell Computer's dynamic network; Acer's cellular form; Sharp's hypertext form; Olivetti's platform organization; or F international's electronic shamrock). The popular business press accounts of new forms serve as an important signpost, but the theory underlying these ideas remains to be more fully developed. In particular, theories of evolution and mutation process of new organizational forms remain to be developed (cf. Lewin, Long, and Carroll 1999, Lewin and Volberda 1999).

In this chapter, we explore the coevolution perspective as a new meta-theoretical lens for research in organization studies and for reintegrating organization theory and strategy. We believe that coevolution frameworks will inform research in organization studies, that spans levels of analyses and involves adaptation or change over time. In our judgment, coevolution frameworks could prove especially useful for progress on bridging the adaptation–selection chasm and for developing insights into the mutation process of incumbent organizations. The coevolution meta-theoretical lens has the potential for integrating micro- and macro-level evolution within a unifying framework, incorporating multiple levels of analyses and contingent effects, and leading to new insights, new theories, new empirical methods, and new understanding.

21.1 KEY THEMES IN ADAPTATION SELECTION RESEARCH

How do firms coevolve with their environment? Most scholars in strategy and organization theory study this question by considering environmental change as an exogenous variable (cf. Baum and Singh 1994; Baum and Korn 1999; March 1994). Moreover, they employ a single theme for describing how and why organizations tend to become isomorphic with their environments through processes of either adaptation or selection. Less frequently examined are questions of how organizations systematically influence their environments and how organizational environments (comprised of other organizations and populations) influence those organizations in turn. In this section, we briefly summarize key theoretical frameworks in sociology, economics, and strategy and organization theory; the dominant themes of these frameworks as they relate to adaptation and selection; and the implications of each approach for firm strategy and adaptation.

Sociology encompasses two dominant views. According to *population ecology* (Hannan and Freeman 1977, 1984; Aldrich and Pfeffer 1976), managerial intentionality should have little or no impact on adaptation. Environments select organizations through resource scarcity and competition. The analysis of this selection process is applied at the population level of organizations, since the distribution of fitness across the population of organizations, rather than the fitness of any single organization, is the object of interest. Furthermore, organizational attempts at restructuring and transformation are taken to be futile and even to decrease firm chances of survival. The inability to adapt is a direct outcome of inertial pressures that prevent organizations from changing in response to their environments. The concept of structural inertia, like that of fitness, refers to a correspondence between the adaptive behavioral capabilities of a class of organizations and their particular environments (Hannan and Freeman 1984: 152; Mason 1949). Organizations accumulate structural and procedural baggage through retention processes, and the ability of an organization to respond to changes in its environment is directly related to the build-up of structural inertia. In population-ecology theory, firm survival is a function of high reliability and specialization. However, selection rates increase as environmental rates of change exceed firm rates of change. The extreme implications for strategy and organization change are that, in the long run, managerial actions make no difference. At best, they cannot affect selection rates. Most likely, such actions can intensify selection rates. The best management can do is focus on the firm's niche, optimize the firm's specialization, and hope for the best. As new entrants define a new environment and the old niche decays, firms in the niche become increasingly isomorphic and are selected out (Miller 1990).

In contrast to population ecology, *institutional theories* focus on why organizations within a population exhibit similar characteristics. The central concern of *institutional theories* is on answering the question 'Why is there such a startling homogeneity of organizational forms and practices?' (i.e. within a population). The emphasis is on the causes and sources of similarity (not variation) in organization forms and managerial practices. This population isomorphism results from coercive, normative, and mimetic isomorphic pressures perceived to be legitimate (DiMaggio and Powell 1983). Population isomorphism allows initiatives that are not driven by necessity or obvious advantage to diffuse through an industry group. Greenwood and Hinings (1996) illustrate the dynamic potential of institutional theory to explain adaptation. The embeddedness of organizations in their institutional context is a basic reason for organizations' resistance to change. The more organizations are coupled to a prevailing organizational template in a highly structured institutional context, the higher the resistance to change. Moreover, internal dynamics of organizations are the reason for differences in the pace of change within sectors. The implications of institutional and neo-institutional theories for strategy and organization change are that longevity and survival are achieved through alignment of organization values and practices with institutional norms and expectations. The implication is that organizations that practice 'fast follower strategies' in maintaining congruence with newly emerging industry norms and shared logics will gain legitimacy sooner than less nimble mimetic firms and survive longer.

Economics has brought forward several theories that inform the selection–adaptation debate. These theories range from industrial organization and the behavioral theory of the firm to recent evolutionary theories of economic change and resource- and knowledge-based theories of the firm.

Industrial organization theorists focus on the selection of industries and the positioning of firms within that industry to achieve sustained competitive advantage (Porter 1980, 1985). The industrial organization approach originated from the structure–conduct–performance paradigm of industrial organization developed by Mason (1949) and Bain (1959). In particular, the structure–conduct–performance paradigm places more emphasis on structure (context) than on conduct (strategy) and on implications for public policy as opposed to firm strategy. Central assumptions of *IO economics* are that market dynamics and structure are exogenous and cannot be affected by the individual firm whose own performance is determined by membership in an industry and adherence to industry conduct. Porter (1980), however, applies the paradigm at the firm level to develop generic strategies of competitive advantage. In this formulation, the focus is on the quest for monopoly rents through industry and segment selection and the manipulation of market structure to create market power. The implications of *IO economics* for strategy and adaptation are that business unit managers should choose an attractive industry and define the frontier for a generic strategy such as cost leadership. Moreover, because greater rivalry will destroy value, managers should erect barriers to entry and use oligopolistic bargains to prevent competitive escalation within an industry.

The *transaction costs theory* (TCE) anchors its analytical development on the transaction as the unit of economic analysis (Commons 1934; Williamson 1975, 1979). The central focus of TCE is on the minimization of transaction costs within and between organizations and achievement of efficiency in transactions. Transaction costs include negotiating, monitoring, and enforcing contracts. The goal of TCE is to align the different types of transactions with the optimal governance structure under different conditions of opportunism and self-interest seeking with guile. TCE implications for strategy and organization change are to minimize transaction costs by matching correct governance structure with appropriate transaction. Specifically TCE would prescribe vertical integration for high asset specific and uncertain transactions and market structures for low asset specific transactions.

The *behavioral theory of the firm* (Cyert and March 1963) has a managerial view of the firm as balancing the resource allocation processes to satisfy multiple stakeholders' demands, while maximizing the personal goals of managers. The overall thesis is that managers are rational in striving to maximize their personal goals while satisfying stakeholder expectations. They seek to avoid uncertainty by negotiating their environment, employing satisficing decision-making, maintaining firm performance relative to industry average, and seeking stability (equilibrium). Organization slack serves to buffer environmental uncertainty. It is also a necessary (but not sufficient) condition for innovation. The theory embodies process description of how structural inertia evolves and grows and provides the rationale for periodic cycles of strategic rejuvenation through restructuring and rationalization. The implications of *The Behavioral Theory of the Firm* for strategy and organization adaptation are threefold. First, a firm should accumulate slack resources for avoiding uncertainty. Second, continued fitness on a rugged landscape requires strategic intent to allocate slack resources to innovation. Third, firm survival and longevity is directly related to scale and organization slack, and ability to undertake periodic rejuvenating through rationalization of slack and reinvesting in new opportunities (Tushman and Romanelli 1985).

Consistent with the behavioral theory of the firm (Cyert and March 1963), *evolutionary theories* assume that organizations accumulate know-how and tacit knowledge in the course of their existence (Nelson and Winter 1982). Organizations become repositories of unique skills that are often difficult to transfer. These skills are the source of both inertia and distinctive competence. The inertia is caused by sunk costs of past investments; escalation of commitment; entrenched social structures; and organization member attachment to cognitive styles, behavioral dispositions, and decision heuristics. The accumulated skills that render firms inert are also the source of opportunities for strengthening firm-unique advantages and furthering and improving their know-how and tacit knowledge. Improvements are realized slowly and incrementally. The potential benefits include greater reliability in delivering desirable and differentiated products, and the advantages from efficiently replicating and extending routines (Miller and Chen 1994: 1). The implications of *evolutionary economics theories* for strategy and adaptation are that firms should replicate and retain successful routines, benchmark competitors' best practices and actively manage updating of internal routines (micro–macro coevolution), leverage and extend past competencies and develop a coherent path-dependent strategy.

The *resource dependence theory* elaborates and extends the behavioral theory of the firm construct of avoiding and controlling environmental uncertainty (Cyert and March 1963). In contrast to institutional theory, resource dependence theory views organizations as actively engaged in structuring exchange relationships to control or reduce environmental uncertainty (Thompson 1967; Pfeffer and Salancik 1978; Oliver 1991) by 'negotiating the environment' (Cyert and March 1963) and by strategically managing interdependencies. Unlike strategic choice theories (Child 1972; Andrews 1971), the theory recognizes that certain environmental constraints cannot be changed and redefined. Thus the implications of *resource dependence theory* for strategy and organization change involve one of two types—dependence reduction and dependence restructuring (Green and Welsh 1988). Dependence reduction might include exit from lines of business, spinning off a business, or more generally choosing to abandon a power relationship. Dependence restructuring might involve vertical integration, mergers and acquisitions, strategic alliances (Koza and Lewin 1998), interlocking directorates and membership in standard-setting bodies (Tushman and Rosenkopf 1992) and industry trade associations (Cyert and March 1963; Pfeffer and Salancik 1978).

In a similar way to evolutionary theories, the firm in the *resource-based theory* is seen as a bundle of tangible and intangible resources and tacit know-how that must be identified, selected, developed, and deployed to generate superior performance

(Penrose 1959; Learned 1969; Wernerfelt 1984). Competitive advantage derives from firm heterogeneity in resources and capabilities (Penrose 1959; Teece *et al.* 1993; Barney 1991; Lippman and Rumelt 1982; Peteraf 1993). The implications for strategy are that competitive advantage can be sustained through barriers to imitation by investing in inimitable idiosyncratic capabilities (Lippman and Rumelt 1982; Winter 1987) and leveraging these firm core specific assets for competitive advantage.

Many studies show that in highly competitive environments a core competence can become core rigidity (Teece 1984: 106; Leonard-Barton 1992; Burgelman 1994; Barnett, Greve, and Park 1994) or a competence trap (Levitt and March 1988; Levinthal and March 1993). Teece, Pisano, and Shuen (1997) suggest that the mechanisms by which firms accumulate and dissipate new skills and capabilities is the source of competitive advantage. They propose that *dynamic capabilities* represent the firm's latent abilities to renew, augment, and adapt its core competence over time. This idea led to the view that knowledge is the most strategically significant resource of the firm (Leonard-Barton 1992; Conner and Prahalad 1996; Grant 1996). In other words, knowledge is the crucial inimitable strategic resource of the firm. The implications for strategy and adaptation are that the organization should maximize *knowledge* creation and integration. Managers should facilitate all sources of knowledge creation such as improvisation and emergent processes, as well as external network relationships (Cohen and Levinthal 1990). Organizations should be designed and managed as learning organizations while at the same time safeguarding unique knowledge capabilities (Nonaka and Takeuchi 1995).

Finally, several theories in strategy and organization design are considered here as they inform selection–adaptation research. These theories encompass contingency, strategic choice, learning and life cycle and punctuated equilibrium theories (Volberda 1998).

Contingency theory considers environmental conditions as a direct cause of variation in organizational forms. Management's task is to achieve 'good fits' with the environment. The proponents of this approach (Burns and Stalker 1961; Donaldson 1988; Lawrence and Lorsch 1967; Woodward 1965) give primary emphasis to reactive adaptation and minimize or ignore the opportunity that firms have for influencing their environment. Successful adaptation of organization to environment is assumed to be directly dependent on the ability of top management to interpret the conditions facing the firm and to align the strategy and organization of the firm to fit the condition of the environment. The implications of *contingency theory* for strategy and organization change are to continuously monitor the organization – environment fit, create organization structures that maximize fit with environmental contingencies by applying routines for differentiation and integration, and by aligning the strategy and organization of the firm to fit the conditions in the environment.

In contrast to contingency theory (Lawrence and Lorsch 1967; Donaldson 1996) that posits that organizations must adapt to their environments (which are controlling and deterministic), the *strategic choice* perspective (Child 1972, 1997; Miles and Snow 1978, 1994; Thompson 1967) assumes that organizations have the discretion and the strategic capacity to select, enact, and shape their environments. In addition *strategic choice theory* views interaction with the environment as the source of new opportunities and strategic alternatives for repositioning the firm (Child 1972). Hrebiniak and Joyce (1985), Khandwalla (1977), Mintzberg (1979), and many other neo-contingency theorists assert that adaptation is a dynamic process subject to both managerial action and environmental forces. The implications of strategic choice theories for firm strategy are that management should take into account the multiple ways in which organizations interact with their environments through the process of mutual adaptation between the organization and its environmental domain. Specifically, managers must select the environment in which the firm should compete, design the organization structure that best fits this environment, actively shape and enact this environment, determine the performance criteria for measuring success, and design the strategies which will maximize organization performance.

Organizational learning theories inform organization adaptation by focusing on the mechanisms and processes by which organizations, groups, or individuals learn (acquire) or unlearn skills, knowledge, norms, or values. Learning takes place at the level of the individual, group, or organization (Fiol and Lyles 1985; Huber 1991; Crossan, Lane, and White 1999). At the individual level the focus has been on acquisition of skills, values, and norms (Argyris and Schön 1978) and on trial and error processes (Miner and Mezias 1996). At the group level the research focused on the role of performance feedback, shared understanding, aspiration level adaptation, social comparison processes, and coordinated behavior (Miner and Mezias 1996; Lant 1992). The behavioral theory of the firm (Cyert and March 1963) introduced the construct of *organizational learning* by defining organizations as adaptive systems and by describing processes, such as problemistic search, through which routines and procedures adapt incrementally and sometimes radically over time. Other theories, especially evolutionary theories embed various learning mechanisms into their dynamic adaptation models. These include integrating learning at the population level with learning at the organization level (Nelson and Winter 1982; Miner and Mezias 1996). Organization learning has important implications for strategy and organization adaptation over time. In particular it has implications for avoiding competency traps and myopic learning by focusing on the long term and by balancing exploitation and exploration learning (March 1991; Hedberg and Jönsson 1978; Lewin, Long, and Carroll 1999). It implies a never-ending emphasis on renewing the knowledge base of the organization, simultaneously driving incremental improvements (single loop learning) and radical innovation (double loop earning), and designing, monitoring, and extending the absorptive capacity of the organization to assimilate internal and external new knowledge. The extent to which organizations' exploration of unknown futures and their exploitation of known capabilities balance each other is of crucial importance to effective learning (March 1991; Hedberg and Jönsson 1978). These forms of learning need not be contradictory processes. They can be complementary, and organizations must learn how to carry out both forms.

Life cycle and *punctuated equilibrium* theories model adaptation and selection over time. Adaptation is assumed to hold during one time period and selection during a different time period. Consequently, several types of temporal relationships may exist among contrary forces. Utterback and Abernathy (1975) suggested that the dominant type of innovation, whether technologically complex or simple, and whether applied to product or process, depends upon the stage of development. Tushman and Anderson (1986) propose, on the basis of a number of product–class case studies, that technology progresses in stages through relatively long periods of incremental, competence-enhancing innovation by elaborating a particular dominant design. These periods of increasing consolidation and learning-by-doing may be punctuated by radical competence-destroying technological innovations. These so-called punctuated equilibrium models, discussed most explicitly by Tushman and Romanelli (1985), posit alternating cycles of preservation 'which elaborate structures, systems, controls, and resources toward increased coalignment', and cycles of fundamental change 'periods of discontinuous transition where strategies, structure, and systems are fundamentally transformed towards a new basis of alignment'. The implications for strategy are that firms should develop organizational forms that are immune to the cycles of technology-destroying competencies and can survive the periodic alternation between incremental and radical change (Duncan 1976; Shepard 1967; Tushman and O'Reilly 1996). The central question is not what technology, structure, or culture to put in place to encourage innovation, but how to manage the dichotomy between routinizing current activities while simultaneously supplanting these same routines.

Table 21.1 summarizes the salient adaptation–selection characteristics of the single-lens perspectives and their implications for firm strategy.

The table clearly demonstrates the fragmented state of the field of organization studies. In a sense the table supports Pfeffer's (1993) view of the domain of organizations theory as more of a weed patch than a well-tended garden. The table also shows that certain lenses, such as industrial organization, the behavioral theory of the firm, and strategic choice perspectives attempt to further elaborate the role of managerial intentionality. Other lenses highlight the limitations of managerial intentionality. Perspectives, such as population ecology, institutionalism, and, to some extent, evolutionary theories, discount the ability of organizations to self-consciously change themselves significantly or repeatedly, or that conscious change initiatives by management are likely to succeed. Instead, using variables such as

Table 21.1 Single-lens theories informing selection–adaptation discourse

Theoretical roots	Dominant paradigm	Selection/Adaptation	Managerial implications
Sociology	Population ecology	Population selection and structural inertia	Management makes no difference; new entrants redefine industries; established firms should focus on what they do best until selected out
	Institutional theories	Population isomorphism based on industry norms and shared logics	Established firms should adopt fast follower strategy for aligning organizational form with prevalent institutional norms and values and the populations dominant logic
Economics	Industrial organization	Level of industry attractiveness and competitive advantage within that industry	Managers should choose an attractive industry; define performance frontier for a generic strategy; reduce intraindustry rivalry and create barriers to entry
	Transaction costs	Minimization of transactions costs within and between firms	Managers should focus on relative coordination costs of transacting inside versus outside the firm by minimizing transaction costs
	Behavioral theory of the firm	Satisfying multiple stakeholders, structural inertia due to satisficing, uncertainty avoidance, and slack	Periodic restructuring and rationalization. Exploration requires strategic intent to allocate slack to innovation. Negotiate environment to reduce uncertainty
	Evolutionary theories	Success reinforces incremental improvements and proliferation of routines as source of inertia (e.g. sunk costs, commitments, social structures)	Managers should overcome preference for improvement of prior and commensurate skills that result in incremental innovations

(continued)

Table 21.1 *Continued*

Theoretical roots	Dominant paradigm	Selection/Adaptation	Managerial implications
	Resource dependence theory	Organizations have discretion and power to shape and enact their environments which themselves represent opportunities for strategic alternatives. Dependence reduction and dependence restructuring are generic strategies for controlling or enacting the environment	Managers should reduce environmental uncertainty by selecting, enacting, and/or negotiating their environment. Control and shape access to resources through a mix of dependence reduction or dependence restructuring strategies
	Resource-based theory of the firm	Idiosyncratic resources basis of sustained competitive advantage, causal ambiguity in evaluating own and competitor core competencies source of suboptimal performance	Managers should maximize unique core competency, correct casual ambiguity in judging own and competitors core competencies
	Dynamic capabilities/knowledge-based theory of the firm	Sustained competitive advantage based on dynamic capabilities and intellectual capital	Management should focus on knowledge creation and integration, continuously renew knowledge base
Strategy and organization design	Contingency theory	Environment source of variation in performance	Top management must interpret and react to changes in environment, maintain fit through changes to organization form
	Strategic choice	Variation in performance results from environmental changes and from firm shaping of environment	Managers should achieve dynamic fit through monitoring and shaping of environment
	Organizational learning	Variation in performance results from changes in environment and organization ability to adapt through learning	Managers need to balance single and double-loop learning
	Life cycle/punctuated equilibrium	Periods of adaptation and consolidation are followed by periods radical competence–destroying change	Managers should anticipate radical change by managing dichotomy between incremental and radical innovation

resource scarcity, industry norms, static routines, and structural inertia, these perspectives focus on the way environments select organizations.

While these various single-lens perspectives have advanced the strategy and organization field, the resolution of the adaptation–selection debate has not progressed very much. We believe that single-theme explanations for the adaptation–selection phenomenon have reached their limit and that strategy and organization theory scholars should adopt research strategies that consider the joint outcomes of managerial adaptation and environmental selection instead of naïve selection or naïve adaptation. Thus, the future of organization studies, we believe, depends very much on developing mindsets, gestalt, and empirical approaches that integrate frameworks across the single-lens silos. Empirical work exists that clearly supports one of the extremes (selection versus adaptation). With a few exceptions (e.g. Baum and Singh 1994; Bruderer and Singh 1996; Lant and Mezias 1990; Levinthal 1997), researchers have tended not to address the interrelationships between processes of firm-level adaptation and population-level selection pressures. Advances in organization studies will derive from the recognition that adaptation and selection are not wholly opposing forces but are fundamentally interrelated and coevolving. Specifically, the meta-theoretical coevolutionary approach assumes that change may occur in all interacting populations of organizations, permitting change to be driven by both direct interactions and feedback from the rest of the system resulting in a dialectic leading to new insights and advances in organization studies.

21.2 COEVOLUTIONARY THEORY AND ADAPTATION SELECTION RESEARCH

Evolutionary theory is not a new idea in organization science. Coevolution was implicit in the early work on the emergence of bureaucracy. Weber (1978) argued that the bureaucratic form of organization arose at a particular time in history in response to the confluence of forces of change that ushered in the industrial age. Chandler (1962) makes a similar coevolution argument, noting that the M-form of organization coevolved with the development of the transportation and communication industries, which enabled business enterprises to manage across time and space and to diversify their business interests. Kieser (1989) describes how medieval guilds were replaced by mercantilist factories as markets and institutions coevolved. He shows how coevolutionary processes resulted in an increase of functional specialization of institutions, de-monopolization of social monopolies, and

Table 21.2 Antecedents of coevolution

Aspects of Coevolution	Contributors
Historical embeddedness	• Replacement of medieval guilds by mercantilist factories (Kieser 1989) • Emergence of bureaucracy (Weber 1978) • Diffusion of M-form (Chandler 1962) • Historical institutional analysis of French and British firms (Calori *et al.* 1997)
Levels of coevolution	• Micro- and macro-coevolution (McKelvey 1997) • Intraorganization, organization, population, and community coevolution (Baum and Singh 1994) • Internal and external context (Pettigrew 1995)
Interaction genealogical and ecological processes	• Enactment, double interacts (Weick 1979) • Variation, selection, retention (Aldrich 1979) • Mutual learning (Nelson and Winter 1982; Levitt and March 1988) • Coevolution of capabilities and competition (Huygens 1999 Huygens *et al.* 2001; Levinthal and Myatt 1994) • Synthesis of ecological and genealogical processes (Baum and Singh 1994; Levinthal 1997; Mezias and Lant 1994)
Zero-sum competitive coevolutionary systems	• Red Queen Race (Beinhocker 1997; Kauffman 1995; Van Valen 1973) • Hypercompetition (D'Aveni and Gunther 1994)
Pluralistic competitive coevolutionary systems	• Adaptation on various fitness landscapes (Levinthal 1997) • Competitive coevolutionary configurations (Baum 1999; Heylighen and Campbell 1995)
Cooperative coevolutionary systems	• Learning alliances (Hamel 1991) • Coevolution of alliances (Koza and Lewin 1998)
Micro-coevolution	• Intraorganizational ecological processes (Burgelman 1991, 1994, 1996) • Selection and adaptation at intracorporate levels of analysis (Barnett, Greve, and Park 1994; Galunic and Eisenhardt 1996)

decoupling of individual motives and organizational goals. Table 21.2 summarizes selected antecedents of coevolution.

Weick (1979) conceptualizes a view of organizing in which organization members are seen as enacting and socially constructing their environment. Weick thus represents the environment simultaneously as endogenous and exogenous. Aldrich

(1979) outlined an evolutionary theory based on processes of variation, selection, and retention. Nelson and Winter (1982) and Levitt and March (1988) have proposed variations of mutual learning frameworks that retain and reinforce learning and incremental improvements of successful routines. Levinthal and Myatt (1994) study the macro-evolution of the mutual fund industry in terms of the coevolution of industry market activities and distinctive capabilities of firms within the industry. These studies, which incorporate both firm- and industry-levels of analysis, subsume possible interactions between genealogical processes (replication of routines, capabilities, competencies) and ecological processes (dynamics of competition and selection).

Firm–industry analysis also points to search behavior potential in moving toward a coevolutionary view of capabilities and competition (Huygens 1999; Huygens *et al.* 2001). In a study on evolution among Illinois banks, Barnett and Hansen (1996) report findings that support dynamic interactions between firm learning and adaptation, on the one hand, and higher levels of competition and selection, on the other. This form of persistent coevolution is dubbed an 'arms race' or 'The Red Queen effect' (Beinhocker 1997; Kauffman 1995; Van Valen 1973) after the comment to Alice, 'It takes all the running you can do to keep in the same place' (Carroll 1946). The concept of hypercompetition (D'Aveni and Gunther 1994), in which escalating competition results in short periods of advantage punctuated by frequent disruptions, represents a similar approach (Ilinitch, Lewin, and D'Aveni 1998). In these coevolutionary models, the assumed symmetry between forces of adaptation and selection results in their canceling each other out. That is, search behavior on the firm level may lead to unique capabilities and competitive advantage, but as a result of increased competitive dynamics, these advantages are quickly eroded. The implication is that all species keep changing in a never-ending race only to sustain their current level of fitness.

Of course, a much larger variety of coevolutionary systems can be studied. Levinthal (1997) shows the relative impact of different levels of firm adaptation and population selection in a changing environment by simulating adaptation on smooth versus rugged fitness landscapes. Moreover, on the basis of Heylighen and Campbell's (1995) competitive configurations, Baum (1999: 120) illustrates various alternatives to zero-sum, purely competitive coevolutionary systems that are supercompetitive (increase in a firm's fitness results in a decrease in rival firms' fitness); partly competitive (some resources are shared and others not); synergistic (an increase in one firm's fitness results in an increase in rival firms' fitness); and independent (an increase in one firm's fitness does not affect rival firms' fitness).

In addition to various competitive coevolutionary configurations, there are several studies that investigate cooperative coevolutionary systems. For example, Hamel (1991) concludes that international alliances that are thought at the start to be synergetic turn out to be supercompetitive. Moreover, Koza and Lewin (1998) argue that strategic alliances are embedded in the firm strategic portfolio and coevolve with firm strategy; institutional, organizational, and competitive environment; and managerial intentionality for the alliance.

Other studies beyond aggregate studies on dynamic competitive and cooperative interactions between firms involve intraorganization evolution or micro-evolution. These studies consider coevolution of intrafirm resources, dynamic capabilities, and competencies in an intrafirm competitive context (Barnett, Greve, and Park 1994; Galunic and Eisenhardt 1996; Burgelman 1991, 1994, 1996). Galunic and Eisenhardt (1996) study selection and adaptation at the intracorporate level of analysis. They used charter changes to align and realign the competencies of various divisions with coevolving markets and opportunities. They report that charter loss in M-form firms involves a mix of selection and adaptation processes. Selection occurs among competing divisions but losses involve purposive action by group executives and major adaptive shifts by divisions. Burgelman's (1994, 1996) intraorganizational process model shifts the locus of selection from the firm as a whole to classes of strategic action inside the firm, and views managing intraorganizational ecological processes as a means by which the firm can achieve the learning benefits of both external and internal selection.

21.3 THEORY AND EXTENSIONS OF COEVOLUTION

The coevolution construct has been gaining adherents over the past few years. In this section we consider some of the essential properties of coevolution and their implications for strategic management and organization adaptation research.

Multilevelness/embeddedness. Coevolutionary effects take place at multiple levels within firms as well as between firms. While coevolution has been studied on a single level of analysis, McKelvey (1997: 360) argues that coevolution takes place at multiple levels. He makes a distinction between coevolution within the firm (micro-coevolution) and coevolution between firms and their niche (macro-coevolution). This approach recognizes that processes of variation, selection, and retention operate within the organization and interact with similar processes operating at the population level. The focus of macro-coevolutionary theory is on firms existing in a coevolutionary competitive context, while micro-coevolution considers coevolution of intrafirm resources, dynamic capabilities, and competencies in an intrafirm competitive context.

Pettigrew (1995), for example, makes a distinction between external context involving economic, political, and social forces and the internal context focusing on resources, capabilities, culture, and internal politics. In a more formal formulation, Baum and Singh (1994) consider coevolution at community, population, organization, and intraorganization level. However, multilevel coevolutionary thinking requires scholars to consider the interactions between multiple levels of coevolution. Nonetheless, McKelvey (1997) as well as Baum and Singh (1994) argue that coevolution by lower levels always occurs in the context of higher levels of coevolution. In other words, micro-coevolutionary order within firms emerges in the context of macro-evolutionary selectionist competitive pressure (McKelvey 1997: 361; Cohen and Stewart 1994). Studies that use such a nested coevolutionary perspective are sparse (Tushman and Rosenkopf 1996; Garud and Van de Ven 1992). An exception is March's (1991) study of the interaction of evolutionary adaptive thinking at both the microstate level (changes in individual beliefs) and the firm level (changes in the organizational code), in the context of environmental turbulence. The volume *Variations in Organization Science* (Baum and McKelvey 1999) contains several chapters on multilevel coevolution (Ingram and Roberts 1999; Rosenkopf and Nerkar 1999; Van de Ven and Grazman 1999).

Multidirectional causalities. Organizations and their parts do not merely evolve. They coevolve with each other and with a changing organizational environment (Baum 1999; Kauffman 1993; McKelvey 1997). Changes may occur in all interacting populations of organizations, permitting change to be driven by mutual direct interactions and by feedback from the rest of the system. In this connection, Baum and Singh (1994), for example, make the distinction between direct coevolution, in which one population evolves in response to another population, and diffuse coevolution, in which one or more populations evolve in response to several other populations in a broader ecological system. In such complex systems of relationships, dependent–independent variable distinctions become less meaningful, since changes in any one variable may be caused endogenously by changes in others.

Nonlinearity. As a consequence of indeterminate feedback paths, changes in one variable can produce quite counterintuitive changes in another variable. For example, as a result of higher order feedback processes, the effects of changes in one variable frequently contradict inferences based on simple cause–effect logic of linear relations between independent and dependent variables (Baum and Singh 1994; Casti 1994). That is, coevolution subsumes nonlinear feedback among interacting populations, and such nonlinearities can substantially complicate attempts to understand evolutionary change. Scholars in strategy and organization research have abstracted away nonlinear interactions for the sake of analytical tractability (Anderson 1999). A coevolutionary approach, however, requires that sets of co-acting organizations and their environments be the object of study, and that changes in all interacting organizations be allowed to result not only from the direct interactions between pairs of organizations, but also by indirect feedback through the rest of the system.

Positive feedback. Organizations systematically influence their environments, and organizational environments fundamentally comprised of other organizations in turn influence organizations. These recursive interactions result in interdependencies and bi-directional causality; each firm influencing the other and in turn being influenced by the behavior of the other. In this mutual interaction feedback perspective, the unidirectional view of cause-and-effect relationships gives way to a recursive bi-directional view of mutual causality.

Path and history dependence. Adaptation in a coevolutionary process is path- or history-dependent (Calori *et al.* 1997; Kieser 1989; McKelvey 1997). Variation in adaptations among constituent firms in a population may reflect heterogeneity in the population of firms at earlier points in time (Stinchcombe 1965; Levinthal 1997), rather than variation in niches in the environment (as suggested in population ecology) or a set of distinct external conditions (as generally suggested by contingency theories).

On the basis of these properties of coevolution, we identify several requirements that distinguish coevolutionary research from non-coevolutionary research. However, not all of these requirements must be satisfied in each study. Under conditions of coevolutionary equilibrium, conventional single-lens perspectives in which the environment is treated as exogenous may be quite appropriate (independent coevolutionary systems). Nonetheless, a large and important class of phenomena involves conditions of simultaneous evolution that persist over long time periods. We conclude that the application of a coevolutionary perspective should at a minimum consider:

(a) studying organization adaptations over a *long period of time* (McKelvey 1997; Levinthal 1997) by using longitudinal time series of microstate adaptation events and measures of rate of change or pace of change;

(b) examining organization adaptation within a *historical context* of the firm and its environment (Calori *et al.* 1997; Kieser 1989, 1994; Stinchcombe 1965);

(c) *multidirectional causalities* between micro- and macro-coevolution (McKelvey 1997), as well as between and across other system elements (Baum 1999). In such systems of relationships among variables, the dependent–independent variable distinction becomes less meaningful. Changes in any one variable are caused endogenously by changes in the other;

(d) incorporating *mutual, simultaneous, lagged, and nested effects.* Such effects are not very likely to be linear, and as a consequence of feedback flows, changes in one variable can produce counterintuitive changes in another variable;

(e) *path dependence, which enables and restricts adaptation* at the firm level and at the population level, thereby driving both retention and variation at different rates;

(f) incorporating changes occurring at the level of *different institutional systems* within which firms and industries are embedded. Change in the regulatory environment can affect the firm and the industry, but the firm and/or the industry may have also influenced these changes;

(g) accommodating *economic, social, and political macro-variables* that may change over time and influence the deep structure within which micro- and macro-evolution operate (for example, the aging of the population is not impacting each of the affected populations of organizations or individual organizations to the same extent). It is necessary to identify and incorporate the simultaneous or lagged effect of such macro-variables.

These properties of coevolutionary systems and requirements for coevolutionary research leads us to reconsider accepted research directions, and to consider fundamentally new research approaches on the role that intentionality plays in organization adaptation and change.

21.4 Empirical Explorations of Coevolution

It is evident to us, that progress in complexity science (Anderson *et al.* 1999; Axelrod and Cohen 2000), emergence (Holland 1999), computational organization theory (Carley 1995), and population ecology are converging toward creating a much needed theoretical footing for coevolutionary research. It appears to us that the pace of theory building, new analytical models, and new theoretical insights are outstripping commensurate progress with empirical approaches. Empirical coevolution research requires longitudinal methods of analyses and time series data. Although the relevance and need for longitudinal research in strategic management and organization adaptation research is widely recognized (Miller and Friesen 1982; Huber and Van de Ven 1995; Henderson and Mitchell 1997; Barnett and Burgelman 1996), such research is far from becoming the norm. For example, *Organizational Research Methods*, a new journal sponsored by the Academy of Management Research Methods Division, has published only one article that directly informs longitudinal research (Chan 1998) in its first two years of publication. Longitudinal coevolutionary research will require a richer arsenal of methods and techniques beyond traditional time series methods and hazard rate models. For example, sequence analyses (Abbott 1990; Sabherwal and Robey 1993) are not often considered in strategic adaptation research where the data could be represented as strings (sequences) of microadaptation events over time. Similarly, the rapid rise of computational organization theory and agent-based modeling (Carley 1995) has not significantly affected empirical methods needed for researching coevolutionary phenomena such as multidirectional causalities, simultaneous and lagged effects, non-linearity and positive feedback loops. These methodological challenges continue to pose thorny obstacles for coevolutionary empirical research.

Measurement issues and accessibility to appropriate time series data also present new challenges—in particular, the use of rates of change and velocity measures. Cross-sectional survey-based studies and economic time series modeling dominate by far the empirical research landscape in strategic management. The PIMS database was a major source for time series research in strategic management and marketing strategy research with a focus on economic model formulations of competitive dynamics (Boulding and Staelin 1995). The cause of empirical coevolution research would advance greatly with the advent of new types of time series data consisting of microstate adaptations (McKelvey 1997).

Efforts at creating such data sources are still in their infancy. Appropriate microstate adaptation data sequences will vary with research questions being investigated and with the particular coevolutionary system under study. Examples of microstate data sequences include product changes and new product introductions (Sanderson and Uzumeri 1997) and strategic adaptations such as mergers, acquisitions, divestitures and green field investments (Barnett, Greve, and Park 1994; Capron, Mitchell, and Swaminathan 2001; Capron, Dussauge, and Mitchell 1998; Greve 2000; Greve and Taylor 2000; Karim and Mitchell 2000; Volberda *et al.* 2001). Combining such microadaptation sequences with other event histories, such as regulatory changes, technological innovations, and demographic changes, with performance time series and founding conditions establishes an organization environment system within which coevolutionary studies can take place. It becomes viable to investigate dynamic phenomena involving firm micro-evolution, industry macro-evolution, environmental and technological evolution and coevolution processes within such a system. Such studies, for example, can reveal new insights into organization failures, seemingly permanent failing organizations, and mutation and emergence of new organizational forms.

Coevolution studies of the type envisioned here are still a rare exception because the required data sequences are not readily available. The research and assembly of such large-scale primary data sequences requires time and resources on a scale not generally available to most researchers in strategic management and organization studies. However, promising progress can be found in the *Organization Science* special issue on coevolution (Volume 10, Number 5, 1999) and the *Organization Studies* special issue on multilevel analysis and coevolution (Volume 22, Number 6, 2001).

Moreover, the time horizon for undertaking coevolution studies remains inde-terminate. Theories and models of coevolution are silent on this issue. Yet the choice of the time horizon can be important in the conduct and interpretation of any longitudinal time series or coevolution study. Barnett and Hansen (1996), for example, create a data set for the years 1900 to 1993.

McKelvey (1997) argues that coevolution studies should use data consisting of rates of change in the variables and measures of interest. The underlying assump-tion is that time series of rates of change capture or reflect adaptation outcomes that are independent of firm microcontextual details. For example, in strategic manage-ment, research contrasting above- and below-average performance over long time periods can be assumed to reflect firm-specific adaptation factors (e.g. exploitation and exploration, absorptive capacity, path dependence) that distinguish between these two subpopulations when founding conditions and environmental change event histories have been incorporated in the coevolutionary analysis. Although such large-scale longitudinal coevolutionary studies are only starting to appear, they point to new directions in empirical research on the selection–adaptation puzzle.

Studies of simultaneous evolution, or coevolution of organizations and their environments are still rare. We define coevolution as the joint outcome of man-agerial intentionality, environment, and institutional effects. Coevolution assumes that change may occur in all interacting populations of organizations. Change can be driven by direct interactions and feedback from the rest of the system. In other words, change can be recursive and need not be an outcome of either managerial adaptation or environmental selection but rather the joint outcome of managerial intentionality and environmental effects.

Historically new developments in management theory and managerial practice have coevolved by 'feeding' on each other through processes of reciprocal relation-ships. Such processes are mediated, for example, by management consultants (Kieser 2000) and by the felt pressure of business schools faculty to demonstrate the managerial relevance of their research (March and Sutton 1997). Advances in organization studies including new theoretical advances in strategic management could emerge from deliberate and collaborative efforts to integrate complementary theoretical frameworks involving adaptation selection research. It should involve combining and recombining multiple theoretical lenses (instead of further increasing fragmentation) and new ways of informing, tracking, and learning from the managerial experiments taking place in the world of practice (see also Volberda and Elfring 2001). In other words, advances in organization studies are not an outcome of research on managerial adaptation or environmental selection but rather the joint outcome of research on intentionality and environmental effects.

In conclusion, we argue that advances in organization studies require moving beyond the adaptation–selection debate and should emerge from building and testing coevolutionary theories. The rate of progress would be attenuated by finding new ways to undertake longitudinal studies of organization adaptations, utilizing common core data sets coupled with links to managerial practice to inform and validate advances in theory.

REFERENCES

ABBOTT, A. (1990). 'A Primer on Sequence Methods'. *Organization Science*, 1/4: 375–92.
ALDRICH, H. (1979). *Organizations and Environments*. Englewood Cliffs, NJ: Prentice-Hall.
—— and MUELLER, S. (1982). 'The Evolution of Organizational Forms: Technology, Co-ordination, and Control', in B. M. Staw and L. L. Cummings (eds.), *Research in Organizational Behavior*, iv. Greenwich, Conn.: JAI.
—— and PFEFFER, J. (1976). 'Environments of Organizations'. *Annual Review of Sociology*, 2: 121–40.
—— and ZIMMER, C. (1986). 'Entrepreneurship through Social Networks', in D. Sexton and R. Smilor (eds.), *The Art and Science of Entrepreneurship*. Cambridge, Mass: Ballinger.
ANDERSON, P. (1999). 'Complexity Theory and Organization Science'. *Organization Science*, 10/5: 216–32.
—— MEYER, A., EISENHARDT, K., CARLEY, K., and PETTIGREW, A. (1999). 'Introduction to the Special Issue: Applications of Complexity Theory to Organization Science'. *Organization Science*, 10/5: 233–6.
ANDREWS, K. R. (1971). *The Concept of Corporate Strategy*. Homewood, Ill.: Irwin.
ARGYRIS, C., and SCHÖN, D. A. (1978). *Organizational Learning: A Theory of Action Perspective*. Reading, Mass.: Addison-Wesley.
AXELROD, R., and COHEN, M. D. (2000). *Harnessing Complexity: Organizational Implications of a Scientific Frontier*. New York: Free Press.
BADEN-FULLER, C., and STOPFORD, J. M. (1992). *Rejuvenating the Mature Business: The Competitive Challenge*. New York: Routledge.
BAIN, J. S. (1959). *Industrial Organization*. New York: Wiley.
BARNETT, W. P., and BURGELMAN, R. A. (1996). 'Evolutionary Perspectives on Strategy'. *Strategic Management Journal*, 17/Special Issue: 5–20.
—— and HANSEN, M. T. (1996). 'The Red Queen in Organizational Evolution'. *Strategic Management Journal*, 17/Special Issue: 139–57.
—— GREVE, H. R., and PARK, D. Y. (1994). 'An Evolutionary Model of Organizational Performance'. *Strategic Management Journal*, 15/Special Issue: 11–28.
BARNEY, J. B. (1991). 'Firm Resources and Sustained Competitive Advantage'. *Journal of Management*, 17/1: 139–57.
BAUM, J. A. C. (1996). 'Organizational Ecology', in S. R. Clegg, C. Hardy, and W. R. Nord (eds.), *Handbook of Organization Studies*. London: Sage.
—— (1999). 'Whole–Part Coevolutionary Competition in Organizations', in Joel A. C. Baum and Bill McKelvey (eds.), *Variations in Organization Science: In Honor of Donald T. Campbell*. Thousand Oaks, Calif.: Sage Publications.
—— and KORN, H. J. (1999). 'Dynamics of Dyadic Competitive Interaction'. *Strategic Management Journal*, 20/3: 251–78.

——and MCKELVEY, B. (1999). *Variations in Organization Science: In Honor of Donald T. Campbell*. London: Sage.

——and SINGH, J. V. (1994). *Evolutionary Dynamics of Organizations*. New York: Oxford University Press.

BEINHOCKER, E. (1997). 'Strategy at the Edge of Chaos'. *McKinsey Quarterly*, 1: 25–39.

BOULDING, W., and STAELIN, R. (1995). 'Identifying Generalizable Effects of Strategic Actions on Firm Performance: The Case of Demand-Side Returns to R&D Spending'. *Marketing Science*, 14/3: 1160–77.

BRUDERER, E., and SINGH, J. V. (1996). 'Organizational Evolution, Learning, and Selection: A Genetic-Algorithm-Based Model'. *Academy of Management Journal*, 39/5: 1322–49.

BURGELMAN, R. A. (1991). 'Intraorganizational Ecology of Strategy Making and Organizational Adaptation: Theory and Field Research'. *Organization Science*, 2: 239–62.

——(1994). 'Fading Memories: A Process Theory of Strategic Business Exit in Dynamic Environments'. *Administrative Science Quarterly*, 39/1: 24–56.

——(1996). 'A Process Model of Strategic Business Exit: Implications for an Evolutionary Perspective on Strategy'. *Strategic Management Journal*, 17: 193–214.

BURNS, T., and STALKER, G. M. (1961). *The Management of Innovation*. London: Tavistock.

CALORI, R., LUBATKIN, M., VERY, P., and VEIGA, J. F. (1997). 'Modelling the Origins of Nationally Bound Administrative Heritages: A Historical Institutional Analysis of French and British Firms'. *Organization Science*, 8/6: 681–96.

CAPRON, L., DUSSAUGE, P., and MITCHELL, W. (1998). 'Resource Redeployment Following Horizontal Acquisitions in Europe and North America, 1988–1992'. *Strategic Management Journal*, 19/7: 631–61.

——MITCHELL, W., and SWAMINATHAN, A. (2001). 'Asset Divestiture Following Horizontal Acquisitions: A Dynamic View'. *Strategic Management Journal*, 22/9: 817–44.

CARLEY, K. M. (1995). 'Computational and Mathematical Organization Theory: Perspective and Direction'. *Computational and Mathematical Organization Theory*, 1/1: 39–56.

CARROLL, L. (1946). *Through the Looking Glass & What Alice Found There*. New York: Grosset & Dunlap.

CASTI, J. (1994). *Complexification: Explaining a Paradoxical World through the Science of Surprise*. New York: HarperCollins.

CHAN, D. (1998). 'The Conceptualization and Analysis of Change Over Time: An Integrative Approach Incorporating Longitudinal Mean and Covariance Structures Analysis (LMACS) and Multiple Indicator Latent Growth Modeling (MLGM)'. *Organizational Research Methods*, 1/4: 421–83.

CHANDLER, A. D. (1962). *Strategy and Structure: Chapters in the History of the American Industrial Enterprise*. Cambridge, Mass.: MIT Press.

CHILD, J. (1972). 'Organization Structure, Environment and Performance: The Role of Strategic Choice'. *Sociology*, 6/1: 1–22.

——(1997). 'Strategic Choice in the Analysis of Action, Structure, Organizations and Environment: Retrospect and Prospect'. *Organization Studies*, 18/1: 43–76.

CIBORRA, C. U. (1996). 'The Platform Organization: Recombining Strategies, Structures, and Surprises'. *Organization Studies*, 7/2: 103–18.

COHEN, J., and STEWART, I. (1994). *The Collapse of Chaos: Discovering Simplicity in a Complex World*. New York: Viking.

COHEN, W. M., and LEVINTHAL, D. A. (1990). 'Absorptive Capacity: A New Perspective on Learning and Innovation'. *Administrative Science Quarterly*, 35/1: 128–52.

COMMONS, J. R. (1934). *Institutional Economics*. Madison: University of Wisconsin Press.

CONNER, K. R., and PRAHALAD, C. K. (1996). 'A Resource-Based Theory of the Firm: Knowledge Versus Opportunism'. *Organization Science*, 7/5: 477–501.

CROSSAN, M. M., LANE, H. W., and WHITE, R. E. (1999). 'An Organizational Learning Framework: From Intuition to Institution'. *Academy of Management Review*, 24/3: 522–37.

CYERT, R. M., and MARCH, J. G. (1963). *A Behavioral Theory of the Firm*. Englewood Cliffs, NJ: Prentice-Hall.

D'AVENI, R. A., and GUNTHER, R. E. (1994). *Hypercompetition: Managing the Dynamics of Strategic Maneuvering*. New York: Free Press.

DAVIDOW, W. H., and MALONE, M. S. (1992). *The Virtual Corporation: Structuring and Revitalizing the Corporation for the 21st Century*. New York: HarperBusiness.

DiMAGGIO, P., and POWELL, W. (1983). 'The Iron Cage Revisited: Institutional Isomorphism, and Collective Rationality in Organization Fields'. *American Sociological Review*, 48: 147–60.

DONALDSON, L. (1988). 'In Successful Defence of Organization Theory: A Routing of the Critics'. *Organization Studies*, 9/1: 28–32.

——(1996). 'The Normal Science of Structural Contingency Theory', in S. R. Clegg, C. Hardy, and W. R. Nord (eds.), *Handbook of Organizational Studies*. London: Sage.

DUNCAN, R. B. (1976). 'The Ambidextrous Organization: Designing Dual Structures for Innovation', in R. H. Kilmann, L. R. Pondy, and D. P. Slevin (eds.), *The Management of Organization Design*, i. New York: North Holland.

FIOL, C. M., and LYLES, M. A. (1985). 'Organizational Learning'. *Academy of Management Review*, 10/4: 803–13.

GALUNIC, D. C., and EISENHARDT, K. M. (1996). 'The Evolution of Intracorporate Domains: Divisional Charter Losses in High-Technology, Multidivisional Corporations'. *Organization Science*, 7/3: 255–82.

GARUD, R., and VAN DE VEN, A. H. (1992). 'An Empirical Evaluation of the Internal Corporate Venturing Process'. *Strategic Management Journal*, 13: 93–109.

GRANT, R. M. (1996). 'Prospering in Dynamically Competitive Environments: Organizational Capability as Knowledge Integration'. *Organization Science*, 7/4: 375–87.

GREEN, S. G., and WELSH, M. A. (1988). 'Cybernetics and Dependence: Reframing the Control Concept'. *Academy of Management Review*, 13/2: 287–301.

GREENWOOD, R., and HININGS, C. R. (1996). 'Understanding Radical Organizational Change: Bringing Together the Old and the New Institutionalism'. *Academy of Management Review*, 21/4: 1022–54.

GREVE, H. R. (2000). 'Market Niche Entry Decisions: Competition, Learning, and Strategy in Tokyo Banking, 1894–1936'. *Academy of Management*, 43/5: 816–36.

——and TAYLOR, A. (2000). 'Innovations as Catalysts for Organizational Change: Shifts in Organizational Cognition and Search'. *Administrative Science Quarterly*, 45/1: 54–80.

HAMEL, G. (1991). 'Competition for Competence and Interpartner Learning within International Strategic Alliances'. *Strategic Management Journal*, 12: 83–103.

HANDY, C. (1995). *The Age of Unreason*. London: Arrow Business Books.

HANNAN, M. T., and FREEMAN, J. (1977). 'The Population Ecology of Organizations'. *American Journal of Sociology*, 82/5: 929–64.

—————(1984). 'Structural Inertia and Organizational Change'. *American Sociological Review*, 49: 149–64.

HEDBERG, B., and JÖNSSON, S. (1978). 'Designing Semi-confusing Information Systems for Organizations in Changing Environments'. *Accounting, Organizations and Society*, 3/1: 47–64.

HENDERSON, R., and MITCHELL, W. (1997). 'The Interactions of Organizational and Competitive Influences on Strategy and Performance'. *Strategic Management Journal*, 18/Special Issue: 5–14.

HEYLIGHEN, F., and CAMPBELL, D. T. (1995). 'Selection of Organization at the Social Level: Obstacles and Facilitators of Metasystem Transitions'. *World Futures: The Journal of General Evolution*, Special Issue: 181–212.

HOLLAND, J. H. (1999). *Emergence: From Chaos to Order*. Reading, Mass.: Helix Books.

HREBINIAK, L. G., and JOYCE, W. F. (1985). 'Organizational Adaptation: Strategic Choice and Environmental Determinism'. *Administrative Science Quarterly*, 30/3: 336–49.

HUBER, G. P. (1991). 'Organizational Learning: The Contributing Processes and Literatures'. *Organization Science*, 2/1: 88–115.

—— and VAN DE VEN, A. H. (1995). *Longitudinal Field Research Methods: Studying Processes of Organizational Change*. Thousand Oaks, Calif.: Sage.

HUYGENS, M. (1999). *Coevolution of Capabilities and Competition: A Study of the Music Industry*, Ph.D. series in General Management, no. 33. Rotterdam School of Management.

—— BADEN-FULLER, C., VAN DEN BOSCH, F. A. J., and VOLBERDA, H. W. (2001). 'Co-evolution of Firm Capabilities and Industry Competition: Investigating the Music Industry, 1877–1997'. *Organization Studies*, 22/6: 971–1011.

ILINITCH, A. Y., LEWIN, A. Y., and D'AVENI, R. A. (1998). *Managing in Times of Disorder: Hypercompetitive Organizational Responses*. Thousand Oaks, Calif.: Sage.

INGRAM, P., and ROBERTS, P. W. (1999). 'Suborganizational Evolution in the U.S. Pharmaceutical Industry', in J. A. C. Baum and B. McKelvey (eds.), *Variations in Organization Science: In Honor of Donald T. Campbell*. London: Sage.

KARIM, S., and MITCHELL, W. (2000). 'Path-dependent and Path-breaking Change: Reconfiguring Business Resources Following Acquisitions in the U.S. Medical Sector, 1978–1995'. *Strategic Management Journal*, 21/10–11: 1061–81.

KAUFFMAN, S. A. (1993). *The Origins of Order: Self-Organization and Selection in Evolution*. New York: Oxford University Press.

——(1995). 'Technology and Evolution: Escaping the Red Queen Effect'. *McKinsey Quarterly*, 1: 118–29.

KHANDWALLA, P. N. (1977). *The Design of Organizations*. New York: Harcourt Brace Jovanovich.

KIESER, A. (1989). 'Organizational, Institutional, and Societal Evolution: Medieval Craft Guilds and the Genesis of Formal Organizations'. *Administrative Science Quarterly*, 34/4: 540–63.

——(1994). 'Why Organization Theory Needs Historical Analyses—and How This Should Be Performed'. *Organization Science*, 5/4: 608–20.

——(2000). 'Matthias Kipping and Ove Bjarnar (eds.).: The Americanisation of European Business: The Marshall Plan and the Transfer of US Management Models'. *Organization Studies*, 21/5: 1015–18.

KOZA, M. P., and LEWIN, A. Y. (1998). 'The Co-evolution of Strategic Alliances'. *Organization Science*, 9/3: 255–64.

LANT, T. K. (1992). 'Aspiration Level Updating: An Empirical Exploration'. *Management Science*, 38: 623–44.

—— and MEZIAS, S. (1990). 'Managing Discontinuous Change: A Simulation Study of Organizational Learning and Entrepreneurship'. *Strategic Management Journal*, 11: 147–79.

LAWRENCE, P. R., and LORSCH, J. W. (1967). *Organization and Environment: Managing Differentiation and Integration*. Boston: Division of Research Graduate School of Business Administration Harvard University.

LEARNED, E. P. (1969). *Business Policy: Text and Cases*. Homewood, Ill.: Irwin.

LEONARD-BARTON, D. (1992). 'Core Capabilities and Core Rigidities: A Paradox in Managing New Product Development'. *Strategic Management Journal*, 13/Special Issue: 111–25.

LEVINTHAL, D. A. (1997). 'Adaptation on Rugged Landscapes'. *Management Science*, 43/7: 934–50.

—— and MARCH, J. G. (1993). 'The Myopia of Learning'. *Strategic Management Journal*, 14/Special Issue: 95–112.

—— and MYATT, J. (1994). 'Co-evolution of Capabilities and Industry: The Evolution of Mutual Fund Processing'. *Strategic Management Journal*, 15/Special Issue: 45–62.

LEVITT, B., and MARCH, J. G. (1988). 'Organizational Learning', in W. R. Scott (ed.), *Annual Review of Sociology*, xiv, Palo Alto, Calif.: Annual Reviews.

LEWIN, A. Y., and STEPHENS, C. U. (1993). 'Designing Postindustrial Organizations: Combining Theory and Practice', in G. P. Huber and W. H. Glick (eds.), *Organizational Change and Redesign*. New York: Oxford University Press.

—— LONG, C. P., and CARROLL, T. N. (1999). 'The Coevolution of New Organizational Forms'. *Organization Science*, 10/5: 535–50.

—— WEIGELT, C., and KIM, J. (forthcoming) *Selection and Adaptation Research*.

—— and VOLBERDA, H. W. (1999). 'Prolegomena on Coevolution: A Framework for Research on Strategy and New Organizational Forms'. *Organization Science*, 10/5: 519–34.

LIPPMAN, S. L., and RUMELT, R. P. (1982). 'Uncertain Imitability: An Analysis of Interfirm Differences in Efficiency under Competition'. *Bell Journal of Economics*, 13/2: 418–38.

MCKELVEY, B. (1997). 'Quasi-Natural Organization Science'. *Organization Science*, 8/4: 352–80.

MARCH, J. G. (1991). 'Exploration and Exploitation in Organizational Learning'. *Organization Science*, 2/1: 71–87.

—— (1994). 'The Evolution of Evolution', in J. A. C. Baum and J. V. Singh (eds.), *Evolutionary Dynamics of Organizations*. New York: Oxford University Press.

—— and SUTTON, R. I. (1997). 'Organizational Performance as a Dependent Variable'. *Organization Science*, 8/6: 697–706.

MASON, I. E. (1949). 'The Current State of the Monopoly Problem in the U.S'. *Harvard Law Review* (June).

MEZIAS, S. J., and LANT, T. K. (1994). 'Mimetic Learning and the Evolution of Organizational Populations', in J. A. C. Baum and J. V. Singh (eds.), *Evolutionary Dynamics of Organizations*. New York: Oxford University Press.

MILES, R. E., and SNOW, C. C. (1978). *Organizational Strategy, Structure, and Process*. New York: McGraw-Hill.

—— —— (1986). 'Organizations: New Concepts for New Forms'. *California Management Review*, 28/3: 62–73.

————— (1994). *Fit, Failure, and the Hall of Fame: How Companies Succeed or Fail*. New York: Free Press.

————— MATHEWS, J. A., MILES, G., and COLEMAN, Jr., H. J. (1997). 'Organizing in the Knowledge Age: Anticipating the Cellular Form'. *Academy of Management Executive*, 11/4: 7–20.

MILLER, D. (1990). *The Icarus Paradox: How Exceptional Companies Bring about Their Own Downfall*. New York: HarperCollins.

—— and CHEN, M.-J.(1994). 'Sources and Consequences of Competitive Inertia: A Study of the U.S. Airline Industry'. *Administrative Science Quarterly*, 39/1: 1–23.

—— and FRIESEN, P. H. (1982). 'The Longitudinal Analysis of Organizations'. *Management Science*, 28/9: 13–34.

MINER, A. S., and MEZIAS, S. J. (1996). 'Ugly Duckling No More: Pasts and Futures of Organizational Learning Research'. *Organization Science*, 7/1: 88–99.

MINTZBERG, H. (1979). *The Structuring of Organizations: A Synthesis of the Research*. Englewood Cliffs, NJ: Prentice-Hall.

NELSON, R. R., and WINTER, S. G. (1982). *An Evolutionary Theory of Economic Change*. Cambridge, Mass.: Belknap.

NONAKA, I., and TAKEUCHI, H. (1995). *The Knowledge-Creating Company*. New York: Oxford University Press.

OLIVER, C. (1991). 'Strategic Responses to Institutional Processes'. *Academy of Management Review*, 16/1: 145–79.

PENROSE, E. T. (1959). *The Theory of the Growth of the Firm*. New York: Wiley.

PETERAF, M. A. (1993). 'The Cornerstones of Competitive Advantage: A Resource-Based View'. *Strategic Management Journal*, 14/3: 179–91.

PETTIGREW, A. (1985). *The Awakening Giant: Continuity and Change in Imperial Chemical Industries*. Oxford: Basil Blackwell.

—— (1995). 'Examining Change in the Long-Term Context of Culture and Politics', in J. M. Pennings and Associates (eds.), *Organizational Strategy and Change*. San Francisco: Jossey-Bass.

PFEFFER, J. (1993). 'Barriers to the Advance of Organization Science: Paradigm Development as Dependent Variable'. *Academy of Management Review*, 18/4: 599–620.

—— and SALANCIK, G. R. (1978). *The External Control of Organizations: A Resource Dependence Perspective*. New York: Harper & Row.

PORTER, M. E. (1980). *Competitive Strategy: Techniques for Analyzing Industries and Competitors*. New York: Free Press.

—— (1985). *Competitive Advantage: Creating and Sustaining Superior Performance*. New York: Free Press.

ROMANELLI, E. (1991). 'The Evolution of New Organizational Forms'. *Annual Review of Sociology*, 17: 79–103.

ROSENKOPF, L., and NERKAR, A. (1999). 'On the Complexity of Technological Evolution: Exploring Coevolution within and across Hierarchical Levels in Optical Disc Technology', in J. A. C. Baum and B. McKelvey (eds.), *Variations in Organization Science: In Honor of Donald T. Campbell*. London: Sage.

SABHERWAL, R., and ROBEY, D. (1993). 'An Empirical Taxonomy of Implementation Processes Based on Sequences of Events in Information System Development'. *Organization Science*, 4/4: 548–76.

SANDERSON, S. W., and UZUMERI, M. (1997). *Managing Product Families*. Chicago: Irwin.

Schumpeter, J. A. (1950). *Capitalism, Socialism and Democracy*. New York: Harper & Brothers.

Shepard, H. A. (1967). 'Innovation-Resisting and Innovation-Producing Organizations'. *Journal of Business*, 40/4: 470–7.

Stinchcombe, A. L. (1965). 'Organizations and Social Structure', in J. G. March (ed.), *Handbook of Organizations*. Chicago: Rand McNally.

Teece, D. J. (1984). 'Economic Analysis and Strategic Management'. *California Management Review*, Spring: 87–110.

—— Pisano, G., and Shuen, A. (1997). 'Dynamic Capabilities and Strategic Management'. *Strategic Management Journal*, 18/7: 509–33.

—— Rumelt, R., Dosi, G., and Winter, S. (1993). 'Understanding Corporate Coherence: Theory and Evidence'. *Journal of Economic Behavior and Organization*, 23/1: 1–30.

Thompson, J. D. (1967). *Organizations in Action: Social Science Bases of Administrative Theory*. New York: McGraw-Hill.

Tushman, M. L., and Anderson, P. (1986). 'Technological Discontinuities and Organizational Environments'. *Administrative Science Quarterly*, 31/3: 439–65.

—— and O'Reilly, I. (1996). 'The Ambidextrous Organization: Managing Evolutionary and Revolutionary Change'. *California Management Review*, 38/4: 8–30.

—— and Romanelli, E. (1985). 'Organizational Evolution: A Metamorphosis Model of Convergence and Reorientation', in B. M. Staw and L. L. Cummings (eds.), *Research in Organizational Behavior*. Greenwich, Conn.: JAI.

—— and Rosenkopf, L. (1992). 'Organizational Determinants of Technological Change: Towards a Sociology of Technological Evolution'. *Research in Organizational Behavior*, 14: 311–47.

—— —— (1996). 'Executive Succession, Strategic Reorientation and Performance Growth: A Longitudinal Study in the U.S. Cement Industry'. *Management Science*, 42/7: 939–53.

Utterback, J. M., and Abernathy, W. J. (1975). 'A Dynamic Model of Process and Product Innovation'. *Omega*, 3/6: 639–56.

Van de Ven, A. H., and Grazman, D. N. (1999). 'Evolution in a Nested Hierarchy: A Genealogy of Twin Cities Health Care Organizations, 1853–1995', in J. A. C. Baum and B. McKelvey (eds.), *Variations in Organization Science: In Honor of Donald T. Campbell*. London: Sage.

Van Valen, L. (1973). 'A New Evolutionary Law'. *Evolutionary Theory*, 1: 1–30.

Volberda, H. W. (1996). 'Toward the Flexible Form: How to Remain Vital in Hypercompetitive Environments'. *Organization Science*, 7/4: 359–74.

—— (1998). *Building the Flexible Firm: How to Remain Competitive*. New York: Oxford University Press.

—— and Elfring, T. (2001). *Rethinking Strategy*. London: Sage.

—— Van den Bosch, F. A. J., Flier, B., and Gedajlovic, E. R. (2001). 'Following the Herd or Not? Patterns of Renewal in the Netherlands and the UK'. *Long Range Planning*, 34/2: 209–29.

Weber, M. (1978). *Economy and Society: An Outline of Interpretive Sociology*. Berkeley: University of California Press.

Weick, K. E. (1979). *The Social Psychology of Organizing*. Reading, Mass.: Addison-Wesley.

Wernerfelt, B. (1984). 'A Resource-Based View of the Firm'. *Strategic Management Journal*, 5/2: 171–80.

WHITTINGTON, R., PETTIGREW, A., PECK, S., FENTON, E., and CONYON, M. (1999). 'Change and Complementarities in the New Competitive Landscape: A European Panel Study, 1992–1996'. *Organization Science*, 10/5: 583–600.

WILLIAMSON, O. E. (1975). *Markets and Hierarchies*. New York: Free Press.

——(1979). 'Transaction Cost Economics: The Governance of Contractual Relations'. *Journal of Law and Economics*, 22: 233–61.

WINTER, S. G. (1987). 'Knowledge and Competence as Strategic Assets', in D. J. Teece (ed.), *The Competitive Challenge: Strategies for Industrial Innovation and Renewal*. Cambridge, Mass.: Ballinger.

WOODWARD, J. (1965). *Industrial Organization: Theory and Practice*. New York: Oxford University Press.

....

CHAPTER 22

AT HOME FROM MARS TO SOMALIA

RECOUNTING ORGANIZATION STUDIES

....

MARTA B. CALÁS

LINDA SMIRCICH

A software glitch, a premature engine shutdown and problems with NASA money and management doomed the Mars Polar Lander to crash into the Red Planet last December, independent experts reported on Tuesday. The Mars Polar Lander project, and the earlier Mars Climate Orbiter, which failed last September due to an embarrassing misunderstanding over English and metric measurements, were examined along with Deep Space 2, a pair of Mars probes that also failed and for which an immediate cause was not named...aside from money problems, there were not enough people to do the work...it was stressed that while some projects will be canceled...the long-term goal to look for evidence of life on Mars will continue. 'The goal is to follow the water,' since water is seen as a prerequisite for life. 'You must know where the water is or was...if it turns out the water all went underground, eventually we'll have to carry drills to Mars...This is not about who's to blame. This is about how to ensure success. We have to put in place a system of checks and balances to ensure success' (Tuesday, 28 March 2000; *Yahoo News*)

Sakorey Faday and Adan Mohammed are young women from two different African countries, but they share experiences as similar as they are tragic. Adan spent 10 days walking 60 miles with her children to a feeding center 360 miles southeast of Addis Ababa. The trek proved too much for her two children. Both died along the way. Faday walked to Baidoa in neighboring Somalia in search of help after drought ended her farm work; the twin to the malnourished baby wrapped in her arms died at birth... The situation is exacerbated by the nomadic life-style of the people who live in the region ...it would take at least 10 years to change local habits...they have been nomads for centuries, and their allegiance is to the land and their clans, not to any state. Most would resist changes... political attitudes and trade regulations need to change...so that the nomads can take their herds to the closest market without being blocked by national borders. In the meantime, donors are being asked for more than 800,000 tons of food to keep famine at bay. (Tuesday, 11 April 2000; *Yahoo News*)

SEVERAL news items will help us illustrate the current state of organization studies and its prospects. Starting with the two items above, we ask: What can organization studies contribute to understanding these situations? What would organization studies have to say? For starters, some versions of modernist organization studies might characterize the first as an instance of sheer mismanagement, an obvious case of ineffective organizational practices, and the second as a tragic result of the resistance to change of those wedded to a nomadic way of life. Another, more critically inclined organization studies would decry the wastefulness of space exploration and the search for water on Mars, while children not too far away die of malnutrition and lack of fresh water.

Organization studies might also tell postmodernist tales about the news items above. For instance, a postmodern story might engage the contemporary discourse about time/space compression to observe that time and space seem to be compressed only on the side of the powerful—for 'the other' of this tale appears

A huge sea of ice lies just under the surface of Mars, ready to be tapped by future explorers as a source of fuel and maybe even drinking water, scientists report...this water is so plentiful it would only have to be heated to 33 degrees F to be usable... astronauts would not drink it—at least not right away. 'If Martian microbes are sitting there waiting to bloom, the last thing we would want is a war of the worlds waiting to blow up in our bellies.' Scientists from across the United States joined up with Russian and French teams to analyze data...It will take much more work to confirm that the substance found on Mars really is frozen water. But the experts seem convinced. (Tuesday, 28 May 2002; *Yahoo News*)

Five African leaders and the U.N. secretary-general have been invited to next month's summit of the eight major industrialized nations to discuss a new plan to help the world's poorest continent—the first time the exclusive G-8 club has opened its annual meeting...G-8 nations are working from the premise 'that 40 years of development assistance in Africa hasn't been enormously successful.' The bottom line today is that every indicator in Africa is going backward instead of forward—from life expectancy to school enrollment to clean water, famine and AIDS. The plan of action presented at the summit will establish 'a broad partnership with all of Africa' to look after basic needs—food, water, education and health care... (Wednesday May 29, 2002; *Yahoo News*)

to inhabit an ever-moving space in which time travels backward. Foucauldian versions might genealogize the discourses and practices of 'success' and 'development', which can co-exist so comfortably side-by-side in the history of our present, as they emerge, placidly randomized, from each one of our textbooks. Or, perhaps, the discourses of globalization could be deconstructed by reading the binaries embedded in 'Martian microbes waiting to bloom and blow up in our bellies' through the blooming bellies of African populations whose life expectancy is going backward.

Organization studies of today can say and do each of these and more, but that is not what we want to do. Rather, as we take stock in the twenty-first century we want to remark on the multiplicity of critical perspectives that our field has at its disposal today, but notice at the same time that despite all these critical analyses, organization studies has contributed little innovation when it came to producing institutions. If anything, the 'organizational logic', of the turn of the nineteenth century, with its penchant for bureaucratizing, rationalizing, and economizing, became entrenched in most social institutions of the 'developed' and the 'developing' world, to the point that it was apparently 'common sense' the world over.

Both sets of news items above, with their attachment to the grounds of man/agerialism, can be characterized as encased in this kind of organizational logic. Under the more common rubrics of 'modernity' and 'modernization', the logic of our institutions has become easily transportable. It was even exported into 'space'. With its ability to 'commodify' every 'thing' and every 'body', the logic of our institutions appears to allow little room for a different conversation, no matter how many theoretical innovations we claim to have produced in organization studies.

Thus, our more general observation is that despite its often triumphalist appearance, the logic of modernity and managerialism has been a failing proposition for all our institutions. As we reread the above examples, they attest to this failure; and, yet the 'solutions' continue to repeat more of the same. In our view, an important aspect of this failure stems from limitations in our own academic domains to produce other possible understandings 'for the world' with all we already have at hand, including other possible understandings for our own academic domains.

Let us look again at the examples and consider the following: Despite evident failures in both, how is it possible for NASA to elicit an appearance of success to the point of obtaining an ongoing mobilization of very material resources? Why is 'the African other' mired in symbols of ongoing failures? In each case one can immediately imagine the 'bodies' involved, and the symbolic value of each of these bodies: 'scientists' vs. 'peasants'; 'white' vs. 'black'; 'maleness' vs. 'femaleness'; 'literate' vs. 'illiterate'; 'knowledgeable' vs. 'ignorant'; 'the West' vs. 'the Rest'. In the rhetoric of each 'news' article one can sense the directional arrow of the modernist narrative of 'progress': NASA moving up and away toward promises of future quests, leaving Earth, and its limits, behind. 'The other' incapable of transcending its own traditions, its dependence on an earth no longer productive, its inability to know any better...

Through sharing their relational conditions both examples stay in their modern place: the two quotes connected by 'technological determinism', 'managerialism', and 'the market', while the 'ignorance' of 'the other' attains for NASA the appearance of 'expertise'. Is this what we teach in organization studies? Unpacking the effects of 'progress' and the value of 'modernization' is a requirement for unmasking modernist failures that hide under the guise of 'success'. It is a requirement for rethinking the institutional 'development' of our world through different understandings. Is this how we teach organization studies? Should not we unpack the logic of our universities and stop all this foolishness by refusing to teach 'organization studies'? But, what else to do?

22.1 FROM MARS TO SOMALIA: THE POST-COLONIAL/FEMINIST/ TECHNOLOGY NEXUS

Leaving NASA aside, let us reflect once again on the images conveyed by Ethiopia and Somalia, and on how these images entrench a sense of despair about the deplorable conditions of the African continent. At the most immediate, the imagery shows a people so 'behind' in their 'development' that they are hardly able to help themselves, unless, of course, they change their (ignorant) ways while being aided by western expertise. Yet today it would be easy to challenge such explanations.

Three theoretical discourses quite at hand, and their intersections, will help: Third World feminist analyses, post-colonial theorizing, and anthropology of technology. Together they can shed some light on the 'backward' construction of 'all of Africa' by 'western knowledge', and then provide a different logic for our institutions.

First, consider 'colonial difference' and 'border thinking' (Mignolo 2000). Much of western civilization spawned from African regions. At the same time Africa has been in continuous interaction with the west over the centuries, and always making significant contributions to the west in those interactions. Historicizing these encounters is a relevant exercise when unpacking modernity, for it not simply reclaims the forgotten history of 'the other', or rejects a misleading assumption about the possibility of a 'people without history'. Further, and more importantly, historicizing these encounters shows how the west needed to forget 'its other' if it were to become 'modern'. Remembering the histories of 'the other' must be part of the project of remembering the history of the west, and what brought us to think in 'modern' ways.

Gender, race, and class analyses provide further help in this enterprise. While there are well-known feminist critiques about the male bias in western philosophy, which equated women with nature and man with reason, naturalizing a hierarchical condition for the sexes (e.g. Lloyd 1993), these critiques are not sufficient for revealing the reproduction of 'subjugated knowledges' (Foucault 1980) beyond those of white women of the west. Several post-colonial feminist analyses, such as Spivak's recasting of the subaltern (1988; 1999) and Suleri's (1992) pluralization of gender in the nexus of colonial and post-colonial discourses, remind us about the continuous intersections of gender/race/class/ethnicity and transnationalism when limiting 'knowledge' to that articulated by certain actors in the west. Some of these works show very directly the implications of western knowledge-making institutions in submerging others' knowledge. For example, in Mohanty's words (1991: 74):

in the context of the hegemony of the Western scholarly establishment in the production and dissemination of texts, and in the context of the legitimating imperative of humanistic and scientific discourse, the definition of 'the third world woman' as a monolith might well tie into the larger economic and ideological praxis of 'disinterested' scientific inquiry and pluralism which are the surface manifestations of a latent economic and cultural colonization of the 'non-Western' world.

From there, however, Mohanty makes the more important point that to acknowledge this is also to acknowledge the possibility that the other of 'the west' is able to represent herself—rather than needing to be represented by western knowledge. Yet, this may be more easily said than done. There is still much western rhetoric to dislodge. Fabian (1983) observes that from the nineteenth century these ways of understanding became articulated in specific rhetorical arguments deployed by anthropologists, often acolytes of colonial ruling.

Fabian traces how evolutionary conceptualizations sustaining modern philoso-phy become dominant tropes in anthropological narratives. He shows that several notions of *time* perform as 'space' or distanciation between the anthropologist (or western knowledge) and his/her 'other' as research subject and object of analysis. In these representations 'the other' is always behind, either through 'naturalized', 'typological', or 'intersubjective' tropes of time. Fabian proposes that only through a notion of *coeval* time—that is, realizing that we all (i.e. us and those who we study) are of the same time/space—can we understand the practices of others, as they exist in relationship to us and to our own (academic and political) practices of knowledge creation.

This is still a quite important point. The concoction of rhetoric within the walls of the academy continues to go far beyond these walls into contemporary practices. For instance, current 'development practices', emerged in academic and other institutions of the United States after World War II, as a political economy engagement with the just named 'Third World' (Escobar 1995). These practices were drawn as policies with clear directions of what needed to be done for the 'under-developed'.

Supported by many of the philosophical notions and rhetoric we have indicated above, conjoined through ideologies of capitalism and liberal political democracy, development policies were meant to bring the rest of the world to the time/space of the west. These policies evolved according to what was perceived as the needs of the 'target countries'. Africa, in particular after the 'end of colonialism' in the 1960s, became a primary target of these programs. Women became, as well, a significant population toward which many programs were directed. Today, perhaps even with more emphasis, women are principal subjects of development policies (e.g. World Bank 2001).

Considering the 'news' about Africa in our excerpts in light of these points may explain why such news stories are usually not surprising or unreason-able. These 'news' items reiterate what 'we already know' about 'the other'. However, in light of these points as well, we can no longer ignore how 'our knowledge'/'what we already know' is being constituted by silencing other know-ledges.

Contemporary feminist anthropologists have attended precisely to this matter by focusing, like Fabian, on the modernist constitution of anthropological under-standings. Some of these writings employ analyses located in feminist materialist variations of poststructuralism and post-colonial analyses in order to reconsider the limitations of prior anthropological knowledge, which often conceals the actual conditions as well as the agency of its subjects (e.g. di Leonardo 1991). These authors are especially concerned that failures of western knowledge, such as the failure of development projects, end up blaming their victims. Thus, in most cases, these reframings of anthropological understandings also reverse the west/ rest location of knowledge by highlighting our own western ignorance. Beyond providing ways of questioning the faulty logic of 'modern knowledge', they also provide ways to begin thinking about the possibilities of other knowledges, operating under different logics.

A specific example may provide some clarification. Warren and Bourque (1991) discuss different ideologies used in development policies directed to fostering change and progress for Third World Women through knowing, understanding, and using 'technology'. 'Technology' here means things as diverse as changes in reproductive practices to cooking utensils, to information technologies, and so on. One early strategy, *integrationist*, followed the western logic of 'equal opportunity' in which women should become educated and structurally incorporated into the 'mainstream' uses of technology, as defined by the west. This strategy proved difficult to implement, for the 'structural barriers' in question are hard to overcome if one follows the 'modern' principles of 'equal opportunity' based on 'gender differences'.

A second strategy, *appropriate technology*, assumed that the technology may have been too complex for the 'less developed'. They focused on what was understood in the (First World) development community to be simpler, closer to the needs of the population and based on their own resources, such as 'small scale' technological changes. Yet, the strategy proved to be appropriate mostly from the perspective of 'experts' from the west, for they demonstrated a failure to understand the needs of the users, resulting in the abandonment of many of these projects. Still, some considered that it was possible to overcome these limitations if women were involved in technology planning.

A third strategy then appeared: *the feminization of technology*, which proposed that 'feminine values' should be included in the design of the technology. It promoted an agenda based on 'women's culture', reclaiming the 'natural' abilities and concerns of women in contrast to men. These strategies are now considered utopian and irrelevant, since their essentialist view of 'feminine values', based on western radical feminism, showed little understanding of different gender configurations and gender relations in the rest of the world.

Warren and Bourque emphasize the limitations of the three approaches in contrast to what they consider a more relevant understanding of women and technology in the context of development: that these issues need to be understood from a *global economy* perspective. In this perspective the focus is on the relationship between the west and the rest through both gender and technology. Issues to be addressed arise around intersections of gender, race, and class, the gender division of labor worldwide, and the relationships between different forms of households and different forms of economies.

Thus, if we recast these different views of gender and technology in the context of the specific example of Ethiopia and Somalia, we could argue that none of the first three approaches would have changed the conditions of these populations. If anything, they may have, and probably did make conditions worse. The global economy approach would, on the other hand, change the focus of understanding. Questions would become more directed to relationships among the current conditions of Ethiopia and Somalia, the women in this context, and the relationship over time between 'western knowledge' and the other's 'ignorance' under colonialism and post/colonialism. Similarly, questions would become more focused on the conditions of these populations in relationship to the rest of the world, including in relationship to the development community that has intervened and continues to intervene for over forty years with much *technological experimentation.*

Yet, we may not have seen all there is to see of the Third World, gender, and technology by stopping at the global economy view. More recently some anthropologists of technology are paying attention to how Third World and other subaltern populations may be reappropriating and re-forming 'advanced technologies' for their own purposes. Scholars, often using constructivist, actor-network theory approaches (ANT), show how new information technologies (e.g. the Internet), are used by groups as diverse as indigenous populations in the Amazon region and biodiversity conservation groups, to connect and interact the world over (Escobar (1999). At the same time these groups resist the homogenization and hegemonization of globalization by remaining situated within their own particular, place-specific political and practical concerns.

Similarly Haraway (1997) promotes a feminism in which women become central actors in the meaning-making of technoscience through 'situated knowledges' that would represent a better world for all. Escobar asks: *Can the world be redefined and reconstructed from the perspective of the multiple cultural, ecological, and social practices embedded in local models and places?* This is perhaps the most profound question that can be posed from a radical networks perspective. What types of networks would be most conducive to this reconstruction? (1999: 44; italics in original)

These latter arguments further change in fundamental ways the epistemological arguments often associated with 'gender and technology' in development studies. First, rather than the typical 'modernist' notion of 'progress' encasing most of the other views, both the *global economy* and the *anthropology of technology* views reposition their arguments in coeval time. The analytical emphasis remains situated in specific places but focuses on change and considers any change relationally (over time and space). They, therefore, call into question how theoretical framing as well as methodological approaches define the issues, and how those definitions limit understanding of 'what's going on'. What's going on in Ethiopia and Somalia?

22.2 COMING BACK HOME TO ORGANIZATION STUDIES

This long detour through multidisciplinary understandings of 'development' and 'technology' via Ethiopia and Somalia brings us back home. The critique of Third World 'gender and technology' paradigms in the anthropology of development is concurrent with the critique of 'gender-technology' theorizing and researching in the First World (Wajman 1991; Grint and Gill 1995; Terry and Calvert 1997). Similar to Warren and Bourque, these scholars criticize the deployment of traditional feminist lenses such as liberal and radical feminism in understanding women and contemporary technologies. These arguments, like Warren and Bourque's, favor a more materialist analysis of the issues or, like Escobar and Haraway, favor a more processual understanding based on constructivists and ANT approaches.

And yet, as we talk about these intersections of the Third and the First World, including some incursions into space, we have not been that far away. All that we recounted has been produced in western institutions, and has served no other purpose than to give us an entry point for our commentary. In this case, we sought to recast Ethiopia and Somalia in a particular critique of modernity, development, and globalization in the context of technology, to show that there may be much to learn from (rather than teach to) these places in the world. At the same time these multidisciplinary conversations have provided a contrast for observing the limitations and weaknesses in much of the NASA stories; an argument to recast these stories as the foibles of modernity rather than its success.

Altogether we have been trying to find a way to recount these stories by maintaining a certain distance from organization studies. Insofar as organization studies frames what and how we can say, insofar as it limits how we can put our stories together, we would have become prisoners of our own productions, talking to each other about our expertise, while conceiving all those monsters that escape our institutions: 'drinking water in Mars' and '40 unsuccessful years of development in Africa'. Can we, instead, escape our institutions?

We find some solace in a recent talk by Bruno Latour (2001), which takes on from his 1993 work. He asks his interlocutors to think quite differently about our world and what we do in it. He urges paying attention to the fact that there is more in the world than can be controlled by any of us, inside or outside the 'laboratories' for we are all participants in 'hybrid forums'. And yet he observes that we act as if that were not the case, as if somebody knew and somebody was in control, because that is how we came to think as 'moderns'. He asks us, thus, to interpret our present time not as modernity or postmodernity, but as non-modernity, because in his view modernity, and its dream of being able to separate facts from values, ends and means, things and people, while always moving towards an ever better future, never really happened.

If such is the case, he adds building on Callon, Lascoumes, and Barthe, then we must replace the idea of 'experts' (some of us) with that of 'co-researchers' (all of us). One way or another 'we are all engaged... into the collective experiments on matters as different as climate, food, landscape, health, urban design, technical communication and so on. As consumers, militants, citizens, we are all now co-researchers' (2001).

And thus, we see this as an option for organization studies. An option for rethinking our institutions, our universities included, as more hybrid forums, as space for co-researching, for enrolling and being enrolled by Ethiopia, NASA, Somalia, water, earth, gender, race, class, ethnicity, sexualities, nationalism, globalization, development, technology... and all the overflows of those encounters. Co-researcher... quite a nice subject position to be in non-modernity.

REFERENCES

DI LEONARDO, M. (ed.) (1991). *Gender at the Crossroad of Knowledge: Feminist Anthropology in the Postmodern Era.* Berkeley: University of California Press.

ESCOBAR, A. (1995). *Encountering Development: The Making and Unmaking of the Third World.* Princeton: Princeton University Press.

—— (1999). 'Gender, Place and Networks: A Political Ecology of Cyberculture', in W. Harcourt (ed.), *Women@Internet: Creating New Cultures in Cyberspace.* London: Zed Books.

FABIAN, J. (1983). *Time and the Other: How Anthropology Makes its Object.* New York: Columbia University Press.

FOUCAULT, M. (1980). *Power/Knowledge: Selected Interviews and Other Writings,* ed. C. Gordon. New York: Pantheon Books.

GRINT, K., and GILL, R. (eds.) (1995). *The Gender–Technology Relation: Contemporary Theory and Research.* London: Taylor & Francis.

HARAWAY, D. (1997). *Modest_Witness@Second_Millennium. FemaleMan©_Meets_Onco-Mouse2.* New York: Routledge.

LATOUR, B. (1993). *We Have Never Been Modern.* Cambridge, Mass.: Harvard University Press.

—— (2001). 'What Rules of Method for the New Socio-Scientific Experiments?' Plenary Lecture for the Darmstadt Colloquium. *http://www.ensmp.fr/~latour/*

LLOYD, G. (1993). *The Man of Reason: 'Male' and 'Female' in Western Philosophy.* Minneapolis: University of Minnesota Press.

MIGNOLO, W. D. (2000). *Local Histories/Global Designs.* Princeton: Princeton University Press.

MOHANTY, C. T. (1991). 'Under Western Eyes: Feminist Scholarship and Colonial Discourses', in C. T. Mohanty, A. Russo, and L. Torres (eds.), *Third World Women and the Politics of Feminism.* Bloomington: Indiana University Press.

SPIVAK, G. C. (1988). 'Can the Subaltern Speak?', in C. Nelson and L. Grossberg (eds.), *Marxism and the Interpretation of Culture*. Urbana: University of Illinois Press.
—— (1999). *A Critique of Postcolonial Reason*. Cambridge, Mass.: Harvard University Press.
SULERI, S. (1992). *The Rhetoric of English India*. Chicago: Chicago University Press.
TERRY, J., and CALVERT, M. (eds.) (1997). *Processed Lives: Gender and Technology in Everyday Life*. London: Routledge.
WAJMAN, J. (1991). *Feminism Confronts Technology*. University Park: Pennsylvania State University Press.
WARREN, K. B., and BOURQUE, S. C. (1991). 'Women, Technology and International Development Ideologies: Analyzing Feminist Voices', in M. di Leonardo (ed.), *Gender at the Crossroad of Knowledge: Feminist Anthropology in the Postmodern Era*. Berkeley: University of California Press.
World Bank (2001). *Engendering Development: Through Gender Equality in Rights, Resources, and Voice*. World Bank: Oxford University Press.

CHAPTER 23

....

NEW TIMES, FRESH CHALLENGES

REFLECTIONS ON THE PAST AND THE FUTURE OF ORGANIZATION THEORY

....

HARIDIMOS TSOUKAS

Thought deals . . . solely with surfaces. It can name the thickness of reality, but it cannot fathom it, and its insufficiency here is essential and permanent, not temporary.

William James (1909/1996: 250)

We are observing the birth of a science that is no longer limited to idealized and simplified situations but reflects the complexity of the real world, a science that views us and our creativity as part of a fundamental trend present at all levels of nature.

Ilya Prigogine (1996: 7)

A version of this paper was delivered as a keynote address at the Joint IFSAM-ASAC Conference, Organization Theory Division, 8–11 July 2000, Montreal, Canada.

As ONE would expect of all social scientific fields, Organization Theory bears the marks of its birth. Ever since Weber, OT has largely been concerned with the study of formal organizations. Organization, instead of being understood as the generic phenomenon of patterned interaction, has been approached from the perspective of how coordinated interaction is authoritatively achieved within formal organizations (Barnard 1968; March and Simon 1993; Thompson 1967). In the imagery of mainstream OT, organizations are places of 'imperative control' (or 'imperative coordination') (Weber 1947: 152, 324), that is cohesive as well as enduring totalities that resist change, have a dominant culture and a hierarchical power structure that ensures conformity and control so that certain behavioral regularities are more probable to occur than others (Bauman 1992: 60; Pfeffer 1997).

Following such imagery, the key phenomena of interest have been the following two. The first is how power and cognitive structures, having the attributes of being independent and logically prior to individual actors and of relative inflexibility, result in 'de-randomizing' the voluntary actions of agents so that individual human behavior becomes *organizational* behavior. In essence, this is the classic Hobbesian problem on a small scale: how order is created out of the actions of diverse actors. The second is how the hierarchy of power and knowledge, empirically manifested in organizational structure, is related to certain key variables for organizational performance, such as the environment, strategy, technology, and societal institutions (Donaldson 1996; Pfeffer 1997). In both instances formal organization is seen as something solid, enduring, and stands in a causal relation to both human agency and its environment. Moreover, humans are conceived in minimalist terms, ex-temporally and ex-spatially, as self-interested information processors following a consequential rationality.

We have learned a great deal from such a synoptic treatment of organization(s). We have been able to learn about different kinds of organizations operating in different environments as well as about the mechanisms through which control is exerted and uniformity of behavior is generated. But there have been some problems. First, the structure of formal organizations is not something originating outside society but constructed from the symbolic 'raw materials' provided by society at a point in time. As such, structure must be thought of as incorporating (or reflecting) the socially recognized myths and metaphors of the society within which organizations operate. Society does not cause organizations to adopt a particular structure, any more than it causes individuals to adopt a particular culture—in both cases society is a supplier of raw materials, not a causal agent. Embeddedness, not causal interaction, is the mode of relating both organizations to their environments and intra-organizational phenomena to one another. The elaboration of this thesis has been the significant contribution of the institutionalist research program (Powell and DiMaggio 1991; Scott 1995).

Secondly, in the imagery of mainstream OT, action and interaction tend to be significantly underplayed. What is neglected is the process through which apparently 'solid' structures are constructed, maintained, and modified in the course of interaction. Weick's (1979) theory of organizing and the associated cognitivist research it has inspired have been an important correction to the mainstream view. Structure has been shown to emerge in the mind, in the gradual reduction of equivocality surrounding human interaction. We encounter here a classic theme running through OT: structure vs. process. Over time the debate has shifted from a single-minded preoccupation with structure (the organization as a 'solid' entity), to the examination of the processes through which structure is generated, although the more demanding task of investigating how structure and process interact has not been taken up as much as it might.

And thirdly, it has been increasingly recognized that individuals within organizations are not mere self-interested information processors; they rather have tangible bonds, attachments, and affiliations to communities, they are emotional beings, and, yes, they have a body. This recognition has had some intriguing implications. Relatively recently, a considerable amount of research has been directed towards exploring the 'communities of practice' and collectively-held meaning systems that sustain individual action at work (Brown and Duguid 1991; Tsoukas 1998a), the emotional side of human beings that inescapably affects what they do and how they act (Fineman 1993), as well as the organizational implications of gender and race (Gherardi 1995; Nkomo 1992).

I hope you can see the picture I am trying to paint: over time, OT has become more complex in its treatment of its object of study. Its initially rigid assumptions have been relaxed and real-life complexity has been let in (March and Olsen 1986: 28). In effect, it has been recognized that (a) organizational phenomena are embedded into, and they derive their significance from, broader patterns of meaning and nexuses of activity; (b) the apparent solidity of organizations is due to social processes at work; and (c) individuals are inherently social and bodily creatures. However, despite the significant conceptual progress that has been made we are still captive of an intellectualist onto-epistemology that fails to recognize the inherent *sociality* of organizational phenomena—that organizations and organizational members are constitutively (not contingently) social entities. I shall have more to say about this later on.

The move towards incorporating greater complexity and, therefore, increasing OT's theoretical sophistication, will be strengthened if it is also recognized that as well as being concerned with the study of formal organizations, OT is par excellence the field which ought to be focusing on *organization* (Chia 1996; Tsoukas 2001). This is important partly because it licenses OT theorists to look around in the non-social realm for patterns of organization that might provide useful insights into social organization—notice, for example, the increasing popularity of notions such as 'complex adaptive systems' and 'dynamical chaotic systems' (Anderson 1999; Morel and Ramanujam 1999). But, more significantly, it is important because it enables us to understand the new network forms of organization and patterns of inter-organizational cooperation that are increasingly emblematic of late-modern knowledge economies (Castells 2000). And finally, focusing on organization enables us to get a clear picture of the dynamic processes through which organization emerges (Tsoukas and Chia, 2002; Weick 1979).

What new patterns of social organization suggest is that it is possible for actors to be organized outside the bounds of 'imperative co-ordination' (Nohria 1992; Gulati, Nohria, and Zaheer 2000; Hardy 1994). We need, therefore, new categories that are appropriate to the analysis of patterned interaction in an extra-organizational space in which there is no dominant culture, imperative control, or a single legitimate authority (Bauman 1992: 61). If we shift our attention from the study of formal organizations to the study of *organization*, we will be able to see authoritative coordination as a contingent empirical manifestation of the broader process of social coordination—authority is one way through which patterned interaction may be achieved; actors following abstract rules or subscribing to the same values are alternative ways of achieving patterned interaction.

More generally, formal organization should be seen as the quest for closure—for contingencies to be eliminated and for meaning to be definitively established so that consistently effective action, across time and space, may become possible—but such a closure is inescapably incomplete (Tsoukas 2001). As several ethnographic studies have shown, human action occurs in necessarily open-ended contexts, whose features cannot be fully anticipated (Hutchins 1993; Orr 1996). And human action *qua* human has the potential to be reflexive, thus leading to new distinctions and meanings. Thus, insofar as actors follow abstract rules, formal organization is an input into human action, while organization at large is an *outcome* of it—a pattern emerging from actors adapting to local contingencies and closely interrelating their actions with those of others (Tsoukas and Chia, 2002). Organization emerges as situated accommodations become heedfully interrelated in time (Weick and Roberts 1993).

The preceding view has several benefits, since it enables us to see more clearly certain hitherto unappreciated aspects of organization. First, new empirical phenomena such as the increasingly distributed character of contemporary corporations and the pervasive agreements and partnerships seen in certain industries can be accounted for. More generally, it makes it possible for us to expand our understanding of organization by focusing on patterns of coordination between actors (or what was earlier called 'patterned interaction'), at several levels of analysis (coordination between individuals, coordination among governments, corporations, and NGOs in all permutations, as well as forms of governance), and how they are produced. Secondly, it helps us enrich our notion of organization to include *self-organization*—immanently generated order. Whereas we have often tended to think of organization as being almost exclusively imposed from the outside, we are now able to see that organization is, partly at least, a self-generating pattern or, to use Hayek's (1982) term, a 'spontaneous order'—a collectively generated outcome as actors improvise to accommodate local contingencies and interweave their actions across space and time (Tsoukas 1996, 2001; Weick 1998).

23.1 AGAINST INTELLECTUALISM: THE INHERENT SOCIALITY OF ORGANIZATIONAL PHENOMENA

A main feature of mainstream OT has been the conceptualization of formal organization as an internal realm of purely 'organizational' operations and, ever since March and Simon (1993), of computations and programs. In this OT has followed similar developments in sociology and, especially, psychology. Just like the mind has been considered as an inner set of mental processes (Harré and Gillet 1994) and society as a collection of mechanisms for establishing and maintaining control (Bauman 1992), formal organization has been seen as a 'pure' mechanism for reducing uncertainty, for making decisions, and generating behavioral regularities. The epistemological strategy behind such an approach has been that of intellectualism (or representationalism) (Tsoukas 1998b).

Intellectualism, as James (1909/1996: 217) perceptively noted long ago, is the turning of experience into a conceptual order, identifying a thing with a concept and a concept with a definition. Our thinking, on this view, aims to represent a pregiven object of study as closely as possible. An object of study is divided into regions of discrete elements, which are isomorphically represented by names (Varela, Thompson, and Rosch 1991: 147). Social scientific analysis aims at finding out the most appropriate names (concepts) to fit the structure of the world. This is a metaphysical stance, which, as Wittgenstein (1958) clearly saw, requires getting 'in front of' everything, 'looking at' our experiences from outside and mirroring them in our concepts (Finch 1995: 33). Since the world consists of discrete elements, rather than complexes or contexts, the task of social scientific analysis, according to the intellectualist view, is to name those elements and find out the contingent connections between them (Chia 1996; Tsoukas 1994).

In OT (and in the rest of the social sciences) such an approach has had the following two implications. First, social phenomena in organizations are thought to merely consist of, or are the product of, interrelated individuals. And secondly, the relationship between social phenomena and individuals is seen as merely external—the properties definitive of individuals are only contingently linked to social phenomena (Schatzki 2000). The first implication signals the difficulty we have had as OT theorists to pay proper attention to the collective nature of organizations and consider them as something more than mere sites of individual action. The second implication signifies our difficulty to appreciate the irreducible sociality of actors; that the possession of mind and performance of action inherently (not contingently) require a social context, a nexus of practice (Schatzki 2000: 94–5).

Both of the above difficulties can be overcome if we grasp the Wittgensteinian point that social practices and institutions incorporate particular self-interpretations, certain ways in which evaluative distinctions are enacted (Taylor 1985a, b). Without such distinctions a social institution would not be what it is, could not have the shape it has. Moreover, a social institution cannot be intelligible unless its constitutive distinctions are grasped (Winch 1958). Consider, for example, organizational decision-making. The typically Anglo-Saxon practice of making decisions manifests a certain self-understanding, a set of evaluative distinctions that are constitutive of 'decision-making' (cf. Taylor 1985b: 32–5; Tsoukas 1998b: 787–8). These are typically bound up with the clarity of expression, the confrontation between different views, and the impersonal analysis of the situation with the view of getting 'at the heart' of the problem. Such distinctions, however, have no place in other societies, such as for example Japan, where the prevailing set of distinctions incorporates compromise, consensus, respect for seniority, and saving face (Dore 1973; Rosenberger 1992). The difference in what constitutes decision-making in both cases is not merely linguistic; more crucially, it is a difference in social reality. As Taylor (1985b: 33) observes, 'the realities here are practices; and these cannot be identified in abstraction from the language we use to describe them, or invoke them, or carry them out'.

If institutions and practices are what they are by virtue of the particular sets of distinctions that are incorporated in them, where do those distinctions get their meaning from? As Wittgenstein (1958) insightfully observed, the meaning of our signs and symbols comes from the uses we put them to. This happens in the context of *discursive practices*—intentional, normatively constrained sets of actions. According to Harre and Gillett (1994: 28–9), 'a discursive practice is the use of a sign system, for which there are norms of right and wrong use, and the signs concern or are directed at various things' (see also Harré 1997: 175; Bruner 1990: 17–19; MacIntyre 1985: 185–90). A crucial feature of discursive practices is that the meanings they embody are not just in the minds of the individuals involved but in the practices themselves; the meanings are the common property of the practice at hand—they are inter-subjective (Bruner, 1990: 12–13; Taylor 1985b: 36–40). This is ontologically important for it shifts attention from the individual to the individual-embedded-in-practice. It is also epistemologically significant because since inter-subjective meanings do not primarily reside in the minds of individuals, they cannot be known with the traditional methods of empiricist science (e.g. individual answers to questionnaires) but with the use of interpretative methods (Taylor 1985b: 40). Inter-subjective meanings are more than just shared in the sense that each of us has them in our individual minds: they are part of a common reference world which is over and above, and is constitutive of, the individual mind (Bruner 1990: 12–15).

For example, if decision-making is seen as a discursive practice—as what people *do* when they take decisions, subject to standards of correctness—,then what decision-making is, what it consists of, is not something the individuals involved define; decision-making has already been defined by the discourse into which individuals participate. The point here is that the condition for an individual to be a competent member of a discursive practice at all is to have taken for granted the meanings constitutive of the practice. This does not mean, of course, that the individual may not bring his/her own beliefs and attitudes in a particular decision-making process. What, however, he/she will not bring is what *constitutes* decision-making—that has already been defined in the discursive practice in which the individual participates (Taylor 1985*b*: 36).

Clearly, without inter-subjective meanings there could not be collective forms of action at all, since individuals would be lacking a common language whereby to engage in a collective activity. The notion of inter-subjective meanings enables us to conceive of a 'collective subject' without thinking of it as a contradiction in terms. This is especially important when it comes to organizations, since the latter are first and foremost *collective* actors. Yet the ontological individualism that has characterized OT has obscured the collective nature of organizations.

For example, March and Simon (1993: 2) have remarked that 'organizations are systems of co-ordinated action among individuals and groups whose preferences, information, interests, or knowledge differ'. Notice that, on such view, in the beginning there was difference, conflict, even discord, which are then turned by the organization into cooperation. In the words of March and Simon (1993: 2), 'organization theories describe the delicate conversion of conflict into co-operation'. This, however, is a limited view of what organizational life is about. The point of departure for individuals is not only difference but also similarity; conflict and cooperation. Prior to becoming members of a particular organization, individuals were members of other organizations; moreover, societal membership is prior to organizational membership. Insofar as individuals are embedded into broader societal systems of meaning, they draw on them to carry out their tasks. And insofar as organizations similarly incorporate the self-understandings of the wider social system, their identity is always already partly defined. Organizations do not just convert conflict into cooperation; they may also convert cooperation into conflict, as for example when organizational members are asked to behave in ways that may not be congruent with some of the dominant societal self-understandings. A more rounded view of organizational life is possible when we discard ontological individualism and begin to appreciate that inter-subjective meanings, manifested in discursive practices, are constitutive of individuals; and, at a higher level of analysis, that societal self-understandings are constitutive of organizations.

As argued earlier, the intellectualist approach leads to thinking of individuals as only *contingently* connected to social practices. A person's actions respond to events in his/her environment, the argument goes, but the fact that the person acts depends solely on the person's characteristics, especially his/her mental conditions. At the individual level of analysis, the mind itself determines actions; at the collective level of analysis, the collective mind (culture) determines collective practices. But the mind is not a mere set of logical operations—whatever those operations are, they must *mean* something. Meanings are deeply implicated in how people act, and we can find out what those meanings are by looking at what people *do*. The mind therefore is inextricably linked to action—it is manifested in action (Bruner 1990; Harré and Gillett 1994; Weick and Roberts 1993). If this point had been fully grasped, a number of harmful dualisms encountered in OT could have been avoided. Consider the following examples.

1. Hofstede's research on the impact of national culture on organizational structure and functioning is based on a conceptual dichotomy between 'values' and 'practices' (McSweeney 2002). 'Values', argues Hofstede (1991: 8), 'are broad tendencies to prefer certain states of affairs than others...they are not directly observed by outsiders'. Practices, on the other hand, are less fundamental and as such 'are visible to an outside observer' (op. cit.). 'Their cultural meaning, however', remarks Hofstede (op. cit.), 'is invisible and lies precisely and only in the way these practices are interpreted by the insiders.' Notice that culture, for Hofstede, is something that only the privileged 'insiders' have access to and are, therefore, capable of describing (this is an argument very similar to the psychologistic claim that only individuals have direct access to the content of their minds) (cf. Rorty 1991). What this view is missing is that just like an individual would need a language in order to describe his/her mental content and that language would necessarily need to be public, so the insiders into a culture would need to describe their values using some public language, and that would render their values public. The metaphysically private self, assumed by Hofstede's view, is unsustainable because it presupposes the existence of a private language, which, as Wittgenstein (1958) ingeniously showed, is impossible. A private language is an illusion, for such a language would need to establish the meaning of its signs independently of the truth it claims to report, which, since it is a private language, cannot be achieved. And if a private language is an illusion, so is a private subject, be it an individual mind or a collective mind. Whatever values are, they are manifested in the practices people are engaged in—values and practices are not—they cannot be—separate. As Finch (1995: 86), an interpreter of Wittgenstein, argues, 'the attempt to ground both self and objects in "in-itselfness" or "own being", in order to guarantee their reality, lies at the very heart of the ratio-mythic "duplication" which created the metaphysical age'.

2. The currently popular split of organizational knowledge in 'tacit' and 'explicit' is another example of problematic distinctions stemming from an intellectualist

epistemology. It is interesting to note that the intellectualist understanding of tacit and explicit knowledge is nowhere to be seen in the work of Polanyi (1962, 1975), who first introduced such a distinction, but has been added later by his interpreters in management studies. Thus, for Nonaka and Takeuchi (1995: 62–3), tacit and explicit knowledge are 'independent' and they 'interact with and interchange into each other in the creative activities of human beings' (Nonaka and Takeuchi 1995: 61). Indeed, the authors' model of organizational knowledge creation is crucially based on the assumption that tacit and explicit knowledge are not only independent but also convertible to one another.

However, very sensibly, this is not what Polanyi had in mind when he introduced that distinction. For him, tacit and explicit knowledge are mutually constituted—they are not contingently linked. Tacit knowledge can be formalized and explicitly communicated *if* we focus our attention to it. And vice versa: explicit knowledge, no matter how explicit and codified it is, is *always* grounded on a tacit component. Tacit knowledge and explicit knowledge are the two sides of the same coin—being mutually constituted, they cannot 'interact', nor can they be 'converted' to one another (Tsoukas 2003). As Cook and Brown (1999: 385) aptly remark, when we ride a bicycle, the explicit knowledge does not lie inside the tacit knowledge in a dormant form; it is rather generated in the context of riding with the aid of tacit knowledge. 'Likewise', remark Cook and Brown (op. cit.), 'if you know explicitly which way to turn but cannot ride, there is no operation you can perform on that explicit knowledge that will turn it into the tacit knowledge necessary to riding. That tacit knowledge is acquired on its own; it is not made out of explicit knowledge. Prior to being generated, one form of knowledge does not lie hidden in the other.'

If we persist with such a misunderstanding of tacit and explicit knowledge, we risk hypostatizing tacit knowledge and treating it as if it were a version of explicit knowledge—a set of quasi-rules waiting to be discovered. However, in a social context, the crucial feature of tacit knowledge is that it provides the unarticulated background—a set of evaluative distinctions—of what is taken for granted, which is a necessary prerequisite for action. Such an unarticulated background is learned through actors' participation into a social practice, a form of life, and that is why the locus of an actor's tacit knowledge is not in his/her head but in the practice he/she is a member of. At both the individual and the collective levels of analysis, tacit knowledge is the process of instrumentalizing experiences—the lapse into unawareness of the manner in which tools, be they physical and/or intellectual, are used (Polanyi 1962: 59–65). There is no conversion of tacit knowledge to explicit, but of a shift of attention from focal awareness to subsidiary awareness.

Thus, more generally, if the above is accepted, it follows that viewing organizational phenomena as aggregates of contingently related elements leads to major distortions in our understanding of those phenomena, since we are prevented from seeing the *internal* relations holding between individuals and social practices as well as between articulated beliefs and unarticulated distinctions.

23.2 EXPLAINING ORGANIZATIONAL ACTION: FROM CAUSES TO REASONS

The task of OT has traditionally been assumed to be the noticing of relevant regularities and their subsequent causal explanation through contingency models of the type 'If A, then B, in circumstances Z'. In a more elaborate form, contingency models take the following form: 'Given any organization X, if X wants to maximize its performance A and X believes that B is a means to attain A, under the circumstances, then X does B' (Rosenberg 1988: 25). Notice that this general statement connects beliefs and desires to actions. The question is what is the nature of such a connection: does it identify causes of action or does it reveal reasons for action? Or, as Rosenberg (1988: 30) asks, 'Does [a contingency model of explanation—CME] underwrite our explanations of actions because it describes causal relations—that is lawlike connections—in virtue of which actions are determined by beliefs and desires? Or does [a CME] underwrite these explanations because it helps us identify the reasons that make a particular action justified, intelligible, rational, meaningful, or somehow significant to us?'

The CME would describe a causal explanation if beliefs and desires could be objectively established, that is if they could be defined independently of the explanandum (i.e. independent of action). But this cannot be done. An action such as 'loyalty', for example, is identified in relation to a belief as to what constitutes 'loyalty' and incorporates a desire as to how to behave in a manner that is recognized by others as 'loyal' (Taylor 1985b: 23). In other words, insofar as human action is constituted by evaluative distinctions and, therefore, involves rule-following, the criteria of its intelligibility must be internal to that action (Winch 1958: 89–91). What is even worse is that an actor's beliefs and desires cannot be straightforwardly inferred from its actions, for the actor may hold quite different second-order or context-dependent beliefs and desires. For example, as Popper (1979: 246) remarked, Kepler's desire in his mathematical work was to discover the harmony of the world order, although we regard his contribution today as a mathematical description of motion in a set of two-body planetary systems. More generally, action cannot be used as a guide to find out an actor's beliefs, unless we hold the actor's desires constant. And in order to use action as a guide for an actor's desires we need to hold its beliefs constant. As Rosenberg (1988: 33) remarks, 'any action can be the result of almost any belief, provided the agent has the appropriate desire'. It follows, therefore, that in explaining action our aim is to render it intelligible, to find out the reasons it happened, by moving into a 'hermeneutical circle' where we aim to show the coherence between actions, beliefs, and desires (Bohman 1991: 27; Rosenberg 1988: 34; Taylor 1985b: 23–4).

It is because of the hermeneutical circle that we find it so difficult to identify causes in OT and, instead, our explanations cite reasons, thus often having a circular character (Rosenberg 1988; Strawson 1992; Taylor 1985a; Tsoukas 1998b). Thus, a significant body of research has shown that organizations reproduce the beliefs and practices of the society in which they are embedded. Interacting with their environments, organizations do not confront independent entities, but rather engage in processes whereby organizations create opportunities for learning and action, and, in so doing, they shape the links with other organizations in their own image. Individual, as well as organizational, action is hardly ever purely instrumental; it also is a display at which actors look to find what they are. As March and Simon (1993: 16) perceptively noted, action is a purpose in itself. Desires are formed by experiencing choices. Goals lead to actions and actions lead to goals. Problems lead to solutions but, also, solutions create problems. Strategy follows structure, but the reverse is also true.

Should we worry about this circularity? Not necessarily, if our purpose is to *elucidate* the phenomena we deal with, that is to bring out the relationships between actions, beliefs, and desires, and how they came to be established. If we conceive of theory as elucidation we would be quite happy to view our inquiry as an elaborate network of connected items, such that each concept could be understood by grasping its connections with other concepts (Strawson 1992: 19). The charge of circularity would not worry us for, in the perceptive words of Strawson (1992: 19–20), 'we might have moved in a wide, revealing, and illuminating circle'. 'This is not to say', Strawson (op.cit.) continues, 'that the charge of circularity would lose its sting in every case. Some circles are too small and we move in them unawares, thinking we have established a revealing connection when we have not. But it would be a matter for judgement to say when the charge was damaging and when it was not.'

23.3 OVERCOMING HARMFUL DUALISMS

As was earlier said, OT has traditionally been assumed to be the study of authoritative coordinated interaction. Our emphasis has largely been on how human behavior is homogenized in organized contexts and how behavioral regularities come about. Hence the emphasis that has often been paid on routines, programs, schemata. What has been less explored is how change and novelty come about in organized contexts. Interestingly, just like 'structure' was taken to be separate from 'process', 'creativity' was thought to be separate from 'repetition'. It was further assumed that we could focus on 'repetition' or on 'creativity' but not simultaneously on both; we could study 'stability' and 'order' or 'change' and 'evolution', but not both. Moreover, even when creativity and change were the foci of study they were approached as phenomena already accomplished not as ongoing processes (Chia 1999). Much of OT is, to use James's (1909/1996: 262) apt phrase, 'a post-mortem dissection'.

The reason for this synoptic approach is the intellectualist stance mentioned earlier, which compels us to transform the perceptual order into a conceptual order. The trouble with concepts synoptically employed is that while they shed light on particular aspects of reality, they obstruct our access to those other aspects that are not pointed at by the relevant concept. For example, 'routine' is an organizational phenomenon we can easily find evidence for. But by describing a particular behavior as routine we fail to notice that, unlike, machine behavior, human behavior is never completely routine and that it always contains the possibility of novelty and change (Feldman 2000). Even the very experience of routine is sufficient to reshape it (Tsoukas and Chia, 2002). As James (1909/1996: 219) remarks, 'once you have conceived things as "independent", you must proceed to deny the possibility of any connexion whatever among them, because the notion of connexion is not contained in the definition of independence'. 'Stability' and 'change' are two independently defined phenomena, as are 'repetition' and 'creativity', and when we proceed on such intellectualist premises we are easily trapped in focusing on the one at the expense of the other, thus ignoring that *both* terms of each pair are part of the same reality (Wallerstein 1999: 166).

The implications of such an intellectualist epistemology is that we fail to properly understand 'change' and 'novelty' in their own terms, rather treating them as special cases of 'stability' and 'routine' (North 1996; Orlikowski 1996: 63; Tsoukas and Chia, 2002; Weick 1998: 551). This failure is a challenge for us to develop more nuanced accounts of these phenomena and how they are interwoven in organizational life (Tsoukas and Chia, 2002). What is crucially missing from OT is, as Porter (1991) has pointed out with reference to Strategic Management, theories of creative action in organizations. This in turn calls for more work on how structure interacts with process over time, how reflexivity functions, and how context and contingencies influence action paths (Garud and Karnoe 2000). To paraphrase Wallerstein (1999: 166), OT ought to be the search for the narrow passage between the determined and the arbitrary, the general and the particular, closure and open-endedness.

If this point is accepted, then OT should not so much be concerned with the study of authoritatively coordinated interaction as the study of *patterned interaction*, of *'chaosmos'* (Edgar Morin's term, cited in Kofman 1996: ch. 5; Castoriadis 1987, 1991). Our ontology must be broad enough to accept that organizations have the features of a *cosmos* (a pattern) but also that, at their roots, they are chaos, a gaping void from which new patterns, a new cosmos, arises. Human imagination and interaction give rise to new forms, enable new practices to emerge. It is precisely the interdependence of *chaos* and *cosmos* that makes organizational life patterned yet indeterminate, and enables the human mind to account for it, although in an irremediably incomplete way (Tsoukas 2001).

Accepting the ontology of *chaosmos* implies that we must discard two of the foundational myths of our field, namely that 'formal organizations are abstract systems' (Barnard 1968: 74; Thompson 1956/57)—sets of formal rules— and that our inquiry should be guided by the pursuit of the 'decontextualized ideal' (Toulmin 1990: 30–5)—the search for the abstract, the timeless, and the universal at the expense of the concrete, the timely, and the local. Since organizations incorporate self-interpretations articulating evaluative distinctions, they do not have a fixed identity over time and space that might be captured in the same way the DNA captures the essence of genes. In the view suggested here, organizations do not have a certain 'inner' logic, a set of intrinsic properties; they rather are constitutively social all the way—discursive practices embedded within discursive practices. Perhaps our motto, if we need one, should be: don't search for the logic of organizing; look for the discursive practices involved in organizing.

References

ANDERSON, P. (1999). 'Complexity Theory and Organization Science'. *Organization Science*, 10: 216–32.

BARNARD, C. (1968). *The Functions of the Executive*. Cambridge, Mass.: Harvard University Press.

BAUMAN, Z. (1992). 'Sociological Responses to Postmodernity', in Z. Bauman, *Intimations of Postmodernity*. London: Routledge.

BOHMAN, J. (1991). *New Philosophy of Social Science*. Cambridge: Polity Press.

BROWN, J. S., and DUGUID, P. (1991). 'Organizational Learning and Communities of Practice: Towards a Unified View of Working, Learning, and Innovation'. *Organization Science*, 2: 40–57.

BRUNER, J. (1990). *Acts of Meaning*. Cambridge, Mass.: Harvard University Press.

CASTELLS, M. (2000). 'Materials for an Exploratory Theory of the Network Society'. *British Journal of Sociology*, 51: 5–24.

CASTORIADIS, C. (1987). *The Imaginary Institution of Society*. Cambridge: Polity Press.

—— (1991). *Philosophy, Politics, Autonomy*, ed. and tran. D. A. Curtis. New York: Oxford University Press.

CHIA, R. (1996). 'The Problem of Reflexivity in Organizational Research: Towards a Postmodern Science of Organization'. *Organization*, 3: 31–59.

—— (1999). 'A "Rhizomic" Model of Organizational Change and Transformation: Perspective from a Metaphysics of Change'. *British Journal of Management*, 10: 209–27.

COOK, S. D. N., and BROWN, J. S. (1999). 'Bridging Epistemologies: The Generative Dance between Organizational Knowledge and Organizational Knowing'. *Organization Science*, 10: 381–400.

DONALDSON, L. (1996). *For Positivist Organization Theory*. London: Sage.

DORE, R. (1973). *British Factory—Japanese Factory*. Berkeley: University of California Press.

FELDMAN, M. (2000). 'Organizational Routines as a Source of Continuous Change'. *Organization Science*, 11: 611–29.

FINCH, H. L. (1995). *Wittgenstein*. Rockport, Mass.: Element.

FINEMAN, S. (ed.) (1993). *Emotion in Organizations*. London: Sage.

GARUD, R., and KARNOE, P. (2000). *Path Dependence and Creation*. Mahawa, NJ: Lawrence Earlbaum Associates.

GHERARDI, S. (1995). *Gender, Symbolism and Organizational Cultures*. Thousand Oaks, Calif.: Sage.

GRANOVETTER, M. (1992). 'Problems of Explanation in Economic Sociology', in N. Nohria and R. G. Eccles (eds.), *Networks and Organizations*. Boston: Harvard Business School Press.

GULATI, R., NOHRIA, N., and ZAHEER, A. (2000). 'Strategic Networks'. *Strategic Management Journal*, 21: 203–15.

HARDY, C. (1994). 'Underorganized Interorganizational Domains: The Case of Refuge Systems'. *Journal of Applied Behavioral Science*, 30: 278–96.

HARRÉ, R. (1997). 'Forward to Aristotle: The Case for a Hybrid Ontology'. *Journal for the Theory of Social Behaviour*, 27: 173–91.

—— and GILLETT, G. (1994). *The Discursive Mind*. Thousand Oaks, Calif.: Sage.

HAYEK, F. A. (1982). *Law, Legislation and Liberty*. London: Routledge & Kegan Paul.

HOFSTEDE, G. (1991). *Cultures and Organizations*. London: HarperCollins.

HUTCHINS, E. (1993) 'Learning to Navigate', in S. Chaiklin and J. Lave (eds.), *Understanding Practice*. Cambridge: Cambridge University Press.

JAMES, W. (1909/1996). *A Pluralistic Universe*. Lincoln: University of Nebraska Press.

JOAS, H. (1996). *The Creativity of Action*, tran. J. Gaines and P. Keast. Cambridge: Polity Press.

KOFMAN, M. (1996). *Edgar Morin*. London: Pluto Press.

MACINTYRE, A. (1985). *After Virtue* (2nd edn). London: Duckworth.

MCSWEENEY, B. (2002). 'Hofstede's Model of National Cultural Differences and their Consequences: A Triumph of Faith—a Failure of Analysis'. *Human Relations*, 55: 89–118.

MARCH, J. G., and OLSEN, J. (1986). 'Garbage Can Models of Decision-Making in Organizations', in J. March and R. Weissinger-Baylon (eds.), *Ambiguity and Command*. Marshfield, Mass.: Pitman.

—— and SIMON, H. A. (1993). *Organizations* (2nd edn). Cambridge, Mass.: Blackwell.

MOREL, B., and RAMANUJAM, R. (1999). 'Through the Looking Glass of Complexity: The Dynamics of Organizations as Adaptive and Evolving Systems'. *Organization Science*, 10: 278–93.

NKOMO, S. (1992). 'The Emperor Has No Clothes: Rewriting "race" in the Study of Organizations'. *Academy of Management Review*, 17: 487–513.

NOHRIA, N. (1992). 'Introduction: Is a Network Perspective a Useful Way of Studying Organizations?' in N. Nohria and R. G. Eccles (eds.), *Networks and Organizations*. Boston: Harvard Business School Press.

NONAKA, I., and TAKEUCHI, H. (1995). *The Knowledge-Creating Company*. New York: Oxford University Press.

NORTH, D. (1996). 'Epilogue: Economic Performance through Time', in L. J. Alston, T. Eggertsson, and D. North (eds.), *Empirical Studies in Institutional Change*. Cambridge: Cambridge University Press.

ORLIKOWSKI, W. J. (1996). 'Improvising Organizational Transformation over Time: A Situated Change Perspective'. *Information Systems Research*, 7: 63–92.

ORR, J. (1996). *Talking about Machines*. New York: ILR Press/Cornell University Press.

PFEFFER, J. (1997). *New Directions in Organization Theory*. New York: Oxford University Press.

POLANYI, M. (1962). *Personal Knowledge*. Chicago: University of the Chicago Press.

—— (1975). 'Personal Knowledge', in M. Polanyi and H. Prosch, *Meaning*. Chicago: University of Chicago Press.

POPPER, K. R. (1979). *Objective Knowledge* (rev. edn). Oxford: Clarendon Press.

PORTER, M. E. (1991). 'Towards a Dynamic Theory of Strategy'. *Strategic Management Journal*, 12: 95–117.

POWELL, W. W., and DiMAGGIO, P. J. (eds.) (1991). *The New Institutionalism in Organizational Analysis*. Chicago: University of Chicago Press.

PRIGOGINE, I. (1996). *The End of Certainty*. New York: Free Press.

RORTY, R. (1980). *Philosophy and the Mirror of Nature*. Oxford: Blackwell.

—— (1991). *Objectivity, Relativism and Truth*. Cambridge: Cambridge University Press.

ROSENBERG, A. (1988). *Philosophy of Social Science*. Oxford: Clarendon Press.

ROSENBERGER, N. R. (1992). *Japanese Sense of Self*. Cambridge: Cambridge University Press.

SCHATZKI, T. R. (2000). 'Wittgenstein and the Social Context of an Individual Life'. *History of the Human Sciences*, 13: 93–107.

SCOTT, R. W. (1995). *Institutions and Organizations*. Thousand Oaks, Calif.: Sage.

STRAWSON, P. F. (1992). *Analysis and Metaphysics*. Oxford: Oxford University Press.

TAYLOR, C. (1985a). *Human Agency and Language: Philosophical Papers*, i. Cambridge: Cambridge University Press.

—— (1985b). *Philosophy and the Human Sciences: Philosophical Papers*, ii. Cambridge: Cambridge University Press.

THOMPSON, J. D. (1956/57). 'On Building an Administrative Science'. *Administrative Science Quarterly*, 1: 102–11.

—— (1967). *Organizations in Action*. New York: McGraw-Hill.

TOULMIN, S. (1990). *Cosmopolis*. Chicago: University of Chicago Press.

TSOUKAS, H. (1994). 'Refining Common Sense: Types of Knowledge in Management Studies'. *Journal of Management Studies*, 31: 761–80.

—— (1996). 'The Firm as a Distributed Knowledge System: A Constructionist Approach'. *Strategic Management Journal*, 17/Winter Special Issue: 11–25.

—— (1998a). 'Forms of Knowledge and Forms of Life in Organized Contexts', in R. Chia (ed.), *In the Realm of Organization*. London: Routledge.

—— (1998b). 'The Word and the World: A Critique of Representationalism in Management Research'. *International Journal of Public Administration*, 21: 781–817.

—— (2001). 'Re-viewing Organization'. *Human Relations*, Special Millennial Issue, 54: 7–12.

—— (2003). 'Do We Really Understand Tacit Knowledge?', in M. Easterby-Smith and M. A. Lyles (eds.), *Handbook of Organizational Learning and Knowledge*. Oxford: Blackwell.

—— and CHIA, R. (2002). 'On Organizational Becoming: Rethinking Organizational Change'. *Organization Science*, 13: 567–82.

VARELA, F. J., THOMPSON, E., and ROSCH, E. (1991). *The Embodied Mind*. Cambridge, Mass.: MIT Press.

WALLERSTEIN, I. (1999). 'Differentiation and Reconstruction in the Social Sciences', in I. Wallerstein, *The End of the World as We Know It*. Minneapolis: University of Minnesota Press.

WEBER, M. (1947). *The Theory of Social and Economic Organization*, tran. A. M. Henderson and T. Parsons, ed. T. Parsons. New York: Free Press.

WEICK, K. (1979). *The Social Psychology of Organizing*. New York: McGraw-Hill.

—— (1998). 'Improvisation as a Mindset for Organizational Analysis'. *Organization Science*, 9: 399–405.

—— and ROBERTS, K. (1993). 'Collective Mind in Organizations: Heedful Interrelating on Flight Decks'. *Administrative Science Quarterly*, 38: 357–81.

WINCH, P. (1958). *The Idea of Social Science and its Relation to Philosophy*. London: Routledge & Kegan Paul.

WITTGENSTEIN, L. (1958). *Philosophical Investigations*. Oxford: Blackwell.

INDEX